M000211737

The Gospel of the Beloved Disciple

A Work in Two Editions

The Gospel of the Beloved Disciple

A Work in Two Editions

Herman C. Waetjen

NEW YORK • LONDON

T & T Clark International, Madison Square Park, 15 East 26th Street, New York, NY 10010

T & T Clark International, The Tower Building, 11 York Road, London SE1 7NX

T & T Clark International is a Continuum imprint.

Grateful acknowledgment is made to the following for permission to reprint previously published material:

Harcourt, Brace and Company, Inc: Excerpt from "East Coker" in FOUR QUARTETS by T.S.Eliot

The Johns Hopkins University Press: Excerpts from The Act of Reading pp.55 and The Implied Reader pp.xiii by Wolfgang Iser.

Human and Rousseau, Cape Town, 1962: In Tristia en Ander Verse from The Great Ode.

Cover design: Wesley Hoke
Book layout: Chora-Strangers (http://www.chora-strangers.org)

Library of Congress Cataloging-in-Publication Data

Waetjen, Herman C.

The Gospel of the Beloved Disciple: a work in two editions /
by Herman C. Waetjen.
p. cm.

Includes bibliographical references (p.) and index.
ISBN 0-567-02781-3 (hardcover)

1. Bible. N.T. John—Criticism, interpretation,etc. 2. Lazarus, of Bethany, Saint. I. Title.

BS2615.52.W34 2005
226.5'066—dc22

2005012893
Printed in the United States of America

06 07 08 09 10 10 9 8 7 6 5 4 3 2

for Thembisa, Elaine, and Dave

But the faith and the love and the hope are all in the waiting.
Wait without thought, for you are not ready for thought:
So the darkness shall be the light and the stillness the dancing.

T.S. Eliot, "East Coker" in Four Quartets

We dare not worship any other gods before This Countenance
Or, allow them to be served.
This, this, at least, we know - keep on knowing.
He is a finger, hand, or gesture,
or complete turn of hand. These are my words.
His words let super-novae burst forth, shine,
shine and glow through rings and light-hours.
But this radiance is seen by us:
and in no other way recognized in its splendour.
This bursting forth then - perhaps even out of love -
without concern for knowing or being known:
This is His. Ours is this: to be (however insignificant),
to carry on being, with: justice, some pride; and lots of
love; and endless forgiveness for everything:
no one has a perfect rendezvous with the universe;
actually we should learn to live ironically; and:
within irony retain love.

From: "The Great Ode" (N.P. Van Wyk Louw),
translated from the Afrikaans by Christo Lombard,
Windhoek, Namibia.

Ons durf geen gode voor Dié Aangesig
aanbid nie, óf: lááf aanbid word, nie.
Dít, dít, ten minste, wéét ons - bly ons weet.
Hy is 'n vinger, hand, of handgebaar,
of han-om-keer. Dit is my woorde.
Sy woorde laat super-novae uitbars, blink,
blink en straal deur ringe en lig-ure.
Maar die blink die word deur óns gesien:
anders nooit ennooit as blink geweet nie.
Bie bars en uit-breek, dan - dalk selfs uit liefde -
en sonder steru aan weet of aan geweet-word:
dié is Syne. Ons s'n is dít: bestáá (hoe klein ook), bly bestaan
met: juistheid, bietjie trots; en heelwat liefde;
en eindeloos vergiffenis vir áls:
niemand tref dit móói met die heelal nie;
eintlik moet ons leer ironies lewe:
én: binne ironie nog liefde hou.

Table of Contents

Preface

The Gospel according to John is a narrative world artistically constructed by an immensely creative and powerful storyteller. It is an integrated narrative in which all of its content is coherently related to itself and constitutes an independent, self-contained and systemic universe with its own structures of time and space. It is not a copy of the world in which it originated, in spite of its reflection of the realities of the distinctive society in which it emerged. Its narrative structure does not necessarily correspond to the historical progression of events in the public career of Jesus of Nazareth, if, in fact, such a construction were possible. It is not a documentary record of the past, and therefore its orientation is neither historical nor mimetic. Accordingly, its truth cannot be validated by historical inquiry or literary criticism; its truth validates itself in the process of reading and its attendant production of meaning.

The Gospel also cannot be interpreted within the referential framework of early Christian thought or its evolutionary development. It is an aesthetic literary creation, and as such it forms its own world. Consequently source and redaction criticism are precluded because they do not lend themselves to a comprehension of the possible inherent literary unity of a synchronic approach to the text and the resulting ontological priority of the experience of meaning.

The paradigm shift in the historical-critical interpretation of the Fourth Gospel that J. Louis Martyn initiated in 1968 with the publication of *History and Theology in the Fourth Gospel* and the synchronic literary-critical reading advanced by R. Alan Culpepper's *Anatomy of the Fourth Gospel* are the grounding of this present study. It is Martyn's demonstration of the two historical-contextual levels that are implicit in the narrative world of the Gospel that elucidates the hermeneutical genius of this literary masterpiece. The text of the Gospel bears witness to the *einmalig* historical career of Jesus of Nazareth in Roman Palestine.[1] At the same time – and this is the second level of the Gospel's narrative world – it places the story of Jesus' ministry into the context and circumstances of a particular community.[2]

What makes this two-level narrative world more complex is the overlay of two editions to which the textual transmission of the Gospel bears witness. This overlapping, discerned by a requisite critical evaluation of certain manuscript variants, coerces a differentiation of two editions of the Gospel. As the introductory chapter will disclose, the two variant readings of the manuscript tradition of John 20:31, 19:35 and 6:29 require a determination of the Gospel's

[1] *Einmalig* is Martyn's term, and it means "unique," or more literally, "happening only once."

[2] D. Moody Smith, "The Contribution of J. Louis Martyn to the Understanding of the Gospel of John," *History and Theology in the Fourth Gospel*, 3rd ed, 18, acknowledges, "Martyn is quite careful to distinguish his analysis of these two levels from John's own awareness or intent. That is, he does not claim that the two levels constitute a deliberate and conscious technique. Indeed, the evangelist would have insisted upon the unity of the two levels." In a footnote Smith refers to p. 131 of Martyn's text.

original addressees. Were they Christians or non-Christians or possibly both? The answer not only depends on the text-critical principle of *lectio difficilior lectio potior* (the more difficult reading is the more probable reading); it necessarily involves a determination of the relationship of chapter 21 to the Gospel and the function that apparently it was intended to perform as an addendum. Only after this issue has been resolved is the interpreter/reader able to proceed to an identification of the context of the original edition of the Gospel. That is, to what audience were chapters 1-20 addressed? And concomitantly, where and when was chapter 21 added and the text of chapters 1-20 altered? And what was the teleological objective of this second edition?

It is the objective of this study to demonstrate that the first edition of the gospel originated in Alexandria, Egypt and, consequently, that the second level of the narrative world into which the ministry of Jesus was projected reflects the context of the Jewish community of Alexandria some time between the Roman destruction of Jerusalem and the Jewish revolt of 115-117.

These two levels of the first edition of the Gospel are so discriminatingly interwoven and intermingled that they form an indissoluble unity. The only appropriate construction of meaning, therefore, is one that is conditioned by a synchronic reading of the Gospel. It is Culpepper's pioneering *Anatomy of the Fourth Gospel* that presents the literary-critical criteria by which the Gospel's component parts can be integrated to constitute an essential unity.

> As one reads the gospel, the voice of the narrator introduces the narrative world of the text, its characters, values, norms, conflicts, and the events which constitute the plot of the story. The narrator conveys the author's perspective to the reader and sends signals which establish expectations, distance and intimacy, and powerfully affect the reader's sense of identification and involvement. The narrator's claims and the norms of the story woo, beckon, and challenge the reader to believe that the story, its narrative world, and its central character reveal something profoundly true about the "real" world in which the reader lives.[3]

The historical ministry of Jesus that is projected into the religious culture of the Jewish community of Alexandria produces an *immediacy* of his deeds and words for the implied readers who, by interacting with the text of the Gospel and the characters and events that are encountered in its narrative world, experience a spontaneous actualization of that past historical reality. While the employment of the imperfect tense generally limits the durative sense of time to the historical career of Jesus, the present tense is used to draw the implied readers into a sense of "belonging" in the story.[4] The immediacy of this sense of belonging is reinforced by the narrator's employment of the perfect tense which projects the significance of

[3] Culpepper, *Anatomy of the Fourth Gospel: A Study in Literary Design* (Philadelphia: Fortress Press, 1983) 4.

[4] For verbs of the imperfect tense that limit the durative sense of time to the ministry of Jesus, see 2:21; 3:22, 23; 4:2; 6:2,66; 7:5; 10:39; 11:8, 36, 56; 12:11, 37, 42; 17:12; 18:15; 19:3, 12, 21; 20:2-3.

Jesus' words out of his past into the ongoing present experience of the implied readers as they navigate their way through the narrative world of the Gospel.[5] Accordingly the past historical reality of Jesus' ministry impacts and interacts with the circumstances of the Gospel's primary context, and the implied readers are drawn out of their own religious culture and its current crises and are confronted with another world, another construction of reality that they themselves constitute through the reading process. Through this dialectical experience of both *immediacy* and *distanciation* and the resulting disclosure of another world, they are enabled to view their own context more objectively and to perceive more critically their own prejudices, perhaps even their blindness, their paralysis and their participation in their society's constructions of living death.[6] Wolfgang Iser's analysis of the implied reader is pertinent here:

> The reader discovers the meaning of the text, taking negation as his starting point; he discovers a new reality through a fiction which, at least in part, is different from the world he himself is used to; and he discovers the deficiencies inherent in the prevalent norms and in his own restricted behavior.[7]

Distanciation from their own religious culture confronts the implied readers of the Jewish community of Alexandria with the reality of a pervasive and penetrating dualism in which they are participating to the impairment of their own humanness. It may be the dualism of Philo's appropriation of Platonic metaphysics in his allegorical interpretation of the Torah that results in his dichotomization of the ideal human being of Gen 1 and the earthly human being of Gen 2. It may be the dualism of rabbinic Judaism that is being constituted by those who are engaged in consolidating Judaism on the basis of the Pharisaic heritage that requires submission to a pollution system that divides the world into the realms of the clean and the unclean. It may be the dualism of Samaritan gnosticism that has emerged under the influence of Simon Magus.[8] Whatever the origin of the dualism may be, it provides a refuge from the terrors of history and therefore a retreat from authentic historical existence.

---

[5] Martyn's judgment, therefore, that the two levels of the Gospel's narrative world should not be construed as a deliberate and conscious technique of the author would appear to be invalid. For verbs in the perfect tense see 1:34; 3:2, 11, 13, 18, 26; 4:38; 5:22, 24, 33, 37, 43, 45; 6:17, 25, 36, 38, 42, 46, 63, 69; 7:8, 28, 30; 8:20, 31, 33, 40, 42, 55, 57; 9:37; 10:29; 11:11, 12, 34; 12:23, 27, 30, 46, 50; 13:10; 14:25; 15:11, 15, 22, 24; 16:1, 4, 6, 25, 27, 33; 17:2, 6, 10, 12, 14, 22; 18:37; 19:28, 30, 35; 20:18, 25. I am grateful to my colleague, Prof. Robert Coote for raising the question of the Gospel's verbs in the perfect tense.

[6]On the opposition between alienating distanciation and belonging – or immediacy, see Ricoeur, "The Hermeneutical Function of Distanciation." *From Text to Action* (Evanston: Northwestern University Press, 1991) 75-88

[7] Wolfgang Iser, *The Implied Reader: Patterns of Communication in Prose Fiction from Bunyan to Beckett* (Baltimore: The Johns Hopkins University Press,1974) xiii. See especially the final chapter of his book, "The Reading Process: A Phenomenological Approach."

[8] See Acts 8:9-13. Also Irenaeus, *Against Heresies*, Book 1, Chapter 23. *The Ante-Nicene Fathers,* ed. by Alexander Roberts and James Donaldson (Grand Rapids: Eerdmans, 1956) I, 347-348

The Fourth Gospel does not espouse dualism of any kind. Its characterization of Jesus' ministry is anti-dualistic. Jesus directs himself towards the duality of personhood that he himself embodies, a personhood that unites the heavenly and the earthly human being as an aporetic indivisibility.[9] Spirit and matter, soul and flesh, are not dichotomized into alien or alienating realities.[10] Cultural ideologies that maintain social disorders, such as racism and sexism, patriarchy and hierarchy, honor and shame, which alienate human beings from each other and generate political oppression and economic and social inequality are abolished. Jesus himself represents the duality of soul (ψυχή) and flesh (σάρζ), an indissoluble union of Philo's heavenly human being, "the Son of Man" who descended from heaven and the earthly son of Joseph from Nazareth. Coincidentally he is also the enfleshment of the Logos-Sophia and the one upon whom God's Spirit descends and remains. As the narrator unfolds the story, Jesus becomes the very embodiment of Judaism. In his physicality he is the living Temple of God. He is the Passover meal of liberation. He is the Light of the first day of creation, and he is the light of the Hanukkah festival. He is the Lamb of God who removes the sin of the world. He incarnates all that these religious institutions signify, all that these religious festivals memorialize. Consequently, the Temple of God is no longer a stone building but a physical human being who houses God's presence. The festivals cease to be external rituals and observances in which Jesus devoutly participates as a faithful Jew. They become the essential reality of his being that motivates him to express their divine purpose through his deeds and words, above all to fulfill God's will for the salvation of the world.[11]

The author projects the ministry of Jesus into the dualistic religious culture of the Jewish community of Alexandria in order to confront the implied readers with another world, a construction of reality that is non-dualistic, that integrates all aspects of life and living: religious, cultural, social, economic and political, into both an individual and communal incarnation of the sacramental celebrations of God's acts in history. The controversy that the Christian witness provokes within the Jewish community is reflected in the conflict that rapidly intensifies between Jesus and the ruling authorities within the narrative world of the Gospel and rises to a heated polarization that spawns murderous rage. But this is an anti-Judaism that is intra-Judaism. It is an intra-Jewish opposition between two orientations that is analogous to the post-exilic clash between two priestly factions that is reflected

[9] An aporia is the opposite of *poros*, a Greek word that means "passage" or "way through," as in Bos*phoros*. Aporia, therefore, means "no crossing," "no way through;" it is a binary opposition that cannot be dichotomized into a dualism.

[10] For an analysis of the aporiai of the human condition, see Douglas R. McGaughey, *Strangers and Pilgrims: On the Role of Aporiai in Theology* (Berlin: Walter de Gruyter, 1997).

[11] It is not too implausible that Jesus' discourse on "the Bread from heaven" in John 6, which culminates in Jesus' self-disclosure as the Passover meal, is a political interpretation of the Eucharist (that is never introduced into the narrative world of the Fourth Gospel) that by analogy is intended to communicate a discipleship that embodies all that the bread and the wine signify in relation to their ingestion.

in Third Isaiah. The Zadokite priests, having returned from their captivity in Babylon with Ezekiel's hierarchically-oriented vision of the restoration of the Temple cult, are excluding the Levitical priests who embrace Second Isaiah's program of a universal and egalitarian reconstitution of Israel's religion.[12] The repudiation that the visionary community of Levitical priests are experiencing evokes the heart-rending lament of Isa 63:16 and 18-19.

> For you are our father, though Abraham does not know us and Israel does not acknowledge us; you, O Lord, are our father, our Redeemer from of old is your name (Isa 63:16).
>
> Your holy people took possession for a little while; but now our adversaries have trampled down your sanctuary. We have been like those whom you do not rule, like those not called by your name (Isa 63:18-19).

The same polarization is dividing the Jewish community of Alexandria. The rabbis are grounded in the practical realities of their Pharisaic heritage, while the Christian Jews, who represent the eschatological perspective of Jesus, are proclaiming the egalitarian and universal vision that is virtually identical to that of Second and Third Isaiah.

The post-modern orientation of Culpepper's *Anatomy* prioritizes meaning in place of analysis and consequently accentuates the original objective of the Gospel; that is, to engender an experience by rhetorically drawing the implied readers' into a narrative world that necessitates existential interaction. In view of the predispositions laid down in the text for the literary work to exercise its effects, in view of the gaps and blanks that the implied readers are expected to fill, to what extent will contemporary readers be able to produce the meaning encoded in the Gospel? Without any fusion of horizons that historical criticism can generate between the text and the contemporary readers and without any literary competence in reading, a purely subjective interpretation of the text will result in a limited and tradition-bound projection arising out of the act of reading. The resulting meaning is nothing more than a recycled repetition of the reader's prejudices projected onto the text. In contrast, the meaning that is potentially constituted by the textual structures of the implied reader can only be actualized by "informed readers" who possess an historical sense of the Gospel's original context and an attendant literary competence.

The Age of Enlightenment's hermeneutics of historical-critical methodology that engages in a critical construction of the Gospel's original context appears to be a necessary prerequisite for an intelligent and informed reading of the Gospel. "Speech acts," as Wolfgang Iser asserts, "are not just sentences. They are linguistic utterances in a given situation and context, and it is through this context that they take on meaning."[13] That involves contemporary readers in the appropriation of essential information about the Gospel's distinctive language and

[12] See Paul D. Hanson, *The Dawn of Apocalyptic: The Historical and Sociological Roots of Jewish Apocalyptic Eschatology* (Philadelphia: Fortress Press, 1975) 71-100.

possibly its relation to a specific context. Words like λόγος (word), κόσμος (world), θέασθαι (to appraise, size up), θεωρεῖν (to observe and give oneself over to what is being observed), βλέπειν (to see with the eyes of the mind), ὁρᾶν (to see empirically) are pivotal for the construction of meaning in the respective literary contexts in which they are used and therefore require an investigation of their employment in texts contemporaneous with the Gospel. That very inquiry reinforces a historical-critical construction of the context in which the Gospel originated.

An intelligent and informed reading of the Gospel also requires a comprehension of the relationship between "the reader's role as a textual structure, and the reader's role as a structured act."[14] The critical reader-response mode of interacting with the narrative world of the Fourth Gospel, as espoused by Culpepper, enables contemporary readers to discern "the different perspectives represented in the text, the vantage point by which they may be joined together and the meeting place where they converge," but only in terms of a synchronic interpretation of the Gospel.[15] Without a knowledge of the Gospel's context and its implied readers, without a sensitivity to the dialectical experience of immediacy and distanciation that pervades the Gospel, and without an understanding of the role of the reader in terms of the textual structures of the implied reader, contemporary readers cannot construe the meaning of the text intelligently. At least two other components of literary criticism must also be included: the New Criticism's insistence on a close reading of the text and "consistency building."[16] Both, of course require a capacity to read the Greek text, for none of the current renditions in English offers a translation that corresponds to the 27th critical edition of the Nestle-Aland *Novum Testamentum Graece*. Formulas, such as: ἐγὼ εἰμί (I AM) and its equivalences in ὅπου εἰμὶ ἐγώ (where AM I), ἐγὼ ἐκ τῶν ἄνω εἰμί (I from above AM), and ἐγὼ οὐκ εἰμί ἐκ τοῦ κόσμου τούτου (I not AM from this world), which are decisively used within the Gospel, require interpretive constructions that are integrated into its coherent unity.

Must a subject/object analysis, therefore, necessarily occur prior to an existential interaction with the Gospel that will make the experience of meaning potentially possible? Perhaps! But is also possible that historical-critical methodology combined with literary-critical skill in reading may interact dialectically to produce the meaning that is potentially laid down in the text. The cinema experience of viewing a movie offers a pertinent analogy for the experience of interpretation that is prior to explanation or analysis. The moviegoers'

[13] Wolfgang Iser, *The Act of Reading: A Theory of Aesthetic Response* (Baltimore: The Johns Hopkins University Press, 1978) 55.

[14] *Ibid*., 35.

[15] *Ibid*., 36.

[16] On a "close reading" of the text, see Jonathan Culler, "Beyond Interpretation," *Critical Theory Since 1965*, ed. by Hazard Adams and Leroy Searle (Tallahassee: Florida State University Press, 1986) 322. On "consistency building," Iser, *The Act of Reading*, 16-18, 118-119, 122-130, 185.

preunderstanding that is projected upon the unfolding images of the film and the accompanying dialogue of the interlocutors produces an immediate experience of existential understanding. Explanation and analysis occur afterwards and often expand and deepen the interpretation that was naturally generated by the moviegoers' preunderstanding.

As desirable as that immediate experience of existential understanding is for a contemporary reader of the Fourth Gospel, the fore-structure of understanding that enables a contemporary reader to experience an immediate construal of a movie is unable to assume the role that is required for an intelligent reading of the Fourth Gospel because of the limitations of the contemporary cultural horizon. Some of the knowledge that tradition provides may open the text and initiate the process of entering into the textual structures of the implied reader. But a greater fusion of horizons, combining historical-critical information of the text's context and literary-critical skill in reading, is essential if the dialectical experience of both the immediacy and the distanciation that the text potentially offers is to be actualized. At the same time, however, the existential interaction of contemporary readers within the narrative world of the Gospel will be individual, pre-determined by their distinctive history, education and life's experiences. Consequently, the productions of meaning will range between the subjectivity of the reader's socialized ideological perspective and the degree of the reader's objective knowledge of the Gospel's historical context, an awareness of the Gospel's dependence on midrashic intertextuality, and literary-critical capability in reading.

All that follows in the subsequent chapters of this book has evolved from countless crossings through the narrative world of the Gospel of John and attendantly interactions with its text that were informed and nurtured by the commentaries, monographs, and essays of Johannine scholars and interpreters. Supplemental readings in hermeneutics, literary criticism, the sociology of knowledge, Philo, Josephus, the Targums, rabbinic literature, Origen, and the New Testament Apocrypha provided a critical depth of comprehension, as interpretation moved back and forth between the existential experience of meaning and analytical explanation. In articulating my comprehension of the meaning that I have derived from my experience of truth as disclosure and truth as correspondence, I have tried to convey both in terms of their inter-relatedness; and I can only hope that I have been successful.

Without the many individuals and communities I have encountered along the way this book would never have come to maturation. I owe much of my understanding of the aporia of spirit and matter and the aporia of the truth of disclosure and the truth of correspondence to my good friend and fellow pilgrim, Professor Douglas R. McGaughey of Willamette University, whose book *Strangers and Pilgrims*: *On the Role of Aporiai in Theology* has exerted an extensive influence on my hermeneutical perspective. I am grateful to Professor James R. Cochrane of the University of Cape Town for his continued inspirational support and comradeship. I thank Professor Christo Lombard, who made it possible for me to spend a sabbatical year at the University of Namibia in Windhoek, Namibia, and who, as a good friend, continues to be a partner in stimulating theological dialogue. He shared with me the Afrikaans poem by N. P. Van Wyk Louw, which he translated for me and which has been a source of inspiration for me throughout the writing of this book.

I am indebted to the students I have taught in the United States and Africa who have challenged me with their perceptive questions and enriched my hermeneutical development with their insistence on reading the biblical text "from their own place." I thank Dr. Theodore Trost and Dr. Cornelia Cyss Crocker for fruitful periods of collaboration on the Fourth Gospel, and I also I thank my former colleagues of San Francisco Theological Seminary for the animated discussions we shared at different times. I want to restate my gratitude to the Board of Trustees of San Francisco Theological Seminary for their generous policy of sabbatical leaves that have abetted my research and writing throughout my 34 years of teaching at San Francisco Theological Seminary and the Graduate Theological Union. Finally, it is with a special sense of gratitude that I acknowledge Henry Carrigan, Jr., the editor of Continuum, and Amy Wagner, the Senior Managing Editor, for their indispensable role in facilitating the publication of this manuscript.

Above all, I am indebted to my wife, Mary, who read several drafts of the manuscript in order to assist me in improving the clarity of my writing, who added various insights of her own to the interpretation of the Gospel, and who at the very end worked with our son Dave to prepare the final draft for the publisher. Without her love and enthusiastic support this book would never have been written.

My final acknowledgment is reserved for my two daughters, Thembisa and Elaine, and my son, Dave, who have enriched my fatherhood by their magnificent unique selves and have enabled me to transcend into a more grace-filled humanization of my being. For their continuous affirmation and inspiration through provocative challenges and stimulating dialogue I am and I shall be forever grateful. To them I joyfully dedicate this book.

Herman C. Waetjen
San Anselmo, CA

The Gospel of the Beloved Disciple

A Work in Two Editions

Chapter One

The Enigmas of the Origin and Authorship of the Fourth Gospel

Two editions of the Fourth Gospel

Of all the attempts to resolve the enigmas of the origin and authorship of the Gospel according to John, the general postulation of two editions appears to be the most compelling. But not all the constructions or reconstructions of either of these two editions of the Gospel's literary history are equally convincing. The genealogical-diachronic theory of origin that posits a pre-Johannine narrative "Signs Source," combined with a Passion story and subsequently with a "Discourse Source" and redacted into the present form of the Gospel, has dominated scholarly efforts to resolve its enigmas, aporiai and riddles.[1] But among them there has been

[1] As an earlier edition of the Fourth Gospel, the so-called "Signs Source" was originally proposed by A. Faure, "Die alttestamentlichen Zitate im vierten Evangelium und die Quellenscheidungshypothese," *ZNW* 21 (1922) 99-121. Rudolf Bultmann, developed his literary-critical theory in his response to Emmanuel Hirsch's essay, "Hirsch's Auslegung des Johannes-Evangeliums," *EvT* 4 (1937) 115-142. See especially, *Das Evangelium des Johannes* (Göttingen: Vandenhoeck & Ruprecht, 1956) with the *Ergänzungsheft* 1967; English: *The Gospel of John: A Commentary* (Philadelphia: Westminster Press, 1971). The Table of Contents reflects his reconstruction of the original edition of the Gospel. His resolutions of the historical and theological riddles that he engaged convinced him that the present form of the Gospel is the work of a later redactor who revised the earlier edition of the Gospel in order to reconcile it to an emerging catholic orthodoxy. By an analysis of the characteristic theological, stylistic, and linguistic changes, and his attendant reconstruction, he claims to have recovered the original composition of the Evangelist. Others have engaged in a similar diachronic interpretation of the Fourth Gospel that utilizes source and redaction criticism: Barnabas Lindars, *Behind the Fourth Gospel* (London: SPCK, 1971) 27-42 and *The Gospel of John* (London: Marshall, Morgan & Scott, 1972) 46-54; J. Louis Martyn, *History and Theology*, 115, 120, and especially 150-151 for a discussion that links his view of a "Signs Gospel" to a number of other diachronically-oriented scholars such as Robert T. Fortna, *The Gospel of Signs: The Chief Narrative Source Underlying the Fourth Gospel* (Cambridge: at the University Press, 1970) and more recently *The Fourth Gospel and Its Predecessor: From Narrative Source to Present Gospel* (Philadelphia: Fortress Press, 1988). Fortna's heroic effort at reconstruction, like that of his predecessors, is based on a form and redaction-critical investigation that presupposes "two very nearly contradictory modes of Jesus' activity – his narrated deeds and the words of his discourses" which, he contends, are not integrated. Much scholarship has been expended here in an attempt to separate tradition from redaction, but, from the perspective of a synchronic approach, the criteria for such a differentiation are questionable and therefore, in spite of Fortna's claim, "its vindication is ... based on probabilities" after all. Martyn, "Source Criticism and Religionsgeschichte in the Fourth Gospel," *The Interpretation of John*, ed. by John Ashton (Philadelphia: Fortress Press, 1986) 99-121, cites a number of disagreements with Fortna's source-critical analysis. He concludes, "John belongs to a dominantly Jewish-Christian milieu." See John Ashton, *Understanding the Fourth Gospel* (Oxford: Clarendon Press, 1991) 199-204; and Ashton, "The Signs Source," *Studying John: Approaches to the Fourth Gospel* (Oxford: Clarendon Press, 1994) 90-113, which also conveys his critique of Fortna. On theories of displacement and redaction, see C. K. Barrett, *The Gospel according to St. John. An Introduction with Commentary and Notes on the Greek Text* (Philadelphia: Westminster Press, 2nd ed. 1978) 21-26.

only one inquiry that has been more influential than others in elucidating the structure of the Gospel's narrative world and is considered by many as the major inroad into the interpretation of the Gospel. It is J. Louis Martyn's proposal of a two-level drama that determines the composition of the Gospel: (1) "a witness to an *einmalig* event during Jesus' earthly lifetime," and (2) "a witness to Jesus' powerful presence in the actual events experienced by the Johannine church."[2] The impact of this thesis in current Johannine scholarship justifies its assessment as a "paradigm."[3] Its dependence on a reconstruction of an earlier edition of the Gospel, the "Signs Source" that consisted of miracle stories and a passion narrative, does not minimize the promise it holds for further exploration.[4]

R. Alan Culpepper's *Anatomy of the Fourth Gospel* may be considered as the other major inroad into the interpretation of the Gospel according to John.[5] His "Study in Literary Design" has pioneered a synchronic "narrative-critical analysis" of the Gospel by utilizing the literary-critical theories of Seymour Chatman, Roman Jakobson, Wayne Booth, Wolfgang Iser, Gérard Genette, Boris Uspensky and Meir Sternberg in order to formulate his own entry into a "mirror and observer, text and reader" interaction with the narrative world of the Gospel.[6] Instead of an *a posteriori* analysis dependent on the subject-object split, Culpepper is oriented to an *a priori* experience that emanates from this "mirror and observer" interaction for the production of meaning.[7] Yet, as D. Moody Smith surmises, Culpepper's construction of the implied author and the implied readers of the Fourth Gospel "is in many respects congruent with Martyn's analytical historical reconstruction," specifically his contention that the original setting of the Gospel was the synagogue in which the followers of Jesus were experiencing the animosity of their fellow Jews.[8]

Martyn's paradigm of a two-level narrative drama and Culpepper's synchronic mode of a "text and reader" interaction lend themselves to a more comprehensive

---

[2] Martyn, *History and Theology*, 40. In contrast to Martyn's two-level drama synchronically present in the Gospel, Raymond E. Brown, *The Community of the Beloved Disciple: The Life, Loves, and Hates of an Individual Church in New Testament Times* (New York: Paulist Press, 1979) conjectures five stages of diachronic literary development in the evolution of the Gospel.

[3] So D. Moody Smith, "The Contribution of J. Louis Martyn to the Understanding of the Gospel of John," in Martyn's *History and Theology*, 14, n. 30.

[4] *Ibid.*, 150-151. It is the source and redaction-critical work of many scholars, but, above all, that of his doctoral student, Robert Fortna, that serves as the basis of Martyn's pioneering proposal. See D. Moody Smith, "The Contribution of J. Louis Martyn to the Understanding of the Gospel of John," in Martyn's *History and Theology*, 9-11. Also Fortna, *The Fourth Gospel*, 224, 242, n. 35, 274.

[5] Culpepper, *Anatomy of the Fourth Gospel.*

[6] *Ibid.*, 3-4.

[7] Stephen Motyer, "The Fourth Gospel and the Salvation of Israel: An Appeal for a New Start," in *Anti-Judaism and the Fourth Gospel: Papers of the Leuven Colloquium, 2000*, ed. by R. Bieringer, D. Pollefeyt, and F. Vandecasteele-Vanneuville (Assen: Royal Van Gorcum, 2001) 92-110, examines the problem of anti-Judaism in the Fourth Gospel from the perspective of "receiver concerns" and "the rhetorical impact of the gospel within the setting of first-century Judaism."

[8] Smith, "The Contribution of J. Louis Martyn," *History and Theology*, 17.

engagement with the Gospel text, but on the basis of an inquiry into *two more or less similar overlapping editions preserved within the literary structure of the twenty-one chapters of the Gospel* simultaneously present in the critical text of the 27th edition of Nestle-Aland's *Novum Testamentum Graece*.[9] In other words, a synchronic construction of the Gospel in spite of the diachronic sequence of the two editions![10]

The first edition consists of chapters 1 through 20.[11] The second originated at the time chapter 21 was attached as an appendix, apparently in order to serve an entirely different community of addressees. Such a postulation is supported by the lack of continuity between chapters 20 and 21, the apologetic character of the content of chapter 21, and some significant inconsistencies between the original version of the Gospel and its addendum. Although the resulting revision altered its fundamental objective, the design and strategy of that earlier edition are still apparent.

This alleged differentiation of two overlapping editions of the Fourth Gospel is supported by the manuscript variants of 20:31, πιστεύητε ("you may continue to believe") and πιστεύσητε ("you may begin to believe").[12] The dramatic difference between them and their respective addressees becomes more obvious when they are juxtaposed in the context of the concluding verses of the original or first edition of the Gospel.

> Now indeed, Jesus did many other signs in the presence of his disciples that have not been written in this book; but these things have been written so that you may continue to believe (πιστεύητε) that Jesus is the Christ, the Son of God, and that believing you may have life in his name.[13]

---

[9] Nestle-Aland, *NTG* (Stuttgart: Deutsche Bibelgesellschaft, 27 ed., 6 printing). Wilhelm Wilkens, *Die Entstehungsgeschichte des vierten Evangeliums* (Zollikon: Evangelischer Verlag, 1958) 7, contends that one should not differentiate between a relatively minimal comprehensive first edition and a comprehensive revision by another hand. The two stages of the Gospel, the "Grundevangelium" and the "Jetztgestalt," he believes, is the work of one and the same author.

[10] This undertaking presumes the legitimacy of C.H. Dodd's presuppositions, not only for the second edition but also for the first, that it is "the duty of an interpreter at least to see what can be done with the document as it has come down to us before attempting to improve upon it." *The Interpretation of the Fourth Gospel* (Cambridge: at the University Press, 1960) 289-291. See Ashton's critique of Dodd, *Understanding the Fourth Gospel*, 79-81.

[11] Ashton, *Understanding the Fourth Gospel*, 199, is directed toward "only [to] what ... I conceive to be the first edition of the Gospel," but for him that first edition is not identical to the present text of chapters 1-20. Chapters 6, 11, 15-17 belong to the second edition and are therefore excluded from his investigation. See pp. 200-204.

[12] Bultmann, *John*, 698; German, 541, dismisses the importance of the two variants on the basis of his philosophically oriented existential interpretation. For the Evangelist "the faith of 'Christians' is not a conviction that is present once for all, but it must perpetually make sure of itself anew, and therefore must continually hear the word anew." Brown, *John* I, LXXVII-LXXIX, in his evaluation of the variants of 20:31, has decided that the Gospel is addressed to the Christian believer without the distinction of whether his/her ethnicity is Jewish or Gentile.

[13] This reading occurs in P^{66vid} ℵ* B Θ 0250 892^s and l 2211. The P^{66} reading of this text is uncertain.

> Now indeed, Jesus did many other signs in the presence of his disciples that have not been written in this book; but these things have been written so that you may begin to believe (πιστεύσητε) that Jesus is the Christ, the Son of God, and that believing you may have life in his name.[14]

The significance of the difference between these two variants is obvious. The first, πιστεύητε, implies that the original addressees of the Gospel were Christians; the second, πιστεύσητε, requires a non-Christian audience. But can it be determined which of these two readings is the original? Which text with its particular subjunctive form of the verb did the author of chapters 1-20 employ as the conclusion of the first edition of the Gospel? It is noteworthy that the identical problem reoccurs in 19:35:

> And the one having seen has testified, and his testimony is true, and that one knows that it is true, so that you may continue to believe (πιστεύητε).[15]

> And the one having seen has testified, and his testimony is true, and that one knows that it is true, so that you may begin to believe (πιστεύσητε).[16]

And again in 6:29:

> Jesus answered and said to them, "This is the work of God, that you continue to believe (πιστεύητε) into the one whom that one sent."

> Jesus answered and said to them, "This is the work of God, that you begin to believe (πιστεύσητε) into the one whom that one sent."[17]

It would seem that the resolution of the original reading of 20:30-31 should correspondingly be applicable to 19:35 and 6:29.

If the text critical principle of *lectio difficilior lectio potior* (the more difficult reading is the more probable reading) is employed, the aorist subjunctive, πιστεύσητε, should be chosen as the original form of the verb used by the author. It is the more difficult reading! Indeed, it is more probable that initially the Fourth Gospel was addressed to non-Christians and was intended to serve as a *Missionsschrift*, an evangelistic writing, to gain converts to the Christian faith.[18]

---

[14] This reading is supported by $\aleph^2$ A C D L W Ψ 0100 $f^{1.13}$ 33 M lat sy.

[15] This reading occurs in $\aleph^*$ B Ψ; Or.

[16] This reading is supported by $\aleph^2$ A D^s L W Θ 054 $f^{1.13}$ 33 M.

[17] This reading is supported by D K W Γ Δ 0145 f^{13} 700 892 1241 1424 M.

[18] D. A. Carson, "The Purpose of the Fourth Gospel: John 20:31 Reconsidered," *JBL* 106/4 (1987) 639-651, has reached the same conclusion, but without including 19:35 or the problem of the Epilogue of chapter 21. On the basis of his analysis of both verbs, the present and aorist subjunctives, he is convinced that the present form of the Gospel was intended to be evangelistic. On the other hand, Christopher Rowland, "John 1:51, Jewish Apocalyptic and Targumic Tradition," *NTS* 30/4 (1984) 498, assumes that the gospel was "directed primarily to those who were believers already … and is intended to dissuade Jewish-Christians from abandoning their new allegiance to Christ." Against Carson it should be said that both John 4:48 and 11:15 should be read as an ingressive aorist. Others who assign an evangelistic purpose to the Fourth Gospel: Karl Bornhäuser, *Das Johannesevangelium: eine Missionsschrift für Israel* (Gütersloh: Bertelsmann, 1928); W. C. van Unnik, "The Purpose of St. John's Gospel," *Studia Evangelica I* (Berlin: Akademie Verlag, 1959) 282-411; J. A. T. Robinson,

Subsequently the Gospel was revised for Christian readers and the aorist subjunctive, πιστεύσητε, was changed to a present subjunctive, πιστεύητε, in order to reinforce their continuation in the Christian faith. But such logic is not in and of itself convincing. The probability of the priority of the aorist subjunctive, πιστεύσητε, is reinforced by the content of the appendix of chapter 21 and by internal evidence within the preceding *twenty* chapters of the Gospel .[19] Accordingly, the original edition of the Gospel, that is chapters 1 – 20, is most appropriately and legitimately read and construed as an evangelistic text addressed to non-Christians.[20] Πιστεύσητε ("you may begin to believe"), therefore, must have been the original verb employed in 20:31, 19:35 and 6:29.[21]

But this is not simply an either/or text-critical determination. The second reading was substituted at a somewhat later time when the Gospel was adopted by and re-directed to a Christian community. Consequently it was necessary to accommodate it to this new readership by changing the aorist subjunctive to the present subjunctive πιστεύητε ("you may continue to believe") in these three texts, but also by inserting appropriately relevant material into chapters 1-20 and by legitimating the Gospel's canonicity by means of the distinctive content of chapter 21. It is also likely that the Aramaisms in the Gospel were translated into Greek so that they would be intelligible to the new addressees: "Rabbi' was rendered as "Teacher" in 1:38; "Messiah" was transcribed as "Christ" in 1:41; Cephas was changed to "Peter" in 1:42; and "Rabbouni" was converted into "Teacher" in 20:16. The discrepancy of translating both "Rabbi" and "Rabbouni" as "Teacher" most likely implicates the work of the editor of chapter 21 who apparently did not know the difference between them.[22]

Undeniably, the editorial motives embedded in chapter 21, relative to the content and objectives of the preceding twenty chapters of the Gospel, have a direct bearing on the determination of which of these variants of 20:31, the aorist

---

"The Destination and Purpose of St. John's Gospel," *Twelve New Testament Studies. Studies in Biblical Theology* No. 34 (London: SCM Press, 1962) 107-125; published earlier in *NTS* 6 (1960) 117-131. Against John Ashton, "The Identity and Function of the ΙΟΥΔΑΙΟΙ in the Fourth Gospel," *NT* 27/1 (1985); and Ashton, *Understanding the Fourth Gospel*, 13-14 and 131-140.

[19] The following chapters will support this conclusion.

[20] The emphasis on "signs," the shift of the so-called Temple cleansing from the end to the beginning of Jesus' ministry, and especially the threat of being excommunicated from the synagogue, point to a community of Jews and Christian Jews, as Martyn contends in *History and Theology*, 46-66.

[21] Brown, *John* II, 1056, considers the present subjunctive to be the best attested reading; also Lindars, *John*, 617. Rudolf Schnackenburg, *The Gospel according to John* (New York: Crossroad, 1982) III, 338, rejects the ingressive character of the aorist subjunctive and therefore also an evangelistic intent by the author. Barrett, *St. John*, 575, maintains that the question of purpose cannot be determined by the two tenses.

[22] *Rabbouni* is a title of greater distinction, according to Arnold Meyer, *Jesu Muttersprache: Das galiläische Aramäisch in seiner Bedeutung fur die Erklärung der Reden Jesu* (Freiburg & Leipzig: J. C. B. Mohr (Paul Siebeck), 1896) 50, and translates the Aramaic term as "mein Gebieter," in English: lord, master, commander. Also G. Dalman, *The Words of Jesus* (Edinburgh: T. & T. Clark, 1902) 335-340, who, on the one hand, claims that John interpreted *rabbouni* correctly as teacher, yet goes on to state thaț רבוּ, a collateral form of רבן was employed in the Targums as "lord" in all its meanings.

subjunctive, πιστεύσητε, and the present subjunctive, πιστεύητε, is the original verb of the purpose clause which terminates the earlier edition of the Gospel.

The addendum of chapter 21

In all likelihood, chapter 21 is an appendix to the Fourth Gospel, and, very probably attached by a later editor.[23] Some effort at continuity has been attempted, but pronounced discontinuity is evident in the movement from chapter 20 into chapter 21. Initially, the opening phrase of chapter 21, "After these things Jesus manifested himself again to the disciples..." attempts to establish continuity with the Easter events of chapter 20. Particularly the adverb, "again", is intended to convey a continuation of the Easter epiphanies, in spite of the intimation of 20:30-31 that the earthly career of Jesus has ended. The episode of 21:1-13 bears the character of being the very first Easter appearance of Jesus to his disciples, but 21:14 states, "This is already the third (time) Jesus was manifested to the disciples after being raised from the dead."[24] If it is the third, it is curious that there is no recognition of the resurrected Jesus, for in 20:25 the disciples had announced to Thomas, "We have seen the Lord!" Here they appear to have no knowledge of Jesus' resurrection from the dead. The form of address Jesus employs in 21:5, παιδία ("Little Children"), is surprising, not only because it occurs nowhere else in the Gospel, but primarily because it is no longer appropriate in view of their empowerment by Jesus with the gift of the holy Spirit for the mission Jesus had entrusted to them in his Farewell Discourse.[25] The encounter between Jesus and the disciples occurs "at the Sea of Tiberius" without any announced transition from Jerusalem to Galilee. The disciples unexpectedly appear as fishers who have resumed their former vocation, the fishing business, without any reference in the

[23] See Bultmann, *John*, 700-706, for his analysis of chapter 21 on style, vocabulary and sentence structure. Linguistic and stylistic differences are also noted by Barrett, *St. John*, 576. Both Bultmann and Barrett offer cogent reasons why chapter 21 should be detached from the previous 20 chapters as the work of another author. Brown, *John* II, 1077-1082, conjectures that the redactor, a Johannine disciple, appended chapter 21 in order to preserve "such important material." Martyn, *History and Theology*, 163, apparently attributes chapter 21 to "the separated Johannine community" from which the final form of the Gospel emerged. Culpepper, *Anatomy*, 96, characterizes chapter 21 as "an epilogue apparently added shortly after the gospel was completed" that "resolves some of the minor conflicts..." Yet his sketch of Peter's role on pp. 120-121 that includes chapter 21 implies that he considers chapter 21 to belong to the narrative world of the Gospel. Fernando F. Segovia, "The Final Farewell of Jesus: A Reading of John 20:30-21:25," *The Fourth Gospel from a Literary Perspective*, ed. by R. Alan Culpepper and Fernando F. Segovia, *Semeia* 53 (1991) 167-190, reads chapter 21 in terms of a synchronic relationship to chapters 1-20 and therefore considers the addendum to be Jesus' "final farewell." His doctoral student, Larry D. George, *Reading the Tapestry: A Literary-Rhetorical Analysis of the Johannine Resurrection Narrative (John 20-21)* (New York: Peter Lang, 2000) 1-6 and 147-152 adds support to this perspective.

[24] The initial tradition of 21:1-14 may be one of the earliest post-Easter traditions originating from the beginnings of the Christian movement. It presupposes that after Jesus' crucifixion the disciples returned to their former vocation of fishing and early in that context experienced the first appearance of the risen Jesus in Galilee. The focus on Peter and his subsequent reinstatement in 21:15-17 corresponds to the tradition that the Apostle Paul cites in 1 Cor 15:5, "He was seen by Cephas."

[25] It is noteworthy that this form of address, παιδία, is used a number of times in 1 John 2:13-18. For the mission that Jesus' entrusts to them in his farewell, see 14:12; 15:26-27; 16:7-11.

preceding 20 chapters that they, or at least some of them, were originally engaged in that trade before they were called to discipleship. Some degree of familiarity with the Synoptic tradition is certainly evident here.[26] Only the Beloved Disciple is able to identify the figure on the shore as the risen Jesus, but *on the basis of the large catch of fish that their net has enclosed.*

In spite of the problematic differences between chapter 21 and the preceding 20 chapters, however, a minimal effort appears to have been made to integrate the repertoire of chapter 21 into the narrative world of the original edition of the Gospel.[27] Three of the named disciples, Simon Peter, Thomas and Nathanael, have played some role in chapters 1-20. Simon Peter is named first. The ambiguity of his last appearance in 20:2-8 requires his reinstatement into apostleship in order to correspond to the stature he had gained throughout the Mediterranean world at the time chapter 21 was appended to the Gospel.[28] Thomas follows, perhaps because the previous chapter ended with the story of his movement from unbelief to confession. Nathanael, who has not appeared in the narrative world since 1:45-49, is identified with Cana of Galilee, although there has been no such reference in the Gospel. Especially significant is the unexpected entrance of "the ones of Zebedee." Of the seven, they are the only disciples who do not inhabit the narrative world of the first edition of the Gospel, either as such or by their individual names, James and John. "Two others of his disciples" are also included but without being named. They could be any of the others, such as "Judas" who is simply referred to as "not the Iscariot" in 14:22, Andrew, or Philip. One of these seven may be the Beloved Disciple, but he is not identified as such until verse 7 when he recognizes the resurrected Jesus and identifies him to Peter as "the Lord." But which of the seven he is remains unclear. "The Twelve," who are named individually in the Synoptic tradition and who are almost always at the forefront among Jesus' disciples, are virtually inconsequential in the narrative world of the

---

[26] Frans Neirynck, "John 21," *NTS* 36/3 (1990) 321-336, interprets John 21 as an expansion of Lk 5:1-11 and concludes that both are Petrine stories.

[27] Larry D. George, *Reading the Tapestry*, has made a valiant effort to establish the coherent unity of these two chapters. For example, he notes the similarity between 21:20 and 20:14; both texts include the actions of "turning around" and "seeing." Although the verb ἐπιστρέφειν is used in the aorist passive in both cases, there is no correspondence between the verbs for seeing. Chapter 21is not an epilogue of the original author of the Gospel, but an addendum by a later editor. As such it conveys another objective and adds little to the resurrection stories of chapter 20 and the motives behind them.

[28] See *Peter in the New Testament*, ed. by Raymond E. Brown, Karl P. Donfried, & John Reumann, (Minneapolis: Augsburg and New York: Paulist Press, 1973) 129-147, for an examination of Peter's character and role in the addendum of John 21 as well as in the previous 20 chapters. There is not much that is insightful here because too much effort has been devoted to comparing Peter in the Fourth Gospel with Peter in the Synoptic tradition. Kevin Quast, *Peter and the Beloved Disciple: Figures for a Community in Crisis* (Sheffield: Sheffield Academic Press, 1989) 135, along with others, considers the focus of chapter 21 to be "the theme of discipleship." "Peter," he concludes on pp. 148-149, "is portrayed in a positive light" and "appears on both the literal and symbolic level as the leader of the disciples, and this is supported by the Beloved Disciple in the boat." In his judgment chapter 21 presents no reversal of the "general picture of Peter" that is encountered in chapters 1-20.

Fourth Gospel. They are not acknowledged in chapter 21, only in two different contexts in 6:67-71 and 20:24.

Certain aspects of this repertoire indicate a familiarity with the Synoptic Gospels or at least the traditions of Luke 5:1-11 and 24:36-43. The inclusion of "the sons of Zebedee" in 21:2 and the association of the disciples with their former vocation of fishing appear to have been drawn from the Synoptic tradition. It is tantalizing, therefore, to conjecture that the author of chapter 21 deliberately intended to weave some aspects of that material into his appendix in order to overcome any resistance that this divergent Gospel might encounter in the Christian community of the Mediterranean world.

According to 21:1-13, seven disciples had been fishing all night without success. In the early morning they see the risen Jesus standing on the beach, but they do not recognize him. He addresses them as "Little Children " and asks, "You don't have anything to eat, do you?" When they reply that they have caught nothing, he directs them to cast their net on the right side of the boat. Their catch, so large that they are unable to draw the net into their boat, instantaneously evokes the recognition of Jesus by the Beloved Disciple, *who at this point, on the basis of Luke 5:1-11, must be identified as John, the son of Zebedee.* As soon as he exclaims, "It is the Lord," Simon Peter, without a moment's delay, ties on his ἐπενδύτην (outer garment) to cover his nakedness or at least his undergarment, flings himself into the sea and swims ashore. The other disciples follow in the boat dragging the net of fish behind them. In spite of the large number of fish, the net remains untorn, signifying perhaps "the indestructible unity of the Church."[29]

Disembarking onto the shore they discover that Jesus has already prepared a meal of fish and bread for them on a charcoal fire. Very likely his breakfast is a eucharistic celebration replicating the feeding of the multitudes in 6:1-13 in which he multiplied five loaves of barley bread and two small fish. But here there is only one fish, indeed a small one, an ὀψάριον.[30] More fish, therefore are needed for the meal, and Jesus orders them to bring some of the fish they have caught. Simon Peter, who must have been the first to greet the risen Jesus by leaping into the sea and swimming ashore, fulfills his command by going up (ἀνέβη) onto the boat and hauling the net ashore. In chapter 21 this is the first step towards his rehabilitation.

The number of fish netted by the disciples is specified to be 153. Because numbers were symbolically representative of different kinds of realities and values in ancient tradition, as all four Gospels testify, far-ranging attempts have been made to determine the significance of this unusual figure. Cyril of Alexandria offers a threefold division of the number: "the hundred represents the fullness of the Gentiles, the fifty the remnant of Israel, and the three the Holy Trinity."[31] Augustine's interpretation is equally whimsical. The number 153 is the sum of all

[29] Bultmann, *John*, 708-709; German, 548-549.

[30] The diminutive of ὄψον, namely ὀψάριον, is used here, and it strikingly corresponds to an earlier use in 6:11.

numbers up to seventeen, "and this signifies the total number of believers saved by the divine grace working through the medium of the law (ten) and Spirit (seven)."[32] Jerome's view, expressed in his commentary on Ezekiel 47:6-12, is the one most frequently cited. The number corresponds to the reckoning of Greek zoologists that there are 153 different kinds of fish and therefore symbolizes the different kinds of peoples who will be drawn into the net of the reign of God.[33] But there is no reference to such a calculation by Greek zoologists. Oppian of Cilicia (ca. C.E. 180) lists 157 species of fish in his *Halieutica*, and Pliny the Elder counts 104.[34] Moreover, prior to the subsequent interpreters of John 21:11, there is no record of any kind of symbolism related to the number 153, neither in the Hebrew Scriptures nor in Hellenistic literature. Yet because some kind of significance must be attached to the number, most commentators generally concede that the "multitude of fish represents the multitude of believers who are won through the apostolic preaching ..." or that the number "symbolizes the breadth or even the universality of the Christian mission."[35] It is in this context that the number of disciples involved in this Easter scene, that is seven, may also bear a symbolic significance. The seven may represent eschatological completeness. For by the inclusion of all kinds of people, Gentiles as well as Jews, the fullness of God's reign is intimated.

When all is ready, Jesus invites his disciples to join him for breakfast. In view of their Easter evening experience of 20:19-23, it is surprising that they are troubled about his identity. They know it is the Lord, and yet they are uncertain who he really is. Nevertheless, they do not presume to question him about his identity. Their recognition of him in the present must be established by specific historical events and experiences shared in the past. The meal to which he invites them will revive those memories and enable them to acknowledge who he is in spite of his transformed appearance.[36] As the host, therefore, he proceeds in a

---

[31] M.F. Wiles, *Spiritual Gospel:The Interpretation of the Fourth Gospel in the Early Church* (Cambridge: at the University Press, 1960) 64.

[32] *Ibid.*

[33] Earlier interpretations are surveyed by H. Kruse, "Magni Pisces Centum Quinquaginta Tres," *VD* 38 (1960) 129-148. See Raymond E. Brown, *John* II, 1074-1076, for this as well as other speculations on the significance of the number. Brown himself thinks "... the origin of the number probably lies in the direction of an emphasis on the authentic eyewitness character of what has been recorded..." Joseph A. Romeo, "Gematria and John 21:11 – The Children of God," *JBL* 97/2 (1978) 263-264. See Schnackenburg, *St. John* III, 357; Bultmann, *John*, 709, n.2; German, 549, n. 1; E. Hoskyns and F.N. Davey, *The Fourth Gospel* (London: Faber & Faber, 2nd ed. 1947) 555-556, for other interpretations of the number 153. Also Craig R. Koester. *Symbolism in the Fourth Gospel: Meaning, Mystery, Community* (Minneapolis: Fortress Press, 1995) 264-268

[34] Brown, *John* II, 1074. Also Pliny the Elder, *Natural History*. *Loeb Classical Library* III (Cambridge: Harvard University Press, 1983) Book IX, 16.

[35] Bultmann, *John*, 709; Brown, *John* II, 1075.

[36] See Richard R. Niebuhr, *Resurrection and Historical Reason: A Study of Theological Method* (New York: Charles Scribner's Sons, 1957) 172-176, who notes the "historical signs" that the Gospels attribute to the risen Jesus in order "to relate the past to the present of the recognizer as his past, but it must also be brought into relationship of contemporaneity to the recognizer, and that he cannot do unaided."

eucharistic mode, reminiscent of his earlier feeding of the multitudes in 6:11, to distribute to them the bread and the fish. Their response is not noted, but perhaps the implied readers of the second edition will have reached a sense of certainty about the continuity between Jesus of Nazareth and the risen Lord, if not in this episode at least on the basis of 20:24-29.

It is noteworthy that Peter's reinstatement takes place after this Easter celebration of the Eucharist. In spite of his threefold denial of Jesus and the absence of any Easter faith, he is not excluded from the fellowship of the meal. Jesus initiates his rehabilitation by addressing him by his original name and patrilineage, as he had done in 1:42, "Simon, son of John," and proceeding to ask, "Do you love me more than these?" His question employs the verb that he has consistently used in his Farewell Discourse, ἀγαπᾶν (to love). But its direction appears to be determined by the Synoptic tradition of Peter's boast in Mark 14:29 and Matt 26:33, "Even if all are scandalized, but not I." No such egotistical superiority had been expressed by Peter in John 13:27. In his response to Jesus' question, he avoids making any judgment about his fellow disciples. He acknowledges Jesus as "Lord," but instead of attempting to convince him of his love by an impassioned avowal, he humbly submits the truth of it to Jesus' own discernment: "*You know* that I have affection for you." Although the two verbs, φιλεῖν and ἀγαπᾶν are used interchangeably throughout the Gospel, they appear to differ in quality and degree in this appendix of chapter 21.[37] They are not "a meaningless stylistic peculiarity."[38] In this context ἀγαπᾶν (to love), the verb that Jesus employs, is the kind of love that Jesus himself manifests in his relationship to "the Father" by observing the "Father's commandments" and therefore the kind of love he charges his disciples to abide in by obeying his commandments.[39] Peter has not observed Jesus' commandments and therefore he has not remained in Jesus' love. In view of all that has happened, he appears to be aware that words alone will have no legitimacy. In his self-effacement, he can only suppose that the truth of his love that Jesus can ascertain is a caring attachment that has expressed itself in his earlier behavior of swimming ashore to be the first to greet Jesus and his fulfillment of Jesus' command to bring some of the fish that had been caught by dragging the net ashore.

In view of his response Jesus charges Peter, "Keep on tending my lambs." The word ἀρνία may designate sheep of any age, as Frederick W. Danker's revision of the third edition of Walter Bauer's lexicon of the New Testament indicates.[40] But Jesus' subsequent uses of πρόβατα (sheep), the word that he had consistently

---

[37] Noteworthy is that ἀγαπᾶν is the only verb used to express love in 1 John, never φιλεῖν. Is it possible that the addendum of chapter 21 was composed and added to the Fourth Gospel in the same community that produced 1 John?

[38] Brown, *John*, 1102-1103. reviews the scholarly discussion on the variation between these two verbs, but chooses to identify himself with ancient and modern scholars who find no clear distinction of meaning between them. Also Schnackenburg, *St. John*, 362-363. Bultmann, *John*, 711, n.5.

[39] See 15:9-10

employed in 10:1-16, suggest that there must be a distinction between ἀρνία and πρόβατα. "Lambs," therefore, is a valid rendering of ἀρνία and may symbolically refer to new Christians or a young age group, perhaps analogous to the "little children," the τεκνία and παιδία of 1 John 2-3. Accordingly, Simon is entrusted with the feeding and safe-keeping of those represented by Jesus' lambs.

Jesus addresses Peter a second time with the same question using the same verb, ἀγαπᾶν, "Simon, son of John, do you love me?" The redundant phrase, πάλιν δεύτερον (again a second time) may in fact be intended to remind the reader that Jesus is not only asking the same question again.[41] That would be the function of πάλιν. But he is also accentuating his employment of the verb ἀγαπᾶν in view of Simon's use of φιλεῖν.[42] Nevertheless, Simon repeats his earlier reply, determined to persist in his use of the same verb, φιλεῖν, "Yes, Lord, you know that I have affection for you." In reply Jesus gives him a second charge, "Keep on shepherding my sheep." If Jesus' characterization of the Good Shepherd in 10:1-16 is applicable to this commission, Simon is being authorized to serve as Jesus' surrogate to lead the sheep out into the green pastures of life and, if necessary, even to lay down his life for them.

When Jesus asks the same question a third time, he appropriates the verb φιλεῖν which Simon has used and relinquishes his own twice-employed ἀγαπᾶν: "Simon, son of John, do you have affection for me?" Evidently he is willing and ready to accept Simon's humble self-limitation of his former self-assurance. Painfully reminded of his three-fold denial of Jesus, Simon, in sorrowful contrition, not only continues to acknowledge Jesus' lordship but also attributes to him at the very least a thorough familiarity with both his inner and outer life, "You know all things. You know that I have affection for you."[43] In his recognition of Jesus' omniscience, Simon uses two different verbs. The first, οἶδα, generally expresses cognitive knowledge in the narrative world of the Fourth Gospel; it is truth oriented to praxis that belongs to the eschatological reality of God's reign.[44] The second verb, γινωσκεῖν, refers to personal knowledge that is acquired through an

---

[40] *A Greek-English Lexicon of the New Testament and Other Early Christian Literature*, revised and edited by Frederick W. Danker, (Chicago: University of Chicago Press, 2000) 133.

[41] The same redundancy occurs in 4:54, and with the same intention. The reader is to take into account that this is not only the second sign of Jesus' ministry, but it is the second sign that takes place "after two days" or on the third day in Cana of Galilee. Both signs, 2:1-11 and 4:46-54, constitute a trajectory of "seeing and believing" and "believing in order to see" that runs through the entire Gospel. See chapter 6.

[42] Contrary to Bultmann, *John*, 711, n. 5, who says, "The exchange of ἀγαπᾶν and φιλεῖν cannot be significant, for in the third question Jesus also uses φιλεῖν instead of ἀγαπᾶν; and Brown, *John* II, 1106, who also considers the differentiation of the verbs unimportant.

[43] It is noteworthy that Simon Peter, who is consistently designated by that double name throughout chapters 1-20, is referred to as "Peter" after his three-fold reinstatement, a feature that corresponds to the single name that he bears after his renaming in the Synoptic tradition.

[44] This is the kind of knowledge that the disciples acknowledge in 16:30, as Jesus reaches the end of his Farewell Discourse. The difference between οἶδα and γινώσκειν is perhaps best exemplified in 13:7.

"I – You" relationship.[45] Any words by which Simon might endeavor to establish his devotion to Jesus are ultimately futile and worthless. It is only Jesus' knowledge of Simon Peter that will authenticate the quality and the degree of the love he bears toward Jesus. This third refusal to utilize any kind of avowal to certify his loyalty to Jesus, accompanied by a sensitive qualification of the feelings he has, decisively establishes his credibility.

Jesus' final charge, "Keep on tending my sheep!" will involve Simon in caring for the needs of the sheep, so that "they might have life and have it abundantly."[46] His pastoral authority as the surrogate of the Good Shepherd, therefore, will include practical service. For the sheep are not his to serve him. They belong to Jesus.[47]

Jesus concludes his rehabilitation of Simon by reminding him of the prediction he made at the beginning of his Farewell Discourse in 13:36, "Where I am going you cannot follow me now, but you will follow me later." In the form of a double asseveration, so characteristic of his rhetoric in chapters 1-20, Jesus adds to this earlier prolepsis, "Amen, amen I say to you, when you were younger, you girded yourself and went about where you wanted. But when you are grown old, you will stretch out your hands, and another will gird you and carry you where you do not want [to go]." Both texts, 13:36 and 21:18, hint at Simon Peter's death by crucifixion.[48] For the benefit of the reader, the narrator of chapter 21 inserts an intrusive clarification, "He said this signifying by what death he will glorify God." Long before the Fourth Gospel was written and chapter 21 was appended, Simon Peter had been put to death by crucifixion. Like the Good Shepherd himself, he had laid down his life for the sheep. Jesus' final summons, therefore, proves to be ironic: "Keep on following me!" For Simon's rehabilitation not only resulted in the fulfillment of his commission to lead, to exercise authority on Jesus' behalf, to evangelize Jews and Gentiles, to tend the lambs and to shepherd the sheep. He also followed Jesus into crucifixion and death.

In the addendum of chapter 21 Simon is restored to a more complete ministry than that which he was originally called to fulfill in the narrative world of the Fourth Gospel. Regardless of whether 21:1-11 and 21:15-17 may originally have been independent traditions, their juxtaposition accentuates the authority and the leadership that tradition believed Jesus had conferred on him. He had drawn the net ashore, unbroken, in obedience to Jesus' command, and in his rehabilitation he

[45] See 1:10, 49; 2:24-25; 10:15; 14:7, 9; 17:25.

[46] 10:10.

[47] Brown, Donfried, Reumann, *Peter in the New Testament*, 143-144. The question is raised whether these three commands that Jesus directs at Peter are intended to establish his rehabilitation, or whether they reflect Peter's stature as a symbol of pastoral authority in the Christian world at that time? In view of the attachment of chapter 21 by the church at Ephesus in order to prepare the Fourth Gospel for a wide spread Christian audience, both possibilities may be valid.

[48] See Barrett, *St. John*, 585, who cites Barnabas (12:4), Justin (1 *Apol* 35), Irenaeus (*Demonstration of the Apostolic Preaching*, 79), and Cyprian (*Test.* II, 20) all of whom interpreted Jesus' words, "You will stretch out your hands..." as a foreshadowing of Simon Peter's crucifixion.

had been appointed to serve as the surrogate of the Good Shepherd. The responsibilities of his reinstatement extend beyond the expectations Jesus had enunciated in his Farewell Discourse: "I appointed you that you go forth and bear fruit and that your fruit remains" (15:16). His disciples would continue the ministry that he, as the incarnate Logos, inaugurated to establish God's rule on earth. But no explicit commission, analogous to Matt 28:19-20, Luke 24: 46-49 and Acts 1:8, has been entrusted to them or to Simon Peter. Because they "believed into him," they would do greater works than those he had performed (14:12); and through the activity of the Paraclete, "the Spirit of truth," which they would receive (20:22), the world would be convicted of its sin and injustice (16:7-11).

Simon Peter and the Beloved Disciple in John 1-20

Peter's reinstatement to serve as Jesus' surrogate to tend the lambs and shepherd the sheep stands in contrast to the perplexing role that he plays in the earlier chapters of the Fourth Gospel. However his function as a character within this narrative world may be evaluated, the historical priority that is attributed to him in the Synoptics, the Acts of the Apostles, 1 Corinthians 15:5, and Galatians 1:18 is displaced by the Beloved Disciple. Unlike the Synoptic tradition, he is not the first to be called to discipleship; he is not the first to confess Jesus as the Messiah. He is led into discipleship through the instrumentality of his brother Andrew, who has left John to follow Jesus. However, in view of the narrator's identification of Andrew as ὁ ἀδελφὸς Σίμωνος Πέτρου (the brother of Simon Peter) even before Simon Peter is introduced, it must be assumed that the implied readers are already familiar with him. Yet how much of his life and career as a disciple of Jesus is known is indeterminable. Significantly, it is Andrew who leads his brother to Jesus on the basis of his christological witness, "We have found the Messiah."[49] Simon is renamed Peter, but only after the narrator has stated that Jesus *looked intently* (ἐμβλέψας) at him. It is the same verb that was used to indicate the transparency of seeing with which John the Witness looked at Jesus in 1:36. The preposition ἐμ (in) that has been prefixed to the compound verb ἐμβλέπειν reinforces the distinctive sense of perspicuity, of perceiving beyond sense perception, that the verb βλέπειν bears.[50] What does the reader surmise Jesus sees as he scrutinizes Simon? He is the only disciple who receives a new name from Jesus, Cephas, or in translation Πέτρος (Rock), and that in and of itself should heighten the expectation of an unusual role or capacity that he will manifest in the course of the story.[51] Will Simon, renamed Πέτρος, manifest a rock-like

[49] But at this point it should be noted that Andrew's identification of Jesus as the Messiah is based on John's witness to Jesus as "the Lamb of God." There is no historical connection between the two titles, but the Gospel will eventually establish a singular relationship between them.

[50] See chapter 5.

[51] Quast, *Peter and the Beloved Disciple*, 39, recognizes that "nearly every interpretation of this naming involves a certain amount of 'grasping at straws' because the evangelist does not provide any

discipleship? What will be the reaction of the implied readers when the narrator continues to refer to him as "Simon Peter," and not "Peter" throughout the Gospel?[52] And to what extent will the reader's expectation, based on his new name, be fulfilled?

In his first exposure as a disciple he serves as the spokesperson of the Twelve in his declaration of loyalty, as he acknowledges Jesus to be "the holy one of God' (6:68-69).[53] It is the only confession of faith that he makes, and it is difficult to determine its significance.[54] There are virtually no parallels of this epithet in the Septuagint translation of the Old Testament, and those that do occur offer no insight into its precise meaning.[55] On the one hand, it is surprising that Peter does not acknowledge Jesus by the very title that his brother Andrew had used in his own confession, that is, "Messiah." On the other hand, in view of all that Peter has experienced up to this point, specifically Jesus' mighty works of feeding the multitudes and walking on the Sea of Galilee and subsequently his self-identification as the Son of the Human Being who descended from heaven as "the living Bread," his confession might be a recognition of Jesus as "the holy one" who exercises God's eschatological rule on behalf of those who in Dan 7:27 are designated "the holy ones of the Most High."[56] Whatever Peter's confession may

---

leads." But he does not maintain this openness to the gradual portrayal of Simon Peter's character in the Gospel. In spite of the text's ambiguity, he assumes that the naming of Peter has "primarily a christological character and it serves a secondary purpose of high-lighting the 'rock-like' character or role that Jesus intended Peter to assume in the Christian community" (p. 41).

[52] Indeed, twelve times! In addition to 1:40; 6:8, 68; 13:6, 9, 24, 36; 18:10, 15, 25; 20:2, 6. Quast, *Peter and the Beloved Disciple*, 72, regards this "as no more than a Johannine stylistic characteristic…" See also p. 30.

[53] See Mark 1:24 and Acts 3:14. It is important to note that Peter, in his christological confession of Jesus (6:69), does not identify him as the Christ or the Messiah or the Son of David. The manuscript tradition may insert "Christ" before "the holy one of God" or substitute "the Son of God" in place of "the holy one of God." These are scribal interpolations drawn from the Synoptics. Accordingly, Peter's confession should not be interpreted in relation to the Synoptics, specifically Mark 8:29-31, as Ludger Schenke does, "Das johanneische Schisma und die 'Zwölf' (Johannes 6.61-70)," *NTS* 38/1 (1992) 120-121. Peter's confession in 6:69 is not being used to validate the confession of a Johannine group. There is no intimation within the Gospel that the schismatic relationship between two different Christian communities, represented by Peter and the Beloved Disciple, is being clarified.

[54] The use of the title by a demonized individual in Mark 1:24 has no significance for the narrative world of the Fourth Gospel. Schnackenburg, *St. John* I, 307, contends that 'the Holy One of God' is one of those titles that designates Jesus' position. 'The Messiah' or 'the Son of man' would do just as well. A closer examination of these latter titles, however, does not support his simplistic conclusion. In *John* II, 77, Schnackenburg considers Simon Peter's confession to be an appropriate response to Jesus' revelatory formula. He counters Jesus' use of ἐγὼ εἰμί **(I AM)** with σὺ εἶ (you are). Quast, *Peter and the Beloved Disciple*, 51, relies on a comparison between the Fourth Gospel and the Synoptics to conclude: "Peter comes out in even a more positive position … in that he is not explicitly identified with Satan as he is in the Synoptics."

[55] Aaron is designated "the Lord's holy one" in LXX Psa 105 (106):17. In Codex B of the LXX Jud 13:7 Samson, at his annunciation, is called "God's holy one" and in 16:17 he refers to himself as "God's holy one."

[56] According to Dan 7:13-27, a υἱὸς ἀνθρώπου (son of a human being), as the representative of οἱ ἅγιοι (the holy ones), was given the "kingdom" or rule of God.

signify, at face value it appears to be an inadequate acknowledgment of Jesus' identity in view of all that he has done and said.

At the foot-washing scene of 13:6-11, Simon Peter represents the kind of discipleship that is shocked by the reversal of the traditional values of honor/shame culture.[57] A host does not stoop to the slavish washing of his guests' feet! In spite of Jesus' promise that eventually he will comprehend the significance of this act, even if he is unable to grasp it at that moment, Peter seems determined to maintain his subordinate status, "Lord, by no means shall you ever wash my feet!" When Jesus asserts that washing is necessary for a continued relationship, he misconstrues and pleads for a complete head-to-toe bath. He does not appear to understand that guests, like himself, who have bathed in anticipation of participating in a dinner, need only to have their feet washed upon entering the household of the host. Nevertheless, at the very least he may have fulfilled a literary function by serving as a foil for the implied readers who should be able to grasp the symbolic significance of this rite of washing, but, who, like Peter, may be overcome by the subversive reversal of roles that Jesus has constituted (13:12-15).[58]

When Jesus announces his imminent betrayal by a disciple at the meal that follows, Peter takes the initiative to inquire about his identity. But for some reason he cannot interrogate Jesus directly, and he is forced to resort to an intermediary. He signals the disciple who is reclining in Jesus' bosom, the Beloved Disciple, to inquire who it is that Jesus is referring to.[59] Nothing up to this point in the narration appears to justify Peter's apparent subordination to someone who appears to have entered into the narrative world for the very first time. It is entirely unexpected! Yet here, if not earlier, it seems that the figure of Simon Peter is being diminished, and his role as spokesperson of the disciples is being eclipsed by the Beloved Disciple.[60] Of all the disciples who are present at this meal, only "the one whom Jesus loved" is privileged to recline in his bosom. If Simon Peter had

[57] John K. Chance, "The Anthropology of Honor and Shame: Culture, Values and Practice, *Honor and Shame in the World of the Bible. Semeia* 68, ed. by Victor H. Matthews and Don C. Benjuamin (Atlanta: Scholars Press, 1994). Jerome H. Neyrey, *Honor and Shame in the Gospel of Matthew* (Louisville: Westminster John Knox Press, 1998) chapter 1, "Honor and Shame in Cultural Perspective." Halvor Moxnes, "Honor and Shame," *The Social Sciences and New Testament Interpretation*, ed. by Richard Rohrbaugh (Peabody, Mass.: Hendrickson, 1996) 19-40; Bruce J. Malina, *The New Testament World: Insights from Cultural Anthropology* (Atlanta: John Knox Press, 1981) 44-45; Douglas L. Cairns, *Aidos. The Psychology and Ethics of Honour and Shame in Ancient Greek Literature* (Oxford: Clarendon Press, 1993).

[58] There is no indication here that Simon Peter is serving as the spokesperson for his fellow disciples, as Quast claims, *Peter and the Beloved Disciple*, 62-63. That might be true, if he were the first disciple to be approached by Jesus for the washing of his feet.

[59] According to Danker's 3rd edition of Bauer's *A Greek-English Lexicon of the New Testament*, 557, "'being in someone's bosom' denotes the closest association." The reading adopted in the 26th and 27th editions of Nestle-Aland's *NTG*, "to inquire who it might be of whom he is speaking" is supported by P^{66} and a great diversity of textual witnesses, but it contains the only occurrence of the optative mood in the Fourth Gospel. The simpler reading, "and he says to him, 'Tell who it is about whom he is speaking," includes Simon Peter both nodding and speaking to the Beloved Disciple. Of the two, the more difficult reading is preferable.

any priority at all, it is being replaced by the stature of the Beloved Disciple. Should this be construed as an anti-Petrine bias? It would seem that he is deliberately being assigned a secondary role among the disciples of Jesus.[61]

But who is this Beloved Disciple who seems to appear for the first time in the narrative world of the Gospel? And what is the basis of the preeminence that he enjoys? It has been claimed by many that he appears for the first time in 13:23, but, if the literary principle of "consistency building" is valid for the Fourth Gospel, his identity has already been signaled to the reader in the 11:1-44. He is none other than Lazarus![62] For the formula that is used of the Beloved Disciple in 13: 23, ὃν ἠγάπα ὁ 'Ιησοῦς (the one whom Jesus loved), corresponds to the

[60] It is particularly this subordination to the Beloved Disciple that suggests an anti-Petrine perspective within the Fourth Gospel. See A. H. Maynard, "The Role of Peter in the Fourth Gospel," *NTS* 30/4 (1984) 535-537. Also Eric L. Titus, *The Message of the Fourth Gospel* (New York: Abingdon, 1957) 220; G. F. Snyder, "John 13:16 and the Anti-Petronism of the Johannine Tradition," *BR* 16 (1971) 5-15; and P. J. Hartin, "The Role of Peter in the Fourth Gospel," *Neot* 24 (1) 1990, 51, 58-59.

[61] Contrary to Oscar Cullmann, *Peter: Disciple, Apostle, Martyr* (Philadelphia: Westminster, 1953) 27; Brown, *John* II, 1006-1007; Brown, Donfried, and Reumann, *Peter*, 138-139; and R. Alan Culpepper, *The Gospel and Letters of John* (Nashville: Abingdon Press, 1998) 249, who contend that the preeminence of Peter is recognized in the Fourth Gospel.

[62] On "consistency building," see Wolfgang Iser, *The Act of Reading*, 16-18, 118-119, 122-130, 185. On the basis of "consistency building" Lazarus is the only viable identification of the Beloved Disciple; but this applies only to the first edition of the Gospel, chapters 1-20. Floyd V. Filson, "Who Was The Beloved Disciple?" *JBL* 68 (1949) 83-88, was an early advocate of Lazarus as the Beloved Disciple. See also Filson, "The Gospel of Life: A Study of the Gospel of John," *Current Issues in New Testament Interpretation: Essays in Honor of Otto A. Piper*, ed. by William Klassen and Graydon F. Snyder (New York: Harper & Brothers, 1962) 119-123. Brown, *Community*, 31-34, on the basis of 1:35-39 contends that the Beloved Disciple was a disciple of John who subsequently followed Jesus. R. Alan Culpepper, *John, the Son of Zebedee: The Life of a Legend* (Columbia: University of South Carolina Press, 1994) 84, similarly, after an analysis of all the relevant texts, concludes that he was an historical figure "who has been given an idealized role in the crucial scenes of the farewell discourse, trial, death, and resurrection of Jesus." For an exhaustive research of the issue, see James H. Charlesworth, *The Beloved Disciple: Whose Witness Validates the Gospel of John?* (Valley Forge, PA: Trinity Press International, 1995) 185-192 and 288-291, where he lists his reasons why Lazarus cannot be the Beloved Disciple. Charlesworth, pp. 127-224, reviews all the scholarly opinions on the identity of the Beloved Disciple, including J. Kreyenbühl, "Der Verfasser des Evangeliums," *Das Evangelium der Wahrheit: Neue Lösung der johanneischen Frage* (Berlin: C. A. Schwetschke und Sohn, 1900) 151-162; K. Kirkendraht, "Ist Lazarus der Lieblingsjünger im vierten Evangelium?" *STZ* 31 (1914) 49-54; B. G. Griffith, "The Disciple Whom Jesus loved," *ExpT* 32 (1920-1921) 379-381; A. E. Garvie, *The Beloved Disciple: Studies of the Fourth Gospel* (London: Hodder & Stoughton, 1922) 231ff.; Vernard Eller, *The Beloved Disciple: His Name, His Story, His Thought* (Grand Rapids: Eerdmans, 1987) 53, "Either the Beloved Disciple is Lazarus – or else we don't have a ghost of a clue as to who is." See also Alv Kragerud, *Der Lieblingsjünger im Johannesevangelium* (Oslo: Osloer Universitätsverlag, 1959) 45, 141, who acknowledges that identifying Lazarus as "the one whom Jesus loved" has a certain validity, but prefers to differentiate the Beloved Disciple as the ideal disciple of Jesus because Lazarus is not identified as a "disciple" in chapter 11. Finally, J. A. Grassi, *The Secret Identity of the Beloved Disciple* (New York: Paulist Press, 1992) 115-116, maintains that the Beloved Disciple was an historical person, adopted and especially loved by Jesus but whose identity remained a secret. Sandra M. Schneiders, " 'Because of the Women's Testimony ...' Reexamining the Issue of Authorship in the Fourth Gospel," *NTS* 44/4 (1998) 520-522, on the basis of her reading of 19:25-26 concludes that the Beloved Disciple is "a textual paradigm realized in the plurality of textual figures who are drawn from real historical characters in the life of Jesus and/or the community." It is above all Mary Magdalene who serves as an eye-witness and who more than any other disciple embodied the role of the Beloved Disciple in the Gospel.

characterization of Lazarus, ὃν φιλεῖ (the one whom you love) that his sisters employed in the message they sent to Jesus while he was sojourning in Transjordan. Jesus' love for Lazarus is accentuated by the narrator's intrusive remark in 11:5, "Now Jesus *loved* (ἠγάπα) Martha and her sister and Lazarus." And it is intensified by the observation of the by-standers who, when they see Jesus weeping, exclaim, "See how he was loving (ἐφίλει) him."[63]

As the narrative moves towards Jesus' passion, the dissimilarity between Simon Peter and the Beloved Disciple becomes more pronounced.[64] Peter's swordsmanship at the moment of Jesus' arrest in the garden may be construed as his attempt to prove that he is willing to lay down his life for Jesus, an avowal he made in 13:37. But in spite of all that Jesus had said in his farewell speech about laying down his life for his friends in obedience to his Father's will, Peter's discipleship manifests itself in meeting violence with violence. Obviously he has failed to understand Jesus' last will and testament. His rebuke, "The cup which the Father has given me, shall I by no means drink it?" conveys his determination to fulfill his divine commission, regardless of any effort by Peter to prevent it.

Two disciples follow Jesus as he is led to an interrogation that will be conducted by Annas, "the father-in-law of Caiaphas, who was High Priest in that year" (18:13). It is natural that Simon Peter should be one of them. He had vowed to offer his own life on Jesus' behalf. The second is unnamed. The narrator refers to him simply as "another disciple who was known to the High Priest and (who) had accompanied Jesus into the High Priest's courtyard." Who this is and whether he should be identified as the Beloved Disciple remains controversial.[65] Ancient scribes, however, appear to have been convinced that the two were one and the same individual. To ensure that identification they interpolated the definite article "the" before the word "other" in 18:15 so that the phrase would correspond to its later occurrence in 20:2 where Peter and the Beloved Disciple are in focus again. Although their insertion of the definite article appears to be a later addition, their supposition seems to be quite correct. The "other disciple" should be identified as the Beloved Disciple.[66] That will be confirmed in 20:2-3, when the narrator

---

[63] 11:35-36.

[64] Arthur J. Droge, "The Status of Peter in the Fourth Gospel: A Note on John 18:10-11," *JBL* 109/2 (1990) 307-311, offers a perceptive analysis of the Fourth Gospel's negative portrayal of Peter's discipleship. In his discussion of the question why only the Fourth Gospel identifies Simon Peter as the one who drew his sword and cut off the ear of the high priest's slave (p. 311), he concludes that "Peter's action reveals that he is not a 'subject' of Jesus' heavenly kingdom, and thereby confirms the truth of his 'denial' of being Jesus' disciple. Peter's denial is really his *confession*." Droge's italics.

[65] See Charlesworth, *The Beloved Disciple*, 336-359, who, after a lengthy survey, concludes that the "other disciple" must be Judas. Bultmann, *John*, 645, n. 4, contends that his identity cannot "be divined." So also Lindars, *John*, 548. J. J. Gunther, "The Relation of the Beloved to the Twelve," *TZ* 37 (1981) 147, characterizes this "other disciple" as "stupid enough to bring Peter into mortal physical and spiritual danger, and disloyal enough to associate with the forces of the unbelieving world at the moment of conflict;" and therefore concludes that he cannot be the Beloved Disciple.

[66] Also Barrett, *St. John*, 525, is inclined towards identifying him as "the one whom Jesus loved." See Quast's discussion, *Peter and the Beloved Disciple*, 78-82, who finally concludes that the "other

employs the same phrase twice, but with the definite article, ὁ ἄλλος μαθητής in order to certify the identification of the Beloved Disciple with "the other disciple".

Who is actually occupying the office of the High Priest is also problematic. Caiaphas is named as the High Priest in 11:49 and 18:13, but in 18:15 the title is ascribed to Annas, "That disciple was known to the High Priest as he entered with Jesus into the courtyard of the High Priest." Although a confusion of the two is possible, the ambiguity of usage may not be so inexcusable as it seems, for the same inconsistency appears in Josephus' *Antiquities of the Jews*.[67] Caiaphas is in fact the High Priest, but Annas, his father-in-law, was called High Priest long after his deposition.[68]

But in what sense is this disciple "known to the High Priest"? What are the implied readers to project in order to fill this gap? The adjective, γνωστός (known, familiar), employed only twice in the Fourth Gospel (18:15-16), may convey a sense of a familiar friend or relative, as its use in the Septuagint texts of 2 Kgs 10:11, Neh 5:10, and Psa 31:11 recommends.[69] But it may also denote someone or something known on the basis of reputation, as the Septuagint texts of Ex 33:16, Isa 19:21, 1 Esd 2:18, 6:8 and Sir 21:7 indicate.[70] If the "other disciple" is indeed the Beloved Disciple, there is no possibility of identifying him with John, the son of Zebedee, for there is no such character in the narrative world of the Gospel. Moreover, it is very unlikely that a Galilean fisherman would be known to the High Priest.[71] If the "other disciple" is "the one whom Jesus loved," the only valid possibility would be the one who reclined in Jesus' bosom at the meal which Jesus shared with his disciples, and he, on the basis of "consistency building" would be Lazarus.

Accordingly then, he, Lazarus, would be known to the high priest by his reputation, namely as the one whom Jesus raised from the dead. But if, as the narrator observed earlier, the chief priests were also planning to put Lazarus to death, is it likely that the "other disciple," the Beloved Disciple, would be permitted to enter the high priest's court? As improbable as it may seem, such a

---

disciple" must be the Beloved Disciple.

[67] Josephus, *Ant.* 18. 34; cited by C.H. Dodd, *Historical Traditions in the Fourth Gospel* (Cambridge: at the University Press, 1963) 94, n. 2.

[68] *Ibid.*

[69] Barrett, *St. John*, 525-526, is inclined to this view and adds a parallel from Homer's *Iliad* xv, 350. Dodd, *Historical Tradition*, 87, notes 1-2, poses parallels from Lk 2:44 and other texts and is inclined towards "relatives" and has no difficulty imagining that "a person of priestly family among the disciples of Jesus." Also Brown, *John* II, 828, who, conjectures that the author may have obtained this detailed knowledge of the high priest's household from the "other disciple" who may be the Beloved Disciple.

[70] Adolf Schlatter, *Der Evangelist Johannes* (Stuttgart: Calwer Verlag, 3rd ed. 1960) 332, maintains that γνωστός may imply nothing more than someone who is not unknown.

[71] Yet on the basis of this particular text, later generations established the tradition that the Beloved Disciple, identified as John, the son of Zebedee, was a priest. Eusebius in *E. H.* III. 31.3 writes, "John, who leaned on the Lord's breast, who was a priest wearing the headband (πέταλον) and martyr and teacher, and he sleeps at Ephesus." See also Eusebius, *E.H.* V. 24. 3. Grassi, *Secret Identity*, 115.

likelihood is supported by a close reading of the narrator's account in 18:15, "Now that disciple was known to the high priest, and he *entered with* (συνεισῆλθεν) Jesus *into* the courtyard of the high priest."[72] He follows Jesus precisely because he has been raised from the dead and, therefore, no longer fears death. But it is not only on the basis of his reputation as the one raised from the dead by Jesus that he gains access to the interrogation before Annas. According to 11:31, 35 the Jews (οἱ Ἰουδαίοι), members of the ruling elite, had mourned his death and witnessed his resurrection. Consequently he would have been known to the high priest.

This is not a trial before the Sanhedrin. Annas, designated as "the High Priest" by the narrator, is still exercising power by conducting a hearing in order to determine if a charge can be brought against Jesus. As verse 19 indicates, he is questioning Jesus "about his disciples and his teaching." At this point, at least, it would be appropriate to allow one of those disciples, indeed, the most publicized one, Lazarus, to accompany Jesus and be present at his interrogation. There appears to be no immediate danger to him or to Peter.

Simon Peter, however, has remained outside of the courtyard. He is there because he intends to follow Jesus. But because he does not have the reputation of the Beloved Disciple and therefore is unknown to Annas, he is unable to gain access to the courtyard. On the other hand, it may also be that fear and apprehension have made him hesitant to accompany Jesus. The narrator simply observes, "But Peter stood towards the door outside." This would be the door of the high priest's courtyard. Unlike the Beloved Disciple, he has not followed Jesus all the way.

It is the "other disciple," the Beloved Disciple, Lazarus, who intervenes by speaking to the porter, a female slave, and requesting that Peter be brought into the courtyard. As she admits him, she asks, "You too aren't one of the disciples of this human being, are you?" The formulation of her question, including the use of the negative particle μή and the additive sense of the conjunction καί, indicates that she knows that the Beloved Disciple is a disciple of Jesus but is surprised that another disciple would want to be admitted to the hearing before Annas.[73] Peter's reply is a simple "I am not."[74] Ironically he has allowed himself to be brought into

---

[72] Quast, *Peter and the Beloved Disciple*, 81, supports this interpretation by citing the use of the same verb, συνεισῆλθεν in 6:22. Even as Jesus *entered into* the boat *with* his disciples, so the Beloved disciple *entered into* the high priest's courtyard *with* Jesus.

[73] Brown, *John* II, 824, has difficulty acknowledging Lagrange and Wescott who interpret the καί (also, too) in 18:17 to indicate that the slave girl knew that the "other disciple" was also a disciple of Jesus. He proceeds to ask the right question: "… why was the other disciple admitted and why was he not in danger…" It may indeed have been dangerous to appear before Annas as a disciple of Jesus. But the Beloved Disciple accepts that risk because of his deep attachment to Jesus. Peter, on the other hand, avoids the danger of identification, even after he is admitted, by standing with the slaves and retainers.

[74] Walter Grundmann, "Das Wort von Jesu Freunden (Joh. XV, 13-16) und das Herrenmahl," *NT* 3 (1959) 65, contends that Peter's twofold employment of οὐκ εἰμί is the negative counterpart to Jesus' earlier twofold use of ἐγώ εἰμί in 18:5,6, 8. However, John the Witness' denial of his messianic identity, "ἐγώ οὐκ εἰμί," is a more precise negative counterpart. Yet John subsequently employs οὐκ

the high priest's courtyard by the intervention of the Beloved Disciple, the same person he had depended on to learn from Jesus which disciple would betray him. But now he disclaims any connection with Jesus or with the disciple who had him admitted to the hearing. Instead of standing with them, he joins the slaves and retainers, who for one reason or another are tarrying in the courtyard, and proceeds to warm himself at the fire that they have made.

As awkward as the ordering of Simon Peter's threefold denial may be, divided as it is between the hearings of two high priests, it accentuates his lack of integrity. Even as he moves from one interrogation to the next, he is unable to find the strength in himself to be "rock-like" and remain in solidarity with Jesus. According to 18:18 and 25, his primary concern is to stay warm. During Jesus' appearance before Caiaphas he arouses the curiosity of those whom he evidently had accompanied from Annas' courtyard, and they question him in a manner almost identical to that of the slave girl. They too use the negative particle μή implying a negative answer and the additive sense of the conjunction καί, "You too aren't one of his disciples, are you?" Apparently they also are aware that he is a disciple of Jesus, yet on the other hand, like the slave girl, they have difficulty believing that a disciple would be present at his teacher's inquisition. The pairing of Peter and the Beloved Disciple during the passion of Jesus may induce the implied readers to suppose that the "other disciple" is present, but it is not indicated by the narrator. For a second time Peter denies with the same words, "I am not." But one of the slaves, a relative of the high priest's slave whose right ear Peter had cut off, presses the issue of Peter's identity as a disciple of Jesus, "Did I not see you in the garden with him?" For a third time Peter denies, but, in contrast to the Synoptic tradition, without curses and oaths. At that moment a cock crows, and Jesus' prediction of his three-fold denial in 13:38 is fulfilled. In contrast to the Synoptic tradition, nothing is said of any regret or guilt that he may have experienced. He remains a member of Jesus' community of disciples, but, in contrast to the Beloved Disciple, he does not follow Jesus to his crucifixion. Unquestionably, therefore, it is the Beloved Disciple who is the primary disciple and indeed the counterpart of Simon Peter, not only in this episode but also in the narrative world of the Fourth Gospel.[75]

His next appearance, therefore, must come as a surprise to the implied readers. It occurs on Easter morning, and once again he is associated with the Beloved Disciple. Together they run to investigate the report of Mary Magdalene that the corpse of Jesus has disappeared. Notably the Beloved Disciple outruns Peter and reaches the tomb first, but he does not enter.[76] When Peter arrives, he steps into

---

εἰμί when he is asked if he is Elijah, so perhaps Grundmann is correct.

[75] Contrary to Quast's conclusion, *Peter and the Beloved Disciple*, 85.

[76] The Beloved Disciple does not outrun Simon Peter because he is young, or unmarried, or because the narrator wants to emphasize the ideal love of the Beloved Disciple. See Quast's discussion, 109-117. Charlesworth and others, who deny that Lazarus is the Beloved Disciple, do not inquire into the significance of these relevant details of 20:2-8.

the tomb without hesitation and proceeds to view the burial strips and the folded face cloth in which the corpse of Jesus had been wrapped. Subsequently the Beloved Disciple follows him into the tomb, and he finally sees the facial cloth folded and set aside, something he had not noted earlier, and, because that reminded him of his own resurrection, "he saw and believed."[77] Two disciples stand side by side and view the same empirical objects, but only one of them, the Beloved Disciple, believes.[78] Although no object is attached to the verb, "he believed," the narrator's intrusive remark of 20:9 indicates that the object of his faith must be the reality of Jesus' resurrection from the dead.[79] His singular response of faith is not attributable to a leap of faith or "spiritual insight" but his own experience of having been raised from the dead.[80] He outran Peter to the tomb because he had a premonition of what had occurred on the basis of his own resurrection, but his hesitation to enter may have been determined by his experience in the tomb. His Easter faith, grounded in his resurrection from the dead, is prior to, but confirmed by, the Scriptures of the Old Testament.[81]

This is the final appearance of both Simon Peter and the Beloved Disciple in the narrative world of chapters 1-20. As an ironic contrast of discipleship they serve as textual structures of the implied readers of the Gospel. The one who was renamed "Cephas" never reaches mature discipleship. He is not present at Jesus' crucifixion and, at the climactic sign of Jesus' resurrection from the dead, he remains unresponsive. B.W. Bacon's comment made in the context of Simon Peter's denial could be shifted to this final moment of his appearance in the first edition of the Fourth Gospel: "Without the Appendix, these passages remaining where they stand, the Gospel would leave Peter under the unlifted cloud of

---

[77] See chapter 18 on 20:1-9. Sandra M. Schneiders, *Written That You May Believe: Encountering Jesus in the Fourth Gospel* (New York: Crossroad, 1999) 185-188, does a close reading of 20:3-8 and discerningly concludes that its was the facial cloth, as a "sign" that engendered faith in the Beloved Disciple.

[78] Quast, *Peter and the Beloved Disciple*, 120, concludes, "No contrast is intended between the faith of the Beloved Disciple and the apparent lack of faith on Pater's part. Rather, the faith of the Beloved Disciple is emphasized for the purpose of encouraging readers to respond in a similar act of faith." But Quast does not explain why the Beloved Disciple, and not Simon Peter, was chosen to serve as an example of faith. The significance of the new name, *Cephas* or *Petros* is never manifested in Simon Peter's discipleship. See also pp. 122-124 for faulty "Conclusions" that rely on redaction criticism.

[79] See the lengthy discussion of 20:8 and its verb πιστεύω in James H. Charlesworth, *The Beloved Disciple*, 79-118, who finally concludes: "leading commentaries for centuries have misinterpreted the verse." Thomas, he is convinced, is the Beloved Disciple, and the verb of 20:8, ἐπίστευσεν (he believed) is "an inceptive aorist," that indicates that Thomas was "not easily persuaded that Jesus has been raised." Furthermore, all the references to the Beloved Disciple were introduced by the author in the second edition of his Gospel or by the editor of chapter 21.

[80] "Spiritual insight," which A. H. Maynard, "Role of Peter," 540, attributes to the Beloved Disciple, is an insufficient basis for the Beloved Disciple's faith. Why should he alone within the narrative world of the Fourth Gospel have this "spiritual insight" and not also Peter?

[81] No Scripture references are given by the narrator. It may be assumed that the implied readers already know them, such as Isa 25:8, 26:19; Ezek 37:1-10; Dan 12:2-3.

disgrace."[82] It is left to the determination of the implied readers whether he eventually believed on the basis of Mary Magdalene's subsequent witness, "I have seen the Lord!" and therefore also whether he was present in the evening of that same day when Jesus breathed God's Spirit upon his disciples.

The Beloved Disciple also fades away, but in view of his Easter faith there is little difficulty in imagining that he is present with his fellow disciples when Jesus appears among them to fulfill John's promise and baptize them with the holy Spirit. The Beloved Disciple witnesses to the necessity of a personal experience of resurrection as the non-epistemic basis of the Easter faith. In this respect especially he may indeed exemplify ideal discipleship.[83] Simon, in sharp contrast, represents a frail and debilitated discipleship that does not fulfill the anticipated possibilities of the new name, Cephas, which Jesus had conferred on him.[84] It appears, therefore, that within this narrative world of chapters 1-20 an anti-Petrine bias is undeniable.[85]

Whether the editor of the appendix is making a conscious effort to correct that prejudice remains controversial. There are other objectives that have motivated the addition of the supplemental traditions of chapter 21, and together with the reinstatement of Simon Peter they constitute a "necessary ending" for the second edition of the Gospel.[86] The original edition of the Fourth Gospel is a *sui generis* narrative that was composed in order to address an entirely different life-world than that of the first three Gospels. As such it is not a reproduction of any given reality. There is no literary or historical necessity that it should concur with the Synoptic tradition that Peter is the undisputed leader of the disciples and later the head of the church. Yet, on the other hand, there may be a historical necessity that the priority of Simon Peter should be displaced by the Beloved Disciple within this narrative world, but that, of course, would be pre-determined by the assessment of his post-Easter apostleship within the context of the Gospel's addressees. Whatever might have contributed to his devaluation within that community remains a matter of conjecture.

---

[82] Bacon, *The Gospel of the Hellenists,* 483.

[83] So Kragerud, *Der Lieblingsjünger*, 42-52, 141-143.

[84] Kragerud's contention that the portrayal of Simon Peter's discipleship in the Fourth Gospel is as favorable as it is in the Synoptics is determined largely by his inclusion of chapter 21 as an original part of the Gospel. See pp. 53-66.

[85] Also Maynard, "The Role of Peter," 531. The relationship between Peter and the Beloved Disciple, as it is characterized by P. J. Hartin, "The Role of Peter in the Fourth Gospel," *Neot* 24/1 (1990) 58, is inadequate. The "distinctive functions" he assigns to each are deficient: for Peter it is the exercise of "pastoral authority" and for the Beloved Disciple it is "an exercise of discipleship of love and witness."

[86] See Culpepper, *Anatomy*, 96-97. But not the "necessary ending" to the first edition of chapters 1-20!

The Beloved Disciple in John 21

It seems natural, therefore, that the addendum of chapter 21 brings these two disciples into focus again. The character of their individual discipleship had manifested itself in stark contrast in the events of Jesus' passion and resurrection. But that disparity that had allowed Simon Peter's discipleship to remain questionable is now resolved by his rehabilitation. It appears to be necessary, therefore, to end the appendix by conveying a final word about the Beloved Disciple; and it is Simon Peter who, having been confronted with his own destiny, takes the initiative and inquires about the future of his fellow disciple. Earlier he could only address a question to Jesus through the latter's mediation. Now he is able to question Jesus directly. Apparently the redactor of chapter 21 wants to release Peter from his earlier subordination to the Beloved Disciple.

> Turning, Peter sees the disciple, the one whom Jesus loved, continuing to follow, the one who at dinner also reclined on his breast and said, "Lord, who is the one betraying you?" Peter seeing this one says to Jesus, "Lord, what about him?" Jesus says to him, "If I want him to remain until I come, what is that to you? Keep on following me."

It is striking that Simon Peter affirms the discipleship of the Beloved Disciple: "Peter turning sees the disciple, the one whom Jesus loved, continuing to follow, who reclined at the dinner at his breast and said, 'Lord, who is the one betraying you?'"[87] The scene has not changed, and very little time has passed in this context of chapter 21. Yet it appears to be vital, even crucial, that Peter validates the discipleship of the Beloved Disciple. He *sees* this. The verb that is employed is βλέπει, and, if it bears the meaning of its earlier uses in chapters 1-20, it conveys discernment, a clarity of insight, that enables Peter to perceive this.[88] On the other hand, in view of the other verb of "seeing" that is used in verse 21, ἰδών, it may simply be an observation that Peter is making in order to learn about the future of the Beloved Disciple. If his own discipleship will end in crucifixion, what is the prospect of the discipleship of the Beloved Disciple? But that, as Jesus' ambiguous response makes very clear, is none of Peter's business. "If I want him to remain until I come, what is that to you?" For Peter, in the light of his rehabilitation there is only one charge, "Keep on following me!" The future of the Beloved Disciple belongs to the jurisdiction of Jesus.

Attendantly noteworthy in this context is the apparent need to identify the Beloved Disciple of chapter 21 with the Beloved Disciple of 13:23. Why is that necessary? Is it to be ascribed to the apologetic strategy to legitimate the Fourth Gospel to the Christians of the Mediterranean world who are troubled by its

[87] The present participle that is used here, ἀκολουθοῦντα, denotes *continued following* and may imply that the Beloved Disciple has never ceased following Jesus. It does not imply that the Beloved Disciple is now represented as being in the fold over which Peter has now been reinstated as shepherd, as P. J. Hartin contends in "The Role of Peter in the Fourth Gospel," 57.

[88] For the distinctive meaning of the verb βλέπει, see chapter 5.

divergent content? Of all the characters in the narrative world of chapters 1-20, none is as consummate a witness to attest to the reliability and truth of the Gospel as the Beloved Disciple. He had been a disciple of John, but, on the basis of John's witness, he, with his companion Andrew, became the first to accept Jesus' invitation to "Keep on coming and you will see." Subsequently distinguished as "the one whom Jesus loved," he was raised from the dead as the culminating sign of Jesus' ministry. He was present at the last supper, present at Jesus' interrogation by Annas, and present at the crucifixion at which he witnessed the piercing of Jesus' side with a spear and the resulting effluence of blood and water. Without any encounter with the risen Jesus he was the first to believe that Jesus had been raised from the dead. No testimony to the trustworthiness of the Gospel could be more effective than his![89] To attribute the authorship of the Gospel to him must be the other motive for attaching this appendix to the Gospel in order to certify its credibility to its new readership of those who already are Christians.

But is the Beloved Disciple of chapter 21 identical to the Beloved Disciple of chapters 1-20? Does this appendix presuppose that Lazarus is the Beloved Disciple?[90] If the first edition of this Gospel was already bearing its present superscription before the addendum was attached to it, the identity of the Beloved Disciple in chapter 21 would necessarily have been determined by it. Since the oldest manuscripts of the Fourth Gospel, P^{66} and P^{75}, that originated in Egypt between 150 and 200 C.E., are superscribed with the heading, εὐαγγέλιον κατὰ 'Ιωάννην (Gospel according to John), the author would be presumed to be John.[91] That same identity, of course, would be ascribed to the Beloved Disciple of chapter 21, and at the same time also to the figure of the Beloved Disciple in chapters 1-20 on the basis of associating him with the Beloved Disciple of 13:23. As a result, the shrouded identity of the Beloved Disciple as Lazarus in the narrative world of chapters 1-20 has been revised by the appendix of chapter 21 to become John, the son of Zebedee. That is why "the ones of Zebedee" were included in the list of seven disciples at the very beginning of the addendum (21:2), and that is also why the Beloved Disciple, identified now as John, is able to recognize the risen Jesus as "Lord" on the basis of the great catch of fish.[92] "The

[89] See Culpepper, *Anatomy*, 122, for a discriminating characterization of the Beloved Disciple as "the link with Jesus" and therefore "the source and authority of the traditions contained in the Gospel."

[90] Floyd V. Filson, "The Gospel of Life," *Current Issues*, 121-123, was convinced that Lazarus continued to be intimated as the Beloved Disciple in chapter 21, and therefore should also be regarded as the author of the Gospel

[91] See Kurt Aland & Barbara Aland, *The Text of the New Testament* (Grand Rapids: Eerdmans & Leiden: Brill, 1989) 87, who date P^{66} around 200 C.E. and P^{75} "at the beginning of the third century." Philip W. Comfort and David P. Barrett, *The Complete Text of the Earliest New Testament Manuscripts* (Grand Rapids: Baker Books, 1999) 366-369 and 491, are convinced of an earlier date, 150 C. E. for P^{66} and ca. 175 C. E. for P^{75}. The superscript of the uncials, A and B, is κατὰ 'Ιωάννην.

[92] Charlesworth, *The Beloved Disciple*, 37, correctly asks which of the disciples named in 21:2 is the Beloved Disciple? Although "the ones of Zebedee" never appear in chapters 1-20, and therefore may offer a clue as to the identification of the Beloved Disciples in chapter 21, he concludes, "He is probably not one of the sons of Zebedee…"

ones of Zebedee" are deliberately not named in order to maintain the veiled identity that characterizes "the one whom Jesus loved" from 13:23, the very verse that is quoted in 21:20, to 20:2-8.

Ironically, it is the superscription that the Fourth Gospel bears that determined not only the identification of the Beloved Disciple as John, the son of Zebedee, but also the identification of the author of the Gospel. For it is "the one whom Jesus loved," now by implication, John, the son of Zebedee, who is declared to be the author of the Gospel in 21:24.

> This is the disciple who testifies about these things and who wrote these things, and we know that his testimony is true.

On the basis of the Synoptic Gospels, John, the son of Zebedee, who in chapter 21 is imputed to be the Beloved Disciple, can be regarded as "a definite historical person".[93] The Synoptic tradition, on which chapter 21 seems to rely, conveys only minimal information about him as the son of Zebedee. He was a fisherman! Jesus named him and his brother James "Boanerges," or "Sons of Thunder" (Mark 3:17), and the character of personality that it implies may have contributed to their early martyrdom, as Mark 10:39 may intimate. The narrator's aside of verse 23, that follows Jesus' reprimand of Simon Peter, is manifestly a confusion that mistakenly identifies John, the son of Zebedee, with another John who lived into old age in the city of Ephesus but who had died by the time chapter 21 was appended to the Gospel.

> Therefore the word went forth among the brothers and sisters that that disciple would not die. But Jesus did not say to him that he would not die but "if I want him to remain until I come, what is that to you?"

Beverly Roberts Gaventa's conclusion is unimpeachable. "John 20 and 21 constitute dual endings for the Gospel of John, each of which has a distinct function and focus, and that at least some of the difficulties interpreters have identified in chapter 21 derive from the difficulties in closure (or nonclosure, in this case).[94] John 21 is best characterized, in the elegant phrase of David McCracken, as an "archive of excess". By means of adding an appendix that rehabilitated Simon Peter and at the same time authenticated the Gospel by identifying the Beloved Disciple and therefore its author with the name John, this remarkable revision of the first edition of the Fourth Gospel was authenticated to a new readership. Already a synchronically structured narrative world of two levels, (1) Jesus' earthly lifetime and (2) the presence of Jesus in the actual events of the implied readers to whom the first edition was addressed, a third level is actualized by adding the appendix of chapter 21 in order to present a new edition of the

[93] Bultmann, *John* 701; German, 543.

[94] Beverly Roberts Gaventa, "The Archive of Excess: John 21 and the Problem of Narrative Closure," *Exploring the Gospel of John: In Honor of D. Moody Smith*, ed. by R. Alan Culpepper and C. Clifton Black (Louisville: Westminster John Knox Press, 1996) 242, and also 245-247. As for her emphasis on "excess," see her final paragraph on p. 249.

Gospel according to John to a new and wider audience. Subsequently ecclesiastical tradition appropriated its revised identification of the author, and, as Irenaeus testifies, utilized it to affirm the canonicity of this singular formulation of the Good News of Jesus Christ.[95]

Who is that John of the superscription of the gospel?

The only John who is named in the Fourth Gospel is John the Witness, who in his interrogation by the ruling elite acknowledges a divine call to "prepare the way of the Lord" by a ministry of baptizing. He appears in the Prologue of 1:1-18 twice, first as the witness to the Word and then as the witness to the incarnate Word. His testimony is momentously crucial for the historical activity of the Word in the world and for its culminating enfleshment in Jesus of Nazareth. Indeed, without his witness to Jesus as "the one who has happened before me, for he was my First," there would be no legitimation for the startling assertions Jesus will make of his relationship to "the Father" in the narrative world of the Gospel. When Jesus actually appears before him in 1:29-34, John strategically declares that he *ascertained* (τεθέαμαι) the Spirit *descending and remaining* on him and proceeds to identify him in terms of two titles that are decisive for the Gospel's christology: "the Lamb of God who removes the sin of the world," and "the Son of God".[96] His prediction, "This is the one baptizing with the holy Spirit" establishes the tensive anticipation of an eventual fulfillment that will in fact occur in 20:22 and engender the enlargement of the living Temple of God that Jesus is establishing. As Franz Overbeck recognized, John is the "primal disciple," the first true witness to Jesus. His testimony already contains the whole message of salvation in a nutshell.[97] But Clement of Alexandria had already distinguished John in this way:

> Does not John also summon to salvation and become totally a voice of exhortation? Well then let us divine of him, "Who are you among men?" He will not say Elijah. To be Christ will be denied. "But," he will confess, "I shall bellow in the wilderness." Who then is John? To take as a figure, it

[95] Already in 1901 P. Corssen relentlessly pursued the second century traditions of the Johannine authorship of the Fourth Gospel. He shows conclusively, I believe, that Papias could not have known the Apostle John and that he, as little as Irenaeus or Polycrates or anyone else of the second century, considered the Presbyter John to be the Apostle John. There is no external witness that the exchange of the identity of the former in place of the latter took place. Neither Papias nor those who followed possessed an external witness who attested to the authorship of the Fourth Gospel, and if Papias did not possess such a witness, then no one else in antiquity did. Corssen's essay ends with the very pertinent question, "Why then was the Fourth Gospel attributed to the Apostle John?" See Corssen, "Warum ist das vierte Evangelium für ein Werk des Apostels Johannes erklärt worden?" *ZNW* 2 (1901) 202-227; especially pp. 211 and 226-227. Also B.W. Bacon, "The Elder John, Papias, Irenaeus, Eusebius and the Syriac Translator, " *JBL* 27/1 (1908) 6, who maintained, "Papias knew of no John in Asia at all, save what he read in Rev 1:4, 9."

[96] See chapter 3. It is not the typology of a "Prophet" and "King," greater than Moses, as claimed by Wayne A. Meeks, *The Prophet-King: Moses Traditions and the Johannine Christology* (Leiden: E. J. Brill, 1967) 319.

[97] Quoted by Hengel, *Johannine Question*, 129. See Franz Overbeck, *Das Johannesevangelium*, ed. by C. A. Bernoulli (Tübingen: J. C. B. Mohr, 1911) 416f.

> is proper to say, a voice of the Logos bellowing exhortation in the wilderness. What do you bellow, O Voice? Say even to us, "Make straight the ways of the Lord!" John, then, the Forerunner and the forerunner voice of the Logos, a summoning voice, preparing beforehand for salvation, a voice exhorting for "the inheritance of heaven."[98]

Accordingly, there cannot be a more appropriate superscription for a Gospel that is intended to convince a Jewish audience that Jesus is the Messiah, the Son of God, than that which bears the name of John, a Jew who was not a Christian, but who on the basis of a divine revelation presents him, Jesus, to the Jewish readers of the Fourth Gospel as the replacement of the Temple cult and its sacrifices by identifying him as the Lamb of God who removes the sin of the world.[99]

On the basis of this formidable role that this John plays in the Fourth Gospel, it is very likely that originally this Gospel was named after him: εὐαγγέλιον κατὰ Ἰωάννην. The Gospel according to John is the Gospel according to John the Witness! That does not mean that he is the author. But he is the illustrious witness who guarantees the original truth in which the entire Gospel is grounded. On the basis of his immense stature and prestige as the witness to the Word and the Word Incarnate, the *Gospel according to John* would be an effective stratagem to induce a readership to interact with a text that introduces Philo's λόγος (Word) and promptly proceeds to pose an alternative to Judaism's devastating loss of the Jerusalem Temple: the reality of a new, living Temple inaugurated by the enfleshed Word.

Presumably a Gospel bearing the superscription, "according to John," that distinguishes John in his fulfillment of the divine commission to bear witness to the Word and its incarnation, intimates the presence of his disciples among its implied readers and, therefore, betokens the membership of an indeterminable number of his followers in the Jewish community of Alexandria.[100] Surely the prestige of the superscription would induce them to enter the narrative world of the Gospel, where their veneration of John would immediately be validated by his momentous testimony. Yet directly afterwards they would also be confronted with his repudiation of any messianic claims (1:19-27), and subsequently they would experience two disciples withdrawing their allegiance to John and attaching themselves to Jesus. Will these followers of John among the implied readers be inclined to emulate them? If their curiosity motivates them to continue to interact with the Gospel, they would eventually learn that one of these two former disciples of John became the Beloved Disciple of Jesus who, by being raised from the dead,

---

[98] Translated from: Clement of Alexandria, *Προτρεπτικος Προς Ελληνας* or *Exhortation to the Greeks*, ed. by M. Marcovich (Leiden: E. J. Brill, 1995) 9.1 on p. 16. See also 10.1 on p. 18, where John is once again named ὁ κῆρυξ τοῦ Λόγου (the herald of the Logos).

[99] I owe this conception to my son, David Waetjen, who, after listening patiently to my recitation of this thesis, came up with this insight.

[100] These disciples of John in Alexandria may have been the source of the Gospel's unparalleled traditions about John.

would succeed John in serving as the primary witness of the ministry of the incarnate Word.[101]

John was not the "light," as the Prologue declares; yet as Jesus asserts in 5:35, "That one was the burning and shining lamp, and you desired to exult for a hour in his light." Modest and self-effacing, he closes his own career by blending his voice with that of the narrator in 3:28-30, acceding that he is not the bridegroom, but only the friend of the bridegroom who "rejoices with joy" at hearing his voice and whose joy, therefore, has been fulfilled. He disappears with the final pronouncement: "It is necessary that that one increases and that I decrease."

Alexandria as the Gospel's place of origin

The only plausible context for this Gospel, at least its first edition of chapters 1-20, would be Alexandria, and the only likely readership would be the Jewish people of Alexandria.[102] They, like the Jewish people everywhere, had suffered the catastrophic loss of their architectonic center, the Temple, in the Roman destruction of Jerusalem in 70 C.E. How would Judaism adapt to the unprecedented cessation of temple sacrifices and worship? What new uniting center would replace its loss? How was this crisis to be resolved?[103]

In Alexandria many Jews would have been drawn to Philo's philosophical synthesis of Judaism and Middle Platonism. His allegorical interpretation of the Torah, determined by his Platonic-Stoic orientation, established a cosmopolitan ideology that would be attractive to Hellenized Jews by enabling them to embrace their ancestral faith and at the same time to live according to the Stoic-Platonic ideal as citizens of the world. Moses' book of *Genesis,* according to Philo,

> contains an account of the creation of the world [implying that] the cosmos is in harmony with the Law, and the Law with the cosmos, and that man who is observant of the Law is immediately a citizen of the cosmos, directing his

---

[101] See Schneiders, "'Because of the Women's Testimony ...'" 534-535, for her "very tentative hypothesis" that the role of the Beloved Disciple as the foremost eye-witness of Jesus' ministry is "a **textual paradigm** derived from and realized in the leading figures in the Johannine school," of whom the most significant is Mary Magdalene. The evangelist's identity remains disguised, but "the **textual alter ego of the evangelist**, whatever her or his actual identity and gender might have been, is the figure of the Samaritan Woman ..." (The bold text is Schneiders.)

[102] This is also the conclusion that J. N. Sanders reached in *The Fourth Gospel in the Early Church* (Cambridge: at the University Press, 1943) 39, "The place of origin which accounts best for this evidence is Alexandria." As an evangelistic Gospel written to gain Jewish converts, see Karl Bornhäuser, *Das Johannesevangelium: eine Missionsschrift für Israel*; W. C. van Unnik, "The Purpose of St. John's Gospel,"; J. A. T. Robinson, "The Destination and Purpose of St. John's Gospel." Martyn, *History and Theology*, 76, n. 100, does not exclude the possibility that the Gospel was written in Alexandria. But on pp. 162-163 he posits a trilateral social configuration: the parent synagogue, secret Christian Jews who have been able to remain in the synagogue, and the separated Johannine community, "a community made up almost wholly of Jewish Christians (also a few Samaritan Christians).

[103] See Jacob Neusner, "Emergent Rabbinic Judaism in a Time of Crisis," *Judaism* 21 (1972) 313-327. Also Lester L. Grabbe, *Judaism from Cyrus to Hadrian* II: *The Roman Period* (Minneapolis: Fortress Press, 1992) 541.

> deeds toward the purpose of nature, according to which the entire cosmos is administered.[104]

Moreover, the virtues of memory, as Philo delineated them, particularly the recognition of God's lordship and the appropriation of divine wisdom as presented in the Torah, would have evoked a receptive response at a time when a rising spirit of nationalism was generating a reclamation of the Jewish tradition among the Jews of Alexandria.[105] The "linchpin of Philo's religious thought," the Logos, who is designated as a mediating agent between the Creator and the creature, might well serve as a substitute for the brokering activity of the temple priesthood, for, according to Philo, " He is the suppliant of sick-at-heart mortality towards the immortal and ambassador of the ruler towards the subject. He exults in this estate and magnifying it describes it saying, 'And I stood between the Lord and you.'"[106]

In the subsequent development of rabbinic Judaism the Torah was invested with qualities proximally like those of the Logos: the Torah was acknowledged to be pre-existent, the Torah was identified with Wisdom, and the Torah was the agent of creation. Pirque Aboth 3:14 attributes to Rabbi Aqiba (c. 130 C.E.) the claim that the Torah served as the instrument by which the world was created:

> Precious are Israelites, to whom was given the precious thing. It was an act of still greater love that it was made known to them that to them was given that precious thing with which the world was made.[107]

According to *Abot de Rabbi Natan*, Rabbi Eliezer ben Jose of Galilee (c. 150 C.E.) declared, "Before the world was made, the Torah was written and lay in the bosom of God, and with the ministering angels uttered a song."[108]

The Prologue of the Fourth Gospel by its summary account of the vocational activity of the Logos would confront the Alexandrian Jews with a decisive alternative. In opposition to Philo's Logos as the intelligible universe and its copy, the universe perceived by the senses, it eulogizes the historical involvement of the Logos as the agent of creation, communication and interpretation but pre-

---

[104] My translation of Philo, *Opificio Mundi* I, 3.

[105] First of all, see Philo, *de Sacrificiis Abelis et Caini,* 55 and *Legum Allegoriae* I, 53-55. According to Victor A. Tcherikover, *Corpus Papyrorum Judaicarum*, ed. by Victor A. Tcherikover in collaboration with Alexander Fuks (Cambridge: Harvard University Press, 1957) 83-83, the arrival of enslaved Jews from Palestine, who had survived the war against Rome, would have reinforced a rising spirit of nationalism, and the intensification of the contact between the Jews of Egypt and the rabbis of Palestine promoted the latter's efforts to reconstitute Judaism on the basis of the Pharisaic heritage. See also Josephus, *BJ* 6. 418, cited by Tcherikover.

[106] Philo, *Quis Rerum Divinarum Heres*, 206.

[107] *The Mishnah: A New Translation*, Jacob Neusner (New Haven & London: Yale University Press, 1988) 680. See also George Foote Moore, *Judaism in the First Centuries of the Christian Era: The Age of the Tannaim* (Cambridge: Harvard University Press, 1954) I, 266-67. Also Dodd, *The Fourth Gospel*, 86.

[108] Cited by Dodd, *ibid.* Dodd includes the Scripture that was used to support this claim, Prov 8:30, a text that presents Lady Wisdom proclaiming her divine origin. See also *Abot R. Natan* 47, 130 B and *Siphre Deut* 307.4.2.

eminently as the incarnational agent of "grace in place of grace," of truth, and finally of world reconstruction.[109]

Perhaps Nathanael, more than any other disciple of Jesus, is representative of the "true Israelites" among the implied readers of Alexandria.[110] He is acknowledged by Jesus as the true Israelite in whom there is no deceit, and in 1:51 Jesus promises him a new architectonic center. He will see "the heaven opened and the angels of God ascending and descending on the Son of the Human Being." If Israel, according to Philo, is "the one who *sees* God," those, like Nathanael, who, in their interaction with the Gospel, will *see* heaven and earth united by the Son of the Human Being, will indeed be qualified as true Israelites.[111] Jesus himself is the first to issue the invitation, "Keep on coming and you will *see*," to two of John's disciples but especially to the implied readers of the Gospel (1:39). Philip subsequently uses the same words, "Keep on coming and *see*" in his response to Nathanael's disparaging remark about Nazareth (1:46). Various kinds of "seeing" are dignified within the Gospel by the employment of different verbs: θεάσθαι, θεωρεῖν, βλέπειν, ὁρᾶν and it is significant that they are employed by Philo with the same nuances of meaning.[112] Moreover, a notable trajectory runs through the Gospel correlating two visual perspectives that are integrated with the dynamic of believing: "seeing and therefore believing" and "believing in order to see."[113]

The other response to the Jewish crisis of 70 that the Fourth Gospel contests is the reconstitution of Judaism on the basis of the Pharisaic heritage that had been initiated under the leadership of Yochanan ben Zakkai.[114] He had escaped the destruction of Jerusalem through an arrangement with the Romans that included the establishment of a school at Jamnia and the governance of the Jewish people.[115] According to *Abot de Rabbi Natan*, he substituted חֶסֶד (loyalty) in place of the demolished Temple and its sacrificial cult on the basis of the divine injunction of Hosea 6:6, "For I desire mercy (חֶסֶד) and not sacrifice, the knowledge of God than

[109] John 1: 16. See Herman C. Waetjen, "Logos πρὸς τὸν θεόν and the Objectification of Truth in the Prologue of the Fourth Gospel," *CBQ* 63/2 (2001) 265-286.

[110] Culpepper, *Anatomy*, 104, aptly correlates the relationship between the Gospel's characters and the implied readers, "The characters represent a continuum of responses to Jesus which exemplify misunderstandings the reader may share and responses one might make to the depiction of Jesus in the gospel." This correspondence is perhaps especially true of the responses of the crippled human being of chapter 5 and the blind man of chapter 9.

[111] For Philo's definition of Israel, *de Mutatione Nominum,* 81. On Nathaniel and "The True Israelites," see Nils Alstrup Dahl, "The Johannine Church and History," *Current Issues in New Testament Interpretation: Essays in Honor of Otto A. Piper*, ed. by William Klassen and Graydon F. Snyder (New York: Harper & Brothers, 1962). For a more extensive treatment of Nathanael's encounter with Jesus in 1:45-51, see chapter 14.

[112] See chapter 5.

[113] *Ibid.*

[114] See chapter 6.

[115] See Jacob Neusner, *The Fathers according to Rabbi Nathan: An Analytical Translation and Explanation* (Atlanta: Scholars Press, 1986) 42-44; also Neusner, *First Century Judaism in Crisis: Yohanan ben Zakkai and the Renaissance of Torah* (Nashville: Abingdon Press, 1975) 145-155.

burnt offerings."[116] The Hebrew חֶסֶד, sometimes also translated as "steadfast love" or "loyalty," combined with obedience to the Law as it was preserved in both the written and oral Torahs, became the foundation of this Pharisaic Judaism.[117]

The academy of Jamnia gradually established itself as the seat of Jewish government, and the Houses of Hillel and Shammai, that may have been historical institutions prior to 70, became Jamnian parties that antagonistically contended for the power and control of reconstituting Judaism on the basis of their individual Pharisaic heritage.[118] This may be a reflection of the οἱ Ἰουδαίοι of the Fourth Gospel, namely the Pharisees, who by no means are a monolithic group within the Gospel's narrative world. Yochanan ben Zakkai identified himself with the House of Hillel, while his successor Rabban Gamaliel II, who may have deposed him, was a Shammaite; and the issues that separated the Houses they represented were ardently debated. The latter, Gamaliel II, the "Patriarch" or president of the academy from approximately 80 to 115 C.E., endeavored to secure "the recognition of all Jewry for the Bet Din at Jamnia and submission to its authority."[119] Under his direction the eighteen petitions of the Shemoneh Esreh were arranged in the order in which they were to be prayed and subsequently made obligatory for daily recitation by every Jew as a bond of Jewish unity.[120] According to *Berakoth* 28b-29a of the Babylonian Talmud, it was also under his authority that Samuel the Little formulated the *birkath ha-minim* as the twelfth petition of the Shemoneh Esreh, a prayer of eighteen benedictions.[121]

---

[116] J. Goldin, *The Fathers according to Rabbi Nathan* (New Haven: Yale University Press, 1955) 34. Cited by Neusner, *First Century Judaism*, 169-170.

[117] Jacob Neusner, "Emergent Rabbinic Judaism in a Time of Crisis," *Judaism* 21 (1972) 313-327. In *There We Sat Down: The Story of Classical Judaism in the Period in which It was Taking Shape* (Nashville: Abingdon Press, 1972) 37-39, Neusner summarizes Yochanan ben Zakkai's program of reconstruction. See also his, *Development of a Legend: Studies on the Traditions Concerning Yohanan ben Zakkai* (Leiden: Brill, 1970); and Emil Schürer, *The History of the Jewish People in the Age of Jesus Christ*, revised and edited by Geza Vermes, Fergus Millar, Martin Goodman (Edinburgh: T. T.Clark, 1986) I, 524-528.

[118] Jacob Neusner, *The Rabbinic Traditions about the Pharisees before 70* (Leiden: Brill, 1971) III, 281-282 and I, 298-302.

[119] Neusner, *ibid.*, III, 276, " … for it was the Yavneans, the Ushans, who developed these offices into important bases for power within the rabbinical group and in Jewish Palestinian government." Martyn, *History and Theology*, 41, n. 29, "… the Pharisees in chap. 9 probably reflect the authority of the Bet Din in Jamnia much more than they reflect a historical 'Pharisaic Sanhedrin' of Jesus' day."

[120] BT *Berakoth*, 28b. Daniel Boyarin, "Justin Martyr Invents Judaism, " *CH* 70/2 (2001) 427-461, argues that third, fourth and fifth century documents, such as the Mishnah, the Tosephta, and the Talmuds cannot be used to account for the historicity of the Jamnia/Yavneh debates and actions. Although the *birkath ha-minim* is not mentioned in the Mishnah, that silence in and of itself does not disprove that the birkath had not become the twelfth petition of the Shemoneh Esreh at the end of the first century. It seems quite probable that by 200 C.E. rabbinic Judaism had established itself, and Christian Jews were no longer a presence in the synagogue.

[121] Although the insertion of the twelfth petition, the *birkath ha-minim*, lengthened the Tephillah to nineteen benedictions, the prayer continued to be referred to as the Shemoneh Esreh, meaning eighteen.

> Rabban Gamaliel said to the sages: "Is there one among you who can word a benediction relating to the *minim* (heretics)? Samuel the Little arose and composed it. The next year he forgot it and tried for two or three hours to recall it, and they did not remove him. Why did they not remove him, seeing that Rab Judah has said in the name of Rab: 'If a reader made a mistake in any of the other benedictions, they do not remove him, but if in the benediction of the *minim*, he is removed, because we suspect him of being a *min* (heretic). Samuel the Little is different, because he composed it.[122]

The wording of the prayer, attested by the Cairo Geniza, is:

> For apostates let there be no hope, and the kingdom of insolence mayest thou uproot speedily in our days; and let the Nazarenes [Christians] and the heretics (*minim*) perish in a moment, let them be blotted out of the book of life and let them not be written with the righteous. Blessed art thou, O Lord, who humblest the insolent.[123]

Although the *birkath ha-minim* was formulated in the years following the destruction of Jerusalem, possibly in the early 80's, there is no certainty that the reading of the Cairo Geniza, that preserves the oldest version of the petition that includes an imprecation against the *notzrim* (Nazarenes or Christian Jews), is original.[124] Yet, whether original or not, the Fourth Gospel bears witness to expulsion from the synagogue on the charge of being guilty of confessing Jesus as the Messiah.[125] Even if Samuel the Little's twelfth petition did not include the word *notzrim* (Nazarenes), the Pharisaic ideology of separation was being put into practice by excommunicating Christian Jews from the Jewish community in Palestine and in cities of the Hellenistic world, such as Antioch and Alexandria. The Gospel according to Matthew, more or less concurrent with the emergence of this twelfth *birkath*, indirectly supports the reality of Pharisaic oppression and ill-treatment after 70 by the diatribe of chapter 23, composed by the author and anachronistically attributed to Jesus.[126]

---

[122] BT *Berakoth* 28-29a. Also cited by Martyn, *History and Theology*, 59. See William Horbury, "The Benediction of the *Minim* and Early Jewish-Christian Controversy," *JTS* XXXIII (1982) 19; and David Instone-Brewer, "The Eighteen Benedictions and the *Minim* Before 70 CE," *JTS* 54/1 (2003) 25-44. Moore, *Judaism*, I, 91.

[123] See Horbury's extensive discussion of the twelfth *birkath*, "The Benediction of the Minim," 19-61, who concludes, "The Jamnian ordinance belongs to this more systematized opposition of the late first century, and probably reinforces an earlier expulsion attested in John, although uncertainties of dating leave open that these two measures may be contemporaneous."

[124] J. Jocz, *The Jewish People and Jesus Christ* (London: SPCK, 1954) 51-57, concluded that the twelfth benediction was composed in the years following the destruction of Jerusalem, and the *minim* against whom it was directed were doubtlessly the Jewish believers in Jesus of Nazareth.

[125] The practice of expulsion by the Pharisees did not originate after 70. Neusner, *First Century Judaism in Crisis*, 86, says, "The Pharisees, led by Yochanan ben Zakkai, were attempting not merely to rule the sanctuary, but to exclude from the Temple all who did not accept their rulings." See also pp. 87-94.

[126] See Waetjen, *The Origin and Destiny of Humanness: An Interpretation of the Gospel according to Matthew* (San Rafael: Crystal Press, 1976), 216-225. Full text available on chora-strangers.org.

> The scribes and Pharisees are seated on Moses' cathedra. Therefore, all such things they should tell you, do and continue to observe, but don't continue to do according to their works. (Matt 23:2-3)
>
> Woe to you, scribes and Pharisees, hypocrites! Because you close the reign of the heavens in front of human beings, for you do not enter, neither do you allow those entering to enter. (Matt 23:13)

Justin Martyr's *Dialogue against Trypho* bears witness to the estrangement between Christian Jews and Jews. The former are being cursed in the synagogue (xvi, xcvi), Jesus is being anathematized as the Christ (xlvii, xcv, cxxxiii), the mockery of Christ is being promoted by "the rulers of your synagogues" (cxxxvii), and converse with Christians is being prohibited (xxxviii, cxii).[127] Justin's testimony, if it does not confirm the usage of the *birkath ha-minim* against Christian Jews, at least reinforces the profound alienation between these two communities.[128]

Before 70 James, the brother of Jesus and the "bishop" of the Jerusalem Church, may have been influential in extending the Jewish-Christian mission to the Jews of Alexandria. "Jerusalem would have been the natural *fons et origo* of Egyptian Christianity."[129] James' role in such an evangelistic undertaking is supported by the prominent position he occupies in the apocryphal work, the *Apocryphon of James*, a Nag Hammadi document that probably originated in Egypt between 125-150 C.E."[130] Scattered throughout its content are traces of the discourses of Jesus that appear to have been derived from the Fourth Gospel. An intimation of the Logos of the Prologue seems to be present in the characterization of the Word as the origin of faith, love and works; and the comparison of the Word to a "grain of

[127] Horbury's essay is a lengthy discussion of the scholarly debate on Justin's accuracy and reliability, the question of the inclusion of "Nazarenes" in the original formulation of the twelfth petition, the witness of the so-called church fathers after Justin Martyr, and the ongoing history of the petition itself. In summary, Horbury concludes, "Justin, the first non-Jewish witness who directly alleges a synagogue curse, was right in supposing that Christians, both Jewish and Gentile, were cursed in synagogue. The curse, one of a number of measures against emergent Christianity, was a form of the benediction of the *minim*. This malediction on heretics was approved at Jamnia under Gamaliel II and incorporated in the Tefillah, which at this time was gaining in importance as a bond of Jewish unity. The wording of the benediction was variable, and no surviving text can be assumed to reproduce a specimen form of the Jamnian prayer. See pp. 59-60.

[128] Boyarin, "Justin Martyr Invents Judaism," 436, accepts "Horbury's conclusion that Justin must be believed when he says that there was a curse against Christians pronounced in synagogues in some places by the middle of the second century. But," he continues, "I argue that this has no direct and genetic connection with the alleged 'Blessing of the *minim*,' allegedly instituted at Yavneh." If there was a curse against Christian Jews and later rabbinic literature attests to such a curse in the twelfth *birkath,* there appears to be a strong probability that there is a connection between the two. Evidently Boyarin wants historical certainty, but even his conclusions, at least some of them, are based on arguments from silence and therefore are equally probable.

[129] Colin H. Roberts, *Manuscript, Society and Belief in Early Christian Egypt*, The Schweich Lectures 1977 (London: Oxford University Press, 1979) 45.

[130] *The Apocryphon of James*, trans. by Dankwart Kirchner, *New Testament Apocrypha*, rev. ed. by Wilhelm Schneemelcher; English translation ed. by R. McL. Wilson (James Clarke & Co. and Westminster/John Knox Press, 1991) 287.

wheat" is reminiscent of the metaphor of "a seed of wheat" that Jesus employs in John 12:24 to allude to the fruitful outcome of his death.

> For the Word is first of all the origin of faith, secondly of love, thirdly of works. For herein life consists. For the Word is like a grain of wheat. If anyone has sown it, he has faith in it, and if it has germinated, he loves it, since he sees many grains in place of one and while he works he is being saved, since he can prepare it for a meal and further has enough over to sow. This is the way whereby it is possible for you to receive the Kingdom of Heaven. If you do not receive it by Gnosis, you will not find it.[131]

The benediction of page 13 corresponds to John 20:29.

> Blessed will be they who have not seen (yet) have be[lieved].[132]

An echo of 14:12 may be conveyed by a command on page 7:

> ... and, if possible, surpass me! For this is how your Father will love you.[133]

Nuances of Jesus' commission to Mary Magdalene in 20:17 and possibly also his rejoinder to his disciples in 6:62 may be combined in the saying on p. 10:

> And proclaim the good tidings that the Son is ascending as he should.[134]

Translated from Greek into a Coptic dialect, The *Apocryphon of James* professes to be the translation of a Hebrew letter written by James to an unknown addressee in which the risen Jesus, prior to his ascension, transmits revelations to James and Peter.[135] Precedence, however, is given to James, who, in response to his plea to be saved from persecution, is addressed by Jesus privately, "Be saved! I have commanded you to follow me, and I have taught you how to behave before the rulers." Jesus' charge to both James and Peter may be an allusion to the martyrdom they suffered, but it may also be a general exhortation to embrace persecutions!

> Or do you not yet know that you have yet to be abused, to be unjustly accused, to be shut up in prison, to be unlawfully condemned, to be crucified <without> reason and to be <shamefully> buried, just like myself, by the evil one?[136]

Peter's crucifixion is implied in 13:36 and 21:18-19. James suffered martyrdom, and as Josephus attests, it was "those who were strict in the observance of the laws," most likely the Pharisees, who not only respected James during his

---

[131] This translation is taken from *The Jung Codex, Three Studies by* H.C. Puech, G. Quispel and W.C. van Unnik and trans. and ed. by F.L. Cross (London: A.R. Mobray & Co., 1955) 46.

[132] Kirchner, *The Apocryphon of James*, 295.

[133] *Ibid.*, 293.

[134] *Ibid.*, 294.

[135] See *The Jung Codex, Three Studies*, 19, 24, 45-47.

[136] Kirchner, *The Apocryphon of James*, 292.

leadership of the Jerusalem Christian Jews but who also protested his being stoned to death at the instigation of the Sadducean high priest Ananus.[137]

That conciliatory relationship ended after 70. As Judaism confronted the possibility of disintegration, conflicting visions for the continuity of the Jewish faith were formulated and propagated. Two opposing alternatives are mirrored in the Gospel according to John, that of the Pharisees and that of the Christian Jews of Alexandria. Whatever accommodation may have existed in Alexandria between Jews and Christian Jews prior to 70, it was principally the vigorous and efficacious consolidation of rabbinic Judaism by the Pharisees and their successors that intensified the alienation between these two Jewish communities. The *birkath ha-minim*, if it already included a malediction against the Nazarenes, would have fractured the Jewish community and escalated the disengagement between Jews and Christian Jews. Although the Fourth Gospel testifies that the confession of Jesus as the Messiah induced expulsion from the synagogue, the Fourth Gospel also reveals that the separation between the synagogue and the Christian movement had not yet been finalized, at least in its Alexandrian context.

By accepting the invitation Jesus issues to the two disciples of John in 1:39, "Keep on coming and you will see!" the original readers of the Fourth Gospel would eventually experience in a mirror-like reflection this conflict between Christian Jews and the Jewish authorities of Alexandria.[138] The narrative world of the Gospel, therefore, as J. Louis Martyn established, is a literary structure of two historical time-periods: (1) the time of Jesus' historical career and, imposed on top of it, (2) the bitter conflict between Jesus, as he is being represented by Christian Jews, and the Jewish authorities (οἱ Ἰουδαίοι) after the destruction of Jerusalem.[139]

In the Gospel according to John the phrase, οἱ Ἰουδαίοι, denotes principally the ruling elite of the Jewish people, the guardians of Judaism, and not the Jewish people themselves.[140] These leaders are easily identifiable by the phrase, οἱ

---

[137] Josephus, *Ant* XX, 200-203.

[138] That the Jews in Alexandria had a separate political organization of their own, a *politeia* and a *politika*, Eric S. Gruen makes quite clear in *Diaspora: Jews amidst Greeks and Romans* (Cambridge: Harvard University Press, 2002) 54-83, esp. 74-78. Also James Tunstead Burtchaell, *From Synagogue to Church: Public Services and Offices in the Earliest Christian Communities* (Cambridge: at the University Press, 1992) 230, n. 20, who cites *Aristeas* 310, Josephus, *Ant.* 12, 108, and Philo, *In Flaccum,* 74.

[139] Martyn, *History and Theology*, 40, 89. Craig S. Keener, *The Gospel of John: A Commentary* (Peabody, MA: Hendrickson, 2003) I, 213, also considers it probable that the *birkath Ha-minim* was composed prior to the Fourth Gospel and that Jewish Christians perceived it as being directed against them.

[140] Johannine scholarship strives to determine the precise meaning and function of οἱ Ἰουδαῖοι, and a wide diversity of perspectives has emerged. See *Anti-Judaism and the Fourth Gospel: Papers of the Leuven Colloquium, 2000*, for a total of 25 essays on the issue of anti-Judaism and the Fourth Gospel. A general consensus appears to emerge in this book that the term usually refers to the ruling authorities, but sometimes also to the Jewish people and sometimes in a neutral sense to the Jews in contrast to the Gentiles. Prior to the Leuven Colloquium of 2000, the bibliography was already extensive: Rudolf Bultmann, *John*, 86, identifies "the Jews" as "the representatives of unbelief (and

'Ιουδαίοι, when it is used absolutely, either in the nominative, dative or accusative cases, without any modifying or qualifying nouns: 1:19; 2:18; probably 3:25; 5:10, 15, 16, 18; 6:41, 52; 7:1, 11, 15, 35; 8:22, 31, 48, 52, 57; 9:18, 22; 10:24, 31, 33; 11:8, 31, 33, 36, 54; 12:11; 13:33; 18:14, 20, 31, 36, 38; 19:7, 12, 14, 20, 21, 31. Three genitive phrases convey the foreboding and apprehension that the authorities generate within the narrative world of the Gospel, τὸν φόβον τῶν 'Ιουδαίων (the fear of the Jews) in 7:13; 19:38; 20:19. One genitive phrase designates those who are employed by the authorities, οἱ ὑπηρέται τῶν 'Ιουδαίων (the retainers/helpers of the Jews) in 18:12. And there are six prepositional phrases that refer to the authorities: ἐν τοῖς 'Ιουδαίοις (among the Jews) in 10:19 and 11:54; ἐκ τῶν 'Ιουδαίων (from the Jews) in 11:19, 45; 12:9; and πρὸς τοὺς 'Ιουδαίους (toward the Jews) in 18:38. All the other occurrences of "the Jews" are modified by various nouns that necessitate an identification with the Jewish people:

καθαρισμὸν τῶν ἐν τῶν 'Ιουδαίων (cleansing of the Jews) in 2:6

πάσχα τῶν 'Ιουδαίων (Passover of the Jews) in 2:16; 6:4; 11:55

ἄρχων τῶν 'Ιουδαίων (ruler of the Jews) in 3:1

σωτηρία ἐκ τῶν 'Ιουδαίων (salvation from the Jews) in 4:22

ἑορτὴ τῶν 'Ιουδαίων (feast of the Jews) in 5:1 and 7:2

---

thereby, as will appear, of the unbelieving 'world' in general)." Erich Grässer, "Die antijüdische Polemik im Johannesevangelium," *NTS* 11/1 (1964) 74-90, contends for both the authorities and the people, but, influenced by Bultmann's perspective, considers them to be representative of the enmity of the world. He concurs with C. K. Barrett that the Gospel is a "church book." Malcolm Lowe, "Who were the 'Ιουδαῖοι?" *NT* 18 (1976) 101-130, argues that they were the inhabitants of the province of Judea, not Jews, but "Judeans." "Judeans" can be substituted for "Jews" in all but four texts, 4:9 (twice), 4:22, 18:20. John Ashton, "The Identity and Function of the ΙΟΥΔΑΙΟΙ in the Fourth Gospel," 40-75, who does not interpret the Fourth Gospel as a coherent, unified, integrated literary composition, utilizes redaction criticism to resolve the problems of the'Ιουδαῖοι. He concludes that it is the pre-Johannine tradition and not the work of the author that explains the presence of the Ιουδαῖοι in the Gospel. Also Ashton, "The Jews in John," *Studying John*, 36-70, in which he continues to make the same source-critical differentiations. See also Wayne Meeks, "Am I a Jew? Johannine Christianity and Judaism," *Christianity, Judaism, and Other Greco-Roman Cults. Studies for Morton Smith*, ed. by Jacob Neusner (Leiden: Brill, 1975) 182. Hartwig Thyen, "Das Heil kommt von den Juden," *Kirche: Festschrift für Günther Bornkamm zum 75.Geburtstag*, ed. by D. Lührmann and Georg Strecker (Tübingen: J. C. B. Mohr (Paul Siebeck) 1980) 180. See especially Urban C. von Wahlde's survey of the scholarship on this issue, "The Johannine 'Jews': A Critical Survey," *NTS* 28/1 (1982) 33-60. On pp. 99-100, von Wahlde offers five identifying characteristics of "the Jews" that indicate they refer to the authorities. The analysis of R. Alan Culpepper, "Anti-Judaism in the Fourth Gospel as a Theological Problem for Christian Interpreters, *Anti-Judaism and the Fourth Gospel*, 68-91, esp. 90, results in the discouraging conclusion, "... John is both thoroughly Jewish and trenchantly anti-Jewish;" and who therefore advocates "a reassessment of Christian anti-Judaism" through education and careful translation of the gospel ..." Finally Tobias Nicklas, "'*Juden' und Jüngergestalten als Charaktere der erzählten Welt des Johannesevangeliums und ihre Wirkung auf den impliziten Leser. Regensburger Studien zur Theologie* (Frankfurt: Peter Lang, 2001) 391-409, after a very detailed analysis of the effect of the "Jews" and the "Disciples" on the implied readers, offers an intricate summary of his investigation amounting to the conclusion that the designation, "the Jews" in the different contexts of the Gospel are comparable but cannot simply be equated with each other.

βασιλεὺς τῶν Ἰουδαίων (king of the Jews) in 18:33, 39; 19:3, 19, 21

ἔθος τοῖς Ἰουδαίοις (custom among the Jews) in 19:40

παρασκευὴν τῶν Ἰουδαίων (preparation of the Jews) in 19:42

Jesus is called a Ἰουδαίος by the Samaritan woman in 4:9, and his people, in contrast to the Samaritans, are referred to as Ἰουδαίοι in 4:9.

Generally, οἱ Ἰουδαίοι are to be construed as the Pharisees, although in some instances they also include the chief priests.[141] They are, as Martyn acknowledges, "a *very strange* combination.[142] The scribes, who generally play an adversarial role in the Synoptic Gospels, are absent, and so are the Elders.[143] This conjunction of Pharisees and chief priests, plotting to destroy Jesus, is historically anachronous and ideologically incongruous.[144] It is the result of the merging of the two historical periods, the time of Jesus *and* the post-70 era of the reconstitution of Judaism during which the chief priests, who had not been killed in the Jerusalem holocaust, disappeared into anonymity.[145]

From the very beginning of the narrative world of this two-level drama the Pharisees and the priests form a coalition of two generations. According to 1:19, the Jews (οἱ Ἰουδαίοι) from Jerusalem sent priests and Levites to interrogate John about his identity and activity.[146] Who these Jews are is clarified by verse 24. If the definite article οἱ (the) is omitted before the perfect passive participle ἀπεσταλμένοι (having been sent), as the earlier manuscripts, P^{66}, P^{75}, א*, A*, B, C*, advocate, verse 24 indicates that the Pharisees were in fact the senders, and not those who were sent: "They [the priests and Levites] were sent from the Pharisees." [147] As anachronistic and incongruous as this is, the Pharisees must be identified as οἱ

---

[141] The Pharisees and the chief priests are identified together as οἱ Ἰουδαίοι in 1:19 and 25; 7:32, 45; 11:47; 18:3. The chief priests appear independently of the Pharisees in 12:10, but from 18:19 through 19:31 they alone are to be identified as οἱ Ἰουδαίοι. The final references to οἱ Ἰουδαίοι in 19:38 and 20:19 probably mark a return to the Pharisees in the context of level two of the narrative world of the Gospel in its Alexandrian context.

[142] J. Louis Martyn, *History and Theology*, 86. The italics are his. Martyn goes on to say, "By mentioning them [the chief priests] John cares for the *einmalig* level of his drama, for they are contemporaries of the earthly Jesus."

[143] For example, Mark 11:27; 14:43, 53; 15:1.

[144] See, for example, Moore, *Judaism* I, 66-70.

[145] Moore, *Judaism* I, 85-86, says, "The classes to which the Sadducees chiefly belonged had been reduced to insignificance. Many had perished in the war or by the daggers of assassins, other had been executed by the Romans or carried into slavery."

[146] The great weakness of a redaction-critical analysis of the Fourth Gospel is evident in the work of Fortna, *The Fourth Gospel and Its Predecessors*, 15-24. He maintains that the pre-Johannine source of 1:19 narrated that " Priests and Levites were sent to ask" John, and the subsequent redactor added "... **the Jews from Jerusalem sent** priests and Levites..." (bold print by Fortna). But he does not explain why the addition was inserted into the pre-Johannine text. Redaction Criticism cannot grasp the unity and coherence of the Fourth Gospel.

[147] That is probably why Paul Schmiedel conjectured that verse 24 is a later scribal interpolation. But no manuscripts support its omission. See the critical apparatus in the 27th ed. of *NTG* ed. by Barbara and Kurt Aland, 248.

Ἰουδαίοι of 1:19.[148] But probably also the chief priests! Although they do not appear until 7:32, in all likelihood they should be included: "The chief priests (ἀρχιερεῖς) and the Pharisees sent retainers so that they might seize him". Later, in 11:47, in view of the growing anxiety about Jesus' success, the narrator observes, "Then the chief priests and the Pharisees called together [the] Sanhedrin." The two groups continue to collaborate in the Gospel's narrative world until 18:3, "Then Judas, taking the cohort and the retainers from the chief priests and the Pharisees comes there with lanterns and torches and weapons." After Jesus' arrest, however, the Pharisees disappear, and the chief priests become the sole antagonists advocating Jesus' death. However, the final references to οἱ Ἰουδαίοι in the phrase, τὸν φόβον τῶν Ἰουδαίων (the fear of the Jews) in 19:38 and 20:19 should probably be related to the second level of the Alexandrian context of the Gospel and therefore identified with the Pharisees. Consequently, οἱ Ἰουδαίοι must be differentiated according to the two epochs that are merged within the narrative world of the Gospel: (1) the chief priests as "the Jews," the ruling authorities, before 70 C.E. *and* the Pharisees as "the Jews," the ruling authorities, in the post-70 years of the conflict in Jamnia and Alexandria to resolve the problem of Jewish identity in view of the loss of the Temple cult. What both constituencies, the chief priests and the Pharisees, have in common in their individual epochs is their collaboration with Roman imperialism.

Except for 1:19-24 and 6:41, 52, Jerusalem is always the location of the confrontation between Jesus and these two collaborating groups of Jewish leadership. The most virulent encounter occurs in 8:12-59.[149] Within that context Jesus acrimoniously indicts the Pharisees:

> You are from your father, the devil, and you want to do your father's desires. That one was a murderer from the beginning, and he has not stood in the truth because there is no truth in him. When he lies, he speaks from his own nature because he is a liar and the father of lies. But because I speak the truth, you do not believe me. Who of you convicts me of sin? If I tell the truth, why do you not believe me? The one who is from God hears the words of God. You do not hear, because you are not from God. The Jews responded and said to him, "Are we not correct in saying that you are a Samaritan and you have a demon?" Jesus answered, "I do not have a demon, but I honor my Father, and you dishonor me" (8:44-49).

[148] Contrary to Francis J. Moloney, *Signs and Shadows: Reading John 5-12* (Minneapolis: Fortress Press, 1996) 191-192, who identifies "the Jews" with the Jewish people.

[149] See Urban C. von Wahlde, "You are of your Father the Devil," 442-443, who, on the basis of his exegetical analysis, concludes that John 8:38-47 is not anti-Jewish. "The gospel was born in a context in which there were opposing points of view on the true meaning and future of the Jewish tradition." "They would have said the synagogue was wrong but they would not have said that Judaism was wrong." He acknowledges that his position is very similar to that of M. De Jonge, "The Conflict between Jesus and the Jews and the Radical Christology of the Fourth Gospel," *PRSt* 20 (1993) 355.

Such a malevolent exchange is historically anachronous. Like Jesus' polemic against the scribes and the Pharisees in Matt 23, it is a post-70 construction.[150] Estrangement, as unyielding as this, was impossible in the heterodoxy of Judaism that antedated the Jewish revolt against Rome. It mirrors the historical opposition between Christian Jews and the Pharisaic guardians of Jewish society after 70 C.E., more precisely perhaps from the time of Gamaliel II's leadership in Jamnia to the time of the Jewish revolt in Egypt between 115 and 117 C.E.[151] The painful consequence that confronted Christian Jews in their allegiance to the Christian faith is expressed in the intrusive remark of the narrator in 9:22:

> For the Jews had already agreed that if anyone confessed him (as) Christ, he/she would become ἀποσυνάγωγος (without a synagogue).

It is also reflected in 12:42:

> Nevertheless, however, many of the rulers also believed into him, but on account of the Pharisees they were not confessing so that they might not become ἀποσυνάγωγοι.

This conflict generated a climate of suspicion and fear within the Jewish community, as 7:12b-13 testifies. "While some were saying, 'He is a good man,' others were saying, 'No, but he is deceiving the crowd.' Indeed, no one would speak openly about him on account of the fear of the Jews." Joseph of Arimathea is characterized in 19:38 as a "disciple of Jesus but kept-secret on account of the fear of the Jews."

Yet there is another rabbinic disposition towards Jesus that is represented by the character and the characterization of Nicodemus, "a Pharisee" and "a ruler of the Jews."[152] His identification as "a ruler of the Jews" may imply that he is representative of the post-70 rabbinic leadership that has established itself at the academy of Jamnia. Moreover, it suggests that Jamnia and Alexandria are in a corresponding relationship in which the rabbis of Jamnia are struggling to establish their control over the Jewish community of Alexandria. Nicodemus himself,

---

[150] See Luke T. Johnson, "The New Testament's Anti-Jewish Slander and the Conventions of Ancient Polemic," *JBL* 108/3 (1989) 434-441, on the use of polemical language everywhere in the fragmented Judaism of the first century. On Matthew's polemical slander against the Pharisees in chapter 23, see Waetjen, *The Origin and Destiny of Humanness*, 216-225.

[151] Also Georg Richter, "Zur Formgeschichte und literarischen Einheit von Joh 6. 31-58," *ZNW* 60 (1969) 45. According to Lester L. Grabbe, *Judaism from Cyrus to Hadrian,* I, 567, "We know that in time Palestine came increasingly under rabbinic control, until finally the Jewish patriarch had considerable power even over the Jewish communities outside Palestine. ... it is also plain that the extension of rabbinic control after 70 was slow."

[152] For studies on Nicodemus see: F. P. Cotterell, "The Nicodemus Conversation: A Fresh Appraisal," *ExpT* 96 (1984-85) 237-242; M. De Jonge, "Nicodemus and Jesus: Some Observations on Misunderstanding and Understanding in the Fourth Gospel," *Jesus: Stranger from Heaven and Son of God* (Missoula: Scholars Press, 1977) 29-47; Jouette M. Bassler, "Mixed Signals: Nicodemus in the Fourth Gospel," *JBL* 108/4 (1989) 635-646. The attempts to identify Nicodemus with an historical figure have proved to be unsuccessful and speculative.

however, as "a ruler of the Jews" may be representative of that faction at Jamnia – or in Alexandria – that in this early context of post-70 Judaism is not hostile toward Jesus and Christian Jews. The clashes, however, as the Gospel discloses, are intensifying and the alienation is deepening.

At the outset of his visit with Jesus at night Nicodemus addresses him as "Rabbi" and acknowledges that he is "a teacher sent from God; for no one is able to do the signs that you do unless God is with him." This is a significant admission, but it will be contested later in 9:16 and 10:19-21 when the Pharisees are confronted with the problem of determining whether Jesus can be regarded as a "human being from God" after he has performed a sign, the healing of a blind man, while at the same time transgressing the Sabbath.

> Some of the Pharisees were saying, "This human being is not from God because he does not observe the Sabbath." But others were saying, "How is a sinner able to do such signs?" And there was a dissension among them. (9:16)

> A dissension again occurred among the Jews because of these words. Now many of them were saying, "He has a demon and is mad. Why do you listen to him?" Others were saying, "These words are not those of one demon-possessed. A demon surely can't open the eyes of blind people, can it?" (10:19-21)

It is noteworthy that Nicodemus' visit with Jesus is located coincidentally in the context of Jesus' act of "cleansing" the sacred precinct of the Temple and substituting his physical body in place of the Temple's sanctuary. It is an intimated acknowledgment that the Pharisees, like the Jewish author of the Fourth Gospel, were intensely concerned about the existential crisis of Judaism's loss of the Temple.

Nicodemus does not seem to take offense when Jesus asseverates, "Amen, amen I say to you [Nicodemus], 'Unless you are born from above you cannot see the reign of God'." Nor does he appear to become alienated when Jesus chides him for not grasping his teaching on rebirth, "Are you the teacher of Israel, and you don't know these things?" Later, in 7:51, when the chief priests and the Pharisees are conspiring to do away with Jesus, he, identified by the narrator as "being one of them," will manifest an independent predisposition toward Jesus by defending him on the basis of a legal principle derived from Num 35:30 and Deut 17:6 and 19:15, "Surely our law doesn't judge a human being unless it first hears from him and knows what he is doing, does it?" The conflict within the ranks of the Pharisees that is emerging here very likely reflects the alienating tension that troubled the rabbinically oriented leadership of the Jewish community of Alexandria and perhaps also the disputes between the two Houses of Hillel and Shammai at Jamnia. Although Nicodemus was characterized earlier by the narrator as "a ruler of the Jews," he is mocked by his fellow Pharisees with the implicating suspicion, "Surely you too aren't from Galilee, are you?" and simultaneously affronted by their imperious command, "Search and see that out of Galilee *the* prophet does not arise." [153] This division among the Pharisees, the chief representatives of οἱ Ἰουδαίοι throughout most of the Gospel, belongs to the second level of the Gospel's narrative world and in all probability reflects the discord and conflict within the Jewish community in Alexandria – and perhaps also in Palestine – at the end of the first century.

Nicodemus appears one more time in the narrative world of the Gospel; he is present at the burial of Jesus (19:39-42). The narrator reminds the implied readers that he is the one who "first came to Jesus at night." He arrives after Joseph of Arimathea had received permission from Pontius Pilate to claim Jesus' body, and he brings with him one hundred λίτρας of a mixture of myrrh and aloes for the entombment of Jesus.[154] Such a remarkably large amount of aromatic spices is "an extraordinary manifestation of respect."[155] Perhaps a royal entombment is implied.[156] At the very least it is Nicodemus' tribute to Jesus, the tribute of a Pharisee, a ruler of the Jews. He and Joseph collaborate to wrap the body of Jesus in linen cloths with the burial spices and to place it in a new tomb "in which no one had ever been laid" in the proximity of a garden in which he had been crucified.[157]

Nicodemus' veneration of Jesus and the apparently agonizing struggle of some of his fellow Pharisees to "believe into" Jesus pose a strong contrast to those Pharisees who, as οἱ Ἰουδαίοι, attempt twice to stone Jesus to death. This rupture within the ruling community of οἱ Ἰουδαίοι is limited to the Pharisees; no such division is evident among the chief priests. The Pharisees, who want to do away with Jesus, appear for the last time in the narrative world of the Fourth Gospel when they collaborate with the chief priests in order to send Judas with a cohort (σπεῖραν) and a group of retainers (ὑπηρέται) to arrest Jesus and bring him to trial (18:3). From that moment, however, the chief priests become the solitary group of the ruling elite represented by the Gospel's general designation, οἱ Ἰουδαίοι. The high priests, Annas and Caiaphas, interrogate Jesus and deliver him to Pontius Pilate and the Romans for execution.

In the context of this religious crisis in the Jewish community of Alexandria and its bitter conflict between Jews and Christian Jews and between Jews and Jews, a

---

[153] On the text critical problem of the definite article placed before 'prophet,' see chapter 6..

[154] One λίτρα is a Roman pound, equal to the troy weight of 12 ounces. One hundred λίτρας, therefore, would amount to approximately 75 pounds of crushed myrrh and aloes to be strewn between the linen cloths that would be wrapped around Jesus' corpse for his burial.

[155] So Schnackenburg, *St. John* III, 297. In footnote 111 on p. 465 he cites a story taken from Strack-Billerbeck, *Kommentar zum Neuen Testament* II, 53, in which a proselyte justified burning more than eighty sticks of aromatic spices at the burial of R. Gamaliel I (around 40-50 C.E.) because he was "much better than a hundred kings." He also refers to Josephus's account of Herod the Great's funeral in *Ant.*, XVII, 199.

[156] Also suggested by Brown, *John* II, 960, who cites other burial accounts to support his intuitive sense that Nicodemus wants to give Jesus a royal burial.

[157] Brown, *ibid.*, citing OT references to the entombment of Israel's kings in a garden, proposes that the Gospel's reference to "a garden" in 19:41 may support the theme of Jesus as a king.

Christian Jew of Alexandria who was familiar with the writings of Philo and the Pharisaic tradition, composed what is canonically called the Gospel according to John, consisting of chapters 1-20, and addressed it to his fellow Jews in Alexandria:

> Now Jesus also did many other signs before his disciples which have not been written in this book. But these things have been written so that you *begin* to believe that Jesus is the Christ, the Son of God and that believing you have life in his name. (20:30-31)

The Gospel's distinctive narrative intertwining of two historical epochs is determined by this religious crisis of the Hellenistic Jews of Alexandria, specifically during the period of the consolidation of rabbinic Judaism under Gamaliel II to the time of the Jewish revolt in Egypt in the years 115 – 117 C.E.[158] There are many distinctive features that disclose the Jewish and the Jewish Hellenistic character of the narrative world of the Fourth Gospel in the textual structures of the implied reader that are commensurate with an Alexandrian origin, but that also hint at some contact with the Jamnian leadership of Palestine that is promoting the Pharisaic reconstitution of Judaism:

1. The Prologue's disclosure of Jesus as the enfleshment of the Word in 1:14.
2. The narrative world's unveiling of Jesus as the Son of the Human Being (ὁ υἱὸς τοῦ ἀνθρώπου) upon whom "the angels of God ascend and descend" in 1:51.
3. Nathanael as "the true Israelite" who "sees".
4. The emphasis on signs, a distinctive Jewish orientation.
5. The three Passovers in the narrative world of the Gospel that are always "near" but never here: 2:13, 6:4 and 11:55.
6. The six stone water jars in 2:6.
7. Jesus' replacement of the sanctuary with his own body in 2:19-21.
8. Jesus' supersession of Moses: 1:17, 3:14 and 6:32.
9. The frequent use of the divine self-disclosure ἐγὼ εἰμί.
10. The imposition of the ideology of separation and the fear of ἀποσυνάγωγος.
11. The significance of the fourth day of Lazarus' death.
12. The time reference of Pilate's sentencing Jesus to death in 19:14.
13. The Jewish necessity of Thomas requiring empirical evidence of the continuity between the crucified and risen Jesus.
14. The Hebraisms and Aramaisms in the Gospel: Μεσσίας, Κηφᾶς, ῥαββί, Ἰσραηλίτης, Γαββαθά, Γολγοθά, Μαριάμ, σουδάριον, ῥαββουνί.

[158] On the Jewish revolt of 115-117 C. E. in Alexandria, see Schürer, *History of the Jewish People*, I, 529-534.

15. At the same time, the preference for certain Greek equivalents: χριστός, Πετρός, Λιθόστρωτος.

As yet, no final separation between Jews and Jews has occurred .[159] The Jewish community of Alexandria appears to have included students of Philo's Judeo-Platonic philosophy, followers of John the Baptizer, partisans of the many ruling authorities who represent the ideology of the Pharisees, and Christians. Samaritans may also have resided among them, for Josephus alleges that Jews and Samaritans in Egypt brought their dispute regarding the true place of worship, Jerusalem or Gerezim, before Ptolemy VI Philometer.[160] The Samaritan woman introduces this controversy in her dialogue with Jesus in 4:20, and, accordingly, reinforces the evidence of the presence of Samaritans in Alexandria. Consequently, the community of Christian Jews cannot be qualified as "a sectarian group of Jewish Christian origin, one that has distinctly introversionist features but one that has not necessarily turned its back entirely on the possibility of mission to the world."[161]

External evidence for the Alexandrian origin of the gospel's first edition

Alexandria is the most plausible setting of the first edition of the Fourth Gospel! Among the more persuasive bits and pieces of evidence that it originated in Alexandria is the Rylands Papyrus 457, generally referred to as P[52], that has preserved a fragment of John 18:31-33 and 37-38. Found in Egypt, it is usually dated between 125 and 150 C.E.[162] Attendantly, the Egerton Papyrus 2, "a fragment of a work which is in the form of a Gospel and has marked affinities with the Fourth Gospel," also lends weight to an Alexandrian context.[163] Ptolemy and Heracleon, both disciples of the Alexandrian Gnostic, Valentinus, attest to the

[159] Martyn, *History and Theology*, 75, n. 99, encounters difficulties in reaching the conclusion that "the Gerousia has already separated the Johannine community from the synagogue." He finds himself compelled to conclude "that in John's milieu Jewish leaders do in fact exercise some kind of authority over those who have been excommunicated." But he explains that on the basis of the authority that these leaders would be able to exercise "*within their own section of the city*." (The italics are his.)

[160] Josephus, *Ant* XIII, 74-79. Also XII, 7-10. See Emil Schürer, *The History of the Jewish People*, III, Part 1, 59-60 for other textual witnesses to the presence of Samaritans in Alexandria.

[161] Contrary to David Rensberger, *Johannine Faith and Liberating Community* (Philadelphia: Westminster Press, 1988). The dualism that emerges in the Fourth Gospel is the dualism of its immediate context, that is, the culture of Alexandria and especially the dualism of Philo. The Gospel, however, is anti-dualistic. Its binary opposites are aporetic not dualistic. This is not recognized by Luise Schottroff, *Der Glaubende und die feindliche Welt* (Neukirchen-Vluyn: Neukirchener Verlag, 1970) 228-289, as she deduces a radical dualism from the Fourth Gospel. See also the critique in Robert Kysar, *The Fourth Evangelist and His Gospel: An Examination of Contemporary Scholarship* (Minneapolis: Augsburg Publishing House, 1975) 215-221.

[162] J.N. Sanders, *The Fourth Gospel in the Early Church*, 38-39, assigns the date of 150 C.E. K. Aland & B. Aland, *Text of the New Testament*, 57, offer a date of ca. 125 C.E. P. W. Comfort and D. P. Barrett, *The Complete Text of the Earliest New Testament Manuscripts*, 355, prefer an earlier date of ca. 100-125 for P[52].

[163] J.N. Sanders, *Fourth Gospel*, 38, n. 4.

Fourth Gospel's early presence in Alexandria "at a time when there is no evidence that any other church accepted it."[164]

It is the New Testament apocryphal writing, the *Epistula Apostolorum*, a document contemporaneous with the *Apocryphon of James*, that bears a more immediate witness to the Alexandrian origin of the Fourth Gospel.[165] According to C. Detlef G. Muller, the content and form of the *Epistula* and its "free handling of the holy scriptures point to lower Egypt. Alexandria ... must come into reckoning at least for its dissemination, if not absolutely for its composition."[166] This anonymous Egyptian text of the early second century, written in the name of eleven apostles, attests to a direct dependence on all four of the New Testament Gospels, but especially the Gospel according to John. Carl Schmidt maintains,

> And as we fly over the entire text, with every step and stride we bump into Johannine material and familiar Johannine conceptions. Indeed, one can directly set up the proposition, that, should our Epistula have originated in the second century, no other transmitted text of the second century makes such a considerable use of the Fourth Gospel as the one under consideration.[167]

Again

> Yes, the Johannine Gospel, ostensibly in the eyes of the author [of the *Epistula*] is the Gospel that conveys the true knowledge of Christ.[168]

---

[164] *Ibid.*, 40.

[165] The Ethiopic text is a complete translation of the *Epistula*. A Coptic version of the 4th or 5th century, however, is the more consequential witness because it is derived from the original Greek. See the discussion of Carl Schmidt, *Gespräche Jesu Mit Seinen Jüngern*, (Hildesheim: Georg Olms Verlagsbuchhandlung, 1967) 156-181, who concludes that in spite of the superiority of the Coptic text, the Ethiopic version is generally trustworthy. Accordingly, he accepts the Ethiopic dating of the Parusia, that is, 150 years after Jesus' disclosure and therefore 180 C.E. Consequently the *Epistula* is to be dated at some time before 180. H. Lietzmann, "Die Epistula Apostolorum," ZNW 20 (1921) 173-174, is critical of Schmidt's dating, prefers the Coptic version of "120 years," and therefore posits a date sometime prior to 150. He proposes that the Ethiopic version of "180 years" may be due to a postponement of the Parousia. Manfred Hornschuh, *Studien zur Epistula Apostolorum* (Berlin: Walter de Gruyter, 1065) 116, assigns the *Epistula* to the first half of the second century.

[166] C. Detlef G. Müller, *Epistula Apostolorum* in *New Testament Apocrypha*, rev. ed. by Wilhelm Schneemelcher and English translation by R. Mcl. Wilson (Louisville: Westminster/John Knox Press, 1991) 251.

[167] Translated from: Carl Schmidt, *Gespräche Jesu Mit Seinen Jüngern*, 224-225. His contention, however, that the *Epistola* originated in Asia Minor seems largely determined by the opening reference to "the false apostles Simon and Cerinthus" and the traditional view that the Fourth Gospel was composed in Ephesus. But ancient testimony not only locates Cerinthus' field of activity in Asia Minor; Irenaeus, Hippolytus, and Theodoret refer to Cerinthus' instruction in the wisdom of Egypt. See his discussion on pp. 407-428. See also Lietzmann, *Epistula*, 175-176, who maintains an Egyptian origin of the letter. Also K. Lake, "The Epistula Apostolorum," *HTR* 14/1 (1921) 15. According to Hornschuh, *Studien,* the preservation of this letter in Ethiopic and Coptic - and a few fragments in Latin - in all probability points to an Egyptian origin. See pp. 103 – 115 for other indications of an Egyptian provenance.

[168] Translated from: Schmidt, *Epistula*, 225. Also W. von Loewenich, *Johannesverständnis*, 57-59, and M. Hornschuh, *Studien*, 9-10, 120.

Instances of this influence are encountered throughout the *Epistula*. In paragraph 31 Jesus, speaking as the exalted Lord, reminds his disciples of "the word that you have written concerning me, that I am the Logos of God and the Father is in me." In another echo of the Prologue, Jesus repeats this earlier identification in paragraph 39, "I am the Logos; I became flesh." As in the Fourth Gospel, but limited to three brief verses, the transformation of water into wine at the wedding of Cana is placed at the beginning of his mighty works. Johannine language is used in paragraph 5 to characterize the holy Spirit as "the Paraclete." In agreement with 19:31 Jesus is removed from the cross along with the two bandits.[169] The Easter story is a conflation of the four Gospels, but the account of John 20 is dominant. Three women proceed to Jesus' tomb in order to anoint his corpse with burial spices. The number but not their names correspond to Mark 16:1. In the Coptic version they are identified as "Mary who belonged to Martha, and Mary Magdalene."[170] They are the only three women who are named in the Fourth Gospel, and significantly they alone are associated with the two occurrences of resurrection, Mary and Martha with the resurrection of Lazarus, and Mary Magdalene with the resurrection of Jesus.[171] According to the Coptic text, Jesus sends Martha, the woman of faith in John 11:27 and 40-41, to bear witness to his disciples, "Our Master has risen from the dead."[172] When she fails to convince them, Jesus sends Mary to repeat the good news of his resurrection. Here it is difficult to determine whether she is to be identified with Mary Magdalene or with the Mary who is associated with Martha.[173] In any case, she too fails, and therefore it is necessary for Jesus himself to visit them and chide them for their unbelief. Surprisingly, Peter is singled out, "You, Peter, you denied me three times before the cock crew, and now you still deny."[174] It is this reference to another denial, beyond the three that occurred during Jesus' trial before the High Priest, that intimates the absence of Peter's acknowledgment of Jesus' resurrection from the dead. Such a failure could only have been derived from John 20, for, according to verse 8, when Peter and the Beloved Disciple stood side by side in the empty tomb eye-balling the burial cloths of the risen Jesus, only the Beloved Disciple believed. There is no response from Peter. That he persisted as a disciple of Jesus can be intimated from Matt 28:16, but it is more explicitly derived from Luke 24:34, and it may have been that verse that contributed to the elaboration of the "Doubting Thomas" story of John 20:24-29 in the eleventh paragraph of the *Epistula Apostolorum*. Peter is the first of three to be invited by Jesus to certify the

---

[169] *New Testament Apocrypha*, C.D.G. Müller, *Epistula*, 254.

[170] C. Schmidt, *Gespräche Jesu*, 232, is convinced that the three Myrophoren (bearers of burial spices) of the Coptic tradition are more original to the *Epistula* than the three: Sarah, Martha and Mary Magdalene of the Ethiopic text.

[171] *Ibid.*

[172] *Ibid.*, 255.

[173] According to para. 9, she is identified as "the daughter of Martha." *Ibid.*, 255.

[174] *Ibid.*

identification of the risen Jesus with the crucified Jesus: "That you may know that it is I, put your finger, Peter, in the nailprints of my hands." Thomas is commanded to follow, apparently for the same purpose, "And you, Thomas, put your finger in the spear-wounds of my side." The epiphany is concluded with a charge to Andrew, one of the two initial disciples of Jesus, to test the objective reality of Jesus' resurrection, "But you, Andrew, look at my feet and see if they do not touch the ground. For it is written in the prophet, 'The foot of a ghost or demon does not join to the ground.'"

This singular account of Jesus' resurrection and its verification by his disciples, affected significantly as it is by John 20, not only provides additional support for the Alexandrian origin of the Fourth Gospel. *More provocatively it promotes the likelihood that the text that the author of the Epistula Apostolorum utilized was the first edition of the Fourth Gospel, the edition that ended at 20:31.* Nothing of the content of John 21 is encountered in the *Epistola.* Moreover, the content of chapter 21, specifically its account of Jesus reminding Peter of his threefold denial by confronting him with his threefold mortifying question, "Simon, son of John, do you love me more than these," would exclude the possibility of a fourth denial that Jesus charges against Peter in the *Epistula.* In all probability, the first edition of the Fourth Gospel, chapters 1-20, originated in Alexandria, and for a period of time continued to exist without the appendix of chapter 21.[175]

The *Epistula Apostolorum* poses and perhaps resolves two other related issues. When might the superscription, εὐαγγέλιον κατὰ 'Ιωάννην (Gospel according to John) or κατὰ 'Ιωάννην (according to John), have been attached to the Fourth Gospel? And to whom does the name John refer? Noteworthy in this respect is the distinctive ordering of the eleven apostles, who present themselves as the authors of the *Epistula*: John, Thomas, Peter, Andrew, James, Philip, Bartholomew, Matthew, Nathanael, Judas Zelotes, and Cephas.[176] The conjecture of a strong Johannine influence becomes a certainty for Carl Schmidt on the basis of the names that follow John, specifically Thomas, Peter, and Andrew.[177] Very likely, then, it would also be the influence of the Fourth Gospel that resulted in the placement of John at the head of the list. But with whom is he to be identified? As already indicated, the only John who inhabits the narrative world of the Fourth Gospel is John the Witness. The "sons of Zebedee" make their first and only appearance in chapter 21, but they are not named. John the Witness, however, could never be regarded as a disciple/apostle of Jesus. Therefore, the John who

---

[175] The apparently dominant influence that the Fourth Gospel manifests in the writings of Clement of Alexandria may also point to the Alexandrian origin of that Gospel. See *The Exhortation to the Greeks*, chapters 1 and 11. See G.W. Butterworth, *Loeb Classical Library* (Cambridge: Harvard University Press, 1950) 15-26 and 235-251.

[176] H. Lietzmann, *Epistula*, 175, disputes C. Schmidt's allocation of the *Epistula* in an Asia Minor context by referring to Eusebius, *E H* I, 12, 2, in which the same differentiation of Peter and Cephas as two separate individuals occurs in the fifth book of Clement of Alexandria's *Hypotyposes* and therefore considers an Egyptian context for the letter more likely.

[177] Carl Schmidt, *Gespräche Jesu*, 241-242.

has been placed at the head of the authors of the *Epistula* must be the disciple John, the son of Zebedee, even though he is not named in the Gospel. The most reasonable conclusion, as already articulated, seems to be that from its very origin the Fourth Gospel bore the superscription, εὐαγγέλιον κατὰ 'Ιωάννην (Gospel according to John) or κατὰ 'Ιωάννην (according to John), referring to John the Witness. The author of the *Epistula*, however, familiar with the superscriptions of the Synoptic Gospels, particularly κατὰ Μαθθαῖον (according to Matthew), would naturally be inclined to identify John as a disciple, like Matthew. On the basis of the multiple references to John the son of Zebedee in the Synoptic Gospels, the John of the Fourth Gospel's superscription would naturally be identified as the son of Zebedee. As the supposed author of the Fourth Gospel, the Gospel addressed to the Jews of Alexandria "so that they might begin to believe that Jesus is the Messiah, the Son of God," the Christian Jewish author of the *Epistula Apostolorum* honored John as the preeminent disciple/apostle of Jesus.[178]

The transmission of the Fourth Gospel into other Mediterranean cities

Theophilus of Antioch and Ptolemy, a disciple of the Alexandrian Gnostic, Valentinus, are the earliest writers who ascribe the Fourth Gospel to 'John'. Theophilus, an apologist who published three books under the title *ad Autolycum* around 180 C.E., appears to have been influenced theologically by the Gospel. He draws the Logos (Word) of John 1:1 into his interpretation of the Genesis account of creation:

> But his Logos, through whom he made all things, who is his *Power and Wisdom* [1 Cor.1:24], assuming the role of the Father and Lord of the universe, was present in paradise in the role of God and conversed with Adam. For the divine scripture itself teaches us that Adam said that he 'heard a voice'. What is the 'voice' but the Logos of God, who is also his Son? – not as the poets and mythographers describe sons of gods begotten of sexual union, but as the truth describes the Logos, always innate in the heart of God. For before anything came into existence he had this as his Counselor, his own Mind and Intelligence. When God wishes to make what he had planned to make, he generated this Logos, making him external, as the *firstborn of all creation* [Col.1:15]. He did not deprive himself of the Logos but generated the Logos and constantly converses with his Logos. Hence the holy scriptures and all *those inspired by the Spirit* teach us, and one of them, *John*, says, 'In the beginning was the Logos, and the Logos was with God' [John 1:1]. He shows that originally God was alone and the Logos was in him. Then he says, 'And the Logos was God; everything was made through him, and apart from him nothing was made' [John 1:1-3].

[178] In view of the differentiation between the Jews and the Gentiles and particularly the favored status of the original eleven disciples/apostles as the original and therefore also legitimate bearers of Jesus' revelation, the anonymous author of the *Epistula,* as Martin Hornschuh stipulates in *Studien*, 81-82, n. 3, must be a Christian Jew.

> Since the Logos is God and derived his nature from God, whenever the Father of the universe wills to do so he sends him into some place where he is present and is heard and seen. He is sent by God and is present in a place.[179]

Noteworthy in this lengthy passage is Theophilus' attribution of the Fourth Gospel to "John" who is simply identified as one of "those inspired by the Spirit."[180] Here is another piece of evidence that the superscription, εὐαγγέλιον κατὰ 'Ιωάννην (gospel according to John) or κατὰ 'Ιωάννην, (according to John) was already attached to the manuscript of the Fourth Gospel that Theophilus possessed, and this John, in conjunction with the teaching of his Gospel, is regarded to be divinely inspired. Whether Theophilus' text of the Gospel included chapter 21 remains indeterminable. In all likelihood he, like the author of the*Epistula*, identified John as the son of Zebedee and therefore as "a disciple of the Lord."[181]

Whether the Alexandrian Gnostics identified the author of the Fourth Gospel on the same basis of the Gospel's superscription, as Theophilus of Antioch appears to have done is indeterminable. According to Irenaeus, Ptolemy wrote a commentary on the Prologue of the Fourth Gospel, in which he attributed the Prologue to "John, the Lord's disciple."[182] Heracleon, his contemporary, as well as a fellow disciple of Valentinus, produced a commentary on the Fourth Gospel, and, although there is no record of whom he identified as its author, it probably was "John, the Lord's disciple."[183]

Although Theophilus and the Alexandrian commentators of the Fourth Gospel were more or less contemporaneous, the authority they attributed to the Fourth Gospel was based on a different perspective of the author. Theophilus evidently did not need the apostolic authority of John as the Lord's disciple to establish the orthodoxy of his doctrine of the Logos. On the other hand, Ptolemy and Heracleon, by linking their philosophical theology to the Fourth Gospel as authored by "John, the Lord's disciple," may have been motivated "to vindicate

---

[179] *Ad Autolycum* II, 22. Text and translation by Robert M. Grant, *Theophilus of Antioch: Ad Autolycum* (Oxford: at the Clarendon Press, 1970) 65-67. It is also noteworthy that in II, 10 Theophilus equates the Logos and the Spirit: "Therefore God, having his own Logos innate in his own bowels [cf. Ps. 109:3], generated him together with his own Sophia, vomiting him forth before everything else."

[180] It is difficult to determine the significance of the conjunction "and" between "the holy scriptures *and* all those inspired by the Spirit." Is John to be identified with "the holy scriptures" or is he one of "those inspired by the Spirit"? Is Theophilus differentiating between the Old Testament and those, like John, who are divinely inspired? Or is John, as one of those inspired by the Spirit" to be regarded as scripture? See W. von Loewenich, *Das Johannes-Verständnis im zweiten Jahrhundert* (Giessen: Alfred Töpelmann, 1932) 54, who rightly, it seems to me, asserts that the prophets of the Old Covenant along with the Evangelists are comprehended by the predicate πνευματοφόροι (spirit-inspired).

[181] Bacon, *The Gospel of the Hellenists*, 90, identifies Theophilus' reference to "John, inspired by the Spirit" with John the apostle.

[182] *Against Heresies* I, 8, 5.

[183] See Elaine H. Pagels, *The Johannine Gospel in Gnostic Exegesis: Heracleon's Commentary on John* (Nashville: Abingdon Press, 1973) 16-17.

their own systems as having *Apostolic* authority."[184] Irenaeus ironically characterizes them in their use of the Fourth Gospel:

> Those, moreover, who follow Valentinus, making copious use of that according to John, *to illustrate their conjunctions*, shall be proved to be totally in error by means of this very Gospel. [185]

Is, then, their identification of John as "the Lord's disciple," simply determined by their need for apostolic validation? That is, did they themselves decide that the "John" of the Gospel's superscription must be identified with "the Lord's disciple" in order "to vindicate their own systems"? Or did they appropriate the identity of John as "the Lord's disciple" from another Christian community that already had made that identification?

Irenaeus, however, who cited their ascription of the Fourth Gospel to "John, the Lord's Disciple" elaborates this identity by associating it with the Beloved Disciple: "Afterwards John, the disciple of the Lord, who also had leaned upon his breast, did himself publish a Gospel during his residence at Ephesus in Asia."[186] Although he does not explicitly name John as the Beloved Disciple, his reference to John as the one who reclined on Jesus' bosom obviously indicates that he would make that identification. To associate "John" of the Gospel's superscription with the Lord's disciple, as the Alexandrian Gnostics did, does not necessarily imply an identification of John with the Beloved Disciple in the narrative world of the Fourth Gospel. Whether Ptolemy and Heracleon, in fact, did that remains indeterminable due to the fragmentary survival of their writings.

Irenaeus' identification of "John, the disciple of the Lord" with the Beloved Disciple requires that his edition of the Fourth Gospel included the appendix of chapter 21. For it is only in 21:20 that it is explicitly stated that the Beloved Disciple is the one who at the last supper reclined on Jesus' bosom, and, attendantly in 21:24, that he is the author of the Gospel. But since the Beloved Disciple is not named in 21:20, 24, there must be another basis for associating John with the Beloved Disciple and simultaneously identifying him as the author of the Gospel. That, of course, would be the Gospel's superscription, εὐαγγέλιον κατὰ Ἰωάννην (gospel according to John) or κατὰ Ἰωάννην (according to John).

---

[184] J.N. Sanders, *The Fourth Gospel*, 65. The italics are his.

[185] *Against Heresies* III, 11, 7. My italics.

[186] *Ibid*., III, 1, 1. Eusebius, *E H* V, 24, 3-4, reports the testimony of Polycrates, the bishop of Ephesus about 190 C.E. who advocated the Johannine dating of the crucifixion on the Day of Unleavened Bread: "Therefore we keep the day undeviatingly, neither adding nor taking away, for in Asia great luninaries sleep, and they will rise on the day of the coming of the Lord, when he shall come with glory from heaven to seek out all saints. Such were Philip of the twelve apostles and two of his daughters who grew old as virgins, who sleep in Hierapolis, and another daughter of his, who lived in the holy Spirit, rests in Ephesus. Moreover, there is also John, who lay on Jesus' breast, who was a priest wearing the headband (πέταλον), and a martyr and a teacher. He sleeps in Ephesus."

Since Irenaeus also testifies that John "*published a Gospel* during his residence in Ephesus," it seems plausible to surmise that this comprehensive tradition of the Gospel's authorship originated in the Christian community at Ephesus.[187] In all likelihood, in fact, the appendix of chapter 21was composed and attached to the first edition of the Gospel in Ephesus, and it was done in order to accord it apostolic authority.[188] If, therefore, the Gospel was *published* in Ephesus, as Irenaeus maintains, it must have been issued in the form of a new edition that included chapter 21 and all the necessary revisions of chapters 1-20. As a result, the first edition of the Gospel, written for a Jewish readership in Alexandria, became a Gospel addressed to those who already were Christians in Ephesus and the entire Mediterranean world. Accordingly, the aorist subjunctive πιστεύσητε (you begin to believe) of John 20:31, 19:35, and 6:29 was changed to the present subjunctive πιστεύητε (you continue to believe).

> ...but these things have been written so that *you continue to believe* that Jesus is the Christ, the Son of God, and that believing you have life by his name.

All the traditions that Irenaeus cites about John's residence in Ephesus support this conclusion:

> John, by writing this Gospel, sought "to remove that error which by Cerinthus had been disseminated among human beings."[189]

> When John was in the bath-house in Ephesus and learned that Cerinthus was also there, he rushed out, exclaiming, "Let us fly, lest even the bath-house fall down, because Cerinthus, the enemy of truth, is within."[190]

From now on, as a Gospel addressed to Christians, its witness can now be viewed as a refutation of false teaching, for as 21:24 adds, "and we know that his witness is true." Even as Simon Peter had been reinstated and commissioned to "shepherd the sheep," so John, in the guise of the Beloved Disciple, was authorized to serve

[187] J.N. Sanders, *The Fourth Gospel*, 38-39, maintains that the tradition of the Fourth Gospel originating in Ephesus by John the son of Zebedee "grew up in the latter half of the second century, when the local pride of the Ephesian Christians, who had already raised their 'Presbyter' John to the Apostolate by identifying him with the son of Zebedee, and their anxiety to have apostolic support in the Quartodeciman controversy induced them to see in the Fourth Gospel a work of the Apostle John."

[188] This is also the conclusion of B.W. Bacon, "John and the Pseudo-Johns," *ZNW* 31 (1932) 137. He rightly argues, "the *literary* tradition [of the Johannine writings] begins at Ephesus, where canonization also made its first beginnings." See also Bacon, *The Gospel of the Hellenists*, 72, who concludes, on the basis of his investigation of the echoes and influences of the Fourth Gospel in the Apostolic Fathers, "Before 150 A.D. the Fourth Gospel is unknown outside of proconsular Asia." Also p. 153.

[189] *Against Heresies* III, 11, 1.

[190] *Ibid.*, III, 3, 4

as "the abiding witness".[191] In this respect Irenaeus' acknowledgment of a privileged status that Ephesus bears is particularly relevant:

> The church in Ephesus, founded by Paul, and having John remaining among them permanently until the times of Trajan, is *a true witness of the tradition of the Apostles*.[192]

Irenaeus' testimony is obviously nothing more than a canon-maker's tradition. Or as B.W. Bacon certifies, "The name of John is used to cover the distinctive contribution of Ephesus to the canon."[193]

But canonization had become a necessity! In view of the growing metaphysical dualism of the Gnostics in Egypt and Asia Minor and the prophetic excesses of Montanism that had originated in Phrygia, a measuring stick, a *kanon*, was required in order to establish the boundaries of Christian theology and doctrine. The non-conformist character of the Fourth Gospel, however, posed a problem in this context.[194] Both its use by the heresiarchs and its perplexing dissimilarity over against the Synoptics generated a widespread suspicion of its authenticity that in some quarters resulted in a repudiation of its authority among representatives of what is generally called orthodox Christianity. The Roman Presbyter Gaius, and his fellow Alogi, out of their hostility toward the prophetic excesses of Montanists, repudiated all the writings associated with the name of John: the Revelation to John, the Johannine letters and the Gospel according to John, even though they were espoused by the Ephesian Church.[195] Their refutation of Montanism and concomitantly the Johannine writings probably was set forth in the "Dialogue of Gaius," in which, according to Eusebius, Gaius sought "to curb the recklessness and audacity of his opponents in composing new Scriptures."[196] Since he, Gaius,

---

[191] Bacon, "John and the Pseudo-Johns," 145. Sanders, *The Fourth Gospel*, 66-84, shows at length how invaluable the teaching of the Fourth Gospel was to Irenaeus in refuting the heretical interpretations of the Valentinians, Ptolemy and Heracleon.

[192] *Ibid.* The italics are mine.

[193] Bacon, "John and the Pseudo-Johns," 140. See also pp. 132-150 where Bacon adroitly debunks the entire tradition of a Gospel published in Ephesus by the Apostle John.

[194] The Fourth Gospel is an exceptionally singular construction of Jesus' career and teaching. There are no birth narratives of Jesus, no temptation in the wilderness, no naming of the twelve males who serve as the representatives of the New Israel. Instead of teaching parables, Jesus speaks in lengthy discourses. There are no exorcisms. No transfiguration occurs; no Lord's Supper is instituted. Seven representative "signs" convey the objective of Jesus' ministry, and two of them, the transformation of water into wine at Cana and the resurrection of Lazarus, do not appear in the Synoptic tradition. The so-called "Cleansing of the Temple" occurs at the beginning of Jesus' career instead of the historically more certain climax of his ministry.

[195] According to B.W. Bacon, "The Elder John, Papias, Irenaeus, Eusebius and the Syriac Translator," 2-3, "Irenaeus and his disciple Hippolytus defended the Fourth Gospel against the Roman presbyter Gaius and his followers. Hippolytus labeled them Alogi (senseless), 'who for the sake of ridding themselves of the Phrygian heresy had emptied out the baby with the bath' by rejecting the whole Phrygo-Asiatic canon: Gospel, Epistles and Apocalypse." On Gaius of Rome and the Fourth Gospel, see Hans von Campenhausen, *The Formation of the Christian Bible*, trans. by J. A. Baker (Philadelphia: Fortress Press, 1972) 238-242.

[196] *E H* VI, 20, 3. See also II, 25, 6.

could not harmonize the Gospel according to John with the Synoptics and determined that it was a counterfeit produced by Cerinthus, he proscribed its being read in the church.[197]

Others, however, who unhesitatingly subscribed to the legitimacy of the Fourth Gospel as the Gospel according to the Apostle John, resorted to different defenses in order to justify its non-conformist character. According to Eusebius, Clement of Alexandria accounted for the uniqueness of the Fourth Gospel by characterizing it as a "spiritual Gospel" deliberately designed to complement the preoccupation of the first three Gospels with the "external facts" of Jesus' ministry.

> But John, last of all, perceiving that external facts had been disclosed in the Gospels, having been urged on by his friends, and divinely moved by the Spirit, produced a *spiritual Gospel*.[198]

Irenaeus, on the other hand, was constrained to make use of the numerical value of the number four in order to justify its parity with the first three Gospels.

> It is not possible that the Gospels can be either more or fewer than they are. For since there are four zones of the world in which we live, and four principal winds, while the Church is scattered throughout all the world, and the "pillar and ground" of the Church is the Gospel and the spirit of life; it is fitting that she should have four pillars, breathing out immortality on every side and vivifying human beings afresh.[199]

The Muratorian Canon resolves the problem of its eccentric character by ascribing it to the disciple John, who wrote at the encouragement of the other disciples but at the same time included their recollections as well as his own. Noteworthy is the role of Andrew, who, with another unnamed disciple of John, according to John 1:35-39, began to follow Jesus after John the Witness had identified him as "the Lamb of God." By revelation Andrew determines that his fellow unnamed disciple, identified now by tradition as John, should write the Gospel in his own name. All the things he records, however, are the memories of all his fellow disciples. By attributing the content of this Gospel to the larger circle of Jesus' disciples, this tradition invalidates any apprehension or anxiety about its unconventional character.

> The fourth gospel is that of John, one of the disciples. When his fellow disciples and bishops exhorted him he said, "Fast with me for three days from today, and then let us relate to each other whatever may be revealed to each of us." On the same night it was revealed to Andrew, one of the Apostles, that John should narrate all things in his own name as *they* remembered them...[200]

---

[197] *Ibid.*, III, 28, 2. See the discussion of Gaius and the Alogi in Carl Schmidt, *Gespräche Jesu*, 435-452.

[198] *E H* VI, 14, 7. Cited by M. F. Wiles, *The Spiritual Gospel*, 8. Italics are mine.

[199] *Against Heresies* III, 11.8. *The Ante-Nicene Fathers* I, 428.

Origen, like Clement, considered the Fourth Gospel to be a *completion* of the record of Jesus Christ. He calls it "the spiritual Gospel," and attributes its uniqueness to the profound truths that originated from the spiritual intimacy that the Beloved Disciple, who is identified as John, enjoyed in his relationship with Jesus, a relationship disclosed by his privileged position of reclining on Jesus' bosom at the last supper.[201] There are discrepancies between it and the Synoptic Gospels that cannot be harmonized because of their contradictory chronological sequences.[202] But these inconsistencies should not undermine faith because they are designed to express spiritual truths.

> They proposed to speak the truth where it was possible both materially and spiritually, and where this was not possible it was their intention to prefer the spiritual to the material. The spiritual truth was often preserved, as one might say, in the material falsehood.[203]

Others, like Eusebius, Epiphanius, and Augustine, attempted to resolve all apparent points of conflict, while Theodore of Heraclea claimed there were no chronological discrepancies because only the Fourth Gospel was chronologically oriented.

Against the Church at Rome that claimed the authority of Paul and Peter, the Ephesian Church appears to have vaunted its own prestige by being the Church "founded by Paul, and having John remaining among them permanently until the times of Trajan." Most likely its authorization of an edition of the Gospel that was now addressed to all Christians, along with the supporting voices of many of the leading theologians of the second half of the second century, advanced its circulation throughout the Mediterranean world. [204]

In spite of the manuscript tradition and its variants of John 20:31, none of these ancient readers and interpreters expresses any awareness of the existence of two editions of the Fourth Gospel. Any copies of the first edition of chapters 1-20 that continued to circulate after the second edition had been issued, would very soon have been emended to include chapter 21 as it circulated among the Christians of the Mediterranean world. Concomitantly, by the time the rupture between the Jews

---

[200] *Documents of the Christian Church*, selected and edited by Henry Bettenson (New York: Oxford University Press, 1947) 40. Italics are mine.

[201] Origen claims, "No one can apprehend the meaning of it (the Gospel) except he have lain on Jesus' breast and received from Jesus Mary to be his mother also." *Commentary on John* I, 6. *The Ante-Nicene Fathers*, trans. & ed. by Allan Menzies (Grand Rapids: Eerdmans) X, 300.

[202] Origen, *Commentary on John* X, 2. *The Ante-Nicene Fathers*, X, 382.

[203] Origen, *ibid.*, X, 4.

[204] Ernst Haenchen, *John. Hermeneia*, I, 14, has observed, "About 200 C.E. the situation is suddenly altered: all at once the 'ecclesiastical tradition' of the son of Zebedee as the author of the Gospel of John appears. This tradition is present on a broad front: the Muratorian Canon, Irenaeus, Theophilus of Antioch, Polycrates of Ephesus, and somewhat later, Clement of Alexandria." See also B. W. Bacon, "The Elder John, Papias, Irenaeus, Eusebius and the Syriac Translator," 1ff., for his discussion on the debate of the authorship and authenticity of the Johannine writings in the late second half of the second century.

and the Christian Jews of Alexandria had become complete, the second edition of the Gospel, that included chapter 21 and circulated under the identification of John as "the Lord's disciple" and was endorsed by the Christian community at Ephesus, had became the dominant version. Evidently Jewish Christianity forgot that it had once authored and possessed a Gospel of its own that had originated within a Hellenistic Jewish community, an evangelistic Gospel that was designed to draw their fellow Jews into a living Temple of God that Jesus, the Jew from Nazareth had pioneered.[205]

In conclusion it needs to be said that there is no reliable historical evidence that there was an Apostle John or John, "the Lord's disciple" in Ephesus in apostolic times. This tradition would presuppose that the son of Zebedee emigrated from Jerusalem (or Pella in Transjordan) all the way to Ephesus, compelled perhaps by the outbreak of the Jewish revolt against Roman hegemony around 66 C.E. In accordance with the Gospel's tradition of 19:26-27, the Beloved Disciple, to whom Jesus had entrusted his mother, would naturally have taken her with him and then, like him, she would have died and been buried in Ephesus. Such a tradition has survived in Ephesus and is represented to this day by a tomb of Mary.

But the name John does not appear among those greeted by the Apostle Paul in Romans 16, the chapter that he added to constitute a second edition of his letter to the Romans to be delivered to the Christians of Ephesus.[206] Ignatius and Polycarp know nothing about the Apostle John at Ephesus.[207] Justin Martyr, who lived in Ephesus around 135 C.E. makes no reference to such an Apostle, and if his Logos doctrine is indeed a development of the Prologue of the Fourth Gospel, it is noteworthy that he does not cite the Gospel by name.[208]

Historically speaking, the Apostle John, who was believed to have resided in Ephesus until the times of Trajan and to have published a Gospel during that period of residency, never lived in Ephesus. Most likely, in fact, he was already dead, having been martyred sometime between the writing of Galatians and the Roman destruction of Jerusalem.[209] Although an impressive sweep of evidence for

---

[205] Walter Bauer, *Rechtgläubigkeit und Ketzerei im ältesten Christentum*, 2nd ed with a postscript by Georg Strecker (Tübingen: J. C. B. Mohr (Paul Siebeck), 1964) 261, comments, "Es ist beachtenswert, dass die judenchristlichen Kerygmen – im Gegensatz zu der Annahme der kirchlichen Häresiologen – eine Kenntnis von einem judenchristlichen Evangelium nicht besitzen."

[206] See T.W. Manson, "St. Paul's Letter to the Romans – and Others," *Bulletin of the John Rylands Library* 31/2 (1948) 16, for his evidence that Paul prepared a second copy of Romans that included chapter 16 and sent it eastward to Ephesus.

[207] Bacon, "John and the Pseudo-Johns," 137, 140-141.

[208] J.N. Sanders, *The Fourth Gospel*, 27-32, has examined the possible parallels between Justin's *Apology* and his *Dialogue with Trypho*, and he concludes that "certain passages may be explained as reminiscences of the Fourth Gospel, ... there are few, if any, which can certainly be said to be dependent upon it." In contrast, von Loewenich, *Das Johannes-Verständnis*, 45-50, has concluded that Justin's doctrine of the Logos may be regarded as a development of his strong Greek philosophical Logos perspective.

[209] See the lengthy essay by Eduard Schwartz, "Über den Tod der Söhne Zebedäi: ein Beitrag zur Geschichte des Johannesevangeliums," *Johannes und sein Evangelium*, ed. By Karl Heinrich

his martyrdom has been assembled by R. H. Charles, much of it unfortunately is circumstantial.[210] The usual starting point is the prediction of Jesus in Mark 10:35-40,

> And Jesus said to them, "The cup which I drink, you will drink, and the baptism with which I am baptized, you will be baptized."

The strongest support for the death of the Apostle John before 70 C.E. is furnished by a Papias tradition reinforced by the North African work *de Rebaptismate*, the testimony of Chrysostom, the Syrian Aphraates *de Persecutione*, and the Syrian Martyrology.[211] Attendantly, therefore, the tradition that the son of Zebedee as the Beloved Disciple, took the mother of Jesus with him when he moved to Ephesus is equally groundless.

The problem of authorship

What, if anything, then, can be said about the authorship of the Fourth Gospel? The reference of 19:35 to the testimony of the one who witnessed the death of Jesus may offer a clue:

> *The one having seen* (ἑωρακώς) has testified, and his testimony is trustworthy, and that one knows that [what] he says is true, so that you begin to believe.

Although the verse is omitted in the Old Latin text of "e" and a number of Vulgate manuscripts, it belongs to the first edition of the Gospel and is intended to confront the implied readers with the historical certainty of this event. But it is difficult to determine if the author of the Gospel is referring to himself as this witness or if the testimony that is being cited was adopted from someone who is being validated as a reliable eyewitness. The demonstrative pronoun ἐκεῖνος (that one) seems to refer to someone other than the eye-witness *who has seen* (ὁ ἑωρακώς) the confluence of blood and water; and it is "that one," probably the Evangelist, who is guaranteeing the truth of the received testimony "in order that you may begin to believe."[212] *That one* (ἐκεῖνος), therefore, writing at a later time, specifically at

---

Rengstorf (Darmstadt: Wissenschaftliche Buchgesellschaft, 1973) 202-272, who maintained that if Jesus' prediction of the martyrdom of James and John were limited to James, and only half of his prediction had been fulfilled, the tradition would not have been included in the Gospel (202, n. 2).

[210] R. H. Charles, *Revelation. The International Critical Commentary* (Edinburgh: T. & T. Clark, 1920, 1956) I, xiv-l.

[211] Johannes Weiss, "Zum Märtyrertod der Zebedäiden," *ZNW* 11 (1910) 167, observes that the Sinaitic Syriac and the Sinaitic Curetonian substitute "You are able to drink" and "You are able to be baptized" in place of Jesus' use of the future tense, "You will drink" and "You will be baptized" and consequently strip Jesus' words of their original prophetic import. That would imply that these translations represent the tradition that John did not suffer a martyrs' death. Weiss rejects this substitution of the Syriac translators.

[212] Bultmann, *John*, 678; German, 526, asks, "Who is the ἐκεῖνος?" And he replies, "It cannot be the eye-witness himself, but must be another who is in a position to guarantee the truth of the testimony." In n. 5 he adds, "... the subject of οἶδεν (he/she knows) must be a different one from that of λέγει (he/she says)."

the end of the first century C.E. is confronting the implied readers of Alexandria with the testimony of someone who was present at the crucifixion. That individual must be one of the four figures that the narrator identified at the crucifixion, most likely the Beloved Disciple to whom Jesus entrusted his mother. More specifically, it would be Lazarus whom Jesus raised from the dead and who has followed him all the way to the cross and will become the first disciple to believe that Jesus rose from the dead. He would be a persuasive witness, especially if he were that unnamed disciple who, with Andrew, after leaving John the Witness, has been present throughout the narrative world of the Gospel.[213]

Lazarus, as the Beloved Disciple, fulfills the function of witness in a variety of ways. He experiences his own resurrection as Jesus calls him out of his tomb and therefore becomes the representation of the here-and-now reality of the resurrection that Jewish apocalypticism continued to project into the future. His unbinding by the bystanders offers a model of the community's ordained ministry to its members in the corporate activity of liberation. His experience at Jesus' empty tomb establishes his non-epistemic faith as the subjective basis of believing that Jesus rose from the dead. His loyalty to Jesus at the interrogation before Annas, his presence at the crucifixion, his undertaking the care of Jesus' mother, and his seeing and believing on Easter morning certify him as the ideal disciple and the consummate witness of the truth of the Gospel.

But how is he to be judged? Is he a fictional construction? That is a captivating possibility, especially in view of the mythical character of the story of his resurrection that is designed to constitute reality for the implied readers of the Gospel. On the other hand, he may be an historical figure who initially followed John the Witness/Baptizer but subsequently became a disciple of Jesus. Yet no disciple by that name appears in the Synoptic Gospels. It is possible, of course, that he could have lived on as an unacknowledged witness of Jesus' ministry within the Jerusalem community of Christian Jews and perhaps even as a participant in the evangelizing mission of the Jerusalem Church under James to the Jewish community of Alexandria prior to the destruction of Jerusalem.

Lazarus, like James, the brother of Jesus, appears to have been esteemed by the Pharisees, if, as ascertained above, the reference to οἱ Ἰουδαῖοι (the Jews) in 11:33, 36, may be identified as the Pharisees. It is noteworthy that they were involved in mourning Lazarus' death, were present at his resurrection and therefore must have participated in his unbinding (11:44). Many of them, according to 11:45, began to believe into Jesus "*sizing up* (θεασάμενοι) that which he did." Is this a fictional construction of the Lazarus story that may be intended to impress the ruling authorities among the implied readers of Alexandria? Or is this an

[213] Brown, *The Community of the Beloved Disciple*, 31-34, acknowledges that since he wrote his commentary on the Fourth Gospel, he has changed his mind about the identity of the Beloved Disciple and no longer considers him to be Jesus' disciple, John the son of Zebedee. Although he is convinced that the Beloved Disciple was an historical figure who is identifiable with the unnamed companion of Andrew who left John and began to follow Jesus, he does not identify him with Lazarus.

historical reality that reflects an event prior to the destruction of Jerusalem? Was Lazarus among the disciples who, like James, was stoned to death after they were condemned by a session of the Sanhedrin that Ananus had convened?[214] According to 12:10, "Now the chief priests deliberated that they also kill Lazarus." Could Annas be deliberately named in 18:13 to recall Ananus, in as far as Lazarus followed Jesus into the interrogation before Annas? Is it possible, therefore, that he, like James, after his martyrdom by the chief priests, was mourned by the Pharisees?

What is the function of the use of the imperfect indicative ἐφίλει (he was loving) in 11:36 and 20:2? Is it intended to limit the protracted action of Jesus' loving to the period of his historical ministry – like other instances of the imperfect tense in the Gospel? This, for example, appears to be the objective of the imperfect tense in 7:5, "For his brothers also were not believing (ἐπίστευον) into him." Beyond the singular career of Jesus, however, his brother James, and in all likelihood his other brothers, were drawn into the Christian faith. If James is the *fons et origo* of Egyptian Christianity, he would certainly be known to the Jewish community of Alexandria as a follower of Jesus and therefore as a Christian Jew; and the implied readers of the Gospel would naturally construe the imperfect tense of 7:5 as a historical reality limited to Jesus' ministry. Is the imperfect tense of ἐφίλει to be interpreted similarly? Was Lazarus a disciple whom Jesus especially loved because of his staunch and unwavering discipleship from the time he left John the Witness and began to follow Jesus? Did the implied author of the Gospel consequently use his death to draw Jewish apocalypticism's myth of resurrection out of the time frame of the distant future into the here and now present? Did the Evangelist anachronously relocate the time of Lazarus' death in order to place it into the context of Jesus' ministry as the seventh and culminating sign of his ministry? At the center of the story of his resurrection is the profound aporia of death, that is constituted by Jesus' resurrection from the dead and predetermined on the basis of the commitment that human beings make to Jesus as the Pioneer of a New Humanity. On the one hand, as Jesus tells his disciples, "Lazarus our friend has fallen asleep." On the other hand, however, he is dead. Jesus' solemn declaration of 11:25 expresses the double-bind of the Christian interpretation of death that, in imitation of Martha, is to be embraced by all who experience the loss of loved ones in death, and also who, like Lazarus, will experience death sooner or later themselves.

> I am the Resurrection and the Life! The one who believes into me if he dies will live, and everyone who lives and believes into me never dies.

However these issues are to be judged, it is conceivable that Lazarus' witness may have been appropriated and elaborated in the composition of the Fourth

---

[214]Josephus, *Ant* XX, 200-203, refers to "James, the brother of Jesus who was called the Christ, and certain others." See also Eusebius, *E H* II, 23, 1-18 and III, 11-12.

Gospel. As for the author himself, his identity remains unknown, concealed behind the "implied author" whom the reader can encounter in the textual structures of the Gospel. But there are a few certainties that are discernible from the text. The author of the Gospel according to John was a Christian Jew of the Jewish community of Alexandria who, in dialogue with the philosophical-theological writings of Philo, creatively formulated his own theological synthesis within the constructed framework of an original narrative world of the Gospel of Jesus Christ. Living and writing within the conflict and antagonism that permeated this Jewish community as it struggled to reconstitute its identity after its unifying Center, the Jerusalem Temple, had been destroyed by the Romans, he composed a Gospel that would address all the constituent members of this larger community: the Jews who were embracing Philo's philosophical theology, the followers of John the Baptizer, the Samaritans, and especially the Jews who were being induced into the Pharisaic heritage by the growing authority of the rabbinic academy at Jamnia. All of these groups are to be included in the textual structures of the implied reader, for, as the closing verse of the Alexandrian edition of the Gospel acknowledges, "... these things have been written so that you begin to believe that Jesus is the Christ, the Son of God, and that believing you have life in/by his name." With the possible exception of the Apostle Paul, no other author and theologian of the New Testament writings can equal the genius and profundity that are manifested in this literary masterpiece.

Chapter Two

The Prologue 1:1-18

The Word of God in the Old Testament

᾽Εν ἀρχῇ ἦν ὁ λόγος. "In the beginning was the *Word*."[1] In all likelihood, the "beginning" to which this opening prepositional phrase refers is indicated by the parallel prepositional phrase, ᾽Εν ἀρχῇ, that introduces the creation account of the Septuagint translation of Genesis 1. This deliberate correspondence intimates that the implied readers of the opening verse of the Fourth Gospel are expected to identify this beginning with the Genesis account of the creation. This is not the beginning of the *Word*, but the beginning of the creation. Prior to the beginning of God's creative act, the *Word* already existed. It was neither created nor begotten! It was![2]

But what or who is the *Word*? Its placement at the beginning of the Gospel indicates that it is a figure that is already known to the implied readers.[3] It is noteworthy that it stands by itself, ὁ λόγος, without any attributes and without the usual accompanying genitive phrase, τοῦ θεοῦ (of God). It seems to be a proper name![4] Apparently it is a self-existing being or entity that, in its relationship to God's creative act of Gen 1, is the repository of God's language and speech activity.

---

[1] The Prologue is interpreted synchronically, without any effort expended to determine its earlier derivation and the possible units of tradition from which it may have been constituted. Consequently, it is not presupposed that "a cultic community hymn" underlies the Prologue that may have been composed in Aramaic and translated into Greek by the Evangelist and developed with his own comments, as Bultmann contends, *John*, 14-18; German, 1-5. Brown, *John* I, LXIX, does not consider the Prologue to be a key to the whole Gospel and, like Bultmann, believes that it was an independent hymn "that was adapted to serve as the introduction to the Gospel." But the Gospel in its entirety presupposes the Prologue as it presents the indispensable history of the Logos from creation to incarnation and with it the paradoxical movement between the Logos and the Creator that is the key to the christological formulation of the identity of Jesus . See Walter Eltester, "Der Logos und sein Prophet," *Apophoreta: Festschrift für Ernst Haenchen* (Berlin: Alfred Töpelmann, 1964) 109-134; especially p. 118, "...er ist eine geschichtstheologische Ausführung über Sein, Wesen und Werk des Logos." See also the critique of Ernst Käsemann, "Aufbau und Anliegen des johanneischen Prologs," *Exegetische Versuche und Besinnungen* (Göttingen: Vandenhoeck & Ruprecht,1964) II, 155-180.

[2] Karl Bornhäuser, *Das Johannesevangelium: eine Missionsschrift für Israel* (Gütersloh: C. Bertelsmann, 1928) 8.

[3] As Rudolf Bultmann has observed, *John*, 19; German, 5. See also pp. 20-36 for his analysis of the history of religions' background of the Logos figure; German, 6-15. Also Bultmann, "The History of Religions Background of the Prologue to the Gospel of John," *The Interpretation of John*, ed. & trans. by John Ashton (Philadelphia: Fortress Press, 1986), first published in *Eucharisterion: Festschrift für H. Gunkel II* (Göttingen: Vandenhoeck & Ruprecht, 1923) 3-26.

[4] Bultmann, *John*, 21.

In the Old Testament the being of God is always identified in relation to speech, דְּבַר יְהוָה (the word of Yahweh) or in the Septuagint, ὁ λόγος τοῦ κυρίου (the word of the Lord), and specifically in two different kinds of speech activity. On the one hand, God's word is the dynamic generating power of creation, as Gen 1 indicates again and again by the monotonous repetition of "And God said, ..." at the beginning of every creative act. This generative power of God's speech is affirmed by the Psalmist in LXX 32:6 (33:6), "By the word of the Lord (λόγῳ τοῦ κυρίου) the heavens were made firm, and all their power by the breath of his mouth."[5] The same generative power is communicated through "the word of the Lord" that the prophet Ezekiel is commanded to speak to the dry bones of Israel:

> And he said to me, "Prophecy to these bones and say to them, 'O dry bones, hear the λόγον κυρίου (word of the Lord)!' Thus says the Lord to these bones, 'See, I bring upon you πνεῦμα ζωῆς (breath of life), and I will bestow sinews upon you and I will bring up flesh upon you and I will stretch out skin upon you and I will bestow my πνεῦμα (breath, spirit) into you and you will live. (Ezek 37:4-5)

On the other hand, God's speech is also an implement of communication and a medium of revelation. Angelic beings, but chiefly judges and prophets, serve as God's messengers to disclose God's will, to enunciate God's promises, to forth-tell the imminent future and to pronounce judgment. Not only are they empowered to speak God's word; God's word itself, which they speak, is a power to accomplish its appointed mission and to actualize its fulfillment in Israel's history.[6]

> For even as the rain or the snow descends from heaven and by no means is returned until it satiates the earth and brings forth and sprouts and gives seed to the sower and bread for food, so will my word be that goes forth from my mouth; it will by no means be returned until it fulfills whatever I will, and prospers your ways and my commandments. (LXX Isa 55:10-11)

Because it is God's word, it is truth (2 Sam 7:28), and those who embrace it can speak an "Amen" to affirm its validity (Deut 27:26). Because it is God's word, as Moses informed the people of Israel in Deut 30:14, it "is not too hard for you, neither is it far off. ... But the word is very near you; it is in your mouth and in your heart that you can do it." And finally, because it is God's word, according to Isa 40:8, "The grass withers, the flower fades, but *the word of* our *God* (ῥῆμα τοῦ θεοῦ) will stand forever."

---

[5] A comparison of the quotations of the Old Testament encountered in the Fourth Gospel reveals that the Septuagint was the Bible of the Alexandrian community of Hellenistic Jews to which the Gospel was addressed, although internal evidence also indicates that some knowledge of Aramaic was assumed.

[6] See 1 Sam 15:23-28, 2 Sam 23:1-5, 1 Kgs 2:27. See O. Procksch, " Wort Gottes im AT" *TWNT*, ed. by Gerhard Kittel (Stuttgart: W. Kohlhammer, 1942) IV, 89-100; English: *Theological Dictionary of the New Testament*, abridged in one volume, ed. by Gerhard Kittel and Gerhard Friedrich, trans. by Geoffrey W. Bromiley (Grand Rapids: Eerdmanns, 1985) 507-509.

God's Word, as the agent of creation, communication and revelation, is also differentiated from God and identified as a separate entity. C. H. Dodd asserts, "We have to observe that for the Hebrew the word once spoken has a kind of substantive existence of its own."[7] God's speech activity, therefore, could be handed down to subsequent generations in the form of oral tradition or a book. Originally communicated by chosen representatives and transmitted orally, it was gradually transcribed into writing and preserved in books. The divinely inspired utterances of the prophets were collected, edited and transmitted in written form as the word of the Lord. Many of them, Hos 1:1, Joel 1:1, Mic 1:1, Zeph 1:1, Mal 1:1, are introduced by the formula דְּבַר יְהוָה (the word of Yahweh) or in the Septuagint, (λόγος κυρίου), signifying that the entire book of the prophet's disclosures was to be read and reverenced as God's word. Accordingly, God's word could continue among human beings in a form that was detached from God, seemingly independent of its divine origin yet bearing God's power and God's judgments. Even the possessive genitive, "of God" that identified the originator and owner of the word, could be deleted, and "the word of God" could simply be referred to as "this word" or "your word" or "the word." It appears in that mode in Deut 1:32. God's word, spoken earlier by God, has continued to exist in its own power, but in this context without achieving its divinely hoped-for objective.

> And in this word (λόγος) you did not trust in the Lord your God who goes before you on the way to elect for you a place (LXX Duet 1:32-33a)

The Psalmist affirms that the covenant that God's speech activity originally established with Israel continues as an ongoing, self-contained word that God had ordered for a multitude of generations.

> He is mindful of his covenant forever, of his word (λόγου) which he commanded to a thousand generations. (Psa 105(104):8)

In the Wisdom of Solomon, a Hellenistic Jewish composition that probably originated in Alexandria, God's word appears to have developed into a substantial being or hypostasis that subsists in a paradoxical or aporetic relationship with God. But it does not appear to be conceived of as the result of an "archetypal generation in the divine sphere", nor does it appear to be an emanation.[8] It is simply acknowledged as "your word" (logos), yet in its surrogate activity it is more than a divine attribute. On the one hand, it serves as God's agent of creation and therefore is dependent on the power that originated from God: "O God of the fathers and Lord of mercy, who made all things ἐν λόγῳ σου (by your Word)." But on the other hand, in its endeavors to fulfill God's will, it appears to have attained a semi-independent status as God's intermediary between heaven and earth. *Because the Word is on the brink of becoming a proper name, attributable*

[7] Dodd, *Fourth Gospel*, 264.

[8] See Bultmann, *John*, 32-33; German, 16-17, for his characterization of the Logos based on the phrase, καὶ ὁ λόγος ἦν πρὸς τὸν θεόν.

notably to its development under the influence of Hellenistic philosophy, it is more appropriate to refer to it by the original Greek term, Logos.[9]

> Your all-powerful λόγος (*Word*) leaped from heaven, from the royal throne, a stern warrior, into the midst of the land that was doomed, bearing the sharp sword of your authentic command, and standing filled all things with death, and touched heaven while established on earth. (Wis 18:15-16)

More significantly than this evolvement of God's Logos, it is Wisdom, or Sophia, that emerges in the Wisdom of Solomon as a substantial partner of God collaborating with God in the activities of creation, revelation and inspiration. Having already been venerated in Prov 8: 22-31 as the first of God's creative acts and associated with God as a "master worker" in creation, Sophia continues to serve in the same divine capacity, but more specifically in the creation and endowment of the human being.

> O God of the fathers and Lord of mercy, who made all things ἐν λόγῳ σου (by your Word) and built a human being τῇ σοφίᾳ σου (by your Wisdom) so that he/she exercises dominion over the creatures made by you and rules the world in holiness and justice... (Wis 9:1-2)

In 7:22-23 Sophia is extolled on the basis of twenty-one attributes that distinguish her divine character. As a mirror reflecting God's activities and as an image of God's goodness, she has attained the status of an hypostasis, and, like the Logos, she is involved in an aporetic relationship with God.

> For she is the steam (ἀτμίς) of God's power and a pure emanation of the glory of the Almighty. On account of this nothing impure intrudes into her, for she is a radiance of eternal light and a spotless mirror of God's action and an image of his goodness. (Wis 7:25-26)

> She glorifies her noble birth by living with God, and the Lord of all things loves her, for she is an initiate of God's knowledge and an associate of his works. (Wis 8:3-4)

In her dependence on God she mirrors the Creator's character and activities. But she also acts independently and spontaneously in the pursuit of her authorized objectives in order to fulfill her identity.

> Being but one she can do all things and remaining in herself she renews all things, and moving into holy souls in every generation, she constitutes friends of God and prophets. For God loves nothing except the one who lives with Sophia. (Wis 7:27-28)

Consequently Solomon prays in 9:4, "Give me Sophia (Wisdom) that sits by your throne."

[9] *Ibid.*, 24-28; German, 9-15, for Bultmann's review of the philosophical tradition of the Logos.

Logos and Sophia according to Philo

Philo of Alexandria appears to have united the Logos of Middle Platonism with the Logos and the Sophia of Hellenistic Judaism in order to constitute a divine hypostasis and intermediary that engages in the activities of creation, revelation and communication.[10] Logos is the ideal hypostasis for Philo because of its correlation with the speech activity that is ascribed to God in the Old Testament, but especially because the Logos is more immediately associated with the unchanging forms or universals of Platonic metaphysics. The two creation accounts of Gen 1 and 2 provided Philo with a fitting basis for the development of his cosmology of the Logos. The former, Gen 1, is a narration of the Logos emanating from God's conceptualization of the ideal world, that is, the totality of the fixed, unchanging universals that will serve as the prototype of the material creation.

> For God, being God, assumed that a beautiful copy would never be produced apart from a beautiful pattern, and that no object of perception would be faultless which was not made in the likeness of an original discerned only by the intellect. So when he willed to create this visible world, he first formed the intelligible world, in order that he might have the use of a pattern wholly God-like and incorporeal in producing the material world, as a later creation, the very image of an earlier, to embrace in itself objects of perception of as many kinds as the other contained objects of intelligence.[11]

> Therefore, even as the city, being prefigured within the mind of the architect, did not have a place in the outer world but was impressed as a seal in the soul of the craftsman; in the same manner the cosmos that [originated] from ideas would have no other place than the divine Logos, the one setting all these things in order.[12]

The Logos, as a divine personification of the forms or universals that God thought into being, is God's ideal construction of the world that culminates in the essence of the Human Being.

Genesis 2, on the other hand, is the account of the production of a material copy of the ideal model of Gen 1. It is in this context that Sophia plays a role in Philo's philosophical theology. She is "the mother and nurse of the All."[13] But Philo places her in a subordinate relationship to the Logos whom he identifies in this context as "the father."

---

[10] See the perspicacious analysis of Philo's doctrine of the Logos in David Winston, *Logos and Mystical Theology in Philo of Alexandria* (Cincinnati: Hebrew Union College Press, 1985) 9-58.

[11] Philo, *de Opificio Mundi*, 16, trans. by F. H. Colson and G. H. Whitaker, *Loeb Classical Library* (Cambridge: Harvard University Press, 1971).

[12] *Ibid.*, 20. My translation.

[13] Philo, *de Ebrietate*, 31.

> Well then, I say that the father is the masculine, perfect, upright Logos, but the mother, the middle circling course of general education, to whom it is good and profitable to be obedient as children to parents.[14]

Sophia as the mother "was the knowledge possessed by its Maker. God had union with his knowledge, not in the manner of a human being, and sowed created being." By relying on Prov 8:22, Philo concludes that Sophia is the feminine principle that gave birth to the "only and beloved son, the one perceived by the senses, the world we see."[15]

For Philo, however, Logos is God's consummate hypostasis because it is a divine union of the Platonic universals and God's speech activity, and he distinguishes it as a second deity. The Logos is God! Not *the* God, but God! Interpreting the words that God spoke to Jacob in LXX Gen 31:13, "I am the God who was seen by you in place of God!" he asks the question whether there are two Gods.[16]

> What, therefore, are we to say? On the one hand, he who in truth is God is One, but those in an analogical application are called more in number. Wherefore also the holy word in the present instance has indicated the one who is truly God through the [definite] article saying, ἐγώ εἰμί ὁ θεός (I am *the* God), but in an analogical application the one without a [definite] article, affirming, 'the one appearing to you in the place' not 'of *the* God' but only 'of God'. Now he calls his eldest Logos God.[17]

Continuing to reflect on this matter and drawing upon Ex 3:14, Philo proceeds to clarify why God can refer to the Logos as God.

> Now he testifies by an oracular utterance to the one inquiring [Moses] if he has a name, ἐγώ εἰμι ὁ ὤν (I am the One that is), so that of the things which are not possible for a human being to comprehend in the case of God, he/she might [at least]recognize his substance. Therefore, to incorporeal and worship-oriented souls, it is reasonable that he reveals himself as he is, dialogging as friend with friends. But to those still in the body, he shows himself in the likeness of angels, not changing his nature, for he is unchangeable, but presenting to those receiving the impression of his glory in a different form, to take the image not as a copy but [to take] the archetype itself to be that form.[18]

There are aspects of God's deity that human beings simply cannot comprehend, but they can nevertheless experience the existence of God. Those, however, who are

[14] *Ibid.*, 33. My translation.

[15] *Ibid.*, 30. See also *Legum Allegoria* II, 49. In *de Cherubim,* 49 God is designated as "the husband of Sophia".

[16] Philo misinterpreted the phrase, "in place of God" (ἐν τόπῳ θεοῦ) somehow unaware that it refers to Bethel, the place where God met Jacob in a dream.

[17] Philo, *de Somniis* I, 229-230. Elated at having found this text, I quickly learned that C.H. Dodd, *The Fourth Gospel*, 72, 276, had already appropriated it in his interpretation of the Fourth Gospel.

[18] *de Somniis* I, 231-232. My translation.

body-less souls engaged entirely in the worship of God, very likely will experience God's being as it is, analogous to a friend communicating with friends. On the other hand, those whose souls are still confined to a physical body will experience God in a different form, but that form will not be a copy of God's image, but the image or archetype itself, namely the Logos. In other words, God does not hesitate to identify the Logos, the very image that God reveals to human beings, as God. In his treatise, "Allegorical Interpretation," the Logos is designated δεύτερος ὁ θεοῦ λόγος (the Logos [is] second/next to God).[19]

In his treatise, "Who is the Heir" Philo offers a distinguished characterization of the divine activities of the Logos:

> To the Logos, chief messenger and most elderly, the Father, who generated all things, gave the special prerogative, so that standing [as] a border he separates the creature from the Creator. He is the suppliant of sick-at-heart mortality *towards* (πρός) the immortal and ambassador of the ruler *towards* (πρός) the subject. Now this one is always suppliant of sick-at-heart mortality towards the immortal, and ambassador of the ruler to the subject. And he exults in this estate and magnifying it describes it saying, 'And I stood between the Lord and you,' neither uncreated as God, nor created as you, but [in the] middle of extreme limits, between the two extremes, having shares in both sides; on the one hand, to the parent (the one planting) towards assurance that the creature never altogether rebels against the rein and revolts, winning disorder rather than order; to the child (the one planted), towards confidence that the merciful God will never overlook his own work. For I am the one sending messages of peace to creation from God, the one always determining to put down wars, always a guardian of peace.[20]

> But if there happens to be any as unworthy to be named a son of God, let him/her hasten to be ordered according to God's first-born (πρωτόγονος), his Logos, the one most elderly among the angels, as angel chief, having many names. For he is ἀρχή (beginning), ὄνομα θεοῦ (Name of God) and λόγος (Word) and ὁ κατ' εἰκόνα ἄνθρωπος (the human being according to his image) and ὁ ὁρῶν,'Ισραήλ (the one who sees, Israel).[21]

In its fixed and static relationship to the Creator, the Logos is essentially a differentiating entity, located in a hierarchically structured order that separates the creature from the Creator. Serving as the intermediary of communication in this condition of *apartheid*, the Logos transmits messages from "the immortal" to "afflicted mortality" and from "afflicted mortality" to "the immortal." In this stationary mode the Logos is also the personification of cosmic law, and therefore it is analogous to the reins that guide a horse, not to the reign of God into which human beings may enter. Consequently, human beings are prevented from

[19] *Legum Allegoria* II, 86. My translation.

[20] *Quis Rerum Divinarum Heres,* 206. My translation.

[21] Philo, *de Confusione Linguarum*, 146. My translation.

completely rebelling against God and choosing disorder rather than order. This legislative capacity enables the Logos to function as a divine sentinel of peace.

The Logos of the prologue

The three-fold reference to the Logos in the opening verse of the Gospel indicates, as already stated, that this figure of a divine hypostasis, uniting God's universals and God's speech activity, was familiar to the implied readers of this Gospel, the Jews and Christian Jews of Alexandria, to whom it was originally addressed.[22] The introductory phrase, "In the beginning was the Logos!" bears a resemblance to the primordial status and capacity that Philo assigns to the Logos: a substantive being co-existing with God the Creator, and, in its origination, bearing the image and likeness of God.[23] Equally significant, the Logos of the Prologue, like Philo's Logos, is God. Not *the* God! Not God the Creator! But God! And as in Philo's cosmology, the Logos of the Prologue serves as the Creator's agent in the dynamic activity of creating a world (κόσμος), even as John 1:10 witnesses, "... and the world came into being through him." The Logos is God's formative power of possibility by which the non-being of chaos is actualized into a world.

Yet before the Logos serves as the divine agent of creation, its ontological and prehistoric relationship to the Creator is prioritized, "And the Logos was *towards* the God."[24] Although the Logos is independent of the Creator, a being in and of itself, unlike Philo's Logos it does not co-exist alongside the Creator as a static entity. Its primordial relationship to God the Creator is πρὸς τὸν θεόν; a phrase that should be translated, "towards the God." The Greek preposition, πρὸς, when it governs the accusative case, denotes motion, and therefore the meaning "towards" conveys a more accurate sense of the original Greek.[25] The preposition,

[22] Bornhäuser, *Das Johannesevangelium*, 5, rejects Philo's writings as a means of understanding the Prologue. Also Bultmann, "The History of Religions Background of the Prologue to the Gospel of John," 27; Lindars, *The Gospel of John*, 39, 83, "John show no acquaintance with Philo's works..." But the role of Nathanael for the implied readers of the Alexandrian Jews as "a true Israelite" who "will see" and the employment of four verbs of seeing that correspond to those encountered in Philo's writings will indicate at least a familiarity with the writings of Philo.

[23] Dodd, *The Fourth Gospel*, 279, does not consider the dynamic relationship between the Logos and God the Creator, particularly in the use of the preposition πρός in verse one, and therefore he writes, "I conclude that the substance of a Logos-doctrine similar to that of Philo is present all through the gospel, and that the use of the actual term λόγος in the Prologue, in a sense corresponding to that doctrine, though it is unparalleled in the rest of the gospel, falls readily into place." It seems more correct to say that there are similarities, but also significant differences.

[24] The use of the definite article before "God" is intended to convey to the reader that God the Creator is the referent.

[25] Philo also employs the preposition πρός, as the quote from *Quis Rerum Divinarum Heres,* 206 indicates. But it is the movement of communication *towards* the creator from a stationary location between the Creator and the creature. See Bo Reicke, "πρός," *TDNT*, VI, 721, who states that πρός denotes movement "towards" and is almost parallel to εἰς (into). Bultmann, *John*, 32-33, does not comment on the preposition, but he rightly contends that no sense of subordination is implicit in the second and third clauses of verse 1. Brown, *John.* I, 4-5, justifies the translation of πρός as "with" in the sense of "communion" and as "towards" in the sense of "relationship" – yet without any clear preference other than opting for "a nuance of relationship". Barrett, *St. John*, 155, acknowledges that

"with," that is usually employed in English translations, signifies an "alongside of" presence, and in that sense it unfortunately supports Philo's conception of an immobile and static Logos.[26] *The movement that the preposition* πρὸς, *denotes in this context is so pivotal that the phrase* πρὸς τὸν θεόν *is repeated in verse 2.*

Primordially the Logos moves toward God the Creator in order to unite with its Originator, so that it may affirm the ontological unity out of which it originated and in which it continually wills to participate. As its movement of πρὸς τὸν θεόν is completed in its union with the Creator, it participates in the being of the Creator and its own being as "God" is validated, "and the Word was God." Not "the God" but "God"! No definite article is placed before θεόν (God) in this final phrase. In this union the Logos does not disappear by being fused or merged into God the Creator. The Logos does not become identical to God the Creator. It continues to remain itself and retain its identity, but in its primordial relationship to the self-existent God, it is always directed towards the union from which it originated. In this aporetic relationship of union and differentiation, the Logos is essentially an interdependent being. Yet as the conjunction of the Creator God's universals and speech activity, the Logos is also directed towards the fulfillment of God's activities of creation, revelation and communication, and ultimately incarnation.[27]

At the beginning of God's creative act, the Logos served as the divine agent by which the creation was called into being. As verse 3 asserts, "All things happened through him, and without him there happened nothing that has happened."[28] The Logos calls into being a world of binary differentiations, all of which reflect the goodness of its Originator. No antagonistic oppositions emerge from this process. Light and darkness, sky and earth, land and sea, women and men are equally good. For if the Logos is initially in movement πρὸς τὸν θεόν, (towards God the Creator), its participation in the divine essence, resulting in its identity as God (θεός), bears immediate consequences for the character of the work it performs.

πρός with the accusative can hardly mean 'in the presence of' in classical Greek, but this meaning is unquestionable in New Testament Greek..." The preposition is employed 95 times in the first edition of the Gospel, and at least 29 occurrences intimate movement towards union

[26] Dodd, *The Fourth Gospel*, 269, prefers to translate πρός as "with." "In the act of creation the word was to go forth from God, but before creation was begun it was 'with God', ἦν πρὸς τὸν θεόν." In Greek "with" as a preposition is conveyed by σύν governing the dative case or by μετά governing the genitive case.

[27] Dodd's characterization of Philo's Logos, *The Fourth Gospel*, 277, is applicable to the Prologue's Logos, "... the meaning, plan or purpose of the universe".

[28] P^{75} and some later manuscripts place a punctuation mark after οὐδὲ ἓν in v. 3. Accordingly, v. 4 would begin with ὃ γέγονεν and read, "That which has happened in him was life ..." This reading has been adopted by Lindars, *The Gospel of John,* 84-85; Francis J. Moloney, *Belief in the Word: Reading John 1-4* (Minneapolis: Fortress Press, 1993) 31; and R. Alan Culpepper, *The Gospel and Letters of John* (Nashville: Abingdon, 1998) 113. But this is a Gnostic punctuation and supports the Gnostic view of "the uppermost circle of the spiritual world," according to Haenchen, *John* I, 113; Barrett, *St. John,* 156-157. Bultmann, *John,* 40-42, accepts the text-critical reading of Aland, but also struggles against it. For a study of the text-critical problem, see E. L. Miller, *Salvation-History in the Prologue of John: The Significance of John 1:3-4* (NovTSup 60; Leiden: Brill, 1989) 17-44.

Arising out of its union with God, the Logos as God's agent must convey something of the divine essence into the world it constitutes.

This must include all the happenings that follow the primordial event of creation. For, as 1:3 also indicates, "... and without him there happened nothing which has happened." The use of the perfect tense, γέγονεν (has happened), at the end of this verse extends the involvement of the Logos to include all the historical events and revelations through subsequent history into the time of the origin of the Fourth Gospel, wherever and whenever the divinely originated light of the Logos was manifested.[29] For the life that the Logos has in itself – independently of the Creator – is communicated to human beings in their existence as primordial light, that first production of its creative activity.[30] As verse 4 states, "In him was ζωή (life) and the ζωή was the φῶς (light) of human beings."

In view of the Jewish Hellenistic identification of the Logos with the pervasive Scriptural reference, λόγος κυρίου (word of the Lord) it seems valid to assume that this "light of human beings" is to be associated above all with the ongoing speech activity of the Logos in the history of Israel.[31] The Psalmist acknowledges this in LXX Psa 119: 105 (119:105), "Your word is a lamp to my feet and light to my path." And again in LXX Psa 42:3 (43:3), "O send out your light and your truth; let them lead me." The formulations of the covenantal law and their contextual interpretation by the prophets are therefore attributable to the revelatory activity of the Logos.[32]

But there is "the darkness" that is also present and active in the context of the historical activity of the Logos. It is not the darkness of the original creative act of the Logos; it is the darkness resulting from the Fall, and therefore the darkness that is the fundamental condition of human existence in society. In verse 5a it appears to be a state or a condition, in 5b a power. Both, of course, oppose the light that the Logos generates. If that light is identifiable with the truth that the keenness of mental intuition and the clarity of understanding that human beings acquire through the Logos to interpret the world, "the darkness" must symbolize all the

---

[29] Peter Cohee, "John 1.3-4," *NTS* 41/3 (1995) 470-477, on the basis of style analysis, contends that the relative clause ὃ γέγονεν was "an intrusive gloss, either on verse 3b, or, more probably, on 4a" that was eventually introduced into the text. That would eliminate the continued activity of the Logos in human history, an activity that corresponds to v. 5, "And the light shines in the darkness..."

[30] Philo, in *de Opificio Mundi,* 30, also connects ζωή and φῶς but prioritizes the latter: "Privilege is accorded both to spirit/breath and light (φῶj), for he [Moses] names the one spirit/breath of God because spirit/breath is most life giving, and God is the reason of life (ζωή) but of light (φῶj) he says that it is beautiful surpassingly, for the mentally perceived of the invisible in brilliancy and radiance."

[31] To Philo, God is the archetype of every other light, older and higher than every other archetype, and the Logos contains the fullness of God's light. See *de Somniis* I, 75; and *de Confusione Linguarum*, 60-63.

[32] Contrary to Bultmann, *John*, 34-36, who contends that the authentic function of the Logos is that of Revealer. There are other functions equally authentic: the Logos is the Creator's formative power of possibility by which the non-being of chaos will be actualized into a world and the Logos is also the agent that draws human beings into union with God.

manipulations of language in society that suppress the truth, distort reality and foster false consciousness.

Nevertheless, "... the light shines in the darkness." It is a continuous actuality, as the present tense of the verb φαίνει (it shines) conveys. But it is not a timeless presence that can be experienced only by those who transcend the dreams and phantoms of physical reality and in and through their intuitive intellect perceive the revelatory light of the eternal Logos. That would be Philo's understanding![33] On the contrary, the light of the Logos is an illumination that manifests itself in the material realities of historical existence and exposes the distortions of human communication that conceal the ongoing pursuit of power, domination and violence.

At the same time the force and vitality of the light that *shines* (φαίνει) in the darkness is dramatically intensified by the contrast that the following verb κατέλαβεν (overcame), poses. The juxtaposition of the two verb tenses, the present φαίνει and the aorist κατέλαβεν is perplexing.[34] What is the connection between φαίνει expressing the ongoing reality of light shining in the darkness and the aorist sense of "the darkness did not overcome (κατέλαβεν) it"? Did the darkness make an attempt to extinguish the light but failed, and therefore the light continues to shine in the darkness? That hardly seems likely because there is no reference to a particular event or episode in the past when such a conflict occurred, not even in the narrative world of the Gospel. The use of the conjunction καί, (and), which links the two statements of verse 5 to each other, suggests that the sense of the aorist κατέλαβεν is constative, that is, "a line reduced to a point by perspective."[35] In other words, the statement, "and the darkness did not overcome it," views both the prolonged struggle between the darkness and the light and the continuous victory of the light over the darkness as "constituting a single fact." Although the darkness is the prevailing condition of human existence, the pronouncement of verse 5a, "and the light shines in the darkness," may be considered the prior and dominant reality.

The testimony of John

Unexpectedly and arbitrarily, it would seem, John, known in the Synoptic Gospels as "the Baptizer," is introduced.[36]

---

[33] As Philo says in *de Opificio Mundi*, 31, "Now that invisible and mentally perceived light has become an image of the divine Logos." Also *de Josepho*, 146, "And indeed, if one be willing to look into the inner realities he will find that heaven is an eternal day, wherein there is no night or any shadow, because around it shine without ceasing unquenchable and undefiled beams of light." See also 143-145.

[34] As Haenchen acknowledges in *John* I, 114; also Bultmann, *John*, 46.

[35] C.F.D. Moule, *An Idiom-Book of New Testament Greek* (Cambridge: at the University Press, 1960) 11.

[36] In spite of the principal role of John as a witness to the Logos, the Prologue is not a "hymn of the Baptist-Community," as Bultmann contends, *John*, 18; German, 5. Originally, the Prologue was not a Gnostic writing in which John was presented as the incarnate Logos. The Prologue has its own

> There happened a human being, sent from God, his name John. This one came for a witness, so that he might bear witness about the light, so that all might believe through it. (1:6-7)

The introduction of John into this unusual context of the Prologue does not presuppose that the preceding verses should be interpreted as cosmological speculations.[37] This is not the stage at which history is reached. While verse 3a, "all things happened through him," is cosmologically oriented toward the instrumentality of the Logos in creation, verses 3b-5 refer to the continuous involvement of the Logos in human history into the very time of the Fourth Gospel.

It would seem natural, therefore, to present John as a witness to that light. For the activity of the Logos has continued into his time, and through his ministry he demonstrates that "the light shines in the darkness, and the darkness did not overcome it." John is a representative of the hermeneutical disclosure of the Logos, and the objective of his witness is to evoke a commitment to the Logos and the light that it generates in the world. It should not go unnoticed that the Greek prepositional phrase δι' αὐτοῦ at the end of verse 7 is ambiguous. Since the pronoun αὐτοῦ is both masculine and neuter in the genitive case, it can be rendered both *through him* and *through it*. The nearest antecedent is the neuter noun φῶς (light), and therefore, grammatically speaking, the pronoun should refer back to φῶς. It is specifically the light that is generated by John's witness that engenders faith. John testifies about the light, but it is through that very light, the light that the Logos – not John – generates, that all will come to faith.[38]

John will reappear before the Prologue is concluded, and once again he will serve as a witness, but in the new context of the incarnation of the Logos. His direct link to the light of the Logos in verses 6-7 serves to establish his subsequent testimony to the incarnation with greater authority. His role in the Prologue, therefore, is formidable, for he stands at the crossroads of history, on the one hand bearing witness to the light and, on the other hand, testifying to the enfleshment of the source of that light, the Logos.

Nevertheless, although he was "sent from God" and serves as the paramount witness to the light, "he was not the light." Could this negation intimate at least a hint at the possibility of incarnation? For if John is "not the light," who then is? Can there be a human being who is more than John, more than a witness to the light?

---

integrity as a history of the Logos from creation through revelation to incarnation.

[37] Contrary to Moloney, *Belief in the Word:. Reading John 1-4* (Minneapolis: Fortress Press, 1993) 34; and Barrett, *St. John*, 159. Contrary to Haenchen, *John* I, 116-117 and Lindars, *John*, 88, verses 6-7 are not a redactional insertion into the Prologue.

[38] Many commentators interpret the ambiguous pronoun αὐτοῦ (him/it) as a reference to John. So Barrett, *St. John*, 160; Lindars, *John*, 88.

The Logos-Sophia and the work of uniting the world with God

The narrator proceeds as if the question that has been begged will receive an immediate answer:

> The authentic light, which illumines every human being, was coming into the world. He was in the world, and the world happened through him, and the world did not know him. (1:9-10)

This is not a reference to Jesus and his subsequent rejection![39] Verse 9 marks a return to verses 3-5 but offers a significant elaboration of the historical activity that has been ascribed to the Logos. "The authentic light" is the subject of verse 9, and its continuous activity in the world is expressed by a periphrastic, the present participle ἐρχόμενον (coming) combined with the past tense of the verb to be, ἦν (was). The durative nature of the light's activity is being emphasized, corresponding to the durative sense of verse 5a, "and the light shines in the darkness." Because the light is identifiable with its divine source, it is interchangeable with the Logos. Verse 10, therefore, undergoes a shift from the neuter noun φῶς (light) to the masculine noun λόγος (Word) in the employment of the personal pronoun αὐτόν (him).

This linear movement of the Logos in history is not what is implicit in the witness of John. A new dimension of the activity of the Logos is being introduced, although it extends all the way back to the beginnings of human history. The Logos not only serves as the agent of creation and the source of hermeneutical illumination. It is also the intermediary of world construction: "... and the κόσμος (world) happened through him." If a world is constituted by the Logos, it must be the result of the linguistic activity of differentiation. In their analysis of the social construction of reality, Peter L. Berger and Thomas Luckmann state, "Put simply, through language an entire world can be actualized at any moment."[40]

As the divine agent of creation and world construction, the Logos was coming into its own sphere of operations: "He was in the world." But his objective in the world is to draw the world into his own primordial gravitational movement πρὸς τὸν θεόν (towards the God) in order to unite it with its Originator. Up to this point the Prologue's account of the activity of the Logos has emphasized revelatory disclosure and world construction by linguistic differentiation. Now the Logos will engage in a new mode of activity, but one that is more characteristic of Sophia than the Logos. For the work of unification, as already noted, is attributed to Sophia in the Wisdom of Solomon.

---

[39] Also Lindars, *John*, 89. Contrary to Hoskyns/Davey, *The Fourth Gospel*, 145-146; Bultmann, *John*, 46-48, 55-60; German, 26-28, 34-38; Dodd, *Fourth Gospel*, 283; Barrett, *St. John*, 161, who interpret these verses as an implied description of the historical appearance of Jesus.

[40] Peter L. Berger & Thomas Luckmann, *The Social Construction of Reality. A Treatise in the Sociology of Knowledge* (New York: Doubleday, 1966) 39. See also pp. 34-46 on "Language and Knowledge in Everyday Life."

> She is the artisan of all things. For she is a breath of God's power and a pure emanation of the glory of the Almighty. On account of this nothing impure intrudes into her, for she is a radiance of eternal light, a spotless mirror of God's action and an image of his goodness. Being but one she can do all things, and remaining in herself she renews all things, and moving into holy souls in every generation she constitutes friends of God and prophets. (Wis 7:22, 25-27)

It is in terms of the being and function of Sophia that the Logos fulfills its divine purpose of being in the world. Because the Logos is not a fixed, static emanation of God but a divine being that primordially gravitates "towards God the Creator," it can undertake this activity. But its interaction with the world, as verse 13 indicates, is to produce "children" or offspring "of God," not merely "friends of God."

In view of this unity of bipolar modes of movement and activity, differentiation and unification, in the divine being of the Logos, it seems appropriate to attribute an androgynous identity to the Logos. As Dodd has recognized, "... it is impossible to confine the term Logos to the meaning 'word'. It is also the divine Wisdom..."[41] Although there is a shift into a feminine mode of activity, that of Sophia, the language remains masculine. For although the term Logos does not appear in verses 9-13, the use of the masculine personal pronoun αὐτόν (him) indicates that it is the Logos that is operative in the ongoing effort to unite the world with God.[42]

The response that the Logos in its Sophia nature and activity encounters in the world is rejection. Here again a constative aorist is employed, ἔγνω (knew), which reduces this ongoing response of denial and rejection to a single fact. If the world does not know the Logos, it is not because the world is inferior as a copy of the Logos that must be kept separated from the Creator, but because, as Jesus will assert in 3:19, human beings love darkness rather than light.[43] Verse 9 as well as vs. 1-13 refer to the history of the Logos-Sophia *prior* to the time of Jesus. The Prologue, let it be stated very clearly, is an account of the being and activity of the Logos-Sophia, both in its relationship to the Creator and its performance from creation to incarnation. "Jesus Christ" appears only incidentally in the culminating witness of John in verse 17. It is the narrative that follows the Prologue that will unfold his career as the enfleshment of the Logos.

Repudiated by the world and its social construction of reality, the Logos-Sophia "came to its own possessions". That would signify an entry into its rightful dwelling place or home among the people of Israel who in their covenantal

[41] Dodd, *Fourth Gospel*, 295.

[42] *Ibid.*, 268-269.

[43] A noteworthy contrast is the apocalyptic orientation of 1 Enoch 42:1-2, "Wisdom could not find a place in which she could dwell; but a place was found (for her) in the heavens. Then wisdom went out to dwell with the children of the people, but she found no dwelling place. So wisdom returned to her place and settled permanently among the angels."

relationship with God had inherited the material manifestations of the Logos-Sophia, the gifts of the Torah of Moses, the writings of the Prophets and the literature of Wisdom. Speaking for herself in the Wisdom of Sirach, Sophia acknowledges this residency in 24:6-12.

> … in the whole earth, and in every people and nation I acquired a possession. Among all these I sought a resting-place. I sought in whose territory I might lodge. Then the Creator of all things charged me, and the One who created me caused my tent to come to rest. And he said, "Put your tent down in Jacob and let your inheritance be in Israel." Before the present age, from the beginning, he created me; and until the present age [ends] I shall never cease. In the tabernacle I ministered before him, and so in Zion I was established. Likewise in the beloved city he caused me to come to rest, and in Jerusalem was my authority. And I took up root among a glorified people, in the Lord's portion, his inheritance.

The Prologue, however, contradicts Sophia's testimony in Sirach. Even those who had received so much through the benevolence of the Logos and who could have acquired even more through its Sophia nature, even they did not embrace this divine personification of God's Wisdom.

And yet some did, as verse 12 acknowledges and as the Hebrew Scriptures testify. There was always a remnant![44] "For as many as received him, he gave them authority to be children of God." Not merely friends, but God's offspring! By their entitlement as God's offspring, they received the right and privilege to exercise authority on God's behalf. Receiving the Logos-Sophia signified "believing into his name." This phrase, consisting of the participle πιστεύουσιν (believing) and the preposition εἰς (into) is a distinctive code employed consistently throughout the Gospel and denotes the reality of a dynamic relationship with the one who is believed. Its force is more adequately rendered as "to make a commitment to," a commitment that involves the whole person.

Such respondents, who have been entitled "children of God," naturally can claim a divine origin. For, as "children of God," they "were not generated from bloods, nor from the will of the flesh, nor from the will of a male, but from God." These three possible origins of human reproduction may have accounted for the physical origin of human beings in antiquity, but none of them can generate "children of God". Neither by the mixing of female and male bloods![45] Nor by the efforts of the flesh and blood power of the human will! Nor by the design and intention of the male whose seed without its fertilization of the female ovum was considered by many to be a self-contained homunculus or tiny human being! On

[44] As Dodd observes, *Fourth Gospel*, 270.

[45] The unusual use of the plural αἱμάτων (bloods) is generally interpreted as an ancient understanding of human conception that involves the commingling of the woman's blood and the male seed. So J. H. Bernard, *A Critical and Exegetical Commentary on the Gospel according to John*, ICC 2 vols. (Edinburgh: T. & T. Clark, 1928) I, 18. Barrett, *St. John*, 164, attributes the plural to the Hebrew *damim*. See also Moloney, *Belief*, 40.

the contrary, those who received and committed themselves to the Logos-Sophia became God's offspring because God gave birth to them.

This entitlement, "children of God," is limited to the Prologue and may therefore designate those Israelites and Jews of the Hebrew Scriptures who embraced the Logos prior to its incarnation. It is not carried over into the narrative world of the Gospel to identify those who follow Jesus and "believe into the Son". Jesus himself will charge his disciples to "believe into the light so that you may be υἱοί, (generically sons and daughters) of light."[46] Although androcentric, this generic term υἱοί, should not be equated with "children of God". For when Jesus eventually identifies his disciples as "my friends," echoing Sophia's activity, as stated in the Wisdom of Solomon 7:27, and thereby establishes a horizontal relationship with them, their rank must be equivalent to the sonship that Jesus claims for himself. Consequently they are no longer "children of God," but, like Jesus, they have become adult daughters and sons of God with all the rights, privileges and response-abilities of this new status.

In John 1:9-13 the Prologue has reviewed and illuminated the entire pre-Christian history of humankind.[47]

The incarnation of the Logos-Sophia

This synopsis of the cosmological and historical activities of God's androgynous Logos, reaches its culmination in verse 14.[48] At this point it also transcends the paradigms that dominate the Hebrew Scriptures. As Dodd observed, "... it takes us beyond the range of Jewish ideas, and we shall not expect anything in the way of Old Testament documentation."[49] Generally the Logos, as the personification of God's speech activity, presupposes one organ of sense, the ear. It is by hearing that the hermeneutical discrimination of truth is determined. Countless instances of the divine injunction to hear are encountered in the Hebrew Scriptures. To cite only two:

> Hear, O Israel! The Lord our God is one Lord! And you shall love the Lord your God out of your whole heart and out of your whole soul and out of your whole strength. (LXX Deut 6:5)

---

[46] John 12:36.

[47] Eltester, "Der Logos und sein Prophet," 131.

[48] Contrary to Moloney, *Belief*, 40, who states that verse 14 is not the culmination of the Prologue because the incarnation was already presupposed in verses 3c-5. But, as argued above, these verses refer to the historical activity of the Logos down to the time of John the Baptizer and the author of the Gospel.

[49] Contrary to Dodd, *Fourth Gospel*, 283, it needs to be stressed that John 1:9-13 does not presuppose the incarnation. Nor do these verses pleonastically refer to the career of Jesus that is elaborated in the Gospel.

> Hear the word of the Lord, O house of Jacob and all the clans of the house of Israel! Thus says the Lord, 'What offense did your fathers find in me that they distanced themselves from me and went after vain things and became vain. (LXX Jer.2:4-5)

Unprecedented and unexpectedly "the Logos happened flesh". For the first time since the opening verse of the Prologue the Logos is cited by name. The momentous event that is being announced dictates its reintroduction, underlining verse 14 as the culmination of the operations of the Logos. For in contrast to its primordial movement of πρὸς τὸν θεόν (towards the God), that united it with its Originator and resulted in its reaffirmation as θεός (God), the Logos has now united with flesh. In this movement it is in terms of the being and function of Sophia that the Logos continues to fulfill its divine purpose in the world. Previously the Logos had served as the agent of various cosmological and hermeneutical activities: engendering a creation, constituting a cosmos, illuminating human beings, utilizing John as a witness to the light, and generating "children of God". Now the Logos, in terms of its Sophia nature, has become a historical actuality by uniting itself in an indissoluble relationship with a flesh and blood human being and consequently also with its frailty, limitations and temporality. The syntactical juxtaposition of the two words, λόγος (Word) and σάρζ (flesh) accentuates the unimaginable relationship between the two. Moreover, the verb ἐγένετο (happened) that expressed John's appearance on the stage of history is used to unite subject and predicate, "And the Word *happened* flesh."[50]

God's speech activity, the Logos, that expresses God's plan and meaning of the creation, *became* flesh, and, as a result, the prototype of humanity, God's idea of the consummate human being, that Philo assigned to the creation story of Gen 1, was united with the clay copy of Gen 2. As a result, Philo's Platonic dualism is negated. The Logos does not cease being itself, nor will its primordial movement of πρὸς τὸν θεόν (towards the God) be terminated. In its union with flesh it will continue to be God's surrogate, but its function as the Logos-Sophia will be fulfilled in drawing all humanity into the same relationship that it enjoys with its Originator. The goal, as Jesus verbalizes it in his Prayer of Consecration, is no longer generating "children of God" but constituting a New Humanity that, like the Logos-Sophia itself, participates in the being of God.

> Not only for these do I ask, but also for those committing themselves to me through their word, so that they may be one, even as you, Father, are in me and I in you, so that they may also be in us... I in them and you in me, so that they may be brought to completion into one. (17:20-21, 23)

[50] It is noteworthy that the aorist ἐγένετο and the related forms of γίνομαι are used throughout the creation myth of Gen 1 and may have influenced the author in the formulation of the Prologue. Philo also makes extensive use of this verb.

Through enfleshment the Logos-Sophia is objectified. God can now be seen, not in metaphysical visions which autonomous reason contemplates, but in the total physical life of a human being.[51] Later, in the narrative world of the Gospel, Philip will say to Jesus, "Lord, show us the Father, and it is enough for us." Jesus will reply, "Am I with you for such a long time and you have not known me, Philip? The one who has seen me has seen the Father."[52] Ears, however, have not simply been converted into eyes, as in Philo's metaphysics, and the works that are intellectually contemplated have not superseded words. Rather the eye has been integrated with the ear, and together these two physical organs of sense constitute the epistemological foundation of the knowledge of God. Consequently, the words and works of the incarnate Logos-Sophia should be interchangeable, manifesting the integrity of the Creator's speech activity, whose words are deeds and whose deeds are words. But that integration and the integrity it discloses must await their manifestation in the day-to-day involvement in human existence, and that is what the narrative world of the Gospel will reveal. In his Farewell Discourse Jesus will tell his disciples:

> The words that I speak to you I do not speak from myself, but the Father who dwells in me does his works. Believe me that I (am) in the Father and the Father in me; and if not, believe the works themselves (14:10b-11).

The enfleshment of the Logos-Sophia is expressed in language that echoes the tenting of God's presence among the Israelites during the forty-year journey to the Promised Land. One of its concrete manifestations was "the glory of the Lord" that filled "the tabernacle of the tent of meeting," according to Ex 40:34-38. More proximally, however, it is the tradition of Sophia that offers an antecedent for the characterization of the incarnation of the Logos-Sophia, καὶ ἐσκήνωσεν ἐν ἡμῖν (and he/she tented among us). According to Sirach 24:8, Sophia pitched her tent in Israel.

> Then the Creator of all things gave me a commandment, and the One who created me caused my tent to come to rest. And he said, "Put your tent down (κατεσκήνωσεν) in Jacob and let your inheritance be in Israel."

In response Sophia declares, " In the holy tabernacle I ministered before him, and thus in Zion I was established."

Notwithstanding this encampment in Jerusalem, the paradigm shift that 1:14a announces is iconoclastic. Sophia, by pitching her tent in Zion, is confined to the stone building of the temple in Jerusalem. But in her happening as flesh, the Logos-Sophia unites with a human being, and that human being will express this very reality when, at the first Passover in 2:19-21, he will substitute his own

---

[51] For Bultmann, *John*, 83, faith is not a "this-worldly" phenomenon in the sense of bringing a disclosure of God into the realm of objectifying knowledge. "It is in his *word* that he, the Logos, is the Revealer."

[52] John 14:8-9.

physical body in place of the sanctuary on Mount Zion and become the living temple of God.

Taking up residence by pitching a tent implies temporality as well as mobility in contrast to the more durable structure of the sanctuary that houses the divine Presence in Jerusalem. Like the tabernacle of the Exodus, a tent can move from place to place and attendantly sanctify time and space. As a result, the boundary lines between the sacred and the profane are dissolved, and any and every pollution system that divides the world into the two realms of the clean and the unclean is subverted. Accordingly, when Jesus journeys through the polluted territory of Samaria in John 4, he, as the tent of the incarnate Logos-Sophia, sanctifies the land and its people.

As in the Exodus journey, the tenting of the Logos-Sophia takes place in the context of a community: "he tented among us." Both the plural of the prepositional phrase "among us" and the use of the first person plural of the verb that follows, ἐθεασάμεθα (we ascertained), most likely refer to the experience of Jesus' disciples and the witness they have transmitted, the witness with which the author identifies and intends to perpetuate. It is from this point of view that the following story will be told, a view that is identical with that of Jesus, for he himself will utilize the same first person plural in his dialogue with Nicodemus in 3:11 and thereby identify himself with this community and its viewpoint.

Like the Israelites of the Exodus journey, these witnesses, including the implied author, perceived in their experience of this enfleshed Logos-Sophia its δόξα (glory). But it is not the glory of the Shekinah or divine Presence that took up residence in the wilderness tabernacle. For the luminosity of that glory prevented Moses from entering that tent "... because the cloud abode upon it, and the glory of Yahweh (fire, according to Ex 40:38) filled the tabernacle." Nor could it be the radiance of Moses' face reflecting the glory of being in the presence of Yahweh for forty days and forty nights, for it engendered apprehension among the Israelites "and they were afraid to come near him."[53]

The glory that the witnesses perceived was not a demonstration of God's glory. It was a glory "*as of*": δόξαν ὡς μονογενοῦς παρὰ πατρός. That is, "a glory as of only one kind from the Father," or "a glory as of an only offspring from the Father." It is the form or idea of God's conceptualization of the consummate human being that in a distinctive manner reflects the radiancy and splendor of the Creator. This one kind or only offspring must still be the Logos-Sophia, but for the first time its Originator is metaphorically identified as a "father" and the Logos as a one-of-a-kind offspring.[54] Although the word "son" does not occur here or

[53] Ex 34:39-45.

[54] Philo does not employ the term μονογενής. In the Wis Sol 7:22 Sophia is indwelled by a spirit that is μονογενές (one of a kind).

elsewhere in the Prologue, the usage of μονογενές elsewhere suggests that it may be presupposed.[55]

In this way a new view is posed of the relationship between the Logos and its Originator, a view that prepares the reader for the metaphorical Father/Son terminology Jesus will employ to qualify his relationship to God. The adjective μονογενής stresses uniqueness of a kind, and, if that uniqueness of kind is παρὰ πατρός (from the Father), its singularity is attributable to God's metaphorical role as father in relationship to the Logos-Sophia. "Son" is a natural extrapolation, but it is to be construed qualitatively as highly valued, cherished, priceless, and not in terms of "procession" or being begotten.[56] It will serve the enfleshment of the Logos-Sophia in the narrative world of the Gospel when its incarnation is manifested in the person of Jesus as "the Son of the Human Being" and "the Son of God". The incarnation of the Logos-Sophia will be translated into the descent of "the Son of the Human Being," the heavenly Human Being.[57]

The glory of this incarnate Logos-Sophia must therefore be in character with this newly introduced relationship of a unique offspring from the Father. If the subsequent christological titles, "The Son of the Human Being" and "the Son of God" are linked to this relationship "as of only one kind from the Father," the glory of the incarnate Logos-Sophia must be the glory of the Human Being who descends from heaven, the glory of the archetypal androgynous Human Being. But because it is not the glory of God, it cannot be disclosed as a shining radiance or a luminosity. The paradigm shift of the Logos-Sophia happening as flesh cancels that kind of manifestation. The glory of this heavenly Human Being, God's offspring, will be an epiphany, but entirely new and unprecedented. And yet it must be an unknown quantity, for it belongs to the enfleshed Logos-Sophia that is one of a kind but as yet has not been unveiled. Its disclosure will occur in the narrative that follows, the story of Jesus' career. At the same time, it will be a glory that is visible in the flesh, not through the flesh or alongside the flesh, as Rudolf Bultmann rightly insists: "If a human being wishes to see the δόξα, then it is on the σάρξ (flesh) that he must concentrate his attention without allowing himself to fall victim to appearances."[58]

The "ascertaining" or "sizing up" of this glory, as expressed by the verb ἐθεασάμεθα is not simply a spectatorship. It is a *looking on* in order to determine the truth of the matter, to learn with certainty what is behind the appearance of things. The revelation may be present in a peculiar hiddenness, but it will manifest itself to a seeing with the natural eye that responds with openness to make an

[55] See 3:16, 18. All commentators seem to agree that the word "son," although not used, is implied. So Dodd, *Fourth Gospel*, 305, n.1, who says, "... but one who is μονογενής relatively to a πατήρ (father) can be no other than the only son..." Barrett, *St. John*, 166; Haenchen, *John*, 120; Moloney, *Belief*, 43. Above all, see the lengthy footnote on μονογενής in Bultmann, *John*, 71-73.

[56] Also Brown, *John* I, 13-14. The word "procession" is taken from Brown.

[57] See Dodd, *Fourth Gospel*, 305.

[58] Bultmann, *John*, 63.

assessment of what has been experienced.[59] The author, who as representative of the Jewish-Christian community in Alexandria, may speak the ἐθεασάμεθα as a believer, but only because he or she, like the others, has scrutinized the phenomenon in order to make a definite judgment. Faith is the end, not the beginning of the experience of ascertaining the glory of the enfleshed Logos, as the conclusion of the episode of the wedding at Cana of Galilee indicates in 2:11.

Those who have sized up the glory of the incarnate Logos-Sophia acknowledge that they have experienced a fullness of grace and truth. The term χάρις (grace) has been interpreted as goodness, kindness, undeserved favor, and unsolicited gift. Given that the word is used only four times in the Gospel – all of them in the Prologue! – and that its sense is assumed by the author, only the story of Jesus that follows can elaborate its meaning. This is also true of the term with which it is connected, ἀλήθεια (truth). Whether the pair, "grace and truth" should be construed as "an accumulation of things" or whether the second term, truth, is an explanation of the first term, grace, is difficult to determine. A strong case has been made for the latter interpretation. In view of the conjunction καί, (and) having been placed between the two terms as a hendiadys, the phrase, "grace and truth" should be rendered as "the unsolicited gift of truth."[60]

Perhaps the subsequent testimony of John in verse 16 will resolve the matter. Ruth B. Edward's compelling argument that the preposition ἀντί at the end of verse 16 should be translated "instead of" or "in place of" acknowledges both the Law given by Moses and "the grace and truth which happened through Jesus Christ" to be manifestations of the fullness of the Logos.[61] The Law was a grace for Israel! But the grace and truth of Jesus Christ is the "grace in place of grace". It is the new expression of grace that supersedes the earlier grace. Accordingly, in the light of this interpretation it would appear that this pair, "grace and truth" in verses 14 and 16, is more appropriately understood as an accumulation of things: unmerited favor and truth. There was truth in the first gift of grace, the Law. But the grace that supersedes it is more. It is truth objectified, incarnated in a flesh and blood human being whose integrity is evidenced in the correspondence of his words and deeds and whose unsolicited gift is nothing less than the ultimate unconcealment of God's will and the dislodgement of ἁμαρτία (sin) from the world.

John's speech and the conclusion of the Prologue

The Prologue ends with a reappearance of John. Earlier, in verses 6-7, he was unexpectedly introduced as "a human being sent from God who came … to testify about the light." His location at that point in the structure of the Prologue suggests

[59] As Bultmann claims, *ibid.*

[60] Moloney, *Belief*, 44-47 follows Bultmann, *John*, 73-74.

[61] Ruth B. Edwards, "Charin anti Charitos (John 1.16): Grace and the Law in the Johannine Prologue," *JSNT* 32 (1988) 3-12.

that he is the paramount witness to the Logos. For he himself is the evidence of the truth of verse 5. His activity of testifying about the light demonstrates that the light has continued to shine in the darkness. Nevertheless, "he was not the light." By negating John as the light, the author tantalizingly hints at the possibility of incarnation, a human being succeeding John as the embodiment of the light of the Logos.

As unexpectedly as before, John is reintroduced, but only after the Prologue has reached its climax in the disclosure of the incarnation. Now it is his voice, not the voice of the author and the author's community, who will be heard. Formerly he witnessed to the light. Now he will identify the incarnation of the source of that light, the Logos, and for the first time link it concretely to the person of Jesus Christ.

His reintroduction, this time as a voice to be heard, is striking: "John testifies about him and has cried out." Two verbs in different tenses characterize this speech event, μαρτυρεῖ in the present tense (he testifies), and κέκραγεν in the perfect tense (he has cried). The former stresses the ongoing juridical testimony to the light, which reaches back to verse 7. In other words, John has not ceased testifying about the Logos: "This is the one of whom I said…" The Logos, now incarnate, is identical to the one John originally testified about, and in its incarnation it should continue to be identified with the light that he proclaimed from the beginning.

Moreover, his witness began as a cry and has continued as a cry into the present. The verb κράζειν (to cry) occurs four times in the Fourth Gospel and denotes a message that is delivered in spite of contradiction and opposition.[62] Contradiction is certainly apparent in his proclamation, "The one coming after me has happened before me for he was my First." This, of course, is the paradox of the enfleshment of the Logos-Sophia and therefore also the paradox of Jesus' identity that the narrative world will amplify. Chronologically Jesus comes after John, but as the latter antithetically enunciates, "… he has happened before me." In its incarnation the Logos-Sophia has not ceased to be itself. Coincidentally its union with the flesh and blood human being, Jesus of Nazareth, is so complete, so perfect, that that human being can claim to be all that the Logos-Sophia is.[63] Accordingly, Jesus will assert, "Before Abraham was **I AM**."

Throughout the Prologue the two different forms of the verb γίνομαι (happen, be) that the implied author has employed: ἐγένετο (it happened) and γέγονεν (it has happened) express cosmological and historical activities and events.

---

[62] In view of the other three occurrences in 7:28, 37 and 12:44, the conclusion drawn by Walter Grundmann is persuasive, "In each case there is reference to definite mysteries of His person and His work, which He solemnly intimates and proclaims." Grundmann, "κράζειν," *TWNT*, III, 901-902.

[63] In this context it should be emphasized that Jesus of Nazareth is nowhere regarded as a preexistent being in the Fourth Gospel. It is the Word that is preexistent, according to John 1:1. But, as already stated, the union between the Logos and Jesus is so complete that Jesus is able to identify himself with all that the Logos is and has. Contrary to Brown, *John*, I, 5, 35, 64, and elsewhere.

1:3 "All things *happened* through him and without him there *happened* not one thing which *has happened*."

1:6 "There *happened* a human being sent from God, his name John."

1:14 "The Word *happened* flesh."

What, then, is the significance of John's use of ἔμπροσθέν μου γέγονεν (he has happened before me)? In view of the earlier uses of ἐγένετο and γέγονεν, it would seem that John is referring to all the previous activities and interactions of the Logos in history. Accordingly, this clause ἔμπροσθέν μου γέγονεν is more appropriately translated as a progressive perfect, "He has been happening before me." Prior to John, the Logos had been actively involved in history from the very beginning.

This interpretation of the perfect tense, γέγονεν, is affirmed by the following verse that is introduced by the adverbial conjunction ὅτι (because) that establishes a causal relationship between the two sentences. The active involvement of the Logos in history is evidenced by the continuous outpouring of grace that has issued from its fullness, "grace in place of grace." That is, the grace of the Law given by Moses and the grace and truth of Jesus Christ.

But before John offers this evidence of the continuous activity of the Logos-Sophia in history, he acknowledges the preeminence of the Logos-Sophia, "... for he was my First." While this is the literal sense of ὅτι πρῶτός μου ἦν, it does not immediately appear to be intelligible. The difficulty is that the word πρῶτος, which is usually translated as "before," is not a preposition but an adjective.[64] John has already affirmed the priority of the incarnate Logos-Sophia, "He has been happening before me." It seems unnecessary to repeat that acknowledgment.[65] The clause, "for he was my First," must have some other significance.

John's reference to the Logos as πρῶτός μου (my first) is an echo of Yahweh's self-predication as πρῶτος in Is 48:12, ἐγὼ εἰμὶ πρῶτος (**I AM** first).[66] Philo also ascribes this predicate to God, derived perhaps from Isaiah or from the Greek world and legitimated by Isaiah, but only to God the Creator, not the Logos. For the Logos is δεύτερος θεοῦ, *God of second rank* and therefore only θεός.[67] God the Creator is πρῶτος θεός (first God), and the knowledge of the One who is πρῶτος (first) is attainable only by the wise and the mature.[68] Those "who live in the knowledge of the One are rightly called sons of God," and for them God their 'Father' would be πρῶτος, their *First*. Those, however, "who are not as yet unfit

[64] Πρῶτος was inserted into 15:18 by ℵ* D 579 it arm; T, where, as in 1:15, it was considered to function as a preposition.

[65] Bultmann, *John*, 76, among others, takes the phrase ὅτι πρῶτός μου ἦν in a temporal sense and concludes that it refers to the preexistence of the Word.

[66] See also LXX Is 41:4 and 44:6.

[67] *Legum Allegoriae* II, 86.

[68] *de Migratione Abrahami*, 181; *de Abrahamo*, 115; *de Vita Mosis* II, 205.

to be called a son of God, let them press to take their place under God's *first-born* (πρωτότοκος), the Logos."[69]

By predicating the Logos as πρῶτός μου (my First), John the Witness is contradicting Philo.[70] If, according to verse 1bc, the Logos was πρὸς τὸν θεόν (towards the God), a movement that results in union – but foreign to Philo! – the consequent identification of the Logos as θεός cannot be denigrated as a God of the second rank. In their union the Logos-Sophia participates in all that God is and God has, and therefore the predication of πρῶτος that Yahweh claims in LXX Isa 48:12 must also belong to the Logos-Sophia.[71]

The Logos-Sophia, however, is designated by John as πρῶτός μου. If the Logos is the true light that illumines every human being, and John is the witness to that light, it is indeed legitimate for him to claim this light-generating Logos as "my First". There is no other way or means by which the Creator God can be disclosed to human beings, except by the Logos-Sophia who has been happening before John and who, as the light to which John bears witness, can be predicated by him as "my First". In bearing this witness, John's stature is exalted as he becomes the first to name the incarnation of this one who is "my First," namely Jesus Christ.

John's speech event ends by going behind the Logos-Sophia and focusing on its Originator, God the Creator.

> God no one has ever seen; only one of a kind God, the one who is into the bosom of the Father, that one interpreted. (1:18)

Surprisingly, in contrast to verse 1b, the definite article is not employed before θεόν (God), although the reference is to the Creator. The two-sentence structure of verse 18, however, precludes any ambiguity or misunderstanding. Syntactically both sentences begin with "God," but without any definite article to differentiate the one God from the other God. Perhaps here the emphasis is on their horizontal relationship in view of the union which they, according to 1bc, share and in view of the relationship of εἰς τὸν κόλπον τοῦ πατρός that is ascribed to the "only one of a kind God," the Logos-Sophia. Nevertheless, in the contrast that is posed, their difference is immediately discernible. In the first sentence θεόν is the direct object of the verb ἑώρακεν, "God no one has ever seen." This is the Originator of all things, including the Logos, who has been referred to only once in the Prologue as ὁ θεός (the God) in 1b. God the Originator is not accessible to visual perception or, for that matter, to any kind of perception. Philo also acknowledges this truth in

---

[69] *de Confusione Linguarum*, 145 and *Legum Allegoriae* II, 207.

[70] "First" as a translation of πρῶτος cannot convey the richness that the word appears to have had in the Hellenistic world. It has titular significance and therefore should at least be put into the upper case as "First". It might even be good to transpose the Greek word into English. See the discussion by Wilhelm Michaelis, "πρῶτος" *TWNT* VI, 865.

[71] Bultmann, *John*, 33, rightly says, "There is therefore no talk of subordination: the status of the Logos is one of equality with God: he was God." At the same time, however, the Logos is not ὁ θεός (the God).

his writings, for the seeing that he promotes is limited to the viewing of the objectification of the Logos by the eye of the mind. [72] Even Moses, the hierophant and mystagogue, did not see God, only God's ὕπαρξις that is, the thatness, not the whatness of God's being.[73]

In the second sentence θεός is preceded by μονογενής, and both words, "God" and "only one of a kind" serve as the subject of the action that is conveyed by the verb ἐξηγήσατο (he interpreted). The phrase, however, is textually problematic because of its manuscript variants:

In P^{66} ℵ* B C* L sy^{P} Ir Or -- μονογενὴς θεός (only one of a kind God).

In P^{75} a1 33 pc CL -- ὁ μονογενὴς θεός (the only one of a kind God).

In A C^{3} Q Y 063 $f^{1,13}$ M lat sy^{CH} -- ὁ μονογενὴς υἱός (the only one of a kind Son).

The stronger witnesses support the first reading, μονογενὴς θεός. The remaining variants are explainable as scribal changes. No definite article is required before μονογενὴς θεός, because the phrase is already qualified by the apposition that follows.[74] The substitution of υἱός for θεός is certainly secondary, for in the light of the incarnation of verse 14 and the explicit use of υἱός alongside of μονογενής in 3:16 and 18, it removes the ambiguity of θεός and makes the identification of μονογενής explicit. Accordingly, μονογενὴς θεός is the more difficult reading and certainly the original reading. As a phrase it combines the μονογενὴς of verse 14 and the θεός of 1c and is therefore identifiable as the Logos.

Verse 18, syntactically juxtaposing θεόν and μονογενὴς θεός, draws God the Creator and the Logos, the two divine beings of 1bc, into the conclusion of the Prologue, but in reverse order. Finally, and for the first time, a statement is made about the Originator of all things, "God no one has ever seen." The one who will make him visible is the Logos who is εἰς τὸν κόλπον τοῦ πατρός (into the bosom of the Father), a metaphorical expression that is used to convey the intimate and loving relationship that results from the movement of the Logos πρὸς τὸν θεόν in 1b.[75] The Logos-Sophia, who now is united with the flesh and blood human being, Jesus Christ, yet also at the same time is "into the bosom of the Father," will continue its hermeneutical activity of interpreting the One whom no one has ever seen, God the Creator.[76] But in view of the paradigm shift of the incarnation, this hermeneutical activity can only be manifested in the form of narrative, the story of Jesus Christ, which the author's narrator will now begin to

---

[72] See Dodd, *Fourth Gospel*, 72.

[73] *Ibid.*, 61-62.

[74] Bultmann, *John*, 82.

[75] Also Moloney, *Belief*, 49.

[76] In John 13:23 the Beloved Disciple is presented as reclining ἐν τῷ κόλπῳ τοῦ Ἰησοῦ (in the bosom of Jesus). Even as Jesus, the incarnate Word interprets God, so the Beloved Disciple will interpret Jesus.

tell. It will serve as the direct object of the verb that ends the Prologue, ἐξηγήσατο (he/she interpreted).

Consequently, the end of the Prologue is not the conclusion of the history of the Logos-Sophia. Its history continues and must reach its consummation. All that the Prologue attributes to the Logos-Sophia will be manifested in the ministry and witness of Jesus. Accordingly, even as the Prologue testifies, "in him (the Logos) was ζωή (life), and the ζωή was the φῶς (light) of human beings," Jesus, the enfleshed Logos-Sophia, will claim to have the same life (ζωή):

> For even as the Father has life (ζωή) in himself, so also he has given the Son to have life (ζωή) in himself.

Moreover, even as the life (ζωή) of the Logos-Sophia is the light (φῶς) of human beings, Jesus, the bearer of this divine ζωή as the enfleshed Logos-Sophia, will avow that he is the light of the world.

> As long as I am in the world, I am the light of the world. (9:5)

> Jesus said to them, "For a little time the light is among you. Walk while you have the light, lest the darkness overtake you. The one who walks in the darkness does not know where she/he is going. While you have the light, believe into the light, so that you may be daughters and sons of light" (12:35-36).

> I have come as light into the world, that whoever believes into me will not remain in darkness. (12:46)

As the incarnate Logos-Sophia, Jesus will declare that he was sent into the world in order to draw all human beings to himself and therefore into union with the Creator God.

> For God did not send the Son into the world to condemn the world, but in order that the world is saved through him. (3:17)

> For the Bread of God is the one descending from heaven and giving ζωή (life) to the world. (6:33)

> And I, when I am lifted up from the earth, will draw all πρός (toward) myself. (12:32)

> For I did not come to judge the world but to save the world. (12:47)

Yet still another implication of the Prologue must be fulfilled in the telling of the story. For the oscillating movement of the Logos between πρὸς τὸν θεόν (towards the Creator God) and ἐρχόμενον εἰς τὸν κόσμον (coming into the world) so that σάρχ ἐγένετο καὶ ἐσκήνωσεν ἐν ἡμῖν (it happened flesh and tented among us) must by the very nature of its aporetic relationship with God the Creator be culminated in reunion. The Logos-Sophia must return to the ontological unity out of which it originated and in which it continually wills to participate. This in fact is the consummation of the incarnation of the Logos-Sophia and the fulfillment of its primordial movement of πρὸς τὸν θεόν!

> No one has ascended into heaven but the one who descended from heaven, the Son of the Human Being. (3:13)
>
> Then what if you were to see the Son of the Human Being ascending where he was before? (6:62)
>
> You heard me say to you, "I go away, and I will come to you." If you loved me, you would have rejoiced, because I go πρός (towards) the Father, for the Father is greater than I. (14:28)
>
> But now I am going πρός (towards) the One who sent me, and none of you asks me, "Where are you going?" (16:5)
>
> ... because I go πρός (towards) the Father, and you will see me no more. (16:10)
>
> I came from the Father and have come into the world; again, I am leaving the world and going πρός (towards) the Father. (16:28)

This penetrating relationship between the Prologue and the body of the Gospel would appear to subvert any and every effort to separate the Prologue from the narrative world of the Gospel either as a later redactional addition in its entirety or as an earlier hymn that was adopted and edited by the author or the later redactor of the Gospel.[77] It may well be that the Gospel, its Prologue and its narrative world, that is, the totality of chapters 1-20, is the work of a Christian Jew who has drawn from a variety of oral and literary sources and adapted the material to his own theological objectives. His work as an author has necessitated the use of his faculty of creativity to serve the purposes of his Gospel, specifically by formulating the discourses of Jesus and the relationship between the discourses and the narrative in such a way that they address the Jewish community in Alexandria in its distinctive historical context.[78]

---

[77] In spite of the efforts to reconstruct an earlier version of the Prologue, particularly along the lines of Semitic poetry which would require excluding "argumentative verses (13, 17, and perhaps 18)," and possibly also the repetition of v. 2, no one as yet has succeeded in making a satisfactory differentiation between poetry and prose. Lindars' conclusion, *John*, 82, is worth noting: "In fact the form and structure of the Prologue are in conformity with John's discourse style... Each fresh phase of the argument takes up what immediately precedes it, but also recaptures the opening statement of verse 1 (verses 9 and 14). The central section (9-13) has the characteristic Johannine pathos and irony. The whole builds up to an impressive climax."

[78] Barrett, *St. John*, 26, offers an attractive summary of the formation of the discourses and their relationship to the narrative material: "Much of the discourse material in the gospel can be readily understood as having been originally delivered in sermons. An incident from the life of Jesus was narrated, and the evangelist-preacher expounded its significance for the life and thought of the church. As this process was repeated and prolonged, a body of material would grow under his hands until it was capable of formation in the shape of a gospel."

Chapter Three

John's Role as Witness in the Narrative World of the Fourth Gospel

Day One: John's self-witness 1:19-28

John emerges from the Prologue as a figure of considerable stature.[1] Of all the living voices who have served as spokespersons of the Logos, he alone is acknowledged as a witness to the light. Indeed, it is his witness that proves that the light has continued to shine in the darkness. His prominence is amplified by offering his oral testimony as the conclusion of the Prologue. His brief discourse not only emphasizes the primacy of the incarnate Sophia-Logos over his own person and witness. More significantly, by enunciating the superiority of the grace and truth of Jesus Christ over the grace of the Mosaic Law as well as the ultimacy of the forthcoming revelation of the Logos-Sophia in its enfleshment, his speech elicits expectations of controversy and conflict. In the course of the narrative that is introduced by his interrogation, these expectations will be fulfilled.

In the narrative world in which John speaks and acts - mostly speaks! - he bears no epithet. In contrast to the Synoptic Gospels he is never designated as "the baptizing one" (Mark 1:4) or as "the Baptizer" (Matt. 3:1). His status is simply that of a witness, but one that is notably enhanced by the reality to which he testifies. In that role he stands as a signpost at the entrance into the narrative world of the gospel:

> And this is the testimony of John when οἱ 'Ιουδαίοι (the Jews) from Jerusalem sent priests and Levites in order that they ask him, "You, who are you?"

No motive is stated for this questioning; no rationale is offered as to why the authorities are interested in John's self-identification. This interrogation appears to

---

[1] Most of the traditions about John accentuate his baptizing activity. This is not only true of the Synoptic Gospels but also Acts 19:1-7, Josephus' *Ant* XVIII, 116-119, and the Mandaean texts. After John's martyrdom, the circle of his disciples continued to expand into other parts of the Mediterranean world, probably also into Alexandria. Like the Christian Jews, these followers of John may have been affected by the 12th Birkath of Samuel the Little condemning all heretics. John's interrogation by those whom the Pharisees sent in 1:19-28 may have a two-fold objective: (1) to have John deny all messianic inclinations in order to protect his followers, and (2) at the same time to intimate the superiority of Jesus. The Gospel's emphasis on John as the witness of the Logos and the Logos incarnate minimizes his historical significance as "the Baptizer" and confers on him a more formidable role. See Dodd, *Historical Tradition*, 250, who surmises, after analyzing the traditions about John that are unique to the Fourth Gospel, "that the evangelist had at his disposal *some* source of information about John the Baptist which is not otherwise known to us." That source may have been John's disciples in the Jewish community of Alexandria.

have two objectives. It is intended to impress upon the implied readers the vigilance that the guardians of society are maintaining. The messianically-oriented identities that John will disclaim have no allowance in the post-70 era of the Pharisaic reconstruction of Judaism. Watchfulness belongs to the order of the day. At the same time John's interrogation also accentuates what the Prologue has already disclosed. As formidable a witness as he is, his denial of any and every eschatological-christological significance that his own person and ministry might have prepares the implied readers for the advent of the one of whom he said, "The one coming after me has happened before me, for he was my First."

This is immediately evident in his repudiation of any messianic identity by a triple pronouncement that has the strength of a judicial oath: "And he confessed and he did not deny, indeed he confessed, ἐγὼ οὐκ εἰμὶ ὁ χριστός (I not am the Christ)."[2] The position of the pronoun ἐγὼ at the beginning of his response makes his confession emphatic. But more significantly the placement of the negative particle οὐκ (not) between the ἐγὼ (I) and the copula εἰμί, (am) stands in contrast to the self-disclosure formula, ἐγὼ εἰμί (I am), which Jesus will employ in various contexts of the Gospel's narrative world and therefore cancels John as any kind of messianic contender. John also avoids adding the εἰμί (am) after the ἐγὼ in his appropriation of the quotation of Isa 40:3 by which he identifies himself to the delegation of the priests and Levites in 1:23.

The implied readers, who must be familiar with the ἐγὼ εἰμί formula of God's self-identification in the Septuagint translation of Ex 3:14, as well as its use as a translation of the Hebrew אֲנִי הוּא in Isa 43:10, 25; 45:8, 18, 19, 22; 46:4, 9; 47:8, 10; 48:12, 17; 51:12; 52:6 are being signaled that there will be no rivalry or competition for the messiahship from John. That dignity is reserved for Jesus, even though it will be redefined fundamentally as a result of his identification as the incarnation of the Logos-Sophia.

The continuation of the interrogation by the representatives of the Jewish authorities makes it possible for John to reject every messianic typology for himself. He is not Elijah; he is not the Prophet. He is not to be identified as the fulfillment of Mal 3:1 and 4:5-6 who, prior to "the great and terrible day of Yahweh" serves as God's forerunner with a call to repentance.[3] He is not the actualization of the promise of Deut18:15 who enacts a new covenant and legislates God's law to God's people.[4] In no way is John to be considered as any kind of eschatological bringer of salvation. Nor is he the forerunner of Jesus, as he appears in the Synoptic tradition.

But what dignity does he then claim for himself? Or, in the confrontative challenge of those pressing him for some kind of self-identification, "You, who are you? What

---

[2] Bultmann, *John*, 88, n. 1; German, 60, n. 3.

[3] On the two types of prophets, see Richard A. Horsley with John S. Hanson, *Bandits, Prophets, and Messiahs: Popular Movements at the Time of Jesus* (San Francisco: Harper, 1988) 136-153, 172-187.

[4] *Ibid.*, 160-187.

do you say about yourself?" After three negative answers John replies with a quotation from Isa 40:3. It is a text that the narrators of each of the Synoptic Gospels apply to the Baptizer in order to express his fulfillment of that voice in the wilderness issuing a call to Israel to prepare for the coming of the Lord.[5] But here in 1:23 John himself is the speaker, and the quotation must be revised to enable him to respond to those who are cross-examining him: "I [am] a voice of shouting in the wilderness. Straighten the Lord's way." The quotation, of course, is explainable as an abbreviated version of the Septuagint text. On the other hand, it must also be edited to accommodate the distinctive summons John must make in order to conform to the anticipated activity of the incarnate Logos-Sophia.

The initial imperative of Isa 40:3, "Prepare the way of the Lord," has been omitted; and the two words of the second imperative phrase, εὐθείας ποιεῖτε (make straight) appear to have been combined to form a new imperative εὐθύνατε (straighten). Both of these commands intimate that God is coming, but they differ in the kind of undertaking they are intended to elicit. To "prepare the way" implies such activities as improving the roadbed, eliminating the potholes, and resurfacing the pavement. Metaphorically that means obedience to God's commands and fulfillment of God's will. To "straighten the way" conveys another image: eliminating the detours and alternate routes and constructing a road that is straight and undeviating. Metaphorically that involves the elimination of all traditions and practices that qualify a human being's relationship to God.

No reason for these alterations is immediately obvious. The object of the verb "straighten" (εὐθύνω) in the Septuagint, the Testaments of the Twelve Patriarchs and Philo usually is "your ways" "your heart" or "a course" (like that of a ship or charioteer). John, however, by employing a verb in his quotation of Isa 40:3 that is generally linked to ethical behavior, apparently intends to evoke actions that make the coming of God more direct, immediate and undeviating. All forms and forces of separation, like Philo's location of the Logos that "stands on the border and separates the creature from the Creator" or the temple cult and its priesthood that serve as the broker between God the Patron and Israel the client, are to be annulled. Jesus, in his forthcoming ministry, will replace the temple institution with his own physical body and negate such habituating social structures as the Sabbath, which prevent or at least retard transcendence. There must be no structures or institutions in society that prevent a human being from being drawn into union with God.

So, according to John's own testimony, he is only a voice, a voice shouting in the wilderness. In fulfilling the prophecy of Isa 40:3, however, he is not calling Israel to repentance. He is invoking his addressees to make God's way straight and unswerving by eliminating all detours and circuitous routes that prevent uninhibited access into God's presence.

The text of verse 24 is problematic because the earlier manuscripts, P^{66}, P^{75}, ℵ*, A*, B, C* omit the masculine plural of the definite article, οἱ (the) before the perfect

[5] For example, see Mark 1:3-4.

passive participle ἀπεσταλμένοι (having been sent). If the definite article οἱ (the), a reading of the later Constantinopolitan tradition, is admitted as original, verse 24 would indicate that those who were sent belong to the Pharisaic party: "And the ones having been sent were from the Pharisees." But that would contradict 1:19 that identifies those who were sent as priests and Levites.[6] If, on the other hand, the definite article, οἱ (the) is omitted, as the 27th edition of the Nestle-Aland advocates on the basis of the witness of the earlier manuscripts, P^{66} and P^{75}, the sense of verse 24 is altered, "They were sent from the Pharisees." The Pharisees, then, are the senders, and therefore they must be identified with the οἱ Ἰουδαίοι of 1:19.[7]

The interrogation continues but moves from the question of John's identity to the problem of his activity. For if he bears no identity that can be related to any biblical typology but is only a voice shouting in the wilderness, why does he engage in the activity of baptism? What relevance does it have for his oracular ministry, particularly if he is not involved in calling Israel to repentance?[8]

This question, of course, is raised for the benefit of the implied readers, most likely because of its implication that they already know about John's traditional role as a Baptizer. His reply, "I am baptizing in/with water" is puzzling, for it does not appear to answer the query.[9] But it is also provocative because, while it conveys a modesty that is characteristic of John, it also intimates another kind of baptism, one perhaps that is superior to his. But that is not made explicit until 1:33, and only then does the antithesis between water-baptism and spirit-baptism emerge. More immediately the implied readers are tantalized with an enigmatic expectation, "Among you there has been standing one whom you do not know, [namely] the one who comes behind me whose strap of his sandal I am not worthy to loosen." John has dropped the topic of baptism abruptly and introduced the mystery of a stranger. No identification is offered; no name is cited. Whether he is aware of his identity at this moment is not clear. But what is mystifying as Day One draws to a close is the striking juxtaposition of water baptism and the presence of a preeminent stranger. Is there any relationship between the two?

It is John's employment of the phrase ὁ ἐρχόμενος (the coming one) that hints at the eschatological/christological significance of this stranger. Its occurrence in the Synoptic Gospels suggests that it is a fixed title.[10] Martha, Lazarus' sister, will use the same phrase in her christological confession of 11:27. John, however, inserts the

---

[6] That is probably why Paul Schmiedel conjectured that verse 24 is a later scribal interpolation. But no manuscripts support its omission. See the critical apparatus in the 27th ed. of *NTG*, 248.

[7] Also Bultmann, *John*, 90-91, n.7; German, 62, n.6.

[8] Bultmann, *John*, 90-91; German, 61-62, asks the question differently. If John is no "bringer of salvation," his baptism can have no validity. Why then does he baptize? In order "to make known the unknown one who is already present."

[9] Dodd, *Historical Tradition*, 267, n.1, struggles with what he considers to be an impaired antithesis between water-baptism and spirit-baptism in this episode because of John's more immediate announcement of the presence of the one who comes after him but who is still incognito. Instead of giving consideration to rhetorical strategy, Dodd ends up conjecturing "a conflation of two different versions of the saying."

[10] Dodd, *Historical Tradition*, 267.

prepositional phrase ὀπίσω μου (after me), as he had in the Prologue (1:15), in order to indicate that this stranger is also his successor. By asserting that he is not even worthy of fulfilling the role of a slave by untying the shoestrap of this stranger, John intensifies the distance between them and thereby heightens the expectation of the implied readers.

This provocative use of enigma and its eventual resolution is widely used throughout the gospel.[11] As a rhetorical strategy it is an effective technique in promoting reader interaction with the text. As in this instance, it evokes questions and arouses projections of expectations that may or may not be actualized as the story unfolds. Inevitably surprises, both fulfilling and shattering, follow in a continuous network of connections challenging the traditional views and prejudices of the reader.

Nothing more is divulged about the priests and the Levites who had been sent by the Pharisees to interrogate John. They simply disappear. Moreover, nothing of John's replies to their questions of self-identification is reported to those who had deputized them. The entire episode was narrated for the benefit of the implied readers! The first day in the narrative world of this gospel is concluded by utilizing the narrative code of geography and identifying the location of this interrogation: "These things happened in Bethany beyond the Jordan where John was baptizing." Perhaps the purpose of noting the place where this confrontation occurred and thereby stressing the distance that the delegation of priests and Levites journeyed – from Jerusalem to Bethany beyond the Jordan – the narrator may be underlining the prominence that is being attributed to John by the ruling authorities. Also the phrase, "beyond the Jordan" will differentiate the place from the other Bethany in the gospel, the home of Lazarus, Martha, and Mary in 11:1.[12]

Day Two: John's witness to Jesus 1:29-34

Utilizing the narrative code of time, the narrator continues the story by recounting a particular event of the following day. In this episode there are no interlocutors. No one is present except Jesus. He enters the narrative world for the very first time, but on this day he remains silent. He and the implied readers are John's only audience.

No reason is given as to why Jesus is coming to John. According to verses 32-33, there appears to have been a previous encounter between them, perhaps more than one. Ostensibly on this occasion Jesus is to be presented to the implied readers. This day is, in fact, the day of revelation! As Jesus approaches, John introduces him, "See, the Lamb of God, the one who removes the sin of the world!" A most unusual identification! The project that is associated with this designation is unprecedented

[11] Other instances of the use of enigma may be found in 2:4, 3:13, 5:15, 6:53-58, 10:9, 11:5-6, 13:36, 19:28-30, 20:8.

[12] For a discussion of the manuscript variants of verse 28 and specifically the location of this confrontation, see Bultmann, *John*, 93-94, n.3; German, 64-65, n.5

and staggering in its magnitude.[13] The noun ἁμαρτία that is usually translated "sin," is in the singular number, and as such it denotes the condition rather than the act of sin. John anticipates nothing less than the eradication of the human infection of ἁμαρτία, an actuality that is anticipated by the millennially-oriented communities of Jewish apocalypticism. The legitimation of this christological identification will depend on its eventual fulfillment in the narrative world of the Gospel. Its function, therefore, is to evoke an expectation in the consciousness of the implied readers. More immediately, however, it is an appellative that does not correspond to the expectation arising out of the disclosure of the previous day. Is this the stranger who is also John's successor?

Without pausing to explain this extraordinary introduction of Jesus as "the Lamb of God," John proceeds to acknowledge that he is in fact the stranger: "This is [the one] on behalf of whom I spoke." Appropriating words he had used before - except to alter the tense of the copula from the past to the present - he reminds the reader of his earlier witness to the incarnation of the Logos-Sophia in 1:15.[14] But here more explicitly than in verse 15, he identifies the objectification of the Sophia-Logos with a particular individual: "There is one coming after me who has happened before me, for he was my First."

Once again John speaks antithetically. Chronologically Jesus is his successor. But because the union of the Logos-Sophia with Jesus is consummate and indissoluble, Jesus can be identified with its interdependent relationship to the Creator. Accordingly, he is also John's predecessor, both as God's surrogate in speech activity and in his personification of the Light of the first day of creation. "For," as John recapitulates his witness of verse 15, "he was my First."

This two-fold identification of Jesus is the first of a conjunction of antithetical christological identifications placed before the reader by the author.[15] On the previous day John had announced a successor who is already present but incognito. Now on the second day, after identifying this stranger as "the Lamb of God," he confronts the reader with a stunning paradox by combining this identification with his earlier witness to the incarnation of the pre-existent Logos-Sophia:

> See the Lamb of God, the one who removes the sin (ἁμαρτία) of the world. This is [the one] on behalf of whom I spoke. Behind me comes a man who has happened before me, for he was my First.

---

[13] Of John's identification of Jesus as "the Lamb of God" and the one "who baptizes with the Holy Spirit," Moloney, *Belief*, 64, says "None of this can be contained within the historical, cultural, or religious expectations of Israel. The reader is challenged to go beyond what he knows and understands." This is true, but there is more here that Moloney does not acknowledge, at least in as far as these actualities were ascribed to God's intervention in history by Jewish apocalypticism. See, for example, 1 Enoch 5:8-10, 91:16-17, and 2 Baruch 73:1-2.

[14] In verse 15 John had asserted, "This was the one of whom I spoke," referring most likely to his earlier witness about the light (1:7).

[15] See 3:13-14.

On the one hand, Jesus is the incarnate Logos whom John identifies with God as "my First". On the other hand, he is "the Lamb of God" who will eventually be sacrificed at the third Passover in the narrative world of the Gospel. But how could the one before whom John is unworthy even to loosen his sandal strap, the incarnate Logos, be a sacrificial lamb? There are no biblical antecedents or typologies that would elucidate this identification.

The lamb, of course, is significant as a sacrificial animal in the religious cult of Israel. The Sinai ordinance of Ex 29:38-39 stipulates a burnt offering of two lambs to be sacrificed daily, one in the morning and one in the evening.[16]

> It will be a continual burnt offering throughout your generations at the door of the tent of the meeting before Yahweh, where I will meet with you, to speak there to you. There I will meet with the people of Israel, and it shall be sanctified by my glory. (Ex 29:42-43)

But, as Dodd has observed, "the lamb is not in the Old Testament the characteristic sin-offering."[17] Moreover, there is no antecedent here of a human being fulfilling the function of a sacrificial animal, specifically that of a lamb that *removes* the sin of the world.[18]

The Suffering Servant of Yahweh in Isa 53 is generally considered to be a possible parallel and sometimes acknowledged to be consonant with the Gospel's portrayal of Jesus as the Lamb of God.[19] Although the Servant is "like a lamb led to the slaughter," the expiatory death he suffers does not correspond to the removal of sin. It is rather an act of a human being fulfilling the role of a sacrificial animal by making himself an offering for sin (Isa 53:10).

> ...Yahweh has laid on him the iniquity of us all. (Isa 53:6)

While the Servant bears the sins of others, he does not eradicate the condition from which they originated. He becomes a substitutionary sacrifice by suffering the punishment of their sins.

The ritual of the Day of Atonement certified reconciliation with God by sacrificing one goat as a sin offering and by releasing a second into the wilderness, a scapegoat, upon which the High Priest had transferred the iniquities and transgressions of the

[16] Hoskyns/Davey, *The Fourth Gospel,* 169, consider the morning and evening temple sacrifice of the two lambs to "provide the proper analogy."

[17] Dodd, *Interpretation*, 233.

[18] As Dodd, *ibid.*, 237, emphasizes, the verb αἴρειν ἁμαρτίαν means "to remove sin," not simply "to bear sin."

[19] See Dodd 's discussion, *ibid.*, 235-236. Although he admits that Isa 53 has much to commend it as an antecedent of "the lamb of God," he concludes that it is not its "primary and constitutive meaning." For the best parallel he chooses "the Messiah, the King of Israel ... grounded in apocalypticism." On p. 237 he goes on to say: "To make an end of sin is a function of the Jewish Messiah, quite apart from any thought of a redemptive death." Brown, *John* I, 61, prefers the parallel of Isa 53, and, in spite of acknowledging that the verb αἴρειν means "to take away," a reality that is not conveyed in Isa 53, he determines that the difference is not of major importance. Schnackenburg, *St. John*, 300, considers a combination of Isa 53 and the Paschal lamb to be more convincing. Lindars, *John*, 109, claims that the taking away of sin is dependent on Christian thinking.

people. Although it removed the sinful acts and offenses that had accumulated since the previous Day of Atonement, it had to be repeated annually (Lev 16:6-22).[20] The cultic institution of sacrifices maintained the relationship between God and Israel and guaranteed God's uninterrupted presence through the expiatory rituals that effected atonement and purification.[21] Sinners could be absolved and transgressions of the law and the purity code, resulting in contamination and broken relationships, could be forgiven. As Psa 103:12 affirms, "As far as the east is from the west, so far he removes our transgressions from us."

Jewish apocalypticism, however, awaits the elimination of the human infection of ἁμαρτία by God's destruction of the old creation and God's subsequent creation of a new heaven and a new earth, that is, a new moral order in which justice and peace will prevail forever. Accordingly, God, by an act of judgment, will remove the sin of the world.

> And then wisdom shall be given to the elect. And they shall all live and not return again to sin, either by being wicked or through pride. But those who have wisdom shall be humble and not return again to sin; and they shall not be judged all the days of their lives, nor die of plague or wrath. (1 Enoch 5:8-9)

> And it will happen that after he (my Servant, the Anointed One) has brought down everything which is in the world, and has sat down in eternal peace on the throne of the kingdom, then joy will be revealed and rest will appear. And then health will descend in dew, and illness will vanish, and fear and tribulation and lamentation will pass away from among human beings, and joy will encompass the earth. And nobody will again die untimely, nor will any adversity take place suddenly. Judgment, condemnations, contentions, revenges, blood, passions, zeal, hate, and all such things will go into condemnation since they will be uprooted. (2 Baruch 73:1-4)

A quotation from the Qumran Manual of Discipline, 1QS 4:20-21, offers a parallel vision:

> Then God will purify through his truth all the deeds of the human being, and cleanse for himself the body of the human being. He will take away completely the spirit of perversity from the midst of his flesh and will cleanse him of all wicked deeds through holy Spirit. He will sprinkle him with the Spirit of truth like lustral water.[22]

Although there are no antecedents of a sacrificial offering that eradicates the human infection of sin, yet according to John's testimony, Jesus' accomplishment as "the

---

[20] Howard-Brook, *Becoming Children of God*, 67, after reviewing "both apocalyptic and paschal associations, " finally concludes, "This Lamb will, according to John, change the situation in which 'the world' finds itself." But he does not explain what that means and how it might be related to an apocalyptic perspective.

[21] See Roland de Vaux, *Ancient Israel. Its Life and Institutions* (London: Dalton, Longman and Todd, 1961) 451-454, on "A Theory of Sacrifice."

[22] Cited by Schnackenburg, *St. John*, I, 305.

Lamb of God" will be nothing less than the abolition of sin.[23] Its fulfillment will be achieved by God's surrogate, the incarnate Logos-Sophia, the paradoxical union of heaven and earth.[24]

John continues his revelatory witness to Jesus by acknowledging that he did not know the one who incarnates the Logos-Sophia, and therefore the one who will remove the sin of the world. Evidently there was no visible luminescence or glory, no outward sign, no external manifestation that would make him immediately identifiable. How then did he eventually recognize Jesus as the one "who has happened before me," indeed, as the one whom he testifies to be "my First." The question is not immediately answered.

In spite of his refusal to consider himself to be an eschatological forerunner like Elijah or the Prophet, he concedes in 3:28, as he nears the end of his career in the narrative world of the Gospel, that he is Jesus' predecessor: "I have been sent before him." He preceded the one who has happened before him in order to serve as the agent by whom the incarnate Logos-Sophia would be revealed to Israel. "But in order that he be manifested to Israel, on account of this I came baptizing in/with water." Through his fulfillment of the divine commission to baptize, the incarnate Logos-Sophia would be unveiled. John's baptism is consequential after all, even if it is only a water baptism, for it is the context in which the identity of the stranger was disclosed to him.[25] John is intimating that prior to this moment, that is, outside of and prior to the narrative world of the Fourth Gospel, Jesus came to him for baptism; and it was in that event that the revelation occurred.[26] Accordingly, the perplexing juxtaposition of water baptism and the incognito presence of the one who will supersede John proves to be existentially meaningful.

It is at this point that John's witness becomes pivotal and decisive. To accentuate the climactic finality of his remaining deposition, the author utilizes the verb μαρτυρεῖν (to witness) that distinguishes John's role in the Fourth Gospel. As 18:23 indicates, it is a juridical term that pertains to the kind of legal testimony admissible in a court of law. It is noteworthy that of the thirty-three occurrences of both the verb and its cognate, μαρτυρία (witness), in the twenty chapters of the original edition of the Gospel, ten are linked to John. Now, at this critical moment of Day Two he culminates his ministry as God's legal witness by disclosing the revelation that he

---

[23] "To remove the sin of the world" is to save the world (3:17). If taking away the sin of the world is not appropriate to the Evangelist's christology, as Schnackenburg, *ibid.*, 1, 53, asserts, it is certainly appropriate to the soteriology of the gospel.

[24] See chapter 17.

[25] Also Barrett, *St. John*, 177.

[26] An analepsis, according to Culpepper, *Anatomy* 56, identifies this recollection of John from a time prior to the events inside the gospel's narrative world. Culpepper adopts Gérard Genette's definition of analepsis: "any evocation after the fact of an event that took place earlier than the point in the story where we are at any given moment." In this case it is an external analepsis since it is an event that occurred outside of the Gospel story.

experienced at his baptism of Jesus: "I have ascertained the Spirit descending from heaven like a dove and remaining on him."[27]

This is the only evidence John offers to substantiate his testimony to the reader that Jesus is the incarnate Logos-Sophia. Is it believable? His use of the perfect tense, τεθέαμαι (I have sized up) indicates that his observation continued over a period of time. That, of course, is the only means by which he would be able to determine whether or to what extent the Spirit "remained on him". Yet how was it possible for John to see "the Spirit descending from heaven like a dove and remaining on him"? What kind of seeing enabled him to identify the experience Jesus was having at his baptism as "...the Spirit [was] descending from heaven like a dove."[28] The verb, θεάομαι, that John employs in this testimony is identical to the one that was used earlier in verse 14, "we *ascertained* (ἐθεασάμεθα) his glory, glory as only one of a kind from the Father." Of the four different verbs for "seeing" that have been used in the Gospel: ὁρᾶν, θεωρεῖν, βλέπειν, and θεάομαι, the last refers to a very distinctive kind of insight, the kind that Philo expounds in *de Abrahamo* 150-157 and *de Cherubim* 96-97. [29]

"A special precedence must be given to sight," he contends, "for God has made it the queen of the other senses and set it above them all, and, establishing it as it were on a citadel, has associated it most closely with the soul."[30] The eye of the soul is analogous to the eye of God who "ascertains (καταθεάσθαι) the unseen even before the seen, for He himself is his own light."[31] Since the soul is imaged according to the archetype of the eternal Logos, as Philo advanced, the eyes must behold the unseen even before the seen.[32] "Ascertaining," or "sizing up," as the English equivalent of θεασάμενος implies, includes an appraisal of the truth of things in order to establish a legal testimony.[33]

Like other philosophers of antiquity, Philo appears to have assumed "the extramission theory of vision".[34] "People and animals do not see by means of light rays that travel from the external object to the eye, as modern optics would have it, but

---

[27] In contrast to Mark 1:10, it is John, not Jesus, who beholds the Spirit descending from heaven like a dove.

[28] Of course, the implied author may have derived this from his repertoire of tradition. However, there are no parallels to John's testimony of what he beheld at the time of Jesus' baptism. Surely it would be necessary to consider how believable this would be to the reader and therefore what kind of response to John's testimony this would evoke.

[29] For an analysis of these four verbs, see chapter 5, "Seeing and therefore Believing."

[30] Philo, *de Abrahamo*, 150.

[31] *Ibid.*, 96.

[32] See *de Plantatione*, 18; also *de Opificio Mundi*, 139 and *Legum Allegoria* I, 37-42.

[33] *Ibid.*, 71. See also 83, 151. In 158 especially, this kind of viewing includes being drawn into a relationship with that which the eyes have brought into focus: "Whenever he θεάσαιτο (observes) a richly spread table, he flings down his whole person and tumbles upon the dishes set out, eager to devour all at once."

[34] The phrase is taken from Joel Marcus, "A Note on Markan Optics," *NTS* 45/2 (1999) 251. Also his references to *de Abrahamo*, 150-157 and *de Cherubim*, 96-97.

by means of beams that come out of the eye, travel to the object of sight and strike it, thereby producing vision."[35] For Philo this extramission theory of vision operated on two levels. On the one hand, the beams that come out of the human eye strike the object of sight and produce empirical vision. On the other hand, the beams of light that originate from the eye of the soul or the mind penetrate into the essence of things.

> For even as the sun, when it has risen, shows clearly the things hidden by night, so the mind sending forth its proper light renders all forms and conditions to be apprehended clearly.[36]

> For the created is approached by sense which can never grasp the nature that is apprehended by the mind.[37]

If John bears witness to the light (1:7), the light that of course is invisible because it is the light of truth, the light of the first day of creation, he must be endowed with the gift of divine perspicacity. His sight must be engendered from within his soul, by which he is enabled to behold the unseen before the seen. It is this kind of insight that John claims (τεθέαμαι) to substantiate his witness. It is an observing that transcends the seeing of the "flesh" (3:6). It is a perspicacious discernment, a visionary seeing that apprehends higher realities and is existentially affected by them.[38] Because this kind of observing does not necessarily displace the use of the natural organs of sight, it can be identified with the seeing of the physical eyes.[39] John, therefore, can replace his use of τεθέαμαι (I have observed) with ἑώρακα (I have seen) in as far as his perception of reality conditions his ocular vision.

The testimony of verse 32 is continued but at the same time repeated and expanded in verse 33. Once more, evidently for emphasis, John insists, "And I did not know him…" Jesus is the incognito presence of the Logos-Sophia to Israel and to John – and as such also to the implied readers. But God, who commissioned John for this revelatory ministry, made known to him personally the sign by which he would be able to recognize this stranger: "… but the one sending me to baptize in/with water, that one said to me…" John reinforces the authority of his testimony by revealing that he had received the sign in a direct communication from God. Furthermore, the disclosure of the stranger would occur in conjunction with his ministry of baptizing in water, and at that moment of unveiling, when he, John, would see the unseen before the seen, "the Spirit descending and remaining on him," he would also know that, "this is the one who baptizes in/with the holy Spirit."

---

[35] Joel Marcus, "A Note on Markan Optics," 251.

[36] *de Posteritate Caini*, 57; cited by Joel Marcus.

[37] Philo, *de Cherubim*, 97.

[38] So also G.L. Phillips, "Faith and Vision in the Fourth Gospel," *Studies in the Fourth Gospel*, ed. by F.L. Cross (London: Mowbray, 1957) 83-96.

[39] This is evident in 2 Macc 2:4 and 3:36, but also throughout Philo's use of θεάσθαι.

John has announced the divinely revealed sign twice: "the Spirit *descending* and *remaining* on him." Its two-fold repetition is pivotal because it contradicts Philo's dualism and refutes the discrimination that he advances in *de Gigantibus*. Regarding the giants of Gen 6:4-5, who multiplied wickedness on the face of the earth, he asserts:

> Among such as these, then, it is impossible that the Spirit of God should *remain* (καταμεῖναι) and make forever its habitation, as also the Lawgiver himself shows clearly. For, so it says, the Lord God said, "My Spirit will not *remain* (καταμένει) forever in human beings because they are flesh." On the one hand, when the Spirit *remains* (μένει), it does not *remain* (καταμένει) with us many forever.[40]

The Spirit cannot remain forever because flesh and blood human beings are composites of body and soul or body and mind "be-souled by God, and therefore are the borderland between mortal and immortal nature, mortal with respect to the body, but immortal with respect to the mind. This holds true even for Moses. Philo acknowledges that "The Spirit on him (τὸ ἐπ' αὐτῷ πνεῦμα) is wise, divine, entire, undivided, refined … and though it is shared with others or is added to others, it is not diminished in understanding and knowledge and wisdom." Yet after he has conceded that, he continues, "Wherefore the divine Spirit can remain in the soul, it cannot continue to remain (διαμένειν)." Why? He cites Moses himself to answer this question:

> And he himself confesses, "Because they are flesh, the divine Spirit cannot remain forever (καταμεῖναι)."[41]

That is, created human beings, like Adam of Gen 2, are construed by Philo to be a dichotomy of spirit and matter, of infinitude and finitude. In his treatise, *de Opificio Mundi* 139, he comments on the creation of Adam:

> Now that in soul he was also most excellent is manifest; for towards its making he [the Creator] employed no other pattern of things in creation, but only, as I said, his own Logos. Wherefore he [Moses] says that *the human being was made a likeness and imitation of the Logos, when the divine Spirit was breathed into his face.* (Italics are mine.)

Similarly in *de Plantatione* 18-19, he says:

> But great Moses compared the form of the reasonable soul to nothing of created things, but said it to be of the divine and invisible Spirit, signed and impressed by the seal of God, of which the representation is the eternal Logos. For he says, "*God in-breathed into his face a breath of life*" (Gen 2:7); so that *by necessity the one receiving is made in the image of the one who sends forth the breath.*[42]

---

[40] *de Gigantibus*, 19-20. The compound, καταμένειν, does not occur in the Fourth Gospel, but μένειν is used thirty-eight times. See also *Quod Deus Immutabilis Sit*, 2, where Philo, using καταμένειν, says the same thing.

[41] *de Gigantibus*, 29.

[42] Italics are mine.

"*Breathed into*," according to Philo's analysis, implies three things: "the one that inbreathes, the one that receives and that which is inbreathed. God is the one inbreathing, the mind is that which is receiving, and the Spirit (τὸ πνεῦμα) is that which is inbreathed.[43] Comparing Gen 1:26 and 2:7 on the basis of his metaphysical dualism, Philo concludes that there is a vast difference between the human being, Adam, formed from the dust of the ground and inbreathed by God's Spirit *and* the archetypal human being that God originated as the culmination of the creation when the world, discernible only by the mind, was constituted and brought to completion.

> There is a vast difference between the human being now formed (Gen 2:7) and the human being, the one having happened earlier according to the image of God. For the one formed, the object of sense, consisting of body and soul, man or woman, is by nature mortal. But the one according to the image is an idea, a type or a seal, an [object] of thought, without a body, neither male nor female, by nature incorruptible.[44]

Philo's determination, however, is opposed by John's testimony: "I have observed the Spirit *descending* like a dove from heaven and *remaining* on him." If this is true, Jesus is distinguished above all his predecessors, including Moses.[45] His baptism, construed as an event of re-creation, would imply the three actualities that Philo attributes to Adam's creation: God sending the Spirit, Jesus receiving the Spirit, and the Spirit recreating Jesus. Consequently, Jesus of Nazareth, the son of Joseph, an embodiment of the aporia of spirit and matter or, to employ the anthropological terms of the Hebrew Scriptures, *nephesh* and *basar*, was transformed, and as a reconstituted aporia of *nephesh* and *basar*, he would henceforth be empowered and sustained by the Power that formed anew in him the image and likeness of God.

Two essentially different origins of Jesus' singular relationship to God converge here in John's witness: incarnation and the gift of the Spirit. According to the Prologue (1:14-15), "the Logos happened flesh," and John identifies Jesus Christ with that event as the one who "has happened before me because he was my First." Furthermore, according to John's testimony in 1:31-33, "I have beheld the Spirit *descending* like a dove from heaven and *remaining* on him." What, if any, is the relationship between these two originations of Jesus' unique identity and status? To all appearances they seem to be a contradiction. Rudolf Bultmann claims, "The Evangelist has clearly not thought out the relation between the Spirit Jesus receives in his baptism and his character as the Logos: in the rest of the Gospel Jesus appears not as the bearer but as the giver of the Spirit."[46]

---

[43] Where the Septuagint reads πνοή (breath) in Gen 2:7, Philo substitutes πνεῦμα (Spirit). Also *de Opificio Mundi*, 135 and *Legum Allegoria* I, 37-39.

[44] Philo, *de Opificio Mundi*, 134.

[45] Contrary to Barrett, *St. John*, 178, who insists that "too much should not be built upon the word μένειν." The implication is that Jesus becomes the abode or home of God's Spirit. See 1:38-39, 4:40, 5:38, 6:56, 8:35, 14:10, 15:4; above all, 2:19-21, when he substitutes his physical body, the abode of God's Spirit, in place of the sanctuary on the Temple mount.

But these are not two discrete, unrelatable occurrences! The event of the Spirit *descending and remaining* on Jesus is, in fact, a correlate of the event of the incarnation of the Logos. If, according to John's testimony, the Spirit *descended* and *remained* on Jesus, Philo's dichotomization of the aporia of spirit and matter is discredited. At least in any application to Jesus! For if the Spirit remained upon Jesus, the "vast difference' between the human being of Gen 2:7, formed from the dust of the earth and divinely inbreathed, and the human being of Gen 1:26, "the one having happened earlier according to the image of God," is invalidated. In a fundamental opposition to Philo's metaphysical dualism, the implied author, under the guise of John's witness, is inferring that Jesus of Nazareth became the archetypal human being at his baptism when God's Spirit descended and remained on him and breathed into him the divine Logos-Sophia. Jesus is the embodiment of Gen 1:26 and 2:7. He unites both in himself. He is the image of God as God's ideal type and seal of thought, and he is simultaneously the physical, earthly human being who is the son of Joseph from Nazareth of Galilee. Consequently, *Jesus' baptism is to be construed as the occasion of his divine re-creation at which the event of the enfleshment of the Logos* (1:14) *and the event of the Spirit descending and remaining on Jesus* (1:32-33) *were united.*[47] This is the key to the aporetic christological identity of Jesus that pervades the entire Gospel of John.[48]

Therefore, what may be intimated in this concurrence of events is the emergence of a new Adam, a new human being, or, to use the christological epithet of the Gospel, the Son of the Human Being (ὁ υἱὸς τοῦ ἀνθρώπου) in whom the incarnation of the Logos-Sophia and the indwelling of the holy Spirit are combined. It is this conjunction that John, the witness extraordinaire to the light of the Logos, *ascertained* (τεθέαμαι) in that earlier episode of Jesus' baptism that he alludes to in 1:31-32, and therefore he is the preeminent witness of both simultaneously occurring events.

John climaxes his testimony on this second day with an eyewitness attestation: "I myself have seen and I have witnessed that this is the Son of God." He replaces his earlier use of τεθέαμαι (I have ascertained) with a verb that accents empirical experience, ἑώρακα (I have seen), and gives voice for the first and only time to the

---

[46] Bultmann, *John*, 92, n. 4; German, 63-64, n. 8. Haenchen, *John* I, 154, speaks of "The difficulty [that] remains ... of combining the doctrine of the logos with a baptismal account similar to the Synoptics."

[47] The italics are mine. Ernst Käsemann, *The Testament of Jesus: A Study of the Gospel of John in the Light of Chapter 17* (Philadelphia: Fortress Press, 1968)8-12, 63-66 unfortunately rejects dialectical formulae and therefore ends up with "an unreflected docetism". On the one hand, "Nowhere in the New Testament do we meet a more rigorous dualism than in John." On the other hand, "The Johannine dualism is nothing but the doctrine of the omnipotence of the Word." In what sense, then, does the light triumph over the darkness? Especially if "the notion of a restored creation is given up." See Günther Bornkamm's critique and defense of Käsemann's *Testament* in his essay, "Towards the Interpretation of John's Gospel: A Discussion of *The Testament of Jesus* by Ernst Käsemann," *The Interpretation of John*, ed. with an Introduction by John Ashton (Philadelphia: Fortress Press, 1986) 79-98.

[48] The "aporia of spirit and matter" is analyzed by Douglas R. McGaughey, *Strangers and Pilgrims: On the Role of Aporiai in Theology,* 213 –240. I owe my understanding of this "fundamental aporia of the human condition" to him.

cognate that the author has used to define his distinctive role, μεμαρτύρηκα (I have witnessed). By employing this juridical term himself, John certifies the truth of his testimony. On the basis of what God has revealed to him and what he himself has observed and seen, this stranger is none other than "the Son of God."

Whatever pre-understanding the implied readers may have had of this divine epithet, this culminating identification completes the Father/Son conjunction that had been implied in the earlier references to the Creator God as a Father of an only offspring (1:14,18). Through John's witness the enfleshed Logos-Sophia has been identified as Jesus, and Jesus, the one who will baptize in/with the holy Spirit, is acknowledged to be "the Son of God." The nature of this Father/Son relationship will be elucidated as the story continues to unfold.

Day Three: The eclipse of John 1:35-42

John has fulfilled his divine mandate as a witness. He has testified about the light (1:7) and about the grace and truth that happened through Jesus Christ as the incarnation of the Logos-Sophia (1:15-17). His baptizing activity has enabled him to continue to bear witness to Jesus as: "the Lamb of God," "the One who has happened before me," "my First," "the one who baptizes with holy Spirit," and "the Son of God." With this comprehensive acclamation of Jesus his witness is concluded. Although his baptizing activity will continue - as 3:23 indicates - his significance for the narrative world of the Gospel is coming to an end.

Two more appearances occur, however, in order to finalize his displacement by Jesus. On this day, Day Three, John is not alone. Two of his disciples are with him. Evidently Jesus has not left the area, and, as he walks by, John fixes his gaze on him (ἐμβλέψας) and identifies him to his disciples. The verb ἐμβλέψας that is used here is a compound of βλέπειν that characterized John's sighting of Jesus on the previous day. The addition of the preposition *εν* or *εμ* - meaning "in" – intensifies the act of seeing by the eyes and denotes a clarity of vision, literally a "seeing into," that makes true insight possible.[49] According to Danker's third edition of Bauer's *Greek-English Lexicon of the New Testament*, it may convey the figurative meaning of grasping transcendent matters.[50] Philo uses the verb in both senses, as he asserts, "For what the intellect is in the soul, this, the eye is in the body; for each of them sees (βλέπει), one the things of the mind, the other the things of sense".[51] Jacob is designated as "the seeing one" (ὁ βλέπων) because he is able to perceive beyond

[49] See chapter 5. Joel Marcus, "A Note on Marcan Optics," *NTS* 45/2 (April 1999) 250-256, offers an interpretation of this verb, ἐμβλέπειν, that is determined by "the extramission theory of vision." "Beams come out of the eye, travel to the object of sight and strike it, thereby producing vision." If that is what determines the clarity of vision, some internal change must take place within an individual to make perspicacious seeing possible. Βλέπειν is used ten times in chapter 9 to express the kind of seeing that generates true insight.

[50] Chicago: University of Chicago Press, 2000, 179.

[51] Philo, *de Opificio Mundi*, 53.

sense perception.[52] Melchizedek is given the epithet of "the seeing one" (ὁ βλέπων), "For as a priest he is Logos, having as his portion the one that is, and [his] reasoning about him [God] is high and vast and sublime."[53]

John's penetrating seeing (τεθέαμαι) enables him to discern the unseen uniqueness of Jesus' identity and to commit himself to all that he perceives. He expresses that commitment during his ministry as the witness to the light and to the incarnation of the light in Jesus Christ, but even more valiantly when he acknowledges to his disciples that he is only "the friend of the bridegroom" who must decrease while the latter increases. At the same time, he is also endowed with an intensity and clarity of vision (ἐμβλέψας) that transcends sense perception. These two kinds of seeing that are attributed to him should persuade the implied readers, at least temporarily, that the witness he is bearing deserves their trust.

By repeating the epithet he employed on the previous day, "Look, the Lamb of God!" John reinforces a particular prospect that awaits Jesus in the course of his ministry. As initially inscrutable as the appellative may be, it should develop a perspective in the consciousness of the reader that will be consequential for the interpretation of the events arising in the context of the third Passover.

Since there are no biblical antecedents for this identification, the immediate response of these disciples is startling: "And the two disciples heard him speaking, and they followed Jesus." There is no indication that they were present on the previous day and heard all that John witnessed about Jesus. Whether they are attracted to him out of curiosity or whether they are tantalized by the mystery of John's identification remains indeterminable. For whatever reason, they are ready to leave John and attach themselves to Jesus! If they have any inclination towards discipleship at this moment, they may be unaware of its motivation. For the moment no clarification is needed! Their sudden and immediate urge to follow Jesus may be nothing more than an inducement to the implied readers to make a similar response, if only temporarily, regardless of misgivings and disbelief.

Jesus, curious about their sudden attraction to him, turns to them and, sizing them up with his own perspicacious observation (θεασάμενος) asks, "What are you looking for?" (τί ζητεῖτε).[54] His very first words in the gospel are formulated as a question. While it may be spoken to these two adherents in the text, it is principally addressed to the implied readers.[55] More immediately the question may seem intended to solicit from them a reply as to why they are following him. But more

[52] Philo, *Legum Allegoria*, II, 46.

[53] *Ibid.*, III, 81. See also III, 110, 172 and *de Agricultura,* 54.

[54] As Howard-Brook, *Becoming Children of God*, 70, notes, the verb στραφείς (turning) is used a number of times (4) in the Gospel and connotes "a movement toward intimacy." It will be used in this sense especially in 20:14, 15.

[55] Schnackenburg, *St. John* I, 308, suspects this. The Fourth Gospel is not analogous to a window that enables us to look back onto the historical career of Jesus, but it is a narrative text that by reading is be constituted into a story world in order to experience the characters that inhabit it. Consequently, the question Jesus asks must necessarily be addressed to the implied readers.

fundamentally it is a challenge to their quest for meaning and purpose in life. A remarkably similar question is raised in Philo's treatise, "The Worse Attacks the Better," in which "the real man," the authentic human being, who supposedly dwells within each of us, asks the wandering soul, "τί ζητεῖς"[56] Among the possible answers that Philo offers in that context are self-mastery, courage, piety, and virtue. Jesus' question, however, remains unanswered. It stands provocatively at the beginning of his ministry to arouse self-critical reflection within the implied readers as the process of reading and interacting with the Gospel continues. Like the two disciples who are initially attracted to Jesus, the implied readers will eventually be compelled to answer the question in the light of the experience that the story will generate.

The response of these first adherents intimates a resolve to accompany Jesus, "Rabbi, where are you remaining/staying?" The verb they use, μένεις (you remain), which has already been employed by John, has a far-reaching significance in the Gospel.[57] They want to sojourn with Jesus, but their form of address, "Rabbi," suggests a certain caution. They are willing to attach themselves to him as their teacher, but at this point they are not prepared for anything more than that. In view of John's cryptic identification of Jesus as "the Lamb of God," which may be unintelligible to them, such restraint seems most appropriate. Jesus' disciples will address him again as "Rabbi" in 4:31, 9:2 and 11:8, but this form of address will gradually disappear, as they are drawn deeper into his ministry, and after the resurrection of Lazarus they will address him only as κύριε (Lord).[58] At that point, to stay or remain with him will also take on a deeper significance.

Jesus responds to these two individuals with a simple invitation, employing a present imperative that denotes continuous action: "Keep on coming and you will see!" No inner eye of the mind, no insight of the soul will be required. Only ocular vision![59] Jesus employs the future tense of ὁρᾶν, a verb which denotes *seeing with physical eyes*.[60] What will be seen and to what extent that seeing will fulfill the expectations that are being evoked requires a continued interaction with the narrative of the Gospel.

---

[56] Philo, *Quod Deterius Potiori*, 22-24. Cited by Barrett, *St. John*, 180.

[57] For example, see 4:40, 5:38, 6:27, 8:31, 12:46, 14:10, 15:4-10. The verb is utilized 38 times within the original edition of twenty chapters.

[58] Brown, *John*, I, 74, observes, "There is no Jewish evidence for the prefixing of 'rabbi' to the name of any of the sages in the period before 70." This, then, is another feature of the Gospel that supports Martyn's discernment of a two level drama in the narrative world of the fourth Gospel. The use of this title points to the second level that reflects the context of the Jewish community of Alexandria.

[59] While Moloney, *Belief*, 68, may be right in stating that "true discipleship is not the result of the initiative of the characters who find and follow Jesus," there must be some kind of beginning to discipleship. The two disciples who hear John's witness and follow Jesus represent one way among others; and their way may have been designed by the author of the gospel to attract and intrigue the implied readers. Moreover, it should not be forgotten that these two men have been disciples of John.

[60] See chapter 5 on "Seeing and Believing..."

Responding to Jesus' invitation, the two men "came and saw where *he stays* (μένει), and *they stayed* (ἔμειναν) with him that day." Even as the Spirit descended and *remained* upon Jesus, these disciples will remain with Jesus, and as the author continues to use the verb μένειν (to stay, remain), it will gradually develop into a spirituality of relationship between Jesus and his disciples that will culminate in a union of interdependence. At the beginning of Jesus' career, according to the narrator, "*they remained with him*" (παρ' αὐτῷ ἔμειναν). In his Farewell Speech (15:4-10) Jesus will draw them into a remaining or abiding in the transcendent reality of his own interdependent relationship with God that will empower them to continue his work as the Logos-Sophia of God: "*Begin to remain in me and I in you*" (μείνατε ἐν ἐμοί, καγὼ ἐν ὑμῖν).[61]

The narrator notes the time the disciples began to remain with Jesus: "The hour was about the tenth." Reckoning from six in the morning, when the Jewish day began, the time would be four-o clock in the afternoon. The day is beginning to wane, and Jesus will be returning to his living quarters for the coming night. Now, however, he is accompanied by two adherents who have relinquished their relationship to their former teacher and have attached themselves to him. The eclipse of John and the debut of Jesus occur simultaneously. If the tenth hour is the time of fulfillment, both of them have arrived at their own individual fullness of time.[62]

Day Three ends with an identification of one of these new disciples: "Andrew, the brother of Simon Peter was one of the two hearing from John and following him."[63] Evidently, even before remaining with Jesus for the remainder of that day, "he first finds his brother Simon and says to him, 'We have found the Messiah!'" But what could be the source of this surprising confession? Typologically messiahship cannot be deduced from John's designation of Jesus as "the Lamb of God." There is no historical, cultural or theological relationship between these christological identities. Consequently, the juxtaposition of these titles on this day of Jesus' debut may engender bewilderment within the consciousness of the implied readers, and perhaps that is the intention of the author. Whatever the perplexity might be, the implied readers are challenged to apprehend the "moving viewpoint" that travels through the narrative world of the Gospel in order to synthesize the textual perspectives of the implied author.[64] At least they know more than these disciples who on this third day of John's witness have begun to follow Jesus. The implied readers have been

---

[61] Bultmann's comment on this verse in *John*, 100; German, 70, is hardly true at this moment, but it will be fulfilled in Jesus' Farewell Speech: "It is essential to know where Jesus lives, for in the place where Jesus is at home the disciples will also receive their dwelling."

[62] Bultmann, *ibid.*, notes that ten is the "perfect number" in the Old Testament and Judaism, in Pythagoreanism and Gnosticism, as well as in Philo (citing *de Vita Mosis* I, 96). In the Fourth Gospel the day is symbolic of the time of Jesus' activity, for in 11:9 Jesus comments that there is still time to work because night has not yet arrived. In 13:30 the narrator observes that, "It was night." Brown, *John I*, 75, also entertains the possibility that the "tenth hour" may signify fulfillment but prefers to introduce the possibility that it is Friday, the eve of the Sabbath, and once the Sabbath begins, they are restricted in their movements.

[63] Andrew will reappear in 6:8 and 12:22.

inhabiting the narrative world of the Gospel prior to the entrance of Andrew and his fellow disciple, and therefore they are aware of John's witness to Jesus' divine re-creation at baptism in which the conjunction of the Spirit descending and remaining on Jesus and the incarnation of the Logos occurred.

What kind of response will they make as they move further into the narrative world of the Gospel and continue to interact with Jesus' disciples on the two levels of the Gospel's narrative world: "the *einmalig* event of Jesus' earthly lifetime" and the reflected context of the Jewish community of Alexandria?[65] As disparate as these christological identifications of Jesus are, it will gradually become evident, as the narrator continues the story, that other characters will voice confessions which they themselves may not comprehend but which the implied readers must carry forward in order to actualize the anticipated synthesis of the Gospel. At this moment the correspondence of all these confessional identities may be perplexing, but as the plot of the narrative continues to be unfolded a gradual integration will eventually be actualized in profound ironic fulfillment.

Simon's willingness to accompany his brother into Jesus' presence appears to be based simply on Andrew's confession of Jesus as the Messiah. The employment of the Hebrew word, *Messiah*, by a new disciple would be a christological title entirely appropriate to the Jewish addressees of Alexandria. It occurs only in the Fourth Gospel and nowhere else in the New Testament.[66] Along with other Hebrew/Aramaic words that are used throughout the Gospel, it may have been intended to convey a sense of authenticity.[67] The Greek translation that is offered, χριστός, although already used by John in 1:20, may possibly have been added by the Ephesian editor of the second edition of the Gospel, but, in view of the fifteen occurrences of ὁ χριστός within the first twenty chapters, it may in fact be the preferable designation instead of Messiah.

Simon remains mute in this encounter with Jesus. He has had no previous contact with Jesus, so there can be no confession of faith or even an affirmation of his brother's identification. Yet Jesus appears to know him. His scrutinizing look (ἐμβλέψας) penetrates the outer appearance of Simon's person and enables him to perceive his essential being.[68] Accordingly he renames him, "You are Simon, the son of John. You will be called Cephas." Why he is renamed without a word uttered by him must be apprehended by the implied readers as a mystery, unless they are already familiar with his discipleship. Apparently Jesus sees something in him that is not yet

---

[64] See Culpepper, *Anatomy*, 15-49, on the implied author and the rhetorical device of the omniscient narrator that conveys the expositional mode and point of view of the actual author. Also Wolfgang Iser, *The Act of Reading* (Baltimore: Johns Hopkins University Press, 1980) 107-134, on how to grasp a text.

[65] Martyn, *History and Theology*, 40.

[66] See also 4:25.

[67] Especially names and titles, such as: Rabbi in 1:38, Cephas in 1:42, Messiah in 4:25, Gabbatha in 19:13, Rabboni in 20:16.

[68] The narrator used the same verb of John's earlier gaze at Jesus in 1:36.

evident. How Simon Peter will fulfill the destiny of his new name is a matter the implied readers will be compelled to evaluate as the narrative moves on to its conclusion.[69]

As of this moment in the fullness of his time Jesus has gained three followers. Andrew has been named and his brother Simon renamed Cephas. Identifying by name the individuals who inhabit this narrative world is characteristic of the narrator.[70] Yet this is only partially true, for only one of the John's two former disciples is named in this context. The other's identity remains a mystery. Some commentators have been inclined to identify him as the Beloved Disciple.[71] If he is identifiable as "the one whom Jesus loved," his testimony as a disciple of John and Jesus may have been an important resource for the Fourth Evangelist. The text, however, does not make this identification; it must be ascertained in the process of reading, if at all.

John's diminution 3:23-30

John makes one more appearance in the gospel but only to acknowledge his supercession by Jesus (3:23-29). The narrator introduces this concluding episode by paralleling the careers of Jesus and John. Both are baptizing, Jesus in Judea and John in Aenon near Salim "because there was much water there" (3:23).[72] It appears that John is still enjoying a relatively successful ministry, for "they were coming and letting themselves be baptized." Yet the immediate future is ominous, "for John had not yet been thrown into prison." In contrast to the Synoptic Gospels of Mark and Matthew, the martyrdom of John is not recounted. But the inauspicious note of his forthcoming incarceration conveys a somber and plaintive sense of ending.

A dispute over purification with an unnamed 'Ιουδαίος (Jew) draws his disciples to him.[73] But who is this Jew? Should he be identified with the ruling authorities? It would seem so because a confrontation appears to be implied involving a controversy

---

[69] See Culpepper's synthesis of Peter's character, *Anatomy*, 120-121.

[70] For example, the High Priest's servant whose right ear was cut off by Peter's sword, "His name was Malchus" (18:10).

[71] See chapters 12 and 17. F. Büchsel's comment in *Das Evangelium nach Johannes, NTD* 4 (Göttingen: Vandenhoeck and Ruprecht, 1935) 41, is worth quoting in this respect: "To tell this story makes sense only if the Evangelist conceals the beloved disciple behind the unnamed companion of Andrew." Also Maynard, "The Role of Peter in the Fourth Gospel," 533; and Hartin, "The Role of Peter in the Fourth Gospel," 50.

[72] The use of the imperfect tense implies that the activity is limited to the time of John and Jesus. Jerome Murphy-O'Conner, "John the Baptist and Jesus: History and Hypotheses," *NTS* 36/3, (1990) 364-365, identifies the location of Aenon near Salim. "Aenon" means "springs," and the name "Salim" is preserved in the Palestinian village of Salim which is located "4.5 kms … east of the site of ancient Shechem." The springs on the eastern slope of Mount Gerezim near Salim, "attests to a mission of the Baptist in the very heart of Samaritan territory."

[73] The manuscript tradition offers an alternate reading: 'Ιουδαίων instead of 'Ιουδαίου. The latter, however, is the more difficult reading, if only because it is the only instance in the Gospel that the singular is employed. Because of the consistent use of the plural it is very likely that a scribe of a later generation substituted the plural in place of the singular. It has been conjectured by a few scholars that the original reading was 'Iησοῦ but in view of the context that seems highly unlikely. See Bultmann, *John*, 169, n. 3; German, 123, n. 2. Also Barrett, *St. John*, 221.

about purification. The narrator's all-too-brief reference to an encounter between "the disciples of John" and a member of the ruling elite may well intimate that the followers of John the Witness, like the Christian Jews, are members of the Jewish community in Alexandria and, by being engaged in baptizing activity, may be under suspicion of being regarded as *minim* (heretics).[74]

This is the context that the narrator utilizes to let John speak for the last time. The question, however, which his disciples raise in 3:26 is not about purification at all.[75] It concerns Jesus and his career, "Rabbi, the one who was with you beyond the Jordan, to whom you have witnessed; look, he is baptizing and all are coming to him." Although their testimony to Jesus' growing success is a more explicit indication of John's supersession, the preceding reference to "purification" intimates the basis for the superiority of Jesus over John. According to the narrator, Jesus, like John is baptizing. But in 4:2 the narrator will reverse himself and inform the implied readers that it was not Jesus but his disciples who were baptizing. In the light of John's earlier witness (1:33), Jesus will baptize in/with the holy Spirit. Consequently, he cannot, like John, baptize in/with water.

What, then, is the rhetorical strategy of this reversal? Water baptism in and of itself may signify nothing more than purification, and that may be the issue between the disciples of John and the authorities in the Jewish community of Alexandria. But in 3:5 Jesus had informed Nicodemus, a Pharisee and a ruler of the Jews, that unless he is generated "from water and Spirit" he cannot enter into the rule of God. Water baptism alone may be nothing more than a rite of purification. But "water and Spirit" together bring about the eschatological event of death and resurrection. Undergoing death in the waters of baptism brings to an end an existence predetermined by the power of sin and its consequence of death. Being raised up by the revivifying power of the Spirit signifies the entry into a new moral order and the commencement of undertaking the rule of God on God's behalf.

John himself enters into the narrative for the last time and, in view of the superiority of Jesus' person and work that he has already acknowledged, he concedes his own supersession.

> A human being is unable to receive one thing unless it has been given to him from heaven. You yourselves witness to me that I said, ' I am not the Christ, but I have been sent before that one. (3:27-28)

Once more he acknowledges that he is not the Christ, but this time in doing so he does not separate the divine **I AM** formula (ἐγὼ εἰμί) with the negative particle οὐκ, as he had done in 1:20. He places the οὐκ before the **I AM** and follows immediately

[74] The presence of John's followers in the Jewish community of Alexandria would reinforce the cogency of choosing John to serve as the monumental witness to the Logos and its incarnation in Jesus of Nazareth. But see von Wahlde, "The Johannine 'Jews'," 49-50, who concludes that this is a neutral use of Ἰουδαίος.

[75] See Bultmann, *John*, 168-169; German, 124-125.

with the messianic appellative: οὐκ εἰμὶ ἐγὼ ὁ χριστός (not **I AM** the Christ). This too is significant because Jesus also utilizes the **I AM** formula in a reverse order, εἰμὶ ἐγώ, in 7:34, 36; 12:26; 14:3; 17:24. In the context of the narrative world of the gospel as a whole, in which Jesus uses both word orders, ἐγὼ εἰμι (**I AM**) and εἰμὶ ἐγώ (**AM I**), John is testifying that it is not he but his successor, Jesus, who is the Christ, but the Christ who is to be identified with the divine self-disclosure, **I AM**.

Drawing from the metaphor of marriage, John, in conclusion, places himself in the role of a groomsman. Jesus is the groom who is receiving his bride, intimated perhaps to be Israel .

> The one having the bride is the bridegroom. But the friend of the bridegroom who is standing and hearing him rejoices with joy because of the voice of the bridegroom. Therefore, this my joy has been fulfilled. (3:29)

The implied readers hear John state publicly to his remaining disciples that he, John, considers his life and work to have been fulfilled. His mission is accomplished. His joy as the friend of the bridegroom has been fulfilled, and without regret he can fade away. In his realistic awareness of what the arrival of the incarnate Logos-Sophia means, he has no hesitation in conceding, "It is necessary for that one to increase, but for me to decrease." This too may be intended to evangelize the followers of John who are members of the Alexandrian community of Jews.[76]

As Jesus increases within the narrative world of the Gospel in the fulfillment of God's will, he, in contrast to John, will impart joy to his disciples. It will be his joy, the joy of accomplishing his divine mission to remove the sin of the world and therefore saving the world.

> And now I am coming towards (πρός) you, and these things I am speaking in the world so that they may have my joy fulfilled in themselves.

Epilogue 3:31-36

In the light of this self-evaluation, it seems ironic that the Fourth Gospel bears his name. The John of the "the Gospel according to John" is not John, the son of Zebedee, or John the Elder of Ephesus. The John of the superscription, κατὰ Ἰωάννην is John the Witness. There is no other John in the narrative world of the Gospel. The monumental witness that he bears: Jesus as the incarnate Logos-Sophia "who has happened before me because he was my First" and Jesus as "the Lamb of God who removes the sin of the world," shapes the self-understanding of Jesus and the course of his ministry in the Gospel.

Problematic in this respect, however, is the closure of chapter 3, specifically verses 31-36. No speaker is identified with this monologue! John the Witness, Jesus and the narrator have been proposed, but the most likely possibilities appear to be John or the

[76] See Brown, *John*, I, LXVII-LXX for a discussion of the possibility that a refutation of John's messiahship is being directed at a community of John's followers. Also I, 46-54.

narrator.[77] John, after announcing his own diminishment, may intend once more and for the last time to enunciate why Jesus is superior. On the other hand, the narrator is may be presenting a reflective supplement in the form of an appendix to the thoughts already expressed in 3:1-21.[78]

As reasonable as that continuity between verses 30 and 31 may be, it is difficult to believe that this pericope, 3:31-36, belonged to the original composition of the Gospel. It may be the only illegitimate text within the first edition of the Gospel. Its authenticity is undermined by a number of incongruities. There is no immediate identification of the speaker. At least two of its words appear only once in the Gospel, specifically the verb ἀπειθέω (disobey) and the noun ὀργή (wrath). In the Gospel the opposite of "πιστεύων εἰς (believing into) the Son" is always "οὐ πιστεύων (not believing)," never the phrase "ἀπειθῶν (disobeying) the Son."[79] And the consequence for not believing is "judgment" (κρίσις) not "wrath" (ὀργή).[80] In 3:34b the subject of the verb is ambiguous; it might be God, but it might also be Jesus, "the one who speaks the words of God." Later scribes attempted to resolve the matter by inserting an explicit subject.[81] But the most significant incongruity is the singular juxtaposition of ἐκ τῆς γῆς (from the earth) and ἐκ τοῦ οὐρανοῦ (from the heaven). The word γῇ (earth) always refers to geographical territory (3:22, 6:21) or earth into which seed is planted (12:24). Throughout the Gospel ἐκ τοῦ κόσμου (from the world) is always the binary opposite of ἐκ τοῦ οὐρανοῦ.

Although it can be argued that there is continuity between verses 30 and 31, a more cogent continuity may be established between 3:30, John's acknowledgment of his own decrease in stature, and the transition of 4:1 that attests to the superiority of Jesus

[77] Bultmann, *John*, 160-169; German, 116-121, locates this passage immediately after 3:1-21 and interprets it as an extension of verses 9-21, but with an emphasis on the Son bearing witness of what he has seen and heard. Consequently, he stresses the role of Jesus as the Revealer who speaks God's word, a theme he encounters throughout the Gospel. Dodd, *Fourth Gospel*, 308-311, after struggling with this text, finally concludes that 3:31-36 is a continuation of 3:22-30. It is an explanatory appendix to the dialogue with Nicodemus and the discourse that grows out of it. Barrett, *St. John*, 224-225, seems to believe that John is speaking in these verses and contrasting himself, as "the one from the earth" and Jesus as "the one from heaven." He assumes that vs. 31-36 belong to the original text of the Gospel. R. Alan Culpepper, *The Gospel and Letters of John*, (Nashville: Abingdon, 1998) 137-138, rightly states that vs. 31-36 "do not read like a continuation of John's testimony to Jesus." He suggests that Jesus or the narrator may also be speaking here. But he does not entertain a suspicion that this text may be an interpolation. Because verses 31-36 are a doublet of 3:11-21, they "bring the chapter to a satisfying conclusion by recapturing some of its leading themes." Lindars, *John*, 169, considers verses 31-36 a "return to the theme of the discourse with Nicodemus for the second supplementary paragraph." W. A. Meeks, "The Man from Heaven in Johannine Sectarianism," *JBL* 91/1 (1972) 55-56, on the basis of "themes" closely related to the Nicodemus dialogue, interprets 3:31-36 as an integral part of the Gospel, a summary of the themes that emerged from the dialogue with Nicodemus. David Rensberger, *Johannine Faith*, 63, n. 30, considers 3:31-36 to be a continuation of John the Baptizer's speech that presents "the most pointed challenge to his disciples."

[78] R. H. Lightfoot, *St. John's Gospel: A Commentary* (Oxford: at the University Press, 1960) 120.

[79] For example, see 3:18; 8:24, 45-46; 10:25-26, 37-38.

[80] See 3:18-19.

[81] Various manuscripts insert a subject for the verb δίδωσι, namely God the Father. The words τὸ πνεῦμα are omitted by Codex B.

in terms of making more disciples and baptizing more than John. It would appear, therefore, that 3:31-36 is a later scribal interpolation intended, perhaps, to finalize John's witness as to why Jesus is superior and therefore must increase in stature.[82]

Such a necessity might have arisen in an Ephesian context in which John's significance and stature continued to compete with that of Jesus. The testimony of Acts 19:1-7 indicates that John's influence extended into other areas of the eastern Mediterranean world outside of Alexandria and Palestine and continued to be effective in propagating his messiahship and therefore his superiority over Jesus. Perhaps 3:31-36 was interpolated by the Ephesian editor.

[82] Bultmann, *John*, 160, n. 2, "3:31-36 did not originally belong to the sayings of the Baptist, as can be seen from the fact that as far as their form and content are concerned, they belong to 3:1-21, and from the fact that v. 32b does not fit the situation described in v. 26."

Chapter Four

The Beginning of Jesus' Ministry

The marriage at Cana 2:1-11

> And on the third day a marriage happened in Cana of Galilee, and the mother of Jesus was there. Now Jesus and his disciples were also invited to the marriage.

Prior to this event that marks the beginning of Jesus' ministry, four days appear to have been differentiated in John 1:19-51 by the use of the adverb ἐπαύριον (on the next day) in 1:29, 35, 43.[1]

1. John's interrogation by the chief priests and scribes, the representatives of the ruling authorities, οἱ Ἰουδαίοι, who prove to be the Pharisees. 1:19-28
2. John's testimony about Jesus. 1:29-34
3. Two of John's disciples attach themselves to Jesus and the number of his followers begins to increase. 1:35-42
4. Jesus' removal to Galilee, new disciples and the promise of a vision. 1:43-51

In view of the narrator's continued use of the adverb ἐπαύριον at the beginning of the second, third and fourth episodes, it might well lead the implied readers to anticipate a continuation of this day to day time frame as the narrative moves into a new episode in 2:1. When, however, a new time reference, τῇ ἡμέρᾳ τῇ τρίτῃ (on the third day) is introduced that seems to have no relationship to the preceding time code, the reaction in all likelihood would be one of perplexity. At least initially!

Ironically, many of the interpreters, who postulate the so-called "Signs Source" as one of the two major originations of the Gospel, are inclined to attribute this phrase to the redaction of the Evangelist and yet to consider its meaning to be "puzzling" or "uncertain."[2] A possible resolution, that could take into account the

[1] John 2:1-11 marks the beginning of Jesus' public ministry, not the episode that follows, as Barrett, *St. John*, 189, claims. Jesus transforms water into wine to signify the ironic character and objective of his ministry.

[2] See the discussion of Fortna, *The Fourth Gospel*, 49-54. For many the phrase is a conundrum, and many resolutions have been posed, some by inserting extra days into the narrative of 1:19-51 in order to arrive at the number six or seven. Lindars, *John*, 128, suggests the day of resurrection, but goes on to consider it to be the eighth day of Jesus' ministry and symbolic of "the beginning of a new era." Compare Bultmann, *John*, 114, n. 3; German edition, 79, n. 3. Finally, see the discussion of Keener, *John* I, 496-498, who admits the possibility of a reference to the eschatological reality of resurrection but is more inclined to a historical time code "allowing some time for Jesus to travel."

Alexandrian Jews as the implied readers of the Gospel, would be to interpret "on the third day" as a reference to Wednesday, the third day of the week, the time the Mishnah stipulates for the wedding of virgins.[3] Another resolution would be to regard it simply as the third day after Jesus' encounter with Nathanael in 1:45-51.[4]

On the other hand, the time reference may have been designed deliberately to puzzle the implied readers. Without any textual indications they are compelled to consider this breach in the narrative time code to be an unexpected shift into another perspective on time. Unlike the time code, "on the next day," this phrase may not be intended as a chronological reference at all. Its significance, in fact, may be eschatological. For "on the third day" is a point in time that bears the symbolic value of deliverance and restoration in the Hebrew Scriptures. According to Gen 40: 20-23, Joseph's fellow inmates were delivered from their Egyptian prison on the third day, one to be hanged, the other to be restored to his position as Pharaoh's butler. Joseph himself was delivered from the same incarceration "after two years," or at the beginning of the third year. "On the morning of the third day," according to Ex 19:16, God descended upon Mt. Sinai and "Moses went up" to enter into a mutual covenant on behalf of the people of Israel.[5] The classic text, of course, that signals the third day as the time of deliverance and restoration is Hos 6:2, "After two days I will heal you; *on the third day* I will raise you up."

The phrase was incorporated into the early Church's creed to express the culminating reality of Jesus' deliverance from death. The Apostle Paul employed such a formulation in I Cor 15:4, "And he has been raised *on the third day*, according to the Scriptures." In the Synoptic Gospels Jesus utilizes the phrase in his passion predictions.

> From then Jesus Christ began to show his disciples that it is necessary that he go to Jerusalem and suffer many things from the elders and the chief priests and the scribes and be killed and to be resurrected *on the third day.* (Matt 16:21)[6]

Although the phrase does not appear in the resurrection narratives of John 20-21, Jesus employs an approximate parallel in 2:19 to foreshadow his resurrection as the living temple of God: "Tear down this sanctuary and *in three days* (ἐν τρισίν ἡμέραις) I shall resurrect (ἐγερῶ) it."[7] Very likely then, "on the third day" is intended to be more than another instance of the gospel's narrative time code. It is

[3] Brown, *John*, I, 98. See the M *Ketubot* 1:1; B *Ketubim* 2a; PT *Ketubim* 1:1; *Pesiqta de Rab Kahanna,* 26:2, cited by Keener, *John* I, 496, n. 39.

[4] Barrett, *St. John*, 190 and Haenchen, *John*, I, 172.

[5] Cited by Moloney, *Belief*, 77.

[6] See also Matt 7:23, 20:19, 27:63; Luke 9:22, 18:33, 24:46. The preposition μετά (after), introduces the phrase in Mark 8:31, 9:31 and 10:34.

[7] The comment of Dodd, *The Fourth Gospel*, 300, is noteworthy in this context: "It is in accordance with the view taken by this evangelist that the whole of the incarnate ministry of the Word should have the character of the 'third day' of His glory."

a textual signal conveying the reality of resurrection. Jesus is commencing his public ministry as though his resurrection has already occurred and he has entered into a reordering of power. That eschatological reality that Judaism has been anticipating is no longer a future event but a reality drawn out of the future into his present existence. As the result of the conjunction of the enfleshment of the Logos-Sophia and the descending and remaining of God's Spirit at his baptism Jesus will understand himself as God's Son and God's apprentice.

By utilizing this eschatological time code, the narrator is signaling the implied readers that Jesus will live and act ironically throughout his career.[8] To live out of the future, when its realities have not yet been actualized and when there is no certainty that they will be, is a bold act of faith. It is comporting oneself to life ironically. For it not only denies the preponderance of actuality over possibility; it also contradicts the supremacy of death over life and therefore the power that death generates in historical existence.

"On the third day" introduces the *first of the signs* (ἀρχὴν τῶν σημείων) Jesus performs in the narrative world of the gospel. The wonder of converting 162 gallons of water into a vintage superior to the wine the wedding guests have been drinking should not be construed simply as a "powerful indication of Jesus' messiahship."[9] The noun ἀρχή (beginning/principle) in 2:11 attaches an archetypal character to this sign. It is not only the inaugural act of Jesus' career. It comprehends and interprets his entire ministry, for in its link with the significance of "on the third day" it foreshadows the paradigm shift that will eventually be constituted. Like the disciples who witness this sign (2:11), the implied readers are drawn into a new understanding of time which this episode signals and which in the subsequent course of the narrative may have a significant affect on their self-understanding. To follow Jesus is to be challenged to live ironically, as though one has already died and been resurrected from the dead and consequently is a participant in a new moral order.

A marriage is taking place in Cana of Galilee, a place that apparently has no biblical or historical significance. A so-called no-place! This too conveys a note of irony. For the event of a marriage as the context of the first sign of Jesus' ministry, which unites two individuals in the dynamic union of a relationship that oscillates between one-ness and two-ness, vibrates with the echoes of the

---

[8] Irony is difficult to define because of its differences in usage. Paul D. Duke appropriates D.C. Muecke's definition in his study of *Irony in the Fourth Gospel* (Atlanta: John Knox Press, 1985) 13-18, and the three criteria that he works with are certainly applicable here, at least the first two: 1. a double-layered or two-storied phenomenon, 2. some kind of opposition between the two levels, and 3. an element of "innocence" or unawareness. See also Gail R. O'Day, *Revelation in the Fourth Gospel* (Philadelphia: Fortress Press, 1986) especially chapter one. Also Culpepper, *Anatomy*, 151-180. Finally also J.E. Botha, "The Case of Johannine Irony Reopened I: The Problematic Current Situation," *Neot* 25(2) 1991, 209-220, who is critical of Duke, O'Day and Culpepper and contends that the whole question of Johannine irony must be reopened. See also his, "The Case of Johannine Irony Reopened II: Suggestions, Alternative Approaches," *Neot* 25(2) 1991, 221-232.

[9] Fortna, The Fourth Gospel, 48.

Prologue's presentation of the dynamic movement of the Logos-Sophia πρὸς τὸν θεόν (towards the God) that results in a union with the Creator. Moreover, marriage, like the opening time reference "on the third day," might well intimate to the implied readers specific prophetic utterances related to the eschatological reality of God's union with Israel. Hosea in particular employs the metaphor of marriage to express the transformation of Israel's relationship with God.[10]

> And it will be on that day, says *Kyrios* (Lord), you will call me, "O my husband," and you will no longer call me Baalim. ... And I shall betroth you to myself forever, and I shall betroth you to myself in justice and in judgment and in mercy and in compassion, and I shall betroth you to myself in faith, and you will know *Kyrios*.[11]

The traditional patriarchal structure of hierarchy in which God and Israel were joined together, analogous to that of husband and wife, will be terminated. God and Israel, in a new intimacy of knowing each other, will collaborate as equals, each contributing unique qualities and capabilities to their interdependence that the other does not possess. Israel's employment of the form of address, "O my husband," stands in contrast to the former usage of "Baalim" and must therefore be construed to express a fundamentally different relationship than that which was common between husband and wife and therefore also between God and Israel. As the master/slave dependency is relinquished, the new union of equality will constitute a new self-understanding for both parties.

This is the nature of the paradigm shift that the marriage in Cana foreshadows. It is specifically Jesus' work of transforming the water in the stone pots, the water that traditionally was used for ritual purification, into a vintage that surpasses the quality of the wine the wedding party had been drinking.[12]

Both the old and the new are represented among those invited to the wedding. First and, indeed, separately, the narrator acknowledges the presence of Jesus' mother: "And the mother of Jesus was there." Jesus and his disciples have also been invited, but as John Ashton has noted in his close reading of the text, "... she

---

[10] Also Ashton, *Understanding*, 272, who says, "Israel's feeling towards God was profoundly coloured by the image of God as husband and lover..."

[11] A translation of LXX Hos 2:18, 21. In the MT, on which the English translation is based, the text is Hos 2:16, 19-20 See also LXX Is 62:1-5 where the metaphor of marriage is used to give expression to a new creation. Verse 5b even hints at a marriage relationship between Yahweh and the disowned of Jerusalem, "...and as the bridegroom rejoices over the bride, so shall your God rejoice over you." Also cited by Ashton, *Understanding the Fourth Gospel*, 272, who rightly claims, "...the heart of the passage remains the transformation of water into wine, another symbol of joyful celebration." Brown, *John* I, 104-105, acknowledges that the wedding is used to symbolize "the messianic times and the new dispensation."

[12] The jars of water do not represent Judaism but the ritual of purification and especially the purity code that divides the world into the realms of "clean" and "unclean". Also Dodd, *Fourth Gospel*, 299, who considers the stone pots to "stand for the entire system of Jewish ceremonial observance..." Against Bultmann, *John*, 120, n. 2, who has concluded that the water represents everything that is a substitute for revelation. This interpretation, of course, corresponds to his reductionism that in the Fourth Gospel Jesus is essentially the Revealer.

was present at the wedding from the start, unlike Jesus and his disciples, who arrived later, as invited guests, from the outside." Consequently, as he rightly concludes, "... she is more closely identified with the scene of the wedding."[13] Accordingly, when the wine has given out, she approaches Jesus with the announcement, "They have no wine." She says '*they*' rather than '*we*,' as Ashton has also observed.[14] All of these aspects of a close reading of the text are related to her nameless but supervisory role in the story.

As is usually recognized by commentators, "the mother of Jesus" is never named by the narrator. In fact, she appears only twice: at the beginning and at the end of the Gospel's narrative world, and at the end she is joined by another character who also is never identified by name, the Beloved Disciple. Yet the narrator appears to have a predilection to identify individuals by name, as is exemplified by the naming of the High Priest's slave, Malchus, whose ear Peter severed with his sword in the garden at the time of Jesus' arrest. Why then are not characters like Jesus' Mother and the Beloved Disciple, whose role in the Gospel's narrative world is certainly more significant than that of Malchus, also named? When these two individuals meet at the foot of the cross in 19:25-27 and are entrusted to each other by Jesus, the narrator becomes suspect of a literary contrivance. Evidently both the Mother of Jesus and the Beloved Disciple, in addition to being formidable characters in the narrative world of the Gospel, are intended to serve as representations of specific communities. The Beloved Disciple is the personification of a New Israel, the new people of God. The Mother of Jesus, on the other hand, is the embodiment of Judaism.[15] She is Mother Israel, and, in terms of this corporate identity, she is playing a "mediating" role in this episode.[16] It is natural, therefore, that she should be *there* at the wedding, above all if "the marriage at Cana" foreshadows the paradigm shift of a new relationship between God and Israel. And it is in terms of her "mediating" role that she says, "They have no wine" instead of "We have no wine." As Mother Israel she is solicitous about her offspring. As Mother Israel she also has given birth to the Messiah, and therefore she is well aware of her son's capabilities. That is why she turns to him, when the wine has given out, and informs him of the wedding

[13] For both of these citations, see Ashton, *Understanding*, 268.

[14] *Ibid.*

[15] Bultmann, 121, n. 2, rejects the identification of "the mother of Jesus" as representative of Judaism. Even though she is not named in the Gospel, he still refers to her as "Mary". German, 85, n. 2. Later, however, in his comment on 19:27, he claims that "his mother," represents Jewish Christianity. German, 84, n. 2. See the discussion of Ashton, *Understanding*, 268-269, who concludes that she is representative of the Jewish readers of the Gospel who are being urged to "declare themselves for Christ." Culpepper, *Anatomy*, 134, proposes that the mother of Jesus is "...in some sense the description of 'the new Eve'." But to consider her as symbolic of Judaism or Jewish Christianity "lacks solid warrants in the gospel". Keener, *John* I, 502, concludes, "... many of John's anonymous characters may help the reader identify with them, functioning as positive models for discipleship."

[16] The word, "mediating" is taken from Ashton, *Understanding*, 268.

couple's embarrassment, "They have no wine!" Jesus as yet has performed no mighty works; he has given no demonstrations of his power and authority. Yet his mother knows of his divine aptitude and prompts his immediate intervention.

His response is perplexing, for on the one hand he rebukes his Mother with the harsh words, "Of what concern is that to you or me, woman? My hour has not yet arrived."[17] On the other hand, he proceeds to fulfill her request immediately after she has instructed the attendants (διάκονοι) to carry out his commands. His reproachful question, τί ἐμοὶ καὶ σοί, literally, "What to you and to me?" is an idiom that is encountered in the Septuagint, the Gospels and the Acts of Thomas.[18] It is intended to convey a difference in perception or orientation that may imply a rift, a disassociation or a disjunction of engagement. Jesus and his mother are speaking to each other from different perspectives.[19] It is an ironic moment between them. Her announcement, "They have no wine!" is her indirect manner of obligating Jesus to deal with the crisis at hand. His messianic intervention is required in order to rescue the wedding couple from the humiliation of having no more wine to serve to the guests. That this is her immediate consideration is confirmed by her charge to the servants, "Whatever he should say to you, do [it]."

It is commonly acknowledged that the form of address, γύναι (woman), that Jesus employs in his response to his Mother is not disrespectful. While that may be true of the culture of the Hellenistic world, it is unusual and startling in the context of Judaism's norms and conventions.[20] Jesus will use it again in 19:26 when, in the final moments of his life, he commits his Mother into the care and protection of the Beloved Disciple. Mary Magdalene will be addressed in the same way by two angels in Jesus' tomb (20:13). Perhaps this form of address is a feature of the Jewish acculturation of a Hellenistic custom. Nevertheless, in this context of a confrontation, Jesus' use of this form of address effectively separates him from his Mother's motherhood and any influence that she might still exercise in his life and ministry. As Gustav Dalman has said, "When one's mother is addressed as 'woman,' it means a relinquishment of physical relationship."[21] He is

---

[17] This is the translation offered by F. Blass and A. Debrunner, *A Greek Grammar of the New Testament and Other Early Christian Literature*, trans. and rev. by R. W. Funk (Cambridge: at the University Press, 1961) 299.3, who cite parallels in the Septuagint.

[18] See Arthur H. Maynard, "TI EMOI KAI SOI (John 2:4)," *NTS* 31/4 (1985) 582-586, who cites the texts in which this idiom is used: Jud 11:12, 1 Kgs 17:18, 2 Kgs 3:13, 2 Chr 35:21, Mark 5:7 as well as the texts in which variations of the idiom appear: 2 Sam 16:10, 19:22; 2 Kgs 9:18; Jos 22:24; Matt 8:29; Mark 1:24; Luke 4:34; Acts of Thomas 5:45.

[19] Contrary to Maynard, *ibid.*, 585-596, the question Jesus addresses to his mother is eschatologically oriented. It is not to be interpreted christologically for his christological identity is presupposed. He is not terminating a historical relationship to his mother and moving into the transcendence of divine revelation.

[20] Schnackenburg, *St. John* I, 328-329.

[21] Gustav Dalman, *Jesus-Jeshua*, trans. by Paul L. Levertoff (New York: KTAV Publishing House, 1971), 182-183, 202.

no longer under her authority; he is no longer limited by the restraints of Judaism that she may embody.

Jesus, however, construes her indirect summons to help, “They have no wine!” as a reference to Israel’s monumental crisis of existential despair. In the historical context of the Fourth Gospel he would be oriented to the destruction of the Temple and the termination of its cultic sacrifices and offerings that have maintained the covenantal relationship between God and Israel. His response to this crisis would involve him in the fulfillment of the prophetic vision of a new covenant and its accompanying new moral order. Confronted with this ironic moment of his mother’s oblique prompting to act messianically, he refuses to undertake an action that would correspond to his own interpretation of her forceful observation, “They have no wine.” He responds to her with a puzzling and enigmatic rationale, “My hour has not yet arrived.” Apparently without understanding what he is referring to, but also without taking offense, she issues instructions to the attendants in terms of her corporate identity as Mother Israel, confident that her son will do something to alleviate the crisis.

Jesus’ enigmatic reply to his mother is, in fact, directed at the implied readers of the Gospel in order to evoke their interactive questioning. What hour is he referring to? Why is it not yet here? This is the critical moment for him to begin his messianic work by relieving the wedding couple of their embarrassment and replenishing the wedding’s supply of wine. If this is not the hour, when will it arrive?

The significance of his “hour” becomes apparent only when the same words are encountered again in the form of “asides” that interrupt the narrative and are offered by the narrator for the benefit of the implied readers in 7:30 and 8:20, “For his hour had not yet come.” In these contexts of increasing hostility against Jesus by the Jewish authorities who endeavor to seize him and stone him to death, the obvious interpretation of his “hour” is the time of his death.[22]

This simple identification, however, is deficient because it does not take into account that the rationale for Jesus' refusal to intervene was spoken as a response to his Mother's prompting to help. Another critical facet of meaning emerges in 12:23 and 27. When certain Greeks request “to see Jesus,” he responds without a direct reply by acknowledging:

> The hour has come so that the Son of the Human Being is glorified. Amen, amen I say to you, unless a seed of wheat falling into the ground dies, it remains alone. But if it dies, it bears much fruit. (12:23b-24)

It is not yet possible for the Greeks to see Jesus. Like a seed of wheat, he must first die in order to make their access to what he has to offer possible. But it will

---

[22] Schnackenburg, *St. John* I, 328-331, discusses the problem of his “hour” at length, considering it from various perspectives but concludes that in 2:4 it “first and foremost ... signifies the Father's sovereignty over Jesus, asserted precisely in view of Mary.”

be a bitter death, for it will involve more than the agony and suffering of crucifixion. In its anticipation Jesus recoils from its horror.

> Now my self (ψυχή) is agitated and what shall I say? Father, save me from this hour. But on account of this I came into this hour. (12:27)

Ironically this "hour" of death has been his objective from the beginning of his ministry, although he inaugurated it as though his death had already occurred, and he was living and acting in the irony of resurrection. His "hour," therefore, is that time when he will remedy the condition that the failure of the wine symbolizes. That "hour" will be his response to this Father's will and not his Mother's.[23] But more immediately he will fulfill his Mother's request, but only as a sign, a sign that pledges that by the fulfillment of his "hour" in death Israel will realize a messianic bounty of an intoxicating vintage that is far superior to anything that has been tasted and drunk in the past.[24]

The extravagance of this new dispensation is symbolized by the huge capacity of the six stone jars, each able to contain "two or three measures," that is, 18 to 27 gallons. Since they were filled to the brim, the total volume would be 162 gallons. These large vessels served as containers of water "for the purification of the Jews". Yet why so many? If drawn water was not normally used for purification, as C. S. Keener observes, the significance of "six stone pots" may be symbolic of the Torah, but more specifically of the *Torah she be al pe* (literally the Torah on the mouth), the oral Torah, codified by Rabbi Judah the Prince in 200 C. E. as the Mishnah.[25] It is divided into six *sederim* or orders of rabbinic jurisprudence.[26] The tractates of these six *sederim* present interpretations and expansions of the written Torah, the Pentateuch; and, as the opening verse of the Mishnah tractate, *Pirque Aboth*, states, they are intended to construct a fence around the (written) Torah in order to keep a human being far from transgression. In short, they serve to maintain the rabbinic ideology of justice and purity. The use of the verb γεμίζειν with the accusative of content αὐτάς (to fill them up) implies that the stone pots are entirely empty.[27] The implication may be that the entire purity code that regulates the system of purification must be replaced by a new moral order.

---

[23] So also Moloney, *Belief*, 82.

[24] Philo, *Legum Allegoria* III, 79-82, poses Melchizedek as God's king of peace and priest, who, in the context of the refusal of the Ammonites and the Moabites to supply Israel in the wilderness with "bread and water," offers the people of God "bread and wine." "But let Melchizedek instead of water offer wine and give souls to drink straight wine so that they are seized by a divine intoxication, more sober than sobriety itself." Also cited by Dodd, *Fourth Gospel*, 298, in this context.

[25] See Keener, *John* I, 511, for a discussion on the problem of purification water found in pots or drawn from a well.

[26] Barrett, *St. John*, 191, relates the number six to the incompleteness of the Jewish tradition, since six falls short of the number representing completeness, seven; also Robert Kysar, *John the Maverick Gospel* (Atlanta: John Knox Press, 2nd ed. 1979) 46.

[27] *A Greek-English Lexicon of the New Testament and Other Early Christian Literature*, 191.

At the command of Jesus the attendants fill the stone jars to capacity, and, as they draw some off and bear it to the chief steward, the water is transformed into wine. The wonderful transformation is not described; the divine act, as Bultmann observed, remains a mystery.[28] After tasting the wine, the chief steward calls the bridegroom and, as the professional who can judge and discriminate, he not only attests to the superior quality of the vintage but also inadvertently hints at a paradigm shift.

> Every human being first offers the good wine, and when they are drunk, the inferior. You have kept the good wine until now. (2:10)

The bridegroom receives the credit for an unprecedented reversal that he knows nothing about. At the same time the chief steward, in spite of his attestation, remains ignorant of the origin of this superior wine. "But," as the aside of the narrator indicates, "the attendants (διάκονοι), those who drew the water, knew." These "ministers," as the word may also be translated, are those who followed Jesus' instructions, and in their obedience to render service they discover they are insiders who are directly involved in the awesome mystery that has occurred. There is no greater reward for those who minister as servers of the new wine.

In this first or archetypal sign Jesus, according to the narrator's conclusion of the story, manifested his glory. The verb ἐφανέρωσεν (he manifested) denotes a visible act and indicates that whatever glory (δόξα) he disclosed was empirically evident to his new disciples. That δόξα is not simply the revelation of the deity of Jesus as the divine Revealer.[29] It is the disclosure of Jesus as the "son of Joseph from Nazareth" who in an ironic act as the enfleshed Logos-Sophia begins to draw the anticipated future of the new moral order into the present and attendantly to contradict the preponderance of actuality over possibility. His divine creativity of transforming the water of six gigantic stone pots intended for ritual purification into a quality and quantity of wine that excels all that had been consumed previously signals the eschatological reality of a new creation.

The vision Jesus promised his disciples in 1:51 is beginning to materialize. The transcendent resources of heaven are being translated into time and place by the one on whom the heavenly ladder rests, the Son of the Human Being. The disciples who have begun to follow him respond to this epiphany: "they believed into him" (ἐπίστευσαν εἰς αὐτόν). What up to this point may have been belief based on tradition becomes existential faith. For with the metamorphosis of water into wine their religious persuasion is radicalized into a vital commitment to his person and work.

---

[28] Bultmann, *John*, 118. German, 82.

[29] So Bultmann, *John*, 119-121; German, 83-85. The same reductionism of Jesus as the revealed Revealer dominates Bultmann's *Theology of the New Testament* (New York: Scribner's sons, 1955) II, 3-32.

The First Passover and the replacement of the Temple 2:12-25

After inaugurating his ministry in the insignificant village of Cana, Jesus descends to Capernaum. He is accompanied by his mother, his brothers and his disciples. Why his brothers are suddenly included is not explained. Evidently they too had been present at the wedding, and this may be a convenient context in which to introduce them into the gospel's narrative world and to prepare the reader for their more significant appearance in Chapter 7 and the narrator's intrusive remark about them in 7:5. "For neither were his brothers believing into him." Like the disciples they have witnessed the first sign of Jesus' ministry, but unlike them they will not respond with a commitment of faith, at least during the ministry of Jesus.[30]

No motive is cited for this journey to Capernaum. Its function may be to serve as an interlude in the movement of the story. For, as the narrator adds, "and they did not remain there many days." On the other hand, to the limited extent that Jesus conducts his ministry in Galilee in the narrative world of the Gospel, Capernaum appears to be the center of this activity. The discourse on the Bread of Life will be presented in the context of the second Passover in the synagogue of Capernaum (6:59).

The first Passover of Jesus' ministry prevents him from initiating any activity in Capernaum. He turns to Jerusalem instead, yet to what extent he participates in the Paschal celebration is not indicated. According to the story that follows, his observance of this Passover is focused on the Temple, and it involves him in an act of world reconstitution.[31]

Traditionally called "the Temple Cleansing," this event occurs at the end of Jesus' ministry in the Synoptic tradition and is a pivotal antecedent of his subsequent arrest, and execution. Its relocation by the Fourth Evangelist immediately after the wedding at Cana elaborates the paradigm shift that the transformation of the water of ritual purification into wine signifies. If the old wine has run out and the new wine that replaces it symbolizes a new moral order, the Temple, the architectonic center of the symbolic world of Judaism and the embodiment of its structures of purity, reciprocity and indebtedness, must also be transformed.[32] In fact, the old wine has run out! A profound religious crisis is confronting the Jewish people as a result of the Roman destruction of the Jerusalem Temple in 70 C.E. There is no center! There is no institution that

---

[30] There is no indication in the Gospel that they eventually responded to Jesus in faith, but the use of the imperfect tense in 7:5, "They were no believing into him;" limits their unbelief to the time of Jesus' ministry, the first level of the two-tiered narrative world of the Gospel.

[31] "World reconstitution" is the transformation of both subjective and objective reality. Haenchen's view, *John*, I, 189, that "the Fourth Gospel was conceived in a community for which the temple cultus was still something reformable" - even though it was no longer in existence –"and for which the realm of the king Jesus was not of this world" is wrong on both counts.

[32] See Fernando Belo, *A Materialist Reading of the Gospel of Mark* (Maryknoll, New York: Orbis Books, 1981) 37-59, on "The Symbolic Order of Ancient Israel," and his analysis of the systems of pollution and debt.

serves as the cornerstone of the Jewish religion to establish the boundaries of purity. There is no priesthood to act in the role of broker and to offer up the divinely ordained sacrifices in order to maintain the covenantal relationship between God as Israel's Patron and the people as God's clients.

> With the destruction of the Temple the image of the universe was rendered defective, the established framework of the nation was undermined, and a wall of steel formed a barrier between Israel and its heavenly Father.[33]

The Pharisees, under the leadership of Yochanan ben Zakkai and Gamaliel II, have taken the initiative to consolidate Judaism by replacing the Temple institution with their heritage of the written Torah and the orally transmitted Torah.[34] More explicitly, the loss of the Temple and its sacrifices can be supplanted by deeds of love. The Tosefta of *Abot de Rabbi Natan* recounts the story of Yochanan ben Zakkai responding to the anguish of Rabbi Hoshua at the loss of the Temple where expiation for Israel's sins was procured. "My son," he said, "Do not be provoked! We have an expiation that is equivalent to it [the Temple]. It is the rendering of love as prescribed by Hos 6:6, 'I will have mercy and not sacrifice.'"[35]

The Evangelist responds to this crisis by presenting an alternative to the Pharisaic tradition that is being championed by the rabbis of Alexandria in collaboration with the academy of Jamnia. A two-fold set of concomitant acts that Jesus carries out in the Jerusalem Temple is placed at the beginning of his ministry and connected in time to the first Passover in the narrative world of the Gospel.

The first occurs in the ἱερόν (sacred precinct) of the Temple. Here Jesus encounters the business enterprises that are being conducted by the priests. On the one hand, there is the sale of animals: oxen, sheep, and doves to be purchased by the people and offered up as sacrifices on their behalf. On the other hand, there is the banking institution that collects the annual Temple tax from every Jewish male and, when necessary, exchanges the Greek and Roman coins with their offensive images of self-aggrandizing emperors and kings for Jewish coinage.[36]

In response to this commercialism Jesus makes a φραγέλλιον ἐκ σχοινίων (whip from ropes) and proceeds to drive "all out of the sacred precinct (ἱερόν), both the sheep and the oxen." The whip, however, is not used on the bankers; instead their banking tables are overturned, and the money is spilled on the ground. "Remove these things from here!" Jesus commands, "Do not make my Father's

---

[33] S. Safrai, "The Temple," *The Jewish People in the First Century*, ed. by S. Safrai and M. Stern (Assen: Van Gorcum and Philadelphia: Fortress Press, 1987) II, 906. In this context, Safrai cites *B Berakoth* 32b.

[34] See Moore, *Judaism* I, 83-92.

[35] Translated from Hermann L. Strack & Paul Billerbeck, *Kommentar zum Neuen Testament aus Talmud und Midrash* (München: C. H. Beck'sche Verlagsbuchhandlung, 1956) I, 500.

[36] In actuality, as is generally acknowledged, the minting of Jewish money had been suspended when Judea became a Roman province in 6 C.E., and therefore Tyrian coinage, which did not bear any human images, served as the medium of exchange.

house a house of trade!" The Temple is to be divorced from all its commercial enterprises. Accordingly, banking, the collection of the Temple tax and the exchange of money are to be terminated. All activities that extract life and livelihood from the people under this institutional system of reciprocity and indebtedness are permanently suspended. Included are the animals of sacrifice, the oxen, the sheep, and even the doves, the offering specifically designated for the poor.[37] The cult and its priesthood, which traditionally have served as the brokering agency between God the Patron and the Jewish people as clients, are abolished. They will no longer be needed. According to John the Witness, Jesus is "the lamb of God who removes the sin of the world." When his hour comes, he will offer himself as the sacrifice that not only inaugurates perpetual reconciliation between God and human beings and consequently eliminates the necessity of a brokering agency in divine-human relationships. His death on the cross will also initiate the eradication of the human infection of sin.[38] That is how the κόσμος (world) will be saved (3:17). Human being in society will be cured of its condition of alienation and all the offenses of injustice that it generates through the attendantly effective process of world reconstruction.[39]

The passion which Jesus manifests in his cancellation of the Temple's commercial enterprises and cultic practices evokes the disciples' memory of Ps.69:10, "The zeal of your house will devour me." This quotation, which is the substance of this intrusive comment by the narrator, is not a literal rendition of the original Septuagint text. The tense of the verb has been changed from the aorist to the future.[40] Although the zeal of "the Father's house" is devouring Jesus at this very moment, it is another manifestation of his passion, one that will be expressed in the future, that will consume Jesus in death and subsequent resurrection.[41]

It is primarily in Jesus' *second act* at this first Passover in the narrative world of the Gospel that his ironic act of world reconstruction is disclosed. In response to the ruling authorities who, in the light of their orientation to world maintenance, ask for a sign to legitimate his radical act of "cleansing the Temple," he changes

---

[37] Questions such as: "Where did Jesus drive the animals?" are irrelevant for the narrative world of the gospel. See Haenchen, *John*, I, 183.

[38] See chapter 17.

[39] Contrary to Bultmann, *John*, 122; German, 85, this episode is not the end and fulfillment of the revelation of Jesus as the divine Revealer.

[40] This is generally not recognized. Keener, *John* I, 528, generalizes about Jesus' zeal to fulfill "his Father's will." Johannes Beutler, "The Use of 'Scripture' in the Gospel of John," *Exploring the Gospel of John: In Honor of D. Moody Smith*, ed. by R. Alan Culpepper and C. Clifton Black (Louisville: Westminster John Knox Press, 1996) 148, mistakenly parses καταφάγεται as a present tense verb and therefore misses the significance of the future tense.

[41] As Bultmann, *John*, 124; German, 87, also has recognized, "… the Evangelist (or the Editor) is looking forward to what is to come – or alternatively at the whole of Jesus' ministry – and he means that Jesus' zeal will lead him to his death." Also Moloney, *Belief*, 97-104, who eventually acknowledges that Jesus is referring to the Temple of his own body after his resurrection from the dead; and Haenchen, John, I, 187. None of them, however, seem to recognize that the Body of Jesus that will be raised is divinely willed to become a cosmic Temple.

his focus from the ἱερόν (sacred precinct) to the ναός (sanctuary), the central structure of the Temple mount in which the Holy of Holies is located and in which the presence of God resides: "Destroy this ναός, and in three days I shall resurrect it." While the authorities may comprehend the significance of Jesus' violent acts of driving out the sacrificial animals and overturning the tables of the bankers, they do not understand the legitimating sign he offers them.[42] The double meaning of his use of the verb ἐγερῶ (I shall resurrect/raise) escapes them. They construe his world in terms of actuality and identify the referent of ναός (sanctuary) with the stone building on the Temple mount, "Forty-six years this sanctuary was under construction, and you will raise it in three days?"[43] Their level of interpretation converts Jesus' sign into an absurdity, but at the same time it exposes their blunted sensitivity to ironic utterances. In fact, they are the unwitting victims of the profound irony of his legitimating sign. They have missed the ironic imperative with which Jesus introduced his sign, "Tear down this sanctuary..."[44] The irony, of course, refers to the two-layered meaning of his use of the word "sanctuary." For it is not only the stone building on the Temple mount that will be destroyed through their complicity, but more immediately Jesus' body as the living Temple of God that at this first Passover is being substituted in place of the ναός. For their guardianship of the Temple institution and its symbolic world will motivate them to destroy the living sanctuary of God's presence that Jesus embodies by delivering him up to the Romans for execution. Ironically that destruction will in turn result in the demolition of the sanctuary of the Temple mount by the Romans.

To make certain that the reader will construe Jesus' legitimating sign from the intended point of view, the narrator suspends the story in order to insert another intrusive remark: "But this one (Jesus) was speaking about the sanctuary of his body." Jesus, who according to the Prologue is the enfleshment of the Sophia-Logos, is now presented to the implied readers as the new Temple of God, indeed, the living temple of God, who replaces the stone structure of the ναός that had been destroyed by the Romans. Heaven and earth are united in him. As he asseverated to his disciples in 1:51, "Amen, amen I say to you, you will see the heaven opened and the angels of God ascending and descending on the Son of the

[42] This is the first instance of a literary device that is characteristic of the Fourth Gospel, namely, misunderstanding. See Herbert Leroy, *Rätsel und Missverständnis: Ein Beitrag zur Formgeschichte des Johannesevangeliums* (Bonn: Peter Hanstein, 1968) 1, 6, who counts eleven of them in John 2-8. See especially Culpepper's scrutiny of "misunderstandings" in the Fourth Gospel, *Anatomy*, 152-165. He lists eighteen such occurrences: 2:19-21; 3:3-5; 4:10-15; 4:31-34; 6:32-35; 6:51-53; 7:33-36; 8:21-22; 8:31-35; 8:51-53; 8:56-58; 11:11-15; 11:23-25; 12:32-34; 13:36-38; 14:4-6; 14:7-9; 16:16-19.

[43] J. H. Bernard, *A Critical and Exegetical Commentary on the Gospel according to St. John* (Edinburgh: T. & T. Clark, 1953) I, 96, refers to Ezra 5:16 where the same verb, οἰκοδομήθη is used to signify unfinished, ongoing Temple construction. For 46 years the building of the Temple has been in progress, and it has not yet been completed.

[44] Bultmann, *John*, 125. Dodd, *Fourth Gospel*, 302, n.1, prefers to regard the verb as a kind of conditional imperative which should be translated, "If this temple is destroyed..." The loss of the second person plural of the imperative "you" diminishes the irony of Jesus' sign. See Duke, *Irony*, 168, n.18, and especially p.50 where he comments at some length on the irony of Jesus' sign.

Human Being." In contrast to the stationary building of the Jerusalem sanctuary, the body of Jesus is mobile. Wherever he goes, he will fulfill the functions of God's Temple. He will make God present to others, and by communicating God's presence, he will be sanctifying their time and space. His movements from place to place, as, for example, through Samaria in 4:4-42, will scramble the traditional lines of the sacred and the secular established by the fixed location of the Jerusalem Temple. There will no longer be *a priori* predetermined boundaries of the holy and the profane that maintain social and economic structures and ossify concomitant religious and cultural patterns of habituation. They will always be in flux, continuously rearranged by the serendipitous movements of the New Adam, "the Son of the Human Being," the Pioneer of God's household. In his itinerancy as the dynamic and mobile Holy of Holies in the flesh, the disciples - and the implied readers – "will see the heaven opened and the angels of God ascending and descending on the Son of the Human Being" (1:51).

In the sign that he offers the guardians of society in 2:19 Jesus makes the startling avowal that he will raise himself within three days. Later, in 10:17-18, he will extend this pledge:

> On account of this the Father loves me because I give my *life* (ψυχήν) so that I may take it again. No one takes it from me, but I give it of myself. I have authority to give it and I have authority to take it again. This commandment I received from my Father.

The Easter phenomenon that Peter and the Beloved Disciple witness in the empty tomb, namely his burial garments folded and lying in their appropriate places, will validate this warrant (20:7). At the same time, the promise he made to his disciples as the embodiment of "the Father's house" in 14:1-2 will be on the verge of reaching fulfillment.

> Let not your heart be agitated! Believe into God! Believe also into me! In my *Father's house* are many rooms. But if not, I would say to you that I am going to prepare a place for you.

At the first Passover in the narrative world of the Fourth Gospel Jesus becomes "the Father's house" as he substitutes his physical body in place of the Jerusalem sanctuary. As his career draws to an end, he will pledge to his disciples at the beginning of his farewell speech that he intends to enlarge "the Father's house" by adding more rooms.[45] Since it is only in 14:2 and 2:16 that Jesus employs the phrase, "my Father's house," consistency building induces a relationship between these two texts. If Jesus has embodied "the Father's house" throughout his ministry, and if, as he asserts, there are many rooms in "the Father's house," those rooms cannot refer to heavenly mansions that Jesus will prepare by his ascension.[46]

---

[45] See chapter 15.

[46] Martyn, *History and Theology*, 139-140, comes very close to this interpretation by focusing on 14:3 and emphasizing that instead of what has been said in verse 2. So he writes, "Jesus tells his sorrowing disciples not to be troubled, assuring them that there are many rooms in his Father's house.

They must be an expansion of the living Temple that he has personified. They must imply a household of a family of sisters and brothers who, as the enlarged living Temple of God continue his ministry of making God present to others, sanctifying their time and space and consequently scrambling the traditional lines of the sacred and the secular. The living Temple of God that replaces the Jerusalem sanctuary is not to be embodied by One, namely Jesus, but by the One and the Many, both Jesus and those who commit themselves to him as the Pioneer of a New Humanity for the undertaking of world reconstruction. "The Father's house" is designed to be a cosmic living and life-giving Temple of many rooms, each constituting a Holy of Holies in which the Divine Presence resides. That in essence is the reality of the incarnation, and the new synthesis of the divine-human union that Jesus acknowledges in his employment of the **I AM** formula of self-disclosure, whether it is spoken as ἐγὼ εἰμί (**I AM**) or as εἰμὶ ἐγώ, (AM I). For as Jesus says in 14:3, "And if I go and prepare a place for you, I am coming again and I will receive you πρός (towards) myself, so that where εἰμὶ ἐγώ, (**AM I**) you also are." It is only because of being where he is, that is, in his **I AM**, and therefore rooms in "the Father's house," that they will be able to fulfill his promise of 14:12, "Amen, amen I say to you, 'The one who believes into me the works that I do that one will do, and greater works than these she/he will do because I am going πρός (toward) the Father.'"

He then changes the terms of the picture radically by saying that he will come again and take them not to those rooms but to himself. … Thus, the problem of separation is ultimately to be met with the preparation not of rooms, but of a room, and that room is not in heaven, but on earth." It is this earth-oriented emphasis that is decisive. The disciples will be where Jesus is, participating in his divine **I AM**.

Chapter Five

Seeing and Believing and Believing in Order to See

The four verbs of "Seeing" in the Fourth Gospel

During his first visit to Jerusalem, at the first Passover in the narrative world of the Gospel, Jesus engaged in other activities besides his principal act of negating the Temple institution and substituting his physical body in place of the Temple's sanctuary. "Now as he was in Jerusalem at the feast of the Passover, many believed into his name, observing his signs that he was doing" (2:23). Those activities are not delineated; they are simply designated "signs." But they are effective in eliciting a response of faith: "...many believed into his name *observing* (θεωροῦντες) his signs that he was doing." The verb, θεωρεῖν, means "to observe, to look on" but it includes the connotation of giving oneself over to that which has been experienced through the sense of sight. The Jews, who are attending this feast, have observed Jesus' signs and have responded to this visual experience by believing into him.

But how is their faith to be evaluated? What kind of faith is it? "Believing into" (πιστεύειν εἰς) on the basis of signs that have occurred is an orientation to the past. To what extent is that kind of faith more than a passive acknowledgment of God's validation of Jesus? Is it a "believing into" that responds in genuine commitment to discipleship? Is it a faith that can move from an orientation to the past to an openness to the future and accordingly act in the face of impossible possibilities? Seeing may lead to believing, but can believing act without seeing?[1]

What kind of faith arises in this context of Jesus' ministry is not manifestly evident. Nevertheless, the narrator's observation of 2:24-25, introduced by the adversative particle δέ (but), cautions the reader to view critically the relationship between the *observing*, (θεωροῦντες) of these Jerusalem people and their "believing into."[2]

[1] As Ashton, *Understanding the Fourth Gospel*, 520, has observed, "there is ... a perceptible tension between the two," that is, between seeing and believing. And "it is possible to witness such prodigies [Jesus' signs] without *really* seeing," but Ashton has neglected to examine the nuances of the different verbs of seeing that are used in the Fourth Gospel. See the discussion on "seeing signs" and "believing" in Robert Kysar, *John,* 67-83.

[2] The narrator does not refer to miracles (δυνάμεις) but to signs (σημεῖα). Bultmann, *John*, 131; German, 92, therefore, has not been sensitive to the text when he states that "... faith should not rely on miracles." He is correct in adding that "... such faith is only the first step towards Jesus," but his reductionistic christological valuation of Jesus as the revealed Revealer appears to be intimated as he adds, "it has not yet seen him in his true significance." If the faith that is produced by Jesus' signs is unsatisfactory, it may be due to a fixed orientation to the past that believing on the basis of seeing promotes an inability to perceive the reference of the signs. Mighty works may serve as signs, but as signs they point to an eschatological reality beyond themselves, and that reality is essentially

> But Jesus was not entrusting himself to them, for he knew all (human beings), and he had no need that any testify about the human being, for he knew what was in the human being.

Faith that is founded on the evidence of signs and therefore is determined by the realities of the past tends to be reasonable because it is considered to be epistemologically convincing. Something is believed to be true because it has been experienced empirically. The sign that has been observed is an actuality, and as an actuality it can all too easily be appropriated as a consummate criterion of truth for all times. But to what extent will that kind of faith be open to change and be motivated to engage in activities that require openness and vulnerability to all the possibilities of the future?

The sensory acts of both hearing and seeing are crucial to the experience of following Jesus in the narrative world of the gospel. Hearing, of course, is the attentive response that the prophetic voices of the Hebrew Scriptures invoke, for the ear is the primary sense organ in Israelite tradition by which truth is perceived and embraced. To the ruling authorities Jesus declares, "The one who is from God hears the words of God" (8:47). Accordingly, he characterizes those who hear his voice and follow him as his sheep.

> … the sheep hear his voice and he calls them by name and leads them out. When he sends them all out, he goes before them and the sheep follow him because they know his voice. (10:3-4)

The hearing of the ruling authorities, however, is impaired by their presuppositions, and, because they do not understand or perhaps refuse to understand, Jesus confronts them with his judgment in 8:47b, "On account of this you do not hear, because you are not from God."

As consequential as hearing is, the act of seeing gains an overriding emphasis in the Fourth Gospel that it never had before in Israelite religion and culture. As a result of the incarnation of the Logos-Sophia, it becomes possible to see the word as well as hear it. Consequently the Greek philosophical tradition of seeing, as it is expressed classically in Plato's Allegory of the Cave, can be appropriated and integrated into the Gospel's eschatological-christological presentation of the ministry of Jesus of Nazareth. The verbs of seeing that are specifically differentiated in the Allegory of the Cave, ὁρᾶν (to see, experience, witness), βλέπειν (to see with the eyes of the mind) and θέασθαι (to ascertain, look intently

---

christological *and* anthropological. See also Ashton, *Understanding*, 520-524, who differentiates between seeing Jesus' signs and reading about them in the Gospel. The signs, he maintains, signify "Jesus' miracles as they are seen by men: viewed rightly they are signs of Jesus' relationship to the Father, whose emissary he is and whose revelation he embodies – signs, in other words, of his glory." The "signs" are Jesus' works! Whether they are validly referred to as miracles is questionable. Of course, as he insists, the implied readers cannot see these signs, but what he does not seem to take into account is that they can interact with them in relation to the eschatological and christological-anthropological realities to which they refer. And, furthermore, are the realities they indicate fulfilled within the narrative world of the Gospel?

at something) are similarly used in the Fourth Gospel.[3] It is doubtful that they were adopted from Book Seven of *The Republic*. More than likely their distinctive usage in the Gospel results from the influence that the writings of Philo of Alexandria exercised in the formulation of the stories of the Gospel. Linked together, then, the ear and the eye constitute the new foundation for the determination of integrity and truth.

However, in view of the reality of the incarnation, the initial injunction is the invitation to see, and Jesus himself issues it. In 1:39 he invites the two disciples who have left John the Witness and have begun to follow him, "Keep on coming and you will see!" For the implied readers, therefore, the exhortation is, "Keep on reading and you will experience!" Philip subsequently repeats the invitation to Nathanael in 1:46, "Keep on coming and see!" If Israel, according to Philo, means "the one who sees God," Nathanael will be the true Israelite, for, as Jesus states, "*You will see* the heaven opened and the angels of God ascending and descending upon the Son of the Human Being." Ὁρᾶν (to see, experience, witness) is the verb that Jesus employs in 1:39 and 50, and it corresponds to Philo's use of ὁρᾶν in *De Fuga et Inventione,* 208 *and De Mutatione Nominum* 81.[4] "*Seeing God* (ὁρῶν θεόν) is the translation of 'Israel'."

Four different verbs related to the sensory act of seeing are encountered in the narrative world of the Fourth Gospel, and each conveys its own distinctive sense and import.

θέασθαι	6
βλέπειν	17
θεωρεῖν	24
ὁρᾶν ἰδεῖν εἶδον	67
	114[5]

Θέασθαι: *to look intently in order to size up*

Θέασθαι is the first verb of seeing employed by the narrator and occurs appropriately in the Prologue's announcement of the enfleshment of the Logos-Sophia. Used only six times, it bears the meaning of *having an intent look at something* with a sense of appraisal or valuation that reaches out in openness and

[3] Plato, *The Republic* VII, 515-516,; trans. by Paul Shorey, *Loeb Classical Library* (Cambridge: Harvard University Press, 1960) II, 120-129.

[4] *De Fuga* and *de Mutatione Nominum*, trans. by G. H. Whitaker. *Loeb Classical Library* (Cambridge" Harvard University Press,1949) V, 122-123 and 182-183.

[5] This list is taken from Brown, *John* I, 501, but revised slightly in order to maintain the relationship of ἰδεῖν and εἶδον with their dictionary form ὁρᾶν. Brown appears to be the only commentator who recognizes the differences in sight that these verbs convey. He has made a valiant attempt to recover their differences in shades of meaning, but without searching for parallels in Philo or in other texts that would elucidate those differences. See I, 501-503.

permits itself to be drawn into a relationship with that which the eyes have brought into focus.[6] Philo employs this verb in the same way. An architect, engaged by a king to found a city, will *gaze intently* in order to *appraise* the position and the climate of a site before he begins to sketch in his own mind the buildings that will eventually be constructed.[7] For Philo, the intelligible world, that of "the patterns and the originals of the things of sense," can be reached by θεασάμενος or the act of contemplating.[8] It is a seeing that includes judgment or ascertainment. Accordingly, the narrator of the Gospel, speaking on behalf of a community of witnesses, claims to have looked intently at the glory of the enfleshed Logos-Sophia in order to ascertain its origin and concluding that it was "glory as of only one of its kind from [the] Father." Similarly the reader, by consenting to be drawn into the dramatic recounting of the story that is to follow, may be rewarded with the same experience.

John the Witness, in his participation in the drama of Jesus' baptism and determined by this kind of intent looking, claims to have *gazed intently* and *sized up* (τεθέαμαι) the Spirit descending and remaining upon Jesus and therefore to have recognized him as "the one who baptizes with the holy Spirit" (1:32-34).

As the drama of discipleship begins, Jesus *gazes intently* (θεασάμενος) at the two disciples of John who have attached themselves to him and scrutinizes or sizes-up their persons (1:37-8). The great crowd of people approaching Jesus at the mountain in 6:5 involves him in an intent *appraising* (θεασάμενος) that is simultaneously a consideration of the resources available to feed them, for he turns to Philip and tests him by inquiring, "How shall we buy bread so that they may eat?" In 4:35 the disciples are directed to raise their eyes and see, in the sense of *sizing up* (θεάσασθε), the dramatic scene of the fields white toward harvest. This kind of *gazing intently* will hopefully induce a discernment of the truth that will correspond to the judgment Jesus has voiced. In 11:45 the narrator relates, "Many of the Jews, who came to Mary and *seeing* and *ascertaining* (θεασάμενοι) what he did, believed into him." This, especially, must be a significant observation for the implied readers who are finally confronted with the reality of a large number of the ruling authorities committing themselves to Jesus on the basis of *sizing up* the mighty work of raising Lazarus from the dead.

Βλέπειν: *seeing beyond sense perception*

βλέπειν is the second of the four verbs of seeing that the implied readers encounter in the Gospel. It signifies a clarity of vision that makes true insight possible.[9] According to Danker's third edition of *A Greek-English Lexicon of the New Testament*, it conveys the figurative meaning of grasping transcendent

[6] So also G.L. Phillips, "Faith and Vision in the Fourth Gospel," 83-96.

[7] Philo, *de Opificio Mundi*, 17; also 46, 71, 151, 158; *Legum Allegoria* II, 5, 40, 61, and many more similar uses.

[8] *Ibid.*, 71. See also 83, 151, 158.

matters.[10] Philo uses the verb in both senses, as he asserts, "For what the intellect is in the soul, this, the eye is in the body; for each of them sees (βλέπει), one the things of the mind, the other the things of sense".[11] Jacob is designated as "the seeing one" (ὁ βλέπων) because he is able to perceive beyond sense perception.[12] As Moses drew back from his rod that had become a snake in Ex 4:3, in the same way, the human being "who sees (ὁ βλέπων) the snake" – as a symbol of pleasure – runs away from it.[13] Melchizedek is given the epithet of *the seeing one* (ὁ βλέπων), "For he is Reason, having as his portion Him that is, and all his thoughts of God are high and vast and sublime."[14] In *De Plantatione* 38, Philo interprets Eden as the "symbol of a soul whose seeing is perfect" (ψυχῆς τῆς ἄρτια βλεπούσης). Diogenes Laertius, who recounts a conversation about ideas between Diogenes and Plato, is also worth citing here:

> "Table and cup I see; but your tablehood and cuphood, Plato, I can in no way see." "That's readily accounted for," said Plato, "for you have the eyes to see the visible table and cup; but not the νοῦς (mind) by which the ideal tablehood and cuphood are *discerned* (βλέπεται)."[15]

This is the perspicuity of John the Witness, for when he *sees* (βλέπει) Jesus coming to him, he is able to perceive an aspect of Jesus' identity that is not evident in his outward appearance: "Look, the lamb of God who removes the sin of the world" (1:29). Jesus especially exercises this transparency of seeing, and it enables him to determine very clearly what "the Father" is doing in the world and to emulate it in his own activity: "Amen, amen I say to you, the Son is able to do nothing of himself except whatever he *sees* (βλέπῃ) the Father doing."[16]

Ten of the seventeen occurrences of βλέπειν in the Gospel appear in the story of Jesus opening the eyes of a blind male in chapter 9. Blindness, of course, precludes the use of ocular vision and consequently also the empirical viewing of the realities of the incarnation. Jesus' ministry includes the opening of eyes, but particularly those that are blind from birth, those that cannot differentiate between appearance and reality, because their seeing has been impaired by the world in

---

[9] Contrary to Brown, *John* I, 501, who asserts, "…in many instances βλέπειν has no special significance." Yet even the uses of the verb in the texts that he cites, 9:1-41, 13:22 and 20:1, convey the meaning of "seeing with discernment."

[10] (Chicago: University of Chicago Press, 2000) 179.

[11] Philo, *De Opificio Mundi*, 53; also *Legum Allegoria* II, 46, 67, 93; III, 81; in III, 109 and110 it is the reasoning faculty that *sees* (βλέπων) and in III, 172 it is the soul that *sees* (βλέπων) the One who is."

[12] Philo, *Legum Allegoria* II, 46.

[13] *Ibid.*, II, 93.

[14] *Ibid.*, III, 81. See also III, 110, 172 and *de Agricultura,* 54,

[15] Diogenes Laertius, *Lives of Eminent Philosophers* VI, 53. *Loeb Classical Library*, trans. By R. D. Hicks (Cambridge: Harvard University Press, 1965) II, 55.

[16] Brown, *John* I, 502, has recognized that βλέπειν is certainly not the lowest form of seeing in the Gospel, but in his own analysis he does not go far enough to modify the conclusion of G.F. Phillips in "Faith and Vision in the Fourth Gospel," 83-96.

which they have been socialized. Such an individual is "the human being blind from birth" of 9:1. After he has washed himself in the Pool of Siloam and experienced a rebirth, the narrator announces, "He came *seeing*" (βλέπων). It is the use of this verb specifically that indicates that the kind of blindness that has afflicted this man from birth is especially the inability to see the light of truth, the light of the first day of creation, and not simply the world that is illuminated by the light of the sun, moon and stars.[17] Jesus concludes the episode of chapter 9 with an avowal of his mission, "Unto judgment I came into this world, so that the ones not seeing (βλέποντες) would see (βλέπωσιν), and the ones seeing (βλέποντες) would become blind" (9:39).

θεωρεῖν: to observe, to be-hold

Perhaps the most ambiguous verb of seeing in the Fourth Gospel is θεωρεῖν. It is ambiguous in the sense that the response that is anticipated as a result of this kind of seeing is not always forthcoming. It designates *spectatorship*, a looking-on that is expected to result in abandonment to what has visually been experienced.[18] In ancient Greece the individual city-states sent θεωροῖ, (onlookers) to represent them at public festivals. But they were more than observers. Through the act of looking on they gave themselves over, surrendered themselves to the celebration that was taking place.[19] Philo characterizes the faculty of vision as one that is "led upwards by light," and as the soul banquets on the sights that are displayed to it, it becomes possessed with an insatiate desire *to be-hold* (θεωρεῖν). Such spectatorship gives itself over to philosophical questioning, "the perfect good that has come into the life of humankind."[20] Θεωρεῖν in the Fourth Gospel conveys the same sense of be-holding, a looking-on that anticipates a faith commitment to what has been visually experienced, but which is not always fulfilled.

At the first Passover in Jerusalem many who *be-hold* (θεωροῦντες) Jesus' signs "believe into his name." Are they observers who, by "believing into," give themselves over to idolizing Jesus because of his display of power and divine legitimation? Or is their "believing into" an abandonment of themselves to a reality that the signs foreshadow, namely the reality of a new moral order? Jesus' disposition of not entrusting himself to them (2:24-25) suggests their spectatorship is focused on the signs themselves and not their referent. This becomes more evident in Chapter 6 when the Galilean crowd follows Jesus across the Sea of Galilee "because they were *looking on* (P^{66} ἐθεωροῦν) the signs he was doing on

[17] See Philo, *De Opificio Mundi*, 29-35, 53-55, for this same interpretation of the light of the first day of creation.

[18] Hans Georg Gadamer, *Truth and Method*, 124, "Thus watching something is a genuine mode of participating. Here we can recall the concept of sacral communion that lies behind the original Greek concept of *theoria* (my italics)."

[19] Gadamer, *Truth and Method,* 124-125, "Theoria is a true participation, not something active but something passive (pathos), namely being totally involved in and carried away by what one sees."

[20] Philo, *De Opificio Mundi*, 54; also 131; *Legum Allegoria* II, 38, 57, 70, 80.

the sick" (6:2). Their watching was "a mode of participating". According to 4:45 these must be the very same people who witnessed Jesus' healing activity at the first Passover in Jerusalem (2:23). Will they now in their involvement in Jesus' feeding of the multitudes surrender themselves to a discipleship that participates in his work of world transformation? When they follow him to Capernaum inquiring how he managed to arrive at this destination without a boat, Jesus confronts them with the truth of their "believing into his name." "Amen, amen I say to you, you seek me not because you saw (εἴδετε) signs but because you ate and were satisfied" (6:26). Their commitment of faith proves to be nothing more than a concerted attempt to enthrone him as their Messiah in order to continue to enjoy an unlimited supply of bread.[21]

Θεωρεῖν occurs three times in chapter 6, and each instance appears to presuppose the ones that preceded it. Fear overwhelms the disciples as they *observe* (θεωροῦσιν) Jesus walking on the Sea of Galilee. Not only should they be reassured by his encouraging words, "**I AM**! Do not keep on being afraid." Their immediate arrival at their destination, after they have taken him into the boat, is such a stunning experience that commitment to Jesus would be a natural expectation. In his subsequent discourse on the Bread of Life Jesus bluntly states, "This is the will of my father that everyone who *looks on* (θεωρῶν) the Son and believes into him has eternal life" (6:40). The disciples have *observed* Jesus, but will they commit themselves to his life and activity? On the contrary, they are scandalized by his summons to eat the flesh and drink the blood of the Son of the Human Being. As they turn away, Jesus inquires, "Does this offend you? What if you *look on* (θεωρῆτε) the Son of the Human Being ascending where he was formerly?" Seeing Jesus walking on the sea did not evoke commitment to the paradigm shift it manifested, and they appear unable to comprehend how that paradigm shift is expressed in the eating of the flesh and the drinking of the blood of the Son of the Human Being? What will they do when they experience the eschatological event of the New Human Being ascending into heaven?

The utterance of 6:40, "...everyone who *observes* (θεωρῶν) the Son and believes into him has eternal life..." is not only reversed in 12:44 but also expanded to negate any and every commitment of faith that is confined to Jesus as a "divine man" or a wonder worker. "The one believing into me does not believe into me but the one who sent me, and the one *observing* (θεωρῶν) me *observes* (θεωρεῖ) the one who sent me." The idolization of Jesus, as it already has manifested itself in the response of the Galilean crowd to his signs, is repudiated. "Believing into Jesus" signifies making a commitment to the reality of the New Humanity that Jesus embodies. God the Creator originated that reality through the incarnation of the Logos-Sophia, and therefore "believing into" Jesus is ultimately a commitment to God the Creator. Jesus himself has acknowledged that his deeds do not originate from him but are an emulation of the work that God is doing (5:19). In as

[21] See chapter 9.

far as his ministry reflects that work, any sensory act of *looking on* him is simultaneously a *looking on* "the Father."

ὁρᾶν ἰδεῖν εἶδον: to see empirically

The most frequently occurring verb in the gospel, ὁρᾶν and its many forms: *ἰδεῖν, εἶδον, ἑώρακα,* etc. denote empirical seeing. According to Philo, the human mind (νοῦς) occupies a place in human beings that corresponds to that which God inhabits in the world. "It is invisible while it itself sees (ὁρῶν) all things."[22] For the soul, that is studying flight from the passions, it includes *seeing* (ὁρῶν) God.[23] Jesus, using this same verb that denotes empirical seeing, will claim that he has seen God, but without limiting that seeing to his mind's eye and without giving any evidence of fleeing from his passions. As though in contradiction to the concluding declaration of the Prologue, "God no one *has* ever *seen* (ἑώρακεν), he will state in 6:46, "Not that anyone *has seen* (ἑώρακεν) the Father except *the one being* (ὁ ὤν) with God, this one *has seen* (ἑώρακεν) the Father." As the incarnate Logos-Sophia who claims to have descended from heaven (3:13), an origin that distinguishes him above Moses, and therefore as the legitimate heir of God's self-disclosure, **I AM**, he discretely adopts the participial phrase that refers to the Logos-Sophia in 1:18b, μονογενὴς θεὸς *ὁ ὤν* εἰς τὸν κόλπον τοῦ πατρός. That participial phrase, *ὁ ὤν*, is the other half of God's self-disclosure in LXX Ex 3:14, ἐγὼ εἰμὶ *ὁ ὤν*. As the incarnate Logos-Sophia, he participates in the primordial movement of being united with God that legitimates his claim to *have seen* the Father.

According to Philo, the objects that are *seen* (ὁρώμενα) by sight, the noblest of the senses, are seven in number: body, extension, shape, size, color, movement, and quiescence. Accordingly, if the Logos-Sophia has truly "happened flesh," it must be readily discernible to the naked eye. Jesus' simple invitation to two of John's disciples seems to presuppose that experience: "Keep on coming and *you will see* (ὄψεσθε)!" Throughout the narrative world of the Gospel, the physical reality of the incarnation requires no more than ocular vision. Surprisingly nothing more than the same kind of empirical vision is needed to *see* (ὄψεσθε) the heaven opened and the angels of God ascending and descending on the Son of the Human Being. Jesus, of course, is speaking metaphorically in utilizing the substance of Jacob's dream at Bethel in Gen 28:12. Certain qualities of his identity as the enfleshed Logos and also as the living sanctuary of God (2:21) should be evident to ordinary physical sight. Jesus evidently anticipates that that kind of seeing with physical eyes, at least in the context of a mighty work like feeding the multitudes, should result in faith. "*You have seen* (ἑωράκατε) me," he says to the crowd he is

---

[22] *Ibid.*, 69

[23] Philo, *Legum Allegoria* III, 172. In the same paragraph Philo will shift to the verb βλέπων that denotes a seeing beyond sense perception.

addressing in the discourse on the Bread of Life (6:36), "and you do not believe." In response to Philip's entreaty, "Lord, show us the Father...," Jesus says, "Such a long time I am with you and you have not known me? The one who *has seen* (ἑωρακὼς) me *has seen* (ἑώρακεν) the Father" (14:8-9).

The same verb is used in all the Easter stories of chapter 20 and bears the same denotation of empirical seeing. Mary Magdalene, after her encounter with the risen Jesus, tells the community of disciples in 20:18, "I have seen (ἑώρακα) the Lord..." In the evening of the same day when the risen Jesus appears to all the disciples - except Thomas! - "they rejoiced *seeing* (ἴδοντες) the Lord." Thomas, who has been told by his fellow disciples, "We have seen (ἑώρκαμεν) the Lord!" not only demands the same experience but insists it must be thoroughly empirical "Unless I see (ἴδω) the mark of the nails in his hands... I will by no means believe."

Seeing in relation to believing

Obviously there are different kinds of seeing in the narrative world of the Fourth Gospel, and each has its own implications. While the reality of the incarnation presupposes empirical seeing (ὁρε῀ιν), blindness from birth or seeing that is distorted by ideology requires the rebirth of baptism that will produce a clarity of vision (βλέπειν). Seeing can also involve appraisal, a sizing up, accompanied by a vulnerable openness to embrace what has been judged to be true, regardless of the cost (θεάσθαι). Finally seeing can be an "observing" or a "looking on" that may eventuate in a commitment of faith, a giving oneself over to the reality that has been apprehended (θεωρε῀ιν).

All these types of seeing, as indispensable as they are in their individual contexts, are oriented to events that have taken place and result in evaluation, insight, and commitment. Faith in these instances comes after seeing. Faith is determined by seeing. At the wedding at Cana Jesus "manifested his glory and his disciples believed into him." Seeing the sign and the glory that it disclosed evoked their commitment of faith.

There is also, however, a seeing that follows faith, a seeing that will occur only if faith has expressed itself in action. That is the keynote of the second sign Jesus performs. Indeed, it is the only other sign that is enumerated by the narrator:

> Now this again (is) the *second/other* (δεύτερον) sign Jesus did coming out of Judea into Galilee. (4:54)

The enumeration itself, δεύτερον, is not necessarily an attempt "to preserve the source's original enumeration of this as the second sign".[24] The adjective δεύτερον may also mean "other", and very likely that is its sense in this context, "This is the *other* sign Jesus did coming out of Judea into Galilee.

[24] As claimed by Fortna, *The Fourth Gospel,* 65, and Lindars, *John*, 205.

Seeing and therefore believing

The first was the sign of the wedding at Cana, and it occurred "on the third day." The second or *the other* also takes place at Cana "after two days" (4:43) or on the third day. The settings of time and place are identical and link the stories together in a circular movement. On the one hand, Jesus manifested his glory in the sign of transforming water into wine. His disciples saw and "believed into him." On the other hand, Jesus censures the nobleman from Capernaum, "Unless you see signs and wonders you will by no means believe" (4:48). If the disciples saw the sign at the wedding at Cana and committed themselves to Jesus, why is it inappropriate or indefensible to believe on the basis of seeing signs and wonders?

Jesus, having testified that a prophet has no honor in his own country, has left Judea and returned to Galilee. In view of his Nazareth origin, Judea cannot be considered as "his own country." No Bethlehem birth is attributed to him. Indeed, he is rejected as the Messiah in 7:41-42 because he does not fulfill the Davidic typology of having been born in Bethlehem. Earlier Philip had identified Jesus to Nathanael as "the son of Joseph from Nazareth" (1:45). Within the narrative world of the Fourth Gospel, Jesus is a Galilean whose origin is linked to Nazareth, and Nathanael's response to Philip's identification characterizes the village's reputation, "Can anything good be from Nazareth?" Therefore, the proverb Jesus applies to himself, "A prophet has no honor in his own country," refers to his standing in Galilee.

Ironically, however, his fellow Galileans receive him upon his return to his home province. But their motive is suspect because they *saw* (ἑωρακότες) "all the things he did in Jerusalem at the feast" (2:45). Their commitment to him, as evidenced earlier, is based on his authentication by the signs he has performed and not on the realities to which they refer.

Believing in order to see

This, then, is the context in which Jesus is approached by a nobleman from Capernaum who has "heard that Jesus is coming from Judea into Galilee" and who entreats him to come down to Capernaum in order to heal his son, "for he was about to die." In view of the critical nature of the nobleman's request, Jesus' response is startling, "Unless you see signs and wonders you will by no means believe." But the nobleman is not asking for a mighty work in order to establish his faith. He already believes in as far as he presupposes that Jesus is able to heal his dying son.

Notable here is the use of the second person plural in the verbs: *you see* (ἴδητε) and *you believe* (πιστεύσητε). Whom is Jesus addressing besides the nobleman with whom he is speaking? He may be expressing his disapproval of the Galileans who *looked on* (θεωροῦντες) the signs he did at the Passover feast in Jerusalem and who consequently were carried away by "believing into him." But in actuality he is addressing the implied readers who evidently must be included in this rebuke. Jesus' censure, "Unless you see signs and wonders you will not believe!" conveys a general critique of any and every commitment of faith that is regulated by events and experiences - like signs and wonders - that have already occurred.[25] Faith that is determined only by the actualities of the past tends to be closed to the possibilities of the future.

The nobleman, however, appears not to have comprehended Jesus' censure. His desperation has intensified and, although he has addressed Jesus as *lord* (κύριε), he contradicts the appellative he has employed and commands him, "Come down before my little boy dies." Jesus replies with a counter-command, "Go! Your son lives!" The nobleman must return to Capernaum alone. Jesus will not accompany him. He must now act in accordance with the faith that drew him to Jesus in the first place. He must believe in order to see.

Finally grasping the meaning of Jesus' earlier reprimand, he submits to his command: "He believed the word which Jesus spoke to him and he was going" (4:50). As he descended to Capernaum, he is met by his slaves with the report that his child lives. In response to his inquiry as to what hour he began to improve, they informed him that it was at the eighth hour that the fever left him. Cognizant that that was the very moment Jesus had said to him, "Your son lives!" he realizes that his faith has been validated.[26] By trusting Jesus' word, he had returned home, but without the accompaniment of Jesus. He had taken the risk of faith. He had made himself vulnerable to the contingencies of the future. He had believed in order to see! Confronted by the evidence of his faith, he affirms the commitment he had expressed in acting on Jesus' word by embracing the circle of faith.[27] "He believed and his entire house" (4:53). He had begun his journey of faith oriented to a particular possibility of the future: the restoration of his son. And the fulfillment that he experienced not only generated new commitment from him but also established a community of faith by drawing his entire household into a similar commitment.

The same circle of faith emerges in the seventh sign, the resurrection of Lazarus. When Jesus arrives at the sepulcher of "the one whom you love" (ὅν φιλεῖς), he gives orders that the stone be removed from the mouth of the cave-like tomb. Martha objects on the grounds that "he is already smelling for it is the fourth day." After death, according to rabbinic myth, "the soul floats above the corpse," and when after three days, as a result of decomposition, it no longer

---

[25] Fortna, *Fourth Gospel*, 62, rightly asks if it is the readers who are being addressed, but, in view of his efforts to reconstitute the "Signs Source," he proposes that these readers are those who are already familiar with the Gospel's predecessor.

[26] A noteworthy parallel to this story, that is contemporaneous with the Fourth Gospel, is found in the BT *Berakoth* 34b and the JT *Berakoth* 9d. See Moore, *Judaism* II, 236.

[27] As Fortna, 63, has stated, "The saying in v. 48, then, is to be understood as setting up a kind of test of human faith, a test that the official clearly passes."

recognizes the body it inhabited, it departs.[28] In view of this condition, Lazarus' reanimation is hopeless. The soul, having left the body, has gone its way; and a reunion of the two is no longer possible.

In the face of such an impossibility Jesus nevertheless reassures Martha, "Did I not say to you, 'If you believe *you will see* (ὄψῃ) the glory of God'" (11:40). At the first sign a certain number of disciples had seen the glory of Jesus, the incarnate Logos, in the sign of the transformation of water into wine; and in response "they believed into him." Mary, however, must believe in order to see! Furthermore, she must take the risk that even the impossible is possible by having the stone rolled away from the entrance of the tomb. Initially, therefore, Lazarus' resurrection depends on her faith and its strength to confront the absurdity of removing the stone from a tomb that contains a radically decomposed corpse in order to realize the resurrection of her brother.

In spite of the hopelessness of this circumstance Martha puts her faith into practice, and the stone is rolled away. Now Jesus is able to act. Indeed, he will disclose the reality of his autonomy as the incarnate Logos-Sophia by taking action according to the self-understanding he expressed in 5:21, "For even as the Father raises the dead and makes alive, so the Son makes alive whom he wishes." But first he pauses to pray:

> Father, I thank you that you heard me. And I know that you always hear me, but I spoke on account of the crowd standing by so that they might believe that you sent me. (11:41-42)

Verbalizing the confidence he has of always being heard by the Father, Jesus explains his motive for speaking loud enough so that the crowd could hear him. His objective here is "that they might believe that you sent me," not self-aggrandizement through the mighty work that he is about to perform.

Martha *believes* in order to *see* and acts accordingly by having the stone rolled away from Lazarus' tomb. Jesus prays that the crowd that *sees* this sign will *believe*. Once again the dynamic circle of faith emerges! Believing in order to see, as hazardous as that may be, can have far-reaching consequences. On the one hand, that which seems hopeless and impossible may be actualized, and, on the other hand, those who have been spectators may be motivated to make a commitment of faith and enter into the community of the New Human Being.

Believing and seeing, and believing in order to see

The culminating episode of this trajectory of seeing and believing and believing in order to see is the so-called story of "Doubting Thomas" that closes the first edition of the narrative world of the Gospel. Thomas, who was not present on Easter evening when the risen Jesus manifested himself to his disciples, refuses to accept their witness, "*We have seen* (ἑωράκαμεν) the Lord!" He insists on having

[28] See M Yebamot, 16:3.

his own experience of the risen Jesus, and for identification purposes it must be thoroughly empirical. For him as a Jew this is absolutely necessary in order to overcome the scandal of Deut 21:23: "Cursed by God is everyone hanged on a tree." Only the validation of Jesus' resurrection can contradict and refute the curse of crucifixion. Consequently, the continuity of identity between the crucified Jesus and the risen Jesus is critical.

> Unless I *see* (ἴδω) in his hands the impression of the nails and I cast my finger into the impression of the nails and I cast my hand into his side, I will by no means believe. (20:25)

There is nothing negative at all about Thomas' refusal to believe that Jesus has been raised from the dead. He is serving in this final episode of the Gospel as a mirror of the implied readers of the Jewish community in Alexandria who undoubtedly are struggling with the same offense of a crucified Messiah.

Eight days later when all the disciples are gathered together and Thomas is among them, Jesus appears standing in their midst. He greets them with a pronouncement of peace and presents himself to Thomas' inspection: "Bring your finger here and *see* (ἴδε) my hands and bring your hand and cast it into my side and do not keep on being faith-less but faith-full!" (20:27). Convinced on the basis of his sensory experience that this person he has examined is indeed Jesus, Thomas submits to his summons to be faith-full and in confession exclaims, "My Lord and my God." Jesus concludes this final Easter episode by observing that Thomas' insistence of an empirical corroboration has been granted: "Because *you have seen* (ἑώρακας), you have believed." He – and the implied readers – have been privileged with the grace of an empirical experience that enables them to overcome the offense of a crucified Messiah. Jesus brings the narrative world of the gospel, the first edition of chapters 1-20, to a close with a benediction that culminates this trajectory of seeing and believing and believing in order to see. Thomas believed because *he has seen* (ἑώρακας). "Blessed are those *who do not see* (μὴ ἰδόντες) and (yet) *believe*." The demand for empirical evidence, before a commitment of faith is expressed, may be necessary, as it was for Thomas. As in his case, it can indeed elicit faith. That kind of faith, however, is oriented to the past. It looks backwards and is established on the basis of that which has already happened, and consequently it is circumscribed by those actualities that define what is possible. Accordingly, it may lose its vitality and become stultified into the passivity of intellectual assent. Very little if any change is engendered by a believing that is preceded by and founded on seeing.

Believing in order to see, its binary opposite, is oriented to the future.[29] By itself, without any relationship to the past, it is irrational, for it is not grounded in any historical reality. It may be bold and daring but it is simply a leap into the

[29] Contrary to Lindars, *John*, 203 and 616, Jesus does not simply commend "faith without sight." Seeing, followed by believing, is not complete until believing has attained the strength to believe without seeing but in the anticipation of a future fulfillment.

dark, for while it commits itself in order to see, it lacks introspection and critical reflection.

Neither seeing and believing *nor* believing in order to see is the orientation that is promoted in the narrative world of the Fourth Gospel. Both perspectives ae essential and together to constitute the circle of faith. Their inter-relationship is disclosed by the only two numbered signs in the Fourth Gospel.[30] Both occur in Cana of Galilee and both "on the third day" or "after two days." The first establishes the validity of seeing a sign and discerning its underlying motive. Jesus "manifested his glory." The disciples obviously perceived it, for "they believed into him." Seeing and being carried away into a commitment of faith is indispensable to genuine discipleship. But eventually the faith that is engendered must be strong enough to believe in order to see. But that believing is predetermined by earlier experiences of seeing. The nobleman of 4:46-53 does not simply believe in order to see. His initial approach to Jesus on behalf of his dying son presupposes some kind of grounding in faith that enables him to take the risk of believing in order to see. The validation of that commitment of faith in the subsequent experience of seeing reinforces both the content of that faith as well as the relationship to the one to whom the commitment was made. Attendantly, the realized outcome of this circle of faith, as has become evident, may arouse faith within others and lead to the formation of a community of faith in and by which the commitment of all its members will be reinforced and their capacity to see augmented and intensified. This existential circle of faith must necessarily determine its belief content in terms of a movement from fides qua (the faith by which) into fides quae (the faith of which), that is, from faith in terms of a relationship to faith in terms of formulation.[31] But the formulations of faith are always related to the historical and existential context of the disciple and the disciple's community in their mutual collaboration in fulfilling God's work of world transformation. The continuous dynamic movement between fides qua and fides quae relative to context and community will preclude the rigidification of faith into hardened dogma.[32]

---

[30] A corresponding but contemporary rendition of these binary opposites of "seeing and therefore believing" and "believing in order to see" would be the aporia of "truth as correspondence" and "truth as disclosure." See esp. Douglas R. McGaughey, *Strangers and Pilgrims*, 328-378.

[31] Robert Kysar, *John the Maverick Gospel* (Atlanta: John Knox Press, 1979) 65-83, has devoted an entire chapter to "Seeing is Believing – Johannine Concepts of Faith," but, as insightful as his discourse on "Seeing is Believing" is, he has missed the other side of the aporetic character of faith, believing in order to see, that makes for a mature faith.

[32] *Ibid.*, 81. "Faith" in the Fourth Gospel does not have "a creedal ring about it." The Fourth Gospel is not even "partly responsible for the beginning of the gradual shift in the early church toward a creedal understanding of faith."

Chapter Six

Jesus, Nicodemus, and Post-70 Pharisaic Judaism

The reflection of post-70 Pharisaic Judaism in the Gospel 3:1-21

In the narrative world of the Fourth Gospel "the Jews (οἱ 'Ιουδαίοι) generally represent the post-70 C.E. rabbis of Jamnia, Alexandria and other locations who, under the leadership of Yochanan ben Zakkai and Gamaliel II, have been engaged in reconstituting Judaism on the foundation of their Pharisaic heritage.[1] They are not, however, a monolithic group. Even at the academy of Jamnia, where Gamaliel II, after Yochanan ben Zakkai's forced withdrawal to Galilee, served as the "Patriarch" or president from about 80 to 115 C.E., the Houses of Hillel and Shammai are in heated conflict, separated by issues that may only have been resolved after the House of Hillel prevailed.[2] The Fourth Gospel bears witness to the dissension that characterizes the Jewish community in the post-70 crisis of unresolved leadership and ideological determination.

The identity of "the Jews" as the *ruling authorities* is manifested already in the opening episode of the narrative world of the Gospel. The Jews" of 1:19, who anachronistically send priests and Levites to interrogate John in the opening episode of the Gospel, are identifiable as the Pharisees. This is confirmed by the omission of the definite article οἱ (the) before the perfect passive participle ἀπεσταλμένοι (having been sent) in verse 24, according to the witness of the earlier manuscripts, P^{66}, P^{75}, ℵ*, A*, B, C*. The Pharisees, therefore, are not those who were sent but are in fact the senders: "They [the priests and the Levites] were sent from the Pharisees."[3] As incongruous as this bilateral cooperation is historically, it is the result of a coalescence of the two levels of the Gospel's narrative world: Jesus' historical

---

[1] There seems to be general agreement that the phrase οἱ'Ιουδαίοι (the Jews) designates principally the representatives of the Jewish people, the Pharisees, and not the Jewish people themselves. So Bultmann, *John*, 87; German, 59. But what he considers to be the "overall portrayal of the Jews," in the Fourth Gospel, "when viewed from the standpoint of the Christian faith" is that they are "the representatives of unbelief and the unbelieving 'world' in general." Ashton, "The Jews in John," *Studying John: Approaches to the Fourth Gospel* (Oxford: Clarendon Press, 1994) 63, tends to opt for Bultmann "because he shows an incomparably greater understanding of the *meaning* of the Gospel;" and relying on source and redaction criticism, and agreeing with Ernst Bammel, he believes "the Pharisees-passages reflect controversies between the Christian community and shades of opinion within the Jewish world. They represent old valuable tradition."

[2] See Neusner's summary "Conclusion" of Yochanan's career, *First Century Judaism in Crisis*, 196-198. Also Neusner, *The Rabbinic Traditions about the Pharisees before 70*, I, 339-340.

[3] Paul Schmiedel conjectured that verse 24 is a later scribal interpolation. But no manuscripts support its ommision. See the critical apparatus in the 27th ed. of *NTG* ed. by Barbara and Kurt Aland, 248.

ministry and the struggle within the Jewish community of Alexandria to reconstitute Judaism after the destruction of Jerusalem.[4]

John's cross-examination by the priests and the Levites on behalf of the Pharisees alerts the implied readers to the vigilance of the ruling elite. Their interrogation begins with an intimidating inquiry into his identity: "You, who are you?" (σὺ τίς εἶ).[5] It is a confrontative challenge to his self-identification that is conveyed by placing the pronoun σὺ (you) first and adding the second person singular of the copula εἶ (you are).[6] John replies with a forceful denial by appropriating the divine **I AM** self-disclosure formula, but with the negative adverb οὐκ inserted between the ἐγώ and the εἰμί. Significantly he chooses the predicate χριστός as his first disclaimer· ἐγὼ οὐκ εἰμί ὁ χριστός (**I** not **AM** the Christ). It is Jesus who uses the divine self-authenticating formula, ἐγὼ εἰμί (**I AM**), both without and with predicates, and it will play a principal role in his effort to convince the guardians of society of his distinctive relationship with "the Father." John, at his interrogation by those whom the Pharisees sent, also denies being Elijah and "the Prophet." All three of these appellations are christological identities that are eschatologically oriented.

Such watchfulness under the authority of the Pharisees during the historical ministries of John and Jesus is anachronistic. It must be ascribed to the context in which the Gospel was composed. Apparently the Pharisaic-Rabbinic post-70 program of reconstitution required a surveillance of any individual or movement that might threaten the efforts of these new guardians of society to consolidate a unified Judaism that would be submissive to their ideological objectives. Their unswerving temperament against heterodoxy of any kind, including that of Christian Jews as well as the followers of John the Baptizer, is attested within the narrative world of the Gospel in 9:22, 12:42, 16:2, and for the latter 3:25. The *birkath ha-minim*, that was formulated by Samuel the Little under the authority of Gamaliel II and incorporated into the Tefillah, may already have pronounced maledictions against the Nazarenes (Notzrim) in its earliest form in the synagogue.[7] In any case, a policy of exclusion was promoted that proscribed all forms of heterodoxy. Loyalty and conformity guaranteed continued membership in the synagogue and therefore also in the Jewish community.[8] The narrative world of

---

[4] Martyn, *History and Theology*, 89.

[5] The Pharisees address the same question to Jesus in 8:25. See chapter 10.

[6] Schnackenburg, *St. John* II, 200, on 8:25.

[7] According to B *Berachoth*r 28b-29a. See Horbury, "The Benediction of the *Minim* and Early Jewish-Christian Controversy," 19. See also Moore, *Judaism*, I, 91.

[8] See Horbury's conclusions, ibid., 47-61. Justin Martyr's *Dialogue against Trypho* bears witness to the estrangement between these communities. Christians are being cursed in the synagogue (xvi, xcvi), Jesus is being anathematized as the Christ (xlvii, xcv, cxxxiii), the mockery of Christ is being promoted by "the rulers of your synagogues" (cxxxvii), and converse with Christians is being prohibited (xxxviii, cxii). Justin's testimony, therefore, confirms the existence and usage of the *birkath ha-minim* in the synagogue in the early part of the second century C.E. while it also corroborates the fracturing of the Jewish community that is reflected in the Gospel according to John.

the Fourth Gospel bears witness to both the fear of excommunication and the fact of excommunication within the Jewish community for the offense of confessing Jesus as the Messiah.[9]

Accordingly, the implied readers in their interaction with the narrative world of the Gospel would experience in a mirror-like reflection the growing alienation between Christian Jews and the Jewish authorities in their own context of Alexandria.[10] Initially, as the interrogation of John indicates, there is no hostility, only the exercise of vigilance. Jesus' radical act of driving the animals of sacrifice out of the ἱερόν (sacred precinct) and expelling the bankers evokes a sense of alarm among the οἱ Ἰουδαῖοι and in accordance with Jewish tradition they demand a legitimating sign. That enables Jesus to pose enigmatically an alternative to their program of substituting the Torah in place of the Temple, "Destroy this sanctuary, and in three days I shall resurrect it." Their material orientation to the actuality of the Temple prevents them from comprehending his ironic response at this first Passover in the narrative world of the Gospel.

Nicodemus 3:1-22

Nevertheless, it may be both the Temple episode and the "signs" that Jesus subsequently performs in Jerusalem that arouse the interest of one of these guardians of society, Nicodemus, a Pharisee and "a ruler of the Jews."[11] His identification as "a ruler of the Jews" intimates that he is representative of the post-70 rabbinic leadership that has established itself at the academy of Jamnia.[12] That, in turn, poses the probability that Jamnia and Alexandria are in a corresponding

---

[9] See chapter 10. Also Martyn, *History and Theology*, 46-66, for his interpretation of John 9, the exclusion of the blind man from the synagogue.

[10] That the Jews in Alexandria had a separate political organization of their own, a *politeia* and a *politika*, Eric S. Gruen makes quite clear in *Diaspora: Jews amidst Greeks and Romans* (Cambridge: Harvard University Press, 2002) 54-83, esp. 74-78. Burtchaell, *From Synagogue to Church*, 230, "There is late evidence that the great synagogue building in Alexandria held seventy-one thrones for its elders and president. Philo makes it a point that this was the number of elders assembled by Moses, thus strengthening the supposition that even in his time his city maintained a *gerousia* of seventy." See also Philo, *In Flaccum,* 74, cited by Burtchaell.

[11] For studies on Nicodemus see: F. P. Cotterell, "The Nicodemus Conversation: A Fresh Appraisal," *ExpT* 96 (1984-85) 237-242; M. De Jonge, "Nicodemus and Jesus: Some Observations on Misunderstanding and Understanding in the Fourth Gospel," *Jesus: Stranger from Heaven and Son of God* (Missoula: Scholars Press, 1977) 29-47; Jouette M. Bassler, "Mixed Signals: Nicodemus in the Fourth Gospel," *JBL* 108/4 (1989) 635-646. The attempts to identify Nicodemus with an historical figure have proved to be unsuccessful and speculative.

[12] Billerbeck in Strack-Billerbeck, *Kommentar* II, 412-417, considers the possibility that Nicodemus may be identifiable with Naqdemon ben Gorion, a wealthy grain merchant, also called Buni or Bunai, and, after citing the passages from various rabbinic texts, concludes that it would have been difficult for him to continue to maintain his influential relations with the official circles of the synagogue to the time of the destruction of Jerusalem in spite of his membership in the Christian community of Jerusalem. See also Joachim Jeremias, *Jerusalem in the Time of Jesus* (Philadelphia: Fortress Press, paper, 1975) 96, who also cites Josephus, *BJ* 4, 159; from Martyn, *History and Theology*, 88, n. 126, who considers linking Naqdemon as a possible Nicodemus to the second level of the Gospel's witness, yet recognizes the difficulty of such an identification because the former was not a teacher.

relationship in which the rabbis of Jamnia are struggling to establish their control over the Jewish community of Alexandria. Nicodemus himself, however, as "a ruler of the Jews" may be representative of that faction at Jamnia that in this early context of post-70 Judaism is not hostile toward Jesus and Christian Jews. But the Gospel discloses that the clashes are intensifying and the alienation is deepening.

Nicodemus chooses the obscurity of night to visit Jesus with the probable intent of interrogating him. The narrator's time reference, "by night," may intimate an effort to avoid detection by fellow Pharisees or possibly a symbolic anticipation of an eventual coming to faith by passing through darkness to come into the light.[13] But that is a judgment that the implied readers will have to make when they reach 3:19-21. Yet whether Nicodemus is one who, "doing the truth, comes to the light," depends on their assessment of his later appearances. Jesus will use the word "night" negatively to correspond to "darkness," in 11:10, "If anyone walks in the night, he/she stumbles because the light is not in him/her." As Jesus nears the end of his ministry, he anticipates the "night" in 9:4, "Night comes, when no one is able to work." Its arrival will be announced in 13:30 when Judas leaves the fellowship of Jesus and his disciples, "And it was night". In the "night," when Jesus' body is being prepared for burial, the narrator will remind the implied readers that Nicodemus was "the one who first came to him by night," but it will serve the function of insinuating that Nicodemus is not walking in the night. Like Joseph of Arimathea he is a secret disciple of Jesus.[14]

In his first meeting with Jesus, Nicodemus, in a post-70 disposition, addresses Jesus with the honorific title "Rabbi" and seemingly on behalf of his community of Pharisees uses the plural "we" to acknowledge him as a divinely commissioned teacher: "*We* know that you have come a teacher from God, for no one is able to do these signs which you are doing unless God is with him."[15] This may have been intended as an introduction to an interrogation, but, in any case, it is an unequivocally favorable acknowledgment based on his apparent persuasion of the heavenly origin of Jesus' signs. It may reflect a perspective toward Jesus that is represented among the authorities of Alexandria.

---

[13] Jean-Marie Sevrin, "The Nicodemus Enigma: The Characterization and Function of an Ambiguous Actor of the Fourth Gospel," *Anti-Judaism and the Fourth Gospel*, 357-369, offers a rather negative assessment of Nicodemus concluding that "Nicodemus is called an ignorant both by his colleagues (7:50-52) and by Jesus." Moreover, he is an "in-between, neither a disciple who has come to faith" nor a Pharisee, like others among his peers, who rejects Jesus.

[14] This is also the conclusion of Schnackenburg, *St. John* III, 297; Brown, *John* II, 959-960. However, Bassler, "Mixed Signals," has concluded, "The result is that Nicodemus falls between the two major anthropological categories in this Gospel: he is defined as neither fully a "Jew" nor fully a disciple, but as somehow bearing traits of both."

[15] Rensberger, *Johannine Faith*, 38, assigns the role of "a *communal* symbolic figure" to Nicodemus. (The italics are his.) He is representative of "secret Christians;" he is symbolic of the "untrustworthy believers" who out of the fear of "losing their position" maintain their faith in secrecy. His portrayal of Nicodemus is basically negative. See pp. 39-41, 55-57. Martyn, *History and Theology*, 88, also considers Nicodemus to be "typical of those in the Gerousia who secretly believe."

Jesus' interrupts Nicodemus' validation with a provocative asseveration that may be intended to anticipate his questioning, "Unless one is born from above, he or she is unable to see the reign of God (ἰδεῖν τὴν βασιλείαν τοῦ θεοῦ)." A stunning interjection![16] Nothing at all has been said about the reign of God up to this point in the Gospel. If this phrase and the eschatological perspective that it conveys is introduced here for the very first time without explanation or clarification, it must be assumed that Nicodemus – and those whom he represents – are familiar with the substance of its meaning. Equally consequential, the phrase must be intelligible to the implied readers who, as a result of their entry into this narrative world, are present as silent listeners to this dialogue. It is correspondingly significant that Jesus introduces the eschatological reality of God's reign to a ruler of the Jews who is a Pharisee.[17] For the community of the Pharisees, whom Nicodemus represents, had been promoting a de-eschatologized ideology of separation both before and after the destruction of Jerusalem.[18] Under the leadership of Yochanan ben Zakkai prior to 70 the Pharisees attempted to exercise power over the Temple – and therefore also over Jewish life – by excluding from the Temple all who did not accept their rulings.[19] In this endeavor they largely failed. Noteworthy, however, is that the policy of exclusion was already being practiced by the Pharisees before 70.

The ultimate success of Pharisaic Judaism was largely due to Yochanan's efforts in undertaking the governance of the Jewish people by establishing an academy at Jamnia with the support of the Roman government.[20] Rejecting any and every millenarian perspective, like that of the more or less contemporaneous apocalyptic texts, II Baruch and IV Ezra (II Esdras), he promoted the ideological position he had been developing before 70: a life of studying the Torah in order to be drawn

[16] Also acknowledged by Wayne A Meeks, *The Prophet-King*, 298, "This apocalyptic notion seems distinctly an alien intrusion in the Johannine context." But Meeks' interpretation of "seeing the Kingdom of God" is defective.

[17] It is noteworthy that the apocryphal infancy Gospel of Thomas tells the story of Jesus as a child outwitting a Galilean teacher by the name of Zacchaeus. If the name, Zacchaeus, is identifiable with Yochanan ben Zakkai, as Jacob Neusner suggests, this story may have been formulated in Galilee after 70 in order to subvert the authority of Yochanan and his teaching and at the same time to acknowledge the superiority of Jesus. Zacchaeus' readiness to acknowledge that Jesus is "not earth-born" and "perhaps begotten even before the creation of the world" echoes both Jesus' dialogue with Nicodemus and the Prologue of the Fourth Gospel. When he goes on to say, "What belly bore him, what womb nurtured him I do not know!" he may be reflecting the absence of a birth story in the Gospel. See Neusner, *First Century Judaism in Crisis*, 64-66. See "The Infancy Story of Thomas" in *Apocryphal Gospels and Related Writings*, I, 445-446.

[18] Earlier, from the time of the Maccabeans to the reign of Alexandra, the wife of Alexander Jannaeus, the Pharisees were a politically oriented party with an eschatological perspective that motivated them to struggle for justice against the ideology of hellenization that was embraced by the Hasmoneans and the Sadducees. See Victor Tcherikover, *Hellenistic Civilization and the Jews*, 253-265.

[19] Neusner, *First Century Judaism in Crisis*, 86-92. Also Neusner, "Josephus' Pharisees: 'The Real Administrators of the State'" *From Politics to Piety: The Emergence of Pharisaic Judaism* (Englewood Cliffs: Prentice-Hall, 1973) 45-66 and 143-154.

[20] *First Century Judaism in Crisis*, 151. See also pp. 145-152.

into a relationship with the word of God that was transmitted in and by the Scriptures.[21] All legal, ethical and ritual matters were to be resolved by Scripture, but in accordance with the perspective of the Pharisaic tradition as it was being developed after 70 in the disputes between the Houses of Hillel and Shammai.

But Yochanan did believe the Messiah would come.[22] A trace of his eschatology is evident in his pre-70 declaration that the messianic age would not begin until Elijah had redressed all the wrongs that had been perpetrated by the Zadokite priesthood.[23] After 70, however, the imminent redemption that Jewish apocalypticism anticipated was postponed into the distant future. "The new age would endure on the foundation of studying the Torah, doing the commandments and especially performing acts of compassion."[24] "Through *hesed* (loyalty) the Jews might make atonement ... and the sacrifices demanded of them were love and mercy."[25]

Yet, in spite of the de-eschatologized ideology of the Pharisees and rabbis, messianic eschatology continued to be pervasive among the Jewish people. Both John 7:40-44 and 50-52 testify to its perpetuation beyond 70. The Jerusalem crowd in 7:40-43, reflecting perhaps the speculation of the Jewish people of Alexandria, debates the possible christological identity that could be ascribed to Jesus.

> Then some of the crowd hearing these words were saying, "This is truly the Prophet." Others were saying, "This is the Messiah." But some were saying, "Surely the Messiah doesn't come out of Galilee, does he? Did Scripture not say, 'from the seed of David' and 'from Bethlehem,' the village where David was, the Messiah comes?" Therefore a division occurred among the crowd on account of him.

Following this dispute, Nicodemus, in an effort to defend Jesus on the basis of "our Law" (7:51), is censured by his fellow Pharisees as though he too were a fellow Galilean and therefore a messianic perspective of the eschatological prophet might be implied in his advocacy:

> Surely our Law doesn't judge the human being unless it first hears from him and knows what he is doing, does it? They answered and said to him, "You're not from Galilee, are you? Search and see that *the* Prophet does not arise out of Galilee."

According to the manuscript evidence of 7:52, later scribal corrections apparently produced a deliberate change in the original word order in order to eliminate the definite article before the word προφήτης (prophet). That produced the textual reading, "Search and see that a prophet does not arise out of Galilee!" that is

[21] *Ibid.*, 115-117.

[22] Neusner, *There We Sat Down*, 38.

[23] Neusner, *First Century Judaism in Crisis*, 89.

[24] *Ibid.*, 170.

[25] *Ibid.*

continued in most translations of this verse. But that would contradict 2 Kgs 14: 25 and Nahum 1:1. Jonah the prophet came from Gath-hepher, a village in the proximity of Nazareth in Galilee, and, if Elkosh was located in Galilee, Nahum also originated in Galilee. Moreover, the rabbinic tradition of Sukk 27b maintained, "There is no single tribe in Israel from which prophets have not arisen." Likewise Seder Olam Rabba 21 avowed, "There is no city in the land of Israel in which there has been no prophet."[26] Both P^{66} and P^{75} include the definite article before the word "prophet," and that must surely be the original formulation, "Search and see that out of Galilee *the prophet* does not arise."

Does Nicodemus' defense of Jesus insinuate a change in his eschatological perspective?[27] In 3:3 Jesus confronts him with the possibility of drawing the postponed eschatological reality of salvation into the present. But, according to Jesus' solemn declaration, he must be born *from above* (ἄνωθεν).

> Amen, amen I say to you, unless one is born from above, one is unable to *see* the reign of God.

Although the reign of God does not originate ἐκ τοῦ κόσμου τούτου (out of this world), as Jesus informs Pilate in 18:36, it is nevertheless divinely willed to be an empirical reality that is manifest to the physical sight of human beings.[28]

Nicodemus, however, misconstrues Jesus' use of the adverb ἄνωθεν. He does not grasp its ironic ambiguity of combining both possible meanings, "from above" and "again". In accordance with his Jewish perspective he interprets ἄνωθεν simply as "again:" "How can a human being be born when [he/she] is elderly: Surely it is not possible to enter a mother's womb a second time and be born, is it?" Nicodemus is presupposing the actuality of Jewish identity. His question, therefore, anticipates a negative answer to what he has construed as a repetition of a human being's first birth. If by physical birth Jews already are daughters and sons of God, they have been "born from above."

As a response to Nicodemus' confusion that his earlier avowal had raised, Jesus clarifies his declaration with a second asseveration: "Amen, amen I say to you, unless one is born *out of* (ἐκ) water and Spirit, he or she is unable to enter into the reign of God." To enter into the eschatological reality of God's reign, as well as to experience it visually, demands more than the actuality of Jewish identity. It requires "a new origin," a heavenly birth, a being born from above, that can only be effected by the baptism of water and Spirit.[29] Jesus' instructions to the blind male in 9:7, "Go, wash into the pool of Siloam!" which results in being able to see,

---

[26] Also cited by Duke, *Irony in the Fourth Gospel*, 68; and Keener, *John*, 734, n. 298.

[27] Schneiders, *Written That You May Believe*, applies 3:21 in her evaluation of Nicodemus' response to his fellow Pharisees and rightly concludes, "... Nicodemus in this scene, although still dependent on the Old Testament, 'does the truth' according to the law."

[28] The preposition ἐκ denotes origin.

[29] Bultmann, *John*, 137-138; German, 97-98, uses the phrase "a new origin" and offers an exceptional exegesis of the point of Jesus' teaching.

makes it evident that the requisite of being born of "water" refers to a baptism of immersion which signifies an eschatological death that terminates participation in the old moral order. If a water baptism betokens an eschatological death, being born "out of water" must naturally be followed by being born "out of Spirit" so that the rebirth "from above" (ἄνωθεν) can be actualized, and Nicodemus can begin to enter and see the reign of God.

For further clarification Jesus adds, "That which has been born *from* (ἐκ) flesh is flesh, and that which has been born *from* (ἐκ) Spirit is Spirit." A human being's first birth is ἐκ σαρκός (from the flesh), and if a repetition of that first birth by re-entering a mother's womb were possible, it nevertheless remains ἐκ τῆς σαρκός (from the flesh) and therefore a continuation in the old moral order that is dominated by "the Ruler of the world" and the darkness that he perpetuates. But that which is born ἐκ τοῦ πνεύματος (from the Spirit) originates from God because it is God's Spirit that has revivified the one who by baptism has experienced eschatological death. Such a human being is born from above and is able to see and to enter into God's reign.

Jesus entreats Nicodemus not to marvel at the words he has spoken. God's Spirit that revivifies the one who has died in the waters of baptism is like the wind: "The wind/Spirit blows where it wills, and you hear its sound, but you do not know where it comes from and where it goes to. So is everyone who has been born ἐκ τοῦ πνεύματος (from the Spirit). The twofold meaning of πνεῦμα, "spirit" and "wind," metaphorically compares the one with the other. God's regenerating Spirit is as indeterminable as the wind in its coming and going. Like the wind, its activity is discernible by its effect, but it is sovereign and free in its movements; and, therefore, like the wind, it cannot be controlled. Accordingly, those who have been born from the Spirit and have entered into God's reign bear the qualities or attributes of the Spirit. Like the wind, the effect of their activity in their exercise of God's reign is perceivable; and, like the wind, they are sovereign and free in their service as surrogates of God's reign. Jesus is the embodiment of the wind-like character of the Spirit, and in his exercise of God's reign it is an essential aspect of his ministry to draw his fellow human beings into this same wind-like character of the Spirit's activity. In his Farewell Speech he will inform his disciples:

> In my Father's house are many rooms; and if not, I would tell you. For I am going to prepare a place for you, and if I depart and prepare a place for you, I am coming again and will receive you *towards* (πρός) myself, so that *where* **AM I** you also are. (14:2-3)[30]
>
> But I tell you the truth, it is expedient for you that I go away. For if I do not go away, the Comforter will be no means come *towards* (πρός) you. But if I depart, I shall send him *towards* (πρός) you … When that one comes, the

[30] The **AM I**, or εἰμὶ ἐγώ is simply the reverse of the **I AM** or ἐγω εἰμί formula that Jesus employs throughout the Gospel, and it is always preceded by the adverb ὅπου, denoting place *where*. Where Jesus is as **I AM**, there his disciples also will be. See n. 47 and also chapter 8.

> Spirit of truth, he will lead you on the way into all the truth. For he will not speak of himself, but such things as he hears he will speak and the things coming he will announce to you. That one will glorify me, for he will receive from what is mine and will announce [it] to you. All such things that the Father has are mine. On account of this I said that he takes from what is mine and will announce [it] to you. (16:7-8, 13-15)[31]

Evidently Nicodemus comprehends the implications of Jesus' metaphor of the wind and inquires, "How can these things happen?"[32] He perceives that it is a question of possibility, not a question of actuality. The community of Pharisees, whom he represents, are legislating their ideology of loyalty and separation with the presupposition that the old moral order that extends back to the Fall of Adam and Eve will continue for an indefinite period of time. Jewish institutions are being perpetuated, but on the basis of adjustments that the Pharisaic leadership is authorizing. The patterns of habituation that tradition prescribes and that the Pharisees sanction are being used to consolidate an orthodoxy by which loyalty will be judged. Being Jewish in this context of reconstitution requires subjection to conformity. Freedom and dissent are limited, and the possibility of transcendence is virtually extinguished. The ethnic isolation that the ideology of separation entrenches prevents participation in any activities that are directed toward the possibilities of personal or world transformation.

How then can a new origin that is generated by being born from water and the Spirit admit human beings into the reign of God? How can a rebirth induct them into a participation in the wind-like character and activity of the Spirit? Jesus will reply to Nicodemus' question as he moves their dialogue into a monologue of instruction. But before he tells him how these things can happen, he chides him and all the Pharisees whom he represents, "You are the teacher of Israel, and these things you do not know (γινώσκεις) ?"[33] By employing the verb γινώσκεις, he is conveying to Nicodemus – and the community of Pharisees – that his inability to understand is due to his deficiency in the existential knowledge of these realities that he, Jesus, has been affirming. How then can he and those whom he represents in his earlier use of "We" be qualified to be Israel's teacher?[34] The implication is that the Pharisees, in their assumed post-70 role as "the teacher of Israel," are fundamentally unable to lead God's people into the transcendence of the wind-like character and activity of the Spirit that a rebirth originating from heaven can actualize. The isolation and conformity to tradition, which they enforce, preclude

---

[31] For further elucidation of these two texts, see chapter 15, "Jesus' Farewell Speech."

[32] Barrett, *St. John*, 211, translates the text in the same way.

[33] Bultmann, *John*, 144, n. 1; German edition, 103, n. 1, is rightly troubled by the definite article in front of διδάσκαλος (teacher), but he proceeds to draw the insightful conclusion: "Probably we should understand, 'In you I encounter the teachers of Israel; you represent them.'"

[34] Bultmann, ibid., 144; German, 103, appears to be saying the same thing: "Rather Jesus' words make it clear that the teachers of Israel can give no answer." But he does not say why.

the realization of the possibilities that the reign of God inaugurates. Consequently the compelling visions and pronouncements of Israel's prophets are vitiated.

Jesus continues to reprove Nicodemus, but in the form of another asseveration. Why, however, he unexpectedly assumes the first person plural "we," is not immediately obvious. Moreover, he shifts from the singular pronoun σοι (you) to the plural "you" in his employment of the verb λαμβάνετε (receive).

> Amen, amen I say to σοι (you singular), that which we know we speak and that which we have seen we bear witness to, and *you all* do not continue to receive (οὐ λαμβάνετε.) our witness. (3:11)

The shift from the singular to the plural "you" indicates that Nicodemus is indeed representative of the fellowship of the Pharisees to which he belongs. Together they are being censured for their rejection of the Christian witness. Jesus' unanticipated use of the plural "we" appears to be intended to include the ongoing witness of all those who have been born from above, perhaps specifically the Christian Jews of Alexandria.[35] In other words, two communities are being juxtaposed. The Pharisees are being reprimanded for their dismissal of the witness of the Christian community that is representative of Jesus.

In his censure of Nicodemus and his fellow Pharisees, "You are the teacher of Israel and these things you do not *know* (γινώσκεις)?" Jesus utilizes the verb γινώσκειν (to know) that denotes a knowledge derived from discernment, personal experience or acquaintance that in turn will serve as the basis of awareness and understanding.[36] The kind of knowing that is attributed to him in 2:24 presupposes a discernment into human nature that may be intuitive or drawn from his own experience. To the members of the ruling elite, who, according to 8:31, have been believing him, Jesus offers a condition with a promise: "If you remain in my word, you are truly my disciples, and *you will know* (γνώσεσθε) the truth, and the truth will set you free." The personal experience of believing and continuing in Jesus' teaching guarantees an understanding of the truth that is liberating. In 14:7 Jesus tells his disciples that in as far as they have gotten acquainted with him during his ministry, they have also gained a existential knowledge of the Father: "If you *have come to know* (ἐγνώκατε) me, you also *will know* (γνώσεσθε) the Father."[37]

---

[35] The reference of the plural "we" has been identified variously: Bultmann, *ibid*., 146; German, 104, "a way of disguising the person of Jesus"; Brown, *John* I, 132, "a rebuttal of Nicodemus in his own words"; Barrett, *St. John*, 212, "the witness of the church"; Lindars, *John*, 155, "Jesus associating himself with those similarly frustrated."

[36] See also 1:10, 49; 2:24, 25; 4:1, 53; 5:6, 42; 6:15, 69, and 44 other occurrences in the Gospel.

[37] There are two sets of manuscript variants for this twofold use of γινώσκειν. The first is a choice between the pluperfect ἐγνώκειτε and the perfect ἐγνώκατε. Since no reproach appears to be intended at this point in Jesus' Farewell Speech, the perfect tense is the preferable reading. The second is a choice between the pluperfect of οἶδα, ᾔδειτε, the pluperfect ἐγνώκειτε and the future γνώσεσθε. The future γνώσεσθε seems preferable because it follows naturally from the premise of the perfect tense ἐγνώκατε. See Bruce M. Metzger, *A Textual Commentary on the Greek New Testament* (London, New York: United Bible Societies, 1971) 243.

In contrast to his use of γινώσκειν in his reproach to Nicodemus, Jesus employs the verb οἴδαμεν (we know) as he solemnly confronts him with his rejection of the witness of the community of those who have been born from water and the Spirit: "… that which we know (οἴδαμεν) we speak and that which we have seen (ἑωράκαμεν) we bear witness to, and you continue not to receive our witness." He has already used this verb in verse 8, "The wind/Spirit blows where it wills and you hear its sound, but you do not know (οἴδας) where it comes from and where it goes to …" Nicodemus himself used the verb in his opening address to Jesus, "We know (οἴδαμεν) that you have come a teacher from God…" In contrast to γινώσκειν, the verb οἶδα denotes cognitive knowledge, knowledge as fact or information, knowledge that has been gained by research or by recalling an earlier activity or event, and this appears to be its meaning throughout the Fourth Gospel.[38]

Philo of Alexandria has employed both verbs repeatedly in his writings, and they appear to bear the same variations of meaning.[39] In *Legum Allegoria* III, 103, he states that Aaron and Miriam, on the occasion of their rebellion, are told, "If a prophet is raised up to the Lord, God will be known (γνωσθήσεται) to him in a vision." Through the medium of a vision a prophet will have the experience of knowing God and with it the certainty of his divine call. Philo interprets Ex 20:19, "You speak to us, and do not let God speak to us, lest we die," with the comment, "For they knew (ἔγνωσαν) that they have in themselves no organ of hearing fit to be employed when God is giving laws to his congregation." The Israelites discern that they are incapable of hearing God speak. Philo's use of the verb οἶδα conveys the meaning of knowledge gained by recall or investigation. In *De Opificio Mundi* 41, he asks a question that assumes the knowledge of facts: "For who does not know (οἶδεν) that sowing and planting are first, second the growth of the things sown and planted." In the same treatise he expresses ignorance of a fact that investigation may not be able to ascertain, "I do not know (οἶδα) if anyone can adequately sing the praises of the number seven."

Because Nicodemus – and the Pharisees he represents – do not understand "these things" to which Jesus is bearing witness, because they cannot discern the truth of his words, they forfeit their self-acclaimed right to be "the teacher of Israel". Jesus intensifies this implied forfeiture by confronting Nicodemus – and, by the use of the second person plural, his fellow Pharisees – with the Pharisaic rhetorical principle of *qal wahomer*, an analogical movement from a minor to a major premise: "If I speak to you all [of] earthly things and you all do not believe, how will you all believe if I speak to you all [of] heavenly things?"[40] Jesus returns to his earlier use of the first person singular pronoun "I." But in the pronouns and

[38] See also 1:26, 31, 33; 2:9; 4:10, 22, 25, 32, 42; and 64 more occurrences in chapters 5 through 20.

[39] The utilization of the verbs of seeing and the verbs of knowing with comparable meanings that are common to Philo and the Fourth Gospel also lends support to an Alexandrian origin for the Gospel according to John.

verbs of the logical comparison that he addresses to Nicodemus he continues to employ the second person plural, indicating that the community of the Pharisees as a whole is to be included. If Jesus' use of earthly analogies and metaphors to facilitate Nicodemus' comprehension of his teaching about entry into the reign of God here on earth does not evoke faith, to what extent would he be able to believe the heavenly truths to which Jesus bears witness?[41]

The conjunction καί (and) at the beginning of verse 13 would lead the implied readers to believe that Jesus continues to address Nicodemus. It appears to be necessary to reinforce Jesus' capacity to bear witness to "heavenly things," but Jesus himself is no longer the speaker. That, of course, is not immediately evident. In fact, the narrator intends the implied readers to assume that he is speaking, although his dialogue with Nicodemus has ended. Verses13-21 present an epitomization of "the heavenly things" that Jesus has distinguished in his rhetorical analogy of verse 11. They present the content of "that which we know … and that which we have seen and bear witness to …" but in terms of a post-Easter epitomization. Verses 13-21 may in fact be the witness of the community that the author of the Gospel represents, perhaps the Christian Jewish community of Alexandria.

Verse 13, however, poses a conundrum that is difficult to resolve:

> No one has ascended into heaven except the one descending from heaven, the Son of the Human Being.

First of all, it cancels the ascension of anyone whose heavenward movement was not initially preceded by a descent.[42] There is no one in biblical tradition who qualifies for this distinction! Neither Enoch or Elijah or Moses first descended from heaven and afterwards ascended into heaven. Only Jesus! Philo's Moses, however, poses a significant contrast, and in all likelihood it is Philo's exalted discrimination of Moses that is being repudiated.

> Why does God say, "Moses alone shall come near to God, and they shall not come near, and the people shall not go up with them?" O Most excellent and God-worthy ordinance, that the prophetic mind alone should approach God and that those in second place should go up, making a path to heaven, while those in third place and the turbulent characters of the people should neither go up above nor go up with them but those worthy of beholding should be beholders of the blessed path above. But that "(Moses) alone shall go up" is said most naturally. For when the prophetic mind becomes

[40] Lindars, *John*, 155, and Keener, *John* I, 559, are among the few commentators who recognize Jesus' strategic employment of the Pharisaic interpretive norm of *qal wahomer*.

[41] Brown, *John* I, 132, asks, "Why are the things spoken of in vss. 3-8 designated as "earthly"? And he correctly answers, "Perhaps it is because they were illustrated by earthly analogies like birth and wind; perhaps it is because they take place on earth …"

[42] Verse 13 has a polemical intent, as Hugo Odeberg recognized, *The Fourth Gospel: Interpreted in its relation to contemporaneous religious currents in Palestine and the Hellenistic-Oriental world* (Uppsala: Almqvist & Wiksells,1929; repr. Chicago: Argonaut, 1968) 72,

> divinely inspired and filled with God, it becomes like the monad, not being at all mixed with any of those things associated with duality. But he who is resolved into the nature of unity is said to come near God in a kind of family relation, for having given up and left behind all mortal kinds, he is changed into the divine, so that such men become kin to God and truly divine.[43]

Moses' sojourn on Sinai, according to Philo's metaphysical dualism, transforms him into "the heavenly human being, [who] having happened according to the image of God is completely free from mortal and earth-like being..."[44] His divinity is manifest in his descent, and is described by Philo in terms of a transfiguration:

> Then, after the said forty days had passed, he descended with a countenance far more beautiful than when he ascended, so that those who saw him were filled with awe and amazement; their eyes were not able to withstand that dazzling light that flashed like the rays of the sun. (*de Vita Mosis* II, 70)[45]

Moses' ascension at the end of his career parallels his Sinai ascent.[46] Philo's commentary on Deut 33-34 at the end of his treatise on Moses states,

> Afterwards the time came when he had to make his pilgrimage from earth to heaven and, abandoning mortal life to be immortalized, being summoned by the Father, who changed his twofold being, body and soul, into a fundamental unity transposing through and through his nature mind as pure as sunlight. (*de Vita Mosis* II, 288)

According to verse 13, therefore, only the one who descended prior to his ascension is certified to communicate heavenly truths.[47] But how then can Jesus be qualified? As yet in the narrative world of the Fourth Gospel no ascension has occurred. Only a descent has been intimated, as 1:14 declares, "And the Logos happened flesh and tented among us." As the enfleshed Logos, Jesus is from above (8:23). As the enfleshed Logos, he came forth from God (8:42). As the enfleshed Logos, he declares, "Before Abraham happened **I AM**," and without an earlier ascension, like Philo's Moses, that would transform him into divinity.

There will be an ascension, but not until Jesus has been resurrected from the dead. In 6:61-62 in response to the offense that his teaching in the synagogue of Capernaum has aroused, Jesus startles his disciples with the possibility of his ascension, "Does this scandalize you? What if you should view the Son of the Human Being ascending to where he was before?" Subsequently he begins to

---

[43] This translation has been taken from Ralph Marcus, *Philo: Quaestiones et Solutiones in Exodum* II,29 (Cambridge: Harvard University Press, 1953) 69-70.

[44] Meeks, *The Prophet-King*, 124. See *Legum Allegoria* I, 31 and II, 4; also *de Vita Mosis* II, 71-76 for Philo's construction of what Moses experienced on Sinai.

[45] This text is taken over from F. H. Colson, *Philo* VI of the *Loeb Classical Library* (Cambridge: Harvard University Press, 1959) 593.

[46] Meeks, *The Prophet-King*, 124.

[47] Also Ashton, *Understanding,* 354.

prepare his disciples for this event in his Farewell Speech (16:5). In 17:11 in his intercessory prayer for his disciples, he is conscious that his ascent is drawing near, "And I am coming *towards* (πρός) you." In the context of his resurrection he tells Mary in 20:17, "Do not keep on holding me, for I have not yet ascended *towards* (πρός) the Father. But keep on going to my brothers and sisters and say to them, "I am ascending *towards* (πρός) my Father and your Father and my God and your God." When the narrative world of the Gospel reaches its culmination, Jesus' ascension has occurred. Verse 13 is referring to this ascent.[48]

However, at this point in chapter 3 there has only been a descent. But from a post-70 perspective, the ascension of Jesus is a past event, a coincidence that discloses the structuring of the two historical epochs to constitute the narrative world of the Fourth Gospel. The descent that has taken place and the ascent that eventually will follow establishes the proposition of verse 13 and invalidates Philo's Moses and the revelations that Philo attributes to him. Jesus alone is qualified to impart heavenly truths because he originated from heaven. His self-differentiation from the ruling elite in 8:23 explicitly asserts this, "You are from below; I am from above. You are from this world; I am not from this world." The heavenly origin of Jesus' descent would intimate that the "Son of God" appellation is the appropriate christological title by which he should be identified. Attached to verse 13, however, is the eschatologically oriented designation: ὁ υἱὸς τοῦ ἀνθρώπου (the Son of the Human Being). Jesus, who as the incarnate Logos originated in heaven and who descended into the world, is to be identified as ὁ υἱὸς τοῦ ἀνθρώπου. It is an ironic reversal of the corporate *bar enosh* of Dan 7:13-14, the eschatological figure of "one like a son of a human being" who ascends into heaven on a cloud to receive glory, sovereignty and kingship.[49] In his descent as the incarnate Logos, Jesus is to be identified first and foremost as ὁ υἱὸς τοῦ ἀνθρώπου. The distinctiveness of this eschatologically oriented title signifies that he is the New Human Being or the First Final Human Being that God has generated.

There is another heavenly truth that is a vital feature of the epitomization of the Gospel in verses 13-21. Between the descent and the eventual ascent of Jesus as ὁ υἱὸς τοῦ ἀνθρώπου there will be a salvation event that will bring healing to the world. The conjunction καί (and) that introduces verse 14 leads the implied readers directly from the descent to the crucifixion:

> And even as Moses elevated the snake in the wilderness, so it is necessary for the Son of the Human Being to be elevated, so that every one who believes into him should have eternal life.

---

[48] So Bultmann, *John*, 150-151 and n. 2; German, 107-108; H. Strathmann, *Das Evangelium nach Johannes: Das Neue Testament Deutsch* (Göttingen: Vandenhoeck & Ruprecht, 1963) 70; Barrett, *St. John*, 213; Marsh, *St. John*, 181; Haenchen, *John* I, 204; Schnackenburg, *St. John*, 392. Brown, *John*, I, 132, seems to remain puzzled. Moloney, *Belief*, 117, passes over it without comment.

[49] Also Ashton, *Understanding*, 355.

Philo's Moses has been invalidated! Now, in his place, the Moses of Num 21:1-9 is introduced, the Moses who produced healing for the Israelites during their Exodus journey when they had been bitten by poisonous snakes. Yahweh sent these snakes to punish the people who had "spoken against God and against Moses" by complaining about the scarcity of food and water in the desert, and as a result many of them died. When the people confessed their sin and begged that the snakes be taken away, God commanded Moses: "Make a poisonous serpent and set it on a pole; and every one who is bitten, when he/she looks at it, shall live." Moses provided healing by fashioning a bronze serpent and suspending it on a stake.

Philo interprets this story in *Legum Allegoria* II, 79, and asks the question, "How, then, does the healing of their suffering happen?" His answer allegorizes the snake into the ethical principle of self-control by referring to the snake that tempted Eve in Gen 3:1-6.

> He constructed another snake opposite to the one of Eve, the principle (λόγος) of self-control. For self-control is opposite to pleasure, a variable virtue to a variable pleasure and makes war against pleasure. God commands Moses to construct the snake, the one that is for the purpose of self-control, and says, "Make for yourself a snake and place it on a sign." You see that Moses constructs the snake for no one else but himself, for God commands, "Make [it] for yourself," so that you may know that self-control is not a possession of all, but only of the one who is God-loved.

Philo affirms the outcome of the story in *Legum Allegoria* II, 81, "... and every one who is bitten, when he/she looks at it, shall live." But the resulting healing, according to his allegorization, is produced by moderation and self-control.

> For it the mind, being bitten by pleasure, the snake of Eve, has the strength of soul to see the beauty of self-control, the snake of Moses, and through this to see God himself, he will live. Only let him look and note carefully!

To Philo, Moses' snake symbolizes temperance, moderation in sensual desires; and because God directed Moses to make it for himself, the resulting salvation is essentially dependent on an individual's imitation of the supreme model, Moses.

Jesus is superior to the Moses of Num 21:1-6 because he did not produce healing by fashioning a snake out of bronze and fastening it to a pole.[50] He himself became the snake that was hung on the cross and actualized healing as a possibility for the whole world. Jesus is also superior to Philo's Moses because he effected salvation for the entire world by offering up his life for the universal healing of sin. The snake that Philo's Moses produced was his own self-mastery, and, while it served as an example for others, it was directed toward his own salvation.

The verb ὑψοῦν, which is used twice in verse 14 does not occur in the account of Num 21:1-9. Its deliberate employment by the narrator in the appropriation of

[50] Also Keener, *John* I, 563.

this analogy of Moses "lifting up" the snake in the wilderness introduces a profound irony into this event between Jesus' descent and ascent. The passive aorist infinitive ὑψωθῆναι bears the twofold sense of "to be lifted up" and "to be exalted". Jesus, by being "lifted up" on a stake like a poisonous snake, will be exalted. As he approaches his imminent passion, conscious that "the hour has come," he petitions the Father, "Glorify your Son so that your Son glorifies you." Here again the mutuality of interdependence is evident. Since the Son can do nothing apart from the Father (5:19), the Father must take the initiative, so that the Son can respond in kind. If the Father glorifies the Son in the forthcoming crucifixion, the Son will also be able to glorify the Father. This will not be another crucifixion like the thousands of crucifixions that the Romans carried out throughout their history. As Jesus declares to the ruling elite in 8:28, "When you lift up/exalt the Son of the Human Being, then *you will know* (γνώσεσθε) that **I AM** (ἐγὼ εἰμί)." Only when the crucifixion is simultaneously acknowledged to be Jesus' exaltation will they be able to discern personally that he is indeed **I AM**.[51] In that eschatological moment of the καιρός (the right time), as Jesus states in 12:23, the Son of the Human Being will be glorified and, at the same time, he will draw all human beings to himself (12:32).[52] But how will his exaltation be manifested? Will the implied readers perceive the **I AM** of Jesus' self disclosure in his crucifixion?

The οὕτως (thus) at the beginning of verse 16 refers back the ironic coronation of Jesus who, after descending from heaven, makes himself the snake that is lifted up on the cross. "For *in this way* God loved the world so that he gave the Son, the only one-of-a-kind, in order that everyone who believes into him should not perish but continue having life everlasting." Like the ascension, announced in verse 13, Jesus' being "lifted up" in crucifixion is a projection of an event that the implied readers will experience narratively when they arrive at the culmination of the Gospel. But already at this moment, in this context of the narrator's epitomization of the Gospel, they are confronted with an indication of the manner in which God loves the world and, therefore, also them. But also at this moment they are challenged by the *qal wahomer* that Jesus addressed to Nicodemus: "... how will you believe if I tell you heavenly things?" The Son of the Human Being, the First Final Human Being whom God generated, will offer himself to be lifted up as the snake that will bring healing to humankind. It will be God's glory as well as Jesus' glory as Jesus, the incarnate Logos, suffers God's judgment by drinking the wine of God's wrath and completing the Exodus for the entire world. Everyone who "believes into" or

---

[51] See chapter 17.

[52] Jesus' words in 12:32, "And if I am lifted up ἐκ τῆς γῆς (from the earth), I will draw all *towards* (πρός) myself!" may also presuppose his ascension, as Barrett, *St. John*, 427, states, "ἐκ τῆς γῆς underlines the ideas both of the death on the cross and of the ascension."

makes a commitment to this Son, the only one-of-a-kind, will continue to have eternal life.[53]

Verse 17, like the previous verse, is introduced by the adverbial conjunction γάρ (for), but its function is to anticipate any misunderstanding that might arise. If the manner in which God loved the world is manifested by Jesus' descent and by his being lifted up on the cross as a snake, God's objective could not have been judgment. "For God did not send the Son into the world in order to keep on judging the world, but in order that the world should be saved through him." Jesus' mission is to actualize the possibility of world transformation.[54]

Nevertheless, even if God did not send the Son into the world in order to judge the world, judgment nevertheless continues to occur. Jesus will inform the ruling elite in 5:22 and 27, " For the Father judges no one but has given all judgment to the Son" and "He gave him authority to do judgment because he is υἱὸς τοῦ ἀνθρώπου(son of a human being)." Verses 18-21 move the implied readers from a cosmic to a personal consideration of the consequences of God's objectives. They, the implied readers, can avoid judgment by believing into (πιστεύων εἰς) the Son, because their commitment to the Son transfers them into the new creation that Jesus will inaugurate by his death and resurrection. But, "The one who does not believe has already been judged because he/she has not believed into the name of the only one of a kind Son of God." The individual who refuses to make a commitment to Jesus and the name that he bears as God's Son simply remains in the old moral order that already stands under God's judgment because it is dominated by the darkness that "the Ruler of the world" proliferates. For, as the narrator asserts in verse 19, "... the Light has come into the world, and human beings loved the darkness rather than the Light for their works were evil." In spite of the Light, the old moral order continues to persist, "For everyone who does base things hates the light and does not come *towards* (πρός) the Light so that his/her deeds may be exposed." But, as 3:21 certifies, those who do the truth come *towards* (πρός) the Light "so that their works are manifested that they are accomplished in God." Doing the truth produces the empirical manifestation of the Light of the first day of creation and, therefore, discloses the reality of the moral order of the New Creation.

Nicodemus, a ruler of the Jews and a Pharisee who, as "the teacher of Israel" is representative of the post-70 fellowship of the Pharisees, initiated a dialogue with Jesus that ended in the monologue of verses 13-21. His nighttime visit with Jesus is concluded with an epitomization of the Gospel that preliminarily conveys to the implied readers the essence of the Good News that will be more fully disclosed

---

[53] See Chapter 17.

[54] Käsemann, *The Testament of Jesus*, 66-63, claims that the Fourth Gospel has given up on the notion of a restored creation. Because the earth no longer belongs to Christ, John's Christianity is "limited to the experience of the individual and of the group." The Gospel's relationship to the world is similar to that of gnosticism. "One is saved from the world through hearing and receiving the Word."

when the narrative reaches its culmination in the death and resurrection of Jesus . Yet even before the Gospel story ends, but in the light of this epitomization, the final verses of this episode, 3:20-21, pose the existential choice that confronts the implied readers: (1) to remain in the darkness by continuing to do evil and therefore already being judged because they remain in the old moral order, or (2) to come towards the light by doing the truth that the Son of the Human Being reveals through his descent, exaltation and ascent.

Chapter Seven

Romancing the Samaritan Woman 4:1-42

For a period of time in the narrative world of the Fourth Gospel, Jesus moves back and forth between Jerusalem and Galilee. After leaving Judea where his disciples had been engaged in baptizing (3:22), he is constrained by divine necessity to travel through Samaria, "It was necessary (ἔδει) that he pass through Samaria." The verb δεῖ (it is necessary) occurs ten times in the Gospel, and in every instance it conveys a sense of constraint, being obliged, being under contract. As the Son of the Human Being, Jesus is under constraint to be lifted up as a snake in the wilderness (3:14). There is a necessity that he increases and that John decreases (3:30). Jesus and his disciples are under contract to do the works of God (9:4). It would seem, therefore, that the necessity to journey through Samaria is not simply due to practicality. It may be the shortest route between Galilee and Jerusalem, and, as Josephus testifies, "It was the custom of the Galileans at the time of a festival to pass through the Samaritan territory on their way to the Holy City."[1] But as Josephus also discloses, hatred persisted between the Samaritans and the Jews;[2] and it may well have been sustained by the Jewish repudiation of the Samaritans as outsiders, people ostracized from God's covenant.[3]

Jesus, with a sense of divine necessity, deliberately passes through Samaria.[4] As the living Temple of God and therefore the bearer of the divine presence he will sanctify the land and its people. But that is not the urgency of his necessity. As will become evident, it will be nothing less than incorporating the Samaritans into the New Israel or the New Humanity that he is constituting.

He and his disciples stop for a rest at "a city of Samaria called Sychar." Although Sychar (Σύχαρ) is not mentioned in the Hebrew Scriptures, the narrator identifies it with a patriarchal event: "next to the piece of land that Jacob gave his son Joseph." In this reference to Gen 48:22, Jacob bestowed on Joseph, as the father of two sons, Ephraim and Manasseh, "one portion more than to your brothers." The Joseph tribes received a double allotment.[5] Like Shechem of the

---

[1] Josephus, *Ant* XX, 118.

[2] *Ibid.* Also XVIII, 30. See also Tacitus, *Annals of Imperial Rome* XII, 54.

[3] That is the perspective of 2 Kings 17:34-40. See also Sirach 50:25-26.

[4] Also Gail R. O'Day, *Revelation in the Fourth Gospel. Narrative Mode and Theological Claim* (Philadelphia: Fortress Press, 1986) 55-56. Pertinent especially is her view that the kind of necessity that is implied here, mundane or theological, cannot be determined until the complete text has been read.

[5] The Hebrew word for portion is שכם, and, as is generally noted, it is a play on the name Shechem, the city associated with the Jacob traditions in Gen 33:18 – 34:31. In the Septuagint translation of Gen 48:22 שכם is transliterated as Sikima. The manuscript variants of Σύχαρ (Sychar) in 4:5, namely Sicar

Old Testament, Sychar is associated with Jacob, the great patriarch of Israel **and** of the Samaritans, and with his son Joseph, the patriarch of the northern kingdom and, in the subsequent course of history, of the Samaritans. In view of this impressive ancient heritage, it should be no surprise that Jesus is under divine constraint to pass through Samaria. If, as 3:17 declared, "God did not send his Son into the world to judge the world, but that the world might be saved through him," there is a necessity to incorporate the Samaritans into God's New Israel.

This localization of Sychar as being "next to a piece of land that Jacob gave his son Joseph" is followed by the announcement of "a spring of Jacob." "Now the spring of Jacob was there." But there is no reference to a spring – or a well – of Jacob in the Hebrew Scriptures! Moreover, what actually exists at the very edge of the city of Shechem (or Nablus, as it is named today) is a well and not a spring; and, as the Samaritan woman stipulates, it is very deep!

It would be very natural for a well of Jacob to be located in or near Shechem. Many of the traditions of the great patriarch are associated with that city, as Gen 33:18 – 34:31 indicates. Yet there is no explicit reference to a well of Jacob in Shechem. There are, however, many traditions preserved in the Jewish folklore of the Targums and the midrashim that link Jacob to a traveling well. The stories recounting the miraculous provision of water throughout the Exodus journey engendered the inference that a well accompanied the Israelites through the wilderness. The "Song of the Well" of Num 21:16-18 ascribes the digging of the well to the leaders and nobles of the people, but Targum Neofiti 1 adds to Num 21: 18, "It is the well which the princes *of the world, Abraham, Isaac, and Jacob,* dug *from the beginning.*"[6] It was the old patriarchal well, restored and given to the Israelites as a gift through the spirit of Miriam.[7]

That well was especially related to the patriarch Jacob, as the Targums of Gen 28-29 indicate. The five miracles attributed to Jacob in Targums Neofiti I and Pseudo-Jonathan include the removal of the great stone from the mouth of the well in Haran and the overflowing of the water from the well throughout his sojourn in Haran and his courtship of Rachel.[8] Later traditions, such as the Midrash of Psalm

---

and Sucem, appear to be attempts to identify Σύχαρ with the Septuagint's Sikima, and Sucem, (the reading found in the Sinaitic Syriac and the Curetonian Syriac), with the Hebrew שכם. Both intimate an attempt to associate the place more precisely with that extra portion that Jacob gave Joseph. But the narrator has pinpointed the location of Sychar as "**next** to the piece of land," and in all likelihood that piece of land would be Shechem. Sychar, however, is definitely the more difficult of the three manuscript variants. Brown, *John* I, 169, contends that Sychar is a corruption of Shechem.

[6] Jerome H. Neyrey, "Jacob Traditions and the Interpretation of John 4:10-26," *CBQ* 41 (1979) 421-23, has drawn together many of these Targum and midrashic traditions. See especially *Targum Neofiti 1: Numbers*, trans. with Apparatus and Notes by Martin McNamara (Collegeville, Minnesota: Michael Glazier, 1995) 119.

[7] It is noteworthy that the Apostle Paul was familiar with this tradition of a traveling well, even though he refers to it as "the spiritual rock" of the Israelite journey through the wilderness. See 1 Cor 10:1-4.

[8] See *Targum Neofiti 1: Genesis*, trans. with Aparatus and Notes by Martin McNamara (Collegeville, Minnesota: Michael Glazier, 1992) 139-140. *Targum Pseudo-Jonathan: Genesis*, trans.

91 and the Pirque of Rabbi Eliezer associate Jacob with the tradition of the peripatetic well.

> Jacob was seventy years old when he went forth from his father's house, and the well went with him.[9]

> And then, leaving behind the well, the well that had hitherto traveled before him, he took one step and in the wink of an eye was in Haran.[10]

Whether or not the well accompanied Jacob to Haran, it appears to have followed or gone before him throughout his life. The well at Shechem, therefore, could only be Jacob's well.

The narrator, however, identifies this source of water as a spring, a πηγή. If in actuality it was a well, why replace it with a spring? If the original reader was familiar with the targumic tradition of the traveling well of Jacob, he or she would certainly be puzzled by this opening reference to a "spring of Jacob." What is the significance of "the spring of Jacob" in contrast to "the well of Jacob"?

Jesus, wearied from the journey, refreshes himself at the edge of the spring, while his disciples venture into the city to purchase food. The phrase, ἐκαθέζετο οὕτως ἐπὶ τῇ πηγῇ, (he sat down thus at the spring) in 4:6b is reminiscent of Moses' arrival in the land of Midian when he sat down at the well (ἐκάθισεν ἐπὶ τοῦ φρέατος) and, after rescuing the daughters of Jethro from the shepherds, watered their flock of sheep and goats and subsequently was given Zipporah, one of the seven daughters of Jethro, in marriage.[11] The patriarch Jacob had entered into a courtship with Rachel at the well of Laban in Haran where he performed two of the five mighty works that the Targums ascribe to him. Targum Pseudo-Jonathan of Gen 29:10 interpolates the following details into the original version of the biblical text:

> And when Jacob saw Rachel, the daughter of Laban, his mother's brother, Jacob drew near and *with one of his arms* rolled the stone from the mouth of the well; *and the well began to flow, and the waters came up before him*, and he watered the flock of Laban, his mother's brother; *and it continued to flow for twenty years*.

The Midrash of Psalm 91, commenting on v. 7 says:

> The angels bore up Jacob, as is said *Angels ... shall bear thee up in their hands* (Ps 91:11-12). And the steps of Jacob were not shortened and his strength was not subdued, and mighty man that he was, he rolled the stone away from the well's mouth, and the well gushed up, the water brimming

---

with Introduction and Notes by Michael Maher (Collegeville, Minnesota: Michael Glazier, 1992) 99. For a discussion of the dating problems of these Targums, see Philip S. Alexander, "Targum, Targumim," *ABD*, ed. by D.N. Freedman (New York: Doubleday, 1992) 6, 320-331.

[9] *Pirque of Rabbi Eliezer* 35, cited by Neyrey, "Jacob Traditions, " 422.

[10] Midrash of Psalm 91:7 in *The Midrash on Psalms*, trans. from the Hebrew and Aramaic by William G. Braude (New Haven: Yale University Press, 1959) 106.

[11] Ex 2:15-21.

> over. The herdsmen looked and were astonished that Jacob had rolled the stone away by himself since all of them together could not roll away the stone ...[12]

Both of these "betrothal type-scenes, that of Moses and that of Jacob, appear to have contributed to the construction of Jesus' courtship of the Samaritan woman.[13]

Jesus, like Moses, is resting beside the spring, when a Samaritan woman approaches to draw water. The anticipation of the reader, on the basis of intertextual associations, would be a betrothal.[14] This expectation is reinforced by the preceding account of John's appropriation of the metaphor of marriage to distinguish between himself and Jesus in 3:29.

> The one having the bride is the bridegroom. But the friend of the bridegroom who is standing and hearing him rejoices with joy because of the voice of the bridegroom. Therefore, this my joy has been fulfilled.

John's divinely appointed activity of bearing witness to Jesus as the incarnation of the Word has been fulfilled. Accordingly, as "the friend of the bridegroom," he must decrease. Jesus, on the other hand, will enact the role of the bridegroom and romance the Jews into a new relationship with God. He has already signaled that intention by his first sign at the wedding at Cana, transforming 162 gallons of water into a vintage that is superior to any that Israel may have enjoyed throughout her past history. By substituting his physical body in place of the sanctuary on the Temple mount and thereby becoming "the Father's House," he has begun to constitute the corporate body of the Son of the Human Being on whom the angels of God ascend and descend. In his dialogue with Nicodemus, "a leader of the Jews," he has disclosed the right of entry into the eschatological reality of God's rule that will enable Israel to recover her divinely ordained sovereignty and its attendant empowerment.

> Amen, Amen I say to you, unless one is born from water and Spirit, one cannot enter into the rule of God. (3:5)

Now a Samaritan woman must be romanced by this bridegroom so that she too will enter into this new marriage relationship with God, a relationship that Hosea had prophesied to the ancestors of the Samaritans.

---

[12] Braude, *The Midrash on Psalms*, 106.

[13] See also the betrothal story of Gen 24:10-49. The common features of these stories are notable: (1) a man is traveling in a foreign land; (2) he goes to a well; (3) there he meets one or more women; (4) water is offered; (5) the woman or women return home to announce the stranger; (6) the man is invited to stay; (7) a betrothal takes place. Also Schneiders, *Written That You May Believe*, 135. See Paul D. Duke, *Irony in the Fourth Gospel*, 101.

[14] Lyle Eslinger, "The Wooing of the Woman at the Well: Jesus, the Reader and Reader-Response Criticism," *JLT* 1 (2) 1987, 168-169. J.E. Botha, "Reader 'Entrapment' and Literary Device in John 4:1-42," *Neot* 24 (1) 1990, 40-41; see also J. E. Botha, *Jesus and the Samaritan Woman: A Speech Act Reading of John 4:1-42* (Leiden: Brill, 1991) 96-187. Sandra M. Schneiders, "A Feminist Interpretation of John 4:1-42," *The Revelatory Text. Interpreting the New Testament as Sacred Scripture* (San Francisco: Harper, 1991) 187.

> On account of this, see, I will deceive her and I will draw her into a wilderness and I will speak to her heart, and I will give to her fields there and the deep valley of Achor to open her understanding, and she will be humbled there according to the days of her childlike innocence and according to the days of her going up out of Egypt. And it will be on that day, says the Lord, she will call me, "O my husband," and she will no longer call me Baal. (LXX Hos 2:16-18)[15]

The scene that unfolds, however, is troublesome and disconcerting. It does not correspond fittingly to the betrothal stories of Ex 2:15-22 and Gen 29. The stated time is the sixth hour, that is, high noon, Uncharacteristically the woman has come to the spring in the heat of the day, and she is alone, unaccompanied by other women. In ancient Middle East culture, as Gen 24:11 indicates, the daily task of obtaining water was discharged by congenial socializing women engaged in noisy but happy conversation as they made their way to a nearby spring or well in the coolness of early morning and evening. Accordingly, from the very beginning the anticipation that the type-scene of betrothal has evoked is distorted.

Why has this Samaritan woman come alone? Undoubtedly she has chosen to draw water in the middle of the day in order to be alone. Is she alienated from her fellow Samaritans? Is it possible that the movement of this betrothal type-scene is intended to parallel the story of Gomer, who after an adulterous affair, signifying Israel's idolatry, was redeemed by Hosea and restored to her former covenantal relationship to him in marriage? Is she perhaps, like Gomer, a representative figure of her people? How is the personage of this unnamed Samaritan woman to be construed?[16] To what extent is she to be regarded as an individual, and to what extent is she a personification of her people, the Samaritans? Nicodemus, "a ruler of the Jews," is representative of the ruling elite, the Pharisees, who are engaged in legislating Jewish society after 70. Yet by being identified by name as Nicodemus, it is natural for the reader to relate to him as an individual. In contrast, the Samaritan woman who remains unnamed may be intended to play a representative role in the story of John 4. Jesus enters into a courtship with her as an individual, and as an individual she will eventually enter into a collaboration with Jesus. But at the same time her past history that Jesus uncovers in verse 18 enlarges her into a personification of the Samaritan people.[17] Accordingly, she is also to be identified as Lady Samaria!

In spite of the past history of alienation between the Jews and the Samaritans, Jesus initiates the courtship by asking her for a drink. It is, as David Daube

---

[15] The Hebrew text of this passage is Hos 2:14-16. A translation of the Septuagint is offered here because the Fourth Gospel reflects its use, and, in all likelihood, it was the Bible of the Jews in Alexandria, Egypt.

[16] In the context of these questions it is beneficent to read Schneiders' "Feminist Critical Hermeneutics," *Written That You May Believe*, 126-134.

[17] So also Schneiders, *Revelatory Text*, 189.

perceived, an act of kindness.[18] Throughout his dialogue with the Samaritan woman Jesus is gentle and courteous. Nicodemus had been rebuked for his lack of understanding; the Samaritan woman is "treated almost with deference."[19] Jesus' apparent lack of propriety surprises her and she suspiciously questions his motives, "How is it that you being a *Jewish male* ask me, a *Samaritan woman*, for a drink?" Her apprehensive response conveys the colliding social realities of race and gender, and it is reinforced by the narrator's intrusive remark, "For Jews do not *use together* with Samaritans." Implied in this aside is the mutuality of sharing vessels, such as the cup or jug from which Jesus would drink the water that he wants from the woman.[20] Jews do not use vessels together with Samaritans because, according to the Mishnah tractate, *Niddah* 4:1, "Samaritan women are deemed menstruants from their cradle."[21] According to rabbinic tradition, Samaritan women are stereotyped as being permanently polluted or unclean, and therefore any and every contact with them is proscribed in order to avoid defilement. It is that prohibition that the Samaritan woman is alluding to in her response to Jesus' demand for a drink.[22] At this moment it would seem that the implied readers must concur with her critical reply.[23]

Jesus ignores her criticism even as he has ignored the rabbinic regulation. He shifts abruptly from his to her need and transposes himself into the dispenser of water. To the reader this is an electrifying moment of ironic reversal. Jesus, wearied from his journey and denied water with a rebuke, startles the woman with a conditional offer. "If you knew the gift of God and who it is that is saying to you, 'Give me a drink,' you would ask him and he would give you living water." Shamelessly he confronts her with her ignorance. She is oblivious to the gift of God, and she does not know who he is. If she had any inkling of these actualities, she would be petitioning him and he would grant her living water.

But what is "living water?" To the reader it might refer to the running water of the spring, the πηγή, at which Jesus has seated himself. The woman, however, construes it as a reference to what she has come to draw; and in her ironic misunderstanding she sarcastically observes that he does not have a vessel by which to obtain it.

---

[18] David Daube, "Jesus and the Samaritan Woman: the Meaning of συγχράομαι," *JBL* 69 (1950) 137.

[19] Laurence Cantwell, "Immortal Longings in Sermone Humili: A Study of John 4:5-26," *SJT* 36 (1983) 81.

[20] Daube, "Jesus and the Samaritan Woman," 144, has recovered the original meaning of συγχράομαι in 4:9 and therefore the original point of the encounter between Jesus and the Samaritan woman.

[21] Cited by Daube, *ibid*. See Jacob Neusner, *The Mishnah. A New Translation*, 1082.

[22] Daube, "Jesus and the Samaritan Woman," dates the proscription of *Niddah* 4:1 around 65 C.E., but offers evidence that the view was prevalent long before that time.

[23] J.E. Botha, "Reader 'Entrapment,'" 41.

> Lord, on the one hand, you have no bucket and [on the other hand] the well is deep. From where do you have living water? Surely you aren't greater than our father Jacob who gave us the well, are you? And he himself drank from it and his sons and his cattle. (4:11-12)

For the Samaritan woman the source of water from which she came to draw is a well. The word she employs in verse 11 is φρέαρ. Jesus' words appear to have confused her. For after jumping to the conclusion that he is referring to the water in the well, she quickly realizes that he must be referring to another source of water, since he does not have a bucket and the well is deep. "From where do you have living water," she asks.[24] "Surely you're not greater than our father Jacob who gave us this well, are you?"

What is it that elevates the patriarch to greatness in her mind? Is it to be presupposed that she is familiar with the five mighty works that the Targums attribute to Jacob, all of them related to his flight from Beersheba to Haran?

> "The *first miracle*: the hours of the day were shortened and the sun set before the time; the *second miracle*: the four stones which Jacob placed under his head-pillow became one stone; the *third miracle*: the earth shrank before Jacob and he was suddenly in Haran; the *fourth miracle*: the stone that the shepherds could not roll away from the mouth of the well Jacob moved with one had; the *fifth miracle*: the well overflowed and was overflowing for twenty years – all the days that he dwelt in Haran.[25]

There is nothing comparable to these mighty works in the biblical traditions of Jacob. Since there is no scriptural reference that links Jacob, his sons, and his cattle to a well, except the well of Gen 29, the Samaritan woman must be familiar with the miracles of Jacob, at least the two that were performed at the well of Laban in Haran. If Jesus does not have a bucket and the well is deep, he could only provide living water by causing the water to rise to the surface and overflow the well. This, of course, could hardly make him greater than Jacob. But the woman's question is rhetorical and implies a negative answer; and yet at the same time it introduces the possibility that Jesus may indeed be greater than Jacob.

Is the differentiation between a spring and a well of any consequence for the story? At the beginning the narrator stated that Jesus had seated himself "at the πηγῇ τοῦ 'Ιακώβ" (the spring of Jacob). Commentators may note the difference between a well and a spring, but the significance of the difference between them is either ignored or dismissed. There are precedents for this in the Old Testament. In LXX Gen 16:7 the angel of the Lord finds Hagar seated at *a spring* (πηγή) in the wilderness; in LXX Gen 21:19 Hagar is in the wilderness again, after Abraham had been compelled to drive her away, and the angel of God opens her eyes to see *a*

[24] Jesus' identity and its eventual disclosure are climactic in this story, but its function is not simply revelatory. The woman's question, "From where do you have living water?" does not necessarily imply the issue of Jesus' identity, as Gail O'Day contends, *Revelation*, 60-62.

[25] See *Targun Neofiti* I, 139-140; *Targum Pseudo-Jonathan*, 99-101, *Midrash on Psalm* 91:7, 106.

well of living water (φρέαρ ὕδατος ζῶντος). The two words πηγή and φρέαρ appear be used interchangeably. Both are also employed interchangeably in the betrothal story of LXX Gen 24.[26] But in this courtship the differentiation is deliberate and therefore also theologically significant.

Jesus has conditionally promised the Samaritan woman *living water* (ὕδωρ ζῶν). The immediate referent would seem to be the running water of the spring, not the stagnant water of the well. Intertextually the referent of Jer 2:13 would naturally suggest itself to the reader, even as Philo called it to mind in his exposition of the betrothal story of Gen 24.

> Because my people committed two evils. They abandoned me, the spring of living water (πηγὴν ὕδατος ζωῆς) and they dug broken cisterns (λάκκους) for themselves, which are not able to hold water. (Jer 2:13)

Jeremiah is referencing " the spring of living water" metaphorically and therefore also theologically to Yahweh, or, according to the Septuagint, the "Lord" (κύριος). Jesus' promise of "living water" in verse 10 and subsequently of "a spring of water that leaps up into life everlasting" in verse 14 echoes Jer 2:13 and metaphorically refers to the very same reality. Philo of Alexandria, in the context of his allegorical interpretation of the romancing of Rebecca in Gen 24, cites Jer 2:13 and characterizes God as *the spring of life* (πηγὴ τοῦ ζῆν).[27] But, as "the spring of life," God is only the cause of the qualitative life that issues from him, especially in terms of "the deep sources of knowledge from which draughts of reason are drawn."[28] Jesus, however, offers more than Philo. The "living water," that he will give is an indwelling resource that is identifiable with the Spirit of God.[29] He will speak of "living water" again on the last day of the Festival of Booths (7:37-38):

> If any one thirsts, let her/him come to me and drink. The one who believes into me, even as the Scripture said, rivers of living water will flow out of his belly.

And the narrator's aside informs the reader of the referent of "living water":

> He said this about the Spirit, which the ones believing into him were going to receive. For the Spirit was not yet given because Jesus was not yet glorified.

The "living water" that Jesus offers the Samaritan woman is the Spirit of God.

In geographical actuality this source of water at Sychar is a well. It is called, "the well of Jacob." But in this story "the well" like "the spring" is used

[26] See LXX Gen 24:11, 13, 16, 20. In LXX Gen 29:2, 10 only φρέαρ is used; in LXX Ex 2:15 there is only a single occurrence of φρέαρ.

[27] Philo, *de Fuga*, 198.

[28] *Ibid*., 200.

[29] Also Brown, *John* 1, 171.

metaphorically. Indeed, its juxtaposition to the "spring" constitutes a binary opposition:

πηγὴ τοῦ Ἰακώβ	spring of Jacob
φρέαρ τοῦ Ἰακώβ	well of Jacob

Metaphorically the "spring of Jacob" at which Jesus has seated himself, "the spring of Jacob" from which "living water" flows, represents the revelation of God that the grand patriarch experienced, embraced and handed down. It is the revelation that God's Spirit imparts. It is the revelation through which God's Spirit operates and communicates "living water."

By continuing to come to "the well of Jacob," the Samaritan woman reinforces her identification with the great patriarch and his tradition. Ironically, however, as significant as that tradition may be for the preservation of her ethnic identity and religious self-worth, it is a desperate will to meaning that is existentially futile. The "well of Jacob" epitomizes what the "spring of Jacob" has become, a stagnant pool of tradition from which water may still be drawn, but which can no longer quench thirst and therefore is no longer able to impart divine life. Nevertheless, the Samaritan woman continues to come to draw up its water. For it is still the heritage of the great patriarch Jacob; and it united him, his sons – including Joseph, the progenitor of the Northern Kingdom and the Samaritans - and even his cattle, as a family under God's reign. In spite of the persistent hostility between the two communities, it is the common heritage of both the Samaritans and the Jews, and therefore also of Jesus and the woman.

Yet, as Jesus points out to her, "Everyone who drinks of this water shall thirst again." The well of Jacob may satisfy thirst temporarily, but its stagnant water has lost its life-giving vitality and empowerment. The "living water" Jesus offers will no longer be drawn from an external spring. It will not be an extension or a modification of that dynamic revelatory tradition that "the spring of Jacob" represents, but whose life-giving potentiality naturally diminishes into "the well of Jacob" in the course of time.

> …but the water that I *will* give her/him will become in him/her a spring (πηγή) leaping up into life everlasting. (4:14)

The "living water" which Jesus promises the Samaritan woman is an internal source of renewal and refreshment that *will become a spring* that bubbles up into life eternal. That living water that becomes a spring is the Spirit of God, who, according to the narrator's subsequent interpretation of Jesus' outcry in 7:37-38, had not yet been given because Jesus had not yet been glorified.[30] The Samaritan woman will have that spring within her, and therefore she will have immediate access to it wherever she goes. As a bearer of the Spirit, she will be like Jesus

[30] According to Philo, *de Specialibus Legibus* I, 303, God is "the perennial fountain of good things"; in *de Fuga,* 197-198, God is "the eldest spring," "the spring of life"; and "God is more than life, the spring in order to live."

who, by replacing the sanctuary of the Temple with his own body, has become "the Father's House" and the residence of the Spirit.

Jesus' romancing of this woman appears to succeed, for she responds favorably to his offer, "Lord, give me this water, so that I don't thirst again nor come here to draw." Initially she came to draw water from "the well of Jacob," but she has been diverted from her objective. Ironically she requests water from Jesus, knowing that he has no bucket and therefore also knowing that the "deep well" cannot be the source from which he will draw that water for her. Although she still does not know who Jesus is, the gift he has promised is too seductive to resist. How he will procure that "living water" she does not know. He has offered it to her as a promise, "… the water I *shall give* …" Since he surprised her by transgressing the Jewish prohibition of avoiding contact with a Samaritan woman, she is ready to move with him. She wants this "living water;" and the reasons she gives for it, "so that I don't thirst again nor come here to draw," should not be construed as a perpetuation of her misunderstanding.[31] As for the implied readers, they must also be moving with Jesus, but more likely because of the intertextual referents of ὕδωρ ζῶν (living water) in Jer 2:13 and possibly the writings of Philo of Alexandria.

The Samaritan woman recognizes the incredible benefits of Jesus' gift. She will never thirst again, and she will never have to return to "the well of Jacob." But as yet she does not know how or when Jesus will fulfill his promise. Evidently, however, she has interpreted Jesus' offer to be immediately applicable to her as she is – without any necessity of change on her part. She has come alone, and she appears to think that she can continue in her self-imposed isolation, but now with this incredible gift of an indwelling source of "living water." But she must be redeemed from her self-imposed isolation before she can receive the gift of "living water" that will become in her a spring leaping up into life eternal.

At this point, as all commentators recognize, an abrupt transition occurs in the movement of the dialogue between Jesus and the woman. Startlingly, Jesus commands her, "Go, call your husband and come here." This shift, as inexplicable as it may appear, must somehow express Jesus' efforts to continue to romance this Samaritan woman by confronting her with the estrangement she has manifested in coming to the well alone. Implicated in her alienated condition may be her religious infidelity as a Samaritan. Jesus' striving with her is comparable to the prophet Hosea's endeavor to lure her ancestors, the Northern Kingdom of Israel, into a renewed covenantal relationship with Yahweh.

Ironically, as Gail O'Day has discerned, the woman, who covets this "living water" so that she will never have to come back to the well of Jacob, is being

[31] As, for example: Bultmann, *John*, 187; Haenchen, *John*, 230; Barrett, *John*, 235; O'Day, *Revelation*, 64; Hendrikus Boers, *Neither on this Mountain nor in Jerusalem: A Study of John 4* (Atlanta: Scholars Press, 1988) 163. Boers' interpretation is determined by a semantic investigation of John 4 that begins at the deepest level with the polarities of the micro-universe that the author shared with his culture and ends with the themes embodied by the characters of the story at the surface level.

placed under obligation to return.[32] Her reply, "I don't have a husband!" enables her to escape that necessity. It is "a masterful example of ironic understatement." Jesus readily acknowledges the truth of her response but proceeds to confront her with the undisclosed truth of her life in "an ironic overstatement:"[33]

> You said correctly, "I don't have a husband." For you had five husbands and the one you now have is not your husband. (4:17-18)

On the surface level Jesus' revelation underlines her fragmented and estranged history. The fact that she has had five husbands and that the one she is presently living with is not her husband does not necessarily imply that she should be characterized as a "prostitute," or "a five-time loser." To the Jews, who under rabbinic legislation were limited to two, possibly three marriages, her history would be viewed as a scandal.[34] But nothing at all is said about the circumstances of those relationships. No details are offered as to whether her five husbands died one after another, whether she was divorced five times, and why, in view of five previous marriages, she continues to want an intimate relationship. It is enough for the implied readers– and for the reader of today! – that she is portrayed as a broken and isolated woman.[35]

But Jesus' "ironic overstatement" is principally metaphorical and alludes to her past history in her personification of the Samaritans. While the identification of the referents of her five husbands is difficult to ascertain, the symbolic character of the number five should not be discounted. The *Midrash Rabbah* of Genesis 28 bears witness to the rabbinic predilection to interpret symbolically the well from which Jacob rolled away the stone and the three flocks of sheep that Jacob encountered at the well.[36] Two historical referents of the identity of the five husbands and the paramour are usually cited.[37] Origen, in his commentary on the Fourth Gospel, allegorized the five husbands as the five books of Moses. Since the

---

[32] O'Day, *Revelation*, 66.

[33] Both quotations of "ironic understatement" and "ironic overstatement" are drawn from O'Day, *ibid.* See also Duke, *Irony in the Fourth Gospel*, 102-103, who characterizes this moment as "situational irony par excellence." Without any explicit reference to Hosea, Duke comes close to describing this woman as a type of Gomer, who, in the prophecy of Hosea, is a type of the Northern Kingdom of Israel.

[34] Strack-Billerbeck, *Kommentar zum Neuen Testament aus Talmud und Midrash*, II, 437.

[35] This is Laurence Cantwell's conclusion, and, from the viewpoint of today's reader, it is quite correct. See "A Study of John 4:5-26," 73-86, esp. 79-80.

[36] *Midrash Rabbah: Genesis*, trans. by H. Freedman (London: Soncino Press, 1951) II, 641-643.

[37] Bultmann, *John*, 188, rejects all allegorical interpretations and declines to speculate about the significance of the number five. Barrett, *John*, 35, prefers to take Jesus' words in 4:18 as a simple fact and "an instance of the supernatural knowledge of Jesus." Haenchen, *John* I, 230, ignores the matter completely. Schnackenburg, *The Gospel according to St. John,* trans. by Kevin Smyth (New York: Herder & Herder, 1968) I, 433, dismisses all symbolic meanings as misleading. O'Day, *Revelation*, 66-67, does not explore any of these possibilities. Cantwell, "Immortal Longings," poses the possibility of 2 Kings 17:29-34 but prefers to view the woman as a representation of all humanity and not merely the Samaritan people. H. Boers, *Neither on this Mountain nor in Jerusalem*, 171, maintains that the figure five is of no significance except "to reveal Jesus' miraculous knowledge."

Samaritan Bible encompasses only the Pentateuch, the five husbands to whom the Samaritan woman, as the personification of the Samaritan nation, was married symbolize the five Books of Moses. In his interpretation of 4:18, Origen comments, ἀνακτέον ἐπὶ τὰ πέντε Μωυσέως βιβλία. Μόνα γὰρ ταῦτα οἱ Σαμαρεῖται δέχονται (One must refer to the five books of Moses. For only these the Samaritans receive.)[38]

A more convincing interpretation, however, is based on 2 Kings 17:24-41. The five husbands could be identified with the five cults that the foreigners from Babylon, Cuthah, Avva, Hamath, and Sepharvaim syncretistically established when they were settled in the conquered land of the Northern Kingdom by the Assyrian king, Sargon. But the correspondence is disputed because seven gods, not five, are named in 2 Kings 17:30-31. Although the counting is problematic, Josephus is probably correct in his retelling of 2 Kings 17: 24-41 that, "… each of their tribes – there were five – brought along its own god, and, as they reverenced them in accordance with the custom of their country, they provoked the Most High God to anger and wrath."[39] If this is the intended referent of the five husbands, it could be the reckoning of Josephus that is used here.[40]

The present paramour of the Samaritan woman is equally problematic. A plausible possibility is that it is an allusion to the worship of the God of Israel super-imposed on the five pagan cults, as 2 Kings 17:32-41 testifies.[41] The concluding indictment of the deuteronomistic historian would naturally be construed by first century readers to be valid into their own time.

> So these nations worshiped Yahweh, but they also served their carved images; to this day their children and their children's children continue to do as their ancestors did. (2 Kings 17:41)

Her illicit partner has also been identified as her involvement with the heresy of Simon Magus, the Samaritan, who appears in Acts 8:9-24 as a contemporary of the apostles. He practiced magic in Samaria and deified himself as "the power of God that is called Great." Irenaeus expands the story of his career by elaborating on his self-representation as "the loftiest of all powers, the Being who is the Father over all," and his Christ-like descent from heaven to deliver the world from the evil of the powers and principalities.[42] According to the Pseudo-Clementines, Simon

---

[38] A. E. Brooke, *The Commentary of Origen on S. John's Gospel*; The Text Revised with a Critical Introduction and Indices (Cambridge: at the University Press, 1896) II, 271. Brown, *John* I, 171, cites Origen, *In Johannem* 13.8 (GCS 10.232).

[39] Josephus, *Ant* IX, 288. Since some of these gods were female, they probably were associated and worshiped with a particular male deity.

[40] Craig R. Koester, "The Savior of the World" (John 4:42), *JBL* 109/4 (1990) 676 conjectures that Jesus' reference to the woman's former five husbands may have been intended to recall Samaria's colonial past and that "'the one whom you have *now*' might refer to the current colonial power – Rome – not to the God of Israel, as many interpreters have suggested."

[41] Hoskyns/Davey, *The Fourth Gospel*, 242-243.

[42] Irenaeus, *Against Heresies* I, 23.

supposedly derived his gnostic orientation and aptitude from Alexandria.[43] In the early centuries of the Christian movement he was regarded as the wellspring of heresy.

All of these figurative identifications are problematic if they are related to the Samaritan woman in her individuality. That would require that she had her five husbands and her paramour consecutively one after another. Instead, however, it must be her corporate identity as Lady Samaria that comes into focus here because both sets of the metaphorical referents, the five Books of Moses and the five syncretistic cults of 2 Kings 17, require that she was living with the five husbands at the same time.[44] And Jesus' disclosure is intended to be censorious of the totality of her syncretistic religious relationships in her symbolic personification of the Samaritan people, not merely her present partner. That would exclude the allegorization of her five husbands as the canon of the Samaritan Scriptures, the five books of Moses, for they could not typify any kind of religious infidelity. Consequently, Origen's allegorization of the five husbands is untenable. But it would include the five syncretistic cults and the contaminated worship of Yahweh that has continued into the present.[45] Hosea had denounced the adulterous idolatry of the ancestors of the Samaritans. By reproaching the Samaritan woman for her five husbands and her present paramour, Jesus is censuring the Samaritan religion. Indeed, his employment of the perfect tense of the verb, εἴρηκας (you have said), after a series of aorist verbs in verse 17, intimates that what she has said continues to be true into the time of the Fourth Gospel.[46] A few moments later he will reinforce his rebuke with the discriminating judgment, "You worship that which you do not know; we worship that which we know because salvation is from the Jews." Jesus' use of the perfect tense of εἴρηκας in the previous verse, implies that its validity is intended to persist into the context of the Fourth Gospel.

His ironic exposure of her history and its insinuation of a pervasive religious infidelity induce her to identify him as a prophet.

> Lord, I perceive that you are a prophet. Our ancestors worshiped on this mountain; and you say that Jerusalem is the place where it is necessary to worship. (4:20)

---

[43] Walter Bauer, *Rechtgläubigkeit und Ketzerei im Ältesten Christentum*, 53, n.3. See especially the chapter on Simon in Hans Jonas, *The Gnostic Religion: The Message of the Alien God and the Beginnings of Christianity* (Boston: Beacon Press, 1958) 103-111. Jonas acknowledges that the Simon of Acts 8 may not be the same person that Irenaeus is talking about.

[44] L. Cantwell, "A Study of John 4.5-26," 78, rejects the Samaritan woman's representation of "Samaritanism." He regards her to be a more universal type, "who reveals an aspect or facet of everyone who has ever read her story." But that is precisely the genius of the story: to represent the Samaritans and simultaneously to be universally representative of all readers.

[45] Also Schneiders, *Written That You May Believe*, 140.

[46] My thanks to Robert B. Coote for calling my attention to this shift in verb tenses from verse 17 to 18. It is noteworthy that P^{75} substituted the aorist, εἶπας (you said) in place of εἴρηκας (you have said), but the latter is the more difficult reading.

The potential gift of "living water" is momentarily forgotten. Confronted with the truth of her past by a singular Jew who has not observed the rabbinic purity code, she defends herself and her religion by placing herself in the continuity to her ancestors: "Our fathers worshiped at this mountain." As a Samaritan she has been faithful to the traditions of the Samaritan patriarchs. At the same time she is aware that this prophet, who has confronted her with the infidelity and idolatry of the Samaritan people, represents a very different religious perspective: "You (ὑμεῖς) [Jews] say that in Jerusalem is the place where it is necessary to worship." She is very aware of this historical age-old conflict of the true architectonic center for the worship of God.[47] But in spite of their history of adulterous spirituality, she and her fellow Samaritans have remained unswervingly loyal to the *axis mundi* of Mount Gerezim that, like the Temple mount in Jerusalem, has united heaven and earth for them as the place of God's presence.

Jesus' response to this age-old controversy of the true architectonic center of God's presence that she has intimated conveys the paradigm shift that he constituted in Jerusalem at the first Passover in the narrative world of the Gospel when he substituted his own body in place of the sanctuary of the Temple. As the new, living Temple of God he invalidates all architectonic centers: "Neither on this mountain nor in Jerusalem!"[48] There will be no more geographical centers where God's presence is confined to a fixed location. But this annulment will not become effective until his death and resurrection have occurred.

> Keep believing me, woman, for the hour is coming when neither on this mountain nor in Jerusalem will you (plural) worship the Father. You (plural) worship that which you (plural) do not know. We worship what we know, because salvation is from the Jews. (4:21-22)

Mount Gerezim at Shechem, the Temple in Jerusalem, and all temples and sacred mountains will be canceled. Geographical location will not determine where and by whom God is to be worshiped. God's presence will no longer be limited to the sacred space and time of architectonic centers. It will be experienced wherever heaven and earth are united in the corporate reality of the New Humanity. As Jesus declared to Nathanael in 1:51, "You will see heaven opened and the angels of God ascending and descending on the Son of the Human Being." The ladder that Jacob saw in his dream, the ladder that unites heaven and earth, will rest on Jesus as the incarnate Logos and all those who commit themselves to him to fulfill God's mandate to constitute a world wide, all-inclusive living Temple of God. For the Samaritan woman and for her fellow Samaritans – since Jesus has employed

[47] On "sacred mountains," temples, and the symbolism of the "Center," see Mircea Eliade, *Cosmos and History. The Myth of the Eternal Return* (New York: Harper Torchbooks, 1959) 12-21. Also *The Sacred and the Profane. The Nature of Religion* (New York: Harper Torchbooks, 1961) 20-50.

[48] According to the *Midrash on Psalm* 91:7, "From the words of Gen 28:17 the Rabbis inferred that when a man prays in Jerusalem, it is as though he prays before the throne of glory, for the gate in heaven is in Jerusalem, and a door is always open for the hearing of prayer, as is said *This is the gate of heaven*." See Braude, *The Midrash on Psalms* II, 105.

the second person plural – and indeed for all humankind, the origin of this salvation, as he insists, is indeed from the Jews! Verse 22b, perhaps an aside added to the voice of Jesus by the narrator, must not be dismissed as a gloss or a later interpolation. It is a centerpiece of the Fourth Gospel that affirms its paramount truth: Salvation is *from* – (ἐκ) in an originating sense – the Jews.[49] God's only one-of-a-kind Son, upon whom the Spirit descended and remained and into whom the Spirit breathed the Logos, the image and likeness of God, is Jesus the Jew, the son of Joseph from Nazareth. And he serves as God's surrogate to confirm to all of humankind that "God so loved the world – the social construction of reality and all the human beings who live in it and participate in it – that he gave his only one-of-a-kind Son, so that everyone who believes into him, should not perish but have everlasting Life." In spite of any anti-Judaic texts that are encountered in the Gospel, such as 8:44, the Gospel is contending for a vision that is believed to fulfill the will of God as it has been expressed in the Hebrew Scriptures, that is, nothing less than the transformation of the world and those who inhabit it.[50]

But the potentiality of the true worship of God is already a present reality. For the Spirit, as Jesus had said to Nicodemus, blows where it wishes. Accordingly, here and now in the context of this encounter between Jesus and the Samaritan woman - and not only in the future beyond the time of Jesus death and resurrection - God can be worshiped in spirit and in truth.

> But the hour is coming and now is when the true worshipers will worship the Father in spirit and in truth. For the Father seeks such worshipers to worship him. God is Spirit and it is necessary that those worshiping him worship him in spirit and truth. (4:23)

God must be worshiped by human beings in accordance with God's transactions with human beings, namely: creation, recreation, revelation, inspiration, and empowerment. All of these operations and their effects are engendered by the Spirit as the life-giving Breath of God. Jesus will characterize this work to his disciples in 6:63: "The Spirit is the one who makes alive." But not simply physically alive, as when God breathed in Adam's nostrils the breath of life! God, as the creative, life-giving Spirit, empowers human beings to enter into the fullness of life by enabling them to live by faith, without the circumscribed boundaries that the architectonic centers of temples and temple mounts impose. Accordingly, the worship that human beings offer must arise out of a relationship with God's Spirit.

[49] Fortna, *The Fourth Gospel*, 263, rightly does not include 4:22b as part of the 'Gospel of Signs'. He follows Bultmann, however, in symbolically identifying "the Jews" with "the world." That relationship can be universalized homiletically, but within the narrative world of the Gospel "the Jews" and "the world" are associated in the second level of the first edition of the Gospel, the Jewish community of Alexandria.

[50] See Gilbert Van Belle, "Salvation is from the Jews": The Parenthesis in John 4:22b," *Anti-Judaism and the Fourth Gospel*, 370-400, for a sterling defense of the authenticity of 4:22b against Bultmann, Odeberg and others. For a list of the commentators who support the originality of 4:22b and those who reject it as the work of redactor or glossator, see his collation on pages 374-376.

It must be a worship of integrity that originates from the interaction between the inspiration of God's Spirit and the authentic self of the human being. This kind of worship is already possible for the Samaritan woman because, as Jesus said, "The hour is coming and *now is*..." Both the future and the present time that Jesus stipulates are true! Confronted with her religious infidelity as the personification of the Samaritan people, she can now choose to become a true worshiper of God; and when the hour finally arrives and the Spirit is given, she, will be able to fulfill the divine constraint to worship God in spirit and truth. In as far as she represents the Samaritans among the implied readers of the Jewish community of Alexandria the hour "*now is*."

Jesus' prophetic pronouncement elicits the Samaritan woman's eschatologically oriented faith perspective: "I know that Messiah is coming, the one called Christ; when he comes, he will announce all things to us." The new order of reality that Jesus has disclosed corresponds to her Samaritan expectations. Although she employs the Jewish designation "Messiah" – which the narrator translates into the Greek "Christ," – she is probably referring to the Samaritan eschatological anticipation of a "Ta'eb," the one who returns.[51] This would be a prophetic figure like Moses, arising from the tribe of Levi, who would fulfill Deut 18:15 and reconstitute the true cultic worship of God.

Commentators generally conclude that the woman remains unaware of who is speaking to her. For example, Gail O'Day says, "Not only has the Samaritan woman missed the significance of Jesus' words about the eschatological hour, she also does not realize that the person *of* whom she speaks is the person *with* whom she speaks."[52] But in fact she has begun to suspect that Jesus might be that Ta'eb or Messiah. There is no other reason for her to introduce her Samaritan christology at this point in their dialogue, "I know that Messiah *is coming*..." Her intuition has begun to grasp the paradoxical eschatology of his pronouncement, "But the hour *is coming* and now is..." Moreover, what she has been hearing from Jesus corresponds to her conception of the awaited Messiah, "Whenever he (Messiah) comes, he will explain all things to us."

As Hendrikus Boers has recognized, "All that is still needed is the sanction that 'the hour which is coming' is already present."[53] Jesus acknowledges that by confirming her intuition, **I AM, the one speaking to you** (ἐγώ εἰμι, ὁ λαλῶν σοι)[54] His confirmation, however, is not simply an affirmation of the identity that

---

[51] Schnackenburg, *St. John* I, 441. Also John Macdonald, *The Theology of the Samaritans* (Philadelphia: Westminster, 1964) 362-371. The absence of a definite article in front of the word "Messiah" has evoked the conjecture that the source from which the story was drawn read, "Ta'eb, the so-called (by you Jews) Messiah." See Bultmann, *John*, 192, n. 2.

[52] O'Day, *Revelation*, 72.

[53] Boers, *Neither on this Mountain nor in Jerusalem*, 180. But the hour that "*now is*," would be immediately relevant to the Samaritans among the implied readers.

[54] Schneiders, *The Revelatory Text*, 189, seems to be the only commentator who recognizes that "the woman suspects his messianic identity..." See also *Written That You May Believe*, 140.

she has posed.[55] It is an epiphany, a moment of revelation not unlike that which Moses experienced at the blazing bush of Mount Sinai, and it corresponds to Yahweh's self-disclosure to Moses as ἐγὼ εἰμί (I AM) in LXX Ex 3:6 and 14. It would be intelligible and meaningful to the Samaritan woman, for this revelation is central to the Samaritan Scriptures of the five books of Moses. And, as already indicated, the Ta'eb or Messiah she and her fellow Samaritans are awaiting will be a new Moses, the fulfillment of Moses' own prophecy of Deut 18:15.

But the one who is speaking these words and using them to identify himself to her is more than a new Moses. As the incarnation of the Logos, Jesus identifies himself in terms of God's self-disclosure to Moses. Moreover, the entire phrase he enunciates in his response is almost identical to Yahweh's self-disclosure spoken to Israel in exile through Second Isaiah:

> On account of this the people will know my name in that day, that ἐγὼ εἰμὶ αὐτὸς ὁ λαλῶν (**I AM he, the one speaking**). (LXX Isa 52:6)

God's name, on the basis of LXX Isa 52:6, is ἐγὼ εἰμί. Its Hebrew original, אֲנִי הוּא (literally "I He") was treated by various representatives of Rabbinic Judaism as the name of God.[56] In all probability its Greek version, ἐγὼ εἰμί, served as an equivalent rendition on the basis of its employment as the translation of the name God revealed to Moses in Ex 3:14, אֶהְיֶה אֲשֶׁר אֶהְיֶה (I will be who I will be). Appropriately, therefore, as God's name, ἐγὼ εἰμί was used to translate אֲנִי הוּא or simply אֲנִי ("I") at least twenty-one times in Second Isaiah.[57]

Jesus' derivation of ἐγὼ εἰμὶ αὐτὸς ὁ λαλῶν from Is 52:6 is an eschatological fulfillment of the prophetic word, " ... the people will know my name in that day." **I AM** (ἐγὼ εἰμί) without any predicates is God's name, and according to Jesus' acknowledgment in John 17:11, it is the name God has given to him, the incarnate Logos: "Holy Father, preserve them in your name which you have given to me..." Accordingly, Jesus' appropriation of the name **I AM** (ἐγὼ εἰμί) without predicates establishes his solidarity with God.[58] By disclosing this name to the Samaritan woman, he is continuing to romance her into a relationship with him that will enable her to recover her religious fidelity and her spiritual integrity. At the same time the epiphany that she is experiencing places her in continuity with Moses, the privileged recipient of God's first self-disclosure at Sinai that constituted Israel as God's people. In contrast, however, she becomes the first to experience the revelation of God incarnate; and, as the end of the story

---

[55] Dodd, *The Interpretation of the Fourth Gospel*, 314-315, interprets 4:26 simply as "an express avowal by Christ that He is the 'Messiah' – with the implication that 'Messiah' means not only the messenger who will 'announce' certain religious truths (iv.25), but the inaugurator of a new era in religion..."

[56] Dodd, *Fourth Gospel*, 94.

[57] See LXX Is 41:10; 43:10; twice in 43:25; 45:8, 18; twice in 45:19; 45:22; twice in 46:4 and 46:9; 47:8 and twice in 47:10; twice in 48:12, 48:17; twice in 51:12; 52:6.

[58] Dodd. *Fourth Gospel*, 96.

will indicate, it will result in the re-constitution of the Samaritans as the new people of God.

At this point the implied readers have been confronted with the eschatological fulfillment of Is 52:6 and shocked by the gender reversed revelation that is as decisive for the New Israel as the epiphany that Moses experienced was for Old Testament Israel. The dialogue between Jesus and the Samaritan woman is terminated abruptly by the return of his disciples with their purchased food. Their shock that their rabbi is conversing with a woman in public may be predetermined by Rabbinic teaching about the dangers of speaking with women.[59] However, the narrator's use of the imperfect tense of the verb ἐθαύμαζον (they were being amazed) conveys their reaction of wonder at this violation of a Pharisaic/rabbinic tradition that in the two levels of the narrative world of the Gospel is limited to the time of Jesus. None of the disciples, however, dare to challenge Jesus with any presumptuous questions, "What are you seeking?" or "Why do you speak with her?" Yet these questions, which express their attentiveness to this unusual circumstance, may continue to engage the implied readers.

The woman, in the meantime, returns to her city, leaving behind her water jug at the sacred place of revelation. She will not need it anymore! In view of the living water that Jesus will give her, she will have that spring within herself leaping up into life everlasting.[60] Accordingly, Birger Olsson's remark is especially relevant: "The waterpot and the drawing of water could to some extent be symbols of her old life, or of her old religion."[61] But contrary to expectation, she does not call her paramour. By this time the reader will have comprehended Jesus' strategy of confronting her with her own religious infidelity and brokenness by summoning her to bring her husband back to this place. As the personification of the Samaritans who, according to God's pronouncement in Hosea 1:9, "You are not my people and I am not your God," she invites her fellow Samaritans to return with her to the place of her encounter with Jesus. "Come, see a human being who told me all the things that I did." While she may be alluding to her own spiritual impoverishment and alienation, she is really speaking of the history of the religious infidelity of the Samaritan people.

---

[59] See M *Pirque Aboth* 1:5, *attributed to Yose ben Yochanan of Jerusalem (150 B.C.E.):* "And don't talk much with women. He spoke of a man's wife, all the more so is the rule to be applied to the wife of one's fellow. In this regard did sages say, "So long as a man talks too much with a woman, he brings trouble on himself, wastes time better spent on studying the Torah, and ends up an heir of Gehenna."

[60] Various other reasons have been proposed for the woman leaving behind her water jug, her ὑδρίαν. According to Barrett, *John,* 240, she left it so that Jesus could use it to quench his thirst. But for water, Jesus would need a bucket, an ἄντλημα, as the woman had said in 4:11. O'Day's comment, *Revelation*, 75, is worth noting, because it may be "the most reasonable explanation" that 'this reference to the jar indicates that the woman is going to return." Schnackenburg, *St. John*, I, 443, contends that the abandonment of the water jar adds nothing to the story.

[61] Birger Olsson, *Structure and Meaning in the Fourth Gospel*. Coniectanea Biblica. New Testament Series 6 (Lund, Sweden: CWK Gleerup, 1974) 156. n.31.

"Surely this isn't the Messiah, is it?" she asks. Her question, which is introduced by the negative particle μήτι that generally invites a negative reply, may reflect her own doubts about the answer. For Jesus' response to her expressed christological expectation was more than an affirmation. It was a pronouncement of the fulfillment of Is 52:6. God's incarnate Logos revealing God's name to God's people! But that disclosure would be intended for the implied readers, not directly for the Samaritan woman. Her Scriptures did not include the Book of Isaiah, only the five Books of Moses. But that at least would be the basis of her recognition of the significance of Jesus' use of the divine **I AM**. Her invitation to her fellow Samaritans, in spite of her own uncertainty about his true identity, succeeds in tantalizing them to follow her: "*Then* they went out of the city and were coming towards him (πρὸς αὐτόν).[62] At that moment she has assumed a Moses-like role in leading her people to the place of Jesus' self-disclosure as **I AM**.[63] In another stunning reversal a female Moses emerges within the narrative world of the Gospel!

At the same time the disciples introduce a scene that stands in marked contrast to the beginning of the story. Jesus had initiated the dialogue with the Samaritan woman by asking her for a drink; his disciples now evoke a monologue from him by urging him to eat the food they had purchased. His refusal to eat intensifies the astonishment that arose among them when they found him conversing with a woman. Because they were not involved in that encounter, they debate with each other whether someone may have offered him something to eat. Moreover, because they were not involved in that encounter, they cannot construe the meaning of Jesus' discourse. Throughout the episode they remain outsiders. As Jesus informs them, "I have food to eat which you know nothing about." His food, however, is unlike the heavenly food that Philo credits to Moses during his solitary mystical sojourn on Sinai. For, in contrast to Moses "having the better food through contemplation," Jesus is nourished by the rich sustenance that he derived from his dialogue with the Samaritan woman.[64] Such spiritual nutrition supersedes the need for material provisions. In all likelihood the implied readers, who have been present from the beginning, would have no difficulty determining the meaning of his words about food and the implied contrast to the food that Philo ascribes to Moses.[65]

---

[62] The adverbial particle, "then" should be included in verse 30. It is attested by the oldest of the manuscripts, P^{66} and many other significant witnesses.

[63] Schneiders, *The Revelatory Text*, 192, compares her leaving her water jar to incidents in the Synoptic Gospels in which the disciples leave the fishing business, family, or tax collecting to follow Jesus into apostleship. Consequently, as Schneiders concludes, the Samaritan woman is fulfilling her own call to apostleship. See also her essay, "Women in the Fourth Gospel and the Role of Women in the Contemporary Church," *BTB* 12 (1982) 40.

[64] See Philo, *de Vita Mosis* II, 69; and also the review of Philo's interpretation of Moses' mystical ascents in Wayne A. Meeks, *The Prophet-King: Moses Traditions and the Johannine Christology* (Leiden: E. J. Brill, 1967) 123-125.

[65] Also O'Day, *Revelation*, 79.

Jesus proceeds to explain his rationale for rejecting the food his disciples have offered him: "My food is that I do the will of the one who sent me, and I shall bring his work to completion." His is the better food of fulfilling God's will through activity and that includes the activity of imparting a divine revelation to the Samaritan woman. This motivation dominates his ministry throughout the narrative world of the Gospel and culminates in his acknowledgment of 17:4, "… completing the work that you gave me to do," and especially in his final words from the cross in 19:30, "It has been completed." The rhetorical question, perhaps derived from a proverb, that Jesus addresses to his disciples probably presupposes a four month period between sowing and harvest: "Do you not say that it is four months more and the harvest comes?"[66] Ironically, however, the sowing and the harvest are happening almost simultaneously. For as Jesus continues, "Look, I say to you, raise your eyes and view the fields, that they are white towards harvest." He has sown the seed of the Gospel in his dialogue with the Samaritan woman, and the harvest, as a result of her sowing the seed among her fellow Samaritans, is already at hand. At the same time her harvesting is rewarding her, for, in the Moses-like exodus in which she is leading her people, she is gathering fruit for everlasting life. Consequently, as a result of their collaboration as sower and as reaper, both she and Jesus "may rejoice together."[67]

For the benefit of his disciples Jesus utilizes what appears to be a proverb in order to differentiate between the workers engaged in farming the field of the world for the sake of the Gospel: one is the sower and another the reaper. They are not the same, as the conclusion of this story will illustrate. Moreover, he proceeds to remind them of their commission to apostleship by relating them to the activity of harvesting, "I sent you to reap that for which you have not labored. Others have labored, and you have entered into their labor." Although Jesus is addressing his disciples, no authorization as yet has been issued to them to engage in either work of sowing or reaping. They have been uninvolved in this episode, and there is no indication that they will be engaged in reaping among the Samaritans. It is the implied readers who are being alerted to those, like Jesus, who have carried out the initial labor of sowing; and they are prompted to remember that, like the Samaritan woman, they can enter into that collaborative labor by doing the harvesting.[68]

Accordingly, as the narrator submits, "Many from that city believed into him on account of the word of the woman testifying, 'He told me all the things which I did.'" A good harvest is taking place. The Samaritan woman, in reaching out to

[66] Barrett, *St. John*, 241.

[67] Also Boers, *Neither on this Mountain Nor in Jerusalem*, 191-192.

[68] See Brown, *John*, 183-84; and Schneiders, *Revelatory Text*, 193-94, as a "post-resurrection event" read back into the life of Jesus in order to account for the Samaritan mission and the problem of a post-resurrection confession. The Samaritan confession of Jesus as "the Savior of the world" has no necessary relation to his death and resurrection. "Savior" was a title that kings and emperors appropriated to promote propagandistically their rule. His ministry among the Samaritans has effected a transformation of their social construction of reality.

her people, finds herself re-involved in communication and communion. She is no longer isolated and disillusioned in her spiritual poverty. In her Moses-like role she has led her fellow Samaritans to the site of her revelatory encounter with the **I AM** of the incarnate Logos. Their experience of Jesus induces them to ask him to remain with them, "and he remained there two days." The twofold use of the verb, *to remain* (μένειν), should remind the implied readers of the two disciples of John the Witness who attached themselves to Jesus and "*remained* with him." To remain with Jesus or to have Jesus remain with them constitutes an involvement with the bearer of God's presence, who, as a result of having substituted his body in place of the Temple on Mount Zion, has became the living sanctuary of God. By remaining with them, Jesus draws them into the holiness and wholeness of his embodiment of God's **I AM**.

During his brief sojourn among the Samaritans "many more believed because of his word." In the presence of Jesus as the **I AM** of the incarnate Logos, they all have equal access to him. They are distinguished by the extraordinary reversal of the original establishment of the Israelites as the people of God. In the context of that earlier revelation, according to LXXEx 19:9, Yahweh informed Moses,

> "I am coming towards you in the pillar of a cloud, so that the people may hear my speaking to you and trust you forever.[69]

No such demonstration is required to persuade the Samaritans to trust their Moses-like fellow Samaritan who led them to the revelatory site of the **I AM**. None is needed, because, as the Samaritans tell her, "No longer do we believe on account of your word, for we ourselves have heard …" They have had direct and immediate access to the same revelation as their female Moses.

In stark contrast the ancient Israelites, who followed Moses to the place of his experience of the **I AM**, were required to consecrate themselves for three days in order to prepare for the descent of Yahweh on Mount Sinai. When Moses brought them out of the camp to meet God, they stood at the foot of the mountain and observed Yahweh's descent in fire and smoke, as the mountain quaked and the blast of the trumpet grew louder. Moses was summoned to the top of the mountain, but initially it was necessary for him to return to warn the people:

> … lest they should draw near to God to observe, and a multitude of them fall down. Even the priests approaching the Lord God shall be consecrated, lest the Lord depart from them. And Moses said to God, "The people will not be able to come up to Mount Sinai, for you made a solemn declaration to us saying, 'Set apart the mountain and sanctify it.'"[70]

---

[69] Translation from the LXX Ex 19:9.

[70] The translation is from the LXX of Ex 19:21-23. The Israelites are warned that approaching God would result in a multitude of them falling down. In John 18:6 a cohort of 600 soldiers and the servants of the chief priests and Pharisees fall down when Jesus identifies himself to them as **I AM** (ἐγώ εἰμί).

When Moses re-ascended the mountain, he alone, according to Ex 24:2, was permitted to approach God and serve as God's mouthpiece to instruct the Israelites in "all the words and ordinances of the Lord."

As this episode reaches its conclusion, another feature of the paradigm shift that emerges in this story surfaces, namely the horizontality of the revelation that all the Samaritans experience in their relationship with Jesus. Reality has been reconstituted. A truly egalitarian unity has been established between Jesus and the Samaritan people.[71] "No longer do we believe on account of your speaking, for we ourselves have heard, and we know that this is truly the Savior of the world." In the new age of God's rule, God is finally accessible through the incarnation of the Logos, and that accessibility is unobstructed by any purity code or pollution system. The new age of God's entry into solidarity with all humankind through incarnation negates all the forms and forces of separation that maintain and promote the injustice and inequality of racism and sexism. God's accessibility to all, regardless of race and gender, is divinely intended to constitute a world of inclusiveness and unity.

As a result of the Moses-like leadership of the Samaritan woman and the response of her fellow Samaritans to the same revelation that she experienced, the words of Jesus in 3:17 have been fulfilled. "For God did not send his Son into the world to condemn the world but in order that the world might be saved." Jesus, through the surrogate activity of the Samaritan woman, has saved the Samaritan world. Hesitantly she had identified Jesus to her fellow Samaritans as "the Christ." But after they have had their own experience of Jesus' revelation, they confess him as "the Savior of the world."[72]

---

[71] Boers' trajectory of binary oppositions culminates in the Samaritan reinforcement of the integration of the values "/ human solidarity/ and / universal salvation/" in *Neither on This Mountain Nor in Jerusalem*, 200. For an incisive analysis of "The Unification Model of the Christian Faith," see Douglas R. McGaughey, *Christianity for the Third Millennium. Faith in an Age of Fundamentalism and Skepticism* (San Francisco: International Scholars Publications, 1998) 83-146.

[72] Koester, "The Savior of the World," 674 and 676-680, observes that Philo called God "the Savior of the world" in *de Specialibus Legibus* II, 198; but he proposes that the title in 4:42 may be "a polemic against the emperor." "The title 'Savior of the world' was used by Caesar, but the Samaritans recognized that it truly belonged to Jesus, whom they received in a manner appropriate for a king."

Chapter Eight

Failure in Jerusalem

Healing a crippled Human Being 5:1-16

Jesus' very brief encounter with the nobleman of Capernaum is the only event that is reported of his return to Galilee in 4:43-54. It is the "second sign" or "other sign" that he performed "coming out of Judea into Galilee," and it took place in Cana "after two days." Since it may be intended to bring the implied readers full circle into the movement from "seeing with the result of believing" (2:1-11) into "believing in order to see," (4:43-54), more than that may not be necessary. The purpose of Jesus' brief sojourn in Galilee, as "the prophet who has no honor in his own country" but whose word has nevertheless been honored by the nobleman, has been fulfilled.

Another "festival of the Jews" draws Jesus back to Jerusalem. In the narrative world of the Gospel it is his second visit. He returns as the living Temple of God, the one on whom the angels of God are ascending and descending. He is "the Son of the Human Being" whom God sent into the world in order to save the world. He is drawn to a pool (κολυμβήθρα) that is surrounded by a multitude of sick and diseased human beings. But whether it is a sheep pool at a place called Bezetha or whether at the Sheep Gate there is a pool that is called Bezetha has been a conundrum for centuries.[1] The oldest manuscripts of the Fourth Gospel, $P^{66}$and P^{75} do not utilize certain aspects of Greek writing by which grammatical forms are identified: iota subscripts, accents and breathing marks. Therefore it is not clear whether the word "pool," by standing in apposition to the word "sheep," is governed by the preposition ἐπί (at) and is in the dative case, or whether it is the

[1] The name of the pool varies in the manuscript tradition of John 5:2, and it is difficult to determine which reading is the original: Bethesda, Bethzatha, Belzetha, or Bethsaida/Bedsaida. Of the four, the last two have the strongest attestation in as far as they occur in the two oldest manuscripts of the Fourth Gospel, P^{66} and P^{75}. But they are suspect because they are variations of the name of a town located on the east bank of the Jordan River at the Sea of Galilee. Bethzatha, or its variation Bezetha, cited by Josephus as a region at the northeast corner of the Temple, tends to be dismissed too quickly because of the influence of Josephus' writings. If the site is named by the narrator in order to draw the addressees of the Gospel into a more dynamic interaction with the text, perhaps on the basis of their familiarity with Josephus, Bethzatha or Bezetha is the preferred reading. Gustav Dalman, *Sacred Sites and Ways* (London: Society for Promoting Christian Knowledge, 1935) 309-313, supports this reading. Bethesda is often dismissed because it is suspected to be a scribal substitute bearing the symbolic meaning of the Hebrew original, בית חסדא, (house of mercy) from which it may have been derived. However, see the discussions of Brown, *John* I, 206, on the discovery of the "Copper Scroll" at Qumran, which refers to a treasure buried "in Bet Eshdatayin, in the pool at the entrance to its smaller basin," and may confirm the originality of the name as Bethesda. The dual form of the Hebrew, Bet Eshdatayin, corresponds to the two regions of the pool that have been excavated in the region northeast of the Temple that appears to have been named "Bet Eshda" or Bethesda.

predicate of the copula ἔστιν and is the nominative case. In either instance a noun seems to be missing. There are two ways in which the problem of verse 2 can be resolved.[2]

> Now there is in Jerusalem at the sheep *gate* a pool, the one in Hebrew called 'Bezetha' having five porticoes.
>
> Now there is in Jerusalem at the sheep pool a *place*, the one in Hebrew called 'Bezetha' having five porticoes.

Neither of the two words, "gate" and "place," are in the Greek text of verse 2. "Gate" has been added as the first possibility because it generally appears in the English translations.[3] It serves to provide a noun to modify the adjective προβατικῇ (sheep), and in turn it assigns the word "pool" to the nominative case so that a predicate is supplied for the copula "there is" and, at the same time, an antecedent for the nominative phrase that follows, "the one called". In the second case, the word "pool" serves as the noun by which the adjective προβατικῇ (sheep) is qualified and therefore becomes the object of the preposition ἐπί (at). "Place" is inserted in order to provide a predicate for the copula "there is" and simultaneously an antecedent for the nominative phrase "the one called."[4]

There is obviously a gap in verse 2 that has to be filled. Since it appears to be an intentional gap, the first of the two alternatives seems to be a more appropriate and possibly also the more probable resolution of the problem. The narrator introduces the story of 5:1-17 by describing the setting in which the cure of a sick human being takes place: "a pool in Jerusalem," "having five porticoes" and "in Hebrew named Bezetha." What is the function of these details? Undoubtedly they have been included to serve a specific purpose. Are they symbolic? Or are they intended to enable the implied readers of Alexandria to enter into the story more existentially because of a degree of familiarity with the place? Since its name is given in Hebrew, Bezetha," in all likelihood the story's setting is designed to draw the original addressees of the Gospel into a more immediate experience of the event that will occur at this site.[5] Some of them may in fact have visited Jerusalem and may even be familiar with this location. At the very least they have learned about a place that is known in Hebrew as Betheza, if only by reading Josephus' history of the Jewish war against Rome.[6] In view of this possibility and the probability of their familiarity with the Septuagint version of Neh 3:1, 32 and

---

[2] See Brown, *John* I, 206; Barrett, *St. John*, 251; also Haenchen, *John* I, 244.

[3] This resolution of the problem is represented by Bultmann, *John*, 240; German, 179-180; and Haenchen, *John* I, 244.

[4] Favoring this resolution are Brown, *John* I, 206; and Barrett, *St. John*, 251.

[5] This would also be true of other references in the Fourth Gospel where the Hebrew or Aramaic name is given, such as 9:7, 11; 19:13, 17. Perhaps the purpose is to enable the implied readers, who may have some familiarity with the Hebrew names of the places in which certain events of Jesus' ministry occur, to feel at home in the narrative world of the Gospel.

[6] See Josephus, *BJ* 2, 328 and 530; 5, 149-151; cited by Haenchen, *John* I, 244. Josephus refers to the place as "Bezetha," but does not mention the presence of a pool in that place.

12:29, namely 2 Esdras 13:1, 32 and 22:39, they would be more naturally inclined to fill the gap in verse 2 with the word "gate" instead of the word "place."

It is noteworthy, in this respect, that Origen of Alexandria, who wrote the first five books of his commentary on the Fourth Gospel before his withdrawal to Caesarea in 231 C.E., filled the gap of verse 2 with the word "gate."[7] In Fragment 61 Origen writes, "In Jerusalem by the Sheep Gate is a pool … For this reason he (Jesus) goes to the pool by the Sheep Gate."[8] Accordingly, the more cogent of the two alternatives appears to be the insertion of the word "gate" into the blank space of v. 2.

To what extent the details of this setting are to be interpreted symbolically depends on the individual reader. In any case the setting evokes a sense of irony. Here in Jerusalem, the architectonic center of the Jewish world, the city of the great Temple in which the Name of God resides, Jesus encounters a profusion of "the sick, the blind, the lame, and the withered." If Jerusalem were indeed what Israelite and Jewish eschatology had hoped for, the city would be a center of health and wholeness. The ancient prophets had predicted that rivers of living water would flow out of Jerusalem for the healing of Israel.[9] As the navel of the earth, Jerusalem would draw all human beings into union with God.[10] But the ideology of separation that the ruling authorities of Judaism promote in the narrative world of the Fourth Gospel cannot fulfill the divine objective of eliminating injustice and disease, poverty and dehumanization.[11] Any religion that is based on separation and therefore is oriented toward world maintenance cannot fulfill the will of God for humanity.[12]

There is no verse 4 in the critical editions of the Greek text, and therefore many English translations omit it. Verse 3b, "waiting for the movement of the water," is usually included, for it serves as the introduction to verse 4, "for at a certain season an angel of the Lord would come down in the pool and the water would be stirred up. Then the first one stepping in after the stirring of the water was healed of whatever disease he/she had." Although verses 3b and 4 are not inappropriate to the story, they are excluded because they are not found in the oldest manuscripts of the Gospel, P^{66} and P^{75}. They may have been marginal notes that a scribe inserted

[7] Allan Menzies, "Introduction to the Commentaries of Origen," *The Ante-Nicene Fathers* (Grand Rapids: Eerdmans, 1956) X, 294.

[8] From Haenchen, *John* I, 244. Barrett, *St. John*, 251, evidently errs, when he states, "… the whole ancient tradition takes together προβατικῇ κολυμβήθρᾳ (sheep pool), and that no ancient writer (none in fact before A.D. 1283) supplies πύλη (gate) with προβατικῇ."

[9] See Ezek 47 and Zech 13:1, 14:8.

[10] See Isa 60:1-22 and 66:10-21; Zech 14:16-21.

[11] For expressions of the ideology of separation, see 5:18; 7:19, 32; 8:59; 9:22, 34; 11:50; 16:2; 19:7.

[12] The Pharisees, as their name in Hebrew indicates (פרושים), are the "separated ones." On the ideologies of separation and unification, see the analysis of the two models in Douglas R. McGaughey, *Christianity for the Third Millennium*, chapters 2-3.

at a later stage in the manuscript transmission of the Gospel in order to explain verse 7.

Among the masses of the sick and diseased, who are at the pool waiting for healing and restoration, there is an individual who has been afflicted with some kind of debilitating illness for thirty-eight years.[13] The number and its possible significance deserve consideration, perhaps especially because they are so easily dismissed by commentators.[14] Of the three occurrences of the number thirty-eight in the First Testament, the most relevant is found in Deut 2:14.[15]

> And the days which we journeyed from Kadesh-Barnea until the time we crossed the brook Zered, thirty-eight years.

After the Exodus from Egypt, the people of Israel journeyed through the Sinai wilderness for thirty-eight years until they arrived at the border of the land of Canaan.[16] Before they could cross over into the Promised Land, Moses delivered his final exhortations and admonitions to them in the form of a farewell speech. His lengthy discourse conveyed the prescriptions involving Israel in a covenant of reciprocity. The observance of God's commandments, the constitution of the covenant, would result in a surplus of blessing.[17] Violations would be punished with severity.[18] Although health is not explicitly cited as one of the benefits of obedience to the Law, it is certainly presupposed. Disobedience, on the other hand, would result in disease and blindness:

> The Lord will smite you with the boils of Egypt, and with ulcers and the scurvy and the itch, of which you cannot be healed. The Lord will smite you with madness and blindness and confusion of mind, and you shall grope at noonday, as the blind grope in darkness, and you shall not prosper in your ways... (Deut 28:27-29)

The irony of this invalid's wretchedness is immense. On the one hand, his entrance into the Promised Land of restoration has never been fulfilled.[19] There have been thirty-eight years of waiting in vain to cross over into the land of health and wholeness. On the other hand, according to Deuteronomy's covenant of

---

[13] See Jeffrey L. Staley, "Stumbling in the Dark, Reaching for the Light: Reading Character in John 5 and 9," *Semeia 53: The Fourth Gospel from a Literary Perspective* (Atlanta: Scholars Press, 1991) 58-64, for another "reading" of the "ambiguities of character" in the story of 5:1-15.

[14] Brown, *John* I, 207, "The suggestion that the number is symbolic is unnecessary." Barrett, *St. John*, 253, "It is very improbable that the number thirty-eight is symbolic." Bultmann, *John*, 242, "Neither the source nor the Evangelist has in mind an allegorical interpretation of the 38 years." Haenchen, *John* I, 245, "The duration of the illness is a way of emphasizing the magnitude of the healing to follow."

[15] The other two are 1 Kings 16:29 and 2 Kings 15:8.

[16] Philo, *de Vita Mosis* I, 238, also cites the 38 years of Deut 2:14, but adds on "the time already spent," to reach the number 40, that for him signifies "the span of a generation of human life."

[17] Deut 7:12-16, 11:13-17, 28:1-14.

[18] Deut 28:15-68.

[19] This individual may be a man or a woman. Verse 5 introduces the person as an ἄνθρωπος, a human being. But I am choosing to identify him as a male.

reciprocity, the infirmity that has afflicted him would be attributable to some transgression of the Law. So he is in Jerusalem, the architectonic center of the world, at a pool, after having passed through the Sheep Gate, hoping to be healed when the waters of the pool are stirred up.

Jesus focuses on this individual, "knowing that he had already been there a long time," and addresses him with the question, "Do you want to become healthy?"[20] After thirty-eight years of a debilitating illness, the answer that might be expected is, "Yes, I've been waiting for more years than I wish to remember." But his response is a recital of self-pity in which the first person pronoun is used four times.

> Lord, *I* don't have a human being so that when the water is stirred up, he might throw *me* into the pool; and while *I* am coming, another descends before *me*.

Without expressing any sympathy, Jesus addresses him with three commands: "Stand up, take your mat and walk." That is the translation of the New Revised Standard Version. But to construct the full significance of each command, a precise grammatical translation is essential: "Keep on rising, take your mattress once and for all, and keep on walking."

For the first command Jesus appropriates the verb that is usually employed in conjunction with resurrection, ἐγείρειν (to resurrect, raise up, arise). It is used in this sense in 2:19, 20, 22; 5:8, 21; 12:1, 9; 21:14. Its meaning in this context is two-fold. The person is not only to get up or to rise; he is also to be resurrected in the sense of entering into a new condition or state of existence. And since Jesus has issued the command in the present tense, this entry into resurrection is to be a continuous state of existence in which he is to live.

The second imperative is spoken in the aorist tense and expresses 'a once and for all' totality: "take up your mattress" and take it up completely. It is an object that belongs to human existence, and it represents a basic necessity for the journey through life. If the earlier command, "Keep on rising" implies a continuous movement into transcendence, this injunction is intended to keep the person related to historical existence, to the practical realities of everyday life. "Mattress" signifies location because it must be placed somewhere in order to be used. As such it also connotes rest because it is used for sleep. But neither the location nor the rest can be permanent, for the Greek word that is employed in 5:8 is κράβατος, and it refers to a straw-stuffed pallet that is easily transported from place to place. To take a pallet and to take it in its totality, therefore, is to place it somewhere in order to establish location for the necessity of rest and sleep, but

[20] Martyn, *History and Theology*, 72-76, focuses on the second level of the two level drama of the narrative world of the Gospel and, therefore, reads the story in its historical context. In place of Jesus he substitutes a "Jewish Christian" [who] "serves to make real in the life of a fellow Jew the healing power of Jesus. At that, the Jewish authorities step in and question the healed man." It may be more effective to read the story in this way than to presuppose the two levels at the same time.

never permanently. For the pallet also connotes mobility. It can be moved from place to place.

The need for mobility is conveyed by a third command that is issued in the present imperative, "Keep on walking." Historical existence is always a forward movement, a journey into an open future. Each moment in the present is also a horizon of expectation that involves projection toward the realization of new possibilities. For the fullness of life, it is necessary to keep on walking, but at the same time to accept the limitations of physical existence and therefore to put down one's pallet for rest and sleep.

The effect of Jesus' commands appears to be instantaneous: "And immediately the human being became well, and he took his pallet and he walks." Jesus, as the living sanctuary of God and therefore the bearer of God's presence, has enabled this individual to begin to enter into the Promised Land of restoration. Whatever his debilitating illness may have been, he is able to pick up his mattress and walk.

It is at this moment that the narrator introduces the reality of time into the story: "Now it was Sabbath on that day." Jesus of course would have been aware of that and would surmise that the fulfillment of his command, "Take your pallet" would constitute a predicament for the man. For the first Table of the Law that Moses issued prior to Israel's entry into the Promised Land demands the observance of the Sabbath:

> Observe the Sabbath day, to keep it holy, as the Lord God commanded you. Six days shall you labor and do all your work, but the seventh day is a Sabbath to Yahweh your God, in it you shall not do any work. (Deut 5:12-13)

His effort to fulfill Jesus' second command, "Take up your mattress!" is immediately challenged by the ruling authorities, "It is Sabbath and it is not legal for you to take up your pallet." Surely he knows that! But what should he do in view of the convoluted predicament into which the Deuteronomic code had placed him? Initially it had confronted him with the judgment that his illness was to be recognized as punishment for whatever transgression of the law he had committed and at the same time it had consigned him to the realm of the "Unclean." As a result, his illness had imposed a burdensome necessity upon him, limiting his freedom of movement and subjecting him to the consequences of his affliction. Now, however, after having been cured and made "clean," he is enabled to be free and to unburden himself of his previous limitations. But once again he is confronted with the legislation of the Deuteronomic code. Its requirement of Sabbath observance will reinforce his membership in Jewish society. Yet to what extent that socio-religious pattern of habituation will interfere with the necessities of his journey that are signified by the mattress that he is carrying, that is not at all clear. Time and reflection are needed to sort that out.

However, Jesus' first command would already have posed difficulty for him. To "Keep on rising!" and therefore to enter into greater transcendence would eventually engender deviations from his society's institutional formations and patterns of habituation. Would he be able to realize the possibilities of the new freedom he experiences as he moves further into a life of resurrection? In this respect the final command, "Keep on walking!" poses no problems for him. As a Jew he is heir to the great traditions of Abraham and Sarah who walked and journeyed throughout their lives. But how he will incorporate the first two commands into his own journey is the critical issue that confronts him. Apparently he is not ready to face these challenges.

His initial response to the ruling authorities is to refuse to take responsibility for his violation of the Sabbath. "The one who cured me, that one said to me, 'Take up your pallet and keep on walking!'" Significantly, in the face of their challenge he omits the first imperative, "Keep on rising!" Perhaps his fear induced him to exclude it. Perhaps he realizes that he is going to encounter difficulties in fulfilling it. In any case, by disregarding the first command, he is in danger of forfeiting the decisive step into a new Exodus. Apparently he has been cured of his affliction, but it is questionable whether in fact he is moving into the Promised Land of health and wholeness.

When the authorities want to know who gave him the commands that he has attributed to the one who cured him, he is unable to identify Jesus by name. Surprisingly he has not taken the initiative to learn who his benefactor is. Jesus, however, according to an intrusive remark of the narrator, had slipped away in order to avoid the presence and publicity of the crowd in that place. But somewhat later, after finding the man in the sacred precinct of the Temple and perceiving what had happened, he censures him with a rebuke, "Look, you have been freed of your affliction! Do not keep on sinning so that something worse happens to you!" For a fourth time Jesus is compelled to issue another command, and the prohibitory imperative that he employs in the present tense implies that the man he has cured has continued to sin.[21] Although he does not stipulate how he has been sinning or what that sin might be, he must be referring to his refusal to take responsibility for his act of carrying his pallet on the Sabbath and faulting Jesus for giving such a command in the first place. What that "something worse" might be that would result from continuous sinning is not stated, but the consequences of refusing to take responsibility for his own actions and the apparent rejection of Jesus' first imperative, "Keep on rising" may well be intimated.

According to the narrator, the man went off and reported to the authorities that the name of the one who had cured him was Jesus. The intention of his act, however, is not immediately clear. How it is to be construed depends largely on which one of the three variant verbs in the manuscript tradition is determined to be

[21] Nicklas, *Ablösung und Verstrickung*, correctly states that the text does not explicitly indicate what the individual's sin is that Jesus is referring to. It is a gap that the implied readers must fill, but on the basis of Jesus' use of the present tense, the sin must be the forfeit of taking responsibility for the new freedom he/she has received by being healed. If there is a paramount critique of Nicklas' work, it is the absence of a close reading of the text.

the original. Of the three: ἀνήγγειλεν, ἀπήγγειλεν, and εἴπεν, the last is the most probable reading. The first two are variations of the same basic meaning: to announce, to proclaim, and they are used in that sense in 4:25, 16:13-15, 25.[22] The more neutral verb is εἴπεν (he said), and it is an appropriate progenitor of the action that follows: "And on account of this the Jews were persecuting Jesus because he was doing these things on the Sabbath." Contrary to expectation, the restored individual is not proclaiming or bearing witness to Jesus. What he is doing is an unequivocally antagonistic act.[23] He is informing the guardians of society that it was Jesus who commanded him to take up his pallet on the Sabbath.

According to 2:23, Jesus had performed signs during his first visit to Jerusalem, although none of them was recounted by the narrator. Nevertheless, many of those who witnessed them had responded by "believing into him." This is the only sign that Jesus performs during his second visit to Jerusalem, and it ends in failure. A human being has been cured of a debilitating illness, but he rejects a journey into an Exodus of new possibilities. Instead of entering into a life of ongoing resurrection, he prefers the safety of world maintenance, and he is willing to betray Jesus to the ruling elite in order to insure his participation in the social order into which he was born.[24] Jerusalem, as an architectonic center of the world, must remain a place of controlled and controlling institutionalization under a divine imprimatur. "Religion legitimates so effectively because it relates the precarious reality constructions of empirical societies with ultimate reality."[25] Any and every effort at self-externalization that involves the exploration and realization of new possibilities is intolerable.

For the first time in his ministry Jesus begins to experience persecution. He is subjected to a forensic process by the ruling authorities in which he is forced to defend himself against the charge that he is subverting the institution of the Sabbath (5:17-47). When he explains that he is simply imitating God in the work that he is doing, he is accused of making himself equal to God and therefore is guilty of blasphemy that is punishable by death.

> On account of this the Jews were persecuting Jesus because he was doing these things on the Sabbath. But he replied to them, "My Father is working up until now, and I am working." Because of this even more the Jews were seeking to kill him because he was not only dissolving the Sabbath but he was saying God (is) his own Father, making himself equal to God. (5:16-18)

---

[22] It is noteworthy that both compound forms of ἀγγέλλω replace λέγοντες, the participle of λέγω in a great diversity of the manuscript readings of 4:51.

[23] Martyn, *History and Theology*, 75, also interprets the healed man's identification of Jesus as a hostile act. His juxtaposition of John 5 and 9 elucidates the differences between the two stories.

[24] World maintenance or reality maintenance is preserving the institutional order, the ongoing "establishment of symmetry between objective and subjective definitions of reality." See Peter L. Berger, *The Sacred Canopy: Elements of a Sociological Theory of Religion* (Garden City: Doubleday Anchor Books, 1969), 29-51, especially p. 32.

[25] *Ibid.*

The opening of a forensic process against Jesus 5:17-47

To dissolve the divine ordinance of the Sabbath and to make oneself equal to God are two aspects of the same mentality: to think of oneself as the Creator God's surrogate and to act accordingly. In this forensic process that the ruling elite are inaugurating, Jesus will defend himself by qualifying his kinship with God in terms of his self-understanding as "the Son," but in accordance with the aporetic realities of union and differentiation that the Prologue ascribed to the Logos-Sophia. His ministry is conducted in the paradoxical relationship of dependence and independence.

Accordingly, Jesus will declare to the authorities, "The Father and I are one" and subsequently to his disciples, "The one who has seen me has seen the Father," but in the Father-Son union in which he conducts his ministry he always affirms his dependence on the Father. From the very beginning of his defense in this forensic process he stresses his subordinate apprenticeship.[26]

> ...The Son is able to do nothing of himself except what he sees the Father doing, for the things that One does, the Son also does likewise. For the Father loves the Son and shows him all the things which he himself is doing, and he will show him greater works than these so that you marvel. (5:19-20)
>
> I am unable to do anything from myself. Even as I hear, I judge; and my judgment is just, because I do not seek my will but the will of the one who sent me. (5:30)
>
> For the works which the Father has shown me so that I shall complete them, these works that I do testify about me that the Father has sent me. (5:36)

Jesus will continue to highlight his dependence on God in subsequent disputes with the ruling elite as well as in his teaching to his disciples.

> My teaching is not mine but his who sent me. (7:16)
>
> I do nothing on my own, but I speak these things as the Father instructed me. (8:28b)
>
> For I have not spoken on my own, but the Father who sent me has himself given me a commandment about what to say and what to speak. And I know that his commandment is eternal life. What I speak, therefore, I speak just as the Father has told me. (12:49-50)
>
> ... All the things I heard from my Father I made known to you. (15:15)

Significantly, in terms of this dependent affiliation in his union with God, Jesus will acknowledge to his disciples in 14:28, "My Father is greater than I."

At the same time, however, on the basis of his differentiation from God, he also accentuates the autonomy that the Father has granted the Son, so that the Son can act independently of the Father and exercise a will of his own.

[26] The metaphor "apprentice" is taken from Lindars, *John*, 221.

> For even as the Father raises the dead and makes alive, so also the Son makes alive whom he wishes. (5:21)
>
> Amen, amen I say to you, 'The hour is coming and now is when the dead will hear the voice of the Son of God and the ones heeding will live. (5:25)
>
> For even as the Father has life in himself, so also he has given the Son to have life in himself, and he has given him authority to do judgment because he is a son of a human being. (5:26-27)

As Jesus continues to exercise his sovereignty in his differentiation from God, he professes that the Father, who has sent him, has complete confidence in the Son's autonomous activity.

> For the Father judges no one, but has given all judgment to the Son, so that all may honor the Son even as they honor the Father. (5:22-23a)
>
> For the works that the Father has given me in order that I complete them, the works themselves which I do testify about me that the Father has sent me. (5:36)

The dynamic oscillating movement between union and differentiation in the Father-Son affiliation in which Jesus participates is a relationship of *interdependence*. But in their union they are not coequal, for Jesus acknowledges in 14:28, "The Father is greater than I." Or as he prays in 17:3, "And this is everlasting life, that *they know you* (γινώσκωσιν) the only true God and the one you sent, Jesus Christ." In his dependence on God for the works that he performs and the words that he speaks he manifests perfect integrity as the incarnate Logos-Sophia. God's Word can be seen and heard at the same time, and it is that integrity that empirically manifests the reality of God. Accordingly, Jesus can declare to his disciples:

> Amen, amen I say to you, the one *heeding* (ἀκούων plus the accusative τὸν λόγον μου) *my word* and believing the one who sent me has everlasting life and does not come into judgment but has passed out of death into life. (5:24)
>
> The words that I say to you I do not speak from myself, but the Father *remaining* (μένων) in me is doing his works. Believe me that I [am] in the Father and the Father [is] in me. But if not, believe on account of the works themselves." (14:10b-11)
>
> **I AM** (ἐγὼ εἰμί) the way and the truth and the life. No one comes toward (πρός) the Father if not through me. (14:6)

It is essentially this paradoxical relationship of interdependence that Jesus is submitting as his defense to the ruling authorities in this forensic process. He is God's apprentice who is only imitating the works that God does. He is God's spokesperson, and the word that he speaks has the illuminating power of God's speech. Accordingly, he deviates from his employment of the Father-Son relationship and his attendant use of the third person singular in verse 24 in order to return to the first person singular for the purpose of stressing his own authority as the speaker of the divine word. Those who hear it and believe the One on whose behalf he, the Son, is speaking, are participating in a new Exodus. They have *passed over* (μεταβέβηκεν) from death into life. Indeed, the hour of this Exodus is already present, at least for the implied readers of the Jewish community of Alexandria. Like the Israelites who listened to Moses and followed him out of Egyptian enslavement, "the dead who hear the voice of the Son of God... will live" (5:25).

Philo also employs this verb (μεταβαίνειν) as he reflects on the Exodus from Egypt to express the change from one state or condition into another. According to his allegorical interpretation, the Exodus is to be construed as "the *mind* (νοῦς) passing (μεταβαίνων) from one condition over to another; that is, from the enslaved condition of being subject to the passions over to "the piety and holiness of the Father."[27] As he states earlier in *The Migration of Abraham*:

> At the time when we were abandoning Egypt, the entire bodily country, hastening to unlearn the passions according of the guiding patterns of the word of the prophet Moses, they [the passions] followed us, seizing hold of the haste with respect to the Exodus and by envy undoing the swiftness of departure.[28]

> Because of this mixed and rough crowd [made up of] of diverse and promiscuous opinions, the mind, being able to escape from Egypt, the country of the body, wears itself out wandering and going around in a circle for the time of forty years.[29]

It is the voice of the Son of God speaking the word of the Father, the One who sent him, that inaugurates a new Exodus, not from the enslavement of the lusts and passions of human nature but an Exodus from living death or the death of living into a life of freedom and possibility. With a double asseveration Jesus enunciates this "passing over" from one state of being into another:

> Amen, amen I say to you, the hour is coming and now is when the dead will heed the voice of the Son of God and the ones heeding will live.

Because the Father has given the Son to have life in himself, Jesus can impart life independently of the Creator! "For even as the Father has *life* (ζωήν) in himself, so also he gave the Son to have *life* (ζωήν) in himself." Consequently in the exercise of his autonomy he speaks the authoritative commands to the crippled human being at the pool of Bethesda, "Keep on rising, take your mattress, and keep on walking," with the result that "... immediately the human being became whole" (5:8).

This sovereignty that the Son exercises includes "... the authority to do judgment."

---

[27] Philo, *de Migratione Abrahami*, 194.

[28] *Ibid.*, 151.

[29] *Ibid.*, 154.

> Even as I hear, I judge, and my judgment is just, for I do not seek my will but the will of the One who sent me.

According to 5:27, God conferred the authority to do judgment upon the Son "because he is υἱὸς ἀνθρώπου (son of a human being)." The appearance of this phrase, υἱὸς ἀνθρώπου, is puzzling because it is the only instance of its occurrence in the Gospel without the usual definite articles, and it stands in contrast to the appellation ὁ υἱὸς τοῦ ἀνθρώπου (the Son of the Human Being). Because the following verses, 5:28-29, echo Dan 12:2, the apparently non-titular designation υἱὸς ἀνθρώπου may be related to the apocalyptic figure of Dan 7: 13-14.

> Do not continue to marvel at this! For the hour is coming in which all those in the tombs will heed his voice and come forth, those doing good into the resurrection of life, those doing evil deeds into the resurrection of judgment. (5:28-29)

The phrase υἱὸς ἀνθρώπου (son of a human being) is an exact rendition of the Septuagint translation of the Aramaic counterpart, **בר אנש** (son of a human being). The implication appears to be that the Son or the Son of God is identifiable with Daniel's apocalyptic figure, υἱὸς ἀνθρώπου (son of a human being). The Septuagint translation of Dan 7:14 supports this: καὶ ἐδόθη αὐτῷ ἐξουσία (he gave him authority) and 7:22 stipulates that it is the authority to do judgment.[30] Yet it must be ironically oriented, for Jesus stated in 3:13, "No one has ascended into heaven except the one who descended, the Son of the Human Being." Unlike Daniel's "son of a human being" who ascended into heaven on a cloud in order to receive glory, sovereignty and rule, Jesus descended as "the Son of the Human Being" prior to his ascension, and he brought with him the legacy that belongs to the prototypical human being.

The same phrase υἱὸς ἀνθρώπου (son of a human being) also occurs in LXX Psa 8:5 as a translation of the Hebrew **בן אָדָם** (son of a human being). In the context of the wonders of the creation the Psalmist asks, "What is a human being that you remember him/her and a son of a human being that you consider him/her?" And the answer that is offered, "You made him/her scarcely less than the angels. You crowned him/her with glory and honor. You appointed him/her over the works of your hands. You subordinated all things under his/her feet." If God has given Jesus authority to do judgment because he is υἱὸς ἀνθρώπου, it is an extension of the sovereignty that, according to Gen 1:28 was conferred on Adam and Eve at creation. Jesus acknowledges authority in 17:2, "… even as you gave him authority of all flesh." And it is stated ironically by the narrator in the context of Jesus washing his disciples' feet:

[30] But according to the LXX Dan 7:22, God gave "judgment," to the community of the saints of the Most High who are represented by "one like a human being".

> …knowing that the Father gave all things to him into his hands, and that he came forth from God and is going back to God, he arose from dinner and placed aside his garments and taking an apron, he tied it around his waist.

In the double asseveration of verse 24 Jesus stated the consequences of heeding his voice as he speaks God's word: to have eternal life and "not to come into judgment." He speaks of judgment again in verse 27 and asserts that it belongs to the authority that God gave him "because he is a son of a human being." What is the function of this unexpected non-titular designation? In relation to the eschatological figure of Dan 7:13-14, who ascended into heaven and received glory, sovereignty and kingship, it is ironic. It is also ironic in relation to the prototypical human beings, Adam and Eve, who, having been made in the image and likeness of God and therefore are little less than the angels, forfeited their sovereignty. If God gave Jesus judgment because he is "a son of a human being," God also gave judgment to him as the Son, the Son of God and the Son of the Human Being who descended from heaven. Jesus therefore is able to judge equitably because he belongs to both creations, the old moral order as υἱὸς ἀνθρώπου (son of a human being), namely the son of Joseph from Nazareth, and the new moral order as the one who descended from heaven, the Son of the Human Being.[31] The ruling elite should not continue to be astonished about this because the new age is about to be inaugurated by the opening of the tombs. Those like Lazarus, who do good things, will enter into the resurrection of life, and those like the authorities, who have begun to think of killing Jesus, will enter into the resurrection of judgment.

The aporetic reality of Jesus as υἱὸς ἀνθρώπου (son of a human being), that is, the son of Joseph from Nazareth, and Jesus as "the Son" and "the Son of God" are designations that are both individual and corporate. Jesus never says, "**I AM** the Son" or "**I AM** the Son of God" or "**I AM** the Son of the Human Being who descended from heaven." The only predicates that he attaches to his **I AM** (ἐγὼ εἰμί) are activities in which he and the Father collaborate. The christological titles, "the Son" and "the Son of God" and "the Son of the Human Being," which unfortunately are masculine in gender, should be construed as appellations of "the One and the Many." Throughout the narrative world of the Gospel they refer to the One, Jesus, the Pioneer of the Many, who by his death and resurrection will enlarge the living Temple of God that he embodies to include the Many.

In 5:30-47 Jesus returns to the use of the first person singular, and, although he continues to speak of "the Father," he no longer refers to himself as 'the Son." The keynote of his defense has been articulated in his discourse on the Father/Son relationship and his work as both "the Son of God" and "a son of a human being." But now, at this point in his defense, he acknowledges that he cannot serve as his

---

[31] See Barrett, *St. John*, 262, who expresses a similar view: "Jesus does not judge *simply* because he is a human being… He judges because he is humanity restored…" (The italics are his.) Lindars, *John*, 225-226, considers this interpretation but dismisses it.

own witness. His double asseverations have conveyed the oath-like formulations of his interdependent apprenticeship with the Father. Further self-testimony would be untenable. Other witnesses are required that will corroborate the truth of the testimony he has rendered in 5:19-29. Accordingly, he calls upon the witness of John (5:33), his works (5:36), "the Father" (5:37), and finally the Scriptures and Moses (5:45).

John's testimony is weighty because 'he was a burning and shining lamp, and you wanted to exult in his light for an hour." He was indeed a formidable witness, both in the Prologue and in his presentation of Jesus to his own disciples – and to the implied readers – in 1:29-36. But there is no evidence within the narrative world of the Gospel that the ruling authorities "wanted to exult in his light for an hour." It must be an external analepsis that would be meaningful to the implied readers and therefore reflect the esteem, perhaps even the adulation that John enjoyed among the Jews of Alexandria.

But there is a greater witness to Jesus' person and work than the imposing testimony of John. It is the substantial attestation that is manifested by the works that the Father has commissioned him to complete as well as in the testimony of the Father himself. However, the intractable problem relative to the witness that is submitted by Jesus' works is the incapability of the authorities to hear and see. For, as Jesus charges, they are unable to recognize that the activities that he engages in correspond to the works of God. Indeed, they cannot make a valid determination because:

> Never once *have you heard* (ἀκηκόατε) his *voice* or *seen* (ἑωράκατε) his *form/ appearance* (εἶδος) , and you do not have his word (λόγον) abiding in you, because you do not believe that one whom he sent. (5:37-38)

Because their hearing and their seeing are impaired, they have been unable to hear God's voice or see God's *appearance* (εἶδος). It is very natural and appropriate, therefore, that he censures them by discrediting their hearing and seeing in as far as their hearing and seeing prevent them from discerning the correspondence between the works of God and the works of Jesus and between the truth of God's word and the truth of Jesus' teaching. At the beginning of this trial he had justified his healing on the basis of discerning God's activity in the world.

> Amen, amen I say to you, the Son can do nothing of himself except what he *sees* (βλέπῃ) the Father doing. For the things that One does, the Son also does likewise. (5:19)

Jesus' deeds and words are determined by his imitation of God's works that he learns by seeing, but it is a penetrating, perspicacious *seeing* that is not determined by the alienated and alienating social construction of reality. The immediate example he cites is the work of resurrection: "Even as the Father raises the dead and makes alive, so also the Son makes alive whom he wills." If God shows him the things that God is doing, Jesus, as God's apprentice, must have the capacity to differentiate that divine activity from all the jumble and mishmash of the industry that characterizes the world. Attendantly, because his works correspond to his words, Jesus, as the incarnate Logos-Sophia, also claims that his teaching originates from God. He defends the truth of what he says on the basis of having *heard* it from God.

> I have many things to say about you and to judge, but the One who sent me is true, and the things that I heard from him, these things I speak into the world. (8:26b)

> And now you seek to kill me, a human being who has spoken to you the truth which I heard from the Father. (8:40)

In his farewell speech he will justify calling his disciples "friends, because all the things I heard from my Father I made known to you" (15:15).

In this respect Moses is Jesus' forerunner, for the capacity to *hear* God's *voice* and to see God's *appearance* is attributed to him in Num 12:6-8.

> And he [God] said to them [Aaron and Miriam], "Heed my words! If a prophet of yours should come to [the] Lord, [that is, to me], I shall be known to him in a vision and I shall speak to him in sleep. Not so my restorer, Moses! He is faithful in my whole house! I shall speak to him mouth to mouth, in *appearance* (εἴδει) and not through enigmas. And he saw the glory of the Lord."[32]

The authorities, who are conducting this forensic process, claim to believe Moses. That, of course, implies that they are convinced that God spoke to Moses and, therefore, in their self-satisfaction they can boast in 9:28b that they are Moses' disciples. Moreover, as Jesus says in 5:45, "they have hoped into Moses," which may insinuate that the ideological future they are projecting for post-70 Judaism is grounded in Moses. Ironically, however, unlike Moses, they have never heard God's voice or seen God's appearance. Furthermore, they fail to remember God's rebuke to Aaron and Miriam for their diminishment of Moses in Num 12:6-8. At least there is no consciousness of how that censure might be applicable to them in their collusion against Jesus.

Philo appropriated this text in order to augment the prestige of Moses. His allegorization of God's instructions to Moses for the construction of the Tabernacle culminates in distinguishing Moses as "the artificer of the archetypes," and an apprentice under God's tutelage. Moses' preeminence is reinforced by God's reprimand of Aaron and Miriam: "For when Aaron, *the word* (ὁ λόγος) and Miriam, *the perception* (ἡ αἴσθησις) rebelled, they heard expressly,"

> If there should be a prophet to the Lord, God will be known to him in a vision and in a shadow, not visibly; but to Moses, who is faithful in his whole house, he will speak mouth to mouth, in *form/appearance* (εἴδει) and not through enigmas.[33]

---

[32] My translation of LXX Num 12:6-8.

[33] Philo, *Legum Allegoria* III, 102-103.

Jesus, God, and Philo all utilize this seemingly opaque word εἶδος. What kind of experience is signified by *seeing God's form* or *appearance*? What is Jesus referring to when he avows that the authorities have never seen God's εἶδος? The last verse of the Prologue, 1:18, declares, "No one *has* ever *seen* (ἑώρακεν) God." Jesus, nevertheless, claims one exception:

> Not that anyone *has seen* (ἑώρακεν) the Father, except *the one being* (ὁ ὢν) from the Father; this one *has seen* (ἑώρακεν) the Father (6:46).[34]

However, nothing is said here of seeing God's εἶδος. What kind of reality, then, is God's εἶδος? Is it empirically invisible? Or is it an actuality that is perceivable by the physical sight of human beings? In the narrative world of the Gospel the perception of God's *form* or *appearance* is not predetermined by Philo's eyes of the mind that are able to take flight and attain to the furthest regions of the air by passing over the borders of the world in order to approach the Uncreated One.[35] That kind of seeing belongs to Philo's metaphysical dualism. In Num 12:6-8, God's use of εἶδος refers to the experience of God's glory that Moses had requested in Ex 33:18-23.

> When my glory passes by and I shall place you in the opening of the rock and I shall cover my hand over you until I pass by, and I shall remove my hand and then *you shall see* (ὄψῃ) my back, but my face will not be seen to you. (LXX Ex 33:22-23)

Similarly Jesus must be referring to a *form* or *appearance* of God that is discernible to the naked eye. But it is a seeing – as well as a hearing – that requires a heavenly rebirth, a being born from above, as Jesus asseverated to Nicodemus, a Pharisee and "a ruler of the Jews". That is why he can avow this deficiency of the ruling authorities so unqualifiedly. The authorities cannot *hear* God's *voice* or *see* God's *appearance* because their hearing and seeing are impaired by their ideological persistence in reconstituting Judaism on the basis of the moral order of the old creation. In the New Creation that Jesus, the New Human Being (ὁ υἱὸς τοῦ ἀνθρώπου) is inaugurating, *God's εἶδος is Jesus himself as the incarnation of the Logos-Sophia.* But God's εἶδος also includes all those who become incarnations of the Logos-Sophia by their participation in the New Creation. Only by being generated by God will the authorities – and the implied readers – be able to *hear* God's *voice* and *see* God's *appearance* in the flesh and blood discipleship of human beings.

Jesus presents his last witness by summoning the ruling elite to "search the Scriptures, because you think to have everlasting life in/by them, and these are the ones testifying about me." He does not want glory from human beings. That is a value of the honor/shame culture of the "world," the social construction of reality, and it has no integrity because it involves human beings in a schizophrenic state of being. In the social contests for honor and glory it is honorable to deceive, to misrepresent, and lie

---

[34] See chapter 9 for an interpretation of this text.

[35] See Philo, *de Plantatione,* 22. Also *Quod Deus Immutabilis Sit*, 45-46.

to outsiders. Only those who are worthy of respect have a right to the truth.[36] If Jesus embraced those values, he would have no integrity, either before God or in his own eyes. What he desires from them is that they would receive him because he came in the Father's name, not his own. But they are locked into the culture of honor/shame, and therefore, as Jesus *has known* (ἔγνωκα), they do not have God's love in themselves; and that, of course, is the result of their inability to *hear* God's *voice* and *see* God's *appearance*.

Jesus, as he stated earlier, has been given the authority to judge. But he will not be their accuser before God. That will be Moses himself, "unto whom you have hoped". Jesus concludes his self-defense by enunciating Moses' anticipation of his work.

> "For if you believed Moses, you would believe me, for he wrote about me. And if you do not believe his writings, how will you believe my words?" (5:46-47)

Moses, he claims, wrote about him! No text is cited, and the implied readers are left to determine for themselves in what way Moses anticipated the coming of Jesus. Possibly Deut 18:15 would come to mind. But he cannot be only a New Moses, a Moses *redivivus*, for, unlike Moses, he will be the snake lifted up on a pole "so that everyone who believes into him has everlasting life." In what way, then, did Moses write about him? Earlier, in 1:45, Philip had conveyed a similar witness to Nathanael, "The one whom Moses wrote about in the Law … we have found." If he is the fulfillment of Deut 18:15, it cannot be in terms of a lawgiver; for as John stated in the Prologue, "… the Law was given through Moses; grace and truth happened through Jesus Christ." In all likelihood, therefore, Moses, in writing about Jesus, was anticipating a New Deliverer who, like Moses, would lead the people of God into a New Exodus.[37] That liberation, as Philo's interpretation of that "Passing Over" (μεταβαίνων) discloses, became a model, an archetype, of an anticipated Exodus into a Promised Land in which a more comprehensive salvation would be actualized. The testimony that Jesus has offered in the form of two sets of double asseverations constructs that redemption as the conquest of the ultimate reality of death and attendantly all the forms and forces of living death that are nurtured and sustained by it.

---

[36] Malina, *New Testament World*, 38.

[37] Meeks, *The Prophet-King*, 292, names the "gifts" that the Fourth Gospel connects with Moses: the Torah, the manna, and the lifting up of the serpent, and states that "Each of these gifts has its parallel in a gift made by God through Jesus". But Meeks has omitted the greatest gift of all, the Exodus. He seems to have difficulty breaking away from typology and the continuity that it establishes. Jesus' gifts are symbolically identical with himself because he gives himself as the one who unites heaven and earth in his self-disclosure as ἐγὼ εἰμί, and therefore his gifts transcend those of Moses. Bultmann, *John*, 273, is correct in judging that Moses' writings about Jesus should not be construed "as consisting primarily in the Messianic prophecies." But he is wrong in concluding that Moses' writings about Jesus refer to the Law. Barrett, *St. John*, 270; and Lindars, *John*, 233, make the same judgment. Keener *John* I, 662, suggests that Moses saw the glory of Jesus on Sinai when he received the Torah.

> Amen, amen I say to you, the one heeding my word and believing the one who sent me has eternal life and does not come into judgment but *has passed over* (μεταβέβηκεν) from death into life. Amen, amen I say to you, the hour is coming and now is when the dead will hear the voice of the Son of God and those hearing will live. (5:24)

Jesus closes his defense with a *qal wahomer*, a syllogism that moves from an ironic minor premise to a major premise and challenges the authorities' faith in the writings of Moses, the one, as Jesus stated, unto whom they have hoped.[38]

> Now if you don't believe the writings of that one, how will you believe my words?

Will the authorities among the implied readers be willing to acknowledge that Moses wrote about Jesus? If, in fact, they will, then they have no choice but to believe Jesus' words. On the other hand, if they refuse to believe that Moses wrote about Jesus as the one whom God would raise up to undertake a new and a final Exodus, can they still claim to believe the writings of Moses? If not, then naturally they also cannot believe Jesus' words. Ingeniously Jesus ends this judicial hearing that the authorities have initiated against him by calling them into question and compelling them to make a judgment about their own faith as to what Moses said and therefore also the truth of Jesus' words and deeds.

---

[38] Keener, *ibid*., also identifies 5:47 as a syllogism from a minor to a major premise.

Chapter Nine

The Second Passover and the Discourse on the Bread from Heaven

Feeding the Multitudes 6:1-13

If Moses wrote about Jesus in anticipation of a New Deliverer who would inaugurate a New Exodus, it is appropriate that Jesus offers a sign and gives evidence of that New Exodus as the second Passover of the Gospel's narrative world draws near.[1]

Jesus has left Jerusalem and returned to Galilee. While it is not explicitly indicated, it appears to be presupposed. The narrator reports that he crossed "the Sea of Galilee of Tiberius".[2] The two genitives that follow each other, "of Galilee" and "of Tiberius," are an awkward combination of names by which to identify the lake, but perhaps the Evangelist is addressing an audience that may be familiar with only one or the other and therefore wants to make sure that the lake is identifiable.[3]

Curiously, Jesus' objective in crossing the Sea of Galilee is to reach a particular mountain. His movement from the sea to the mountain in verses 1 and 3 is interrupted by the report of verse 2 that a great crowd was following him, "because *they were observing* (ἐθεώρουν) the signs that he was doing upon the sick." These are the Galileans who had viewed Jesus' signs in Jerusalem (2:23) and who, upon his return to Galilee, received him, "having seen all the signs that he did in Jerusalem at the feast" (4:45). Perhaps they are a mirror image of at least some of the implied readers of the Gospel, who, as Jesus declared in 4:48, unless they see signs and wonders, will by no means believe. In any case, the narrator's employment of the verb ἐθεώρουν implies that they are continuing to be drawn to

---

[1] Bultmann, *John*, 209-210; German, 154-155, contends that the order of chapters 5 and 6 cannot be original because nothing has been said about Jesus return to Galilee. At the close of chapter 5 he is still in Jerusalem. Chapter 6, he believes, would follow chapter 4 very well. The original order must have been chapters 4, 6, 5, 7. Barnabas Lindars, *Behind the Fourth Gospel: Studies in Creative Criticism* (London: Talbot, 1971) 47-50, argues that chapter 6 did not belong to the first edition of the Gospel, but to the second. Ashton, *Understanding*, 200, supports Lindars' view on the basis of "internal evidence," claiming that chapter 6 conveys "disputants ... from the ranks of the Christian group itself."

[2] P[66] and a few other manuscripts refer only to "the Sea of Galilee"; N, 0210, a few others and the Bohairic Coptic substitute "the Sea of Tiberius;" and a large number of manuscripts read, "the Sea of Galilee into the regions of Tiberius." Very likely C. K. Barrett, *John*, 273, is correct in concluding that "The clumsy text is no doubt the original."

[3] Only the Fourth Gospel refers to the lake as "the Sea of Tiberias." Since Josephus uses this name to refer to this body of water, those who are familiar with his writings may know it only by this name.

Jesus on the basis of the signs he is performing. But what will be the outcome of their observation? Will they be drawn into a committed discipleship?

Upon reaching the other shore – wherever that may be – Jesus proceeds to go up "into the mountain" (εἰς τὸ ὄρος) and there seats himself with his disciples. It is at this point that the narrator announces the time: "Now the Passover was *near*, the festival of the Jews." In view of this conjunction of details, it is difficult to avoid the supposition that the narrator intends the implied readers to project a new Exodus as well as to draw a parallel between Jesus and Moses:

1. Crossing the sea in order to reach a specific mountain
2. Followed by a great throng of people
3. Ascending into the mountain
4. Near the time of the Passover

After the very first Passover Moses led the Israelites through the Red Sea to Mount Sinai; and there, as the representative of the people, he ascended the mountain in order to enter into covenant with God on behalf of Israel.[4] At that architectonic center Israel was born as the elect people of God.[5]

Now at this imminent Passover, the second in the narrative world of the Gospel, Jesus does not go up to Jerusalem, as he had done earlier in 2:13. There is no religious necessity to undertake that journey in order to be present at this festival, for the Jerusalem Temple is no longer the center of the world where the divine presence resides. Jesus, as the incarnate Logos-Sophia, having substituted his physical body in place of the sanctuary of the Temple, has become "the Father's House." As the New Human Being (ὁ υἱὸς τοῦ ἀνθρώπου) on whom the heavenly ladder rests and the angels of God ascend and descend, he crosses the Sea of Galilee, ascends "into the mountain" and there, near the time of the Passover, he seats himself with his disciples. As the Passover draws near and a great crowd has followed Jesus to this navel of Galilee, a New Exodus is being projected as a sign of fulfillment. Will these Galileans, who have been *observing* (ἐθεώρουν) the signs Jesus was doing, abandon themselves to what they have experienced visually?[6] Will they commit themselves to accompanying Jesus into a New Exodus?

Raising his eyes and *looking at* (θεασάμενος) the approaching crowd, Jesus apparently is ascertaining what resources are needed to feed them. For he immediately turns to Philip and inquires, "From where shall we *buy* bread so that these may eat?" It is a question that parallels the one that Moses addressed to God

---

[4] See Ex 20: 21, 24:1-2 and 9-18.

[5] Here again see Mircea Eliade, *Cosmos and History: The Myth of the Eternal Return* (New York: Harper & Brothers, 1959) 12-17 and *The Sacred and the Profane* (New York: Harper & Row, 1961) 36-47.

[6] See the analysis of the verb θεωρεῖν (to observe) in chapter 5.

during the Exodus, "From where am I to get meat to give to all these people?"[7] Before Philip is able to answer the question, the narrator pauses to insert an intrusive remark for the benefit of the reader, "But he was saying this testing him, for he already knew what he was going to do." Yet if bread is to be *bought*, it must require money. Philip's reply, therefore, is determined by Jesus' question, "Loaves of bread in the value of two hundred *denarii* are not sufficient so that each might receive a little."[8]

On the one hand, Philip cannot be faulted for his response to Jesus' question. Buying bread presupposes the necessity of money, and he, Philip, is aware of the inadequacy of funds for the needs at hand. But on the other hand, Jesus was asking a rhetorical question, for, in view of their ascent "into the mountain," he was very aware that no bread would be available for purchase in that vicinity. "*From where* shall we buy bread so that these may eat?" Jesus is conscious of the limitations of the place; Philip is sensitive to the limitations of their resources. But why be concerned about the limitation of resources? Should he not have remembered how Moses had asked a similar question and, as a result of God's provision, had provided the Israelites with a virtually endless supply of meat?[9] Earlier he had witnessed to Nathanael, "The one whom Moses wrote about in the Law and [the one whom] the prophets [wrote about] we have found" (1:45). If Jesus is indeed the fulfillment of Moses' prophecy of Deut 18:15, it would be a natural inference that Jesus has a Moses-like capability to feed the hungry masses. Moreover, he had been present at the wedding at Cana and had witnessed Jesus' wonderful transformation of 162 gallons of water into wine when the supply of wine had run out. Evidently Philip's assessment of the circumstance is restricted to the actuality of material resources. Jesus' ascertainment, on the other hand, moves beyond the actualities of sense and contemplates the possibilities latent in the moment.

Andrew, originally a disciple of John and the brother of Simon Peter, announces that a *youth* (παιδάριον) is present who has "five loaves of barley bread and two very small fish."[10] If three loaves, as Luke 11:5 indicates, are an adequate meal, the five loaves of the youth, along with the two tiny, sardine-like fish, would be enough to satisfy the hunger of one person. Yet Andrew's evaluation, "But what are they among so many?" is no different than that of Philip's. The material resources that are available – like the two hundred *denarii* – are too limited to be of any use in this situation. Yet would not Andrew have remembered a context in the career of Elisha in which somewhat similar resources were wonderfully multiplied? These responses, of course, are intended for the evaluation of the implied readers.

[7] Num 11:13; but also 11:4-32.

[8] A denarius, a silver Roman coin, is generally considered to be a day's wage. See Matt 20:2, 9-10. Two hundred denarii, as the New Revised Standard translates, is equivalent to "six months' wages."

[9] LXX Num 11:13.

[10] A παιδάριον is a double diminutive of παῖς (child, boy), but in LXX Gen 37:30 it refers to seventeen year old Joseph. Barley bread is the bread of the poor.

This feeding of the multitudes in the context of an imminent Passover, after an Exodus-like crossing of the Sea of Galilee and an arrival at a Sinai-like mountain, is comparable to Moses providing manna for the Israelites in the wilderness (Ex 16:4-16).[11] It is also remarkably parallel to Elisha's feeding of one hundred men in the Septuagint translation of 2 Kings 4:42-44.[12] When the prophet receives twenty loaves of *barley bread* and cakes of preserved fruit, he orders the food to be set before the people. His servant, Gehazi, who in the Septuagint version of 2 Kings 4:12, 14, 15 is designated a παιδάριον (youth), reacts in a manner similar to Andrew, "How can I set this before one hundred men?" Elisha repeats his command and adds, "For thus says the Lord, 'They will eat and they will have [some] left.' And they ate and had [some] left, according to the word of the Lord."

As Jesus directs the people to recline on the grass that was abundant in that place, the narrator once again intrudes into the story to inform the reader that the number of those reclining was five thousand males. In contrast to the Synoptic tradition, there is no reference to women and children. Jesus takes the loaves and the fish and, after speaking a blessing over them, distributes both to the people, "as much as they wanted." The narrator deliberately does not include his disciples in the distribution of the food. Why only Jesus dispenses the bread and the fish will be elucidated when Jesus delivers his discourse on the Bread of Life.

The disciples are reintroduced after all have been satisfied, and they are charged with the task of gathering together the leftover fragments of food: "Gather together the overabounding fragments so that nothing is lost."[13] When the task has been completed, the leftover crumbs and pieces from the five barley loaves fill twelve baskets, intimating perhaps that there is enough to feed the twelve tribes of Israel. As earlier in Jesus' ministry, the narrator also designates this mighty work as a sign, and those who have experienced it and have *seen* (ἰδόντες) the twelve baskets full of leftovers immediately identify Jesus as "the Prophet, the one coming into the world." This is the first christological identity that the crowd ascribes to Jesus in the narrative world of the Gospel. On the basis of what they have witnessed, they are ready to regard Jesus as the New Moses, the fulfillment of Deut 18:15, who, like his predecessor, will lead them into the Promised Land of abundance.[14] Jesus, however, sensing that the people want to seize him in order to

---

[11] Bertil Gärtner, *John 6 and the Jewish Passover* (Lund: C. W. K. Gleerup, 1959) 18-19, makes a "noteworthy connection between John 6 and the Jewish Passover, namely that the Jewish texts [like Mekhilta Ex 2:99] connect the manna with the Passover." See also Josh 5:10-12.

[12] Also Brown, *John*, I, 246; Barrett, *St. John*, 275; Haenchen, *John* I, 271.

[13] A noteworthy typology on "scattering" and "gathering" is developed by Meeks, *The Prophet-King*, 93-98, who links Jesus "separate command" in 6:12 to a relationship between *Didache* 9:4, "... so let your church be gathered together from the end of the earth into your reign" and John 11:52, "... so that the scattered children of God are gathered together into one" and ties them together in Jesus' self-identification as the Shepherd in 10:16.

[14] Meeks, *ibid.*, 87-99 and especially 318-319, relies on his interpretation of this feeding episode to begin to reach the conclusion that although Jesus fulfills the Moses typology in various ways, he is more than a new Moses. For Meeks, the central christology of the Fourth Gospel is summarized in the title of his book, "The Prophet-King". However, in his focus on the Moses traditions in the Fourth

make him a king, a Bread Messiah upon whom they can depend for their physical needs, withdraws "into the mountain" where he had begun to constitute a new people of God. In view of their misinterpretation of the sign, the Galileans are not yet ready to participate in the Passover of a New Exodus.

Walking on the Sea of Galilee 6:14-21

Jesus is on the mountain alone, and in the evening, when he does not appear, the disciples *descend* to the sea, embark into their boat and "*were trying* to go across the sea to Capernaum" (6:17).[15] The sequence of action, described by the narrator in verse 17, may intimate that the disciples are already at sea.[16] Darkness had fallen, and they had been waiting for Jesus to appear. But it is only when he does not show up, that they begin to make their way across the sea toward Capernaum. When they had rowed about twenty-five or thirty "stades," that is, about three or four miles, or half-way across the lake, "*they observe* (θεώρουσιν) Jesus walking on the sea and approaching the boat, and they were frightened."[17] The verb, θεώρουσιν, is a faculty of vision that is "led upwards by the light," to cite the meaning that Philo attributed to it.[18] It refers to a spectatorship or a looking at that anticipates a commitment to what has been visually experienced, as Jesus himself will state in 6:40, "For this is the will of God that everyone *observing* (ὁ θεωρῶν) the Son and believing into him has everlasting life." But the visual experience of the disciples evokes alarm and fear. They do not appear to recognize him, and, if they did, there is nothing in their past experience as his disciples that would enable them to make sense of what they are experiencing. But he reassures them, "**I AM**, stop being afraid!"

This is the second time in the Gospel that Jesus uses this phrase of self-identification, ἐγὼ εἰμί (**I AM**). Earlier he had spoken it to the Samaritan woman in order to establish his union with God by appropriating God's self-identification in the Septuagint translation of Is 52:6.[19] Here his solidarity with God is already evident in his walking on the sea, for it is in Job 9:8 that God is characterized as the one who "trampled the waves of the Sea."[20] If the sign of his mighty work of feeding the multitudes by multiplying the loaves and the fish evoked the fulfillment

Gospel, he does not include 6:16-21 in his final determination of the Gospel's christology.

[15] The imperfect middle indicative, ἤρχοντο, may be a conative imperfect, as Brown and Barrett suggest, and should therefore be translated, "they were trying to go." Brown, John I, 251; Barrett, *St. John*, 280.

[16] Brown, *John* I, 251.

[17] Keener, *John* I, 672, cites various ancient divine heroes, philosophers, and others who walked on water or calmed storms. This episode of Jesus walking on the sea may not be a close parallel to the exodus event, as Keener acknowledges, but it is necessary in order to prepare the implied readers for his forthcoming discourse on the Bread of Life.

[18] Philo, *de Opificio Mundi,* 54. See chapter 5.

[19] See the discussion of 4:26 in chapter 7.

[20] The **I AM** of 6:20 is not simply an identification, 'It is I/me'. Contrary to Barrett, *John*, 281; and John Painter, "Tradition and Interpretation in John 6," *NTS* 35/3 (1989) 431.

of Deut 18:15, this act of emulating God by "trampling the waves of the sea" transcends any and every attempt to identify Jesus in terms of Old Testament typology. It is his self-disclosure to his disciples as **I AM** without predicates, as he walks on the sea, that will authenticate his self-identification to the Galileans in 6:51, "**I AM** the living Bread which descended from heaven. If anyone eats of this Bread, she/he will live forever, but now the Bread which I shall give is my flesh on behalf of the life of the world."

As soon as the disciples recognize Jesus, according to the narrator, "they were wanting to take him into the boat." Their *looking at* (θεώρουσιν) Jesus walking on the sea has resulted in receiving him, in taking him into the boat with them. They are committed to him! Apparently that desire to have Jesus join them in the boat results in the astonishing outcome of a sudden arrival at their destination: "and immediately the boat happened at the land toward which they were going." Such a marvelous realization is anticipated in Psa 107:30, "... and he brought them to their desired haven." When the disciples experience the coming of Jesus, the one who tramples the waves of the sea and expresses his solidarity with God by his self-disclosure as **I AM**, they have reached their destination. They have realized their destiny. As Jesus will say to them later in 12:26, "If anyone would serve me, let him/her follow me and *where **I AM*** (ὅπου εἰμὶ ἐγώ), there will my servant be." In 14:3 he will promise his disciples, "Again I am coming and I will receive you to myself, so that *where **I AM*** (ὅπου εἰμὶ ἐγώ) you also are." Finally in his culminating prayer of chapter 17, he will entreat God, "Father, that which you have given me, I want that *where **I AM*** (ὅπου εἰμὶ ἐγώ), these may be with me, so that they *observe* (θεωρῶσιν) my glory which you have given me." The reality of incarnation that Jesus embodies is to be imparted to his disciples so that they will participate in his divine **I AM** and therefore also in his union with God.

Jesus' discourse on the Bread of Life 6:22-71

In the meantime, the crowd of Galileans, for whom Jesus had multiplied the loaves and the fish, are still on the far side of the sea. On the following morning they become aware that there had been only one boat at that place, and Jesus had not embarked in it with his disciples as they left to row towards Capernaum. When they do not find Jesus or his disciples among the boats from Tiberius that had landed nearby, they get into those boats and sail to Capernaum in search of Jesus. Upon finding him, they ask, "Rabbi, when did you get here?" Implied in their interrogation may also be the question, "How did you get here?"[21]

Jesus responds with his double asseveration, accentuating the truth of what he wants to say to his audience, peremptorily, of course, to the implied readers of the Gospel (6:26). "Amen, amen I say to you, 'you aren't looking for me because you saw signs but because you ate of the loaves and were filled'." Originally the Galileans had followed him because they were impressed by his legitimating signs.

---

[21] Brown, *John* I, 261.

Now, according to Jesus' indictment, they are pursuing him because his multiplication of the loaves and the fish demonstrates to them that he obviously has access to an inexhaustible supply of food. This is the first of several misconceptions that they disclose, namely, the bread they ate is an end in itself. Jesus censures them for their mistaken interpretation, " Do not keep on working for the food that perishes!" As vital as physical sustenance is, it must not be the only or the ultimate objective of human existence. As physical as human beings may be in their flesh and blood existence, nothing that is material in its actuality can ultimately satisfy their hunger and thirst. The phrase, "food that perishes" refers to more than the bread and fish that Jesus multiplied for the people. It comprehends all the material things that human labor produces and acquires and consumes.

Beyond the physical and material needs of human existence is "the food that remains into eternal life." That is the food that they should work for, and that is the food that the New Human Being (ὁ υἱὸς τοῦ ἀνθρώπου) offers. Here, for the first time, Jesus indirectly professes to the Galileans that he is the Son of the Human Being, but they would not know what the implied readers have already learned, that "No one has ascended into heaven except the one who descended, the Son of the Human Being." He will give them the food that endures forever because he is the Son of the Human Being who descended from heaven, and that is the food they should work for. God guarantees its authenticity because God set his divine seal of approval on the one who makes it available.[22]

Obviously affected by the authoritative pronouncement Jesus has addressed to them, the Galileans inquire, "What do we do so that we work the works of God?"[23] At this point the response that the implied readers might expect the Galileans to make would be: "Give us this food."[24] They will indeed ask for it later, but at the moment that question is inappropriate, if only because more must be said about the kind of food that "the Son of the Human Being" offers. Jesus has admonished them to *work* for "the food the remains into eternal life." If their labor is not to be directed toward the food that perishes, that is, the production of material things that do not fulfill human aspirations, what then are the works that they should engage in? What kind of food should they pursue that fulfills God's will? Of course, as God's elect people, they already know, or at least should know, the works that

---

[22] Different interpretations are offered by commentators to account for Jesus' use of the aorist tense, ἐσφράγισεν (he sealed). Brown, *John* I, 261, refers back to 3:33 and suggests that it is the believer who, by accepting Jesus' testimony, certifies that God is truthful. But that is not what Jesus states in 6:27. Barrett, *John*, 287, proposes that it "should probably be found in Jesus' baptism." For the implied readers of the Gospel, the life of Jesus that is recounted in the Gospel occurred in the past. Therefore, his resurrection from the dead would be God's seal of approval.

[23] As a parallel to the Galileans' question, Haenchen, *John* I, 290, points to LXX Num 8:11, in which God tells Moses that Aaron shall present the Levites before the Israelites as those who will "work the works of the Lord".

[24] This is Bultmann's judgment, *John*, 220; German, 162, and he goes on to say, "Rather one would expect them to ask, as in fact they do in v.34 (in the same way that 4:15 follows 4:14): 'Give us this bread.'"

they, as participants in the divine covenant, are obligated to fulfill. Their question, therefore, must be rhetorically directed to give Jesus the opportunity to make an unprecedented response that will move the dialogue to a more intense and penetrating degree of enlightenment. Neither Moses nor any of the great prophets of ancient Israel would have replied to their question in this way.

Jesus answered and said to them, "This is the work of God, that you believe into him whom that one sent." Enunciating implicitly that he was sent by God, Jesus summons them to "believe into him." On various occasions previously he disclosed the benefits of that kind of faith. Here for the very first time he invokes his Galilean audience to "believe into him." As elsewhere in the Gospel, his employment of the verb, *believe* (πιστεύειν), is followed by the preposition *into* (εἰς) and conveys the force of "commitment." "Believing into" is not an intellectual assent to a set of doctrines or a verbal confession of Jesus as "Lord" and "Savior". "Believing into" is a commitment that involves the total person in following Jesus into thinking and doing and fulfilling the will of God as a steward of the creation.

Here, however, as in 19:35 and 20:31, the manuscript tradition of the Fourth Gospel offers two variant readings in the subjunctive mood: πιστεύητε in the present tense (you continue believing) and πιστεύσητε in the aorist tense (you begin to believe). Both of them are valid, but specifically in their individual historical contexts. The aorist subjunctive, πιστεύσητε, belongs to the original edition of the Gospel that was addressed to the Jews of Alexandria in order to draw them into a commitment to Jesus as the Founder of a New Israel. The present subjunctive, πιστεύητε, was substituted in Ephesus when the addendum of chapter 21 was added, and the intention of the Gospel was reoriented to serve those who already were Christians. In either case, the distinctive combination of πιστεύειν εἰς is the summons to make a commitment to Jesus as the embodiment as well as the pioneer of a New Humanity.

In view of the role that signs play in the Old Testament, the Galileans' response is typically Jewish: "What sign, then, do you do so that we may see and believe you? What work do you do?"[25] Ironically the Galileans have already experienced a sign, as the narrator acknowledged in 6:14, and they interpreted it as the fulfillment of Deut 18:15, the coming of "the Prophet" or a New Moses. But Jesus does not want his feeding of the multitudes to be interpreted as a sign that corresponds to the work of Moses. By referring to himself and his work in terms of the christological title, ὁ υἱὸς τοῦ ἀνθρώπου (the Son of the Human Being), he subverts their earlier identification of him as "the Prophet." But if he is indeed the Son of the Human Being who is summoning them to make a commitment to him, that requires a validation of its own. Accordingly, the Galileans want a sign of divine authentication to certify that the work of God is to believe into the Son of the Human Being whom God has sent and sealed and who will give them the food

[25] As the Apostle Paul also acknowledges in 1 Cor 1:22, "The Jews ask for signs…"

that remains into eternal life. Moreover, that validation must be empirical: "so that we may *see* (ἴδωμεν) *and believe* you." Believing will be based on the experience of empirical seeing. But whether their believing will be the commitment of "believing into" or only an acknowledgment of credibility is at this point indeterminable. Significantly, there is a shift here from "food" to "bread."

Moses had validated himself to their ancestors by providing them with manna in the wilderness. To that end they cite Scripture: "*Bread from heaven* he gave them to eat." If, in contrast, the bread and the fish that Jesus multiplied is to be characterized as "the food that perishes," at least in the light of his rebuke of the Galileans for craving more of the same, what work is he able to do that compares with the bread that came *from heaven*? The Scripture that they quote is derived from the Septuagint translation of Ps 77 (78): 24, but it may also be a conflation of various Old Testament texts. The referent of the pronoun "he" that is the subject of their citation appears to be deliberately ambiguous. Is it God or is it Moses? In all the possible texts that may have been combined, God is clearly the one who gave the manna:

Ex 16:4	I am going to rain bread from heaven for you.
Ex 16:15	It is the bread Yahweh has given you to eat.
Psa 78:24	He rained down on them manna to eat and gave them the grain of heaven.
Neh 9:15	For their hunger you gave them bread from heaven
Wis 16:20	Instead of these things you gave your people food of angels, and without toil you supplied them from heaven with bread ready to eat.[26]

In the light of these texts it would seem that the referent of the pronoun "he" in the Galilean citation must be God. Yet in all likelihood the intended referent of their citation, "Bread from heaven *he* gave them to eat*,"* while it may be deliberately ambiguous, is Moses. If the Galileans are challenging Jesus to do a sign that is comparable to the manna that the Israelites ate in the wilderness, it must be Moses, and not God, who originally validated himself by this sign. Jesus' response to their challenge in the form of another double asseveration supports this identification of

[26] Of these five texts that may have contributed to the composite version of the Galileans, the one that corresponds more immediately than the others is LXX Ps 77(78): 24. Yet the Wisdom of Solomon 16:20 may be the closest to the context in which this encounter between Jesus and the Galileans is taking place. There is little verbal correspondence between it and the quotation of the Galileans, but the emphasis of the former on bread "ready to eat" and "supplied *without toil*" may account for their ideological perspective that interpreted Jesus' feeding of the multitudes as a sign of the fulfillment of Deut 18:15. No work was involved. Bread was supplied without toil and ready to eat. In this light Jesus' emphasis on *work* may also be accounted for. His negative prohibition: "Don't work for the bread that perishes but the bread that remains into eternal life;" is followed by the unequivocal qualification: "This is the work of God, that you believe into the one whom that one sent."

Moses as the referent of the pronoun "he" in their scriptural quotation, "Amen, amen I say to you, not Moses gave you the bread from heaven."[27]

By negating Moses as the giver of bread from heaven, Jesus appears to be correcting the Galileans' interpretation of Scripture. God, not Moses, provided that manna from heaven.[28] Yet at the same time, because the issue here is the demand for a validating sign, Jesus replaces Moses as the referent of the pronoun "he" with the referent that Ps 77(78): 24 and all the other possible texts related to this quotation imply, namely, "my Father."[29]

> … but my Father gives you the true Bread from heaven. For the Bread of God is the one descending from heaven and giving life to the world. (6:32-33)

Moses cannot be validated by the manna from heaven, because that manna was not the true bread that God gives; it did not give life to the world. God validates Jesus because God gives him as the true Bread, the Bread that descends from heaven and gives life to the world.

For the moment the issue of doing the works of God is set aside. At last the reader's expectation is fulfilled. The Galileans, in their response to Jesus, plead for this bread: "Lord, at all times give us this bread." But they do not yet grasp that he is referring to himself as the true bread. Their misunderstanding is like that of the Samaritan woman who petitions Jesus for that internalized spring of living water that bubbles up into everlasting life that he has offered. If God validated Moses through the giving of manna, and that was not the true bread from heaven, then God must be legitimating Jesus as the intermediary who is dispensing the true bread from heaven. Jesus corrects their misunderstanding with an **I AM** avowal that is followed by a predicate: "**I AM** the Bread of Life." For the first time in the Gospel he links his self-disclosure as the divine ἐγώ εἰμί, by which he had revealed himself to his disciples while walking on the Sea of Galilee, with a predicate that designates him as the true Bread from heaven that gives life to the world. He is not God's intermediary – like Moses – dispensing the true bread. He himself is the true Bread who descended from heaven. On the basis of that self-designation he promises his fellow Galileans, as well as the readership of the

---

[27] Jesus' use of the perfect tense verb δέδωκεν (he has given) in 6:32 is problematic. It seems more likely that his response to the Galileans' quotation in which the aorist tense, ἔδωκεν (he gave) is used, would deliberately employ the same verb in order to emphasize the past tense of the giving of that bread in contrast to Jesus' subsequent use of the present tense, δίδωσιν (he gives). But the perfect tense is the more difficult reading, and is supported by P^{75} and other manuscripts. Its use indicates that Moses has continued to give that bread from heaven. That would imply that Moses' bread is to be construed as more than the manna of the wilderness, perhaps as an allegorical reference to the Law that Moses handed down to Israel. Barrett, *St. John*, 290, does not hesitate to draw the Law given by Moses into this context.

[28] Barrett, *St. John*, 289-290. But there is no implication here that the manna in the wilderness is to be allegorized as "a type of the heavenly bread given by Jesus."

[29] Also Brown, *John* I, 262. But the true bread from heaven is Jesus himself, and not merely his teaching, as Brown states. His "flesh and blood" will be the new Passover meal!

Fourth Gospel, "The one who comes *towards me* (πρὸς ἐμέ) will by no means hunger, and the one who *believes into* me will by no means thirst forever." His references to "hunger" and "thirst" anticipate his eventual summons to the Galileans to "have life in themselves" by eating his flesh and drinking his blood."

Yet he knows that in spite of what they have seen, they do not believe. Accordingly he acknowledges, "*You have seen* (ἑωράκατε) [me] and you do not *believe*." Once again the significant relationship between seeing and believing is emphasized. But the use of the pronoun με (me) is somewhat surprising. Since its authenticity is supported by P^{66} and possibly also P^{75}, as well as the remaining manuscripts, it may be original. In 4:45 the narrator had stated that the Galileans had *seen the things* he did in Jerusalem. Consequently, Jesus' reference to himself, "You have seen me…" may refer to the things they have seen him do. But now, at this critical juncture, when they have experienced his wonderful multiplication of the loaves and the fish, seeing no longer leads into believing. The relationship between them has been severed, perhaps already at the time when Jesus confronted them with the truth of why they were pursuing him, "You seek me not because you saw signs, but because you ate of the bread and you were filled." In the face of this disappointing outcome, Jesus is forced to speak collectively in acknowledging the emerging reality of disbelief.[30]

> Everything that the Father gives me will come *towards* (πρός) me, and the one coming *towards* (πρός) me, I will by no means throw out, for I descended from heaven not so that I do my own will but the will of the one who sent me. And this is the will of the one who sent me, that everything that he has given me I do not lose of it, but I shall raise it at the last day. For this is the will of my Father, that everyone who *observes* (θεωρῶν) the Son and believes into him has eternal life, and I will raise him at the last day. (6:37-40)

God's will corresponds to that which is visually manifested (θεωρῶν) and experienced in the ministry of Jesus. But will those who are *observing* the incarnate Logos-Sophia, the New Human Being, as he discloses God's will through his deeds and words, be induced into a faith commitment to all that he, Jesus, embodies: "the Father's house" and "the Bread of Life"? Those who give themselves over to this "perfect good that has come into the life of humankind" have eternal life here and now, and the Son of the Human Being (ὁ υἱὸς τοῦ ἀνθρώπου) as "God's Son" will resurrect them when the Last Day arrives.

Among these Galileans, according to 6:41, there are individuals who are identified as οἱ Ιουδαῖοι. They are considered by some commentators to be the

[30] The neuter, as Barrett, *St. John*, 294, correctly observes, emphasizes "the collective aspect of the Father's gift of believers."

"common people" or "the people of Galilee."[31] Others identify them as "Judeans."[32] Verse 41 is also construed as a mirror reflection of Jewish opposition to the Christian perspective on Jesus.[33] But they are members of the ruling elite, who have "penetrated" into Galilee.[34] This is their only appearance in Jesus' homeland, and they seem to be introduced deliberately as interlocutors who are aroused because Jesus has avowed, "**I AM** the Bread, the one descending from heaven." Again it is a matter of his aporetic self-identification, and the conflict it arouses within the context of the Fourth Gospel. Jesus is known and identified in terms of his family relationships: "He is Jesus, the son of Joseph, isn't he, whose father and mother we know? How does he now say, "I have descended from heaven?" Their "grumbling" calls attention to a significant gradation that has begun to unfold in this discourse on "the Bread of Life." The use of the verb ἐγόγγυζον (*they were grumbling*) may also remind the reader of the grumbling of the Israelites against God during their wilderness journey in LXX Ex 16:8-12 and Num 11:1.

Jesus has moved beyond the witness he gave in the forensic process before the ruling elite of Jerusalem. In 5:17-47 he had testified that his activity as God's Son is simply an imitation of the work that the Father does, and because of this mutuality he, as the Son, should be honored in the same way as the Father is honored. In this discourse of chapter 6, he re-introduces his descent from heaven that he had voiced earlier in his dialogue with Nicodemus, but now relating it to his self-disclosure as "the Bread of Life." Moses may have provided Israel with bread from heaven during the journey through the wilderness, but he is the Bread that descended from heaven. His hearers, the grumbling authorities (οἱ'Ιουδαῖοι), as well as the implied readers of the Gospel, – all of them! – should know this, that as unwilling or even incapable as they are of moving themselves into a faith commitment to him, those who do come *towards* him, that is, for union and not separation, are in fact being moved, pulled, and drawn by God.

> No one is able to come *towards* (πρός) me unless the Father, the one who sent me, draws him/her, and I will raise her/him up at the last day. (6:44)

---

[31] Brown, *John*, I, 270; von Wahlde, "The Johannine 'Jews'," 44. Keener, *John*, I, 685, offers another point of view, proposing that these 'Galileans,' because of their grumbling against Jesus, "finally receive the ironically pejorative title, "Jews," that is "Judeans."

[32] Ashton, "The Jews in John," *Studying John*, 49-51, is inclined to agree with Malcolm Lowe, "Who were the 'Ιουδαίοι," *NT* 18 (1976) 101-130, that originally these "Jews" in Galilee were Judeans, inhabitants of Judea, and not Pharisees; and this section of chapter 6 was composed when the regional connotations of the name had faded. In his essay, "The Identity and Function of the ΙΟΥΔΑΙΟΙ," 54, he attributes the "Jews" of 6:41 and 52 to tradition history rather than the literary integrity of the Gospel.

[33] Henk Jan De Jonge, "The 'Jews' in the Gospel of John," *Anti-Semitism and the Fourth Gospel*, 246.

[34] Also Fortna, *Fourth Gospel*, 303; and the verb "penetrate" is taken from him. See also chapter 1 on the identification of οἱ'Ιουδαίοι (the Jews).

Indeed, it must be God who draws those who come *toward* Jesus, for God is acting in and through the union that is embodied in Jesus' self-disclosure as ἐγὼ εἰμί (**I AM**). He is the incarnate Logos-Sophia and his teaching, therefore, is the Word of God. Accordingly, as he himself announces, one of the realities of the new covenant that the prophets envisioned is being fulfilled through his words and deeds, "All will be taught of God." The quotation that he cites is a paraphrase of Isa 54:13, καὶ πάντας τοὺς υἱούς σου διδακτοὺς θεοῦ (and all your sons taught of God), a text that is drawn from Second Isaiah's pledge that God is faithful to "the covenant of peace" and will deliver Israel from exile. Conversely, everyone who is taught by God through the ministry of the incarnate Logos-Sophia "hears and learns *from alongside* (παρά) the Father" and comes *towards* (πρός) Jesus. Because Jesus is the bearer of God's presence, to come *towards* him for union is, at the very same time, to be, to hear and to learn in the presence of the Father.

Moreover, the spontaneous result of being drawn by God into a union with the enfleshed Logos-Sophia is the assurance of resurrection at the last day. For resurrection, as it is envisioned by Jewish apocalypticism, is a corporate event, and union with Jesus, who will be resurrected after his death on the cross, guarantees participation in this corporate reality.[35]

Because his own union with God is so intimate and complete, the claims that he unhesitatingly makes as the Bread that descended from heaven correspond to the paradoxical realities of union and differentiation that are attributed to the Logos in the Prologue, paradoxical realities he alluded to in the forensic process of the previous chapter. Consequently, as the enfleshed Logos-Sophia who has come into the world as the New Human Being (ὁ υἱὸς τοῦ ἀνθρώπου), he can assert, as he does in 6:38, "I have descended from heaven." By implication, therefore, he can also claim that which distinguishes him above Moses, who, according to LXX Ex 33:23, was given the privilege of seeing τὰ ὀπίσω μου (the things related to the backside of God). Jesus, in contrast, professes: "Not that anyone has seen the Father, except *the one who is* (ὁ ὤν) *from alongside* (παρά) God, this one has seen the Father." But he does so only indirectly, in contrast to his outright declaration of 6:38. Distinctive in this oblique formulation is his use of ὁ ὤν (*the one who is*), a masculine singular present participle of the copula "to be" (εἶναι) that may have been derived from LXX Ex 3:14 in which "God said to Moses, Ἐγώ εἰμι ὁ ὤν (**I AM** *the one who is*). Even as he employed the divine formula of self-disclosure to his disciples as he walked on the sea and attached the predicate "Bread of Life" to it in his discourse to the Galileans, here in 6:46 he appears to be discretely identifying himself with the participial phrase that referred to the Logos in 1:18, "Θεὸν οὐδεις ἑώρακεν πώποτε; μονογενὴς θεὸς ὁ ὤν εἰς τὸν

[35] As the Apostle Paul stated in 1 Cor 15:22, "For as in Adam all die, so also in Christ shall all be made alive. In Ezek 37:1-10 Israel is viewed as a collection of bones, and when God's breath blows upon them, they arise into life as a great host. See Isa 25:6-9; 26:19; Dan 12:2; 1 Enoch 62:7-16. Also 1 Thes 4:15-17; 1 Cor 15:51-55.

κόλπον τοῦ πατρός, ἐκεῖνος ἐξηγήσατο (God no one has ever seen; only one of a kind God, *the one who is* into the bosom of the Father, that one interpreted).[36] Jesus, in his oblique assertion of 6:46 and its use of ὁ ὤν, may be echoing 1:18 and LXX Ex 3:14, as he intimates something that could never be attributed to Moses. He, as the incarnation of the Logos-Sophia, "who is into the bosom of the Father," and therefore God's interpreter, *he has seen* (ἑώρακεν) God. The verb he employs is the same as the one used in 1:18, ἑώρακεν, the perfect active indicative, third person singular of the verb ὁράω, which throughout the Gospel denotes "to see or to experience empirically."

With his typical double asseveration he adds, "Amen, amen I say to you, 'the one who believes has eternal life'." No predicate accompanies the verb "believe," but the prepositional phrase εἰς εμε (*into me*), which is regularly combined with it, appears extensively in the manuscript tradition of 6:47. More than likely, however, in the light of his provocative intimation that he has seen God, Jesus is simply invoking a faith that believes that what he has implied is true. According to Gospel's Prologue, "descending from heaven" and "having seen God" characterize the activity of the Logos-Sophia. If, according to Philo, "seeing God (ὁρῶν θεόν) is the translation of Israel," it is all the more true of Jesus as the New Human Being (ὁ υἱὸς τοῦ ἀνθρώπου) who descended from heaven. Believing this startling disclosure has a direct bearing on the legitimacy of Jesus' self-disclosure as the Bread of Life, and therefore he repeats his earlier pronouncement.

> **I AM** the Bread of Life. Your ancestors ate manna in the wilderness and died. This is the Bread descending from heaven, so that anyone who eats of it will not die. **I AM** the Living Bread, the Bread descended from heaven. If anyone eats of this Bread she/he will live forever. (6:48-51b)

In this summary conclusion, he elicits what he had already implied in 6:35, "**I AM** the Bread of Life. The one who comes *towards* (πρός) me will by no means hunger, and the one who believes into me will by no means ever thirst." If he is "the Bread that descended from heaven" and therefore "the Bread of Life," those who come *towards him* and enter into a commitment to him that culminates in union, they must necessarily partake of him and his divine life. This, then, is the answer to the Galileans' question, "What do we do that we work the works of God?" It is to commit themselves to Jesus by eating the bread that he offers, "the Living Bread, the Bread descended from heaven."

Provocatively Jesus proceeds to identify the predicate of his divine self-designation, "**I AM** the Bread of Life," with his flesh: "And the Bread which I shall give is my flesh on behalf of the life of the world." These words evoke a conflict among the ruling authorities (οἱ Ἰουδαίοι) who had been aroused earlier by Jesus' pronouncement, "**I AM** the Bread that descended from heaven." Now they dispute among themselves how he is able to give his flesh to eat. Once again

[36] See chapter 2 on the Prologue of the Gospel.

their adversarial role enables Jesus to reach a climactic gradation in his discourse on "the Bread of Life." In response to their questioning he pointedly confronts them with a conditional prospect, reinforced by his typical introductory double asseveration,

> Amen, amen I say to you, unless you eat the flesh of the Son of the Human Being and drink his blood, you do not have life in yourselves. The one who chews my flesh and drinks my blood has eternal life, and I will raise him/her at the last day. For my flesh is true food, and my blood is true drink. (6:53b-55)

These words may presuppose the tradition of the Eucharist, but they are not a direct or an immediate reference to it.[37] "In other words, the 'eucharistic overtones' of the passage are secondary and negative in import."[38] In view of the imminence of the Passover, the second in the Gospel, and the feeding of the multitudes, 6:51c-58 is oriented to the Passover meal.[39] Here the words are σάρξ (flesh) and αἷμα (blood).[40] The terms that are encountered in the eucharistic traditions that have been transmitted by Paul and the Synoptics are: σῶμα (body) and τὸ αἷμα μου τῆς διαθήκης (my blood of the covenant) or ἡ καινὴ διαθήκη ἐν τῷ αἵματι μου (the new covenant in my blood).[41] *Flesh* and *blood*, as Jesus utilizes them in this context, refer to physical corporeality, the finitude and limitation of the human being. "… σάρξ in John is always used to designate the

[37] Among those who argue for a eucharistic interpretation of 6:51b-58 are: Eduard Schweizer, "Das johanneische Zeugnis vom Herrenmahl," *EvT* 12 (1952/53) 341-353. Günther Bornkamm, "Die eucharistische Rede im Johannes-Evangelium," *ZNW* 47 (1956) 161-169. Oscar Cullmann, "The Meaning of the Lord's Supper in Primitive Christianity," in O. Cullmann and F. J. Leenhardt, *Essays on the Lord's Supper* (Atlanta: John Knox, 1958) 8-16; R. H. Lightfoot, *St. John's Gospel: A Commentary* (London: Oxford University Press, 1960) 162. In contrast, Bultmann, *John*, 234-237, attributes verses 51-58 to an ecclesiastical redactor because it differs doctrinally from the earlier edition of the Gospel. Brown, *John* I, 274, claims that "there is a secondary, eucharistic reference in 35-50, and this reference will become primary in 51-58. Barrett, *St. John*, 297, and Keener, *John* I, 690, who like Barrett proposes that "John's eucharistic language applies directly to Jesus' death." Also Meeks, *The Prophet-King*, 93. Rudolf Schnackenburg, *St. John* II, 56-69; David Rensberger, *Johannine Faith,* 70-81; Ludger Schenke, "Das johanneische Schisma und die 'Zwölf' (Johannes 6:60-71), *NTS* 38/1 (1992) 115-116. Among those who argue against a eucharistic interpretation: James D. G. Dunn, "John VI – A Eucharistic Discourse?" *NTS* 17/3 (1971) 328-338.

[38] Dunn, "John VI – A Eucharistic Discourse?" 337. Barrett, "Sacraments," *Essays on John* (Philadelphia: Westminster Press, 1982) 89-91, separates verse 52 from verse 51c and asserts, "It is here, not in verse 51c, that a new paragraph begins, and here (in verse 52) that the introduction of blood points beyond the mere image of bread to the sacrament (if that is the right word – it is not John's) of the Lord's Supper. He follows Brown in differentiating verses 35 to 51 as sapiential and "verses 53 (or thereabouts)" as sacramental.

[39] Contrary to Wilhelm Wilkens, *Die Entstehungsgeschichte des vierten Evangeliums* (Zollikon: Evangelischer Verlag, 1958) 75-76, who seems to assume that the word "flesh" is identical to the word "body" and contends that 6:51c-58 had its origin in the Synoptic tradition of the Last Supper.

[40] Georg Richter, "Zur Formgeschichte und literarischen Einheit von John 6. 31-58," *ZNW* 60 (1969) 46, interprets "flesh" from the christological debate in which the author is engaged against those who rejected the Eucharist or were content to interpret it symbolically and spiritually, and employs Ignatius' *Letter to the Smyrnaeans* 7:1b to support his contention that "flesh" was a eucharistic term and therefore can be interpreted as such in John.

[41] See Mark 14:24, Matt 26:28, Luke 22:20; also 1 Cor 11:25, which is similar to Luke 22:20.

sphere of humanity in its weakness and helplessness."[42] But this is the σάρξ of the incarnate Logos![43] It is the authentic humanity of the Son of the Human Being who descended from heaven.

At the first Passover Jesus replaced the stone sanctuary of the Temple in Jerusalem with his physical body, and consequently he became the new Temple, the living Temple of God, "the Father's house." Similarly, at this second Passover he is substituting his physical self in place of the Passover meal. As he conducts a new Exodus, he presents himself as the new Passover meal of liberation. The bread he gives is his flesh on behalf of the life of the world. A sacrificed lamb is the flesh that is eaten at the Passover meal. At the third and culminating Passover Jesus will fulfill the role that John the Witness ascribed to him. He will become "the lamb of God that removes the sin of the world"; and he will do so in the reality of his flesh and blood humanity.[44] As he says in 6:51c, "And the bread which I shall give is my flesh on behalf of the life of the world." His death as the lamb of God will terminate the old moral order that is dominated by the human infection of sin and simultaneously open the door to a new age of freedom and wholeness, justice and equality – everything that the original Exodus was intended to actualize.[45] On the one hand, therefore, "To eat Jesus' flesh and drink his blood is nothing other than to accept his true humanity."[46]

But on the other hand, there is more that is comprehended in his substitution of his physical self in place of the Passover meal, and it is expressed in his solemn declaration, "Amen, amen I say to you, unless you eat the flesh of the Son of the Human Being and drink his blood, you do not have life in yourselves." It is noteworthy that these words are addressed specifically to the ruling authorities, and therefore it is plausible that they should have a *political import*. But how will they, the ruling authorities, construct the intent and meaning of his words? The literal sense of cannibalism is naturally improbable. Drinking blood is prohibited by the purity code of Lev 7:26-27, and eating human flesh is as abhorrent to the Hellenistic world as it is to the Jewish religion.[47] Jesus is speaking metaphorically. But in the light of his subsequent disclosure in 6:63, he is also speaking ironically.

---

[42] Dunn, "John VI – A Eucharistic Discourse?" pp. 336, 331.

[43] Peder Borgen, *Bread from Heaven: An Exegetical Study of the Concept of Manna in the Gospel of John and the Writings of Philo* (Leiden: Brill, 1965) 186, "The purpose is not to give doctrinal instruction about the Eucharist as such, but rather to use the eucharistic ideas to throw light upon the reality of the incarnation." Again, "Eating and drinking in the Eucharist means that the believers become united with the historical Jesus." But it is more than that! It is to be united with the historical Jesus as "the Son of the Human Being" who united heaven and earth and therefore in the work that he wants his disciples to continue – as in 14:12.

[44] Contrary to Wilkens, *Entstehungsgeschichte*, 11-29, the Fourth gospel is not a "Passion Gospel."

[45] See chapter 17.

[46] Dunn, "John VI – A Eucharistic Discourse?" p. 336.

[47] Dodd, *Fourth Gospel*, 341, "The bare idea of attaining eternal life by 'feeding upon the σάρξ' was, as the author well knew, a 'scandalous' idea to his Hellenistic public."

Initially 6:63 appears to contradict verse 53.[48] For if it is true that, "The Spirit is the one giving life; the flesh benefits nothing," how can eating his flesh and drinking his blood communicate life? How can his flesh and blood serve as the new Passover meal of liberation?

As already noted, "flesh" and "blood" are anthropological designations that imply life, but life in terms of finitude, limitation, and necessity.[49] Yet ironically, according to 6:53, they communicate eternal life. It must be, therefore, that "the essence of life" resides in Jesus' flesh and blood. But what is "the essence of life" that vivifies or animates his flesh and blood? He names it in 6:63, "The Spirit is the one giving life."

Philo of Alexandria, confronting these same anthropological terms, "flesh" and "spirit" in his allegorical interpretation of the Pentateuch, resolved the issue of "the essence of life" on the basis of his platonically oriented dualism by constructing them as binary oppositions.

> In many passages of the Law Moses pronounces blood (αἵμα) to be the essence of life, saying in plain words, 'for the life of all flesh (σάρξ) is the blood' (Lev 17:11). Yet, when first after the creation of heaven and earth and of what lies between them, the Framer of living beings fashioned the human being, we read, "He breathed into his face the breath of life (πνεῦμα ζωῆς) and the human being became a living soul" (Gen 2:7) showing hereby, on the contrary, that the essence of life is breath (πνεῦμα).[50]

He concludes:

> Each one of us, according to immediate analysis, has happened two in number, both an animal and a human being. To each of these its own relative power is distributed, to the one [αἵμα] maintaining life, according to which we are alive, to the other reasoning, according to which we have become reasoning beings.[51]

The human being, as a body of flesh and blood is the seat of sense perception and, according to Philo, "The exact name for sense perception is 'woman'."[52] The human being as soul, identifiable with mind, is the authentic human being, superior to the human being whose life principle is based on the essence of blood that

---

[48] Against Bornkamm, "Die eucharistische Rede im Johannes-Evangelium," 166-167. In the words of Dunn, "John VI – A Eucharistic Discourse?" 331, a wedge must not be driven between the σάρξ of vss. 51c-56 and the σάρξ of v. 63.

[49] Regarding "flesh," see Hans Walter Wolff, *Anthropology of the Old Testament* (Philadelphia: Fortress Press, 1974) 30-31. Regarding "blood," see pages. 60-62, especially 62. Blood, like breath, belongs to God, "... and therefore life without a steady bond with him and an ultimate tending towards him is not really life at all."

[50] Philo, *Quod Deterius Potiori,* 80. *Loeb Classical Library* (Cambridge: Harvard University Press, 1958) II, 257.

translated by F. H. Colson and G. H. Whitaker. See also *Legum Allegoria* III, 161, where Philo employs the terms soul (ψυχή) and body (σῶμα).

[51] *Quod Deterius Potiori*, 82.

[52] *Ibid.*, 84.

empowers the body of flesh. Philo appropriates the figure of the High Priest and allegorizes his entry into the Holy of Holies in order to characterize the piety of the reasoning human being.

> The God-loving soul, disrobing the *body and the things dear to it* and fleeing far away from these receives a firm and assured solidity in the complete ordinances of virtue.[53]

> Because the soul, residing with intelligence and spending time in the house of wisdom is unable to function with any of the friends of the body and spends its days in the house of wisdom. For then it is nourished by food more divine in knowledgeable things, on account of which it also neglects the *flesh*.[54]

In his reflections on Israel's post-Exodus journey through the wilderness, he interprets the heavenly provision of manna as "the soul's food."

> You see that the soul is not nourished with earthly things and corruptible things, but with such words as God shall have poured like rain out of that nature, raised from the ground and pure, which he has called "heaven." To continue: let the people, and let all that goes to constitute the soul, gather together and make a beginning of knowledge, not all at once but 'that of a day for a day.[55]

For Philo, the nourishment of the human being, who is oriented toward πνεῦμα (*breath* or *spirit*) as the essence of life, is food that is celestial and imperishable. It is knowledge that is constituted by the eternal forms, but above all by an upward gazing contemplation of God. Jacob's son, Levi, is the prototype who "forsakes father and mother, his mind and material body, for the sake of having as his portion the one God for the Lord himself is his portion" (Deut 10:9).

Jesus, like Philo, acknowledges that "the flesh benefits nothing," but at the same time he refuses to denigrate flesh and blood. Although they represent the sphere of humanity's finitude and vulnerability, they nevertheless characterize authentic historical existence. Moreover, the flesh and blood that he is distinguishing is the flesh and blood of the eschatological reality of the Son of the Human Being who "descended from heaven." It is the flesh and blood of the Son of God on whom John the Witness saw the Spirit (πνεῦμα) descending and remaining and who therefore is "the Father's house."[56] It is the flesh and blood of the Son of the

[53] *Legum Allegoria* II, 55. Italics are my emphases.

[54] *Ibid.*, III, 152. See also III, 161. Italics are my emphases.

[55] *Ibid.*, III, 162-163.

[56] Here is a major contrast between Philo and the Fourth Gospel. When God breathed into Adam, according to Philo, Adam became a "living spirit." In Gen 2:7 the Septuagint translates the Hebrew נִשְׁמַ (breath) as πνοή (breath), but Philo replaces πνοή with πνεῦμα (spirit). Either he is reading another Greek translation of the Hebrew text or he is making his own substitution to suit his immediate purpose. On this basis Philo is able to identify the human spirit as a fragment of the divine Logos. See *Quis Rerum Divinarum Heres*, 230-236. In the Fourth Gospel Jesus is not a fragment of the divine Logos. He is "the son of Joseph from Nazareth" upon whom the Spirit descended and remained.

Human Being on whom the angels of God are ascending and descending, and who therefore unites heaven and earth. It is the flesh and blood of the Son of the Human Being who is supercharged with the heavenly life of God's ζωή, and who therefore declares, " **I AM** the Bread of Life."

Therefore, to come *towards* (πρός) Jesus, the incarnate Logos-Sophia, is not to be associated principally with "eating" and "drinking."[57] The preposition πρός implies a movement when it governs the accusative case, especially in1:1-2 and 14:3, 6, 12, 18, 23, 28; 16:5, 7, 10, 17, 28; and it is a movement that initiates an entry into union with Jesus in order to enlarge the community and communion of the Son of the Human Being. This is authenticated by the closing petitions of Jesus' prayer in 17:20-24.

> Not only for these do I ask, but also for those believing into me through their word so that all are one, even as you, Father, [are] in me and I in you, so that they also are in us, so that the world believes that you sent me. And the glory that you have given me I have given them so that they are one even as we [are] one. I in them and you in me, so that they are completed into one, so that the world knows that you sent me and loved them even as you loved me. Father, that which you have given me, I want that *where **AM I*** (ὅπου εἰμὶ ἐγώ), these are with me…

This movement into union is also confirmed by the same use of εἰμὶ ἐγώ in 12:26, and 14:3.[58]

If "to come *towards* Jesus" signifies a movement into union with the New Human Being, what is the meaning of eating his flesh and drinking his blood? How or in what sense is the eating of his flesh and the drinking of his blood to be construed as a new Passover meal? Even if verse 53 is interpreted metaphorically, the words themselves seem to promote the class realities of the old moral order, the κόσμος or *world* in which the ruling authorities whom Jesus is addressing, participate.[59] The hierarchical structures of that realm foster and sanction the kind of cannibalism that the dominant and the dominators of this world practice on those whom they subjugate. To one extent or another they exploit, dispossess and marginalize the lower classes, and, in effect, eat their flesh and drink their blood. The apocalyptic analysis of 1 Enoch 7:3–5 employs these very words in its condemnation of the old moral order. The mythical giants, who represent the systemic structures of society, specifically the institutions and organizations and the alliances between them that are constituted by the rich and the powerful:

> These devoured all the toil of human beings, until they were unable to sustain them. And the giants turned against them in order to devour them.

[57] As Peder Borgen claims, *Bread from Heaven*, 154-155. Nor does it mean "the eating and drinking of wisdom (and the Torah) in spite of the possible parallel of Sirach 24:21. This would be a capitulation to Philo's perspective.

[58] See also 7:34, 36 for the denial of this participation in Jesus' εἰμὶ ἐγώ.

[59] John 8:23 should be remembered in this context: "You are from below, I am from above. You are from this κόσμος (*world*); I am not from this κόσμος."

> And they began to sin against birds and against animals and against reptiles and against fish, and they devoured one another's flesh and drank the blood from it.[60]

But Jesus is not supporting the status quo of the κόσμος or the old moral order, as he addresses these words to the ruling authorities: "Unless you eat the flesh of the Son of the Human Being and drink his blood, you do not have life in yourselves." For this is the flesh and blood that is offered as the new Passover meal, and therefore it must be a meal of liberation. Those who are drawn into union with Jesus in his eschatological identity as "the Son of the Human Being" are where he is. They participate in the corporeality of his self-disclosed divine **I AM**, as he himself informs his disciples in 12:26, "If anyone would render service, let her/him follow, and *where **I AM*** (ὅπου εἰμὶ ἐγώ) there also my servant will be." The blind male, whose sight Jesus restored and who through his rebirth in baptism lost all the predicates that defined him in the past and became a naked **I AM**, is a prototype of a participant in the **I AM** of Jesus.[61] In this horizontally constituted community in which every member is a bearer of God's Spirit and therefore, a room in "the Father's house," there can be no cannibalism. There can be no victimization of others by eating their flesh and drinking their blood. Like Jesus, those who participate wield the same kind of autonomy over their own lives that he claimed for himself in 10:17-18.

> On account of this the Father loves me because I lay down my life (ψυχήν), so that I take it again. No one takes it from me, but I lay it down of myself. I have authority to lay it down and I have authority to take it again. This is the commandment I took from my Father.

The new people of God that Jesus is inaugurating as "the Son of the Human Being" is a community in which all of its members, out of their own individual sovereignty, offer themselves in service to each other as well as to the society in which they live. In and through this mutuality of self-giving a reciprocal nourishing takes place that is mutually energizing and liberating and that in the course of time generates a divine humanness that manifests the glory of God. Jesus of Nazareth is the glory of God in the narrative world of the Fourth Gospel because out of his sovereignty he uses his body of flesh and blood, empowered by God's Spirit, to serve his society and to minister to the needs of its people.

Jesus heightens the provocative condition that he has laid down to the authorities by inflating its offensiveness:

> The one who chews my flesh and drinks my blood has eternal life, and I will raise him/her up at the last day. My flesh is true food, and my blood is true drink. The one chewing my flesh and drinking my blood remains in me and I in him/her. (6:54-56)

---

[60] *The Ethiopic Book of Enoch. A New Edition in the Light of the Aramaic Dead Sea Fragments*, trans. and ed. by M .A. Knibb and E. Ullendorff (Oxford: Clarendon Press, 2 vols., 1978) II, 78-79.

[61] See chapter 11.

The new Passover meal of his flesh and blood requires chewing. It cannot simply be swallowed whole. The process of mastication is involved. Metaphorically construed, reflection or deliberate consideration is necessary in order to determine when and how a particular service is to be rendered to others that will nourish and energize, unbind and set free. The flesh is true food and the blood is true drink because, unlike the cannibalism of the κόσμος (*world*), they are not being extracted from others in order to increase possibility and extend the life of the rich and the powerful. They are offered in the freedom of sovereignty to terminate all forms of domination, to deliver from oppression, to enhance self-worth, to enable the fulfillment of potentiality, to end all poverty.[62] Ironically, anyone who chews Jesus as the Bread of Life that descended from heaven, who offers his or her life as a Passover Meal of liberation, will live forever. For Jesus himself lives because of his union with God, as he declares in 6:57.

> Even as the living Father sent me, and I live because of the Father, so also that one who chews me will live because of me. This is the bread descending from heaven, not like that which the ancestors ate and died. The one chewing this bread will live forever.

The first Exodus failed because the ancestors did not eat the true bread and therefore they died. The Passover Meal they continued to eat did not promote liberation. The hierarchical society they constituted proved to be cannibalistic, and, as the Hebrew prophets testified, the lives of the weak and the powerless were devoured by the dominators. Micah 3:1-3 and 3:9-10 offer a pertinent witness:

> And I said, "Hear, you heads of Jacob and rulers of the house of Israel! Is it not for you to know justice? You who hate the good and love the evil, who tear the skin from off my people, and their flesh from off their bones; who eat the flesh of my people, and flay their skin from off them, and break their bones in pieces and chop them up like meat in a kettle, like flesh in a cauldron."
>
> Hear this, you heads of the house of Jacob and rulers of the house of Israel, who abhor justice and pervert all equity, who build Zion with blood and Jerusalem with injustices.

Jesus concludes his discourse by uniting the beginning and the end of his teaching: "The one chewing this bread will live forever." He is the Living Bread. He is the Bread that descended from heaven. Those who masticate this true bread, this heavenly manna, will live forever because they have believed into him and are moving towards union with him as he lives forever in union with the Creator.

According to 6:4, "the Passover, the feast of the Jews was near." Jesus' feeding of the multitudes takes place in that context, indeed, with an intimation of an Exodus. Should his multiplication of the loaves and the fish be considered to be a

---

[62]To ingest the bread of the Lord's Supper is to take into oneself identification with the Body of the New Human Being that the bread represents. To drink of the cup of the Lord's Supper is to identify oneself with the New Covenant and therefore particpation in all its responsiblilties.

Passover meal? Probably not! But at the very least it is a foreshadowing, a sign – as Jesus himself says in 6:26 – of the new Passover meal that he is inaugurating. In this respect, the Passover, as 6:4 states, is only *near*. The true Passover, that is, the New Passover will be celebrated when this corporate "Son of the Human Being," or the living Temple of God is established by Jesus' death and resurrection, when he gives his flesh on behalf of the life of the world.

For the readers of the Gospel it would be important that Jesus delivered this homily in a synagogue in Capernaum. They are being drawn into a reconstitution of Judaism by a Pharisaic-rabbinic leadership that is competing for the control of the synagogue institution in Alexandria. As the dominant elites, they want to determine the future of Judaism by subordinating their ethnic community to their ideology of an ethical dualism that promotes purity and separation. Conformity to the religious and social order that they are constituting hierarchically is nothing more than a continuation of world maintenance that characterizes the old moral order that has persisted for generations. In place of the traditional Passover Meal that failed in nurturing liberation and perpetuated only living death, Jesus, with great irony, is offering a new Passover Meal in which its participants sacrifice themselves for the liberation of each other and all their fellow human beings, but always out of their own liberated sovereignty.

Accordingly, the negative response that Jesus receives from his disciples in the Capernaum synagogue may well mirror the effect that the author would anticipate among the implied readers of the first edition of the Gospel in Alexandria: "This is a hard word. Who is able to hear it?" In all likelihood their offense would not be based on a literal interpretation of his words. They are familiar with the tradition of ὁ υἱὸς τοῦ ἀνθρώπου or at least υἱὸς ἀνθρώπου (son of a human being), originating from Wisdom tradition or from the eschatology of Jewish apocalypticism, but this is an unrealistic expectation. To give one's flesh and blood, the substance of a human being's limited mortality, for the liberation of others is unreasonable and, in view of the stark cannibalistic realties of the old moral order, even preposterous.

Perceiving the grumbling that is going on within them, Jesus replies with a perspective of "the Son of the Human Being" that raises the level of his offense-evoking instruction to a greater challenge to his scandalized audience: "Does this offend you? If then you should *observe* (θεωρήτε) the Son of the Human Being ascending where he was formerly?" His sentence remains unfinished. There is no apodosis that follows the condition that Jesus has formulated. Will their offense be increased or diminished? Will that experience of *observing* or *looking at* (θεωρήτε) the Son of the Human Being returning to his place of origin evoke greater outrage or will it challenge them into a committed participation in his divinely empowered life? It is the reality of Jesus as the incarnate Logos-Sophia, Jesus as the bearer of God's Spirit, that guarantees that the eating of the flesh of the Bread that descended from heaven and the drinking of his blood results in everlasting life.

> The Spirit is the Life-Making One; the flesh benefits nothing. The words that I have spoken to you are Spirit and Life. But there are some among you who do not believe. (6:63)

Many have been scandalized and in their continuing offense refuse to believe.[63] The narrator reinforces Jesus' observation by an intrusive remark that accentuates his capacity as the bearer of God's Life-Making Spirit to discern who, among his followers, would eventually defect and even betray him and who would remain committed to him. He then adds, "On account of this I have spoken to you, for no one is able to come *towards* (πρός) me unless it has been given to him from the Father." The words he has spoken were intended to determine who would continue to follow him and who would defect.[64] The commitment of faith is essential for an entry into the eschatological reality of the Son of the Human Being. Once again, therefore, Jesus uses the preposition *towards* (πρός) in order to emphasize that the movement into a union with him as the Son of the Human Being is ultimately initiated by God.

The offense of his words has its anticipated effect: "For this reason many of his disciples turned back and no longer were walking with him."[65] But not all of them! For the very first time the reader is introduced to a group of "the Twelve," who may be representative of the new Israel. None of them, in contrast to the Synoptics, has been named previously, and, no attempt is made here to account for them. It is not necessary. There are only four references to the Twelve in the narrative world of the Fourth Gospel, three in verses 67, 70 and 71, and a final reference in 20:24. The function of the three at the end of chapter six is to underline the reality of a new Israel that is following Jesus into a new Exodus. Many disciples have turned away and abandoned him, but there are still Twelve who in this context serve as the core of God's new people. The fourth and last

---

[63] Contrary to Kikuo Matsunaga, "Is John's Gospel Anti-Sacramental? – A New Solution in the Light of the Evangelist's Milieu," *NTS* 27/4 (1981) 517 and 520, Simon Peter does not represent those who accepted 'the word of Jesus' and remained in John's church, nor does the Gospel's negative portrayal of Judas mirror the hostility of John's church against the "drop-outs."

[64] Rensberger, *Johannine Faith*, 78-80, who is oriented toward John's 'liberating community' is not correct in his contention that "Participation in the Eucharist is here made a criterion for inclusion in or exclusion from 'life' in a manner that brings its function as a boundary into prominence." It is participation in following Jesus into becoming the Passover meal, of giving one's flesh and blood for the liberation of the world.

[65] Contrary to Brown, *Community of the Beloved Disciple*, 82-84, who maintains that the two groups that are emerging in 6:66-68 represent Jewish Christians who left the synagogue but then drew back because Jesus declared that the Bread of Life was his flesh and blood; and they subsequently constituted the churches of inadequate faith. In contrast Peter and the Twelve, who refuse to abandon Jesus are "the Apostolic Christians." Yet "they do not reach the heights of the Johannine understanding of Jesus" that is represented by the Beloved Disciple. Both groups, however, are reflections of the Jewish community in Alexandria and may well be represented among the implied readers.

occurrence of the number 12 in 20:24 should remind the implied readers that there are still Twelve in spite of Judas' betrayal, and they continue to embody the new Israel that has been constituted by the death and resurrection of Jesus. Turning to these Twelve, Jesus inquires, "Surely you also don't want to go away, do you?" Simon Peter responds on behalf of the Twelve, "Lord, *towards* (πρός) whom shall we go? You have the words of eternal life, and we have believed that you are the Holy One of God."

For the implied readers of Alexandria, Peter's rock-like loyalty would be impressive. In spite of the large number of followers who have begun to turn away from Jesus – undoubtedly reflecting the continuing loss of disciples among the Jews after 70 C.E. – the central core, representing the new Israel would convey a vital reassurance to the implied readers that a new Israel has been established and there are still some who have remained faithful. Perhaps they would find themselves identifying with Peter. His titular designation of Jesus as "the Holy One of God" is certainly feeble, but on this occasion, at this moment, it may be adequate.

Jesus' response is directed to all of the Twelve apparently acknowledging that Peter's confession was also made on their behalf: "Did I not select you Twelve for myself? Yet one of you is a devil." Even among the Twelve, whom Jesus had chosen for his own purpose, there is one who will defect. Evidently Jesus is already aware of his association with the devil and therefore does not hesitate to designate him as "a devil." Because it is a member of the Twelve who as yet has not been named, the narrator steps into the story to inform the reader who it is: "Judas, the son of Simon Iscariot." At the same time he also specifies the evil that he will perpetrate, "for he was going to betray him." Later, in the context of the third Passover at the pre-Passover meal that Jesus celebrates with his disciples, the narrator will remind the implied readers that "… the devil had already entered into the heart of Judas, son of Simon Iscariot, in order to betray him." Yet it is only after Jesus has identified him as the betrayer by giving him the piece of bread that he has "dipped into the dish," that "then," according to the narrator, "Satan entered into him." Although the devil had already entered into the heart of Judas, as the narrator has indicated, it is only after Jesus himself has identified him as the betrayer that he leaves the fellowship of the community in order to fulfill his intention.

There is a new Israel, in spite of Jesus' identification of one of the Twelve as a "devil." It was posed as a sign on the other side of the Sea of Galilee on "the mountain" where Jesus seated himself with his disciples. In the context of an approaching Passover he has signaled a new Exodus out of the old moral order and its stark cannibalism into a new order of being in which its participants, living in freedom and guarding their sovereignty, would devote their physical existence, charged with the divine life of God's Spirit, to the salvation of the world.

Chapter Ten

Jesus at the Festival of Booths in Jerusalem

Controversy and increasing alienation 7:2-52

Jesus resumed his ministry in Galilee after his discourse in the synagogue at Capernaum, and, as 7:3 implies, he continued to do his mighty works. Galilee, after all, is "his own country." At the same time, as the narrator states, "he was not willing to walk about in Judea because the authorities (οἱ Ἰουδαῖοι) were seeking to kill him." Obviously the defense that Jesus delivered at the forensic process that they initiated in Jerusalem has not altered their outlook or their intention.

As the Festival of Booths approaches, his brothers challenge him to show himself to the world and display his works to his followers in Judea.[1]

> Now the feast of the Jews, the Festival of Booths, was near. His brothers, therefore said to him, "Leave here and go into Judea so that your disciples also observe your works that you are doing. For no one who seeks to be open to the public does anything in secret. If you do these things, show yourself to the world." (7:2-4)

Evidently they are taunting him, for they know that his ministry is directed towards the people and his works are intended for their well-being and wholeness.[2] They may have become aware of his transformation of water into wine during their attendance at the wedding at Cana (2:13). They also know that he has disciples in Judea, for that is the rationale they offer as they urge Jesus to promote himself: "so that your disciples (in Judea) observe your works." Whether, however, they are aware that the guardians of society intend to kill him is indeterminable. Perhaps, as some commentators suggest, they are to be regarded as representative of the "world."[3] But more specifically, they may be captives to the dominant honor/shame culture of their society, and that necessarily requires that recognition and honor are to be pursued aggressively as the greatest good.[4] The narrator conveys their outlook by observing, "...his brothers were not believing into him."

---

[1] On the Feast of Booths, see Paul Billerbeck's excursus in Strack-Billerbeck, *Kommentar* II, 774-812. Also George W. MacRae, "The Meaning and Evolution if the Feast of Tabernacles" *CBQ* 22 (1960) 251-276. J. Jeremias, *TDNT*, IV, 281-282. Sukkôt, as it is called in Hebrew, commemorates Israel's post-Exodus wandering in the Sinai wilderness and sojourning in tents. See Lev 23:39-43 and Deut 16:13-15.

[2] Lindars, *John*, 283.

[3] Bultmann, *John*, 290; German, 218; Barrett, *St. John*, 311.

[4] On Mediterranean honor/shame culture see *Honor and Shame in the World of the Bible: Semeia* 68; especially Chance, "The Anthropology of Honor/Shame Culture, Values and Practice," pp. 139-149. Also Malina, *New Testament World*, 25-50. On honor/shame culture in Judaism, see Claudia V. Camp, "Honor and Shame in Ben Sira: Anthropological and Theological Reflections," in *The Book of Ben Sira in Modern Research*, ed. by Pancratius C. Beentjes (Berlin: Walter de Gruyter, 1997).

The use of the imperfect tense of ἐπίστευον (they were believing) preceded by the negative particle οὐδέ (neither) in the narrator's aside in verse 5 is notable because it denotes the *ongoing* unbelief of Jesus' brothers *in the past*. The post-70 implied readers of Alexandria, who would have some knowledge of the post-Easter role of his brothers in the Jerusalem Church, would construe verse 5 as an actuality that is ascribable to the first level of the Gospel's narrative world, the level of Jesus' earthly ministry. By including the unbelief of his brother in the past, the Evangelist may have projected that many of these Alexandrian addressees would experience a similar movement from unbelief to faith when they reached the culminating narration of Jesus' death and resurrection and finally were confronted with the objective of the Gospel: "... but these things have been written so that you begin to believe that Jesus is the Christ, the Son of God, and so that by believing you have life in/by his name."

In response to their challenge Jesus confronts his brothers with a critical differentiation, "My καιρός (right time) is not yet present, but your καιρός (right time) is always here. The world cannot hate you, but it hates me because I testify about it that its works are evil" (7:6-7). He urges them to go up to the feast, but he will not go "because," as he tells them again, "my καιρός has not yet been fulfilled." The *right time* for him to enter into his passion has not arrived. By exercising his autonomy as the New Human Being who descended from heaven he will determine when he should go up to Jerusalem. Since he will not return to Galilee, this journey will be his last, ending in the fulfillment of the authorities' conspiracy to kill him.

Soon after his brothers have departed for Jerusalem, Jesus also goes up "not openly but as in secret" (7:10).[5] The inclusion of the comparative particle ὡς indicates that Jesus wants to be inconspicuous, not surreptitious. Apparently, as unexpected as this may be, he has determined that this is the right time. His unobtrusive arrival in Jerusalem may signify a temporary delay or postponement of his καιρός. His need for being under cover for a period of time is vindicated by the continued hostility and the malice of the authorities, for, as verse 11 indicates, they were searching for him at the feast: "Where is that one?" Jerusalem is pulsating with hearsay and chatter about Jesus, but covertly, as the rumors circulate that he has been marked for death. "Among the crowds there was much secret discussion about him. Some were saying that he is good; but others were saying, 'No, but he is misleading the people.' No one actually was speaking about him openly on account of the fear of the Jews."[6] In all likelihood the controversies and the conflicts that are being narrated in chapters 7 and 8 are a mirror-like reflection of the disputes that have been unfolding within the Jewish community of Alexandria after the destruction of Jerusalem.

In the middle of the feast Jesus quietly yet boldly enters the sacred precinct of the Temple.[7] Presupposed, of course, since 2:19-21, is his replacement of the stone sanctuary on the Temple mount with his own body and therefore his embodiment as

---

[5] The inclusion of the comparative particle ὡς is supported by P^{66}, P^{75} and an extensive number of other manuscripts, and probably should be acknowledged as original.

[6] John 7:12-13.

"the Father's house." Ironically, therefore, he who has become the living sanctuary of God in the narrative world of the Gospel bears God's presence into this architectonic center of Judaism and begins to teach. The authorities (οἱ Ἰουδαίοι), who hear him, are astonished at his learning, since it appears that he had received no formal education.[8] Jesus responds to them as though he has overheard their puzzlement, and, as he had stated earlier at the beginning of the forensic process of 5:17-47, he acknowledges his dependence on "the One who sent him." His teaching originates from God, not from himself; and anyone who does God's will, will discern (γνώσεται) its divine authenticity. By teaching the truth that originates from God (7:16), Jesus proves that he is seeking God's glory and not his own; and that evidence, in view of the ruling elite's determination to kill him, establishes that "he is true and there is no injustice in him."

Although the authorities had attempted to subject him to the role of defendant in the judicial process of 5:17-47, he ended that hearing by calling them into question and compelling them to make a critical judgment about their own faith in what Moses said and therefore also the truth of Jesus' words and deeds. Now, upon his return to Jerusalem, he initiates an offensive against them by charging them with their own violation of the law: "Did not Moses give you the law? And none of you does the law! Why do you seek to kill me?" The crowd, that evidently has continued to be a silent listener to this exchange but appears to have no awareness of the growing plot to kill him, censures him harshly, "You have a demon! Who is seeking to kill you?" In reply he refers to his previous action on the Sabbath: "One work I did and you all are astonished!" Enabling a crippled human being to walk should be no different than breaching the Sabbath to perform a circumcision. In his defense Jesus appeals to an analogy drawn from Mosaic legislation.

> *On account of this* Moses has given you circumcision – although it is not from Moses but from the fathers – and you circumcise a human being on the Sabbath. If a human being receives circumcision on the Sabbath so that the law of Moses is not abrogated, are you angry with me because I made a human being healthy on the Sabbath? Don't judge according to appearance, but render a just judgment. (7:22-24)

The ordinance of circumcision prescribes that this religious duty is to be performed on the eighth day. Accordingly, a child that is born on the Sabbath will necessarily have

[7] Bultmann, *John*, 237-238; German, 177-17; and others place 7:15-24 before 7:1-14, after relocating chapter 6, in order to connect chapter 7 directly to chapter 5. That transposition would make Jesus' question in 7:19 more abrupt than it is because it would precede the narrator's announcement of 7:1. Moreover, chapter 6 is a necessary intrusion between chapters 5 and 7 in order to introduce the new Exodus that Jesus is inaugurating at the second Passover after the forensic process of 5:17-47. Also Schnackenburg, *St. John* II, 130-131. Fortna, *The Fourth Gospel*, 302-303, explains the rearrangement of chapters 5 and 6 in place of the earlier sequence of 6 and 5 as the redactive work of the later or final evangelist. Lindars, *John*, 234, considers the present order to be suitable because chapter 6 offers an illustration of 5:39, 46-48.

[8] Against Schnackenburg, von Wahlde, "The Johannine 'Jews,'" 44, rightly concludes that "the Jews" of 7:15 and 7:35 "cannot be taken as the people." In both verses they are the ruling authorities.

to be circumcised on the Sabbath. Circumcision, therefore, overrides the Sabbath! The Mishnah preserves a tradition that supports the minor premise of Jesus' syllogism. Rabbi Aqiba stated it as an "operative principle," that circumcision and all the work involved to prepare for its enactment outweigh the Sabbath law, except that labor which can be completed on the eve of the Sabbath.[9] But why does Jesus introduce his argument with the prepositional phrase, διὰ τοῦτο (on account of this)? Rabbinic interpretation judges circumcision to be a realization of human completeness and wholeness, even when its enactment occurs on the Sabbath. If the performance of circumcision overrides the Sabbath, the major premise of Jesus' syllogism must be even more valid because his act of healing on the Sabbath restored a human being to divinely willed wholeness and activity. Such a *qal wahomer* was formulated by Rabbi Eleazar ben Azariah around 100 B.C.E. that extended the principle drawn from circumcision to include the whole body, "If circumcision, which attaches to only one of the 248 members of the human body, suspends the Sabbath, how much more shall [the saving of] the whole body suspend the Sabbath."[10] If it is "*on account of this* that Moses has given ... circumcision," why should one work of restoration that has enabled a human being to reach wholeness on the Sabbath be an infraction of the law any more than the continuous transgressions of the Sabbath by the circumcisions that are performed on this sanctified day?[11]

Jesus' incisive reasoning in defense of his Sabbath healing stirs up an inquisitiveness among "some of the the Jerusalemites." They are puzzled because, on the one hand, they are aware that the authorities are seeking to kill Jesus, but, on the other hand, no attempt is being made to prevent him from continuing his teaching. Consequently they ask: "Surely the rulers don't think this is the Christ, do they? But we know where this one is from. Now when the Christ comes no one will know where he is from" (7:26-27). It is an ironic moment! They are in the presence of the Christ, yet they refuse to accept him as the Christ because they think they know who he is and where he is from. Evidently, like Philip in 1:45, they know that Jesus is the son of Joseph from Nazareth, and that origin does not correspond to their traditional categories of messiahship.

Somewhat later, the crowd will debate the authenticity of Jesus' messiahship, and there will be some among them who will dispute it because his patrimony does not correspond to the Davidic typology derived from Scripture. In the narrative world of the Fourth Gospel Jesus is "the son of Joseph from Nazareth". That is the identity that Philip cites, as he bears witness to Nathanael in 1:45, "We have found the one whom Moses and the Prophets wrote about, Jesus, the son of Joseph from Nazareth."

---

[9] M *Shabbat* 18:3g – 19:3.

[10] *Yoma* 85b; taken from Barrett, *St. John*, 320.

[11] See M *Nedarim* 3,11. Lightfoot, *St. John*, 179; Barrett, *St. John*, 320; Bultmann, *John*, 277-278. Meeks, *The Prophet-King*, 47, appears to be correct in identifying Jesus' argumentation here as a *qal wahomer*.

Galilee, therefore, is his homeland, not Judea or Jerusalem or the Temple.[12] And that is one of the offenses of his christological identity in the Gospel according to John.

As though in response to their dismissal Jesus acknowledges the basis of their judgment, "You know (οἴδατε) me and you know (οἴδατε) where I am from." Yet in spite of the cognitive knowledge they have, the irony is that they really do not know him at all because they do not know the One who sent him.

> I have not come of myself, but the one sending me is genuine, whom you do not know (οἴδατε). I know (οἶδα) him because I am with him and he sent me. (7:28-29)[13]

Here Jesus employs the verb οἶδα, that, as indicated above, denotes cognitive knowledge, knowledge as fact or information that has been gained by seeing or by recalling an earlier activity or event that has been experienced. He is claiming to know God in terms of knowledge that is based on his own experience of seeing God, as he obliquely claimed earlier in 6:46, "Not that anyone has seen (ἑώρακεν) the Father, except the one who is from the side of God (ὁ ὢν παρὰ τοῦ θεοῦ). This one has seen the Father."[14] He will make the same claim to the ruling elite in 8:55, "… but I know (οἶδα) him. If I said that I do not know (οἶδα) him, I would be a liar like you." This self-assurance of his relationship to God and the mission that he claims arises from it arouses another effort to seize him. But no one lays a hand on him because, as the narrator remarks in verse 30, "His hour had not yet come."

Jesus' teaching, however, elicits a positive response, "Many from the crowd believed into him, and they were saying, 'When the Christ comes, will he do more signs that this one did?'" To what extent their faith is conditioned by the signs Jesus has been performing is inconclusive. Yet the quantity of signs they attribute to him appears to be a factor in their measurement of his stature and their willingness to make a commitment to him.

This response of faith that Jesus evokes from the Jerusalem crowd alarms the ruling authorities who are now more precisely identified as the chief-priests and the Pharisees. They send retainers, that is, the Temple police, to seize Jesus, and he tantalizes them by speaking enigmatically about his imminent departure: "Still a little while I am with you. You will seek me and not find, and *where* **AM I** (ὅπου εἰμὶ ἐγώ) you are unable to come" (7:33-34).[15] In all the instances of the

[12] Contrary to Judith Lieu, "Temple and Synagogue in John," *NTS* 45/1 (1999) 63-69.

[13] In these verses Jesus employs the verb οἶδα, that, as already indicated, denotes cognitive knowledge, knowledge as fact or information. Jesus knows God in terms of a face-to-face experience just as the people know him as Jesus, the son of Joseph from Galilee, because they have met him in person. But, as 17:25 indicates, he also knows God in terms of personal communion.

[14] The preposition παρά when governing the genitive case, signifies "from the side of" or "from," and it is in terms of that relationship that Jesus can intimate that he has seen God.

[15] Lightfoot, *St. John's Gospel*, 181, includes the adverb ὅπου (where) that precedes the formula, "where I am" and says, "The words 'where I am" are found on the Lord's lips in John not only at 7:34, 36 but also at 12:26, 14:3, 17:24. The same truth is expressed in another form in His words 'whither I

occurrence of the **I AM** formula in reverse (7:34, 36; 12:26; 14:3; 17:24) Jesus employs it in reference to himself and in relation to those who will or will not be with him or have a share in his relation to the Father.[16] The Temple police do not grasp his words or his unusual employment of the **I AM** formula. In bewilderment they repeat what he has said, but without understanding (7:36). Consequently they interpret the announcement of his imminent departure as a possible journey into the Jewish dispersion to teach the Greeks. Ironically, however, as 12:20-21 indicates, the Greeks will approach Philip requesting, "We want to see Jesus." Their entreaty will be denied, yet beyond the narrative world of the Gospel his disciples will journey into the dispersion to teach the Greeks.[17] But as they go, Jesus' promise of 14:3 will have been fulfilled by his death and resurrection and by his breathing the holy Spirit upon them, "Again I am coming and I will receive you *towards* (πρός) myself, so that ὅπου εἰμὶ ἐγώ, (*where* **AM I**) you also are."

"On the last day of the great feast," as the Feast of Booths reaches its climax, Jesus stands up and as the living Temple of God he *was crying out* (ἔκραζεν) an invitation to all who are present.[18] "If any one thirsts, let her/him come *towards* (πρός) me and drink. The one who believes into me, even as the Scripture said, rivers of living water will flow out of his/her belly" (7:37-38).[19] He has water to offer, as he stated earlier in his dialogue with the Samaritan woman, "... but the water that I shall give her/him will become in her/him a fountain leaping up into eternal life." Now in the context of Sukkot he appropriates the invitation of Isa 55:1 in order to make that water that springs up into eternal life more universally available: "Those thirsting, you go to the water, and as many as do not have money, going buy without money and [without] price wine and milk!"[20] But instead of adapting Isa 55:1 completely to his

go' at 8:14, 21, 13:13, and the present tense in the words, 'where I am' may perhaps be loosely used for the future." But it seems more probable that a spiritual truth is being expressed both in terms of motion ('whither I go') and in terms of rest ('where I am'). Barrett, *St. John*, 325, considers the possibility that εἰμί should be accented εἶμι and translated, "whither I am about to go". He concludes, "... the present passage stresses rather the temporal limitation of Jesus' ministry; he will not always be accessible as he is now." Unfortunately, Lightfoot, Barrett, and others have not recognized the use of the **I AM** formula in reverse.

[16] Philo, *de Vita Mosis* I, 84, uses the **I AM** formula in reverse in the context of God acknowledging the gifts of the organs of communication: mouth, tongue, and throat by referring to himself αὐτὸς εἰμὶ ἐγώ (**myself AM I**).

[17] Lightfoot, *St. John*, 181. Bultmann, *John*, 309; German, 233.

[18] Verse 37 of P^{66} and other manuscripts use the imperfect tense of κράζω rather than the aorist, and it is this reading that is adopted here. This is another instance in which the time of this event is limited to the ministry of Jesus, the first level of the narrative world of the Gospel. The same is true of the use of the imperfect tense of ἔλεγεν, the reading of P^{66} and other manuscripts in place of εἶπεν.

[19] J. Blenkinsopp, "John vii.37-39: Another Note on a Notorious Crux," *NTS* 6/1 (1959) 95-98, analyzing the difficulties of "this particularly dangerous spot of the mined terrain of the Fourth Gospel," raises the appropriate questions, and finally cites Origen's interpretation as "one strand" that offers "some interesting light on the Gospel as a whole."

[20] Michael A. Daise, "If Anyone Thirsts, Let That One Come to Me and Drink": The Literary Texture of John 7:37b-38a," *JBL* 122/4 (2003), 689 and 699, is quite right to connect Isa 55:1 to John 7:37. But 7:38a, "The one believing into me, even as the Scripture said" is not related backwards to 7:37 but forwards to 7:38b. Also the infinitive ἔρχεσθαι (to come) is not intended "to pick up on the

context by commanding them to "go to the water," he invites them to come *towards* (πρός) him in order to quench their thirst.

What effect, then, will the water that he offers have on those who drink and quench their thirst? Will that water motivate them to believe into Jesus? Will they be willing to make a commitment to him? Jesus appears to assume that it will happen and proceeds to disclose the outcome: "The one believing into me, even as Scripture said, 'Rivers of living water will flow out of his/her belly'." The substantive participle ὁ πιστεύων (the one believing) is "the head of a new construction."[21] The stunning condition that results from believing into him is established by 2:19-21. As the "Father's house," and as "the Lamb of God" Jesus will enlarge God's living Temple that he embodies by his death and resurrection and by breathing the holy Spirit upon his disciples in 20:22. As he promises his disciples at the beginning of his Farewell Speech, they will become rooms in the living Temple that God wills to constitute and that he, Jesus, is pioneering.[22] Accordingly, those who come to him and drink of the water he offers are potential members of the "Father's house," the living Temple of God that he at this moment embodies.

The formula, "as the Scripture said," is directly connected to 7:38b, "Rivers of living water flowing out of her/his belly," and its scriptural orientation is the prophetic text of Zech 14 – and probably also Ezek 47:1-12 – which is intimated by the context of the Feast of Booths in which Jesus is extending his invitation. Sukkot, according to Zech 14:19, is specifically named as the feast of the new creation, the new moral order that will be inaugurated by God after the judgment of "the day of the Lord" has occurred.[23] "Yahweh will become king over all the earth" (14:9) and the families of the earth will go up to Jerusalem to worship the King and to celebrate the New Exodus at the Festival of the Booths (14:16). When God stands on the Mount of Olives, "the Mount of Olives will be split in two" (14:4) and "on that day living water shall flow out from Jerusalem, half of them to the eastern sea and half of them to the western sea; it shall continue in summer as in winter" (14:8).[24]

---

discourse in 7:33-36." It is determined by Jesus' invitation in the context of Sukkot that is oriented toward the transcendence of 7:38b. Joel Marcus, "Rivers of Living Water from Jesus' Belly (John 7:38)," *JBL* 117/2 (1998) 328-330, contends that one of the scriptures that the formula of 7:38a presupposes is "the eschatological prophecy in Isa 12:3, "With joy you shall draw water from the wells of salvation." As appropriate as it is, in view of its association with Sukkot in the Talmudic texts of B *Sukk.* 48b, 50b*; and* P *Sukk.* 5:1 (55a), the popular etymology that he derives from the Hebrew text of Isa 12:3 is contrived.

[21] Brown, *John* I, 320-321, 327, is correct in reading the text in this way, and he supports it with the punctuation in P[66]. He also links Zech 14 and Ezek 47 to Jesus as the living Temple of God. But he rejects the conclusion that the believer can also be a source of living water: "… there is little reason for supposing that the "him" of the citation is the believer."

[22] John 14:1-3 refers to Jesus' imminent going into death and resurrection in order to enlarge the Father's house by adding many more rooms in order to establish a new Temple on earth that consists of countless human beings. See chapter 15.

[23] MacRae, "The Meaning and Evolution of the Feast of Tabernacles," pp. 268-275, acknowledges the "messianic" character of Zech 14. So also Lightfoot, *St. John*, 182, but without drawing in the identity of Jesus as the living Temple of God and his work of enlarging "the Father's house."

Ezekiel has a vision of a growing river that originates from the Temple and flows out "toward the eastern region" irrigating the desert and making the waters of the Dead Sea fresh and alive (47:1-12). Both the land and the sea will be productive for God's people. As verse 12 promises:

> And on the river there will go up on its bank on this side and that side every eatable tree. By no means will anything decay on it, neither will its fruit fail. It will bring forth new fruit because their waters proceed from the Sanctuary and their fruit will be for food and for their ascent into health. (LXX Ezek 47:12)

It is the rabbinic hermeneutical principle of *gezerah shawah* that unites these two texts in the construction of an analogy.[25] Zech 14:8 features "living waters flowing from Jerusalem to both east and west" in the context of a new creation, and Ezek 47:1 contributes the aspect of "water flowing from the Temple" and growing into a river that produces "fruit for food and for their ascent into health" in the context of a new Temple. Combined they constitute an analogy of a new moral order in which living water flows out of a new Jerusalem Temple and becomes a river that is beneficial to humanity. Jesus adopts this hermeneutical construction as Scripture and adapts it to his self-understanding as God's new living Temple, but with the prospect that this living Temple that he embodies will be enlarged to include many more rooms. The promise of 7:38b will be fulfilled when his disciples become "rooms in the Father's house" by their incorporation into the living Temple that Jesus is constituting through the gift of the holy Spirit. From that moment "rivers of living water will flow from their bellies."[26]

Unexpectedly the narrator steps into the story to make an intrusive remark to the implied readers in order to insure their understanding, "But this he *was saying* about the Spirit which the ones believing into him were going to receive, for the Spirit was not yet, because Jesus was not yet glorified" (7:39).[27] The promise of 7:38-39 is a prolepsis, and when it is fulfilled in 20:22-23, the living Temple of God, which Jesus embodies, will have been expanded through the addition of more rooms (14:2).[28]

---

[24] During Jesus' seven-day sojourn in Jerusalem for the celebration of the Feast of Booths, water was brought from the Pool of Siloam in a golden pitcher and poured out on the altar of sacrifice in order to petition for a good rainfall in the forthcoming rain season to quench the thirst of the land and the people. See H. Strathmann, *Johannes* NTD, 134. Also Lightfoot, *St. John*, 182; Aileen Guilding, *The Fourth Gospel and Jewish Worship* (Oxford: at the Clarendon Press, 1960) 92-93, also cites the T *Sukkot* 3:3, linking the libation of water to the prophecy of Ezek 47.

[25] Brown, *John* I, 323, refers to these texts in his lengthy discourse on 7:32, but without reaching any insightful conclusions. For the rabbinic principle of *gezerah shawah* as an "argument from analogy" see Günther Stemberger, *Introduction to the Talmud and Midrash*, trans. and ed. by Markus Bockmuehl (Edinburgh: T & T Clark, 2nd ed. 1996) 18-19. Also J. W. Doeve, *Jewish Hermeneutics in the Synoptic Gospels and Acts* (Assen: Van Gorcum, 1954) 66-67.

[26] Barrett, *St. John*, 328, says, "... but it is a valid inference that the believer, being joined to him, is also, in a secondary way, a source of living water."

[27] Here again the use of the imperfect tense ἔλεγεν (he was speaking), the reading of P[66] refers to the time of Jesus' career, the first level of the narrative world of the Gospel.

[28] On 'prolepsis,' see Culpepper, *Anatomy*, 61-70.

Because each disciple will be a "room" in which the Spirit dwells, the water of life can indeed cascade from this living Temple of the One and the Many.

Jesus' cry elicits a favorable response from the Jerusalem crowd, and two christological identifications are posed: "the Prophet" and "the Christ." These may be the predominant titles that are circulating in the Jewish community of Alexandria, and they are being introduced in order to reflect the world in which the implied readers live. Some were saying, "This is truly the Prophet." Their identification corresponds to the earlier designation of the Galilean crowd that experienced his mighty work of feeding of the multitudes in 6:14, "This is truly the Prophet, the one coming into the world." Jesus' pronouncement of 5:46, "For that one [Moses] wrote about me!" appears to support this christological outlook. Jesus' declaration of 7:16, "My teaching is not mine but [that] of the One who sent me!" corresponds to Deut 18:18 and could also serve as a basis for his identification as the Prophet.[29] But there are no allusions to Deut 18:15 that would indicate that the Gospel according to John is affirming Jesus as the Prophet like Moses.[30] Posed by the Jerusalem crowd and therefore mirroring the Gospel's Alexandrian context, this christological interpretation of Jesus may have been influenced by Philo's characterization of Moses:[31]

> Thus he beheld what is hidden from the sight of mortal nature, and, in himself and his life displayed for all to see, he has set before us, like some well-wrought picture, a piece of work beautiful and godlike, a model (παράδειγμα) for those who are willing to copy it. Happy are they who imprint, or strive to imprint, that image (τύπον) in their souls. (*de Vita Mosis* I, 158-159)

> A partner of God's own possessions who also shares God's possessions who has received the whole world as his portion. (*de Vita Mosis* I, 155-157)

> Again, was not the joy of his partnership with the Father and Maker of all magnified also by the honor of being deemed worthy to bear the same title? For he was named god (θεός) and king (βασιλεύς) of the whole nation. (*de Vita Mosis* I, 158)

> Moses, the holiest of those ever yet born. (*de Vita Mosis* II, 192)

In certain respects Jesus may resemble Philo's Moses. Yet whatever those similarities may be, the supremacy of Jesus is the point of view that dominates the Fourth Gospel. If, as he himself states in 3:13, "No one has ascended into heaven except the one who descended," Moses' ascension is canceled because it was not preceded by a descent. Moses, as 3:14 intimates, brought healing to the Israelites by fashioning a serpent from bronze and suspending it on a pole, but Jesus offers himself as the snake that will be elevated and exalted on the cross to bring salvation to the world. But it is in 6:32-33 that Jesus explicitly enunciates his superiority to Moses, "Amen, amen I say to you,

---

[29] According to Meeks, *The Prophet-King*, 46.

[30] Contrary to Meeks, *ibid.*

[31] Philo, *de Vita Mosis*, the translations are by F. H. Colson's translation in *Philo*, VI of the *Loeb Classical Library* (Cambridge: Harvard University Press, 1959).

Moses did not give you the bread from heaven, but my Father gives you the true bread from heaven. For the bread of God is the one descending from heaven and giving life to the world" (6:32-33).

Others among the Jerusalem crowd, however, insist that he is "the Christ." That was posed as a possibility in 7:26. Here it appears to be a conviction, in spite of the earlier disallowance: "When the Christ comes no one will know where he is from." There are others, however, like Nathanael in 1:46, who object to this appellative (7:41b-42). They contest Jesus' messiahship on the basis of the Davidic typology, "Surely the Christ doesn't come out of Galilee, does he? Didn't Scripture say 'out of the seed of David' and 'from Bethlehem, the village where David was,' the Christ comes?" (7:41-42). Dissension breaks out within the crowd as Jesus is discredited as the Christ on the basis of Scripture, and nothing is postulated that could challenge this orientation.[32] In the narrative world of the Gospel the messianic Son of David typology plays no role in establishing Jesus' messiahship.[33] That kind of material continuity cannot capture or convey the complexity of his person and his achievement of salvation to which the Gospel is bearing witness.

The Temple police attempt to take advantage of the ongoing christological dispute by seizing Jesus, but, according to the narrator, no one was able to lay hands on him. Challenged by the chief priests and the Pharisees as to why they did not take Jesus' captive, the Temple police admit their powerlessness in the face of his authority, "Never did a human being speak like this!" Their report evokes an anxious interrogation that reveals their apprehension of a loss of control. "You also aren't deceived, are you?" they ask the Temple police. "Surely none of the rulers or Pharisees believed into him, did they?" They acknowledge that the response of the fickle crowd is understandable; they simply don't know any better. They are ignorant of the Law, and therefore they are cursed (7:49).

Ironically the chief priests and the Pharisees, particularly the latter, violate and therefore also invalidate their ideology of *loyalty* (חֶסֶד) by imposing their pollution system upon the common people. Yet they separate themselves from them because they "do not know the Law" and therefore are unclean and cursed. Throughout this interaction between Jesus and the guardians of society, Nicodemus, the Pharisee and "a ruler of the Jews" has been absent. He resurfaces after the retainers, who had been dispatched to seize Jesus, return empty-handed; and his fellow Pharisees

---

[32] Duke, *Irony*, 67, claims that the ironic technique of the Gospel "favors John's knowing the Bethlehem tradition and expecting his readers to know it." But if that is true, why would Jesus have affirmed the knowledge of the Jerusalem crowd in 7:28, "You know me and you know where I am from." In the light of 7:41b-42, that can only correspond to Philip's witness to Nathanael in 1:45, "Jesus, the son of Joseph from Galilee" and Nathanael's reply, "Can anything good come out of Nazareth."

[33] It is the offense of the Fourth Gospel that Jesus originated from Nazareth. Whether the Gospel's implied readers were familiar with the Matthean and Lucan traditions of Jesus' birth in Bethlehem is indeterminable. Contrary to Duke, the irony of 7:42 does not presuppose a Bethlehem tradition. Jesus' possible birth in Bethlehem and his Davidic ancestry have no significance whatsoever in this narrative world.

anxiously inquire whether any of their colleagues have believed into him. Perhaps Nicodemus is under suspicion as a secret believer? He is aware of their murderous design and insists on due process; "Isn't it true that our law does not judge a human being until it first hears from him and knows what he is doing?" But they contemptuously dismiss his legal principle as a possible partisan maneuver on behalf of a fellow Galilean, "You too aren't from Galilee, are you?" At the same time they perceive that a messianic perspective may be implied in his advocacy of Jesus, and they respond with a denigrating rejoinder: "Search and see that the Prophet does not arise out of Galilee."

The manuscript evidence of 7:52 indicates that later scribal corrections produced a change in the original word order apparently in order to eliminate the definite article before the word προφήτης (prophet). That produced the textual reading, "Search and see that a prophet does not arise out of Galilee." But that would contradict 2 Kgs 14:25 and Nahum 1:1. Jonah the prophet came from Gath-hepher, a village in the proximity of Nazareth in Galilee, and, if Elkosh was located in Galilee, Nahum also originated in Galilee. Moreover, the rabbinic tradition of Sukk 27b maintained, "There is no single tribe in Israel from which prophets have not arisen." Likewise Seder Olam Rabba 21 avowed, "There is no city in the land of Israel in which there has been no prophet."[34] The word order attested by P^{66} and P^{75}, which includes the definite article before the word "prophet," must surely be the original formulation, "Search and see that out of Galilee *the prophet* does not arise." The phrase "out of Galilee," is emphasized by being placed before "the prophet" so that the identification of Jesus as the eschatological prophet is precluded. Nicodemus' fellow Pharisees reject the identification of Jesus as the Prophet on the basis of their interpretation of Scripture. Their material typology controls their interpretation of the biblical text so that they are no longer open or receptive to divine revelation. Any insecurity they might experience is suppressed by their self-legitimation as divinely appointed brokers between God as the divine patron and the people as clients. Nicodemus, however, is the exception; as "a ruler of the Jews" he displays an integrity that will not tolerate any misuse of the law.[35]

The scribes and Pharisees, the woman, and Jesus 7:53--8:11

This tradition of the scribes and Pharisees testing Jesus by confronting him with the issue of imposing the death penalty on an adulterous woman, is missing in both the oldest and best manuscripts of the Fourth Gospel and is generally considered to be a later scribal interpolation.[36] Yet in spite of the discontinuity that it introduces

[34] Also cited by Duke, *Irony,* 68; and Keener, *John* I, 734, n. 298.

[35] See also Bultmann, *John*, 309-312; German edition, 234-236.

[36] The tradition of John 7:53-8:11 also appears in manuscripts of Mark (after 12:17) and Luke (after 20:39). See Walter Grundmann, *Das Evangelium nach Markus,THzNT* (Berlin: Evangelische Verlagsanstalt, 1959) 245-247. Lindars, *John*, 306-308, traces the pericope in the non-canonical and ecclesiastical writings of the 3rd and 4th century Church. Brown, *John* I, 333-338, offers an analysis

between 7:52 and 8:12, a certain integrity is evident in its placement into this context by later scribes. Although the interpreters of the Law, the οἱ γραμματεῖς, never appear in the narrative world of the Fourth Gospel, the Pharisees of 7:52-8:11 do provide some continuity between 7:45-51and 8:13 in as far as they challenge Jesus to respond to the law regarding the punishment for committing adultery. Instead of answering their question, however, he stoops down and writes in the sand. As they persist in their questioning, he straightens up briefly saying only, "Let the one without sin first cast a stone on her!" and then stoops down again to continue writing in the sand.[37] "By writing on the ground and not responding immediately or directly to [their] question, Jesus nullifies the presumed control of the scribes and Pharisees and places them on the same level as the woman."[38] It is a most appropriate action in view of the condescending arrogance that the Pharisees manifested in 7:49 as they condemned the crowd for its ignorance of the Law.

> Both stand under the power of the old ways, the power of sin, to use the rhetoric of the text, but the present moment (απὸ τοῦ νῦν) invites both to a new way of life. The woman is invited to participate in a new future for herself that will allow her to live, not as a condemned woman but as a freed woman. The scribes and Pharisees are invited to give up the categories by which they had defined and attempted to control life.[39]

Accordingly, the introductory clause of 8:12 could be viewed as referring back to Jesus' response to the religious leaders in 8:7 and thereby providing at least an indirect continuity into the dynamics of the growing hostility between Jesus and the ruling elite.

Hostility and murderous intent 8:12-59

Apart from verses 1-11, chapter 8 may be divided into three gradational episodes: 12-20, 21-29, and 30-59.[40] The first, verses 12-20, reintroduces Jesus who has not

of the problems of authorship, canonicity and meaning. See also Barrett, *St. John*, 589-592, who cites an unpublished manuscript by David Daube in which Daube states, "... in its original context, the slogan 'He that is without sin among you, let him be the first to cast a stone at her' is directed specifically against the unfair treatment of women by men and their laws; and that it is representative of a strong movement in Tannaitic Judaism." Above all, see Gail R. O'Day, "John 7:53-8:11: A Study in Misreading," *JBL* 111/4 (1992) 631-640, who offers a critique of the three major types of mis-readings: that of Augustine, Calvin, and those that have attempted to discover what Jesus wrote on the ground. All of them have "reshape[d] the text away from Jesus' treating the woman as a social and human equal of the scribes and Pharisees." See also her conclusions on pp. 638-640.

[37] See T. W. Manson, "The Pericope de Adultera (Joh 7:53-8:11) *ZNW* 44 (1952-53) 255-256, who explains Jesus' act of writing in the sand by utilizing the practice of the presiding judge in a Roman criminal case to write down the sentence and then read it aloud. "Jesus by this action says in effect: 'You are inviting me to usurp the functions of the Roman Governor. Very well, I will do so; and I will do it in the approved Roman manner'."

[38] O'Day, "John7:53-8:11," 636-637.

[39] *Ibid.*, 637.

[40] Manfred Diefenbach, *Der Konflikt Jesu mit den "Juden": Ein Versuch zur Lösung der johanneischen Antijudaismus-Diskussion mit Hilfe des antiken Handlungsverständnis* (Münster: Aschendorff Verlag, 2002) 118-119, offers an outline of the structure of 7:1 through 8:59 that occurs

spoken since 7:37-38.[41] Verse 12, however, is an awkward transition from 7:45-52, if only because the antecedent for "them" is ambiguous until verse 13 identifies "them" as the Pharisees, unless, of course, the introductory clause of verse 12, πάλιν οὖν αὐτοῖς ἐλάλησεν ὁ 'Ιησοῦς λέγων (therefore again Jesus spoke to them saying...) is construed as a changeover from the episode of 7:53-8:11 into 8:12bc. Nevertheless, the hostility of the Pharisees that intensified in chapter 7 has not diminished. There is no inclination to test Jesus. There are determined to kill him, and that establishes the unity between chapters 7 and 8.[42] The narrator began chapter 7 with two reports: (1) "The Jews were seeking to kill him," and (2) Jesus is compelled to go up to Jerusalem for the Feast of Booths in secret. The controversies and conflicts that occur after he begins to teach in the Temple produce a gradation that reaches its climax at the end of chapter 8 when the earlier announced objective of the authorities to kill Jesus manifests itself in an attempt to stone him to death, and he is forced to hide. The time frame may still be the Feast of Booths and, if 8:20 refers all the way back to 7:14, the location continues to be the treasury of the Temple.

Gradually, as the story has moved forward, the implied readers have encountered Jesus assimilating into himself the entire cultural tradition of the Jewish religion. He is the new Temple of God (2:19-21); he is the new Passover meal (6:48-52); he is the source of living water that springs up into everlasting life (4:14, 7:37-38); and he is the prophetically anticipated eschatological reality of the Temple as the source of "rivers of living water" (7:37-38). By absorbing all these religious-cultural realities into himself, Jesus, as the New Human Being (ὁ υἱὸς τοῦ ἀθρώπου) and therefore God's offspring, will do for the world what religion has always attempted but never succeeded in achieving. Through the abolition of the fear of death, the eradication of the human infection of sin and the alienation it generates, he will constitute a transcendence of human existence that will enable human beings to become incarnations of the glory of God and therefore also fully alive.

Jesus' previous interaction with the ruling authorities occurred in 7:15-19 soon after he began to teach in the sacred precinct of the Temple. In the face of their intention to kill him he defended himself by pleading his innocence: "But the one seeking the glory of the One who sent him, this one is true and there is no injustice in him." Now, after having engaged the crowd, the Jerusalemites, and the Temple police, and after having been repudiated as "the Prophet" and "the Christ," he returns to confront the authorities, specifically the Pharisees who with the chief priests have been plotting his death, with the qualification that legitimates the teaching that he offers, "teaching" that he insisted earlier, "is not mine but of the One who sent me". It is appropriate that he discloses this at the Temple treasury, for the treasury was

in the context of Sukkot and contains various dialogues between Jesus and the crowd, Jesus and the Jerusalemites, Jesus and the ruling authorities; and culminates with three discourses on the last day of Sukkot in 8:12-59.

[41] On John 8:12-59 and its relationship to the Feast of Booths, see Guilding, *Fourth Gospel and Jewish Worship*, 107-110.

[42] Brown, *John* I, 342.

located in the Court of the Women where four golden candlesticks would burn at night during the Feast of Booths.[43] In this context he declares, "**I AM** the Light of the world. The one who follows me will by no means walk in darkness but will have the light of life."

For the second time at a Jewish festival he combines the divine **I AM** formula of self-disclosure with a metaphor that characterizes the activity in which he is engaged. Earlier, in the context of the second Passover (6:4), he had announced to the authorities (οἱ Ἰουδαίοι) in Galilee, "**I AM** the Bread, the one descending from heaven" as he proceeded to substitute his flesh and blood in place of the Passover meal.[44] Now the implied readers are confronted with a new self-identification that is addressed to the guardians of the Jewish social construction of reality, "**I AM** the Light of the world." The Prologue informed them that divine *life* (ζωή) resided in the Logos, and that life transmitted divine illumination to human beings (1:4). Jesus, the incarnation of the Logos-Sophia, to whom "the Father gave... to have *life* (ζωή) in himself" (5:26), communicates the divine light of revelation to the world through his divine life. He is not only the Revealer; he is also the revelation that he reveals.[45] His deeds and words, which expose the darkness and disclose the will of the Creator for the world, make him the embodiment of light. Those who follow him will have "the light of life." They will participate in the divine life that he makes possible by breathing God's Spirit upon them and, like him, they too will become the Light of the world.

This is the possibility that he offers the ruling elite. It is a possibility that they of necessity should actualize in their capacity as the guardians of their society. Their ideological identification with the Law, however, has induced them to preserve their society by the political control of the people who, in their judgment, are damned because they do not know the Law and who therefore must be saved from themselves. It is in that frame of mind as the representatives of the Law that they respond to him juridically by censuring him for his self-authentication, "You testify about yourself, your testimony is not true." It appears to be an echo of M Ketubot 2:9, "But a person is not believed to testify in his own behalf."[46]

Already in 5:31 Jesus had acknowledged, "If I testify about myself, my testimony is not true." Now, however, in a surprising reversal he replies, "If I testify about myself, my testimony is true." The forensic process of 5:17-47 has not exonerated

---

[43] See Guilding, *Fourth Gospel and Jewish Worship*, 93; also Brown, *St. John*, I, 344; also Lindars, *John*, 315, and Barrett, *St. John*, 335.

[44] See chapter 9.

[45] Contrary to Bultmann, *John*, 342-344, who continuously stresses Jesus' role as the Revealer who makes God visible. Yet from his neo-Kantian perspective, he refuses to objectify the revelation that Jesus is revealing because any objectification produces knowledge that would "characterize the realm of the human and the realm of 'works' and of law." See the critique of Anthony C. Thiselton, *The Two Horizons: New Testament Hermeneutics and Philosophical Description* (Grand Rapids: Eerdmans, 1980) 205-217.

[46] Jacob Neusner, *The Mishnah: A New Translation* (New Haven: Yale University Press, 1988) 382.

him. Evidently the four witnesses he had cited in 5:32-47, namely John, his works, "the Father who sent him," and Moses, have not convinced the ruling authorities of the heavenly origin of his activity and teaching. Consequently, to defend the truth of his witness he turns, for the first time, to the shrouded side of his identity and discloses to them their ignorance of his origin, "I know where I came from and where I am going to, but you do not know where I come from and where I am going to." That origin is the basis of his defense and the truth of his witness, "**I AM** the light of the world." It is an ironic differentiation from his earlier acknowledgment to the Jerusalemites, "You know me and you know where I am from." The truth of the two establishes the aporetic character of his identity: the Son of the Human Being who descended from heaven and Jesus, the son of Joseph from Nazareth.

The ideology of these ruling authorities, however, predetermines them to an empirically oriented perspective: "You judge according to the flesh." To them he apparently is only an uneducated Jew, "Jesus, the son of Joseph from Nazareth." At this critical juncture, confronted by the rulers of society for whom due process of law is no longer a sacred trust but who ironically require legal protocol, Jesus contradicts his earlier acknowledgment of the invalidity of self-authentication and insists on the truth of his self-affirmation.

> Even if I testify about myself, my testimony is true, for I know where I came from and where I am going to. But you do not know where I came from and where I am going to. You judge according to the flesh, but I judge no one. And if I do judge, my judgment is true. (8:14-16)

Here the outcome of the trial of 5:17-47 is exposed. Jesus' efforts to authenticate himself are failing because the ruling authorities continue to judge him on the basis of their separationist ideology of the old moral order. On the one hand, their ideology prevents them from engaging in a critical inquiry into the origin of his deeds and words, and, on the other hand, their categories of messianic typology prevent them from seeing beyond the external appearance of the "flesh." In their eyes – in spite of his appeal to four witnesses – he is a Jew from Galilee whose ancestry and geographical origin cannot be correlated to any biblical antecedents. They do not live ironically, and they have no ironic perspective by which they interpret the world.

For Jesus, on the other hand, there is no necessity to judge, for, as he stated earlier in 3:18, "the one who does not believe is judged already because he/she has not believed into the name of the only one-of-a-kind Son." By not making a commitment to the reign of God that Jesus is inaugurating, by preferring to remain in the old moral order, they are imposing their own judgment on themselves.

Nevertheless, if it is necessary for Jesus to judge, for, as he asserted earlier, "the Father has given all judgment to the Son," his judgment is true because he is not alone. He is supported by the One who sent him. That fulfills the legal requirement of two witnesses for his legitimation: his own testimony and the testimony of the one who sent him. To reinforce his own witness Jesus employs the divine self-authenticating formula: " **I AM** the one testifying about myself, and the Father who sent me testifies about me" (8:18). When the Pharisees demand, "Where is your father?" they betray once more their inability to hear with understanding. All that Jesus has said about the Father/Son relationship has fallen on deaf ears. Consequently, since they manifest no comprehension of the divine origin of his activity and teaching, he can only conclude, "You know neither me nor my Father. If you knew me, you also would know my Father" (8:19). The narrator ends this incident by locating it "at the treasury" and informing the implied readers once again of the inability of the authorities to seize him "because his hour has not yet come."[47]

The next episode, verses 21-29, intensifies the confrontation between Jesus and the ruling elite, as the narrator repeats the same form of introduction used in 8:12: "Then he said to them again..." The dialogue must be continued because the empirically oriented perspective of the authorities prevents them from knowing where is from and where he is going, and that will have far-reaching consequences for them. As the plaintiff Jesus has defended his work on the basis of his collaboration with the "Father (5:17-47) and attributed the origin of his teaching to the One who commissioned him. Now, in this gradational movement of the ongoing dialogue, Jesus assumes the role of a judge and introduces the consequences they will suffer when he leaves.[48] "I am going away and you will seek me, and you will die in your sin. Where I am going you are unable to come." Their empirically oriented perspective that tends to foster a literalistic interpretation of what they hear and see precludes their comprehension, and they speculate, "Surely he won't kill himself, will he? For he says, 'where I am going you are not able to come'." What he tells them of course is true. They cannot follow him into crucifixion, for that is where he is going, as the implied readers should be able to perceive by now. He will not kill himself, but ironically he will be killed when these authorities hand him over to the Romans for execution.[49] Jesus charges that they are guilty of being captive to the social construction of reality, the world that lies in darkness: "You are ἐκ τῷν κάτω (from below) ... you are ἐκ τούτου τοῦ κόσμου (from this world)."[50] Light has come into the world, incarnated in Jesus, but they

[47] Ludger Schenke, "Der 'Dialog Jesu mit den Juden' im Johannesevangelium: ein Rekonstruktionsversuch," *NTS* 34/4 (1988) 573-603, offers a redaction-critical analysis of John 3-12 in order to recover from the fragmented character of the present dialogical structure of Jesus' interaction with "the Jews" what he considers to have been the original unity of the source that the Fourth Evangelist utilized. Already at the very outset, 8:20 is adopted from Bultmann's source analysis and identified as a redactional frame. But no effort has been made to analyze the literary style of the author. Verse 20 is simply used to separate two episodes of Jesus' dialogue with the authorities in order to enable the narrator to move that dialogue into a gradational shift in which Jesus takes the offensive and assumes the role of judge.

[48] So also Jerome H. Neyrey, "Jesus the Judge: Forensic Process in John 8,21-59," *Bib* 68/4 (1987) 509.

[49] See also Duke, *Irony*, 85-86.

[50] The Fourth Gospel's employment of κόσμος (world), appearing 76 times, can cogently be interpreted as "the social construction of reality". See Berger and Luckmann, *The Social Construction of Reality: A Treatise in the Sociology of Knowledge,* 56ff. Also Peter L. Berger, "Religion and World Maintenance," *The Sacred Canopy,* 29-51. W. A. Meeks, "The Man from Heaven in Johannine Sectarianism," *JBL* 91/1 (1972) 70, has reached a similar conclusion.

remain imprisoned within the world that they have been engaged in constituting, and they have identified themselves with it so completely that they are no longer transparent to themselves. Entombed in a closed system of meaning, they will die within the old moral order that their ideology maintains. As Jesus said in verse 21, "I'm going away and you will seek me and you will die in your sin." His phrase, "you will die in your ἁμαρτίᾳ (sin)" refers to sin as a condition, the human infection that activates disobedience and acts of transgression and generates both the death of living and the death of dying. They will die from the disease of alienation that extends back to Adam and Eve and that has continued to dominate the old moral order.

Jesus differentiates himself from them by utilizing the divine **I AM** formula to accentuate his heavenly origin: ἐγὼ ἐκ τῶν ἄνω εἰμί (**I** from above **AM**). Between the personal pronoun ἐγώ and the copula εἰμί he inserts the prepositional phrase ἐκ τῶν ἄνω that denotes where he is from. As the New Human Being he has not originated from this social construction of reality (ἐκ τοῦ κόσμου τούτου). Accordingly, he had declared to Nicodemus in 3:13. "No one has ascended into heaven except the one who descended, the Son of the Human Being." Confronting the authorities as their judge in terms of this divine self-authentification, he pronounces his sentence upon them as the consequence of their continuing unbelief, "Therefore I said to you that you will die in your sins. For unless you believe that **I AM** (ἐγὼ εἰμί) you will die in your sins." In contrast to verse 21 Jesus employs the plural ἁμαρτίαις (sins). The ἁμαρτία (sin) that permeates the old creation in which they participate propagates acts of injustice, oppression and dehumanization that also produce death. They will remain in the darkness and die in the sins of their transgressions (8:24).

This is the second time in the narrative world of the Gospel that Jesus uses the absolute form of the sacred self-authenticating identification, **I AM**.[51] Believing that he is simply **I AM** without any predicates means that he is not to be differentiated from the Creator in terms of his person and his work. In his **I AM** "the Father" and "the Son" are inextricably linked together. When Jesus employed the divine formula with predicates, as in 6:41-42 and 8:12, "**I AM** the bread that descends from heaven" and "**I AM** the light of the world," the authorities appear to focus on the predicates. When, however, he employs it without a predicate, as here in 8:24, they confront him with the question of identity, "You, who are you?" (σὺ τίς εἶ). It is a critical moment. The same question had been addressed to John the Witness in 1:19 by priests and Levites at the behest of the Pharisees; and its distinctive formulation, by placing the pronoun σύ (you) first and adding the second person singular of the copula εἶ (you are), intimates a challenge.[52] In his reply John had inserted the negative particle οὐκ into the **I AM** formula and added a predicate: ἐγὼ οὐκ εἰμὶ ὁ

[51] The implied readers are already familiar with his use of **I AM** without a predicate. They encountered it in 6:20 when he identified himself to his disciples as **I AM** while walking on the Sea of Galilee, and in 18:5, 6, 7. All the other occurrences of **I AM** are followed by a predicate of one kind or another: 4:26; 6:35, 41, 48, 51; 8:12, 18.

[52] See Schnackenburg, *St. John* II, 200.

χριστός (**I** not **AM** the Christ).[53] Jesus, who in contrast to John, employs the absolute form of ἐγώ εἰμί (**I AM**) but without the negating adverb οὐκ, is nevertheless expected to add a predicate. The two titles that John had disavowed, "the Christ," and "the Prophet" have been repudiated as possible christological identifications of Jesus. What predicate would he employ to identify himself now?

Jesus' response is difficult to construe. It does not form a sentence, and it is possible that the text is corrupt: τὴν ἀρχὴν ὅ τι καὶ λαλῷ ὑμῖν (literally: "the beginning what I also speak to you").[54] Different constructions have been posed to resolve its contextual meaning, but generally without drawing upon verses 28-29. The scribe of P[66], evidently puzzled by the text, inserted the words εἶπον ὑμῖν (I said to you) at the front of Jesus' response in order to make it intelligible.[55] By adopting the P[66] interpolation and construing the phrase τὴν ἀρχήν (the beginning) as an adverbial accusative denoting time, the text could be rendered as a statement, "*I said to you* from *the beginning* what I am also speaking to you."[56]

Another construction is offered by the Greek Fathers, who interpreted τὴν ἀρχήν adverbially as ὅλως (at all) and rendered the text as an exclamation, "That I speak to you at all!"[57] This rendition seems to be favored by more recent commentators who add the adverbial conjunction "why" and consequently transform the exclamation into a question: "Why do I speak to you at all?"[58] A third construction takes the liberty of including the **I AM** formula (ἐγώ εἰμί) that Jesus used in the previous verse and places it at the beginning of his reply as an affirmation, "I am what I tell you from the beginning" or, "From the beginning I am what I tell you."[59]

Of these three interpretations, the first, which corresponds to the reading of P[66] and construes Jesus' words as a statement, is supported by the continuation of his discourse. In spite of the ambiguity of his response: "I told you at the beginning what I am also speaking to you," it is an answer to their question. Because of their inability to understand what he told them at the beginning, specifically at the forensic process

---

[53] Also 3:28.

[54] Bultmann, *John*, 352, and n. 5, posits that the text may be corrupt and speculates what the original sense may have been: "At the beginning, no matter how much I may talk to you, you will not believe; but there will come a time ..." German, 268 and n. 2.

[55] For the P[66] text of 8:25, see Comfort and Barrett, *Earliest New Testament Manuscripts*, 408. But see especially Robert W. Funk, "Papyrus Bodmer II (P[66]) and John 8, 25," *HTR* 51 (1958) 95-100, who acknowledges that the two words, εἶπον ὑμῖν, are a marginal correction but nevertheless are to be attributed to the original scribe. Furthermore, he contends that there is a "strong possibility that these two words, εἶπον ὑμῖν, stood in the text from which P[66] was copied" and points out that the appearance of εἶπον with λαλῶ is Johannine, as in 12:49 and 16:4.

[56] This is essentially Funk's rendition, *ibid*., 100. See Funk's helpful analysis of the problematic phrase, τὴν ἀρχήν, pp. 98-99. Brown, *John* I, 348, also adopts most of Funk's translation.

[57] *Ibid*.

[58] Bultmann, *John*, 353, prefers this construction. So also R. Schnackenburg, *St. John* II, 200; J. Becker, *Johannes* I, 295; Francis J. Moloney, *Signs and Shadows: Reading John 5-12* (Fortress Press: Minneapolis, 1996) 100. This is also the translation of 8:25 in the NRSV.

[59] Barrett, *St. John*, 343. Also Lightfoot, *St. John*, 191; Lindars, *John*, 321. But Jesus has not repeated the ἐγώ εἰμί in verse 25.

of 5:17-46, he has said it to them again, but in terms of the divine self-authenticating formula, **I AM**. Because of their continuing inability to understand, he addresses them in the role of their judge:

> I have many things to speak about you and to judge, but the One who sent me is true, and the things I heard from alongside of him, these things I speak into the world (κόσμος). (8:26)

At this point, 8:27, and for the benefit of the implied readers, the narrator interrupts Jesus' discourse with an intrusive remark: "They did not *discern* (ἔγνωσαν) that he was speaking to them [about] the Father."

Jesus, therefore (οὖν), on the basis of the narrator's comment discloses the implication of his response to the authorities' question, "You, who are you?"

> When you lift up/exalt (ὑψώσητε) the Son of the Human Being, then you will know that **I AM (**ἐγώ εἰμί). (8:28)

Once again no predicate follows **I AM**. Jesus has none to offer. He never attaches identity predicates to his use of this self-authenticating formula. He never says, "**I AM** the Son of the Human Being" or "**I AM** the Son" or "**I AM** the Son of God." He speaks only in terms of the third person:

> And no one has ascended into heaven except the one who descended, the Son of the Human Being. (3:13)

> And even as Moses lifted up the snake in the wilderness, so it is necessary for the Son of the Human Being to be lifted up. (3:14)

> The Son can do nothing from himself, except whatever he sees the Father doing. (5:19)

> For the Father loves the Son and shows him the things he is doing. (5:20)

> Even as the Father raises the dead and makes alive, so also the Son makes alive whom he wills. (5:21)

> For even as the Father has life in himself, so he has also given the Son to have life in himself. (5:26)

> My teaching is not my own but of the One who sent me. (7:16)

> And if I judge, my judgment is true, because *I am* (εἰμί) not alone, but I and the One who sent me. (8:16)[60]

I AM, without predicates, is all that he is as the incarnate Logos and as "the one who descended from heaven, the New Human Being." His use of **I AM** without any predicates denotes both his union and his collaboration with God, and it is precisely in this strain as God's apprentice that he continues in 8:28, "And from myself I do nothing, but even as the Father taught me, these things I speak. And the One who sent

[60] It is noteworthy that Jesus also employs the copula εἰμί (I am) without the first person pronoun ἐγώ (I). Other occurrences are found in 7:28, 29, 33; 13:13, 33; 14:9; 16:32; 17:11 and 18:37, but in these instances, naturally, it has no christological significance.

me is with me; he did not leave me alone because I always do the things pleasing to him." It is only in terms of this union and collaboration with God that Jesus attaches predicates to his use of the self-authenticating **I AM** in the narrative world of the Fourth Gospel:

I AM the bread of life.
I AM the bread that descends from heaven.
I AM the light of the world.
I AM the one testifying about myself.

This union and this collaboration with the Creator that he intimates in his employment of **I AM** will be discernible at his crucifixion, when he is enthroned and exalted on the cross, and it will be visible to the implied readers who continue to be present at this forensic process of 8:21-59.

The third episode (8:30-59) in this gradational series of interaction between Jesus and the ruling elite is introduced by the narrator's report, "Many believed into him." In a surprising turnabout some of the authorities appear to have been induced to make a commitment to him on the basis of what they have heard him say in 8:21-29. Jesus has experienced such a response from the Jerusalem crowds, but now, for the first time, officials of government (οἱ Ἰουδαίοι) have begun to "believe into him."[61]

Since they belong to the fellowship of the ruling elite who have been plotting to kill him, Jesus challenges them in order to determine the authenticity of their commitment.

> If you remain (μείνητε) in my word, you are truly my disciples, and you will know (γνώσεσθε) the truth and the truth will liberate you. (8:31-32)

The integrity of Jesus' word, which originates from his being and personhood as the enfleshed Logos, ordains him as the Truth, the source of God's revelation. Their continuance or "abiding" in his teaching, therefore, will sustain them in their discipleship and guarantee not only their personal knowledge of the truth but also their effective liberation.

But freedom, according to their perspective, is already a present reality in which they participate as the offspring of Abraham: "We are the seed of Abraham and to no one have we ever been enslaved. What do you mean by saying, 'You will become free.'" The very fact of their Jewish identity, based on their descent from the grand Patriarch of Israel, is the grounding of their freedom.

Jesus responds to their superficial accreditation of freedom to their identity as Abraham's offspring, with a double asseveration, "Amen, amen I say to you, 'Everyone who does sin (ἁμαρτία) is a slave of sin'." As the underlying condition of human existence in the old moral order, ἁμαρτία is a power that engenders

[61] Because of this surprising development, it is claimed by some commentators that this belief is "unwarranted" and inconsistent with the context of 8:21-29. Bultmann, *John*, 433; German, 332. On the basis of the inconsistencies, von Wahlde, "The Johannine 'Jews'," 50-51, attributes this text to the work of a redactor.

injustice, oppression, exploitation and therefore the dehumanization of those created in the image and likeness of God. It is the disease that predestines human beings to both the death of living and the death of dying. As Jesus had warned these authorities earlier, "I am going away and you will seek me, and you will die in your sin (ἁμαρτία)." The self-understanding that they have verbalized is founded on physical kinship, and physical kinship, as Jesus told Nicodemus, is simply "that which is born of flesh is flesh." To be the physical offspring of Abraham, therefore, is to be predetermined to be a participant in the same moral order in which Abraham existed, the moral order dominated by the condition and power of sin (ἁμαρτία).

Moreover, as Jesus adds, "The slave does not remain (μένει) in the house forever; the Son remains forever. If, therefore, the son liberates you, you will be free indeed." Are there allusions here to Abraham's two sons, Isaac and Ishmael?[62] According to Gen 21:10, the latter, the son of a slave woman, was cast out; the former, the son of Abraham and Sarah, remained "in the house." Isaac, the free-born son, may have remained in the house forever, but he as well as Ishmael, like their father Abraham, were embedded in the realm of ἁμαρτία (sin) and therefore subject to its power. Consequently Jesus' differentiation between "the slave" and "the son" cannot be applied to them, and therefore the authorities who claim to be free, based on their identity as Abraham's seed, cannot simply be identified with the slave son, Ishmael.

The Son, who remains forever, is the Son of the Human Being who descended from heaven and who, by his union and collaboration with God, will liberate all who are enslaved, those who are Abraham's seed as well as those who are not. Set free by the Son and therefore like the Son, they will remain forever; and if it is "in the house" that they will remain, it will be the "Father's house" that the Son embodies and will eventually enlarge through his death and resurrection.

Jesus concludes by acknowledging that they are indeed Abraham's offspring, "but," he continues, "you are seeking to kill me because my word does not have room in you." In the chiastic structure of 8:31b-38, the narrator has disclosed to the implied readers that these members of the ruling authorities are not remaining in his word and therefore are truly not his disciples.[63] Jesus draws the contrast between himself and these members of the ruling elite in 8:38, "The things I have seen in the presence of the Father I speak; and you therefore, the things you heard from the father you continue to do."[64] Acknowledging that the authorities are the offspring of Abraham is an affirmation of their Jewish identity, but to insinuate that they have a father from whom they have heard the things they are doing is to imply

[62] This is the conclusion of Neyrey, "Jesus the Judge: Forensic Process in John 8:21-59," 521-527.

[63] Neyrey, *ibid.*, 520, has identified this chiastic structure and, in terms of his demonstration of the forensic character of 8:30-37, has disclosed the falsehood of their commitment to Jesus.

[64] The Hesychian and the Byzantine textual traditions witness to the scribal insertion ὑμῶν (your) in front of the second use of "father" in verse 38, an interpolation that clarifies the direction of Jesus' word.

another patrimony. Since they suspect that Jesus has referred to another father, they name their ancestor again in order to overcome the ambiguity, "Our father is Abraham." But Jesus contradicts their claim,

> If you were children of Abraham, you would continue to do the works of Abraham. But now you are seeking to kill me, a human being who has spoken the truth to you that I heard from God. This Abraham did not do. You continue to do the works of your father. (8:39b-40)

Their identity and activity do not correspond, for their self-identification as Abraham's offspring is invalidated by their intention to kill Jesus.[65] But what are the works of Abraham to which Jesus is alluding? It is Philo who, more specifically than the Genesis stories of Abraham, ascribes "works of justice and kindness to human beings" to Abraham, and very likely that is the underpinning of Jesus' reference.

> "So, then, he was not only peaceable and a justice-lover but courageous and warlike, not in order to wage war, for he was not combative or perverse but to secure peace on behalf of the future that the opponents were destroying.[66]

Accordingly, Abraham cannot be their father. They have another father to whom they have been listening and from whom they have been learning. Jesus continues to base his refutation of their claim on the revelation he has derived from his own experience, but he shifts from the sense experience of "the things *I have seen* (ἑώρακα) *in the presence of the Father*" (παρὰ τῷ πατρί) to the sense experience of "the truth I *heard* (ἤκουσα) *from alongside of God*" (παρὰ τοῦ θεοῦ). By using the preposition παρά in relation to the dative case, he is citing location or position: being "in the presence of." As the Logos incarnate he is affirming what he has learned by the things he has seen and heard in God's presence. His experience as God's apprentice stands in sharp contrast to the charge he brought against the authorities in 5:37b, "Not ever have you heard his voice or seen his appearance," while at the same time it affirms 6:46, "Not that anyone has seen the Father, except *the one being from alongside of God* (ὁ ὢν παρὰ τοῦ θεοῦ)." But here in 6:46, as in 8:40, Jesus is employing the preposition παρά in relation to the genitive case in order to convey a sense of

---

[65] See von Wahlde, "'You Are of Your Father the Devil' in its Context: Stereotyped Apocalyptic Polemic in John 8:38-47," *Anti-Judaism and the Fourth Gospel*, 423-437, for an analysis of the structure of the argument in 8:38-47 that he compares with other late Jewish and early Christian literature, including the Dead Sea Scrolls, the Testaments of the Twelve Patriarchs and 1 John. He concludes on pages 440 and 442 that this pattern of argument employed in 8:38-47 is stereotypical in as far as it had "a much wider circulation in the first century than the Johannine community." "[John] is using a series of categories which his reader would immediately recognize as a standard type of apocalyptic argument. ... They would also recognize that the argument had no more hostility to it than any other case in apocalyptic polemic." But on p. 443 he claims that the term οἱ Ἰουδαίοι (the Jews), "refers to 'those in Judea', i.e. the religious authorities in Jerusalem with whom the Johannine community saw themselves in conflict and who were ultimately responsible for the exclusion of the Johannine community from the synagogue."

[66] *de Abrahamo*, 225. See also 232, 261 and especially 262-265.

source or direction. Both location and source are true. As the incarnate Logos who descended from heaven, he has seen things in the presence of God, and the revelation to which he is bearing witness originates from God.

Ironically, the authorities revise their self-identification as Abraham's offspring that Jesus has repudiated and appropriate the claim that he has been making for himself, "We were not born out of prostitution! God is the one Father we have." They reject his insinuation that they are the product of adultery and, at the same time, ascribe to themselves the descent that Jesus has been professing. Their dismissal of his indictment by contesting, "We were not born out of prostitution" should not be judged as "a covert counter-attack against Jesus."[67] He is not being vilified. This is not an attempt to redirect his insinuation of their illegitimacy back to him; it is simply a rejection of the charge he has made against them.

But Jesus refuses to acknowledge the legitimacy of their new claim. He countercharges, "If God were your Father, you would love me, for I issued from God and I am here. I did not come of myself but that One sent me." He has stated this repeatedly. Yet, as he despairingly inquires, "Why do you not "discern with understanding" (γινώσκετε) my speech?" The word λαλία that he uses here, refers to the "content of his speech" but particularly to his "way of speaking," namely, that quality of authority that he manifests in both his speaking and teaching.[68] Without waiting for a reply, he answers his own question by revising the charge he made earlier in verse 37, "Because you are unable to hear my word." They have difficulty discerning the truth of his revelation, but they have no difficulty hearing "the things from their father." The latter, therefore, the one whom they are heeding, must be someone in opposition to God. Jesus unhesitatingly draws the logical inference, "You originate from your father, the devil, and you will to do the cravings of your father." Since the craving they want to fulfill is killing Jesus, they must be the devil's offspring, because "That one was a murderer from the beginning and he did not stand in the truth because there is no truth in him. When he speaks the lie, he is speaking from his own realm because he is a liar and the father of lies."

Are there allusions here to Cain, who murdered his brother Abel? It is contended by some interpreters that a later editor interpolated the phrase τοῦ πατρός (of the father) at the beginning of 8:44. If that insertion were eliminated, the original text would read, "You originate from the devil and want to do the cravings of your father..."[69] That father, whose cravings the ruling authorities

[67] Also Schnackenburg, II, 212, who draws upon Hosea's charge against Israel as "children of whores."

[68] *Greek-English Lexicon of the New Testament and Other Early Christian Literature*, 583.

[69] Günther Reim, "Joh. 8. 44 – Gotteskinder/Teufelskinder. Wie antijudaistisch ist 'Die wohl antijudaistischste Äusserung des NT'?" *NTS* 30/4 (1984) 619-624, reviews various interpretations of this text and contends for such an editorial revision and, following N. A. Dahl, concludes that "the father" with whom Jesus is associating the ruling elite is Cain, basing his conclusion on the readings of Targum Neofiti and 1QH VII,3 and the Samaritan text, the Malef. Also Neyrey, "Jesus the Judge: Forensic Process in John 8:21-59," 527-528. See especially, N. A. Dahl, "Der Erstgeborene des Satans

want to fulfill by killing Jesus, is identifiable as Cain, for, "On principle Jews can never be children of the devil."[70] But more than likely the genitive phrase, τοῦ διαβόλου, (the devil) stands in apposition to τοῦ πατρός (of the father) that immediately precedes it, and therefore there is no need to conjecture that τοῦ πατρός is a later editorial interpolation. Jesus is identifying the authorities who desire to kill him by drawing upon the myth of Gen 3:1-6. Like the devil who, by lying, robbed Adam and Eve of life with God and subjected them to the curses of the Fall, the ruling elite have constituted a social construction of reality, founded on the Pharisaic heritage of the loyalty and separation, in which the possibility of transcendence is virtually unrealizable. The conformity that is legislated and the excommunication that is threatened promote a society of living death.

If these authorities, who have claimed to be his disciples, would continue in his word, they would know the truth, and the truth would set them free. But, as he is aware, their rejection of his word and the truth that it promises to reveal pivots on his self-identification with "the Father."[71] Accordingly, he confronts them with the charge, "But I, because I am telling you the truth, you do not believe me." The emphasis on the "I" (ἐγώ) at the beginning of his censure, indicates that he is the pretext of their rejection. They refuse to acknowledge that he is that eschatological fulfillment that "Moses and the prophets wrote about," that he, as the son of Joseph from Nazareth, is also New Human Being who descended from heaven. It is the aporia, the paradox of his identity that prevents them from affirming the truth of his revelation. If he places himself before them as a plaintiff instead of a judge, what crime would they be able to charge against him: "Who of you," he asks, "convicts me of sin? If I am telling the truth, why don't you believe me?" If all the charges against him are groundless, why do they refuse to believe him? Why do they want to kill him? If God is their Father, as they have claimed, they, like anyone "being from God" would take heed to the pronouncements of God. Once again he determines that there is only one valid inference that can be drawn, "On account of this you do not hear, because you do not originate from God."

The authorities, affronted by his bitter accusations: "You originate from the devil" and "You do not originate from God," retaliate with spite: "Do we not say rightly that you are a Samaritan and you have a demon?" Their countercharge implies that he, like the Samaritan people, is guilty of apostasy. He is no longer to be regarded as a loyal Jew. Moreover, he is under the spell of an unclean spirit. The Jerusalem crowd had made the same charge in 7:20. Both are grounds for excommunication. Jesus in turn accuses them of defamation and defends himself against their libel by declaring that he has only one objective in his ministry: "to honor the Father." He is not pursuing the values of the honor/shame society in which they live; he is not seeking

---

und der Vater des Teufels (Polyk. 7:1 und Joh 8:33)" in *Apophoreta: Festschrift für Ernst Haenchen*, ed. by W. Eltester (Berlin: Alfred Töpelmann,1964) 70-84.

[70] Reim, *ibid.*, 622.

[71] As in John 5:18.

his own glory. By slandering him because he has told them the truth, they are guilty of dishonoring him. Consequently they should be wary, for "There is One who seeks [his honor] and he judges." The peril that this reality poses for the authorities, who evidently have abandoned their commitment to him, induces Jesus to return to the promise he had made to them earlier. What he had said in 8:31 he now enunciates in terms of a double asseveration, "Amen, amen I say to you, 'If anyone keeps my word, he/she will by no means *look on* (θεωρήσῃ) death forever'." That assurance, spoken with a double *amen* to guarantee its certainty, evokes from them their earlier charge, "Now we know (ἐγνώκαμεν) that you have a demon. Abraham and the prophets died and you say, 'If anyone keeps my word, he/she will not taste (γεύσηται) death forever'."

Once again these guardians of society have misunderstood Jesus. He did not say, "… he/she will by no means *taste* death forever." He is not guaranteeing the eternal continuation of temporal existence to those who keep his word. The entry into physical death is not precluded for anyone, not even for those who know the truth and have been liberated by it. The verb Jesus employed, θεωρήσῃ denotes "giving oneself over to that which has been observed or beheld." It is a special verb of seeing for Philo who characterizes it as "a faculty of vision that is led upwards by light."[72] Θεωρήσῃ preceded by a double negative, denotes that those who guard Jesus' word will behold the reality of death, both the death of living and the death of dying, and will by no means give themselves over to either one. Because Jesus has set them free by delivering them from death in all its forms, they know that death is no longer the supreme determinant of human existence either in their participation in the social construction of reality or at the point of their physical demise.

Ironically, however, the verb γεύσηται that the authorities substituted in place of his θεωρήσῃ conveys another reality that is equally true. Those who keep Jesus' word will indeed taste death, but not forever. As was stated in the epitomization of the Gospel in 3:16, "For in this way God loved the world that he gave his Son, the only one-of-a-kind, in order that every one believing into him should not perish but have life everlasting."

The authorities extend their misunderstanding of Jesus' promise into the issue of his identity, "Surely you aren't greater than our father Abraham who died and the prophets who died, are you?" Their use of the negative particle μή indicates that they anticipate a negative reply to their question. How could he be greater than Abraham or the prophets? They tasted death. By what powers of possibility is he able to prevent that? Their confusion and their perplexity about his identity induces them to raise the question of his self-identification, "Whom do you make yourself?" Once again Jesus avoids their challenge to submit a predicate of self-understanding or self-identification. He insists that he has no desire to glorify himself, "If I glorify myself, my glory is nothing" and, as he indicated moments ago in verse 50b, "It is the Father who glorifies me, whom you say, 'He is our God'."

[72] Philo, *de Opificio Mundi*, 54.

Assuming the role of judge once more, he repeats his indictment, "And you have not known (ἐγνώκατε) him." They originate from the devil because they want to kill him. They do not originate from God because they do not hear and heed him. Accordingly, they have not known him in terms of personal acquaintance. Jesus counters their deficiency in their experiential knowledge of God by accentuating his own cognitive knowledge of God, "But I know (οἶδα) him. If I said I do not know (οἶδα) him, I will be like you, a liar. But I know (οἶδα) him, and I keep his word." The knowledge of God that he claims for himself is based on earlier experiences, such as seeing "the things of God" that he referred to in 8:38 or "the truth that he heard from God" (8:40). It is a "knowing of" that is predetermined by a mutually constituted ongoing personal familiarity.

Jesus' dialogue with the ruling authorities, in which he has been both defendant and judge, reaches its culmination as he takes up their reintroduction of Abraham whose offspring they have claimed to be, "Your father Abraham exulted to see my day, and he saw and rejoiced." The great Patriarch of Israel, being a human being of faith, believed that God's word would be fulfilled and his offspring would inherit the Promised Land.[73] Once again the authorities misunderstand what Jesus has said. Non-plussed, they ask, "You are not fifty-five years old and you have seen Abraham?" But he did not claim that he saw Abraham or that Abraham saw him. Abraham, from his context and life-style as a sojourner long ago, glimpsed the day of the actualization of God's promise, the possession of the Promised Land by God's people, and he gloried in it.

Jesus' replies to their disbelief with a closing double asseveration, "Amen, amen I say to you, 'before Abraham happened, **I AM** (ἐγὼ εἰμί)'." Before Abraham was born, the union that Jesus' **I AM** conveys was already present, the union that the opening verse of the Prologue announces, "In the beginning was the Logos, and the Logos was towards God [the Creator], and the Logos was God." Jesus boldly identifies himself with that union because he, as the enfleshed Logos-Sophia, is drawn into that harmonious union of oneness.

To what extent the ruling authorities have understood Jesus' solemn declaration remains unclear. The murderous intent that they have retained reaches a climax as they make their first attempt to punish Jesus by stoning him to death. Ironically, he, as the living Temple of God, is forced to withdraw from the Jerusalem Temple and to escape into hiding. This will not be the last attempt of the authorities to stone him to death.

[73] Compare with Philo, *de Abrahamo*, 262-276, whose reflections on Abraham's faith, especially in paragraph 268, are oriented toward "improvement of the soul in all things, [the soul] being fixed firmly and set upon the One who is the cause of all things and able to do all things but willing only the best."

Chapter Eleven

Paradoxical Success in Jerusalem

Enabling a blind man to see 9: 1-12

After a virulent confrontation with the ruling authorities that ended with an attempt to stone him, Jesus retreats from the sacred precinct of the Temple. As he leaves he encounters a man, a male, born blind.[1] Evidently it is a physical affliction because he has been forced to make his living by begging. Since he is "blind from birth," as the narrator states, his blindness also appears to be a spiritual incapability to see the light of truth.[2]

The story, therefore, may presuppose the implied readers' familiarity with the "Allegory of the Cave" in Book Seven of Plato's *The Republic*. From that perspective, the man's condition of blindness has been engendered by the process of socialization in his society that has been established and maintained by the ruling elite who construct reality (κόσμος) according to their ideological values. From the very beginning of his life he has been taught to believe that the "world" (κόσμος) of the society into which he was born constitutes the truth of things.[3] In his case that would include the truth of his uncleanness resulting from an earlier known or unknown violation of the divinely sanctioned purity code of Leviticus or the Deuteronomic Covenant of reciprocity.[4] Consequently, like the individual who had been suffering a debilitating illness for thirty-eight years in 5:5, he would be consigned to the realm of the "Unclean." That is implied in the question that the disciples raise regarding this affliction and its etiology, "Rabbi, who sinned? This man or his parents that he was born blind?"

[1] Bultmann, *John*, 239; German, 178, is correct in recognizing that John 5 and 9 share a common pattern and are to be interpreted from the same historical situation. But that is not simply a relation between a young Christianity and a hostile Judaism. Both stories reflect conflict within the Jewish community of Alexandria as the struggle continues to replace the Temple with a new unifying center for the people of God. If, as Brown contends in *The Community of the Beloved Disciple,* 72, "this blind man is acting out the history of the Johannine community," it is in the context of a Jewish and not a Christian community. Brown's view has been adopted by David Rensberger, *Johannine Faith,* 42, "The blind man, it seems clear, symbolizes the Johannine Christians." Above all, see Martyn, *History and Theology*, 35-89, for the trail-blazing interpretation of John 9, that is the starting point of this construction of the story. Staley, "Stumbling in the Dark,," 64-69, offers a characterization of the blind male that, in contrast to the individual of chapter 5, is considered to be "comical." Nicklas, *Ablösung und Verstrickung*, 336, acknowledges the legitimacy of a synchronic interpretation of 9:1-41, after concluding that the text shows itself to be a coherent unity.

[2] This is confirmed by Jesus' concluding words of judgment in 9:39.

[3] Here also see P. L. Berger and T. Luckmann, *The Social Construction of Reality*, 45-118.

[4] Bultmann, *John*, 330, n. 8, explicitly refers to Ex 20:5 and Deut 5:9; German, 251, n. 2.

Like Plato's followers, they want to determine the origin of his blindness. As members of that society, their perspective is determined by their Deuteronomic heritage, the transmission of a sinful condition from an earlier generation or possibly the result of the man's own culpability. Was he born blind because his parents ate sour grapes and set his teeth on edge?[5] Or is he guilty of eating sour grapes and setting his own teeth on edge? Was he was raised by parents who were blind to the truth of things and therefore could not differentiate between reality and appearance? Or is he himself the origin of his own disability?

Jesus repudiates their proposed analysis of cause and effect. Neither the purity code of Leviticus nor the Deuteronomic Covenant of reciprocity determines the orientation of his ministry. The affliction of blindness or, for that matter, any illness must not be interpreted as retribution of sin.[6] "Neither he sinned nor his parents, but in order that the works of God are manifested in him." For him this is an opportunity to act on behalf of God and enable someone to see the light of truth, as well as the empirical world of sight, that is, both the light of the first day of creation and the physical light of the fourth day of creation. Such work is not to be limited to Jesus alone! For the first time in his ministry he draws his disciples – and the implied readers -- into his mission to ensure the continuation of his work: "It is necessary that *we* work the works of the One who sent me while it is day; the night comes when no one is able to work." Utilizing proverbial wisdom, Jesus stresses the necessity to maximize the activity of God as long as daylight lasts and – in as far as daylight may be metaphorically representative of the span of a lifetime – as long as a person's life and physical vitality endure. The coming of night, like the arrival of death, marks the cessation of all activity.[7]

The work that he accentuates is oriented to his self-understanding of being light and therefore generating light in the world: "When I am in the world, φῶς (light) I am of the world." He had enunciated this understanding of his being earlier at the outset of his conflict with the Pharisees and, as in all instances of the **I AM** formulation, had placed the **I AM** (ἐγὼ εἰμί) at the beginning of his self-disclosure in relation to the divine activity in which he is engaged: "**I AM** the light of the world." Here, however, the typical **I AM** formula is not used. The pronoun "I" does not appear before the copula "am." Instead the word "light" (φῶς) begins the second clause of his declaration, probably for the sake of emphasis, "When I am in the world, *light* I am of the world."[8] Jesus is identifying himself with primordial light, the light of the first day of creation.[9]

---

[5] See the Hebrew proverb that conveys what might be called the biblical understanding of "original sin" in Jer 31:29 and Ezek 18:2.

[6] Dodd, *Historical Tradition,* 187.

[7] *Ibid*., 186, where Dodd cites examples of this proverbial wisdom.

[8] The adverbial conjunction "when" simply denotes the duration of Jesus' ministry in the world.

[9] Schnackenburg, *St. John* II, 257, on the basis of Jesus' self-disclosure as "the light of the world" determines that main theological purpose of this story is christological. But it is both soteriological, christological and ecclesiological.

According to Philo of Alexandria, the "light of the world" is the light of the first day of creation, and it is an image of the divine Logos who makes itself intelligible by means of interpretation.

> Now that invisible light falling in the province of the mind has come into being as an image of the divine Word (θείου λόγου), the one interpreting its origin.[10]

Philo had differentiated between two kinds of seeing in his discourse "On the Creation," the spiritual sight that belongs to the light of the first day of creation and the physical sight that relates to the fourth day of creation.

> The *breath* (πνεῦμα) and *light* (φῶς) are deemed worthy of privilege. For the one he names [the breath] of God, because breath is most life-giving, and God is the author of life, but of light he says that it is surpassingly beautiful (Gen 1:4): for the intelligible is more radiant and more brilliant than the visible even as sunlight, I think, [is more brilliant and more radiant] than darkness and day [than] night.[11]

> According to necessity, the Maker decorated the heaven on the fourth day with a very beautiful and a most divine structure, namely the light-giving stars; and knowing that of all beings, light is best, he displayed it as the instrument of sight, the best of the senses; for what the intellect is in the soul, this the eye is in the body; for each of them *sees* (βλέπει), one intellectual things, the other the things of sense.[12]

In the Fourth Gospel the two kinds of seeing that Philo differentiated and disconnected, the seeing of the soul and the seeing of the eyes, are not disengaged from each other. The light of truth, the light of the first day of creation is not limited to the perceptibility of the soul. Opening the eyes of a human being born blind, therefore, does not require a movement from the corporeal world of the senses into the incorporeal realm of the intellect in order to discern the Word of God.[13] Of the four verbs of seeing, it is ὁρᾶν that bears the sense of eye-balling, using physical eyesight to perceive the truth of things. Jesus employs the verb in 1:39 when he invites the two disciples of John, "Keep on coming and *you will see* (ὄψεσθε)." If the Logos-Sophia has become incarnate in Jesus, it should be possible for these disciples, as well as the implied readers, to see it as well as hear it. In his bitter conflict with the guardians of society in 8:56, Jesus claims that the grand Patriarch of Israel, Abraham, exulted because he was enabled to see Jesus' day, and *he saw* (εἶδεν) and he rejoiced. According to 20:8, the Beloved Disciple viewed the burial garments in Jesus' tomb, "and *he saw* (εἶδεν) and he believed."

The verb that Philo employs for both kinds of sight, βλέπειν, is used ten times in this episode. The man born blind lacks both kinds of sight, the ability to see the

[10] Philo, *de Opificio Mundi,* 31.

[11] Philo, *de Opificio Mundi*, 30.

[12] *Ibid.*, 53.

[13] See Philo, *de Opificio Mundi*, 19-24.

light of the fourth day of creation and more significantly the light of the first day of creation, the light of truth. Jesus, unlike Philo's Logos, makes it possible for him to see, not by enabling his mind to discern the "incorporeal objects" of ideas and their senses to "apprehend bodily forms," but by directing him to a baptism of rebirth as an entry into a new being in which both kinds of seeing will be united in the quest for the truth of things.

The blind man has remained mute throughout Jesus' interaction with his disciples. He makes no request for the recovery of his sight. Nevertheless, Jesus addresses the condition of the man's blindness by spitting on the ground, making a ball of clay, and applying it to his blind eyes.[14] To make a ball of clay requires the act of kneading in order to mix the spittle and the earth.[15] But what function the clay is intended to serve is not clear.[16] Perhaps Jesus wants to remind him of his participation in the humanity of Adam, made from clay, but a humanity that is limited in its capacities because it is fallen and therefore incapable of seeing the light of truth, the light of the first day of creation. On the other hand, he may want to evoke from the blind man the realization that eliminating blindness is as much a work of God as the original creation of Adam from the clay of the earth.[17]

Both of these rationales of smearing clay on the blind man's eyes illuminate the purpose of the washing that Jesus prescribes. The blind man must bathe himself "into the pool of Siloam." He must be immersed in its water. He must be baptized![18] Jesus himself will not lead him to the pool in order to baptize him. He does not baptize in water (4:2). But the blind man's immersion will signify his "being born out of water."

Whether the interpretation of "Siloam" that is offered, namely "having been sent" applies to Jesus or to the blind man is difficult to determine. Certainly in this episode the blind man is being sent to Siloam for a bath. But throughout the

---

[14] Contrary to J. Becker, *Johannes* I, 316, Jesus is not using this opportunity to demonstrate his power. His objective is soteriological; he wants the man to see the light of truth. The outcome of the washing does not demonstrate Jesus' power. It proves that a rebirth has taken place, a rebirth that has begun to change the man's life forever.

[15] It is the act of kneading that is forbidden on the Sabbath, according to M *Shabbat* 7:2 and 24:3. See Strack-Billerbeck, *Kommentar* II, 530.

[16] In the Mediterranean world, spittle was believed to have the power of healing, as Mark 8:23 seems to imply. Lindars, *John*, 343, suggests, "Jesus does exactly what was done at the creation of man in Gen 2:6-7; ...the healing is a creative act."

[17] Irenaeus, *Against Heresies* V, 15,2, saw an allusion to Gen 2:7, maintaining that Jesus intended to point out "the original fashioning of the human being, how it was effected , and manifesting the hand of God to those who can understand by what the human being was fashioned out of the dust." In other words, Irenaeus interprets Jesus' act as a sign that God's hand is at work here as it was in Gen 2. C. K. Barrett, *St. John*, 358, dismisses Irenaeus' interpretation.

[18] Virtually no commentators refer to this washing as an act of baptism. Schnackenburg, *St. John* II, 257-258, reviews the arguments from the text to determine if baptism is intimated and reaches a negative conclusion. Howard-Brook, *Becoming Children of God*, 217, acknowledges: "The words suggest engaging in the very act that Nicodemus could not do: to be born ἄνωθεν in water and spirit (3:5)." Nicklas, *Ablösung und Verstrickung*, 347, follows Irenaeus and other ancients in acknowledging the allusion to Gen 2:7 and the interpretation of Jesus' act as a new creation.

narrative world of the Fourth Gospel Jesus declares that he has been sent into the world by the Father: 3:17; 5:36, 38; 6:29, 57; 7:29; 8:42; 10:36; 11:42; 17:3, 8, 18, 23, 25. Furthermore, even as he has been sent, so in turn he also sends his disciples into the world (17:18). However, the Hebrew form of Siloam, *Shiloaḥ*, may or may not be derived from the root שלח, and even if it were, *Shiloah* is not a passive participle meaning "sent."[19] Because there is no certain correspondence between Siloam and the parenthetical expression that translates it as "having been sent," it is very likely that it was inserted into the story at the time the second edition of the Gospel was prepared for a Gentile Christian readership in Ephesus.[20]

The man followed Jesus' instructions. He went off and through his immersion in the water of Siloam he experienced a rebirth, and he returns to his neighbors and friends able to see.[21] But it is more than physical sight that he has gained. Βλέπειν is the verb of seeing that is employed here, and it signifies a perspicuity that makes true insight possible.[22] This transparency of seeing will enable him to differentiate between reality and appearance.[23] He will begin to see the light of the first day of creation, the light of truth. Because his baptism has transformed him, his life has been changed, so changed that his neighbors no longer recognize him. At least they are not certain that this is the same person, the one whom they knew as a beggar. They speculate about his identity. Is he or isn't he? Some were saying, "It is he!' Others were saying, "No, it's not he; it's someone like him!" To all of them he identifies himself with the words, ἐγώ εἰμί (**I AM**). Not "I am he" and not "I am the man."[24] Simply "I am." This is the only instance in the narrative world of the Fourth Gospel that someone other than Jesus employs this phrase.

It is the same formula that Jesus has used in 4:26; 6:20; 7:34,36; 8: 24, 28, 58; and he will use it again in 12:26; 13:19; 14:3; 17:24; 18:5, 6, 8. It corresponds to the Septuagint's rendering of Yahweh's self-identification, אֶהְיֶה אֲשֶׁר אֶהְיֶה to Moses in Ex 3:14 as ἐγώ εἰμί ὁ ὤν (**I AM** the One who is). A somewhat similar translation of אָנֹכִי אֱלֹהֵי occurs in Ex 3:6 as ἐγώ εἰμί ὁ θεός (**I AM** God). Because Jesus is united with the Creator as the Logos incarnate, he is privileged to

---

[19] Brown, *John* I, 373.

[20] Bultmann, *John*, 333, also surmises that the name was added by the later editor and observes that the name of the pool is raised to the level of allegory; German, 253.

[21] An aorist middle indicative has been used in order to express a reflexive action.

[22] See chapter 5. βλέπειν is used 10 times in John 9, always bearing the connotation of perspicuity: "To grasp transcendent matters," or "to see with the eyes of the νοῦς." *A Greek-English Lexicon of the New Testament and Other Early Christian Literature*, 179.

[23] As Brown, *John* I, 502, has recognized, βλέπειν is certainly not the lowest form of seeing in the Gospel, but in his own analysis he does not go far enough to modify the conclusion of G.F. Phillips, "Faith and Vision in the Fourth Gospel," 83-96.

[24] This is Schnackenburg's translation, *St. John* II, 246, without any further consideration of the ἐγώ εἰμί. Bultmann, *John*, 333-334; German, 253-254; Martyn, *History and Theology*, 36, 41; and Rensberger, *Johannine Faith*, 41-49, do not comment on it. Nicklas, *Ablösung und Verstrickung*, 378, recognizes that the man who now sees could have responded to his friends and neighbors with a simple εἰμί (I am), and therefore he asks the appropriate question whether there is an allusion here to something deeper. Disappointingly, he leaves it unanswered.

appropriate God's self-disclosure, ἐγώ εἰμί and to express his union with God by walking on the Sea of Galilee and exercising divine sovereignty over chaos. But does this divine formula bear the same significance when this man, who is now able to see, identifies himself as ἐγώ εἰμί? Commentators have expressed different views:

> This is an instance of a purely secular use of the phrase.[25]
>
> ... it is a mistake to read them [the grand overtones of Jesus' **I AM**] into it.[26]
>
> The author is writing simple narrative.[27]
>
> ... simply establishes his identity.[28]

However, a rebirth has occurred in the waters of Siloam. The past life of this beggar ended eschatologically in the death experience of his immersion and with it any predicates of the past that would identify or characterize him. Consequently, he can no longer say "I am the beggar!" because it is no longer a predicate that defines his new existence.

The man, as a result of "being born from above" and therefore becoming a new human being, is simply "I am."[29] In that very respect he has become like Jesus, who, as **I AM** (ἐγώ εἰμί) refuses to attach any predicates to his self-disclosure, because, as the New Human Being, there are no predicates except those that express the activities in which he and God are collaborating. To be born from above, as Jesus said to Nicodemus in 3:3, enables a human being "to see the reign of God." To be born of water and the Spirit enables a human being to enter into the reign of God (3:5). The man who has gained sight will begin to see God's reign and, by entering into it, he will be drawn into union with Jesus, the enfleshed Logos-Sophia, who will draw him into the same kind of union with God that he himself enjoys.

> Father, that which you have given me, I want that *where **I AM*** (ὅπου ἐγώ εἰμί) those also may be with me, so that they *look on* (θεωρῶσιν) my glory which you have given me. (17:24)

As a new human being, he is no longer a sinner in the sense of being polluted or unclean because of his physical blindness. But he will need to have his feet

---

[25] Brown, *John* I, 373.

[26] Lindars, *John*, 344.

[27] Barrett, *St. John*, 359.

[28] Lightfoot, *St. John's Gospel,* 203.

[29] No one has said this better than Beatrice Bruteau, "Prayer and Identity," *Contemp Rev* 1982, 9. "When you are perfectly empty of all predicates – including the descriptions of yourself as a "receiver" – then you are intensely full of pure "I am," and just as this point is reached, it explodes into creative outpouring energy, 'May all of you be and be abundantly!" This is the point at which God is closer to you than 'you' – meaning your descriptions – are to yourself, as St. Augustine said. God irrupts in the center of your being, as that fountain of living water that makes you to be. But since God cannot be objectified, cannot be experienced as an object, you have to experience this from the subjective side, as if it is your own self-being."

washed continuously, for, as Jesus said to Simon Peter in 13:10, "The one who has bathed has no need to be washed, except for the feet." On the one hand he is clean, yet on the other hand, he is still a sinner because his old nature has not yet been absorbed into his new humanity. In this aporia or double bind of being both a new human being and a sinner, his self-understanding and with it his use of the word "I" will have no one fixed meaning. It will be a continuum moving between the binary oppositions of his humanity that will continue to subject him to acts of injustice and dehumanization and his union with God that will now be expressed in his own self-disclosure as **I AM.**

Another forensic process 9:13-39

After his neighbors and friends have learned how his eyes were opened, they lead him to the Pharisees. It is at this point in the story that the narrator pauses to inform the reader of the time, "Now it was Sabbath on the day Jesus made clay and opened his eyes." Since it was necessary to knead the spittle and the earth in order to make clay, the informed readers now know that Jesus has desecrated the Sabbath. But he is not charged, and no forensic process is opened against him. Instead an interrogation is conducted in which the man whose eyes Jesus opened is compelled to take on the role of a defendant and explain how he is now able to see.[30] His testimony produces a conflict among the Pharisees, a conflict that may mirror a split within the fellowship of the ruling elite that became evident in their put-down of Nicodemus in 7:52. One faction judges that Jesus cannot be from God because he did not observe the Sabbath. Others, however, are puzzled that someone who is obviously a sinner – because he transgressed the Sabbath – is nevertheless able "to do such signs." When they ask the man, who now sees, "What do you say about him?" he unhesitatingly identifies Jesus as a prophet.

The Pharisees, who are now confronted with the quandary of a mighty work having been performed on the Sabbath, move into an offensive mode by attempting to discredit Jesus. Identified now by the narrator as οἱ Ἰουδαίοι (the Jews), they dispute that the man was actually blind and has gained his sight. In order to settle the issue, his parents are called into the trial in order to testify: "Is this your son, whom you say that he was born blind? How then does he now see?" They willingly answer the first two questions in the affirmative: "He is our son and, yes, he was born blind." But they refuse to give evidence as to how he is now able to see or who may have opened his eyes. Fearful lest they incriminate themselves and be subject to expulsion from the synagogue, they force the authorities to return to the interrogation of their son. "Ask him!" they urge, "He is of age; he will speak for himself." For, as the narrator informs the reader in another intrusive remark, "... the Jews had already agreed that if anyone confesses him [as] Christ, he/she

[30] Martyn, *History and Theology*, 40, begins his dramatization of this story by interpreting it on the second level of the narrative world, the world of the implied readers: "Through a faithful witness *in the Johannine church*, the healing power of Jesus touches a poor Jew, afflicted many years with blindness. His sight is restored!" (The italics are his.)

would be *without a synagogue* (ἀποσυνάγωγος)." Evidently the parents are more anxious about losing their membership in the Jewish community than they are about remaining in solidarity with their son.[31]

Consequently, he is called back for a second interrogation. The authorities are now willing to acknowledge the recovery of his sight, but it is to be endorsed as the intervention of God, and not the work of Jesus. "Give glory to God!" they charge. At the same time they attempt to coerce him into assenting to their verdict that Jesus is guilty of desecrating the Sabbath and therefore should to be denounced as a sinner. But un-intimidated by their authority, he insists on the validity of his own experience: "Once I was blind but now *I see* (βλέπω)."

For the second time, as though wanting to wear him down, they inquire, "What did he do to you? How did he open your eyes?" Undaunted and resolute, he takes the offensive and begins to interrogate them, "I already told you and you did not hear. Why do you want to hear again? Surely you don't want to become his disciples, do you?" Since he refuses to be intimidated by their status and authority, they resort to verbal abuse. "You are a disciple of *that one*," they declare contemptuously without naming Jesus, "but we," they put forth with great self-importance, "we are disciples of Moses. We know that God spoke to Moses, but we do not know where *this one* is from." Ironically, they are certain that he is not from God, yet they do not know where he is from. They claim to believe Moses, but as Jesus had said to them in an earlier confrontation, "If you believed Moses, you would believe me, for he wrote about me."

Now, with growing confidence, the defendant taunts their incongruous reasoning by reminding them of the biblical tradition that they have in common and at the same time appropriating their earlier uses of the phrase "We know." "This is marvelous! *You do not know* where he is from, and he opened my eyes. *We know* that God does not hear sinners, but he does hear anyone who is God-fearing and does his will." They have claimed to be Moses' disciples, yet they refuse to acknowledge the truth of the Mosaic legacy of the Deuteronomic covenant that he recalls to them. Obedience to God's will results in God's responsive blessings, while disobedience brings about punishment and rejection.[32] Continuing in the same vein, the defendant expands his deuteronomically oriented contention by asserting that nothing like this has ever happened before. There is no recorded healing of a human being born blind in the Old Testament.[33] The only valid conclusion, therefore, is that Jesus is from God. "From earliest time it was not heard that anyone opened the eyes of one who was born blind. If this one were not from God, he would be able to do nothing."

---

[31] Rensberger, *Johannine Faith,* 47, considers the "perfidy" of the parents to be "the most shocking thing in the whole story."

[32] For example, see Deut 7:12-16, 11:8-17, 28:1-29. Barrett, *St. John*, 363, lists other pertinent texts: Isa 1:15, Psa 66:18 and 109:7, Prov 15:29; Job 27:9 and 35:13. Also John 16:23-27.

[33] Brown, *John*, I, 375.

Affronted by his bold scripturally based reprimand in defense of Jesus, the ruling authorities discredit him with a stinging insult, "You were born completely in sins, and you are teaching us?" Ironically, they contradict their own previous acknowledgment of his former blindness and of the divine origin of his recovery of sight, and by relegating him back into the realm of uncleanness in which he had stagnated as a blind man, they reject him as a possible source of divine truth: καὶ ἐξέβαλον αὐτὸν ἔξω (and they threw him out). Neither of the two ban formulas, however, the less severe *niddui*, a disciplinary action that amounted to a ban of thirty days and was used primarily against the "free spirits" among the learned sages, and the more rigorous ban, the *cherem*, that imposed community shunning upon the individual that had economic consequences and could include confiscation of goods, neither of them involved excommunication.[34] It is the removal from the synagogue, the ἀποσυνάγωγος that his parents feared, that is inflicted on him, and he is expelled and consequently ostracized from his Jewish community.[35]

Jesus learns that he has been excommunicated and therefore searches for him, even as he, Jesus, had sought out the individual whom he had healed of a debilitating illness in 5:5-14. When he finds him, he confronts him with a question of faith and commitment: "Do you believe into the Son of the Human Being?" Once again Jesus uses the very first title that he had appropriated for himself in 1:51. As throughout the Gospel, "the Son of the Human Being" is both an individual epithet and a corporate designation. Initially and foundationally, according to 3:13, it refers to Jesus as the one who descended from heaven. But, if the corporate interpretation of the υἱὸς ἀνθρώπου of Dan 7:13 that is given in Dan 7:27 may be applied to Jesus' reference to υἱὸς ἀνθρώπου in 5:27 and carried over to the titular ὁ υἱὸς τοῦ ἀνθρώπου, "the Son of the Human Being," as Jesus employs it in the Fourth Gospel, it is at least potentially corporate in its meaning. It may, therefore, imply a new People of God. Jesus, therefore, is offering the individual, who has been expelled from his community, the prospect of being incorporated into a New Israel. When he inquires who this Son of the Human Being is, Jesus discretely informs him, "You have seen him and the one speaking with you is that one." Without a moment's hesitation the man, who now sees, embraces his commitment to this new People of God by simply affirming, "I

---

[34] In Strack-Billerbeck, *Kommentar*, IV, Part I, 297-333, Billerbeck reviews the two types of bans in the rabbinic literature and contends on pp. 329-331, that the "synagogue bans had nothing to do with exclusion from the synagogue. It was not until the 9th century that the *cherem* ban was used for excommunication.

[35] Billerbeck, *ibid.*, 331, at the end of his lengthy excursus, concludes that Christians were excluded from the synagogue by the 12th Birkath of the Shmone Esre, and not the practice of banning. Also Martyn, *History and Theology*, 46-66, who, after a lengthy analysis, reaches essentially the same conclusion. Brown, *John* , I, 374, incorrectly refers to three types of banning and wrongly claims that the *cherem* ban "permanently excluded one from Israel." But, in spite of that, he concludes, "John is referring to the exclusion of Jewish Christians from the synagogue."

believe," and, with an acknowledgment of Jesus as κύριε (Lord), he prostrates himself before him.

Jesus comes to Jerusalem to fulfill his mission of saving the world (3:17), by introducing restoration and regeneration and by opening the reality structures of society to new possibilities. In chapters 5 and 9 two different Jerusalem pools are juxtaposed. His saving activity at Bezetha, ends in betrayal and persecution. His healing of a male born blind at the pool of Siloam produces a devoted disciple but at the same time intensifies opposition. The ruling authorities are promoting a religion that maintains "an all-embracing sacred order," and they are ready to expel anyone from their society who threatens that sacred order. In this socio-religious climate Jesus encounters animosity and recognition, rejection and commitment.

The paralyzed human being of 5:1-15 chooses to identify himself with the guardians of society who maintain the reality structures that guarantee the continuity of his security in the face of a journey into new possibilities. Although Jesus has enabled him to walk again, he does not hesitate to betray him to the authorities. On the other hand, the blind male of 9:1-39 is transformed by his bath in the pool of Siloam and commits himself to Jesus as the Light of the world who has enabled him to see. The truth of things that he has begun to experience enables him to defy the guardians of society even to the extent of suffering expulsion and consequently losing his ethnic roots.

Jerusalem is the center of the world, traditionally the place where God, or God's name, resides on earth. Yet, in the narrative world of the Fourth Gospel, it continues to be a place of paralysis and blindness, sickness and disease. Eschatologically it awaits the time of prophetic fulfillment when it will become that divine center within which justice and reconciliation, wholeness and well-being, will flourish and at the same time be projected into the world beyond.

Jesus culminates this episode of opening the eyes of a male blind from birth with an ironic declaration of his mission, "For judgment I came into this world, so that those *not seeing* (μὴ βλέποντες) *would see* (βλέπωσιν) and *those seeing* (οἱ βλέποντες) would become blind." It is here in this summation of his ministry that "blindness" and "seeing" are clearly presupposed to be more than physical realities. In this context the adverbial conjunction, ἵνα, unquestionably expresses purpose. Jesus' objective is to end all blindness by enabling human beings to see the light of truth, the light of the first day of creation. At the same time, however, those in society who would prevent this fulfillment, particularly the ruling elite, are blinded when they are confronted with the truth that calls their reality constructions and their reality maintenance into question.

Some of the Pharisees, who happen to be with him and hear his categorical indictment of those who claim to see, are unwilling to be included among those who are blinded by the truth, "Surely we also aren't blind, are we?" Their question presupposes that they believe they are able to see. Evidently the bitter controversy that has resulted in the expulsion of a man who has seen and witnessed to the light of truth has not aroused any suspicion within them that they might indeed be blind. Jesus, therefore, confronts them with the gravity of their tragic condition: "If you were blind, you would not have sin. But now that you say, 'We see,' your sin remains." Their sin is not their blindness, but rather the self-deceiving condition of being convinced that they see, when in reality they are really blind and in that diseased condition oppress, abuse, torture and even kill those who see and speak the truth.

The shepherd discourse 10: 1-42

Jesus' career is moving inexorably toward its anticipated fulfillment. He has desecrated the Sabbath by kneading clay in order to open the eyes of a man born blind, yet he is not charged with a transgression of the Law. The authorities have turned their attention to the man who, as a result of Jesus' mediation, is now able to see the light of truth, and they have excommunicated him from the synagogue, although he has broken no laws, and is guilty only of defending Jesus . What has happened here is, in all likelihood, a mirror reflection of the turmoil within the Jewish community of Alexandria.

The episode ended with Jesus' pronouncement of judgment on the Pharisees who, as the representatives of the Law, have misused their power and committed a grave offense against a member of God's people by removing him from the Jewish community because he defended Jesus. Incensed at the injustice they have perpetrated, Jesus proceeds to charge them to be false shepherds of God's people.[36] He addresses them in 10:1-3 with his characteristic double asseveration that serves as an introduction to a παροιμία, a figure of speech, as the narrator characterizes it in verse 6a.[37]

> Amen, amen I say to you, 'The one who does not enter into the fold of the sheep through the door but climbs over from another place, that one is a thief and a bandit. But the one entering through the door is the shepherd of

[36] Ulrich Busse, "Open Questions on John 10," *The Shepherd Discourse of John 10 and its Context*, ed. with introduction by Johannes Beutler and Robert T. Fortna (Cambridge: at the University Press, 1991) 6, cites most of the problems of John 10 that are disputed: form, structure, wording, and place in context, but concludes on p. 16 that the chapter is "a coherent literary composition and flow of argument in so far as the main interest of the author is christological-soteriological." He also acknowledges that "The image of the legitimate and illegitimate shepherds can be understood properly only against the background of events reported in chapter 9." See p. 13. See also Robert Kysar, "Johannine Metaphor—Meaning and Function: A Literary Case Study of John 10:1-8," *Semeia 53: The Fourth Gospel from a Literary Perspective* (Atlanta: Scholars Press, 1991) 81-111, who analyzes the relationship between the images the implied author utilizes in order to "victimize" the implied reader by strategies of confusion, suspense, and the tension generated by shifting from one metaphorical field to another. "While not debilitating the reader, the implied author keeps the reader off-balance by challenging any smugness and annihilating any complacency." On the five "participatory, shocking, and paradoxical qualities of the images," see especially pp. 94-101. As he correctly states on p. 99, "the author is trying to ... create a reader experience of a world at the center of which stands the Christ figure."

[37] In 16:29 the disciples will use this word, παροιμία, expressing their relief that Jesus is no longer speaking to them with a figure of speech.

> the sheep. To this one the gatekeeper opens, and the sheep hear his voice, and he calls his own sheep by name and leads them forth.

Accordingly, 10:1-5 must bear the essence of this figure of speech, namely a comparison between two types of shepherds: the one who climbs into the sheepfold by another way and the one who enters the sheepfold through the door and, therefore, is admitted by the gatekeeper.[38]

It is noteworthy that Philo uses the two names of Moses' father-in-law, Jethro and Raguel, to contrast two types of shepherding.[39] On the one hand,

> He is Jethro when vanity is thriving, for by the interpretation [of his name] he is unnecessary. ...Jethro prefers human things above divine things, customs above laws, profane things above sacred things, mortal things above immortal things and on the whole supposing instead of being. For daring to come self-bidden into the post of counselor he gives instructions to the wise not to teach the only things [that are] worthy to learn, the ordinances and the law of God.[40]

On the other hand, when Jethro becomes Raguel, a significant change occurs:

> Yet often this one [who] seems wise changes his way of thinking and, leaving the sheep which he received to manage [while] blind, he seeks the divine herd and becomes a component without reproach, marveling at the nature of a herdsman and revering the authority by which he manages the charge of his own flock. For Raguel is to be interpreted as shepherding of God.[41]

According to Philo, Moses guarantees this interpretation of the name Raguel by describing him as one who "brings forward judgment and justice."[42] The kind of shepherding, therefore, that God wills, is shepherding that "brings forward judgment and justice."

The Pharisees, as intimated by Jesus' comparison, are like the shepherd who does not enter through the door but climbs over from another place. Yochanan ben Zakkai and his Pharisaic colleagues "advanced their own candidacy as Roman supporters" and under Roman approval and authority, established their hegemony

---

[38] See Johannes Beutler, "Der altestamentlich-jüdische Hintergrund der Hirtenrede in Johannes 10," *The Shepherd Discourse of John 10 and its Context*, ed. with introduction by Johannes Beutler and Robert T. Fortna (Cambridge: at the University Press, 1991) 22-30, for a determination of the historical background. Working out of source and redaction criticisms, he proposes a line of development from Jeremiah, Ezekiel and Zechariah through the apocryphal writings and the Damascus Document into the New Testament. The image of the Good Shepherd in this discourse, however, is based on Jesus' self-disclosure as the Door, and it has no parallels in the LXX or the NT. Beuler believes there may be a connection with the veil of the Temple sanctuary, especially in Heb 10:19-21.

[39]Philo, *de Mutatione Nominum,* 103. The English translations generally render Raguel as Reuel, but, according to Num 10:29, Raguel or Reuel was the father of Hobah. The other name of Jethro, therefore, is Hobah. See Ex 3:1, 4:18, 18:1-12; Num 10:29; Jud 4:11.

[40] Philo, *ibid.*, 104.

[41] *Ibid.*, 105.

[42] *Ibid.*, 106.

over the Jewish people by constituting "a new center of autonomous government" at Jamnia.[43] Like Philo's characterization of the name Jethro, they "come self-bidden into the post of counselor," and, by ingratiating themselves to the Romans, they are granted the management and control of God's sheepfold.[44] They are, therefore, like the *thief* (κλέπτης) who entered the courtyard by devious means. At the same time, they are also like the *outlaw* (ληστής) in as far as they have employed violent means to maintain the *loyalty* (חֶסֶד) of God's people by threatening them with expulsion *from the synagogue* (ἀποσυνάγωγος) if they should confess Jesus as the Christ (9:22).

However, there is another level of meaning that Jesus' comparison conveys by the use of the word αὐλή in 10:1 and again in 10:16. Although it is usually rendered as "sheepfold" in the English translations, αὐλη designates an "open space" or a "courtyard," as in 18:15 where it refers to the courtyard of the high priest. In the light of Jesus' comparison of two types of shepherds and especially his reference to "the door," αὐλή bears the twofold sense of "courtyard" and "sheepfold."[45]

The Pharisees are illegitimate shepherds not only because they climbed into the sheepfold from another place but also because they did not go through the door. But what is the door into the "courtyard of the sheep"? The Pharisees' inability to apprehend his comparison of the two kinds of shepherds and their dissimilar entries into the sheepfold, as verse 6b indicates, may be intended to serve as a foil for the incomprehension of the implied readers in order to enable Jesus to clarify the two central images of his figure of speech, the courtyard and the door.[46]

Jesus addresses the Pharisees again with a double asseveration, "Amen, amen I say to you, '**I AM** the Door of the sheep. All such who came before me are thieves and bandits, but the sheep did not hear them."[47] Earlier in 10:1, Jesus used "thief"

[43] Neusner, *ibid*., 135-155.

[44] See Jacob Neusner, "Yochanan's Policy at Yavneh," *First Century Judaism in Crisis*, 189-192, especially 191, Yochanan attempted to endow his new court with prerogatives hitherto reserved to the sanctuary – to preserve the memory and sanctity of the Temple, on the one hand, while providing for its temporary inaccessibility, on the other."

[45] In the literature on John 10 αὐλή is not construed as a figure of speech that as an enclosure or courtyard metaphorically represents the outer court of the Temple as God's sheepfold. See for example: Bultmann, *John*, 358-391; Schnackenburg, *St. John* II, 275-293; Brown, *John* I, 385-393, Barrett, *St. John*, 367-378; as well as the essays in *The Shepherd Discourse of John 10 and its Context*.

[46] Against Schnackenburg, *St. John* II, 288, who contends that 10:7 introduces a "fresh discourse by Jesus" that implies a new audience, neither the Pharisees nor the Jews but the believing readers. The adverb πάλιν (again) refers to the double asseveration. For a second time Jesus addresses the Pharisees with a solemn declaration, but one that will clarify the image of "the door of the sheep". See John Painter, "Tradition, History and Interpretation in John 10," *The Shepherd Discourse of John 10 and its Context*, 61,

[47] P^{75} and the Sahidic Coptic manuscripts substitute "shepherd" in place of "door." It must be a scribal correction because "door" is the more difficult reading. Because of its critical significance, Jesus will repeat this self-disclosure in verse 9. See Busse, "Tradition, History and Interpretation in John 10," 10; and Johannes Beutler, "Der altestamentliche-jüdische Hintergrund der Hirtenrede in Johannes 10," *The Shepherd Discourse of John 10*, 20.

and "bandit" metaphorically to characterize the Pharisees who did not enter through the door but climbed over from another place. They are illegitimate shepherds. Now, however, on the basis of his self-disclosure as the Door, he designates all those "who came before him" as thieves and bandits. These are, speaking symbolically, "illegitimate doors," not unauthorized entrants or illegitimate shepherds.[48] Jesus is referring to all those who, preceding him, have predicated themselves as doors opening into redemption and liberation. But none is named. That is a gap that the implied readers must fill. If they have read the writings of Josephus, they may identify them as the messianic claimants who surfaced in times of calamity and crisis, opportunists who aggrandized themselves by exploiting God's people with promises of deliverance and emancipation. Jesus, in his second self-disclosure as "the Door" in verse 9, returns to his characterization of these "pseudo-doors" as thieves and, using the singular "thief," represents them as those who victimize "the sheep" by stealing, slaying and destroying. In stark contrast, he asserts that his objective in coming is that they might have ζωή (life), the very same ζωή that, according to his testimony in the forensic process of 5:26, the Father gave him to have "life (ζωή) in himself," and to have it more abundantly.

This self-disclosure as the Door appears to have no reference to any previous events or actions of his ministry up to this point in the narrative world of the Gospel. At the first Passover Jesus became the living Temple of God by substituting his physical body in place of the stone sanctuary on the Temple mount. At the second Passover he became the Passover meal, "Amen, amen I say to you, 'Unless you eat the flesh of the Son of the Human Being and drink his blood, you do not have life in yourselves.'" Now, as he approaches the third Passover, the feast at which he will be crucified, he declares that he is the Door of the sheep. But this self-disclosure, like the ascent of the Son of the Human Being that he referred to in 3:13, awaits its actualization at the culmination of the narrative world. When Jesus fulfills his role as the Lamb of God at the third Passover, he will activate his self-disclosure as the Door.[49] In response to his cry, "I thirst," a sponge filled with wine-vinegar will be lifted to his lips on a branch of hyssop, and he will symbolically become the Passover Door through which a new Exodus is inaugurated.[50]

Consequently, if Jesus is the Door, the αὐλή must be the *courtyard* of the Temple, the great enclosure where God's people gather for worship and sacrifice that metaphorically represents God's sheepfold. This identification of the αὐλή is supported by Jesus' reference in 10:16 to "sheep who are not from this courtyard," namely the Gentiles who primordially do not belong to God's sheepfold and

[48] Barrett, *St. John*, 371, identifies the "thieves and bandits" as those of verse 1 who "climb up some other way."

[49] See Barrett, *St. John,* 371-373, for other interpretations of Jesus as the Door.

[50] See chapter 17.

therefore have no place in the courtyard of the Temple. Jesus, therefore, must be the Door or the gate that opens into the sanctuary that he embodies. To go through the Door, therefore, is to enter into "the Father's house." A possible correlation between Jesus as the Door into the courtyard and Jesus as the Vine-stock of 15:1 is intimated by Josephus' description of the door or gate into the sanctuary of the Temple.[51]

> The gate ... was completely overlaid with gold, as was the whole wall around it. It had above it those golden vines from which grape clusters were hanging to the height of a man."[52] "Now the doors at the entrance with the lintels, equal (in height) to the sanctuary, he decorated with many colored hangings. ... Above these under the cornices there was spread a golden vine having grape-clusters hanging [from it].[53]

Everyone must enter through the Door! Including the Pharisees, who represent the ruling elite, so that they may become the legitimate shepherds of Israel! But also God's people, Israel, all those who are in the courtyard of the sanctuary![54] By entering through the Door, they will have access to God's presence and have life more abundantly.[55] As Jesus states in his second self-disclosure as the Door in 10:9-10,

> **I AM** the Door! If anyone enters through me, he/she will be saved and she/he will go in and go out and find pasture. The thief does not come except in order to steal and to slay and to destroy. I came in order that they have life and have it more abundantly.

Moreover, as already indicated, by entering through the Door, they will be incorporated into the living Temple of God that Jesus will constitute through his forthcoming death and resurrection.

Because he entered the courtyard of God's sanctuary through the Door that he himself will embody, he is also the Good Shepherd.[56] That is his self-disclosure in his clarification of his figure of speech. As he said in 10:2,

> The one entering through the door is the shepherd of the sheep. To this one the gatekeeper opens, and the sheep hear his voice, and he calls his own sheep by name and leads them out. When he drives all of his own out, he

[51] See Lawrence D. Sporty, "Identifying the Curving Line on the Bar-Kokhba Temple Coin," *Biblical Archeologist*, 46/2 (1983) 121-124.

[52] Josephus, *BJ* 5, 210.

[53] *Ant* XV, 394.

[54] Contrary to Schnackenburg, *St. John* II, 289, who favors the translation of the genitive, τῶν προβάτων, as "to the sheep." But the door is not Jesus' access to the sheep, but the sheep's access to the Exodus to which the door opens. That is confirmed by 10:9-10.

[55] Psa 117 (118):20 in its Septuagint translation is sometimes cited as a background text:, but the Greek word πύλη (gate) is used instead of θύρα (door).

[56] Bultmann, *John*, 358, claims that the image of the shepherd was drawn from Gnostic tradition. His rearrangement of the discourse on the Good Shepherd is unconvincing. Introduced in 10:22ff. and concluded in 10:31-39, the misplaced section, 10:1-18, which is not "an ordered whole," is divided into two parts. The restructuring that he offers is: 10:22-26, 11-13, 1-10, 14-18, 27-29.

> goes before them and the sheep follow him because they know his voice. A stranger they will by no means follow, but they will flee from him because they do not know the voice of strangers.

Because he will enter through the door into the courtyard of God's sanctuary in order to offer himself as "the Lamb of God who removes the sin of the world," God, the Gatekeeper of the courtyard/sheepfold, admits him as the Shepherd of the sheep. "The good shepherd," as Jesus states in 10:11, "offers his ψυχή (life) on behalf of the sheep." Because he will enter through the door and by his sacrifice become the Door into the new Exodus, he can declare, "**I AM** the Good Shepherd."[57]

Philo idolized Moses as the good shepherd, but specifically as "a shepherd in training" for kingship, "for one who is going to command the most civilized herd of human beings."[58]

> Moses became more skilled than any of his time in managing flocks and providing what tended to the benefit of his charges. His capacity was due to his never shirking any duty, but showing an eager and unprompted zeal wherever it was needed, and maintaining a pure and guileless honesty in the conduct of his office.[59]

Because he manifested self-restraint, continence, temperance, shrewdness, good sense, knowledge, endurance of toil and hardships, contempt of pleasures, justice, advocacy of excellence, and because he renounced wealth, God rewarded him with the wealth of the whole creation.

> For making him worthy to appear as a partner of his own sphere, he gave the whole world as an acquisition adapted to his heir.[60]

> Was not the pleasure of partnership towards the Father and Maker of all things greater by being made worthy of bearing the same title? For he was named god (θεός) and king (βασιλεύς) of the whole nation.[61]

Philo also notes that Moses interceded for the people of Israel when they were being attacked by Pharaoh and his chariots at the edge of the Red Sea, and he was empowered by God to divide the waters for their safe passage. But there is no

---

[57] Jerome H. Neyrey, "The 'Noble Shepherd' in John 10: Cultural and Rhetorical Background," *JBL* 120/2 (2001) 267-291, employs the honor/shame model of the "noble shepherd, derived from the Greek rhetorical literature on "noble death" and utilized in 4 Macc to express the nobility of dying "unconquered" or "conquering death" in order to interpret Jesus' words of "laying down his life on behalf of the sheep." "Exalted honor should be accorded Jesus" especially because he claims to have the authority to take his life again after he has offered it in sacrifice." But it is precisely this claim, based on his distinctive authority as the incarnation of the Logos-Sophia, that negates the honor/shame model of a "noble death." The ethical dualism that honor/shame promotes is transcended in the narrative world of the Fourth Gospel.

[58] Philo, *de Vita Mosis* I, 61.

[59] Translation of F. H. Colson, *Philo: Loeb Classical Library* VI, 309.

[60] Philo, *de Vita Mosis* I, 155.

[61] *Ibid.* I, 158

reference to Ex 32:32 and his attempt to make atonement for Israel's idolatry. It is the rabbinic Mekhilta on Exodus 12:1 that interprets his intercession as an offering of his life on behalf of Israel.[62]

However, even as Moses did not give the true bread from heaven, he also did not "offers his ψυχή (life) on behalf of the sheep." Jesus alone is the Good Shepherd because he will enter through the door of God's courtyard, and by his sacrifice he will become the Door into a new Exodus that will bring healing and wholeness to the whole world.[63]

In contrast to Jesus – and ironically Moses as well! – the Pharisees have proved themselves to be like the hired hand. They *observe* (θεωρεῖ) the predator threatening the flock and, instead of responding to their safety and well-being, they save themselves, believing, perhaps, that it is expedient that they remain alive in order to care for the sheep that survive. Jesus is the Good Shepherd because he *knows* (γινώσκω) his sheep personally, and *they know* (γινώσκουσι) him personally in the same manner as the Father *knows* (γινώσκει) him and *he knows* (γινώσκει) the Father. On the basis of this intimate relationship between him and the sheep and between him and the Father, he repeats the qualification of being a good shepherd that he stated in 10:11, "... and I offer my life on behalf of the sheep."

Moreover, he declares, "And I have other sheep that are not from this courtyard/sheepfold. It is necessary that I lead those, and they will hear my voice, and they will become one flock, one shepherd." For the first time in the narrative world of the Gospel Jesus speaks universally. These sheep are the Gentiles, those who are outside of the courtyard of God's people, and it is a divine *necessity* (δεῖ) that they too are incorporated into God's sheepfold, so that together they will constitute one flock escorted and guided by one shepherd.

This, as he discloses to the Pharisees, is why God loves him. As the Good Shepherd he has the freedom and sovereignty to offer his life so that he may take it again. He can enunciate this with confidence because of his self-understanding as "the Son" to whom "the Father gave to have life in himself" (5:26).

> No one takes it [my life] from me, but I offer it of myself. I have authority to offer it, and I have authority to take it again. This commandment I received from my Father.

---

[62] See Meeks, *The Prophet-King*, 312. He observes that "The phrase נתן נפש is the precise equivalent to τὴν ψυχὴν τιθέναι," which occurs in 10:11. See also pp. 108, 161, 196-197.

[63] Bultmann's judgment that the discourse of the Good Shepherd, especially 10:7-10, conveys "the exclusiveness and the absoluteness of the revelation" that Jesus brings, is invalid in the light of his self-disclosure as the Door and its activation in 19:28-30. His sacrifice does not make him the Revealer; it makes him the consummator of God's new creation. See *John*, 375-391; German, 386-398. Schnackenburg, *St. John* II, 295, after examining the Mandaean texts that Bultmann relies on, rightly concludes, "Jesus' sacrifice of his life, however, is not a subsequently added feature but a distinguishing mark of the 'good shepherd' right from the start."

But how can this be a commandment from the Father, if he has divine life in himself and the divinely imparted authority to offer it and then take it again? Here once again the paradoxical character of the relationship that Jesus has with the Creator emerges. He and the Father are one, yet in that union, as he will tell his disciples, "The Father is greater than I." Jesus himself is an apprentice who is imitating God's works. As the incarnate Logos-Sophia, the New Human Being who descended from heaven, he has been given to have life in himself. But integrated into the sovereignty that he has received is God's commandment to offer his life on behalf of the sheep of God's courtyard and also on behalf of those outside the courtyard and then to take it again. This sovereignty will be manifested to the implied readers when Simon Peter and the Beloved Disciple have entered the empty tomb and witness Jesus' burial garments folded and lying in their individual places (20:6-7).

Jesus' words evoke a division among these authorities whom he has been addressing: "Many of them were saying, 'He has a demon and he is mad. Why do you hear him?'"[64] They had repudiated Jesus earlier on the basis of the same charge (8:48). But in this context there are others among them who dissent: "These are not the words of one who is demon-possessed. Surely a demon isn't able to open the eyes of the blind, is it?" Once again the implied readers are confronted with a split within the body of the ruling elite. With which group will they be inclined to take sides?

Hanukkah, the Feast of Lights, and escalated conflict 10:22-42

The scene changes abruptly. According to the narrator, it is now winter, and God's people are in Jerusalem celebrating Hanukkah, the Feast of Lights. Jesus is also present, and, as he walks about in the sacred precinct of the Temple, he is surrounded by the ruling authorities who apparently have continued to be tantalized by the question of his christological identity: "How long will you keep us in suspense? If you are the Christ, tell us openly!"

Ironically they appear to have shifted their perspective. From that moment in his ministry when they charged him with relaxing the Sabbath and making himself equal to God, they have been plotting to kill him. But now at this juncture in the continuing controversy and conflict between them and Jesus, they are acknowledging for the first time that they are tantalized about his identity. What if he is indeed the Messiah?

Jesus responds to their demand as ambiguously as before. He will not use predicates by which to classify or label himself. Moreover, "the Christ"

---

[64] Contrary to John D. Turner, "The History of Religions Background of John 10," *The Shepherd Discourse of John 10 and its Context*, ed. with introduction by J. Beutler and R. T. Fortna (Cambridge: at the University Press, 1991) 34, who contends that 10:19-21 was the original conclusion of chapter 9. Turner searches Hellenic and Hellenistic literature for parallels to "sheep and shepherds" and "shepherd and sheepfold" but does not perceive the metaphorical sense of αὐλή and therefore also Jesus' self-disclosure as the Door that is the basis of his self-disclosure as the Good Shepherd.

designation has its own history, and they, the ruling elite, have their own interpretation of it. What would be their response if he answered with a simple affirmation? Eventually they will deliver him to the Romans on the charge of being the Christ. Jesus simply repeats what he has told them earlier. The judgment of who he is belongs to them, and it should be based on: "The works that I do in the name of my Father, these testify about me." That should be relatively easy for them because they know the Scriptures, and they can determine to what extent the deeds he performs correspond to the works that the Scriptures attribute to God. To what extent do his acts differ from those that the prophets enunciated to be the works that God requires of Israel? But they decline to engage in that critical analysis and therefore they refuse to recognize his claims that he is an apprentice of God who does God's will and acts with God's authority because he originated from God.

Jesus therefore concludes, "But you do not believe because you are not of my sheep." They are not his sheep because they have not entered through the Door; and they have not entered through the Door because they refuse to believe. They are deadlocked in their own ideology. In contrast, those who are his sheep are able to live in confidence even if, like the man whose eyes Jesus opened, they are ostracized from the Jewish community.

> My sheep hear my voice, and I know (γινώσκω) them personally, and they follow me, and I give them eternal life, and they will by no means ever perish, and no one will snatch them from my hand. My Father who gave [them] to me is greater than all, and no one is able to snatch [them] from the hand of my Father.[65] (10:26-29)

Jesus concludes his response to the suspenseful question of the authorities by asserting for the first time what has only been implicit, "I and the Father are one." It is the logical conclusion of all that he has stated about his imitation of God's works and his fulfillment of God's will. Moreover, it is an answer, although an oblique answer to their challenge, "If you are the Christ, tell us openly."

It is this declaration of his union with God that provokes the authorities to make a second attempt to stone him to death: "They picked up stones so that they might stone him." Jesus does not withdraw from them and hide himself, as he did earlier in 8:59. He challenges the legitimacy of their intended act on the basis of his apprentice activity, "Many good works I showed you from the Father. Because of which work of them are you stoning me?" Their response reveals the pivotal difficulty they have had with Jesus' self-disclosure as "the Son" and his relationship to "the Father." It is a relationship that calls into question their own

[65] Verse 29 poses a tangle of text-critical problems: combinations of masculine and neuter relative pronouns and masculine and neuter comparative adjectives. The strongest attestation is offered by the oldest papyri, P^{66} and P^{75}, and K f^{1} f^{13} 33 M; but in contrast to the other manuscripts P^{66} and P^{75} use the aorist instead of the perfect tense. This textual reading makes better sense than the other readings: "My Father who gave to me is greater than all…" The other readings, preferred by B. M. Metzger et al., *A Textual Commentary on the Greek New Testament* (London: United Bible Societies, 1971) 232, may be determined by 6:39 and 17:2. See also Barrett, *St. John*, 381-382.

self-understanding as the guardians of Israel and their incarnation of that self-understanding in their abusive and dehumanizing governance of God's people. They are the kind of shepherds that Ezekiel condemned:

> Thus says the Lord God, "O shepherds of Israel, surely shepherds should not feed yourselves, should they? Should not shepherds feed the sheep. Look, you devour milk and [with] wool you clothe yourselves and the well-nourished you slaughter and you do not feed my sheep." [66]

Because they refuse to draw the necessary conclusion about Jesus' identity on the basis of the works he does, works that contradict their ideology of *loyalty* (חֶסֶד) and simultaneously subvert their leadership, they are ready to put their ideology of separation into practice by eliminating Jesus from their society, even as they excommunicated the blind man whose eyes Jesus opened.

Earlier their charge against Jesus was "making himself equal to God." Now the charge has been gradated to "making yourself God."

Jesus responds with a text drawn from Psa 82:6,

> Is it not written in your law, "I said, you are gods?" If he called those gods to whom the word of God happened, and Scripture cannot be torn down, you say [to] the one whom the Father sanctified and sent into the world, "You are blaspheming," because I said, "I am God's Son."

Here Jesus does not employ the divine self-disclosure **I AM**, only the simple copula εἰμί (I am). But he has utilized the rhetorical principle of *qal wahomer*, a syllogism that moves from a minor to a major premise. He does not apply Psa. 82:6 to himself as a justification of his self-disclosure as "the Son." If, on the one hand, it is true that God said this to those to whom the word of God happened, *how much more* is it not justifiable for Jesus to assert, "I and the Father are one!" on the basis of the works of God that he performs?[67]

> If I don't do the works of my Father, don't believe me! But if I do, if you don't believe me, believe the works so that you *know personally* (γνῶτε) once and for all and *keep on knowing* (γινώσκητε) that the Father is in me and I in the Father. (10:37-38)

The reaction of the authorities does not change in spite of Jesus' plea. "Therefore they were seeking to seize him, and Jesus went out from their hand." His hour has not yet come.

---

[66] Translated from LXX Ezek 34:2.

[67] Jerome H. Neyrey, "I said 'You are gods": Psalm 82:6 and John 10," *JBL* 108/4 (1989), 647-663, interprets the word "one" in Jesus' declaration, "I and the Father are one," as meaning "equal". But in 14:28 Jesus tells his disciples, "The Father is greater than I." The word "one," therefore, cannot mean "equal". Jesus and the Father are one in the sense of being united and in that union Jesus serves as God's apprentice, exercising power on God's behalf to do God's work. As the enfleshed Logos-Sophia, Jesus conducts his ministry in an interdependent relationship with the Creator, but because the Creator is the source of his power and authority, he cannot and does not claim equality with God.

The restoration of the crippled human being in 5:1-16, the first of two explicit healings in Jerusalem, ended in failure. The individual reported Jesus to the authorities, and Jesus was subjected to a forensic process on the charge of "relaxing the Sabbath and making himself equal to God." His mediation of sight to a man born blind, the second restoration in Jerusalem, that climaxed in the individual's excommunication from the synagogue because he dared to defend Jesus, proved to be a paradoxical success. The injustice of excommunication motivates Jesus to take the offensive against the guardians of society by utilizing a figure of speech that implicates them as illegitimate shepherds. He is the Good Shepherd because he enters through the door and becomes the Door into a new Exodus. The authorities press him to reveal to them unequivocally whether in fact he is the Christ. When he continues to relate himself to God as God's apprentice, who imitates the works of God, they make a second attempt to stone him. His defense by means of a syllogism, based on Psa 82:6, that justifies the possibility of being able to say, "I am God's Son," ends in their second frustrated effort to seize him.[68]

Once again Jesus is forced to withdraw. Evidently Galilee is not an option. Now, because of the growing threat to his life, he retreats to the other side of the Jordan River "into the place where John was first baptizing, and he was remaining there." Yet even there, large numbers of people are drawn to him. Although, as the narrator recounts, "They were saying, 'John, on the one hand, did no sign, but, on the other hand, everything that John said about him was true'." It is crucial that Jesus is linked again to the formidable personage of John, in spite of this accent on the lack of signs in his ministry. The absence of divine legitimation on the basis of signs does not diminish John's testimony; he himself had claimed to be nothing more than "... a voice of shouting in the wilderness," and legitimation, therefore, was superfluous.[69]

However the implied readers may be judging Jesus' integrity and the rectitude of the ruling elite at this point in the narrative world of the Gospel, they are confronted again by John's witness that is confirmed by "the many," who crossed the Jordan River in order to be with Jesus. Perhaps as a concluding challenge to the implied readers, the narrator ends the episode with the observation, "And there many believed into him."

---

[68] See 7:32 and 7:45-46.

[69] Schnackenburg, *St. John* II, 315, is wrong in his judgment that the witness of the "many" that "John did no sign" betrays hostility toward the Baptizer. On the contrary, the reiteration of John's witness is critical at this juncture to the implied readers. He has served as the formidable witness to the Logos and to the enfleshed Logos, and now the implied readers are reminded of his witness by the people who have crossed the Jordan to be with Jesus.

Chapter Twelve

The Resurrection of Lazarus

Raising Lazarus from the Dead 11:1-44

The second effort by the governing authorities to seize Jesus, after their second attempt to stone him failed, compels him to withdraw from Judea and cross the Jordan River to the place where John began his ministry of baptism. A re-connection with John's original sphere of activity introduces an occasion for the reaffirmation of both individuals in their relation to each other. Jesus, out of harm's way, attracts large numbers of people. Their testimony suggests that he must have engaged in some kind of activity: "John did no sign, but all the things he said about this one are true." John's witness is corroborated by the common people and, over against the opposition of the rulers, it authenticates Jesus and confirms the commitment that the masses are willing to make to him: "... and many believed into him."

Into this context a certain "Lazarus from Bethany" is introduced, and with him his two sisters, Mary and Martha.[1] Although the latter of the two will play a more consequential role in the following episode, Mary is named first and identified by her proleptic act of "anointing the Lord and wiping his feet with her hair."[2] In the context of the raising of Lazarus and whatever response-ability Martha may fulfill in conjunction with it, the implied readers are to anticipate the loving and extravagant gesture of Lazarus' other sister, Mary.

In his place of refuge beyond the Jordan, Jesus receives a message from these two sisters, "Lord, see, *the one whom you love* (ὃν φιλεῖς) is ill." His immediate response is verbal, and, although it is reassuring, it is also ironic, "This sickness is not

---

[1] Lazarus is the first and only individual in the narrative world of the Gospel , who, as a recipient of Jesus' mighty work of resurrection, is named. Perhaps he was known to some of the members of the Jewish community in Alexandria. The identification of his home, "Bethany" may be intended to provide a location with which the implied readers are familiar. It is noteworthy that, like "Lazarus of Bethany" various individuals in the Gospel are named in relation to their home: "Jesus of Nazareth," "Philip from Bethsaida, from the city of Andrew and Peter." See Schnackenburg, *St. John* II, 321. Commentators usually connect the name Lazarus with the poor man of Jesus' parable in Luke 16:19-31 who bore the same name, but there is no certainty that the author of the Fourth Gospel was familiar with Luke's Gospel or the tradition of the parable.

[2] For an analysis of the literary character of this story: context, form, plot, deep structure, mode, prolepses, narrator, characters, source, tradition and style, see Mark W. G. Stibbe, *John's Gospel* (London: Routledge, 1994) 75-106. The source analyses of Bultmann, *John*, 395, n. 4; German, 301, n. 4; Schnackenburg, *St. John* II, 317-321; Fortna, *The Fourth Gospel*, 94-108, contribute nothing to the interpretation of 11:1-44. See also Barnabas Lindars, "Rebuking the Spirit: A New Analysis of the Lazarus Story of John 11," *NTS* 38/1 (1992) 89-104, who is convinced that "the source [of this story] must be reconstructed before we can begin to think of it in historical terms." What the phrase "historical terms" signifies is not clear.

towards death but on behalf of the glory of God, so that the Son of God may be glorified through it." Since the disciples will not be addressed until verse 7, Jesus' more immediate audience would be the implied readers.[3] They are to know that Lazarus will not die. His sickness will not terminate his life. If this is what Jesus' words are intended to convey, it is not clear in what sense Lazarus' sickness can serve to disclose the glory of God or in what way the Son of God can be glorified through it. At least it should be transparent at this point that Jesus' apprenticeship as the Son who is doing the works of the Father establishes their mutual glorification.

But whatever ambiguities Jesus' words might bear, there is no obscurity about his relationship to these people. By means of an intrusive remark the narrator assures the implied readers that Jesus bears great affection for this family of three: "*Jesus, on the one hand, loved* (ἠγάπα δὲ ὁ 'Ιησοῦς) Martha and her sister and Lazarus." His consequent behavior, however, is unexpected and disconcerting. It does not correspond to the narrator's intrusive remark: "As therefore he heard that he is sick, *then, on the other hand* (τότε μὲν) he remained in the place in which he was two days." The particle μέν (on the other hand) that follows τότε (then) at the beginning of the second clause of verse 6 is a startling reversal of the general usage of the two particles of correlation, μέν and δέ. Ordinarily μέν (on the one hand) is followed by δέ (on the other hand), but here the two are reversed. The narrator's aside that follows Jesus' response, therefore, should be rendered as, "On the one hand, Jesus loved Martha and her sister and Lazarus. As therefore he heard that he is sick, he then, on the other hand, remained in the place in which he was two days." Jesus is intentionally deferring his intervention.[4] Apparently, since "this sickness is not towards death," there is no need to rush to Lazarus' bedside.

After waiting two days, Jesus sets out for Bethany on what is evidently the third day. Once again the timing of Jesus' activity appears to be determined deliberately by the eschatological significance of the biblical code of the third day and its connotation of deliverance or resurrection, especially as it is anticipated in Hos 6:2, "After two days he will revive us; on the third day he will raise us up." Jesus' first sign of transforming water into wine at the beginning of his ministry, signifying a paradigm shift, occurred "on the third day."[5] When he substituted his own body in place of the sanctuary on the Temple-mount (2:20), he predicted that in the event of its destruction he would resurrect it in three days. Now, in this seventh and culminating sign of his ministry, the eschatological reality of resurrection will be drawn out of the future into the present. It will no longer be the objective toward which history moves; it will no

[3] Also Bultmann, *John*, 397, n. 3; German, 303, n. 1, who claims that the message intended for the reader is," ... death is not the end and meaning of the illness". For a utilization of the Lazarus story in order to introduce "the analytical and interpretive tools of modern and postmodern rhetorical criticism," see Wilhelm Wuellner, "Putting Life back into the Lazarus Story and its Reading: the Narrative Rhetoric of John 11 as the Narration of Faith," *Semeia 53: The Fourth Gospel from a Literary Perspective*, 113-132.

[4] Also Barrett, *St. John*, 390.

[5] See chapter 4.

longer be the goal that will culminate history. It will become a reality into which human beings can enter in the here and now of the present, a reality in which they can begin to actualize the possibility of a new creation in the face of the finality of death. This is how the raising of Lazarus will glorify God and the Son of God.

When, however, Jesus voices his intention to return to Judea, he is rebuffed by the disciples with the grim reminder, "Rabbi, just now the Jews were seeking to stone you, and you are going there again?" But he overrules their objection with a rhetorical question that validates his intention but at the same time forewarns them about the dangers they will face as they return to Judea and Jerusalem.

> Are there not twelve hours of the day? If anyone walks in the day, he/she will not stumble because *he/she sees* (βλέπει) the light of this world. (11:9)

Jesus is ready and willing to return to Judea in spite of the threatening situation because there is still time within the framework of the twelve hours of daylight to respond to the summons he has received from Mary and Martha to save Lazarus. Moreover, because he walks in the day and is attentive to the light of this world, the light of the first day of creation, he will not stumble, even when the night eventually comes. For when Judas leaves the community of Jesus and his disciples in order to betray Jesus, the narrator will announce to the reader in 13:30, "And it was night."

The verb βλέπει (*he/she sees*) that Jesus employs in this context denotes clarity of vision that makes true insight possible.[6] Ostensibly it would appear that Jesus is referring to the light of the sun, the heavenly luminary that was created on the fourth day (Gen 1:14-19). But the verb βλέπει, as its ten-fold use in the story of a male born blind indicates (9:1-41), bears the sense of a seeing that is enabled to grasp the transcendent realities of truth. Jesus, therefore, is referring to the light that generates a seeing beyond physical vision, a seeing that perceives the light that God created on the first day of creation. It is the light of truth, and it is this light that he himself embodies and re-presents in his ministry, "While I am in the world, I am the light of the world" (9:5). Consequently authentic discipleship is circumscribed by "walking in the day," for it is only "in the day" that the light of truth, the light of the first day of creation, is visible and therefore discernible. This first advisory condition of 11:9 is reinforced by the earlier promise of 8:12, "The one following me will by no means walk in darkness but will have the light of life."

Yet at the same time the possibility of another condition is posed:

> But if anyone walks in the night, he/she stumbles, because the light is not in him/her. (11:10)

The luminaries that God created on the fourth day, the moon and the stars, cannot generate the light that is required to prevent stumbling. But that is not the condition that Jesus is posing. To walk in the night is to be devoid of all light, to be without the light of truth. Walking in the night corresponds to the absence of

[6] See chapter 5.

incarnated light that enables a human being to differentiate between truth and falsehood and therefore also between good and evil.[7] As Jesus said, "The light is not in him/her."

The darkness of Judea and Jerusalem to which Jesus and his disciples are returning will be especially hazardous for those of his disciples – or the implied readers of the Gospel in their own context of darkness – who are walking in the night and consequently have no light in themselves to empower them to discern the realities of evil.

It is only after issuing these advisory conditions that Jesus vindicates his intention to return to Judea: "Lazarus our friend has fallen asleep, *but* (ἀλλά) I am going in order that I might awaken him." The employment of ἀλλά in verse 11b is disconcerting because the expectation of the reader is continuity based on the natural relationship between "falling asleep" and "being awakened," continuity which would be expressed by the conjunction "and" (καί). As a coordinating conjunction, however, ἀλλά connects two equal but opposite elements. "Being awakened," therefore, is discontinuous with "falling asleep"; the one evidently does not naturally follow the other.[8]

The disciples, however, do not apprehend this, and consequently they construe Jesus' words literally: "Lord, if he has fallen asleep, *he will be saved"* (σωθήσεται). The verb which they employ in the passive voice, σωθήσεται , conveys the sense of "getting on well" or "being restored to health."[9] Ironically, in spite of their misunderstanding, what they have said is nevertheless true and, in a sense, echoes what Jesus had enunciated in verse 4.[10] However, as in earlier instances of misunderstanding, the narrator interrupts the story momentarily in order to inform the implied readers of the meaning of Jesus' words, "Now Jesus had been speaking of his death, but those thought that he is speaking about the sleep of slumber." If "being awakened" is discontinuous with "falling asleep," the condition that "being awakened" is intended to alter must be a different kind of sleep. And indeed it is the sleep of death! Jesus utilizes "sleep" as a euphemism of death, not to minimize the reality of death but in order to communicate his paradoxical understanding of that reality: on the one hand, death as the termination of life; on the other hand, sleep as a continuation of life. Since he first referred to Lazarus' death as "sleep," the accent is intended to fall on the possibility that is concealed behind the actuality of expiration, that is, the possibility of the continuity of life.

---

[7] Barrett, *St. John*, 392, "Absence of light without is matched by absence of light within."

[8] Barrett, *ibid.*, who, in view of Jesus' "supernatural knowledge" that Lazarus had died, asserts that "… disciples might therefore have been prepared for a rather more than commonplace remark." But Jesus' use of *but* (ἀλλά) falls on deaf ears. Will the implied readers grasp it? Schnackenburg, *St. John* II, 326, simply states, "The saying, however, is worded ambiguously and leads to a misunderstanding…" See Bultmann, *John*, 399, n. 6, who maintains this is not a "Johannine misunderstanding."

[9] See *A Greek-English Lexicon of the New Testament and Other Early Christian Literature*, 982.

[10] Also Barrett, *St. John*, 393, but without noting the irony.

Initially Jesus could respond to the message of Lazarus' sisters, "This sickness is not towards death but for the glory of God." Ironically, however, it is a sickness towards death! Lazarus will die; his life will be terminated; but at the same time the truth of death will be disclosed. Its apparent finality will be unconcealed to be the triumph of life; and in that reconstitution the glory of God will be manifested. That is also why Jesus, after correcting his disciples' misconstrual of his euphemism, can exult in his absence at Lazarus' bedside: "I rejoice on your account so that you might believe because I was not there." Another ironic note! Jesus can be glad that he was not present at Lazarus' bedside to prevent him from dying because his disciples will experience the eschatological reality of the resurrection. The first sign of Jesus' ministry had occurred "on the third day," signifying that he was acting as though the resurrection had already occurred. In this seventh and culminating, end-of-the-age sign, the earlier words of Jesus are being fulfilled, "...the hour is coming and *now* is when the dead will hear the voice of the Son of God and those hearing will live..." [11] The reality of the resurrection, anticipated by Jewish apocalypticism at the end of history, will be actualized in the present; and it is imperative that his disciples - and the implied readers! - witness this event. Accordingly Jesus urges his disciples, "Let us go to him."

One of them, Thomas, is introduced here for the first time.[12] His entry into the circle of Jesus' disciples has not been noted and is apparently unimportant. Why he appears here as the spokesperson for his fellow disciples is puzzling. In some way perhaps he may be a mirror image of some of the Gospel's implied readers. His name is translated into its Greek equivalent as Δίδυμος (Didymos), probably for the benefit of the implied reader, even as the Aramaic name Κηφᾶς, which Jesus bestowed on Simon in 1:42, was rendered into Greek as Πέτρος.[13] Both names, Thomas and Didymos, mean "twin," but whether this is intended to have any significance for the implied readers remains indeterminable. Ancient tradition identified him as the twin brother of Jesus, but there is no explicit acknowledgment of such a relationship here.[14] Nevertheless, such an identification may have been derived from the narrator's introduction of Thomas as "Didymos" (Twin), not as the twin *brother* of Jesus, for the word "brother" is not used here, but as the "twin" in the sense of being a disciple who has identified so completely with his teacher that he is like him in his attitude and

[11] Dodd, *Fourth Gospel*, 366, "... the evangelist has taken an event associated with the 'last day', and transplanted it into the historic ministry of Jesus, thus making of it a 'sign' of the ζωοποίησις which that ministry (when consummated) brought into effect."

[12] For a tradition-historical account of Thomas and the unfolding roles that the church assigned to him in its literature, see Barrett, *St. John*, 393; Schnackenburg, *St. John* II, 327-328.

[13] See also 20:24 and 21:2.

[14] In the apocryphal book, *The Acts of Thomas*, Thomas is named "Judas Thomas, who is also (called) Didymus." The name "Judas" may be the result of the effort of ancient tradition to identify him as Jesus' brother by relating him to the same name in Mark 6:3. In para.31 he is specifically identified as "the twin brother of Christ." *New Testament Apocrypha*, ed. by E. Hennecke & W. Schneemelcher, trans. by R. Mcl. Wilson (Philadelphia: Westminster, 1963) II, 339, 352. In *The Gospel according to Thomas*, ed. by A. Guillaumont, H. Puech, G.Quispel, W. Till, Y. A. Al Masih (Leiden: Brill, 1963) 3, he is called "Didymos Judas Thomas."

outlook. He too realizes that Jesus' return to Judea will result in his death. Nevertheless, his devotion and loyalty to Jesus are so all-embracing that he has no hesitation in exhorting his fellow disciples, "Let us also go so that we die with him!" As stouthearted and fearless as his proposal may appear, he is voicing a heroism that is naive and ignorant of the kind of death that Jesus will suffer and what it may achieve. Yet ironically, the objective that his exhortation obviously intends may intimate a second level of signification: following Jesus all the way into death is a necessary prerequisite of discipleship.[15]

Like other characters in the narrative world of the Fourth Gospel, Thomas, "the one called Didymos," serves as a purposeful figure to fulfill the rhetorical objective of the implied author in his role as narrator. For Thomas, as the Twin, by exhorting his fellow disciples to join him in following Jesus into death confronts the reader with a radical discipleship that identifies with Jesus so completely that it is willing and ready to die with him.[16] For the very first time the reader is alerted to a possible prospect of the future: dying with Jesus as a mark of discipleship. At this point in the narrative world, however, there is only the bravado of Thomas and the irony of its negation by another kind of participation in the death of Jesus.

Later, when Jesus enigmatically informs his disciples of his imminent departure in the opening statement of his Farewell Address (13:33-36), the objective that he intends his exodus to achieve for his disciples is finally articulated:

> In my Father's house are many rooms; and if not, I would tell you, for I am going to prepare a place for you. And if I go and prepare a place for you, I am coming again and I will receive you to myself so that *where* **I AM** (ὅπου εἰμὶ ἐγώ) you also are. And where I am going you know the way. (14:2-4)

In this context Thomas again serves as an interlocutor, and, in response to Jesus' pledge to fulfill these objectives, he complains that he has not understood his enigmatic response to the question Simon Peter had raised in 13:36. By repeating the unresolved issue of where Jesus is going, Thomas is purposely serving as a spokesperson for the implied readers in order to gain an unambiguous clarification of Jesus' intent, "Lord, we do not know where you are going! How do we know the way?" By pressing Jesus to be more transparent about his designs, he seems to have forgotten his earlier discernment that Jesus' return to Judea and Jerusalem would result in his death. Evidently he is unable to make a connection between his previous realization and Jesus' announcement of his forthcoming departure.

Jesus does not answer his first question; he does not tell Thomas and his fellow disciples where he is going. But in response to the second, "How do we know the way?" he declares: "**I AM** (ἐγὼ εἰμί) the way, the truth and the life. No one comes

---

[15] Duke, *Irony*, 59, also regards Thomas' exhortation as an ironic remark, but only in the sense that he is making a "false promise." However, it is a proposal and not a promise that he is voicing! Duke rejects the irony of "dying with Christ" as the second level of signification.

[16] Culpepper, *Anatomy*, 123-124, aptly characterizes Thomas as "the clear-eyed realist," but does not acknowledge the naive heroism of his willingness to die with Jesus and the irony that it expresses.

towards (πρός) the Father except through me." Although Jesus continues to keep his disciples – and the implied readers! – in suspense about where he is going, he establishes a course, a journey, that moves through multiple experiences of the disclosure of truth towards authentic life in all of its fullness. Nothing is said about a departure into death and therefore also nothing about a discipleship of "the way" that necessitates a participation in his death. Nevertheless, even if Jesus' disciples have not as yet grasped the reality of his forthcoming crucifixion, the reader has been privy to the prophecy of Caiaphas, the High Priest, that "Jesus was going to die on behalf of the nation and not only on behalf of the nation but also that the scattered children of God be gathered together into one." Consequently, it is only on the basis of a radical discipleship that participates in Jesus' death that his response to Thomas' question about "the way" has any ethical integrity, "No one comes *towards* (πρός) the Father except through me." No one can enter into God's kingship except by being born from above. No union with God is possible except by being united with Jesus in his death and resurrection. Thomas has expressed a willingness to die with Jesus, but as yet he has no comprehension of the kind of death Jesus will suffer or the consequences that it will hold for him and his fellow disciples.

When Jesus arrives at the outskirts of Bethany, he learns that Lazarus has already been in the tomb for four days. If Lazarus had died on the day or the day after Jesus received the sisters' message that their brother is ill, and Jesus had waited until the third day to begin the journey to Bethany, it is conceivable that Lazarus might have been in the tomb four days by the time Jesus reaches Bethany. It is more likely, however, that the specified time period in the tomb is an anticipation of Martha's objection to Jesus' command to remove the stone from the tomb, "Lord, he is already smelling, for it is the fourth day." That would imply the impossibility of raising Lazarus from the dead. For, according to rabbinic tradition, legal testimony about the identity of a corpse is given only during a period of three days after death.

> They derive testimony [concerning the identity of a corpse] only from the appearance of the whole face with the nose, even though there are signs of the corpse's identity on his body or garments. ...They give testimony [about the identity of a corpse] only during a period of three days [after death].[17]

In other words, the fourth day is considered to be that time in the process of physical decomposition when the face of the corpse is no longer recognizable. Consequently the soul, which has remained close to the corpse, no longer recognizes the body to which it belonged and therefore abandons it and "goes its way."

The narrator, therefore, intends the reader to be aware that Jesus, from the time of his arrival at the outskirts of Bethany, is cognizant of the hopeless condition of

[17] M *Yebamoth* 16:3, *A New Translation*, by Jacob Neusner (New Haven: Yale University Press, 1988) 376. See the discussion of the Mishnaic text in "Yebamoth" 16:3, *The Talmud of Babylonia: An American Translation*, trans. by Jacob Neusner (Atlanta: Scholars Press, 1992) 174-175.

Lazarus. He is not only dead; his state of being as a corpse is unequivocally terminal.

At the same time, by interrupting the story at this point with another "aside," the narrator informs the implied readers that Bethany is approximately "fifteen stades" or nearly two miles from Jerusalem. Not only would it appear that Jesus has come so far for nothing; because of Bethany's proximity to Jerusalem, he has also jeopardized his life by exposing himself to the hostility of the governing authorities in the capital city. At this moment, however, he is on the verge of entering into a context of extensive grieving. Martha and Mary are in mourning, and they are surrounded by "many from the Jews" who have come to offer their consolation and support (11:19). But who are these "Jews"? "Consistency building" would induce their identification with the ruling authorities, like those who appear in Galilee among the addressees of Jesus' discourse on the Bread of Life.[18] It is consequential that they are present to witness this culminating sign of Jesus' ministry. If this is a valid conclusion, Lazarus must be considered to be a person of importance within the Jewish community, having access into circles of power. It is significant that "the other disciple," who *accompanied* (συνεισῆλθεν) Jesus *into* courtyard of the high priest, was known to the high priest (18:15). It is another implication that Lazarus is identifiable as the Beloved Disciple.

Martha has left her sister Mary at home and immediately upon meeting Jesus reproaches him for the consequence of his late arrival, " Lord, if you had been here, my brother would not have died." At the same time, unaware of his deliberate delay in responding to her and her sister's call for help, she voices her perception of the intimacy of his relationship with God and therefore the possibility of receiving from God whatever he requests.

> *But* also now I know that whatever *you will ask* God, God will give you.[19]

To what extent Martha is prepared to believe in order to see is not yet evident. Her confidence in Jesus, however, seems to enable her to be open to unrestricted possibility. Nevertheless, when Jesus tells her, "Your brother will rise again," she replies with a characteristically Jewish perspective that projects the eschatological reality of resurrection to the end of time, "I know that he will rise in the resurrection at the last day." In the light of this futuristic eschatology it is difficult to assess the extent of her expectation on the basis of her expressed confidence in Jesus, "...I know that whatever you ask God, God will give you."

---

[18] See 6:41 and 52. Bultmann, *John*, 401, German, 306; and Schnackenburg, *St. John* II, 329, conclude that "the Jews" are "the judging public," "needed as witnesses of the miracle."

[19] Two variants in verse 22 are difficult to evaluate. "But" (ἀλλά) stands at the very beginning of the verse in P^{66} and P^{45}, as well as in many uncials and minuscules. It may be a scribal attempt to reinforce the discontinuity between Martha's reproach and her expression of faith that immediately follows. Yet without the conjunction "but," the continuity between Martha's reproach and her confession of faith is too easy and unconstrained. The verb αἰτήσῃ (you will ask) is attested by a strong representation of the manuscript tradition and is evidently the more difficult reading. Yet, the particle ἄν, which expresses indefiniteness, requires the use of the subjunctive mood and is supported by the alternative reading, αἰτήσῃς, in P^{66}, P^{45}, Codex W and a few others. Both the preposition ἀλλά (but) and the aorist subjunctive αἰτήσῃς are probably original. Compare 2:7.

Jesus responds to her futuristic perspective with a pronouncement on the paradoxical reality of resurrection. Utilizing once again the **I AM** (ἐγώ εἰμί) formula of self-disclosure, he links himself to this paradoxical reality of resurrection, "**I AM** the resurrection and the life..." As the incarnation of the Logos-Sophia he embodies the eschatological expectation of the New Humanity who in collaboration with God makes all things new and establishes life as the supreme reality of human existence.

> The one who believes into me, even if he or she dies, will live; and the one who lives and believes into me will by no means ever die. (11:25-26)

The first half of his declaration expresses nothing more than the futuristic eschatology that Martha has voiced. Lazarus, the one whom Jesus loves, has believed into Jesus; he has made a commitment to Jesus, and although he has died, he will live. He will rise again!

On the other hand, however, "... the one who lives and believes into me will by no means ever die." Lazarus, therefore, has not died. As Jesus said earlier, "This illness is not towards death;" and again, "Lazarus our friend has fallen asleep." In life Lazarus lived by his commitment to Jesus and therefore already participated in the everlasting life of the New Humanity that Jesus has been constituting. Consequently, the impossibility of his resurrection, in the light of the fourth day reality of his terminal state of being, is rendered possible![20]

Martha affirms Jesus' pronouncement with a declaration of faith that accounts for the confidence she expressed earlier in the possibility she perceives that Jesus is able to receive from God whatever he asks:

> Yes, Lord, I have believed that you are the Christ, the Son of God, the one coming into the world. (11:27)

Her confession corresponds to Nathanael's acknowledgment of Jesus at the beginning of the gospel: "Rabbi, you are the Son of God, you are the King of Israel!" It is also a confession that anticipates the stated objective of the narrator at the conclusion of the gospel, "But these things have been written so that you may begin to believe that Jesus is the Christ, the Son of God, and so that believing you might have life in his name" (20:31). It would seem, therefore, that Martha's statement of faith, which is spoken in the context of the seventh and culminating sign of Jesus' ministry, expresses the credo that is central to the gospel's christological perspective. By joining together the two christological titles, "Messiah" and "the Son of God," she, like Nathanael, transcends the rejection of Jesus as the Messiah that is expressed in 7:42 and is based on his non-fulfillment of the Messiah typology by not being from "the seed of David" and not being "from David's village, Bethlehem." Moreover, her addition of the concluding participial phrase, "the one coming into the world," echoes the Prologue's presentation of the incarnational movement of the Logos-Sophia as "the true light, ...

---

[20] As Schnackenburg says, *St. John* II, 331, in his critique of Bultmann's one-sided emphasis on Jesus as the Revealer, "... he is not just the revealer, but also the giver of this indestructible life." Compare Bultmann, *John*, 402-403; German, 307-308.

(which) was *coming into the world*," and links that dimension of the gospel's christology to her statement of faith. Martha, therefore, in spite of her futuristic eschatology and its projection of the reality of resurrection to "the last day," discloses a capacity to be open to new possibilities. After enunciating her faith, she returns home and informs her sister that Jesus has arrived and summons her as well.

Mary responds to his call by rising quickly from her grief-stricken posture of sitting and going out of the village to meet Jesus.[21] Perhaps the use of the resurrection verb ἠγερθη (*she arose*) intimates a kind of resurrection experience; that is, her response to Jesus' summons raises her up from her state of desolation and mourning. She is followed by "the Jews," the ruling authorities, who had been grieving with her in her home, but who had assumed that she was going to bewail Lazarus' death at his tomb. They will be present at the exchange between Jesus and Mary and at the raising of her brother, Lazarus. When she encounters Jesus, she falls at his feet in an intensity of devotion but at the same time voices the same rebuke her sister had uttered in view of the consequence of his late arrival, "Lord, if you had been here, my brother would not have died."

As Jesus witnesses her grief and the wailing of her fellow mourners who had followed her, the reality of Lazarus' death overwhelms him and he begins to feel an emotional rage swelling and surging through him. The narrator employs two verbs to convey his agitated condition. The first is ἐνεβριμήσατο, a verb that is often translated "to be deeply moved" or "to be greatly disturbed," but a verb that is stronger than ὀργίζω (*be angry*), and in Greek literature is more generally used to signify the noise that horses make when they are about to move into battle; that is, "to snort."[22] The other is ἐτάραξεν, from ταράσσω, which means "to stir up," or "to agitate," and is usually expressed in the passive voice. Here it is employed in the active voice and is followed by the reflexive pronoun ἑαυτόν (*himself*) as a direct object. Jesus is both the acting subject and the object that is being acted upon. He is troubling himself! The rage that is welling up within him becomes the agent that unsettles him, shakes him up, and in turn stirs up more rage. These overpowering emotions are not engendered by or directed at Mary and her fellow mourners because of their lack of faith or because their grief may be "forcing a miracle upon him."[23] It

---

[21] Of the two manuscript variants, ἠγέρθη and ἐγείρεται, the former is probably the original, following the aorist verb ἤκουσεν (*she heard*) and is attested by P^{75} and the majority of the manuscripts. As an intransitive verb in the passive voice, ἠγέρθη is translated as "she arose," which, in view of 11:20b, includes the implication of "from her sitting position," most likely the posture of being grief stricken.

[22] Εμβριμάομαι, expressing strong emotions, occurs five times in the NT: Matt 9:30; Mark 1:43, 14:5; and John 11:33 and 38. See H. G. Liddell and R. Scott, *A Greek-English Lexicon* (Oxford: at the Clarendon Press, 9th ed., 1966) 540.

[23] See Barrett, *St. John*, 398f, who considers both possibilities, concluding that it is "not necessary (though not impossible) to take unbelief as the cause of Jesus' anger, but at the same time also considers it plausible that his anger may be generated by his perception that "the grief of the sisters and the Jews are almost forcing a miracle on him." Bultmann, *John* 406, interprets Jesus' agitation as being directed at "the lack of faith, expressed in the wailing that is raised about the death of Lazarus in his [Jesus] presence." Also Schnackenburg, *St. John* II, 335-336.

is rather the fact of Lazarus' death that Jesus is experiencing in and through the desolation of the two sisters and their fellow mourners that evokes his overpowering emotions. Jesus is enraged at the reality of death![24] While still at a distance from Bethany he could say, "I rejoice on your account ... that I was not there." But as he confronts the death of the one he loves, he is seething with emotions. When he inquires where Lazarus is buried and is invited to view Lazarus' tomb, he bursts into tears. Rage turns into weeping.

Moved by his tears, the mourners exclaim, "See how he was loving him!"[25] This is the third reference to Jesus' love for Lazarus that is expressed in this story. There is no one else in the preceding narrative world of the Fourth Gospel of whom this is said. When, therefore, the relative clause ὅν ἠγάπα ὁ 'Ιησους (the one whom Jesus loved), which is similar to the message which the sisters sent Jesus in 11:3, Ἴδε ὅν φίλεις (see the one you love), is encountered in 13:23, and again in 19:26 and 20:2, the identification that logically emerges is that Lazarus is the Beloved Disciple in the narrative world of the Fourth Gospel.[26]

Discerning the love for Lazarus that Jesus has manifested by his tears, the ruling authorities, who are aware of the episode of 9:1-41, wonder why he, who was able to open the eyes of the blind, could not have prevented him from dying. Jesus himself, however, is still seething with emotions, and, as he reaches the tomb, his tears turn into *a rage within his spirit*, ἐμβριμώμενος ἐν πνεύματι. Once again the narrator employs the verb ἐμβριμᾶθαι (*to snort*) in order to convey the emotions that are boiling within him.

At this point the narrator pauses once again to introduce an "aside" for the benefit of the reader: "Now it (the tomb) was a cave, and a stone was laid upon it." Caves of

---

[24] Lindars, "Rebuking the Spirit: A New Analysis of the Lazarus Story of John 11," 103, conjectures that the author derived the verb ἐμβριμᾶσθαι from "Synoptic-type traditions" and "characteristic of his method of narrative composition to build on words or phrases in his courses," used it a second time in 11:38. He contends that in the sources, the phrase ἐνεβριμήσατο τῷ πνεύματι was used in exorcisms and meant "rebuking the spirit," but the author altered its meaning "to command Lazarus to come out of the tomb." Unfortunately, Lindars has missed the aporetic character of the entire story. Stibbe, *John's Gospel*, 65, rightly says, "Death is Jesus' enemy in John 11:1-44."

[25] The use of the imperfect indicative ἐφίλει (he was loving) in 11:36 and 20:2 is puzzling. Like other verbs in the imperfect tense, it is intended to indicate that this reality is to be limited to the first level of the narrative world of the Gospel, that is, the career of Jesus? Can it be extrapolated from this that Lazarus' death, perhaps before 70, was utilized to serve as the seventh sign that dramatizes the drawing of Jewish apocalypticism's future projection of resurrection into present historical existence? The truth of Jesus' paradoxical declaration of 11:25 can be applied to Lazarus' death even if the story itself is a myth in the sense of building world. Lazarus believed into Jesus and even though he died, he will live, and everyone who lives and believes into Jesus will never die.

[26] This identification is denied by Schnackenburg, *St. John* II, 322 and 514, n. 18. But it is affirmed by Mark W. G. Stibbe, *John as Storyteller: Narrative Criticism and the Fourth Gospel* (Cambridge: at the University Press, 1994) 78. R. Alan Culpepper, *John, the Son of Zebedee*, 72-85, reviews the evidence for various possible identifications of the Beloved Disciple: the Apostle John, Lazarus, John Mark, Matthias, the Rich Young Ruler, Paul, Benjamin, Gentile Christianity, an Itinerant, Prophetic Community, and the Elder who wrote 2 and 3 John, and finally concludes that the Beloved Disciple is John the son of Zebedee. Lazarus is rejected because of the discrepancy within the Gospel, that is, if the Beloved Disciple is identified as Lazarus in chapters 11-12, why should his identity be hidden in the subsequent chapters of the Gospel?

course served as burial places, but there may be more to the significance of this intrusive remark than a simple identification of Lazarus' tomb as a cave.[27] At this moment the narrator may be enlarging the scope of this seventh and culminating sign of Jesus in order to relate the eschatology of resurrection to the reality of living death and the living dead. The cave of Lazarus' tomb is also identifiable with Plato's cave of non-being, a burial place for the living dead as well as the physical dead.[28] Lazarus, therefore, may serve as a paradigmatic figure of the non-being of both the living and the physical dead; and accordingly the resurrection that he experiences is applicable to both conditions. It may, in fact, be more applicable to the non-being of the living than the non-being of the dead. Although Jesus had announced, "Lazarus *died*" (ἀπέθανεν), and Martha is described as "the sister of the one *having come to an end* (τετελευτηκότος), the narrator never states that Lazarus is νεκρός (dead).[29] Consequently it would seem that the ambiguity is determinate, and the fourth day reality of decomposition may also be ascribed to the condition of the living dead.

Upon arrival at Lazarus' burial place, Jesus commands the stone to be removed from the mouth of the cave-tomb. Martha, who had expressed her confidence in Jesus that "whatever you will ask God, God will give you," and who had subsequently revealed the basis of that conviction by confessing Jesus as "the Messiah, the Son of God, the One coming into the world," objects, "Lord, he is already smelling, for it is the fourth day!" Putrefaction and the attendant departure of the soul that is no longer able to recognize the face of the corpse to which it belonged would guarantee the impossibility of resurrection.

In response Jesus reminds Martha of the need in this context to believe in order to see: "Did I not say to you, 'If you believe you will see the glory of God'." Nothing of the kind had been said in the earlier dialogue between them, but Jesus may have implied it in his **I AM** pronouncement on the paradoxical reality of resurrection. In any case, it belongs to a trajectory that runs through the gospel and culminates in the final benediction Jesus speaks to Thomas, "Blessed are those not seeing and believing!"[30] Martha cannot look back into the historical past to locate a tradition or a prototype that would establish the reasonability of such a possibility. There are no antecedents for this historical singularity! Therefore Martha must make herself vulnerable and open herself to the possibilities of the future, possibilities that are constituted by the incarnation of the Logos-Sophia in Jesus of Nazareth, the son of Joseph, and in those who follow him into a new creation. Martha must believe in order to see! She must have the stone removed from the entrance to the cave-tomb, if

---

[27] Barrett, *St. John*, 401, links this narrator's aside to "epigraphical evidence for its use as 'grave'."

[28] See Plato, *The Republic* VII, 1-2 (514-517a), *Loeb Classical Library*, trans. by Paul Shorey (Cambridge: Harvard University Press, 1970). In Book X, 13 (614b-e) Plato recounts the myth of Er, something of a parallel to the story of Lazarus, in which the warrior Er, whose corpse was still intact after he had been slain in battle ten days before, subsequently revived on the twelfth day as he lay upon the funeral pyre.

[29] This is recognized by Barrett, *St. John*, 401, but without attaching any significance to it.

[30] Chapter 5, on "seeing and believing" and "believing in order to see."

Jesus is to fulfill his objective. To that extent the resurrection of Lazarus depends on her.

Without hesitation she acts according to the faith and confidence she had expressed earlier. The stone is rolled away; and Jesus can proceed to manifest the glory of God by drawing the reality of resurrection out of the future and actualizing it in a circumstance of apparent impossibility. But first he looks heavenward and voices a prayer:

> Father, I thank you that you heard me; and I knew that you always hear me. But I spoke on account of the crowd standing by so that they might believe that you sent me. (11:41-42)

No prior prayer has been spoken, so the use of the aorist tense, ἤκουσας (*you heard*), may simply express Jesus' confidence that God has heard what he has just said to Martha. Moreover, at the time he spoke he knew that God always hears him. For the union that he enjoys with God as the apprentice Son, the incarnate Logos-Sophia, assures him of continuous communion and communication and therefore also of the freedom in which he can act in accordance with the self-understanding he disclosed in 5:20-21,

> ...the Father loves the Son and shows him all the things he is doing, and greater works than these he will show him, so that you marvel. For even as the Father resurrects the dead and makes alive, so also the Son makes alive whom he wishes.

What he said to Martha, however, was also intended for the benefit of the by-standing crowd, and that includes the authorities (οἱ Ἰουδαίοι) of verses 31 and 36, and, of course, also the implied readers, so that they might believe that God sent him. For, while Martha must *believe in order to see*, the crowd, the authorities, and the implied readers who witness the reality of resurrection being drawn out of the future into the present, will hopefully *see and believe*, and consequently be drawn into the journey of faith.[31]

At last, with the cave-tomb open, Jesus, turning his gaze from heaven to the cave-tomb, bellows with a booming voice, "Lazarus, come out!" The dead man, whose state of being was terminal, whose decomposition was so advanced that his soul no longer hovered above its corpse, heard his shout, and with bound hands and feet and a burial cloth covering his face he somehow succeeds in exiting from the tomb, his cave of non-being. How he could manage to do that is difficult to imagine. But he came forth! Jesus' double asseveration of 5:25 has been fulfilled:

> Amen, amen I say to you, 'The hour is coming and now is when the dead will hear the voice of the Son of God and those hearing will live.

[31] Jesus' prayer of 11:41-42 may be intended to be heard by the by-standers, but, as Schnackenburg, *St John* II, 339, has recognized, it is primarily intended for the "readers." Its function, however, is not "that they should understand the miracle as God's testimony to his [Jesus] mission," but in order that, by seeing, they might commit themselves to him.

Death has been vanquished, the death of living and the death of dying. As Jesus had promised his disciples in 11:4, "This sickness is not towards death, but on behalf of the glory of God so that the Son of God is glorified through it." The divine collaboration of "the Father" and "the Son" has resulted in a manifestation of divine glory.

For Lazarus, however, that transcendence over the death of living and the death of dying must be more fully realized. He has exited from the tomb bound hands and feet and unable to see because his face is covered with a burial cloth (σουδάριον). He must be unbound. Accordingly, Jesus turns to the by-standers, including the authorities (οἱ Ἰουδαίοι), who have witnessed this resurrection, "Loose him and let him go forth." Lazarus has responded to Jesus' bellowing summons, "Come forth." But in order to be free he needs the gracious aid and helping hand of those around him. Jesus' liberation from the death of living and the death of dying requires a two-fold response: the act of Lazarus himself to hear and exit, but also the caring involvement of his community.

Lazarus has experienced the resurrection power of the incarnate Logos-Sophia, Jesus of Nazareth. He believed into the one who disclosed himself as "**I AM** the Resurrection and the Life," and even though he died, he lives. And, as the one who lives and believes into Jesus, the New Human Being, he will by no means (οὐ μή) die forever." That is the aporia, the paradox of faith in its confrontation with the powers of death and life.

But Martha and the surrounding by-standers have also been actors and agents in Lazarus' resurrection. Before Jesus could call him out of the tomb, the stone had to be rolled away, and for that to be done it was necessary for Martha to "believe in order to see." After Lazarus responded to Jesus' call and exited from his cave, those present participated in his resurrection by releasing him from his restrictive garments and enabling him to enter into the possibilities of his new existence.

The Sanhedrin's condemnation of Jesus 11:45-57

Included in the outcome of this seventh and culminating sign is the fulfillment of Jesus' prayer of 11:42, "And I knew that you hear me always, but on account of the crowd standing by I spoke, so that they might believe that you sent me." According to 11:45, "Therefore, many of the Jews, those who came to Mary and θεασάμενοι (sizing up) what he did, believed into him." The earlier division among the ruling authorities continues to manifest itself. While some of them believe that Jesus is demonized and mad, others have expressed doubts that a demon-possessed human being could open the eyes of the blind (10:20-21). Still others who witnessed Lazarus' resurrection, but who refuse to believe that Jesus was demented, make a commitment to him. Some of them, however, went off to the Pharisees and informed them of the things Jesus had done. They are comparable to the formerly paralyzed individual of 5:15 who identified Jesus to the guardians of society as the one who had commanded him to carry his pallet on the Sabbath. The same verb, εἶπαν (they said), is used in 11:46 that the narrator had employed in 5:15, εἶπεν (he said).

Consequently (οὖν), the chief priests, who are also to be included among the οἱ Ἰουδαίοι (the Jews), and the Pharisees join together to convene a meeting of the Sanhedrin (11:47). This is the first collaboration between the chief priests and the Pharisees since 7:32, but their apprehension has escalated into a convocation of the supreme court of Judaism. They were saying:

> What shall we do, for this human being is doing many signs? If we allow him thus, all will believe into him, and the Romans will come and remove both our place and our nation.

Jesus' signs are powerful and convincing. If he continues to gain a greater following without being suppressed by the authorities, indeed, if all will commit themselves to him, they, the accomplices of Roman colonialism, will lose their power and their control. According to their reasoning, that would necessitate Roman counteraction that would result in the loss of the Temple and the nation. The narrator confronts the implied readers with the irony of the Sanhedrin's ignoble effort to avoid the holocaust that occurred in 70 C.E.[32] Caiaphas, who is introduced for the first time as "the High Priest in office that year," arrogantly censures his fellow members of the Sanhedrin:

> You know nothing whatsoever, neither are you considering that it is profitable *to you* that one human being dies *in place of/on behalf of* the λαός (People) and that the entire nation is not destroyed.[33]

Various charges have been leveled against Jesus: relaxing the Sabbath and making himself equal to God (5:18), having a demon and being demented (8:48, 10:20) and making himself God (10:33). But none of them are cited in the deliberations of the Sanhedrin. Their alarm is focused on the "many signs" he is doing and the attendant possibility of all the people committing themselves to him. Typically, as collaborators with colonial imperialists, their concern is the continuation of the Temple cult they administrate as the divinely-appointed brokers between God and Israel and the systemic structures that the Temple cult maintains.

Their resolution for this potential crisis is terminating Jesus' ministry by condemning him to death. He will be that "one human being" who will die *in place of* (ὑπέρ) the *People of God* (λαός) and, as a consequence, the *nation* (ἔθνος) will be preserved.[34] But the preposition ὑπέρ, when it governs the genitive case, can mean *on behalf of* as well as *in place of*. Caiaphas, of course, intends the meaning: *in place of*. He wants Jesus to die instead of the People of God. Jesus, indeed, will die

---

[32] Also Duke, *Irony*, 86-87. See the discussion of 11:48 in Paul Winter, *On the Trial of Jesus* (Berlin: Walter de Gruyter, 1961) 39-42.

[33] *A Greek-English Lexicon of the New Testament*, 1031, "Sometimes the meaning, *in place of* merges with *on behalf of, for the sake of*."

[34] The word λαός is the term that the Septuagint employs to designate the Jewish people as the elect people of God, and that is its denotation in the Fourth Gospel. On the other hand, ἔθνος signifies the nation as "a race united by a common descent". See Hoskyns/Davey, *Fourth Gospel*, 412.

in place of the People, even as the first-born of the Egyptians died in place of the Egyptian people at the time of the first Exodus. But the ambiguity of the preposition permits the narrator to use Caiaphas' speech to intimate the irony that their objective will disclose. For Jesus will also die *on behalf of* or *for the sake of* the People of God in an enactment of the ritual of the Day of Atonement that will be imposed on him when he is handed over to the Romans for execution.[35] Like the he-goat of Lev 16:10 upon whom the High Priest pronounces the sins of the People of God (λαός), he will be sent into the wilderness, to Azazel, in order to transfer their sins into oblivion. Ironically, however, Jesus, in the role of the scapegoat, will break the cycle of violence by his death, but as its instigator and not as its victim.[36]

The narrator, aware of this immense irony, interrupts the scene with an intrusive comment intended for the implied readers that supplements the irony that has already been expressed:

> But he did not say this of himself, but being High Priest of that year he was prophesying that Jesus was going to die ὑπέρ (on behalf of) the nation, and not on behalf of the nation alone but also in order that he gathers together into One all the scattered children of God. (11:51-52)

It is essentially this digression that indicates that the narrator uses Caiaphas' speech to intimate the irony that Jesus will die *on behalf of* the People. Here, additionally, the word ἔθνος, designating a people united by a common descent, is substituted in place of Caiaphas' use of λαός (People of God) in order to reconstrue his "prophesy." Jesus is not only going to die *on behalf of the People of God*. The post-70 implied readers are to know that he is also going to die *on behalf of* the nation that was destroyed by the Romans in 70, in spite of the efforts of the Sanhedrin to save it by condemning Jesus to the role of a scapegoat. Moreover, as the narrator's intrusive remark amplifies, "and not only on behalf of the nation alone but also in order that he gathers together into One all the scattered children of God." In the first edition of the Fourth Gospel that was addressed to the Jews of Alexandria, these words must signify that Israel is to be restored as a nation of twelve tribes, and that all those scattered in the world-wide Jewish dispersion will be reunited with this reconstituted people of a common descent in a

---

[35] Duke, *Irony*, 88, perceives a double irony here: the ambiguity of the preposition ὑπέρ, and the ambiguity of the word λαός (People of God). "Caiaphas thinks of one *laos*, the author means quite another." The second irony here, however, is the enactment of the Day of Atonement upon Jesus.

[36] Similarly Stephen Motyer, "The Fourth Gospel and the Salvation of Israel: An Appeal for a New Start," *Anti-Judaism and the Fourth Gospel* (Assen: Royal Van Gorcum, 2001) 99. On René Girard's theory of the scapegoat, see his books: *Violence and the Sacred* (Baltimore: Johns Hopkins University Press, 1977) and *The Scapegoat* (Baltimore: Johns Hopkins University Press, 1986). In this respect Walter Wink's application of Girard's theory to the death of Jesus is defective. See his *Engaging the Powers: Discernment and Resistance in a World of Domination* (Minneapolis: Fortress Press, 1992) 144-147. The same holds true for Robert G. Hamerton-Kelly's interpretation of Jesus' death in Mark's Gospel in *The Gospel and the Sacred: Poetics of Violence in Mark* (Minneapolis: Fortress Press, 1994) 1-14.

community of the One and the Many.[37] For the second edition of the Gospel that was prepared in Ephesus for Gentile Christian readers, the narrator's digression would be construed more universally. Most likely "All the scattered children of God" would be interpreted to refer to all Christians everywhere.[38]

Caiaphas' counsel is decisive and is ratified by the Sanhedrin; "Therefore, from that day they conferred with themselves so that they might kill him." Although the authorities have been motivated to do away with Jesus earlier in his ministry, they now undertake their objective in earnest under the jurisdiction of the Sanhedrin.

Jesus, evidently aware of their intention, removes himself from public scrutiny, specifically the notice of the guardians of society (οἱ 'Ιουδαίοι). Earlier, at the time of the Feast of the Tabernacles (7:1), he had remained in Galilee before secretly journeying to Jerusalem because the authorities (οἱ 'Ιουδαίοι) were seeking to kill him.[39] Now he withdraws into a city named Ephraim in the vicinity of the desert, and there he continues to remain with his disciples.[40]

Dinner with Mary, Martha and Lazarus in Bethany 12:1-8

It is in this context that the narrator announces the nearness of the "Passover of the Jews."[41] Many of the people would travel from their homes in the country in order to purify themselves in preparation for the celebration of the Passover. While they are in the sacred precinct of the Temple engaged in their rites of purification, they search for Jesus, questioning each other whether he would come to the feast. Apparently they are aware of the peril he is confronting, for the chief priests and the Pharisees had issued orders that anyone who knew his whereabouts should inform them so that they might arrest him (11:57).

Six days before the Passover Jesus returns to Bethany "where Lazarus was whom he resurrected from the dead". This appears to be a turning point in the Gospel. In 2:13, 6:4 and 11:55 the narrator had announced, "the Passover of the Jews was near." "Six days before the Passover" would indicate the seventh day,

---

[37] Schnackenburg, *St. John* II, 350, interprets the aside of 11:51-52 to refer to "the idea of the eschatological Israel, which will once more include the twelve tribes and will be gathered out of the dispersion." For the second edition of the Gospel that was prepared in Ephesus for Gentile Christian readers, the narrator's digression would be construed more universally. Most likely "All the scattered children of God" would be interpreted to refer to all Christians everywhere.

[38] Hoskyns/Davey, *Fourth Gospel*, 528.

[39] In view of the possibility of a contradiction between 11:54 and 7:1, von Wahlde, "The Johannine 'Jews'," 51-52, identifies these οἱ'Ιουδαίοι as the common people and concludes that it is a neutral use of this term. James H. Charlesworth, "The Gospel of John: Exclusivism Caused by a Social Setting Different from that of Jesus (John 11:54 and 14:6," *Anti-Judaism and the Fourth Gospel*, 490, believes that οἱ'Ιουδαίοι should be translated as "some Jewish leaders."

[40] Ephraim, according to Gustav Dalman, *Orte und Wege Jesu* (Gütersloh" C. Bertelsmann, 1921) 191, is to be identified with the present-day village of et-taijibe. It was equivalent to a county-seat in Samaritan territory when, at the time around 145 B.C.E., it was ceded to Judea. At a 2,600 foot elevation, it lies at the eastern edge of the Judean highlands about 12 miles northeast of Jerusalem.

[41] As in 2:13 and 6:4, the genitive construction, τῶν'Ιουδαίων, refers to the Jewish people and not only to the ruling authorities.

that is the Sabbath, when the feast of the Passover will be celebrated. Since Passover is the day after the Day of Preparation, it will the day after Jesus' death, the day of his entombment.[42] This corresponds to 19:31,

> Then the Jews (οἱ 'Ιουδαίοι), since it was the Day of Preparation, so that the bodies did not remain on the cross on the Sabbath, *for great was the day of that Sabbath*, asked Pilate that their legs be broken and they be taken away.

The imminence of the Passover has been announced, but the day of its actual arrival is never noted. For at Jesus' death the Passover will have been superseded because he substituted his flesh and blood in place of the Passover meal at the time of the second Passover, and because Jesus fulfills the role of the Passover lamb in 19:28-30.[43]

Jesus returns to Bethany because he wants to be with those whom he loves. Martha serves a dinner in his honor, while Lazarus reclines at table with Jesus and his disciples. Mary, the third member of the family, takes this opportunity to express her sentiments by anointing his feet with a pound of pure, expensive oil of nard and by wiping his feet with her hair. This may be her demonstration of gratitude and devotion for her brother's resurrection. But it is also more! The inexplicable intrusive remark of 11:2, that it was Mary who "anointed the Lord and wiped his feet with her hair" – stated prior to the message the two sisters sent Jesus notifying him of their brother's sickness – intimates to the implied readers that there is a correlation between her loving act of anointing Jesus' feet and the resurrection of her brother, Lazarus.

In the context of the third and culminating Passover of the Gospel, Jesus' act of raising Lazarus has established the possibility of actualizing the future reality of resurrection, that Jewish apocalypticism projects as an event of the Last Times, in the present here and now. The interdependence between the first sign of transforming water into wine and Jesus' replacement of the Temple sanctuary with his own physical body at the first Passover foreshadowed the salvation of a new Exodus. The dehumanizing limitations that hierarchically structured institutions, such as the Temple cult, impose on human beings have been abolished. Similarly, the correlation between the feeding of the multitudes and the episode of Jesus walking on the Sea of Galilee at the second Passover signals the new possibilities of historical existence resulting from the interdependent relationship between God and humanity that the new Exodus will establish. The association between the seventh sign of Lazarus' resurrection and Mary's anointing of Jesus' feet at the third Passover accentuates the historically-materially oriented ministry of Jesus that

[42] Brown, *John* I, 447, dates the Bethany scene on Saturday evening, observing that if Martha could be serving dinner, the Sabbath must have come to an end. Accordingly, the Passover would be celebrated on Friday evening/Saturday. P^{66}, however, reads "five days."

[43] Bultmann, *John*, 414; German, 316; and Schnackenburg, *St. John* II, discern no special significance in the narrator's phrase, "Six days before the Passover."

will culminate in his Passion as he becomes priest-like in offering himself as the Lamb of God that removes the sin of the world.[44] She may be the only one at this scene who understands this, and, in an act of genuine discipleship, she is expressing her veneration of Jesus in anticipation of the world transformation that Jesus will achieve through his death.[45]

Philo, in his treatise on Moses' ordinances regarding the temple cult, its priesthood and the sacrifices they offer on behalf of Israel, spiritualizes the prescribed ritual of ordaining priests for their service in the Temple cult by washing their feet.

> Now by the washing of the feet the walking is no longer on earth but is ether-skimming. For the soul of the lover of God is towards truth leaping upwards towards heaven and winging [its way] by busying oneself with high things, striving for and joining in the dance with the sun and moon and the all-holy, all-harmonious host of the other stars, ordered and governed by the God whose kingship is indisputable and undiminished, by which everything is justly presided over.[46]

This, of course, is the direction of Philo's general interpretation of the Greek translation of the Old Testament: a backwards movement from the material creation of Gen 2 to the archetypal realm of the Logos that is attributed to Gen 1.[47]

Mary does not wash Jesus' feet; she anoints them. In view of the soteriological significance inferable to his feet, she does not anoint his head, as the unnamed woman does in Mark 14:3 and Matt 26:7.[48] Kings, as the First Testament indicates, are anointed on the head. The christological interpretation of Jesus as Messiah is featured in Mark and Matthew, but specifically his messiahship in death. The woman's lavish anointment is not merely an anticipation of his burial. It is above all an acknowledgment of his royalty in crucifixion as he dies on behalf of his subjects' sins. Jesus, therefore, is not to be acknowledged as a typical king in the tradition of Israel's history. Because the woman has anointed him as Messiah in death, he – in contrast to his earlier rejection of that title in Mark 8:30 – will affirm his messianic kingship at his trial before the Sanhedrin.[49]

Jesus' feet, instead of his head, has a distinctive significance in the narrative world of the Fourth Gospel! Of the two sisters, Martha and Mary, it was the latter who fell at Jesus' feet (11:32). It is his feet that brought him to Bethany and to

---

[44] See chapter 17.

[45] On Mary as a "genuine disciple of Jesus," see the discussion of S. Schneiders, *Written That You May Believe*, 108-110.

[46] Philo, *de Specialibus Legibus* I, 207.

[47] Compare Philo, *de Opificio Mundi,* 69-71 with 134-139.

[48] Barrett, *St. John*, 412, is correct in his judgment, "... the anointing of a messianic king of a kind inconsistent with his [John's] understanding of Jesus." But it is invalid to conclude that by combining the Marcan and Lucan narratives with each other, the Fourth Evangelist has ended with "some confusion."

[49] Waetjen, *A Reordering of Power: A Socio-political Reading of Mark's Gospel* (Minneapolis: Fortress Press, 1989) 204-206.

Lazarus' tomb and, as a consequence, he is able to glorify God and to be glorified himself as God's apprentice by raising Lazarus from the dead. His feet, therefore, bring salvation. Indeed, they will bring salvation when he, in the ministry of a priest, will be lifted up on a cross instead of leaping upwards towards heaven and joining in a dance in concert with the sun, moon and stars as they are ordered and governed by God. The salvation that his feet bring is directed towards authentic historical existence, not towards the archetypal realm of the transcendent Logos. Mary, therefore, may be acknowledging the fulfillment of the Septuagint text of Isa 52:7.

> I am present, as [the] right-time on the mountains, as [the] feet of one proclaiming a report of peace, as one proclaiming good things, because I will make audible your salvation, saying to Zion, "Your God will reign."

By coming to Bethany, in spite of the on-going threats on his life, Jesus is not only making the good news of God's salvation audible. By raising Lazarus from the dead, he is also making God's salvation visible. It is a sign that God will reign. Mary acknowledges this soteriological reality by anointing Jesus' feet with an expensive pure oil of nard that is subsequently priced at "300 denarii," approximately a one-year's wage.[50] Attendantly she also wipes his anointed feet with her hair.[51] Both acts convey a sense of intimacy and adoration and, in the circumstance of men reclining at dinner in a context of honor/shame culture, her loving devotion might be regarded as shameless.[52] The narrator, however, observes, "the house was filled from the fragrance of the oil". Mary's expensive nard ointment has permeated the house, and its wonderful aroma intensifies the pleasure of the reclining guests. Perhaps a symbolic significance is also being

---

[50] Howard-Brook, *Becoming Children of God*, 271, raises the question, "Where did she get such an incredibly valuable pound of perfume?" The narrator reports in 18:15 that "the other disciple," who entered into the courtyard of the high priest, was known to the high priest. If this "other disciple" is Lazarus, as is contended in this book, it suggests, as Keener does, *John* II, 864, that Lazarus and his sisters may have been "a well-to-do Bethany family". The presence of authorities (οἱ Ἰουδαίοι) at the mourning of Lazarus indicates that they may also have had connections with the upper class.

[51] These features are also encountered in the Lucan story of a penitent woman washing Jesus' feet with her tears, wiping them with her unbound hair and anointing them with myrrh (7:36-50). The Johannine version may be "secondary," in its dependence on it, as Schnackenburg, *St. John* II, 367, contends, but it has been creatively revised for its incorporation into the Gospel. Schneiders, *Written That You May Believe*, 108, considers Mary's act to be "a combination of the Mark-Matthew account of the anonymous woman's (messianic?) anointing of Jesus' head. See her other comments, pp. 107-110.

[52] Schnackenburg, *St. John* II, 522, n. 15, notes that "Anointing of the feet by a woman during a meal was definitely improper in Jewish eyes." See also Howard-Brook, *Becoming Children of God*, 271. Nevertheless, this community, consisting of the family of siblings, Martha, Mary and Lazarus, who by honoring Jesus and perhaps with him his disciples, are joined together in a new grouping, neither "voluntary" nor "natural" but in a reconstituted moral order, "the reign of God." Therefore, the structures of relationships and the attendant ethical values would transcend those of Mediterranean honor/shame culture. Compare Bruce J. Malina, *The New Testament World: Insights from Cultural Anthropology* (Atlanta: John Knox Press, 1981) 40-42.

intimated to the implied readers: the fragrance of the ointment that fills the house will diffuse into the world as the good news of the salvation that Jesus actualizes.[53]

In this festive context Judas Iscariot is introduced to the implied readers for a second time. In 6:71 the narrator had identified him as one among the disciples whom Jesus had referred to as "a devil." Acknowledged again as "one of his disciples, the one who is going to betray him," he censures Mary's loving act by questioning, "Why was this oil not sold for 300 denarii and given to the destitute?" Its apparent altruistic motive is negated by the narrator's intrusive aside:

> But he said this not because he was concerned about the destitute, but because he was a thief and he was carrying the money-box containing the things deposited. (12:6)

No such accusation is raised against Judas in the Synoptic tradition, and its basis in fact remains indeterminable.

Jesus defends Mary by relating her demonstration of love eschatologically to his anticipated entombment: "Let her alone! [The ointment was not sold] so that she may observe it for the day of my burial." The adverbial conjunction, ἵνα, introduces the reply to Judas' question, "Why was this ointment not sold ...?" Jesus accepts her act as an anticipation of the last rite of his entombment that she is observing at this moment. For it is by his death, certified by his burial, that he will have completed the soteriological work for which he was commissioned as the Son of the Human Being who descended from heaven and who as the Son of the Human Being will be lifted up and exalted as "the snake in the wilderness" (3:13-14).

Moreover, as Jesus adds, "The destitute you have always with you, but me you do not have always." His disciples will continue to be able to show their solicitude for the poor, but the time-frame in which they can affirm their love and devotion to Jesus is limited.

The narrator shifts the scene to the ruling authorities who, according to 11:57, had ordered that anyone with information about the whereabouts of Jesus should report to them. At last Jesus has been located. "Then a large crowd from the Jews (οἱ Ἰουδαίοι) knew that he was there ..."[54] For the first time the narrator acknowledges that there is a large crowd of people who identify with the guardians of society and willingly submit to their jurisdiction. They report Jesus' whereabouts to their leaders, and out of curiosity they come to Bethany "not only on account of Jesus but in order that they might see Lazarus whom he raised from

[53] A perspective that Bultmann, *John*, 415, n. 3, draws from "older exegetes" like Ignatius, *Ephesians* 17:1.

[54] There are a number of manuscript variants for the difficult reading of the first eight words of verse 9: Ἔγνω οὖν [ὁ] ὄχλος πολὺς ἐκ τῶν Ἰουδαίων. As the subject of a verb ὁ ὄχλος πολὺς is unusual Greek, and therefore B. M. Metzger's *A Textual Commentary on the Greek New Testament*, 237, is inclined to enclose ὁ in brackets. P^{66*} and P^{75} do not include the definite article before ὄχλος and therefore may offer the more difficult reading. As Schnackenburg, *St. John* II, 524, n. 31, observes, "It is a sign that the copyists were not sure about the ὄχλος."

the dead". Their captivation by this culminating sign of Jesus' ministry heightens the apprehension of the chief priests, and in their state of alarm they conspire to kill Lazarus as well, "for on account of him many of the Jews were going off and believing into Jesus." In 11:45 the narrator reported that many of the Jews, who came to Mary and saw the things Jesus did, believed into him. Now others among the leaders of the people, after seeing the resurrected Lazarus with their own eyes, enter into a commitment to him. Lazarus himself, therefore, who, because of his resurrection, is no longer captive to the ultimate threat of death that the authorities can impose, endangers their rule and control of society.

Jesus' triumphal entry into Jerusalem 12:12-19

On the following day Jesus enters Jerusalem, and a great crowd, hearing that he is coming, welcomes him with palm branches and with bellowing words drawn from Psa 118:25-26, "Hosanna! Blessed is the one coming in the name of the Lord, the king of Israel!"[55] For the first time since Nathanael's confession in 1:49, Jesus is acknowledged as the king of Israel. But, as the implied readers may already have perceived, or at least will soon perceive, his coronation to kingship will take place in his crucifixion, in his being lifted up and exalted on the cross. In the narrative world of the Fourth Gospel the messianic kingship of Jesus is a reality of supreme irony.

The palm branches, which the people are waving as they greet Jesus, signify victory, the victory over death that he manifested by raising Lazarus from the dead, as the narrator acknowledges by the intrusive remark of 12:17-18. According to 2 Macc 10:7, the purification of the sanctuary and the rededication of the Temple was celebrated "in the manner of the festival of the booths."

> Therefore, carrying ivy-wreathed wands and beautiful branches and also fronds of palm, they offered hymns of thanksgiving to the One who had given success to the purifying of his own holy place.[56]

Proleptically, the palm branches may also signify Jesus' final victory over death that is manifested by his own resurrection from the dead.

In response to the bellowing greeting of the crowd, Jesus finds a donkey and seats himself on it in order to ride into the city and ultimately to his coronation on the cross. The narrator leads the implied readers to believe that he chose this demonstration deliberately in order to fulfill Zech 9:9.

---

[55] The crowd's acclamation may have been drawn from the Septuagint, but in view of the added "Hosanna" at the beginning of their cry, and the attachment of "the king of Israel" at the end, this benediction may have been adapted from Synoptic tradition.

[56] See also 1 Macc 13:51, where, as Brown, *John* I, 461, has noted, the word Livonia (palm branch), occurring only here in the LXX, is used in John 12:13. Also Josephus, *Ant* III, 245 and XIII, 372. See W. R. Farmer, "The Palm Branches in John 12,13," *JTS* 3 (1952) 62-66, who notes that the palm branches represented a victory symbol at the time of the Maccabees and also during the revolts of 66-70 and 135 C.E. Also Howard-Brook, *Becoming Children of God*, 274, on other references to palm branches.

> Stop fearing, daughter of Zion! See, your king is coming, seated on the colt of a donkey. (12:15)

According to the narrator's aside, the correlation between the entry into Jerusalem on a donkey and the prophecy of Zech 9:9 eluded Jesus' disciples at that moment. They remembered that these things were written of him and the things they did to him after his resurrection from the dead.

The jubilant welcome that Jesus received from the people who had come to Jerusalem for the Passover continues to alarm the ruling authorities. With exasperating resentment the Pharisees acknowledge their own impotence to each other, "*Keep on observing* [it] (θεωρεῖτε)! You are accomplishing nothing! See, the world has gone after him!" In this infuriating moment the Pharisees are forced to acknowledge that, temporarily at least, they have to abandon themselves to the reality they are perceiving. There is nothing they can do.

Chapter Thirteen

Jesus Closes His Ministry

The glorification of the New Human Being 12:20-36

After the Pharisees have acknowledged that the whole world has gravitated toward Jesus, the narrator introduces "certain Greeks among those going up in order that they might worship at the feast."[1] They are not Hellenistic Jews, but Gentiles as the Greek word, Ἕλληνες, denotes. Very likely they are God-fearers who are admitted to the synagogue but are excluded from the inner courts of the Temple. They want an audience with Jesus, but they are reluctant to address him directly.[2] So they approach Philip, the disciple from Bethsaida, with their request, "Sir, we want to see Jesus!" Philip consults with Andrew, and together they bring this petition to Jesus. Since they are the only disciples with Greek names in the narrative world of the Gospel, it is appropriate that they submit it to Jesus on behalf of the Greeks.[3] His response to his disciples expresses *a closure of his ministry* and at the same time implies a rejection of the entreaty of the Greeks.[4]

> The hour has come so that the Son of the Human Being is glorified. Amen, amen I say to you, "Unless the seed of wheat, falling into the ground, dies, it remains alone. But if it dies, it bears much fruit." (12:23-24)

Jesus must complete the work he has begun by constituting a new Exodus before the Greeks can be evangelized. The fruitfulness of the salvation that he foresees is dependent on the necessity of his death.[5] But at the same time, the deliverance that he will achieve and the possibilities that it will actualize must be published and actualized in the lives of his fellow Jews – and, indeed, in the lives of all human beings. Consequently Jesus attaches a general tenet to his metaphor of a seed

---

[1] Many commentators attempt to overcome what appears to them to be a puzzling arrangement of texts and conclude that this section of chapter 12 is explicable only on the basis of "unordered fragments" and "later additions" redacted by the Evangelist. See Bultmann, *John* 420-433; German, 321-331. Also Schnackenburg, *St. John* II, 381; and Fortna, *The Fourth Gospel*, 280-283. But this section is a single unit, regardless of source and redaction criticism. All that follows Jesus' announcement of the closure of his ministry is teaching directed at his disciples and at the crowd about his forthcoming exaltation as "the Son of the Human Being."

[2] On "proselytes" and "God-fearers" and their rights in Judaism, see K. G. Kuhn, *TWNT* VI, 730-745; in the one volume English translation by G. W. Bromiley, *TDNT* 941-946.

[3] Schnackenburg, *St. John* II, 382.

[4] Also Fortna, *The Fourth Gospel*, 280-281.

[5] Contrary to G. Nicholson, *Death as Departure: The Johannine Descent-Ascent Schema* (Chico, CA: Scholars Press, 1983) 152, who maintains that Jesus' metaphor of a seed of wheat is not "a direct reference to his death." Ashton, *Understanding the Fourth Gospel*, 494, considers 12:24-26 to be a later interpolation.

bearing fruit by dying that leads directly into a characterization of discipleship that is congruous with his "fruit-bearing" death and that will continue the work of world transformation that he has inaugurated.

> The one loving his/her life (ψυχή) destroys it, and the one hating his life (ψυχή) in this world will safe-guard it into everlasting life (ζωήν).[6] (12:25)

Although the prepositional phrase, "in this world" is missing in the first half of Jesus' pronouncement, it must be assumed, for life cannot be lived apart from this world. Although Jesus is the son of Joseph from Nazareth and, therefore, ἐκ τοῦ κόσμου (from the world), the origin that he prioritizes is ἐγὼ ἐκ τῶν ἄνω εἰμί (**I** from above **AM**).

He is the New Human Being whom God sent *to save the world.* The "world," then, must be the realm of brokenness, dis-ease, alienation, indeed, the region in which death rules. Jesus' self-disclosure as "the Light of the world," implies that the world must be a principality of darkness. If "the ruler of this world" will be cast out, as Jesus will declare shortly in 12:31, the world is the domain of a sovereignty that is opposed to God. Consequently, the world cannot engender the kind of human beings that fulfill God's original design and purpose.

The word ψυχή (soul) that Jesus uses is a translation of the Hebrew נֶפֶשׁ, an anthropological term that originally referred to the physical organ of the "throat" and became representative of the human being in the mode of "desiring, striving or yearning."[7] Ψυχή, like נֶפֶשׁ, designates the whole person but in terms of that vitality that craves possibility, freedom and life.[8] Since there is no antithesis between soul and body in biblical anthropology, ψυχή can become a synonym for the personal pronoun, as in the Septuagint translation of Gen 27:25 and Jer 3:11. Because it is the life that God gives, as Gen 2:7 indicates, and because God wills its fulfillment in truth and integrity, human beings as ψυχή are held accountable for the kind of life they lead and for the relationships they carry on with their fellow human beings.

Accordingly, "those who love their life," as they live it in the world, refers to human beings who are untroubled by the world's institutions and structures that are opposed to God's will for human freedom and possibility. Those who love their life are conscience-less about the injustices that impose living death on their fellow human beings. They are self-satisfied and comfortable in a political order that maintains social-economic structures that promote inequality, poverty and

---

[6] Dodd, *Historical Tradition*, 338-343, after a comparison of this saying with the parallels encountered in the Synoptic tradition, concludes, "There is nothing against the view that the couplet, simple, rhythmical, and genuinely biblical in its language, was handed down by tradition substantially in the terms preserved in John xii.25 (without the qualifying clauses)."

[7] Wolff, *Anthropology of the Old Testament,* 10-15.

[8] *Ibid.*, 16; Also Eduard Schweizer, "ψυχή," *TWNT*, IX, 631-632; English 639-640. On the differentiation of body and soul in Greek thought, see 632-633; English, 633-34.

exploitation, while at the same time they serve the rich and the powerful. In their insensitivities and hard-bigheartedness they will destroy their lives.

On the other hand, those who hate their lives as they live it in the world are scandalized by the domination of the rich and the powerful that deprives the majority of human beings of the kind of life, freedom and possibility that God wills for all human beings. They are affronted by the materialistic values that determine society's culture and the profiteering capitalism that multiplies injustices and resulting alienation. Such persons will safe-guard their lives because their rejection of that "world" and the evil that it generates will motivate them to work for reform and the redemption of life.

As he closes his public ministry and prepares for his imminent work of saving the world by his death and resurrection, Jesus invites those who are safe-guarding their lives by entering into solidarity with the poor and the degraded, the exploited and the dispossessed, to follow him. For they are naturally his agents, his intermediaries, in as far as they engaged in the same activities of world transformation to which he has been committed; and therefore they will have a share in his participation in the divine **I AM**, both in the present and in the future.[9]

> If any acts in service to me (διακονῇ), let her/him follow me, and *where **AM I*** (ὅπου εἰμὶ εγώ) there also my agent (διάκονος) will be. (12:26)

Moreover, he insists, such agents and intermediaries will be honored by "the Father" because their participation in Jesus' work, and therefore also his **I AM,** will unite them with God the Creator.

Philo's Platonic body/soul dualism predetermines his perspective of "the world" and its social construction of reality. Since human beings are made in the image and likeness of the λόγος (Word), when divine breath is breathed into their face, the Creator's will for every human being is to live in accordance with the Logos.[10] That requires a backward movement from the physical world to the realm of the Logos, from the material copies of creation that the senses experience to the spiritual world of sovereign Reason and the forms that it contemplates.

> Every human being, according to the mind, is related to the divine Logos, having originated as a copy or a fragment or a radiance of that blessed nature, but according to the structure of the body [is] related to all the world (κόσμος).[11]

---

[9] It is not merely "the heavenly world," the home to which Jesus is going that the disciples will reach through their deaths, as Schnackenburg contends in *St. John* II, 385. The disciples will participate in Jesus' transcendence in the here and now after Jesus' ascension. The reverse of Jesus' **I AM** self-disclosure in 12:26, "*where **AM I*** my agent also will be" echoes Isaiah's response to God's summons, after seeing a vision of God sitting on a throne, and subsequently being cleansed of his sin, 'Ιδού εἰμι ἐγώ, απόστειλόν με (See, **AM I**, send me).

[10] Philo, *de Opificio Mundi*, 139.

[11] *Ibid.*, 146.

In terms of their origin as a copy of the Logos, human beings who live in accordance with their identity as "Sons of God" will be disposed to think that moral beauty is the only good, so that, like veteran warriors, they erect counter-fortifications against pleasure as the goal of life.[12] On the other hand, as structures of physical bodies, they are related to the world and that requires world citizenship.

> [The good human being] is a world citizen, and therefore not enrolled in any of the cities of the inhabited world for he/she has received no allotment of land but has received the whole world (κόσμος) as a share.[13]

World citizenship, therefore, requires the practice of training in wisdom to cultivate courage, for, as Philo recognizes:

> ...there are many conditions in life admittedly hard to bear, poverty and disrepute and disablement and sickness in its manifold forms, in view of which those of small minds show weakness, unable to be raised from their cowardice. But those of intelligence and nobility staunchly strip for combat vigorously, zealously striving against the boastful promises and threats with all their strength.[14]

Human beings who as world citizens live in accordance with Logos will encounter misfortune, deprivation and disease, but Philo is convinced that "if the soul is healthy, the diseases of the body do very little harm."[15] Philo offers no evidence of a comprehension of the many forms of living death that are generated by the institutions of government and law, the exploitation of human labor, and the power structures of religion. His ideology of living and acting in submission to the Logos, whether in war or in peace, guarantees a spiritual health that overcomes the world.

> The soul that loves God, having disrobed itself of the body and the objects dear to the body and fled away from these, gains a fixed and assured settlement in the perfect ordinances of virtue.[16]

Reason must be in command, subjecting itself to the lessons and instructions of the Law. Despising the things of the body and pursuing a life of virtue and everything that is congruous with it is the only true goal of human existence.[17] Moreover, the Logos is concurrently active in human affairs pledging the Creator that "the creature should never altogether rebel against the rein and choose disorder rather

---

[12] Philo, *de Confusione Linguarum*, 145.

[13] Philo, *de Vita Mosis* I, 157.

[14] Philo, *de Virtutibus*, 5. In paragraph 6, Philo claims that "not a single one is in want, for his needs are supplied by the wealth of nature."

[15] *Ibid.*, 13.

[16] Philo, *de Specialibus Legibus* II, 55. See also II, 56 and III, 152 and 161.

[17] Philo, *de Virtutibus*, 8.

than order." The Logos is "the harbinger of peace to creation from that God whose will is to bring wars to an end, who is ever the guardian of peace."[18]

The Pharisaic Judaism that was being established in Alexandria would harbor little, if any, antipathy towards Philo's allegorical interpretation of the Septuagint Scriptures. Jacob Neusner's characterization of Yochanan ben Zakkai's courage after the destruction of Jerusalem would endorse a common bond, a kind of complementarity, between these two ideological perspectives.

> Here then were the sage's chief concerns: the humble daily life of this world with its laws and ethical demands, and the metaphysical realities beyond to be reached through mystical experience. The pious man must love his neighbor and cherish his honor, property and dignity. He must also seek a true perception of the Godhead in all the concrete imagery of the astral mysticism of the day.[19]

Both orientations, that of Philo and that of Pharisaic Judaism, exalt the Law and, without any prophetic perspective that is directed toward world transformation except the visions of the Prophet Ezekiel, they presuppose that the virtue that results from submission to the Law will generate the justice that will uphold the structures of society.

The public career that Jesus is concluding has been directed toward "saving the world," that is, transforming the social construction of reality so that the eyes of the blind will be opened, the crippled will keep on rising into the fullness of life, and human beings will be resurrected from the living death that they are suffering in the world. His anticipation of death and his invitation to the implied readers who are willing to hate their lives in this world, in this context of the closure of his ministry, arouse overpowering emotions similar to those he experienced when he was confronted more directly with the reality of Lazarus' death in 11:33.

> Now my *soul* (ψυχή) *has been agitated* (τεταράκται), and what should I say? Father save me from this hour! But on account of this I came into this hour. Father, glorify your name! (12:27-28a)

This, the second of three prayers that Jesus addresses to God, is spoken at the closure of his public ministry.[20] In this context of 12:27-28a, after expressing his dread of the ordeal that awaits him, Jesus shifts quickly into an acknowledgment of the ultimate objective of his coming and petitions God to glorify his name. It is a moment of immense irony! After a plea for deliverance, Jesus commands God to glorify himself through the death into which he, Jesus, will enter.

God responds to Jesus' ironic cry and speaks to him a word of reassurance, "I glorified, and I will glorify again." It is the first and only occurrence of God's self-disclosure through speech in the Gospel. In rabbinic Judaism it is called a *bath*

---

[18] Philo, *Quis Rerum Divinarum Heres*, 206.

[19] Jacob Neusner, *First Century Judaism in Crisis*, 133.

[20] The first was uttered in the context of the seventh and greatest sign, the resurrection of Lazarus. The third prayer, in 17:1-28, is enunciated immediately prior to the beginning of his Passion.

qôl, "an articulate and intelligible sound proceeding from an invisible source."[21] God's *bath qôl* is both an affirmation and a promise, acknowledging that all that God's name comprehends has been glorified during Jesus' ministry. Although nothing is specifically cited for support, the implied readers, in all likelihood, will infer that God's glorification has occurred through the fulfillment of God's will by the works of restoration and resurrection that Jesus has accomplished. God also warrants that God will continue to be glorified into the future, above all through Jesus' imminent death. How that will be actualized will not be disclosed until the narrator's account of Jesus' crucifixion has been told.[22]

The crowd has also heard the *bath qôl*, but the interpretations that are verbalized by its members "illustrate their remoteness from the event of revelation."[23] Some claim that it was thunder; others maintain, "An angel has spoken to him." Although God's *bath qôl* was an immediate reply to Jesus' prayer, Jesus responds to the deficient interpretations of the crowd by informing them that the voice "has happened not on my account but on your account." This reversal is unexpected, but the implied readers are confronted with the crowd's incomprehension of the message and the deplorable remoteness of its members from this revelation.[24] Jesus' employment of the perfect tense, γέγονεν (it has happened), would draw them into this moment of a divine disclosure and impress on them the necessity of being alert for the eventual actualization of God's glorification in Jesus' death.[25]

In the light of the crowd's failure to comprehend the message of the *bath qôl*, Jesus proceeds to pronounce judgment "on the ruler of this world" whose domination of the social construction of reality is the source of their deafness and blindness.

> Now is the judgment of this world! Now the ruler of this world will be cast out, and I, if I am lifted up (ὑψωθῶ) from the earth, I shall draw all towards (πρός) myself. (12:31-32)

---

[21] Moore, *Judaism* I, 422, notes occurrences of the *bath qôl* in Dan 4:28 and Matt 3:17. See also Matt 17:5; Mark 1:11, 9:7; and Luke 3:22, 9:35.

[22] Schnackenburg, *St. John* II, 388, looks beyond Jesus' crucifixion to the ascension when God reinstates the Son in heavenly glory and makes Jesus' death fruitful for the work of human beings. These realities are undoubtedly to be included, but God will already be glorified in Jesus' death. Brown, *John* I, 476-477, offers various alternatives. Barrett, *St. John*, 426, acknowledges an alternative interpretation: "the completion of Jesus' work in death." Strathmann, *Johannes*, 182, also acknowledges that God will be glorified through the death of Jesus.

[23] Barrett, *St. John*, 426, assumes that the crowd heard the speech but did not recognize its source, and, therefore, he does not understand how Jesus could say that the voice happened for their sake. The interpretation Schnackenburg offers, *St. John* II, 389, resolves that difficulty.

[24] Brown, *John* I, 477, and Strathmann, *Johannes*, 183, claim that 12:28-30 are not fully coordinated.

[25] Here is another instance in which the narrator's employment of the perfect tense, γέγονεν (it has happened), proved to be puzzling to ancient scribes. The aorist ἦλθεν (it came) has been substituted by P[66] and Codex D, but the perfect tense is the more difficult reading and can be explained, along with the many other uses of the perfect tense, as the effort of the implied author to extend the first level of the narrative world, the time of Jesus, into the time of the implied readers of the Alexandrian Jews.

Jesus has already announced, "The hour has come in order that the Son of the Human Being is glorified". Now, in view of his proximate experience of the darkness of the world (κόσμος) that is reflected in the inability of the crowd, his fellow Jews, to grasp the revelation of the *bath qôl*, he elucidates God's imminent glorification by relating the event of his being lifted up (ὑψωθῶ) in crucifixion in order to terminate the dominating power of "the ruler of this world." Here, for the first time, Jesus refers to this indeterminate being, "the ruler of this world." In his Farewell Discourse he will speak of this entity again. In 14:30 he will inform his disciples of its imminent arrival, "... for the ruler of the world is coming ..." and in 16:11 he will announce its impending judgment. It seems reasonable to associate both "Satan" and "the devil" with this unnamed reality in spite of the absence of this identification within the narrative world of the Gospel.[26] If, as the narrator states in 13:27, "Satan entered into Judas Iscariot," the reality that has become incarnate in Judas is the power of evil that Satan represents, the power of the totality of society's institutions that generate unclean spirits that take possession of human beings.[27] According to 13:2, it is this power that gains control of Judas, and therefore in 6:70 Jesus can proleptically refer to him as a "devil." Because of the power that the ruling elite wield in their control of society's institutions and their concomitant domination of the masses under their rule, Jesus can refer to them as the offspring of the devil (8:44).

The necessary relationship between death by crucifixion and the ejection of "the ruler of this world" that is intimated by 13:31 is corroborated by Jesus' earlier declaration of 3:14, "And even as Moses lifted up (ὕψωσεν) the snake in the wilderness, so it is necessary that the Son of the Human being be lifted up (ὑψωθῆναι)..."[28] "Being lifted up" does not refer to Jesus' exaltation by his ascent and return to the "Father." It is his coronation and exaltation on the cross. For the benefit of the implied readers, the narrator inserts an intrusive remark at 12:33, 'Now this he was saying signifying by what death he was going to die."[29]

In response to Jesus' expectation of "being lifted up," the crowd acknowledges that "they heard from the Law" that the Christ remains into the age – forever! Although they may not apprehend the double-edged meaning of "being lifted up,"

[26] "Satan" occurs only in 13:27 and "the devil" in 6:70, 8:44 and 13:2.

[27] If the "giants" of 1 Enoch 7:2-6 are identifiable as systemic structures and institutions, and if, according to 1 Enoch 15:8-12, they generate evil spirits; the reality of evil is personifiable in mythical figures like "Satan" or "the devil". See Paul W. Hollenbach, "Jesus, Demoniacs, and Public Authorities: A Socio-Historical Study," *JAAR* 49/4 (1981), 567-588.

[28] See Judith L. Kovacs, "'Now Shall the Ruler of This World Be Driven Out': Jesus' Death as Cosmic Battle in John 12:20-36," *JBL* 114/2 (1995) 227-247. Kovacs makes this same connection between 12:31 and 3:14, as well as other verses in order to establish the relationship between Jesus' death and the ejection of "the ruler of this world". But the language game of the Fourth Gospel is derived from Wisdom tradition and not Jewish apocalypticism and its mythology of the Divine Warrior, as she contends in pp. 236-246. Schnackenburg, *St. John* II, 392, does not exclude the possibility of such mythological conceptions.

[29] In view of the narrator's aside, it is difficult how Schnackenburg, *ibid.* II, 393, can connect the "being lifted up" with the ascent of "the Son of the Human Being."

they appear to perceive one side of its significance as an intimation of death, for they proceed to introduce their own concept of "the Christ," as a figure who rules forever. But why the Christ? Have they moved beyond their earlier uncertainty about Jesus and now regard him to be the Christ? What is the author's motive behind this misunderstanding, perhaps the most critical misunderstanding in the Gospel?[30] To the crowd, at least, Jesus' words, "being lifted up from the earth" do not correspond to their preconceptions of the Christ, and therefore they inquire:

> How do you say that it is necessary that *the Son of the Human Being* (ὁ υἱὸς τοῦ ἀνθρώπου) is to be lifted up? Who is this Son of the Human Being? (12:34b)

But Jesus has not employed this figure of *the Son of the Human Being* (ὁ υἱὸς τοῦ ἀνθρώπου) in his disclosure of being lifted up from the earth. At least not here! Jesus used the phrase in his response to Andrew and Philip in 12:23, but there was no indication in that context that the crowd was present to overhear it. Why then this sudden, unexpected reference to ὁ υἱὸς τοῦ ἀνθρώπου? Is the crowd's inquiry to be construed as a rhetorical device of misunderstanding in order to confront the implied readers with that very question? Are they being challenged at the conclusion of Jesus' ministry to determine the relationship between the Christ who remains forever and the Son of the Human Being who will be lifted up and draw all towards himself?

Here it is more evident than elsewhere that the Gospel presupposes readers who are expected to engage in "consistency building" in their interaction with the forward-moving narrative of the Gospel. The narrator assumes that the implied readers will have remembered the two christological titles that emerged at the beginning of the Gospel but appear to have no historical relation to each other: the Christ or Messiah appellation from its earliest manifestation in Isa 9:6 and 11: 1-10 and "a son of a human being" of Dan 7:13-14.[31] At this midpoint in the narrative world of the Gospel, before Jesus enters into his passion, it is vital that the implied readers remember the problem of the relationship between these two christological-eschatological designations and remain alert to their eventual coalescence when Jesus is lifted up from the earth in crucifixion.[32]

Jesus responds by ignoring the crowd's question and issuing instead an existential exhortation to them – and to the implied readers:

---

[30] See Culpepper, *Anatomy*, 163, who attributes the misunderstanding of the crowd to their inability to understand Jesus' death. Attendantly, however, there is also a misunderstanding about the interconnection between "the Christ," who remains forever, and "the Son of the Human Being" who will be "lifted up."

[31] In 1:41 Andrew evangelizes his brother Simon by acknowledging Jesus to be the "Messiah" or "Christ," apparently inferring it from John's witness, "Behold the Lamb of God." Jesus, however, consistently employs the title, "the Son of the Human Being" in 1:51, 3:13-14." There are no historical correlations between these christological trajectories, yet they will be integrated at the culmination of the Gospel.

[32] See chapter 17.

> Still a little while the light is *among you* (ἐν ὑμῖν). Walk as you have light so that the darkness does not overtake you. The one who walks in the darkness does not know where he/she is going. As you have the light, believe into the light so that you become sons and daughters of light. (12:35-36)

It is an appropriate charge to the implied readers, for, in view of Jesus' closure of his ministry and his imminent entry into his passion, the critical issue is the fleeting presence of the Light. Jesus, the Light of the world, is about to enter into the darkness of his Passion. The charge that he gives his audience, therefore, befits this crisis: "Walk in the light so that the darkness does not overtake you." They are not to be overcome by the darkness of the passion that he will suffer. They can avoid being overtaken by the darkness by believing into the Light. Indeed, by making a commitment to the Light, they will grow into the Light; and as the Light and its truth intensifies within them, they will become daughters and sons of the Light. Consequently, they will also be enabled to see the relationship between Jesus as the Christ and Jesus as "the Son of the Human Being." His going away, first into death and resurrection and subsequently into ascension, necessitates the continuation of the presence of Light in the world. Accordingly, the commitment of the disciples – and the implied readers – will enable them to continue the work that Jesus has inaugurated by becoming – like him! – the Light of the world.

An assessment of Jesus' ministry 12:37-50

With these words Jesus closes his public discourse and departs into seclusion for a second time. His ministry to his fellow Jews has ended, and he is troubled by the truancy of their response. They have witnessed the signs that he has done before them, but "they were not believing into him." Here is another use of the imperfect tense that conveys a continuing action in the past and therefore refers to the time of Jesus' ministry and not the circumstances within the Jewish community of Alexandria.[33] Jesus' contemporaries have refused to commit themselves to the truth that he has been disclosing to them through his deeds and his words as the incarnate Logos-Sophia. In view of the failure that he has continued to experience, the narrator intervenes to confront the implied readers with the deplorable fulfillment of Isaiah's word. How will they view this depressing reality?

> Lord, who believed our report? And to whom is the arm of the Lord revealed?

To answer these interrogative quotations, the narrator proceeds to cite another text from Isaiah in order to explain why "they were unable to believe."

---

[33] Although P^{66} f^{13} and a few other manuscripts attest to the aorist tense of the verb, ἐπίστευσαν (they believed), the imperfect tense, ἐπίστευον (they were believing) probably is the more difficult reading.

> He has blinded their eyes and dulled their heart so that they might not see with the eyes and understand with the heart and turn, and I would heal them.[34]

Ironically, in spite of the possibilities of seeing – as well as hearing – that the incarnation of the Logos-Sophia actualizes, they have not seen. But their failure to see and apprehend should not be attributed to God's direct intervention. This blindness, accompanied by a hardening of the heart, should not be interpreted as a God-inflicted necessity.[35] It is rather a manifestation of the wrath of God that is at work in historical existence. God is not the originator of this disastrous condition. It is initiated within society, usually by the dominators, the ruling elite, who constitute an ideology, *a world* (κόσμος) like that which is reflected in the narrative world of the Gospel, that engenders the epidemic conditions of blindness, crippledness and living death. This self-destructing, cause-and-effect syndrome is a form of divine retribution, and God delivers such a dehumanizing and dehumanized society to the consequences of its own deeds.

This stark characterization of God's wrath that would serve as an admonition to the implied readers of Alexandria is followed by a startling pronouncement, "Isaiah said these things because *he saw* (εἶδεν) his glory, and he spoke about him." Isaiah envisioned Jesus' glory! A stunning disclosure to the implied readers! In view of the narrator's witness to the unbelief that Jesus encountered during his ministry, what will be their response to Isaiah's farsighted revelation?

But when did the prophet *see* the glory that Jesus has manifested in his ministry, and where did he speak about him? The only possible context is Isa 6. Yet nothing that is written in the Masoretic text of Isa 6 or in its Septuagint translation indicates that Isaiah viewed God's glory. Both of these versions state that he saw "the Lord seated on a throne, exalted and magnified, and the house full of his glory." This enunciation, however, contradicts John 1:18, "God no one has ever seen." By accentuating the radical transcendence of God, the Fourth Gospel accommodates the orientation of intertestamental Judaism as it simultaneously bears witness to the incarnation of the Logos-Sophia and attendantly, therefore, to the empirical manifestation of the glory of God.

On what basis, then, can the narrator claim that Isaiah "saw his glory and spoke about him"? The only source from which this remarkable disclosure could be drawn is the *Targum of Isaiah* 6:1.[36]

---

[34] This text is not a direct quotation of the Septuagint translation of Isa 6:9-10 but the author's deliberate revision in order to accommodate Isaiah's characterization of the condition of the people of Israel to the Gospel's emphasis on the priority of sight as a result of the objectification of the Logos-Sophia. This includes, as Schnackenburg, *St. John* II, 415, has observed, the significance of the story of the man born blind, whose eyes Jesus opens in chapter 9.

[35] The English translation of Bultmann, *John*, 452, reads, "a necessity ordained of God". The German, 346, "gottverhängte Notwendigkeit" or "God-inflicted necessity" is scarcely more intelligible. Is God the immediate originator of this condition?

[36] Here is further evidence, in addition to the Samaritan woman's reference to Jacob's mighty works in 4:12, that the Targums were accessible to the Evangelist, and that he made use of them. Also

> In the year that Uzziah was struck with it [leprosy], the prophet said, 'I saw the glory of the Lord resting upon the throne, high and lifted up in the heavens of the height, and the temple was filled by the brilliance of his glory.[37]

According to verses 5-6 of the Targum, Isaiah goes on to say:

> And I said, 'Woe is me! For I have sinned; for I am a man liable to chastisement, and I dwell in the midst of people that are defiled with sins; for my eyes have seen the glory of the Shekhinah of the eternal king, the LORD of hosts! Then there was given to me one of the attendants and in his mouth there was a speech which he took before him whose Shekhinah is upon the throne of glory in the heavens of the height, above the altar.[38]

Previously the Shekhinah had resided in the sanctuary of the Jerusalem Temple, but prior to Isaiah's vision, God had declared in the Targum of Isa 5: 5, "I will take up my Shekhinah from them." As the result of its removal from the Jerusalem Temple, Isaiah can see the Shekhinah located in the transcendence of "the heavens of the height" and enthroned in the glory of God's heavenly sanctuary. If, then, the narrator enunciates that Isaiah "saw his glory and spoke about him," it must be inferred that God's Shekhinah is identifiable with Jesus as he has been disclosed in the narrative world of the Gospel. For it is only on the basis of this correspondence that the narrator is able to assert that Isaiah spoke about Jesus. The Shekhinah has returned to earth and is incarnate in Jesus of Nazareth! The coincidence is consummate because Jesus, having replaced the stone building of the Jerusalem sanctuary with his own body, has become the living Temple of God on earth, and throughout his ministry he has been showing forth the glory of God, and he will continue to manifest it during his crucifixion.

However, in spite of Isaiah's foreboding of the failure of Jesus' ministry, the narrator reports a moderate success among "the rulers."

> Yet actually many also among the rulers believed into him. (12:42)

But this is a reference to the second level of the narrative world of the Gospel, that is, the circumstances of the implied readers of the Jewish community of Alexandria. Many among the ruling elite did commit themselves to him. Yet, "on account of the Pharisees they were not confessing so that they would not become synagogue-less (ἀποσυνάγωγοι)." They have believed into him, but lamentably – in contrast to the male of 9:34 whose eyes Jesus opened – they are ambivalent about disclosing their commitment externally in words and deeds. The narrator

---

Brown, *John* I, 486-487, and I, 90, 322, on the basis of 1:18a, 51; 6:46 and 12:41. Barrett, *St. John*, 432, who poses the possibility of "some such version" but rejects the possibility "that it was the reference to the *shekinah* of God that made him say that Isaiah saw the glory of *Christ* and spoke of him." Schnackenburg, *St. John* II, 416-417, considers the narrator's identification of Jesus with the glory that Isaiah saw as "a natural development of his Logos Christology."

[37] *The Isaiah Targum: Introduction, Translation, Apparatus and Notes. The Aramaic Bible*, vol. 11, by Bruce D. Chilton (Collegeville, Minnesota, Liturgical Press, 1990) 14.

[38] *Ibid.*

voices his own judgment as an aside, "For they loved the glory of human beings more than the glory of God." If Isaiah, in his vision of God's glory, already foresaw the glory that Jesus would manifest as God's apprentice throughout his ministry, these members of the ruling authorities are denying their call to give evidence of their commitment by participating with Jesus in the transformation of the social construction of reality. To the extent they continue to divorce their commission from their commitment they are contributing to the blindness, crippledness and living death of those they govern and concomitantly to the relentless cause-and-effect syndrome of divine retribution.

For a third time in the narrative world of the Gospel Jesus cries out with a loud voice in order to gain a hearing of his response to the circumstances of the immediate context. In 7:28 he challenged the Jerusalemites' dismissal of him as the Christ on the grounds that they know him as the "son of Joseph" and his place of origin as "Nazareth." In 7:37 he uttered a cry of invitation on the last day of the Feast of Booths summoning all who thirst to believe into him so that by their commitment to him as members of the living Temple of God they will become channels of living water that gives life to the world.

In this context, at the close of his public ministry, his resonating communication is addressed to the implied readers who include members of the ruling elite of the Jewish community in Alexandria. Like their counterparts during the ministry of Jesus, they are concealing their discipleship by limiting their commitment to a private faith. It is vital that they are aware of the implications of the commitment they have made by believing into Jesus.

Their commitment to him is nothing less than a commitment to God. Their beholding him (θεωρῶν) is nothing less than beholding God (θεωρεῖ) and therefore an abandonment of themselves to God on the basis of what they have experienced. Jesus has come into the world as "Light," the Light of the first day of creation, the Light of truth, and, therefore, those who believe into him will not remain in the darkness that is perpetuated in and by the social construction of reality, the world. As he promised in 12:36, by believing into the Light, they will become sons and daughters of the Light. They will know the truth and the truth will make them free.

On the other hand, those who hear Jesus' words (ῥήματα) but do not safe-guard them by committing themselves to him will not be judged by him. In an echo of 3:17 he declares that he came to save the world, not to judge it. Nevertheless, God has given him authority to do judgment (5:22, 27), and if he judges, his judgment is valid because he is God's apprentice (8:16). Moreover, as he asserts in 8:26, "I have many things to say about you and to judge, but the One who sent me is true, and the things I heard from him, these things I speak into the world." In these earlier utterances Jesus is referring to the divine authority he has received to censure and rebuke as well as to make perspicacious determinations and forensic verdicts of the social construction of reality and the authorities who engage in "world maintenance". But there will also be a final judgment that will take place at the consummation of history.[39] The Word (ὁ λόγος) that he has spoken, as the incarnate Logos-Sophia, will judge those who reject him and do not receive his words. For, as Jesus, in retrospect, affirms once more, "I did not speak from myself, but the Father who sent me has given me a commandment what I should say and what I should speak."

By these concluding words of warning Jesus is inducing the implied readers to remember two corresponding texts, texts that correspond to Philip's witness to Nathanael, "We have found the one Moses wrote about in the Law and the prophets [wrote about]." The Septuagint of Deut 18:18-19 and Isa 59:21 forth-tells the divine origin of the words that the successor of Moses and Isaiah as God's voice will speak.

> A prophet I shall raise up for them among their own people, like you, and I shall give my word (ῥῆμα) in his mouth, and he will speak them even as I commanded him, and the human being who does not hear whatever such things the prophet speaks in my name, I shall punish. (Deut 18:18-19)
>
> My Spirit, which is upon you, and my words (ῥήματα) which I gave into your mouth will by no means fail from your mouth … (Isa 59:21)

Jesus is God's apprentice, and in the role of the prophet like Moses, he has spoken the words that God commanded him to speak. He is God's apprentice, and in the role of Isaiah as God's mouthpiece – but the one upon whom the Spirit remains (1:33)! – he has spoken the words that God put into his mouth. In contrast to these representatives of the Law and the Prophets, however, the words that he speaks at the command of "the Father" communicate everlasting life. "*Therefore*," once more as a reminder and as a final warning to the implied readers, Jesus enunciates, "the things that I speak, even as the Father has told me, so I speak." With this final pronouncement the narration of his public career comes to an end.[40]

---

[39] Barrett, *St. John*, 434, does not make this differentiation. Schnackenburg, *St. John* II, 424, considers Jesus' not judging and yet judging to be a dialectic because Jesus judges only according to what he has heard from "the Father." But there is judging that Jesus does throughout his ministry and there is the judging that will occur "at the last day."

[40] There seems to be a consensus that 12:50 marks the end of the first part of the Fourth Gospel. Bultmann, *John*, 419, says, "It ought to be clear that the retrospect on the public ministry of Jesus in 12:37-43 must originally have formed the conclusion of the whole first half of the Gospel." German, 321.

Chapter Fourteen

The Aporetic Christology of the Fourth Gospel

Incarnation and the descent of the Spirit at Jesus' baptism

According to the monumental witness of John, the Logos-Sophia has been enfleshed in the person of Jesus Christ, and God's Spirit has descended and remained on him. The conjunction of this epochal event occurred at Jesus' baptism by John outside of and prior to the narrative world of the Gospel, as John himself intimates in 1:31-33. It must have happened quietly and unobtrusively, for only John was aware of it; and he had been alerted to it earlier in a private revelation from God.

> And I did not know him, but the One sending me to baptize in water, that one said to me, "Upon whom you see (ἴδῃς) the Spirit descending and remaining on him, this is the one baptizing in the holy Spirit." (1:33)

> And John testified saying, "I have ascertained (τεθέαμαι) the Spirit descending like a dove from heaven and remaining on him." (1:32)

As the result of "the Spirit descending and remaining on him," Jesus becomes the dwelling place of God's Spirit. Philo would acknowledge the first of these two events, "the Spirit descending" upon Jesus. But Philo's anthropological dualism necessitates a repudiation of the second reality: "the Spirit remaining" on Jesus. In his treatise, "On the Unchangeableness of God," he states:

> It has been said before concerning the divine Spirit that the trouble of the things of the flesh make it a heavier burden and harder [for it] to remain forever in a fractured and manifold soul.[1]

> Wherefore the divine Spirit is able to remain (μένειν) in the soul, but it is unable to remain continually (διαμένειν).[2]

This temporal duration of God's Spirit within the human being is predetermined by Philo's dualistic differentiation between two minds. On the one hand, "the mind that was made after the image and archetype," the Logos, alone partakes of the divine Spirit (πνεῦμα θεοῦ).[3] Philo reinforces this in *Legum Allegoria* I, 29, "... so the mind is the sovereign of the soul: to this only God inbreathes." On the other hand, "...the mind that was made out of matter must be said to partake of

---

[1] Philo, *Quod Deus Immutabilis,* 2.

[2] *de Gigantibus*, 28.

[3] *Legum Allegoria* I, 42.

unsubstantial and lighter air."[4] "The formation of the human being, the object of sense, is a composite made up of earthly substance and of divine breath."[5]

The Fourth Gospel, among its various objectives, is directed towards subverting Philo's anthropological dualism. There is no antithesis between soul and body or between the mind made according to the image of the Logos and the mind made from matter. The word ψυχή (soul) occurs ten times, and, like the Septuagintal translation of the Hebrew נֶפֶשׁ, it denotes the total human being in the existential craving for the life that God gives and attendantly, therefore, the human being striving for possibility, freedom and life.[6] A significant instance is encountered in 12:25, "The one who loves his/her ψυχή (soul/life) destroys it, and the one hating his/her ψυχή (soul/life) in this world will safe-guard it into life everlasting." Jesus is not censuring that part of the soul that is inbreathed by air (πνοή) and therefore is oriented to the material world and its physical pleasures, while at the same time he is sanctioning that constituent of the soul that is inbreathed by God's Spirit and disrobes itself of the body in order to gain virtue. Those who love their soul/life direct themselves to possibility and freedom at the expense of their fellow human beings. Those who hate their soul/life in this world (κόσμος) are very aware that the world they live in is a realm of living death for countless human beings, and consequently their pursuit of life is determined by their commitment to justice and reconciliation.[7] This is the very same commitment that Jesus embraces as "the Bread that descended from heaven" or as the Son of the Human Being who gives his flesh and blood for the life of the world.[8] There is no mind/body or soul/flesh dichotomy that is discernible in his Jewish perspective within the narrative world of the Gospel.[9] Although the context of the narrative world is dualistic in the differentiation between "this world," the κόσμος, and the world that is being saved by its incorporation into the eschatological reality of "the reign of God" (ἡ βασιλεία τοῦ θεοῦ), the anthropological, christological, and the sociological orientation of the Evangelist, as it is expressed in the ministry of Jesus is aporetic.[10]

[4] *Ibid.*

[5] *de Opificio Mundi*, 135.

[6] Wolff, *Anthropology*, 10-25. Also Edmond Jacob, "ψυχή," *TWNT* IX, 614-629; *TDNT* IX, 617-631.

[7] Rensberger develops this orientation in chapters 4-6 in *Johannine Faith and Liberating Community*.

[8] John 6:33-58. See chapter 9.

[9] Bultmann, *John*, 9, is grossly mistaken in contending that "John is directly dependent on Gnostic traditions, and he uses these traditions in far greater measure than Philo and the other late Jewish writers."

[10] It is the aporiai of the human condition that determines the Gospel's presentation of the incarnation of the Logos in ministry of Jesus, particularly the aporia of spirit and matter, or the aporia of soul and flesh. The tension between these binary oppositions cannot be dissolved into a dualism without destroying the integrity of the Gospel's theology. On the "aporia of spirit and matter," see McGaughey, *Strangers and Pilgrims*, 213-240. Contrary to Bultmann, ibid., 9, there is no "Entscheidungsdualismus," a dualism of decision or an ethical dualism in Jesus' call to be "born from above." That is a mistaken interpretation of the Gospel that imposes the dualistic context of the

Accordingly, if John's vision of "the Spirit descending and remaining on him," is true, the Gospel's presentation of Jesus of Nazareth and its attendant development of christology cannot be construed in terms of Philo's Platonic dualism or a possible contemporaneous Gnosticism.[11]

There is a correspondence between the two apparently disconnected originations that are ascribed to Jesus by John's witness at the very beginning of the Gospel: the enfleshment of the Logos-Sophia (1:14-17) and the Spirit "descending and remaining on him." Ironically, it is Philo's interpretation of Gen 2:7, but divorced from his Platonic dualism, that establishes the aporetic conjunction of these two events at Jesus' baptism by John.

In his treatise, "On the Creation," Philo combines the employment of the Logos as the archetype of the human being with the divine act of inbreathing:

> Now with respect to the soul (ψυχήν) it is manifest that he was the best, for God employed no other pattern of the things in creation towards its construction but only, as I said, his own Logos. Wherefore he [Moses] says that the human being, imaged and having been made a likeness of that one [Logos], was inbreathed into his face.[12]

His construction of Gen 2:7 in "Noah's Work as a Planter" is almost identical, but the image of the Logos that is stamped upon the human being is communicated coincidentally with God's inbreathing:

> Now our great Moses compared the form of the reasonable soul (ψυχῆς) to nothing of the things having been made, but he said it to be a genuine coin of that divine and invisible Spirit signed and impressed by the seal of God, the stamp of which is the eternal Logos. For he says, "God breathed into his face the breath of life" (πνοὴν ζωῆς), so that, as a necessity, the one receiving is to be imaged towards the one sending. Wherefore it is also said that the human being has been made according to the image of God and not according to the image of the things created.[13]

---

narrative world upon Jesus and therefore also upon the Evangelist. The same mistaken projection of dualism is encountered in Brown, Schnackenburg, Schottroff, Käsemann, Ashton, and others. See especially the concluding reflections of Schottroff, *Der Glaubende und die feindliche Welt*, 289-296.

[11] For example, Bultmann's christological interpretation of Jesus as 'the Revealer". See especially his *Theology of the New Testament* (New York: Scribner's Sons, 1955) II, 3-92. Jesus is not merely a "Revealer," and his work cannot simply be limited to "a revelation of divine glory." As he continually emphasizes in his encounters with the ruling elite, "The works that I do in the name of my Father, these testify about me." They bear witness to a turning of the ages and the emergence of an aporetically oriented New Humanity pioneered by Jesus. Compare with Nils Alstrup Dahl, "The Johannine Church and History," *Current Issues in New Testament Interpretation: Essays in Honor of Otto A. Piper*, ed. by William Klassen and Graydon F. Snyder (New York: Harper & Brothers, 1962) 124-142.

[12] *de Opificio Mundi*, 139.

[13] *de Plantatione*, 18-19. By concentrating on the soul in this interpretation of Gen 2:7, Philo ignores the Septuagint reading, "... ἐνεφύσησεν εἰς τὸ πρόσωπον αὐτοῦ πνοὴν ζωῆς (he [God] inbreathed into his face the breath of life) and appears to view the creation of the human being according to the archetypal Logos. However, in his treatise, "On Noah's Work as a Planter," he reverts to the Septuagintal reading of Gen 2:7 and employs the phrase πνοὴν ζωῆς.

This conjunction of the incarnation of the Logos-Sophia and God's Spirit descending and remaining on Jesus occurred at his baptism by John, for the event of "being born of water and the Spirit is to be construed as being "generated from above" and therefore a rebirth. Jesus, therefore, "impressed by the seal of God, the stamp of which is the eternal Logos, and inbreathed by God's Spirit, is, as the adjective, μονογενῆς, in 1:14 denotes, the "one and only" or the "only one of its kind." Μονογενῆς, is used again in 1:18 where it refers directly back to the Logos of 1:1, but stipulating more dramatically the union of the Logos "into the bosom of the Father," and defining its activity as that of an interpreter. According to 3:16, Jesus is the "one and only Son"; in 3:18 he is enunciated to be "the only one of a kind Son of God." As such he is the εἶδος (form, pattern) of the human being that God conceived before creation, the human being who reflects the image and likeness of God and, therefore, who is "the Son of God." Both of these christological phrases, "one and only Son" and "the only one of a kind Son of God," characterize his uniqueness and authenticate the self-understanding that he expresses to the authorities in 8:23, "**I** from above **AM** (ἐγὼ ἐκ τῶν ἄνω εἰμί) … **I** not **AM** from this world (ἐγὼ οὐκ εἰμὶ ἐκ τοῦ κόσμου τούτου).

As peerlessly distinguished as Jesus is represented in the Fourth Gospel, he nevertheless attributes the same origin to his disciples that he embraces for himself.[14] In his Prayer of Consecration he acknowledges:

> … for they are not *from the world* (ἐκ τοῦ κόσμου) even as ***I not AM from this world*** (ἐγὼ οὐκ εἰμὶ ἐκ τοῦ κόσμου τούτου). I do not ask that you remove them from the world but that you preserve them from the Wicked One. They are not *from the world* (ἐκ τοῦ κόσμου) even as ***I not AM from this world*** (ἐγὼ οὐκ εἰμὶ ἐκ τοῦ κόσμου τούτου).

[14] Contrary to W. A. Meeks, "The Man from Heaven in Johannine Sectarianism," 44, who claims that in the Fourth Gospel "there is no such *analogia entis* between redeemer and redeemed." His essay also appears in *The Interpretation of John*, ed. by John Ashton (Philadelphia: Fortress Press, 1986) 141-142.

Evidently his disciples also have been born from above, although their "being born of water and the Spirit" in baptism is not reported. The same birth is assumed of many of the implied readers who are inhabiting the narrative world of the Gospel. The same conjunction of the incarnation of the Logos-Sophia and the descending and remaining Spirit of God must be attributed to the event of their regeneration. They are qualified, therefore, to be united with Jesus in his peerless distinction as "the only one of a kind Son of God" (3:18). This epithet, like the designation "son of God" in the Old Testament, refers to individuals as well as communities. The king of Israel is named God's son in Psa 2:7, but in Hos 11:1 "my son" designates God's people Israel. God's daughters, "Virgin Israel" and "the Daughter of Zion," are representative of the faithful among God's people. Rachel is the personification of the motherhood of Israel in Jer 31:15. These singular representations of God's elect lend support to the likelihood that the title, "the Son of God," is to be construed corporately, as well as individually, as God's offspring.

It is consequential that only the implied readers, who inhabit the narrative world of the Gospel are aware of John's witness and, according to their familiarity with the philosophical theology of Philo, are confronted with this conjunction of the incarnation of the Logos-Sophia and the descending and remaining of the Spirit on Jesus at his baptism. Only they, as they continue to interact with the narrative, are aware of the significance that this determination conveys for the comprehension of the Gospel's development of the christological interpretation of Jesus and, as they will eventually experience, their own participation in it.

The appearance of the newcomer Jesus 1:29-51

Jesus' entry into the narrative world is quiet and unobtrusive. He steps out of the shadows of Jewish society unexpectedly as a stranger. There has been no previous activity that would publicize his presence. His obscure origin and his shrouded life up to the moment of his presentation to Israel may be intended to correspond to the concealment of "that Son of Man" until the eschatological time of his disclosure,[15] or, perhaps, to the hidden origin of the Messiah prior to his public appearance.[16] Noteworthy in this respect is the postulate that is voiced by the Jerusalemites in their mutual exchange in 7:27, "But the Christ, when he comes, no one will know where he is from." Jesus accentuates this tenet in his self-disclosure to the Pharisees in 8:14, "I know where I came from and where I am going to, but you do not know where I come from and where I am going to." Earlier he had attributed the origination of this self-understanding to the holy Spirit:

[15] See 1 Enoch 48:6.

[16] Justin Martyr, *Trypho* viii,4. John Ashton, *Understanding the Fourth Gospel*, 305, also refers to Justin's *Dialogue with Trypho*, citing the words that are attributed to Trypho: "Even if the Messiah is already born and in existence somewhere, he is nevertheless unknown …"

> The Spirit blows where it wills, and you hear its sound; but you do not know where it comes from and where it goes to. So is everyone who is generated from the Spirit. (3:8)

Emerging into the narrative world as a stranger, Jesus is introduced to his contemporaries – and to the implied readers – by his precursor John in terms of a clashing variety of identifications. He is "the Lamb of God who removes the sin of the world." He is paradoxically John's successor and predecessor, and because he is also his predecessor as the incarnate Logos-Sophia, he is designated as "my First." He is "the one who baptizes with [the] holy Spirit," and he is "the Son of God." These appellatives bear the weight of divine authority in as far as they are articulated by John who was appointed to serve as God's mouthpiece in identifying and presenting the incarnate Logos and the perpetual bearer of God's Spirit to Israel – and to the implied readers.

In quick succession, however, another set of identifications emerges, acclaimed by those who become Jesus' disciples. The first two seem to be attracted to Jesus on the basis of John's identification, "the Lamb of God." Ironically, one of them, Andrew, appears to have concluded from this designation that Jesus is the Messiah, and he proceeds to make the claim to his brother Simon, "We have found the Messiah." Like other interlocutors in the Gospel, he serves as the spokesperson of two titles that have no historical or political relationship to each other. But the significance of their coincidence will eventually emerge in profound irony when Jesus is enthroned on the cross as "the King of the Jews" and dies on the Day of the Preparation of the Passover as "the Lamb of God that removes the sin of the world."

Philip, whom Jesus himself calls into discipleship, gives notice of fulfillment in his witness to Nathanael, "The one whom Moses in the law and [the one whom] the prophets wrote about we have found, Jesus son of Joseph from Nazareth."[17] No christological identification is drawn from tradition. Jesus is simply acknowledged to be the fulfillment of the entire Hebrew Scriptures, but specifically in relation to his human origin: "son of Joseph from Nazareth." The Jewish authorities will cite this identity in their reaction to Jesus' self-identification as "the bread that descended from heaven," in 6:42.

> Is this not Jesus, the son of Joseph? Don't we know his father and his mother? How does he now say, "I have descended from heaven?"

Jesus himself will allude to this identity in 7:28 when he tells the Jerusalemites, "You know me and you know where I am from."[18] John had designated him "the

[17] Contrary to Moloney, *Belief*, 17, Philip is not lying when he exclaims, "We have found..." the one who fulfills the Law and the Prophets. Even though he was found by Jesus, he in his enthusiasm is expressing the conviction he has heard and now supports.

[18] An interesting parallel is offered by Justin Martyr, *Apology* I, 29, who comments on Hadrian's lover, Antinous, whom Hadrian himself elevated to Godhood and worshiped, "And it is not out of place, we think, to mention here Antinous, who was alive lately, and whom all were coerced to worship as a god through fear, though *they knew both who he was and what was his origin*." My thanks to

Son of God." Philip identifies him as "the son of Joseph from Nazareth." Yet another paradox of Jesus' identity is placed before the implied readers as Jesus enters into his ministry.

These designations stand in contrast to those verbalized by John and reflect an effort to identify Jesus in terms of biblical antecedents and typologies. There is naturally no awareness among the disciples what the implied readers have learned from John, namely that Jesus is the union of the incarnate Logos-Sophia and the one on whom the Spirit descended and remained. These disciples, who inhabit the narrative world of the Fourth Gospel, know nothing about that conjunction. At the same time the implied readers learn for the first time that Jesus is "the son of Joseph out of Nazareth." As the offspring of Joseph, he is not only a Jew; he is completely and fully a human being, and this is a datum that must be carried forward in order to comprehend the rapidly emerging, aporetic character of Jesus' identity.[19]

What christological designation Philip is ascribing to Jesus as the fulfillment of the Law and the Prophets is not indicated. Whatever it may be, Nathanael refuses to acknowledge that there could be any kind of christological congruence between this "Jesus, son of Joseph from Nazareth" and the Hebrew Scriptures. No Nazareth origin is anticipated by any kind of messianic typology.

Undisturbed by this inconsistency Philip simply extends to Nathanael essentially the same invitation Jesus issued earlier to John's followers, "Keep on coming and see!" In spite of any misgivings Nathanael might have, he at least appears to be open to seeing for himself. Naturally this would be an encouragement to the implied readers who might share his doubts. For if Nathanael's perspective is comparable to that of the implied readers, that is, a Jew who is familiar with the Scriptures and its messianic typologies, the objective of this exhortation, like that of Jesus, appropriately coincides with the general orientation of this Gospel that is determined by the objectification of the Logos-Sophia. If the Logos happened flesh, then it must be apprehended empirically. It must be seeable as well as hearable.[20]

Nathanael heeds Philip's invitation; he comes in order to see. Jesus, however, is already aware of him as he approaches and exclaims, "Look, truly an Israelite in whom there is no guile!" His seeing, whether purely empirical or an insight engendered by the perspicacity of the soul, appears to be a penetrating discernment that enables him to perceive Nathanael's integrity as a member of God's chosen

---

Cornelia Cyss Crocker for calling my attention to this text. See *The Ante-Nicene Fathers*, ed. by Alexander Roberts and James Donaldson (Grand Rapids: Eerdmans, 1956) I, 172.

[19] Contrary to Moloney, *Belief*, 71, who says that Nathanael, like the other disciples, is mistaken about Jesus' origin out of Nazareth. But there is no mistake about this! These disciples are the narrator's spokespersons for Jesus' earthly origins. See Thomas Söding, "'Was kann aus Nazareth schon Gutes kommen?' (Joh 1.46). Die Bedeutung des Judeseins Jesu im Johannesevangelium," *NTS* 46/1 (2000) 21-41.

[20] See Philo's evaluation of seeing versus hearing, *de Abrahamo* 150, 153-159 and 164.

people.[21] This quality of direct perception, of keen insight into human personality, will manifest itself again.[22] In an intrusive remark, a little later, the narrator will comment on his intuitive knowledge of human character:

> Jesus himself did not entrust himself to them (the Jerusalemites) because he knew all things and had no need that any testify about the human being, for he himself knew what was in the human being. (2:24-25)

It is with this same insightfulness that Jesus views Nathanael and demonstrates his capacity to look into human hearts. It is noteworthy that Jesus characterizes Nathanael as a guileless "Israelite." As the only use of this appellation in the Gospel, it stands in contrast to the regularly employed denomination, "the Jews." The designation "Israelite" can hardly be coincidental, for, in view of Jesus' subsequent promise to Nathanael, "You will *see* the heaven opened..." it corresponds to Philo's interpretation of "Israel" as "one who *sees* God."[23]

Amazed at being recognized, Nathanael asks, "From where do you know me?" Jesus surprises him again with the disclosure, "Before Philip called you, while you were under the fig tree, I saw you." Ostensibly it would seem that Jesus' penetrating seeing is able to gauge character even at a distance. But to what extent did his "being under the fig tree" determine Jesus' awareness and scrutiny of his person? Does the fig tree have any symbolic significance that is linked to Jesus' characterization of Nathanael as a "guileless Israelite"? On the one hand, connecting him with a specific place, such as "under a fig tree," may be nothing more than the evidence Jesus is citing to prove that he did indeed notice him.[24] On the other hand, there may be a correlation between Nathanael's identity as a "guileless Israelite" and "being under the fig tree" that is determined by Hos 9:10:

> "Like a bunch of grapes in the wilderness I found Israel; like one watching in the fig tree early I saw your ancestors.[25]

---

[21] Tobias Nicklas, "'Unter dem Feigenbaum': Die Rolle des Lesers im Dialog zwischen Jesus und Natanael (Joh 1.45-50)," *NTS* 46/2 (2000), cites both the renaming of Jacob in Gen 32:28 and LXX Psa 31:2b to account for the Jesus' characterization of Nathanael as "a true Israelite in whom there is no guile," but without the additional insight that Philo's interpretation of the renaming of Jacob offers.

[22] In 4:17-18, 6:70-71, 13:10 and 38.

[23] Philo, *de Mutatione Nominum,* 81. Barrett, *St. John*, 185, notes this parallel but considers it to be unimportant. Philo continues, "The task of him who sees God is not to leave the sacred arena uncrowned, but carry off the prizes of victory. And what garland more fitting for its purpose or of richer flowers could be woven for the victorious soul than the power which will enable him to behold (θεωρεῖν) the Existent with clear vision." As already noted, it is another indication, that the Fourth Gospel originated in Alexandria and that the author is familiar with the writings of Philo. In *de Specialibus Legibus* III, 184, Philo declares, Nature "... has given the lordship of the senses to the eyes."

[24] C.F.D. Moule, "A Note on 'under the fig tree' in John I 48, 50," *JTS* 5 (1954) 211, concludes, "'Under the fig tree' indicates something far more prosaic, namely accurate knowledge of a person's whereabouts and movements. ...Jesus knew all about Nathanael." See also J. W. Wenham, "The Fig Tree in the Old Testament," *JTS* 5 (1954) 206-207.

[25] Cited is a translation of the LXX text of Hos 9:10a. The Fourth Gospel attests that the LXX was the Scriptures of the Jewish community in Alexandria.

The Septuagint version of Hos 9:10a seems to allude to those who are vigilant in their expectation of the fruit of the fig tree, a metaphorical reference to those anticipating the fulfillment of God's promises. Jesus, who saw Nathanael "under a fig tree" and characterized him as a "guileless Israelite," is identifying him with his ancestors who, according to Hos 9:10a, were under the fig tree watching for the appearance of its fruit.[26] Nathanael, perhaps a mirror image of the implied readers – or at least some of them – is an Israelite, who, without deceit, has been waiting for the fulfillment of God's promises, but equipped with the messianic typologies of the Scriptures, as his response to Philip's witness and his subsequent confession of Jesus indicate.[27]

Nathanael, like the two disciples of John, addresses Jesus as "Rabbi." Unlike them, however, he forgets his earlier apprehensiveness and ecstatically utters a christological confession that climaxes the discipleship that is growing around Jesus, "Rabbi, you are the Son of God, you are the king of Israel." These titles are correlates of the Messiah typology that had evolved in Jewish messianism. "The king of Israel" is simply another designation for the Messiah; and, as the voice of David proclaims in Ps 2:7, the king of Israel is God's Son. Nathanael's messianic identification of Jesus makes him comparable to his Israelite ancestors, "the first fruit on the fig tree in its first season." Notwithstanding, his confession of Jesus as "the king of Israel" will eventually be disputed and repudiated by others. Yet it will ultimately be vindicated, but in profound irony.

Jesus does not correct Nathanael. In time and as a result of his experience of discipleship he may revise his understanding of Jesus' messiahship. In the meantime, however, he has come and seen, and simply on the basis of Jesus' recognition of his character and disposition he has manifested an unexpected leap of faith that he has verbalized in his christological confession. That will not go unrewarded. Nathanael will *see* greater things.

> Because I said to you, "I saw you under the fig tree," do you believe? Greater than these things *you will see* (ὄψῃ)! (1:50)

Jesus promises him a vision that will have unforeseen consequences for the forthcoming journey of discipleship through the narrative world of the Gospel. To emphasize the momentous character of this promise he employs for the first time the distinctively Johannine double asseveration, "Amen, Amen," a formula that conveys a solemn guarantee that what he is going to say is avowedly true. He will utilize it as a preface twenty-five times for the pronouncements he utters in the course of his ministry.

---

[26] Tobias Nicklas, "Unter dem Feigenbaum," rejects the reference to Hos 9:10 on the basis of the difference between "under the fig tree" and "on the fig tree." But even as he does not refer to Philo, he also does not take the LXX version of Hos 9:10a into account. Consequently, his analysis of the textual structure of the implied reader is finally flawed, as he concludes that, as long as the riddle of a deeper knowledge of Jesus that Nathanael desires to unlock remains insoluble, the reader's complete identification with this Israelite is hindered.

[27] For other interpretations of the significance of the fig tree, see Brown, *John* I, 83.

ἀμὴν ἀμὴν λέγω ὑμῖν, ὄψεσθε τὸν οὐρανὸν ἀνεῳγότα καὶ τοῦ ἀγγέλους τοῷ θεοῦ ἀναβαίνοντας καὶ καταβαίνοντας ἐπὶ τὸν υἱὸν τοῦ ἀνθρώπου. (1:51)

Although Jesus is speaking to Nathanael, as the text indicates: καὶ λέγει αὐτῷ (and he says to him), this asseveration is directed at all those who have become his followers: Nathanael, Philip, Simon Peter, Andrew, the companion of Andrew who also left John but remains unnamed, and especially the implied readers.

Amen, Amen I say to you (ὑμῖν), you will see (ὄψεσθε) the heaven opened and the angels of God ascending and descending on the Son of the Human Being.[28]

In his formulation of this promised vision, Jesus combines the pivotal feature of Jacob's dream at Bethel (Gen 28:12), the ladder joining heaven and earth with ascending and descending messengers, and the figure of the Son of the Human Being (ὁ υἱὸς τοῦ ἀνθρώπου). The image and the figure are united but not merged. The Son of the Human Being does not become the ladder, nor does the Son of the Human Being replace the ladder.[29]

According to Gen 28:10-22, the ladder was set up on the earth, and its top reached to heaven. Jacob named the site Bethel, and it served as an aetiological legend to validate the origin of the sanctuary that Jeroboam I set up at Bethel soon after he became the regent of the northern kingdom.[30] As an *axis mundi* or architectonic center, it represented the navel of the earth from which creation originated.[31] Jerusalem became the new resting-place of the ladder when David moved the tabernacle to his newly established capital and his son Solomon subsequently replaced the tabernacle with the construction of a temple.[32] The rabbinic midrash, *Genesis Rabbah* 69:7, identifies the Jerusalem temple as the very location at which Jacob's ladder rested.

---

[28] Contrary to B. Lindars, "The Son of Man in the Johnannine Christology, *Essays on John*, 36; and Lindars, "The Son of Man in the Theology of John," *Essays on John*, 156, John 1:51 is not an addition to the original composition of 1:19-49, and it is also not a symbolic description of the baptismal experience of Jesus.

[29] So also Nils Alstrup Dahl, "The Johannine Church and History," *Current Issues in New Testament Interpretation: Essays in Honor of Otto A. Piper*, 136. Also Ashton, *Understanding*, 347, "The angels do not clamber up and down on the Son of Man but on the ladder." Whether this means, as he continues to say, "… it is simply that there is no other *route* between heaven and earth than the Son of Man …" requires further qualification. Contrary to Moloney, *Belief*, 74. See Dodd, *Fourth Gospel*, 245-246, for a discussion of the problem.

[30] Dodd, *ibid.*, 245, cites a rabbinic tradition of the early 3rd century C.E. in which Gen 28:12 is interpreted as the angels ascending and descending on Jacob, or Israel. But Gen 28:12 explicitly states that the ladder is set on the earth, not on Jacob. See Ashton's discussion of the ladder resting on Jacob or Jacob as a heavenly being, *Understanding*, 342-348.

[31] On mountains and temples as navels or architectonic centers, see Mircea Eliade, *Cosmos and History*, 12-21, on "The Symbolism of the Center". Also his companion volume, *The Sacred and the Profane*, 36-42, on "Sacred Space and Making the World Sacred."

[32] Eliade, *ibid.*, 58-65.

Now, at the very beginning of his ministry, Jesus displaces the location of the ladder once more. It will no longer rest on the Temple in Jerusalem where it had united heaven and earth for generations and thereby constituted the architectonic center of the world, the place at which God's presence is experienced and divine-human communication occurs.[33] Henceforth the ladder will be situated upon the dynamic reality of the New Human Being instead of an immovable stone building.[34] Nathanael will *see* this, and it is in this respect that he is equated with Jacob, because Jacob, according to Philo, is renamed Israel, and Israel is "he who sees God."[35] Accordingly, wherever the community of the New Human Being happens to be at any given time and place, heaven and earth will be united, God's presence will be experienced and divine-human messages will be exchanged. Here, at the very threshold of his ministry, Jesus relocates the heavenly ladder and situates it on the eschatological-christological figure of ὁ υἱὸς τοῦ ἀνθρώπου. This is the image that the implied readers are to take with them as they continue to inhabit the narrative world of the Gospel.[36] Will it eventually be fulfilled before the Gospel ends?[37]

There is at least one context in which earth and heaven are in communication.[38] At the closure of his ministry Jesus, after voicing the agitation of his soul, prays, "Father, glorify your name!" and receives heavenly assurance by means of a *Bat Qol*, "I gloried and I shall glorify." But there is also the vision of the two angels that Mary Magdalene observes (θεωρεῖ) in the tomb of Jesus in 20:12; one is located "at the head" and the other "at the feet" where the body of Jesus had been placed. These are the heavenly messengers who facilitate the communication between heaven and earth and who, after Jesus' resurrection, are representative of his unification of the heavenly and the earthly human being.[39] But because this

---

[33] According to Midr Psa. 91:7, "From the words of Gen 28:17 the Rabbis inferred that when a man prays in Jerusalem, it is as though he prays before the throne of glory, for the gate of heaven is in Jerusalem, and a door is always open for the hearing of prayer, as is said: *This is the gate of heaven*." Braude, *The Midrash on Psalms*, II, 105.

[34] Contrary to Ashton, *Understanding*, 347, the ladder does not fuse with "the Son of Man," and Jesus is not the way up and down. Contrary to Lindars, " The Son of Man in the Theology of John," 158, the ladder is not a third person self-reference to Jesus. The same essay is in B. Lindars, *The Son of Man: A Fresh Examination of the Son of Man Sayings in the Gospels* (Grand Rapids: Eerdmans, 1984) 149.

[35] Philo, *de Mutatione Nominum*, 81. See Ashton, *Understanding*, 348, who draws this equation but without linking it to Philo's interpretation of Jacob the supplanter as Israel.

[36] It is "a programmatic statement pointing to the significance of the story that is to be unfolded," as Lindars states, *John*, 157, but not a later addition attached to the original composition of 1:19-49, as Lindars conjectures, "The Son of Man in the Johannine Christology," 36.

[37] This is the question that Ashton, *Understanding*, 348, asks and rightly answers "... to a larger audience, not just the disciples present at the scene, but the readers of the Gospel."

[38] Angelophanies are not necessary for the fulfillment of 1:51. As Meeks, "Man from Heaven," 51, asserts, "... angels are merely a 'symbol' of the union of the celestial and terrestrial worlds." Above all in the area of communication, especially if the Logos-Sophia also "happens flesh" in the corporate "Son of the Human Being."

[39] See chapter 20.

programmatic, prophetic utterance is also intended for the implied readers, as the plural of the verb ὄψεσθε (you all will see) implies, it is designed to reach beyond the narrative world of the Gospel.

Who is "the Son of the Human Being"?

That is the question the crowd addresses to Jesus in 12:34, "Who is this ὁ υἱὸς τοῦ ἀνθρώπου?" But that could just as well have been asked in the context of 1:51 as Jesus entered into his ministry. Curiously, however, it is raised after he has closed his public ministry. When "the Greeks," who have come to Jerusalem for the Passover, request "to see Jesus," he discloses to his disciples – and to the implied readers, "The hour has come in order that the Son of the Human Being is glorified." This is the hour that has been anticipated since the beginning of his ministry at the wedding at Cana when he informed his mother, "My hour has not yet come." It is the hour that he postponed when his brothers urged him to go up to Jerusalem and "manifest himself to the world."[40] It is the hour that continues to be deferred even when attempts are made to seize him.[41] Finally, as the third Passover approaches, and he has been anointed by Mary and has been welcomed by the crowd as "the King of Israel" – echoing Nathanael's confession in 1:49 – as he enters Jerusalem riding on a young donkey, the time has arrived for the glorification of the Son of the Human Being (12:23).

But why would this question be introduced by the Jerusalem crowd at the closure of Jesus' public ministry, particularly when he did not employ the title in his announcement of being lifted up from the earth?

> We heard from the Law that the Christ remains forever, and how do you say that it is necessary for the Son of the Human Being to be lifted up? Who is this Son of the Human Being?

Although the question was raised by the crowd, it is intended for the implied readers of the Gospel, for they alone have heard Jesus' earlier pronouncements of 3:14 and 8:28 and therefore are able to engage in consistency building.[42] By correlating 12:32, "And if I am lifted up from the earth I will draw all to myself!" with the title, "the Son of the Human Being" that Jesus employed in 3:14 and 8:28 when he originally enunciated the necessity of being lifted up, they are confronted with the question for the first time, "Who is this Son of the Human Being?"[43]

But coincidentally they are confronted with the question in conjunction with the Christ title that the crowd introduced. To them there is no correlation between the

---

[40] John 7:3-8.

[41] John 7:30; 8:20.

[42] Ashton, *Understanding*, 366-367, also acknowledges that 12:34 "relies upon the reader's memory," and "to expand the messianic faith of the community's beginnings into the fuller, richer, faith implied in the title 'Son of Man'." Unfortunately, however, he ignores the juxtaposition of the Christ and the Son of the Human Being titles.

[43] Bultmann, *John*, 349, 354; German, 265, 269-270, insists that 12:34 follows 8:28, and there is a correlation. But 3:14 is not to be excluded and is, in fact, a closer parallel.

Christ who rules forever and the Son of the Human Being who, by being lifted up on the cross, will die. Apparently the narrator intends to prompt the implied readers into remembering the problem of the relationship between the two paramount christological titles that emerged at the beginning of the Gospel but have no typologically historical relation to each other: the Christ or Messiah appellation and the Son of the Human Being.[44] At this midpoint in the narrative world of the Gospel, before Jesus enters into his passion, the implied readers must remain alert to the forthcoming coalescence of these typologies when Jesus is lifted up from the earth in crucifixion.[45]

The question, therefore, persists: "Who is the son of the Human Being"? This eschatological-anthropological title, ὁ υἱὸς τοῦ ἀνθρώπου, occurs thirteen times in the narrative world of the Gospel. Significantly twelve of them frame Jesus' public ministry. The first is enunciated at the very beginning as a promise to his disciples – and the implied readers.

> Amen, amen I say to you, 'You will see the heaven opened and the messengers of God ascending and descending upon the Son of the Human Being. (1:51)

The following nine convey various aspects of Jesus' self-understanding of his origin and his destiny, his mission, his divinely mandated authority, his relationship to God, and the corporate character of this christological designation.

> And no one has ascended into heaven, except the one descending from the heaven, the Son of the Human Being. (3:13)

> And even as Moses raised the snake in the wilderness, so it is necessary that the Son of the Human Being be raised up. (3:14)

> And he gave him authority to do judgment because he is a son of a human being. (5:27)[46]

> Do not work for the food that perishes but the food that remains unto everlasting life, which the Son of the Human Being will give you. (6:27)

> Amen, amen I say to you, unless you eat the flesh of the Son of the Human Being and drink his blood, you do not have life in yourselves. (6:53)

> Does this offend you? What then if you should view the Son of the Human Being ascending where he was before? (6:62)

[44] In 1:41 Andrew evangelizes his brother Simon by acknowledging Jesus to be the "Messiah" or "Christ," apparently inferring it from John's witness, "Behold the Lamb of God." Jesus, however, consistently employs the title, "the Son of the Human Being" in 1:51, 3:13-14." There are no historical correlations between these christological trajectories, yet they will be integrated at the culmination of the Gospel.

[45] See chapter 17.

[46] This is the only occurrence of υἱὸς ἀνθρώπου in the Fourth Gospel, apparently derived from the Septuagint translation of Dan 7:13.

> When you raise the Son of the Human Being, then you will know that **I AM**. (8:28)
>
> Jesus heard that they threw him out and finding him he said, "Do you believe into the Son of the Human Being?" (9:35)
>
> But Jesus responds to them saying, "The hour has come in order that the Son of the Human Being is glorified." (12:23)

The eleventh and twelfth are spoken at the closure of his public ministry, and they are the only instances of the title that are voiced by the crowd.

> We heard from the Law that the Christ remains forever, and how do you say that it is necessary for the Son of the Human Being to be lifted up? Who is this Son of the Human Being? (12:34)

The thirteenth and last is spoken by Jesus as the introduction of his Farewell Discourse:

> Now the Son of the Human Being is glorified and God is glorified in him (13:31).

What is the unity – if any at all – that integrates this great diversity of Jesus' pronouncements of "the Son of the Human Being" into a comprehensible and meaningful synthesis?[47] In view of all the diverging characterizations of the status and activity of ὁ υἱὸς τοῦ ἀνθρώπου, how is the question of the Jerusalem crowd to be answered? There may be no common features that all of the sayings share, but a unity eventually emerges that is inferred from the aporetic origination that is attributed to Jesus within the Gospel.

Nothing is gained by engaging in a quest for the source of this title; the possibilities are limited. The cluster of these sayings is so distinctive and unparalleled that no enlightenment can be drawn from the Synoptic tradition.[48] The Mandaean parallels that have been posed offer no encouragement toward a comprehension of their unity.[49] There is no convincing evidence that the appellation was drawn from Book Two of the Ethiopic apocalypse of Enoch, "The Similitudes of Enoch."[50] However, the singular, anarthrous employment of υἱὸς

---

[47] All of "the Son of Man" sayings can be considered as a cluster, constituted by the author himself. So also Schnackenburg, *St. John* I, 532. However, they have not been drawn from 'a florilegium of logia.' They have an internal consistency and integrity that are determined by Jesus' distinctive identity in the narrative world of the Gospel.

[48] Also Ashton, *Understanding*, 341. To quote Martyn, *History and Theology*, 131, "... the christological movement from the Mosaic Messiah to the Son of Man is John's own creation. We cannot place it alongside a comparable phenomenon in other literature."

[49] As Meeks contends, *The Prophet-King*, 297, and "The Man from Heaven," 44, 46. Johannine christology is determined by Jewish Wisdom myth, but it is not derived from or based on Gnostic mythology.

[50] Contrary to Siegfried Schultz, *Untersuchungen zur Menschensohn-Christologie im Johannesevangelium* (Göttingen: Vandenhoeck & Ruprecht, 1957) 179, the Fourth Gospel does not utilize the "Son of the Human Being" sayings to confess that the prophecies of late Jewish apocalyptic have been fulfilled. If these texts can be included in Philip's confession to Nathanael, "We have found

ἀνθρώπου (son of a human being) in 5:27 corresponds to the Septuagint version of Dan 7:13-14 and Psa 8:4. Both of these texts convey aspects of the self-understanding that Jesus verbalizes in different contexts of his ministry. The authority to do judgment that he claims for himself in 5:22, 27 may be based on Daniel's vision of one like a human being (υἱὸς ἀνθρώπου) who receives "glory, authority, and kingdom". Jesus, however, did not ascend into heaven in order to recover these benefactions that the Creator willed for humanity.[51] In fact, as he declares in 3:13, "... no one has ascended into heaven except the one who descended, ὁ υἱὸς τοῦ ἀνθρώπου. He is *the* Son of *the* Human Being who descended from heaven, not "one like a human being" who ascended.[52] Moreover, his descent did not result in distributing these endowments to his fellow human beings. He descended in order to serve as God's apprentice for the purpose of saving the world by inaugurating a new creation through his death and resurrection. It is only ironically, therefore, that Jesus relates himself to the figure of "one like a human being" of Dan 7:13-14. Similarly, it is only ironically that he also may link himself to the υἱὸς ἀνθρώπου of Psa 8:4, who, as the representative of humankind, was crowned by God with glory, honor and sovereignty. For although he is "the son of Joseph from Nazareth" and therefore a descendant of Adam and Eve, he is preeminently the one who descended from heaven.[53]

Jesus' self-identification with "the Son of the Human Being," is evident in the juxtaposition of 3:13 and 3:14, for he is unable to tell Nicodemus – and the implied readers – of "heavenly things" unless he himself is identifiable with "the Son of the Human Being" who descended from heaven.[54] He relates himself to ὁ υἱὸς τοῦ ἀνθρώπου, in 9:37, albeit indirectly. His appropriation of this appellation must be based on his origination of "being born from above," that moment when he was, "impressed by the seal of God, the stamp of which is the eternal Logos, and inbreathed by God's Spirit" at his baptism by John. This event established his primary identity in the Gospel as "the Son of the Human Being," an eschatological-anthropological figure that is comparable to the Apostle Paul's characterization of "the last Adam" as "a life-giving spirit."[55] Jesus, by being re-created by God, is ὁ υἱὸς τοῦ ἀνθρώπου, and correspondingly a New Adam, the founder and pioneer

the one whom Moses and the prophets wrote about," Schultz' conclusion cannot be denied. But the sayings themselves are based on the origination that is ascribed to Jesus within the Gospel, based on anti-Philo polemics and Wisdom literature.

[51] Gen 1:26-30 and Psa 8:4-8.

[52] The appropriation of the figure of Dan 7:13, υἱὸς ἀνθρώπου, in John 5:27 is not titular, as Lindars, "The Son of Man in the Theology of John," 164, contends.

[53] Contrary to Ashton, *Understanding*, 363, Daniel's "son of a human being" does not serve "to sum up the extraordinarily bold and novel theology succinctly but enigmatically expressed in John 3:13."

[54] Although Jesus reveals the "heavenly things" of 3:14-21 and elsewhere, he is more than a Revealer, and also more than one who reveals that he is an enigma, as Meeks claims, "Man from Heaven," 57.

[55] 1 Cor 15:45; also 15:22.

of a New Humanity. Consequently, as an eschatological-anthropological figure, ὁ υἱὸς τοῦ ἀνθρώπου is more adequately rendered as "the First Final Human Being" or "the New Human Being" and, like its predecessor, υἱὸς ἀνθρώπου, in Dan 7:13-14, it is the eschatological-anthropological reality of "the One and the Many."[56] It is a corporate personage that includes both Jesus and his disciples. It is the pioneering community of a New Humanity, and throughout the Gospel Jesus is its embodiment. His origin as the incarnate Logos-Sophia and the permanent bearer of God's Spirit qualifies him alone as the New Human Being (ὁ υἱὸς τοῦ ἀνθρώπου) in the narrative world of the Gospel. He descended from heaven (3:13) and he, as God's apprentice, actualizes God's reign on God's behalf. As ὁ υἱὸς τοῦ ἀνθρώπου, he correlatively bears the epithet ὁ υἱὸς τοῦ θεοῦ (the Son of God) or simply ὁ υἱός (the Son).[57] But the vision that Jesus promises Nathanael – and the implied readers – is the paradigm shift of the ladder eventually resting on the corporate body of the New Human Being and uniting heaven and earth.

In 2:19-21 Jesus will offer the implied readers another image of this community of the New Human Being, when he replaces the stone sanctuary of the Temple with his own physical body as "the Father's house" and subsequently promises that "many rooms" will be added by his death and resurrection. On Easter evening the living Temple of God will be enlarged when Jesus breathes God's Spirit upon his disciples. At that moment Jesus' asseveration of 1:51 will have been fulfilled corporately, and the ladder that rests on this New Humanity, God's living Temple, will unite heaven and earth, and the ascending and descending messengers will constitute the communication that will flourish between God and human beings.

Jesus will achieve this incorporation of a New Humanity, as 3:14 forecasts its eschatological realization, by being lifted up on a cross analogous to Moses suspending a snake on a pole in order to bring about the healing of the Israelites who had been bitten by poisonous snakes. The juxtaposition of verses 13 and 14 intimates the profound irony of the these two events that stand in opposition to each other: the glory of "the Son of the Human Being" who descends from heaven and the ignominy of "the Son of the Human Being" who dies presaged as a snake on the cross.[58] This conjunction that is more explicitly expressed in 12:23-34 is anticipated in the juxtaposition of the two verbs, ὑψοῦν and δοξάζειν in the

[56] Evinced in the interpretation of Dan 7:13 in 7:27. See also Kenelm Burridge, *New Heaven New Earth: A Study of Millenarian Activities* (New York: Schocken Books, 1969) 153-164, on prophetic figures personifying "the one and the many."

[57] Dodd, *Fourth Gospel*, 230, states: "It is however the titles 'Son of God' and 'Son of Man' that the evangelist has selected to bear the weight of his interpretation of the Person of Christ." According to J. L. Martyn, *History and Theology*, 193, the titles 'Son of Man' and 'Son of God' are interchangeable. Contrary to Ashton, *Understanding the Fourth Gospel*, 337, there is no paradoxical contrast between the titles "Son of God" and "Son of Man." Both are individual and corporate, as Psa 2:7 and Hos 11:1 indicate for the title "Son of God," and Psa 8:4 and Dan 7:13, 27 intimate for the "Son of Man." Both can represent the One and the Many. See also Edwin D. Freed, "The Son of Man in the Fourth Gospel," *JBL* 86/4 (1967), 403, who, on the basis of his analysis, maintains there is no separate Son of Man christology apart from the other titles, "the Son of God" and "the Son."

opening verse of the Suffering Servant of LXX Isa 52:13,"Look, my Servant will understand, and *he will be exalted* (ὑψωθήσεται) and *he will be glorified* (δοξασθήσεται) exceedingly. It is an intimation of the effect that Isa 52:13-53:12 will have in the Gospel's interpretation of Jesus' death at the third Passover in the Gospel.[59]

At the second Passover, in the context of the foreshadowing of a New Exodus, Jesus substitutes his flesh and blood, the flesh and blood of the New Human Being, in place of the Passover meal.[60] It is the flesh and blood of "the Son of God" upon whom John ascertained the Spirit descending and remaining. It is the flesh and blood of "the Son of the Human Being" upon whom the angels of God are ascending and descending. It is the flesh and blood of the one who "tramples the waves of the sea" and identifies himself to his disciples as ἐγώ εἰμί (**I AM**). As the New Human Being who descended from heaven, Jesus predicates himself as "the Bread who descended from heaven and gives life to the world" (6:33).

> **I AM** the Bread of Life. (6:35, 41, 48)
> **I AM** the living Bread. (6:51)

In this context of his discourse on the Bread of Life he unites – for the first time – his self-disclosure as ἐγώ εἰμί (**I AM**) with his appropriation of the eschatological-anthropological figure of ὁ υἱὸς τοῦ ἀνθρώπου. The bread that he will give is his flesh on behalf of the life of the world (6:51).

> Amen, amen I say to you, unless you eat the flesh of *the Son of the Human Being* (ὁ υἱὸς τοῦ ἀνθρώπου) and drink his blood, you do not have life in yourselves. The one who chews my flesh and drinks my blood has eternal life, and I will raise him/her at the last day. For my flesh is true food and my blood is true drink.

To come *towards* (πρός) him as the New Human Being (ὁ υἱὸς τοῦ ἀνθρώπου) and the self-disclosed ἐγώ εἰμί (**I AM**) signifies a movement into union with him and therefore to participate in the authentic humanity that he embodies and wills to extend to all of humankind. But will the implied readers, as Jesus challenges them in 6:62, observe (θεωρῆτε) the New Human Being ascending into heaven and be drawn into an abandonment *toward* him in order to be membered into his divine humanity?

---

[58] As Ashton, *Understanding*, 365, observes, the primary meaning of ὑψοῦν is "exalt," but 3:14 indicates that it is intended to convey a more ironic significance. So also Lindars, "The Son of Man in the Johannine Christology," 38.

[59] Lindars, "The Son of Man in the Theology of John," 154, rightly considers the lifting up on a stake in 3:14 to be a reference to Jesus' crucifixion and designates this to be the "primary meaning" of 3:14. His claim that the two notions of crucifixion and exaltation are combined in the single ambiguous verb ὑψοῦν (to lift up) is also faultless.

[60] See chapter 9.

Ironically, when the New Human Being is *lifted up* and *exalted* (ὑψώσητε) on the cross, then "You *will know* (γνώσεσθε) that **I AM** (ἐγὼ εἰμί)."[61] This is a pledge, a guarantee, that is intended for the implied readers, for no such recognition would be possible outside of a participation in the narrative world of the Gospel. Only by inhabiting the story of the Fourth Gospel will the implied readers perceive in the narration of the crucifixion that the New Human Being is a partaker of God's **I AM**.

The significance of this conjunction of Jesus' **I AM** (ἐγὼ εἰμί) and Jesus' embodiment of the eschatological-anthropological ὁ υἱὸς τοῦ ἀνθρώπου (the New Human Being) is dramatically disclosed in the story of John 9. Following Jesus' instructions, the male, blind from birth, undergoes a baptism in the pool of Siloam and returns to his friends able to see. But he has not only gained physical sight. Through his baptism he has experienced a rebirth, and coincidentally he is now able to begin to see the light of truth, the light of the first day of creation. Because he has changed, as a result of this experience, his friends and neighbors are uncertain of his identity and speculate as to who he really is. He responds, as the narrator indicates in 9:9, "He kept saying, ἐγὼ εἰμί." All the predicates that relate him to his past existence as a beggar have died with him in his baptism. He is a new human being, and therefore he is only an **I AM**. In this new state of being he is drawn into a forensic process by the ruling authorities, and because he challenges them, as he defends Jesus, he is excluded from the synagogue. Jesus, sensing what has happened to him, pursues him and confronts him with the reality of the New Human Being: "Do you believe into τὸν υἱὸν τοῦ ἀνθρώπου?"[62] By a confession of faith, "I believe, Lord!" he, as only an **I AM**, is incorporated into the New Humanity that Jesus embodies.

This conjunction between the divine self-disclosure, ἐγὼ εἰμί, and membership in the community of the New Human Being (ὁ υἱὸς τοῦ ἀνθρώπου) emerged in Jesus' discourse on the Bread of Life as he moved from his own self-disclosure, ἐγὼ εἰμί ὁ ἄρτος τῆς ζωῆς (**I AM** the Bread of Life) in 6:35, 48, 51 to his self-identification as the embodiment of ὁ υἱὸς τοῦ ἀνθρώπου in 6:53. It would appear, therefore, that ἐγὼ εἰμί (**I AM**), either without a predicate or with a predicate, and the corporate figure of ὁ υἱὸς τοῦ ἀνθρώπου are bound together in a unity that is grounded in Jesus' identity as the incarnate Logos-Sophia and the permanent bearer of God's Spirit. "The Son of the Human Being," therefore, as the eschatological-anthropological community of a New Humanity that Jesus embodies participates in the very same union with God that he experiences. It is a union that establishes a co-enthronement with God and therefore authorizes a participation in the divine **I AM**. The commission to serve as God's apprentice emerges naturally from this union and, with it, the empowerment to fulfill the

[61] John 8:28.

[62] Jesus' question, "Do you believe into the Son of the Human Being?" does not mean, as Lindars, "The Son of Man in the Theology of John," claims, "Do you believe in the Revealer?"

objectives of God's will. Accordingly, new predicates are eventually joined to the absolute use of the divine **I AM** (ἐγὼ εἰμί), as Jesus' apprenticeship exemplifies. They are metaphorical predicates that characterize the activity in which he engages as God's apprentice:

6:35 **I AM** the bread of life.
6:41 **I AM** the bread that descends from heaven.
8:12 **I AM** the light of the world.
10:7 **I AM** the door.
10:11 **I AM** the good shepherd.
11:25 **I AM** the resurrection and the life.
14:6 **I AM** the way and the truth and the life.
15:1 **I AM** the true vine.

All, or almost all, of the predicates that Jesus attaches to his self-disclosure as ἐγὼ εἰμί may have parallels in other religious texts, perhaps especially in the Mandaean literature, as Eduard Schweizer has demonstrated.[63] But this does not necessarily imply that the **I AM** sayings of Jesus in the Gospel according to John have been derived from the Mandaean texts or more likely, as Schweizer contends, from an earlier oral or written form (Urform) that was adopted by the Fourth Evangelist in order to distinguish Jesus above all the gods of the Hellenistic world and establish him alone as the true Lord.[64] All the predicates of Jesus' **I AM** declarations have been appropriated from the religious and culture life of Judaism and are directed finally toward drawing the implied readers of Alexandria out of their religious piety and passivity into a dynamic membership in the New Humanity that is committed to world transformation.

Jesus' self-disclosure, "**I AM** the Bread of Life," identifies him as the true manna, the manna that is superior to the bread that Moses provided for Israel in the wilderness, and those who come *towards* (πρός) him and enter into communion with him must necessarily begin to engage in a ministry like his. The flesh and blood of "the Son of the Human Being" is the New Passover meal, and those who partake of it participate in the New Exodus of the New Human Being. They are, therefore, not only liberated but are engaged in the work of liberation. The "rivers of living water" that flow out of the belly of those who believe into Jesus must result from his breathing God's Spirit upon them and thereby incorporating them into "the Father's house" that he embodies. Jesus as the Light of the World transcends the festival of Hanukkah, and those who are drawn into the light of the truth, like the blind male of John 9, will cultivate that perspicuity that enables them

[63] Eduard Schweizer, *EGO EIMI: Die religionsgeschichtliche Herkunft und theologische Bedeutung der johanneischen Bildreden, zugleich ein Beitrag zur Quellenfrage des vierten Evangeliums* (Göttingen: Vandenhoeck & Ruprecht, 2nd ed 1965).

[64] *Ibid.*, 62-88. Schweizer's argument that the Fourth Gospel could not have been a source for the Mandaeans is unpersuasive when he contends that they had the entire New Testament at their disposal and therefore, in addition to the Johannine **I AM** sayings of Jesus, would have appropriated other christological titles.

to determine the truth of things and to personify it in their lives. Jesus is the Door, who, by dying as the Lamb of God, saves all those who are members of God's household.[65] Jesus, as the Resurrection and the Life, draws the apocalyptic expectation of resurrection out of the future into the present, and those, like Lazarus, who are raised from the dead will no longer be intimidated by society's ultimate threat of punishment, death. Jesus, and not a repository of Law or Scripture, is the Way by which human beings journey *towards* (πρός) union with God. Jesus is the Truth because he embodies the Light of the first day of creation. He is the Life because as the incarnation of the Logos-Sophia, God's never-ending Life resides in him. He is also the Vine who, by personification, replaces the golden vine with grape clusters that adorned the entrance-doors of the Temple.[66]

Both the **I AM** declarations of Jesus and his employment of the eschatological-anthropological figure of "the Son of the Human Being" are not directed towards his self-legitimation as the Christ. There are not merely "recognition formulas" that distinguish him christologically as the unparalleled Savior of the world.[67] Nor are they "unconcealed messianic self-attestations" that, in contrast to human necessities and wants, establish the singularity of Jesus.[68] They are formulated by him to articulate the arrival of Jewish apocalypticism's long-awaited "new heaven-new earth" with its New Humanity and attendantly Jewish Wisdom's prayers and hopes for Sophia's renewal of all things by passing into holy souls to make them "friends of God and prophets."[69]

Jesus inaugurated his ministry with an avowal of the glory that his disciples will see as they participate in his community of the New Human Being upon which the ladder rests that unites heaven and earth. He closes his ministry with the enunciation of the glory that the New Human Being will manifest as the awaited "hour" and its anticipated actuality of his death draws near. "The hour has come so that the New Human Being is glorified" (12:23). This is voiced again as the introduction of his Farewell Discourse to his disciples in 13:31, but with the added note, "and God is glorified in him."[70] This is an echo of the *Bat Qol* that responded to Jesus' petition in 12:28 and assured him that even as God has been glorified in his past ministry, God will be glorified in his Passion. This, then, is the supreme irony of Jesus' career as the New Human Being. In the scandal of his death by crucifixion, his being lifted up on the cross is coincidentally his glorification. That can only be the result of the objective he achieves by his death:

---

[65] See chapter 16.

[66] Josephus, *BJ* 5, 210-211. Also Lawrence D. Sporty, *Biblical Archeologist* 46/2 (1983) 121-123.

[67] Schweizer, *EGO EIMI*, 126-127.

[68] *Ibid.*, 129. Also contrary to Elaine Pagels, "Gospels in conflict," in *Beyond Belief: The Secret Gospel of Thomas* (New York: Random House, 2003) 30-73.

[69] Wisdom of Solomon 7:27; see also 10:1-11:1.

[70] Verse 32 is suspect as a later scribal interpolation. Its exclusion is supported by P^{66} and a large number of other mss. See Bruce M. Metzger, *A Textual Commentary on the Greek New Testament*, 242.

nothing less than the eradication of the human disease called sin. This actualization is attainable only because he, as the New Human Being (ὁ υἱὸς τοῦ ἀνθρώπου), is the enfleshed Logos-Sophia and the permanent bearer of God's Spirit.

Who, then, is "the Son of the Human Being"? He is Jesus, the son of Joseph from Nazareth, the one who was born from above, the incarnate Logos-Sophia and the one on whom the Spirit descended and remained. He is the one whom Moses and the prophets wrote about, the one who fulfills the Scriptures and becomes the living Temple of God, the new Passover meal, and the Lamb of God who removes the sin of the world. Paradoxically, in and through all of these appellations, he is, ironically, also the Christ. Through the medium of the narrative world of the Gospel, as J. L. Martyn has recognized, "In John's own time and place Jesus somehow makes effective his presence as the Son of Man."[71]

All these sayings of "the Son of the Human Being," spoken from the beginning to the closure of Jesus' ministry, are offered to the implied readers as a foreshadowing of the New Humanity that will be established at the Easter event by Jesus' resurrection from the dead.[72] The apprenticeship that Jesus fulfills will be transferred to the New Humanity he has pioneered – with the promise and the expectation of 14:12.

> Amen, amen I say to you, the one who believes into me, the works that I do, he/she will do and greater that these she/he will do because I am going to the Father.

[71] *History and Theology*, 134; see also the last paragraph of p. 143.

[72] Contrary to Meeks, "Man from Heaven," 68, that being "from above" is the exclusive property of "the Son of Man." The corporate character of this eschatological-anthropological figure of "the Son of the Human Being" is supported by 15:19 and 17:14-16.

Chapter Fifteen

The Farewell Discourse

Jesus hosts a farewell meal 13:1-30

John 13:1-30 composes the setting of Jesus' Farewell Discourse.[1] The time is the evening before the Day of Preparation or, more generally as the opening verse indicates, "Before the feast of the Passover."[2] Jesus is hosting a farewell meal for his disciples, but there is no intimation that it should be construed as a Passover celebration. The Passover was foreshadowed in an Exodus-like event in conjunction with the feeding of the multitudes in 6:1-13 when, as the narrator stated, "the Passover of the Jews was near." But the Passover itself, although it is anticipated in 11:55, 12:1 and 13:1, never occurs in the narrative world of the Gospel. Jesus' death on the cross as "the Lamb of God who removes the sin of the world" is the great event of the Passover.[3] He becomes its very embodiment.

In a chain of participial clauses the narrator affirms certain anticipated events and the attendant realities that have begun to unfold. It is in this context of the third Passover of the narrative world of the Gospel that Jesus knows that "his hour came." It *came* (ἦλθεν) when Jesus closed his ministry by announcing the hour of his glorification and relating it to a grain of wheat falling into the ground and dying in order to bear much fruit.[4] In this new context the narrator looks beyond Jesus' death and associates "his hour" with his departure "out of this world *towards the Father* (πρός τὸν πατέρα)."

Jesus of Nazareth, the incarnation of the Logos-Sophia, will complete his apprenticeship by an ascent that will culminate the primordial movement of 1:1, καὶ ὁ λόγος ἦν πρὸς τὸν θεόν (and the Word was towards the God).[5] The

[1] R. Alan Culpepper, "The Johannine *Hypodeigma*: A Reading of John 13," *The Fourth Gospel from a Literary Perspective: Semeia* 53, ed. by R. Alan Culpepper and Fernando F. Segovia (Atlanta: Scholars Press, 1991) 133-152, offers a synchronic reading of the entire chapter 13 in order to understand it in its narrative context and to determine "how it elicits responses from those who seek to read it". Verses 31-38 are not differentiated as the beginning of Jesus' farewell discourse, but only as "further instruction" and "the second conversation with Peter."

[2] As Fernando E. Segovia calculates, *The Farewell of the Word: The Johannine Call to Abide* (Minneapolis: Fortress Press, 1991) 3, "All of John 13-17, therefore, focuses on this one meal in Jerusalem on the day before the feast of Passover ..."

[3] See chapter 17.

[4] Various substitute readings in place of the aorist ἦλθεν are encountered in the manuscript tradition; but this is the reading that takes account of Jesus' use of ἐλήλυθεν (it has come) in 12:23, and, because it is supported by P[75] and the majority of the manuscripts, it very likely is the preferable reading.

[5] Jesus will acknowledge this heavenward movement twice in his Prayer of Consecration (17:11, 13).

phrase of 13:1, πρός τὸν πατέρα and the phrase of 13:3, πρός τὸν θεόν (towards the God), may be intended to remind the implied readers of the opening verse of the Gospel. The objective of the descent of the Son of the Human Being, that is, to be lifted up on a cross in order to actualize the healing of humankind, will have been achieved. The context of his ascent, therefore, stands in opposition to that of Philo's Moses. For, according to Philo, the divinely inspired Moses, when summoned heavenward "by the Father," was "transformed into mind, pure as the sunlight" and left behind a heritage for Israel in the form of oracles and inspired sayings.[6] The legacy of the ascending Son of the Human Being will not be a set of Scriptures but an empowered new people of God that is divinely willed to continue, not for its own sake but for the fulfillment of the work of drawing all human beings into a new era of salvation that Jesus will actualize as God's apprentice through his death and resurrection.

Accordingly, as the narrator accentuates by the two-fold use of the verb ἀγαπᾶν (to love), the aorist participle ἀγαπήσας (loving) and the main verb ἠγάπησεν· *loving his own, the ones in the world, he loved them unto the end* (εἰς τέλος). He loved them to the very culmination of his apprenticeship.[7] The employment of the nominal adjective, τοὺς ἰδίους (his own) echoes the Prologue's history of the Logos-Sophia in its movement into the world and more particularly to God's elect people, Israel, in order to give them authority to be God's children. Even as some received the Logos-Sophia by believing into his name and therefore being engendered by God (1:12-13), there are those who have believed into Jesus and have been drawn into the New Humanity that he embodies.

A meal, a farewell dinner, takes place in order to enable Jesus to express his love for "his own" and to unite them around him in a continuing fellowship. Yet even within this community of a new people of God, there is one who will betray him, Judas, the son of Simon Iscariot. The narrator had identified him in the same way in relation to his father in the intrusive remark of 6:71. He has also been implicated as a thief who stole from the funds deposited in the community's treasury.

In this context of the fellowship of a community meal, Jesus washes his disciples' feet.[8] To insure an awareness of the significance of this subservient act,

---

[6] Philo, *de Vita Mosis* II, 288-291.

[7] Culpepper, "The Johannine *Hypodeigma*," 136, construes the phrase, εἰς τέλος (unto the end) to mean both "completely" and "to the end"; and both appear to be expressed in the footwashing.

[8] G. Richter, *Die Fusswaschung im Johannesevangelium* (Regensburg: Pustat, 1967) 305-307, contends that 13:12-20 is a later redaction and therefore incompatible with 13:1-11. The footwashing is a polemicizing against all rites of cultic cleansing because Jesus' death effects a complete cleansing once and for all. See pp. 294-295.

James D. G. Dunn, "The Washing of the Disciples' Feet in John 13 1-20," *ZNW* 61 (1970) 247-250, interprets the foot-washing as a "sign" intended to convey "a figure of the cross". J. N. Sanders, *A Commentary on the Gospel according to St. John*, ed. and completed by B. A. Mastin (New York: Harper & Row, 1968) 308, claims that Jesus' foot-washing symbolizes baptism.

the narrator introduces the event by confronting the implied readers with Jesus' consciousness of his origin, his autonomy as God's apprentice, and his destination.

> Knowing that the Father gave all things in his hands and that he came forth from God and goes back *towards God* (πρὸς τὸν θεόν), he rises from dinner and places [aside] his garments and, taking an apron, he tied [it] around himself. Then he throws water into the wash-basin and he began to wash the feet of the disciples and to dry them with the apron that was tied around him. (13:3-5)

By washing his disciples' feet Jesus is subverting the hierarchical structures of patron-client relationships and the honor/shame culture of the Mediterranean world.[9] Simon Peter, conscious of Jesus' paramount singularity, addresses him as "Lord" and questions the appropriateness of his slavish subordination.[10] "Lord, you are going to wash my feet?" In response, Jesus informs him that this reversal will be unintelligible to him in the present: "That which I do, you do not *know* (οἶδας) now." "But," he assures him, "you will *know* (γνώσῃ) after these things." The temporal reference, "after these things," naturally pertains to that time beyond Jesus' forthcoming death and resurrection.[11] But Simon Peter will not arrive at a personal enlightenment of the significance of Jesus' act within the narrative world of the Gospel. Here he is serving as a foil for the implied readers. They must fulfill that understanding of Jesus washing his disciples' feet.

But Peter is adamant in his hierarchically ordered cultural perspective. He refuses to let Jesus subordinate himself by washing his feet: "By no means shall you ever wash my feet!" Jesus' reply makes the symbolic significance of washing indispensable to membership in the new community of God's people that he is constituting: "If I do not wash you, you have no share with me."[12] Simon, stunned by the possibility of exclusion from Jesus' community perseveres in addressing Jesus as "Lord," and invokes him to wash "... not my feet only but also my hands and my head." If washing is indispensable, it seems to Peter that a complete

---

[9] Also Culpepper, "The Johannine *Hypodeigma*," 142. See Jerome H. Neyrey, "Despising the Shame of the Cross: Honor and Shame in the Johannine Passion Narrative," *Semeia* 68, 115-118; also John K. Chance, "The Anthropology of Honor and Shame: Culture, Values and Practice," *Semeia* 68. Moxnes, "Honor and Shame," *The Social Sciences and New Testament Interpretation*, 19-40. Bultmann, *John*, 468, does not refer to Mediterranean patron-client relationships or honor/shame culture but views Peter's resistance from the perspective of "the natural man" and human pride. German, 356.

[10] D. F. Tolmie, *Jesus' Farewell to the Disciples: John 13:1-17:26 in Narratological Perspective* (Leiden: Brill, 1995) undertakes a narrative criticism of Jesus' farewell, utilizing Levi-Strauss and Greimas to analyze the surface and deep structures of the events recounted in these chapters, and Seymour Chapman's conception of character to analyze the character traits of Jesus' disciples, but substantive insights into the kind of discipleship that Jesus is inculcating do not emerge.

[11] As Culpepper, "The Johannine *Hypodeigma*," 138, indicates, it is a "prolepsis" referring to the time "after Jesus has completed his mission."

[12] Also Culpepper, *ibid.*, 139. Contrary to Francis J. Moloney, *Glory Not Dishonor: Reading John 13-21* (Minneapolis: Fortress Press, 1998) 14, the footwashing is not a veiled reference to the practice of baptism in the early church. Baptism is an entry into a new creation; footwashing is the continuous cleansing that follows.

washing from head to toe is a necessity. But Jesus assures him, "The one who has been bathed has no need to be washed, except the feet only, but he/she is completely clean." The manuscript variants of verse 10 pose a fundamental issue that induces two basically different interpretations. The shorter text excludes the phrase, εἰ μὴ τοὺς πόδας (except the feet) and is supported by the Codex Sinaiticus, the Old Latin, the Vulgate and Tertullian and Origen.

> Jesus says to him, "The one who has been bathed has no need to be washed but is completely clean; and you are clean." (13:10)

This reading emphasizes the bathing that is intimated in verse 8, a bathing that effects a complete cleansing; "he/she is completely clean."[13] "The washing of the feet has signified the complete cleansing of the cross."[14]

The longer text that includes εἰ μὴ τοὺς πόδας (except the feet) and is attested by a great majority of the manuscripts, intimates that foot-washing and being completely clean as the result of having been bathed are two differentiable events.[15] Indeed, the two verbs that Jesus uses, λούειν (to bathe) and νίπτειν (to wash) convey this distinction.

> Jesus says to him, "*The one who has been bathed* (λελουμένος) has no need to *be washed* (νίψασθαι) except the feet, but is completely clean; and you are clean." (13:10)

P^{66} adds the adjective μόνον, (except the feet *only*), perhaps because of its use in the previous verse, but it may in fact be original because the objective of Jesus' act is the washing of the feet, and only the feet. There is no indication that the feet are symbolic of the whole human being. The aporia of being bathed and therefore being wholly clean, on the one hand, and the necessity of having the feet washed, on the other hand, defines the human condition that characterizes membership in the New Humanity Jesus is establishing. Its paradoxical nature has been adopted and expressed in the letter of 1 John:

> Everyone who remains (μένων) in him does not sin. Everyone who sins has neither seen him nor known him. (3:6)

---

[13] Dunn, "The Washing," has adopted this reading and contends that "Jesus in washing his disciples' feet is acting out what his death will accomplish for his disciples. His death washes them clean." Apparently also Dodd, *Fourth Gospel*, 401-402; and Barrett, *St. John* 441-442, on the basis of assuming that the two verbs, λούειν and νίπτειν are synonymous. Culpepper, "The Johannine *Hypodeigma*," 140, chooses the shorter reading, but without considering the difference between the verbs.

[14] Dunn, "The Washing," 250. This is also Culpepper's interpretation, "The Johannine *Hypodeigma*," 139, 147, linking Jesus' death with Peter's ignorance of the significance of the footwashing. But the footwashing is not "a proleptic and metaphorical interpretation of Jesus' death". As an example (ὑπόδειγμα), it signifies the replacement of the predominant patriarchal and hierarchical culture with the New Humanity that embodies the many rooms of "the Father's House."

[15] See Metzger, *A Textual commentary on the Greek New Testament*, 240.

> If we say that we have no sin, we deceive ourselves and the truth is not in us. If we confess our sins, he is faithful and just so that he forgives our sins and cleanses us from every injustice. (1:8-9)

The paradigm of foot-washing that Jesus offers his disciples presupposes a prior condition of wholeness and health that is established on the basis of membership in the community of the New Humanity. Incorporation into that membership may occur by being born from above "out of water and Spirit," a baptism through which an eschatological death is followed by the Spirit's re-creation that makes a human being completely clean. Jesus' pronouncement, "And you are clean" is affirmed in 15:3 when he declares to his disciples, "Already you are clean through the word that I have spoken to you."[16]

However, even as the feet touch the earth and require continuous washing, the disciples of Jesus, like Simon Peter, live in a fallen world of systemic structures and institutions and, therefore, cannot refrain from doing injustices of one kind or another that require forgiveness and reconciliation. Those who participate in the community of the Son of the Human Being and wash each other's feet symbolically engage in acts of cleansing that close the past and open the future to greater wholeness and integrity.[17]

Jesus' additional remark, "Yet not all" elicits from the narrator an aside for the benefit of the implied readers, "For he knew the one betraying him. On account of this he said, 'Not all of you are clean'."

In this subversion of the hierarchical ideology of honor/shame culture Jesus makes himself representative of the horizontally constituted community of the New Humanity he is founding.

> Do you *know* (γινώσκετε) what I have done for you? You call me "the Teacher" and "the Lord," and you are right, for *I am* (εἰμί). If, therefore, I, the Lord and the Teacher, washed your feet, you also ought to wash each other's feet. For I gave you a model so that even as I did to you, you also do. (13:12b-15)

But at the same time, by a double asseveration, he also issues a warning to those who would subvert this horizontal structure of God's new people by constituting a new hierarchy in which the servant supplants the master or the disciple supersedes

[16] See Bultmann's discussion, *John*, 471-472; German, 359-360. He considers two possibilities: verse 10 is directed against any attempt to supplement Christian baptism with other washings, *or* the cleansing through his word that Jesus acknowledges in 15:3 is directed against every sacramental purification, including baptism. He concludes, "... the sacraments are superfluous for him [John]." But they are not superfluous. They may be intimated: baptism in 3:3-5 and 9:7; the Eucharist possibly in 6:3-13 and 13:2-17. The point is that they, like Jesus' embodiment of the Passover meal, are to be absorbed internally in order to become and be what baptism and the Eucharist symbolize.

[17] Sandra M. Schneiders, "The Footwashing (John 13:1-20): An Experiment in Hermeneutics," *CBQ* 43 (1981) 84-86, construes the footwashing as a model of service between friends. Certainly Jesus' loving act constitutes a new structure of relationships that will be articulated in 15:14-15. But the washing of the feet, in contrast to the whole body, intimates the need for continuous confession and forgiveness.

the teacher. There may be some among the implied readers in Alexandria to whom especially these words are addressed.

> Amen, amen I say to you, the slave is not greater than his lord nor is an apostle greater than the one who sent him. If you know these things, fortunate are you if you do them. (13:16-17)

In contrast to Simon Peter, there is one who, although he has had his feet washed by Jesus, refuses to enter into the horizontal relationship that Jesus is constituting between himself and his followers. Consequently Jesus circumscribes what he has said to his circle of disciples by adding, "I am not speaking about all of you. I know whom I chose. But so that Scripture is fulfilled, 'The one chewing my bread raised his heel against me'." Of course, he is referring to Judas who will betray him, and, by betraying him will elevate himself above his Lord and teacher. The Septuagint quotation of Psa 40:10 that Jesus cites has been adapted to the larger context of the Fourth Gospel.

> The human being of my peace, upon whom I hoped; the one eating my loaves of bread, has exalted a supplanting against me.[18]

Only the second half of Psa 40:10 is utilized, and certain revisions have been made to accommodate the text to the narrative world of the Gospel. The nominal participle, ὁ τρώγων (the one chewing) has replaced ὁ ἐσθίων (the one eating), perhaps in order to remind the implied readers of Jesus' startling use of this verb in 6:54, 56, 58. The singular, ἄρτον (loaf of bread) has been substituted for the plural ἄρτους because Jesus is ὁ ἄρτος τῆς ζωής (the bread of life). The main verb, ἐπῆρεν (he lifted) and its object, πτέρναν (heel) have replaced ἐμεγάλυνεν ... πτερνισμόν (he exalted a supplanting). "... the words are not used primarily to stress the fact that the dreadful event had been foreseen or pre-determined by God, but to state the incredible fact that the betrayer eats at the same table as Jesus, and belongs to the circle of his friends."[19] More concretely, Judas, by chewing Jesus' bread, has been participating in the flesh and blood life of the enfleshed Logos-Sophia and therefore has experienced the authentic existence of God's ζωή (life) and φῶς (light) that Jesus communicates. His betrayal implies that he has elevated himself above Jesus – who as his Lord and Teacher has washed his feet – and judged him to be worthy of being put to death.

Jesus is enunciating the fulfillment that Judas' betrayal will actualize so that the faith of his disciples will not be devastated when the events of his Passion begin to unfold.

> I tell you from now before it happens so that when it does happen *you continue to believe* (πιστεύητε) that ἐγὼ εἰμί (**I AM**). (13:19)

[18] H. G. Liddell & Robert Scott, *A Greek-English Lexicon*, 1546, translates πτερνισμός as *supplanting*, citing LXX Psa 40 (41):10. It is derived from the verb πτερνίζω meaning *trip up, supplant*. The narrator has used πτέρναν, which is given the meaning *heel*.

[19] Bultmann, *John*, 478; German, 364-365.

Once again the problem of the original tense of the verb πιστεύειν (to believe) emerges. In 20:31, 19:35 and 6:29 the aorist subjunctive πιστεύσητε (you begin to believe) was adopted as the reading of the original edition of the Gospel.[20] Of the same two alternatives, the present subjunctive, πιστεύητε (you continue to believe) appears to be the original verb in this context of the first edition of the Gospel. Jesus is addressing his disciples – and the implied readers – who already believe so that they will not renounce their commitment to him in his disclosure to them as ἐγώ εἰμί (**I AM**).

In 12:44 he confronted the ruling elite who believed into him but refused to confess him openly with the reality of his affiliation with God, "The one who believes into me does not believe into me but into the one who sent me." Now in this context in which he prepares his disciples for his imminent death that will be initiated by the betrayal of Judas, he resorts to another double asseveration in order to remind them of the same alliance.

> Amen, amen I say to you, 'The one who receives anyone I shall send, receives me. But the one who receives me, receives the One who sent me.

It is above all the implied readers who are being addressed here, for Jesus is speaking in anticipation of sending forth his representatives in order to continue the work that he has inaugurated. There may be Judas-like informers in the Jewish community of Alexandria who are betraying those who confess Jesus as the Messiah. To them Jesus warrants the solemn truth that those who identify themselves as his disciples have been sent by him and therefore ultimately also by God.

For a second time following the closure of his ministry Jesus gives voice to his emotional state as he approaches his imminent death. Earlier, in 12:27, he expressed his inner turmoil arising from the dreadful ordeal of crucifixion and the stark attendant realities that await him. Now, in profound distress that a bosom friend in whom he trusted and who ate his bread is going to betray him, he again employs a double asseveration to announce to his disciples, "Amen, amen I say to you, 'One of you will betray me'." His disciples *were looking at* (ἔβλεπον) each other trying to discern who that might be.[21] In this context the narrator introduces "the one whom Jesus loved (ὃν ἠγάπα ὁ Ἰησοῦς), utilizing the same relative clause that was employed in 11:3, "Lord, look, ὃν φιλεῖς (the one whom you love) is sick."[22] It is a demeanor that is reinforced by the narrator's intrusive remark in 11:5 and by the exclamation of the by-standers in 11:36. On the basis of consistency building the Beloved Disciple must be Lazarus, a disciple who is dear

---

[20] See chapter 1, Introduction.

[21] As in other uses of the imperfect tense, denoting an ongoing action in the past, ἔβλεπον may imply the level of Jesus' earthly career in the narrative world of the Gospel.

[22] Like others, Culpepper, "The Johannine *Hypodeigma*," 145, contends that it is at this point that the Beloved Disciple is introduced.

to Jesus because he raised him from the dead and perhaps also because the chief priests have been planning to kill him too.

Simon Peter beckons to him to ask Jesus to identify that disciple. Emphasizing his posture as the one reclining in Jesus' bosom, the narrator implies that the Beloved Disciple, in the light of 1:18, should be recognized as the one who interprets Jesus. Because he had been a follower of John who bore witness to the Logos, and because he was raised from the dead as "the one whom Jesus loved," he is privileged to occupy a position of honor by reclining on Jesus' bosom. If the Logos, according to 1:18, is "into the bosom of the Father and interprets (the Father)," Jesus as the enfleshed Logos-Sophia becomes the historical interpreter of "the Father;" for as he tells Philip in 14:9, "The one having seen me has seen the Father." Analogously, therefore, the Beloved Disciple, who reclines in the bosom of Jesus, becomes the interpreter of Jesus, the incarnate Logos. His fearlessness of death, as a result of his resurrection, will enable him to follow Jesus into his trial, to be present at his execution, and to become the first believer in his resurrection from the dead.[23] Consequently, he is the only disciple in the narrative world of the Gospel who is qualified to supersede John by becoming the interpreter of the incarnate Logos-Sophia.

In response to the Beloved Disciple's question, "Lord, who is it?" Jesus answers obliquely, "It is that one for whom I shall dip the piece of bread and give to him." Dipping the bread, he gives it to Judas and, after he has received it, "*then* Satan entered into him." In this act of receiving the piece of bread, the Scripture of LXX Psa 40:10 is also fulfilled, "The one chewing my bread lifted his heel against me." At the beginning of the meal the narrator had informed the implied readers: "the devil had already cast into Judas' heart the notion of betrayal." After receiving the morsel of bread from Jesus, Judas is conquered by the design that he has been harboring to betray Jesus. Perceiving this overpowering resolution unfolding in Judas, Jesus charges him, "Do quickly that which you are going to do!" In an aside the narrator notes that the disciples reclining with Jesus misconstrued what he had said to Judas. Since they knew that he was in charge of the community treasury, they supposed that Jesus was bidding him to purchase whatever was needed for the feast or that he should give something to the destitute. So taking the morsel, Judas left the fellowship; and the narrator quickly adds, "and it was night." Finally that time in the narrative world arrives when "no one is able to work." But more significantly, at the departure of the betrayer this night also ushers in the effective fulfillment of the objective of the powers of darkness, Jesus' death. For him,

---

[23] Sandra M. Schneiders, " 'Because of the Women's Testimony …' Reexamining the Issue of Authorship in the Fourth Gospel," *NTS* 44/4 (1998) 520-522, on the basis of her reading of 19:25-26 concludes that the Beloved Disciple is "a textual paradigm realized in the plurality of textual figures who are drawn from real historical characters in the life of Jesus and/or the community." It is above all Mary Magdalene who serves as an eye-witness and who more than any other disciple embodied the role of the Beloved Disciple in the Gospel.

therefore, it is the time to enunciate his last will and testament and to take leave of his disciples.[24]

Jesus' farewell discourse[25]

Unit 1[26] • "Lord, where are you going?" 13:31 – 14:31

Jesus introduces his last will and testament by affirming his declaration of 12:23 and the confidence that he had derived from the heavenly attestation of 12:28, "Now the Son of the Human Being is glorified and God is glorified in him." For the last time in the narrative world of the Gospel he appropriates the figure of ὁ υἱὸς τοῦ ἀνθρώπου (the Son of the Human Being). It is from this eschatological-christological-anthropological perspective of the New Human Being that the implied readers are to hear his farewell speech. His glorification as the New Human Being has begun and with it also God's glorification because, as God's apprentice, he is now moving toward the fulfillment of his commission of saving the world.

But there is a glorification that will occur in the future, beyond the completion of his work through his death and resurrection. That glorification includes the work of his disciples – including those among the implied readers who have committed themselves to him – that will begin to be fulfilled on Easter evening when Jesus breathes the holy Spirit upon them in order to empower them to fulfill their commission.[27] All of them, as he intimates in 17:24, will be participating in his divine **I AM** as they *observe* (θεωρῶσιν) his glory and are apprehended by it and drawn into it. This continued fulfillment of God's work is valued so highly by God that God, as Jesus states, will glorify him, Jesus, immediately. That is the immense confidence that God has in Jesus' actualization of God's plan and purpose for the world.

---

[24] Farewell discourses in the form of a last will and testament are numerous in Jewish tradition. The Book of Deuteronomy is Moses' farewell speech. Jos 23-24 may be Joshua's farewell, and 2 Sam 22-23, the last words of David may be his farewell. The book of the Testaments of the Twelve Patriarchs presents the farewell speeches of Jacob's twelve sons. Segovia, *Farewell*, 5-20, reviews the various analyses of the genre of "Farewell Type-Scenes and Their Motifs." As a genre or type, farewell discourses are structured to convey: (1) an announcement of an imminent departure, (2) comfort for those being left behind, (3) recounting blessings, (4) exhortation to keep commandments, (5) a look to the future, (6) a possible choice of a successor. Ashton, *Understanding*, 470-471, considers the "true literary antecedent of John 14 [to be] the combined testament/commission form that appeared in Hebrew literature as early as the tenth century (1 Kings 2:1-9) and was taken over by the Deuteronomist (Deut 31:1-6, 6-8, 14-15, 23; Jos 1:1-9). See also Moloney, *Glory*, 5-7.

[25] The present structure of Jesus' Farewell Discourse can be interpreted intelligibly without a diachronic analysis of its component traditions. As Segovia says, *Farewell*, 20, "John 13-17 is a coherent and self-contained narrative section of the Gospel ..." Also Moloney, *Glory*, 4.

[26] Segovia, *Farewell*, 62, 125, 170, 215, also divides Jesus' farewell discourse into four units. The first, 13:31-14:31 conveys a three-part structure: 13:31-38, 14:1-27 and 14:28-31. See pp. 64-68.

[27] *Ibid.*, 73, rightly interprets 13:32 in terms of "the Son of the Human Being" but limits this eschatological-christological-anthropological figure to Jesus alone.

These opening verses of Jesus' farewell address, 13:31-32, encapsulate all the aspects of his last will and testament that involve him and his disciples – and the implied readers – in the glorification that has begun and in the glorification that will be realized in the future. Having stated these realities of the present and the future, Jesus announces his imminent departure:

> Little children, yet a little while I am (εἰμί) with you. You will look for me, and, even as I told the Jews, "Where I am going, you are unable to come," and I tell you now. (13:33)

As in 7:34 and 8:21, when he informed the ruling elite of his eventual departure, he does not disclose the destination of his going away. His qualification, "Where I am going, you are not able to come!" is not necessarily an ambiguous reference to the *Parousia*, the so-called second coming. Jesus may disappear from them, and for a brief time they will be left without any security, except for their commitment to him.[28] But he will reveal the destination of his departure soon enough. More immediately his disciples are to know that they will be left alone, without his presence, and any search for him will be fruitless.[29] This is a new time, and in this crisis of separation it is imperative that they support each other. Jesus, therefore, issues a new charge, a new commandment by which they will be able to establish their solidarity:

> A new commandment I give you, that you love one another, even as I loved you, so that you also love one another. (13:34)

In this open-ended duration of separation they are to love each other as completely and unreservedly as Jesus has loved them. His love for Lazarus, manifested by risking his life to return to Judea in order to raise him from the dead, serves as a paradigm of the divine unqualified love that his disciples are commanded to express to each other in deeds and words. Moreover, by communicating this kind of love to each other, "… all will know that you are my disciples, if you have love among each other." *Agape* is the hallmark of Jesus' discipleship. The love that he is eliciting is not "a personal emotion, but is the service that liberates; and the response to it is not a mystical or pietistic intimacy with Christ, but the ἀλλήλους ἀγαπᾶν" (to love one another).[30]

Simon Peter interrupts Jesus' farewell speech, perhaps to serve as the spokesperson of the anxiety of separation that Jesus' announcement has evoked, "Where are you going?" he inquires. Surely his great love that he offered a

[28] Bultmann, *John*, 524-525; German, 402-403, recognizes that their "… future is subjected to an imperative," but he seems to have neglected the faith commitment that the disciples bring with them up to this very moment; and it is on the basis of that faith commitment that Jesus issues a new commandment to them.

[29] See Segovia, *Farewell*, 75, n. 34, who acknowledges "the similar status accorded to both Jews and disciples with regard to the departure," but, as his interpretation of 14:1-3 indicates, that similar status is based on Jesus' eventual ascension.

[30] Bultmann, *John*, 526; German, 404.

moment ago as a model for his disciples requires that he disclose the destination of his departure. But for the moment at least his response is as enigmatic as his earlier announcement of departure, but with the stipulation that is specifically addressed to Peter: "Where I am going, you are not able to follow me *now*, but you will follow me later." This one exception, "You will follow me later," that stands in contrast to 13:33c, must imply his eventual martyrdom by crucifixion.[31] But Peter wants to follow him into his departure now. Whether he has an inkling of where Jesus is going is not clear. In mindless abandonment he expresses a readiness to sacrifice himself on Jesus' behalf, "I will offer my life (ψυχήν) on your behalf." In an ironic response Jesus exposes his empty pledge by juxtaposing his avowal with a forecast of his eventual threefold denial that he warrants with a double asseveration, "Amen, amen I say to you, 'By no means will the cock crow until you deny me three times'."

Jesus' love for his disciples, however, requires an answer to Peter's question; but, in view of the destination of his departure, a word of consolation and encouragement is essential. He employs the verb that expressed his own emotional state in 12:27 and 13:21 in order to alleviate the anxiety of his disciples: "Don't let your heart be agitated!"[32] The courage that is vital in this time of crisis originates from and is renewed by faith: "Keep on believing into God and keep on believing into me!"[33] Their continued commitment will draw them into the monumental consequences of his departure.

Jesus follows these words of comfort with a promise: "In my Father's house are many rooms (μοναί). If not, I would tell you, for I'm going away to prepare a place for you." For the second and only other time in the Gospel Jesus speaks of "the Father's house." In 2:16, after he had driven the animals of sacrifice and the bankers from the sacred precinct of the Temple, he rebuked the guardians of society, "Don't make my Father's house a house of business!" His violent action evoked his disciples' memory of LXX Psa 68 (69):10. But the quotation of this Septuagint text has been edited by the implied author, and the verb in the aorist tense, κατέφαγεν (it consumed), has been replaced by the future καταφάγεται (it will consume): "The zeal of your house *will consume* me." As a result of his replacement of the Temple's sanctuary (ναός) that houses God's presence with his own physical body, Jesus' becomes "the Father's house." He will be its embodiment throughout the narrative world of the Gospel. Consequently, it will be the zeal of the Father's house that will consume him in fulfilling his apprenticeship.

---

[31] Also Barrett, *St. John*, 453. Segovia, *Farewell*, 78, acknowledges Jesus' use of the second person singular of the verbs δύνασαι (you are able) and ἀκολουθήσεις (you will follow), yet he applies them to all the disciples. See Bultmann, *John*, 596-597; German, 460-461, who separates the two verbs, ὑπάγειν (to go away) and ἀκολουθεῖν (to follow) in order to differentiate between Jesus' eschatological act in which Peter cannot follow and the discipleship of following Jesus into "world-annulment and beyond that into "glory" that can only be realized through faith.

[32] Contrary to Moloney, *Glory*, 29, the farewell proper begins with 13:31, not 14:1.

[33] Both verbs are formulated in the present imperative denoting continuous believing.

When, therefore, he tells his disciples that there are many rooms in the Father's house, he is anticipating the enlargement of that house that he has been embodying as the residence of God's Spirit.[34] His departure, therefore, is oriented towards the incorporation of his disciples into "the Father's house," and it is by his death and resurrection, not his ascension, that a place for them in the Father's house will be actualized. Consequently, Jesus' earlier announcement, "... where I am going you are not able to come," more immediately refers to his death and resurrection.[35] After he has prepared a place for them in the Father's house that he has embodied, and after his preliminary ascension, he will return on Easter evening to complete the work of enlarging the Father's house by adding more Spirit-filled rooms. When he breathes the holy Spirit upon his disciples, they are incorporated into the living Temple of God and they become bearers of God's presence. The Father's house is not a supramundane condominium or place of the heavenly mansions beyond historical existence.[36] It is the historical reality of a dynamic expanding, mobile House of God consisting of many rooms, represented by those who commit themselves to Jesus, in whom the presence of the Creator resides.[37] Perhaps *the Father's house* (οἰκία τοῦ πατρός) is the self-designation of the Christian Jews in the Jewish community of Alexandria.[38]

The duration of Jesus' departure will not be long: "And if I go and prepare a place for you, I am coming again, and I shall receive you to myself, so that *where **AM I*** (ὅπου εἰμὶ ἐγώ), you also are."[39] This too is not a reference to his anticipated ascension![40] Jesus will return to them after his resurrection and

---

[34] Like other commentators, Moloney, *Glory*, 33, does not engage in "consistency building" and therefore does not connect 14:2 with 2:16 and the change of tense in the quotation of Psa 69:10 that has a bearing on 14:2, 23.

[35] Contrary to Bultmann, *ibid.*, 600-601; German, 463-464, Ashton, *Understanding*, 461, who identify "the Father's house" as "the heavenly home"; also Lindars, *John*, 470. Dodd, *Interpretation*, 404-405, correctly acknowledges "the first intention of the words, the journey of death." But he misconstrues the place that Jesus is preparing for his disciples as heaven and therefore also his return "to bring them home" as a reference to the second coming.

[36] Robert H. Gundry, "In my Father's House are many Μοναί," *ZNW* 58 (1967) 70, says, "We are not at first to regard the 'abodes' as rooms in heaven." The more immediate meaning therefore is: "... not mansions in the sky, but spiritual positions in Christ, much as in Pauline theology." However, " ... a natural, even a necessary inference that Jesus means he will go to the Father in heaven, will therefore prepare a place (or abodes) for his disciples, and afterwards will return to receive them so that they may be – to use his own words – "where I am."

[37] Barrett, *St. John*, 456, rightly construes "the Father's house" as communion with God, but also infers that it refers to heaven, "to which Jesus is now returning". Segovia, *ibid.*, 82-83, in spite of his fine close reading of the text, has not engaged in consistency building and therefore interprets 14:2 traditionally as an ascension. Jesus is going to the Father's house to prepare a place for his disciples.

[38] David E. Aune, *The Cultic Setting of Realized Eschatology in Early Christianity* (Leiden: Brill, 1972) 130, interprets 14:2 as "the self-designation of the Johannine community."

[39] Philo, *de Vita Mosis* I, 84, seems to have had no difficulty in reversing the divine self-disclosure ἐγὼ εἰμί to εἰμὶ ἐγώ. He revised the Septuagint's translation of God's self-acknowledgment, ὀυκ ἐγὼ ὁ θεός (Is it not I God?) as the author of the organs of communication by substituting αὐτός εἰμὶ ἐγώ (**I** myself **AM**).

[40] Bultmann, *John*, 602, n. 1; German, 465, n. 1, who rightly contends that the eschatology here is not that of "the Jewish-Christian hope," that is the so-called second coming. But neither is it "the

ascension.[41] He and his disciples – and his disciples among the implied readers – will be reunited after his death and resurrection as the expanded and expanding incorporated living Temple of God. As co-embodiments of God's house, Jesus and his disciples will be in communion with each other, and his disciples, therefore, will also be participants in his divine εἰμὶ ἐγώ. It is this orientation to a historically constituted, ever-growing Temple of God incorporating Jesus and his disciples that determines the meaning of 14:4-24.

Jesus, having informed his disciples why he is going away, and having stipulated more specifically the outcome of his departure, assumes that now at least they know the way to his destination, "And where I am going you know the way." On the basis of his announcement at the closure of his ministry in 12:23-24 they should know the way, "Except a seed falling into the ground and dies, it cannot bear much fruit." Unless Jesus goes into death and resurrection, rooms cannot be added to the Father's house and attendantly the disciples will not be able to be united with him in his **I AM**.

But, as Thomas' response indicates, he and his fellow disciples have not comprehended what Jesus has been telling them and therefore they still have no notion of where he is going. So he asks, "How do we know the way?" For this ultimate historical destination of being united with God through Jesus' divine **I AM**, there is no other way except in terms of his self-disclosure: "**I AM** (ἐγώ εἰμί) the Way, the Truth and the Life." To be drawn *towards* God and therefore to be united with God in the historical existence of the present time can only be realized through Jesus, the enfleshed Logos-Sophia, "No one comes *towards* (πρός) the Father except through me."[42] Jesus is the Way precisely because in and through

---

individualistic eschatology of the Gnostic myth," as he claims. It is the corporate reality of being united with Jesus in the living Temple of God and therefore also in Jesus' εἰμὶ ἐγώ. Gundry, "In my Father's House are many Μοναί," 72, concludes, "According to the first meaning Jesus speaks of his going to the cross, his preparing by his death spiritual abodes in the Father's household or family, his return to the disciples immediately after his resurrection, and the sending of the Spirit to minister his continuing presence until he comes to receive those who are already in him so that they may be with him eternally. And all of that anticipates the second meaning according to which Jesus speaks of his going to the house of heaven, his preparing there abodes for believers, his return, and his taking believers to be with him in heaven forever since they have already come to be in him in faith."

[41] According to Lindars, *John*, 471, "Jesus will first go and prepare the rooms, and then go back to welcome the guests. It is natural to think of this as the Parousia, or Second Coming. But if Jesus' departure is his death, then the return is his resurrection, and the reception of the guests is the mutual indwelling which will obtain in the post-Resurrection situation of the Church." But Barrett, *St. John*, 457, continues to vacillate between the *Parousia* and present, on-going communion with Christ.

[42] On 14:6b, see Charlesworth, "Exclusivism Caused by a Different Setting,"506, who concludes that "exclusivistic theology that denies salvation, a way to God, except through Jesus is founding the Gospel of John only in 14:6b". Verse 14b is not a later interpolation! And in 14:6ab Jesus is not speaking about salvation or "a way to God". Charlesworth has not taken into account the significance of the preposition in 14:6b and 1:1-2. Jesus is presenting himself as the pioneering incarnate Logos-Sophia who is fulfilling God's will by constructing the way into a union of "awesome intimacy" with the Creator. This by no means forecloses the way to God through prayer and worship by any human being, regardless of religious faith or denominational membership. Salvation is not to be construed as going to heaven after physical death; it is recovering human health and wholeness by exiting from the cave of non-being at Jesus' call and being unbound by one's bystanders. Beyond that there is

him the objective of the Logos, who primordially moves *towards* (πρός) God in order to unite with God, is to fulfill God's will for creation by drawing human beings into a union of intimacy with God. Jesus is the Truth because, as the Light of the first day of creation, he, by his deeds and words, is the Truth of God. He is the Life because the divine, never-ending Life (ζωή) of God resides in him as the result of the incarnation of the Logos-Sophia and the permanently abiding Spirit of God. Consequently, Jesus is united with the Father so completely, so consummately that he can say to his disciples – and the implied readers – "If you *have known* (ἐγνώκατε) me, you also would *know* (ἤδειτε) the Father."[43] Knowing Jesus experientially and existentially engenders a cognitive knowledge of God, for Jesus, as the incarnate Logos-Sophia, exegetes God (1:18). His disciples, who have accompanied him during his ministry and have witnessed his work as God's apprentice, already *know* (γινώσκετε) "the Father." In fact, they have eye-balled him, they have *seen* (ἑωράκατε) God (14:7).

Philip, one of Jesus' original disciples, enters as another interlocutor in order to enable Jesus to elucidate the meaning of what he has said: "Show us the Father, and it is enough for us!" If Jesus can give them a glimpse of God, their faith will be affirmed and all that Jesus has enunciated as the Way, the Truth and the Life will be credible and trustworthy. Representing his fellow disciples, Philip, like his fellow Galilean Jews of 4:48, wants empirical evidence to confirm the truth of Jesus' relationship to the Father.. But the endorsement of the primacy of seeing promotes the establishment of truth on the basis of sense experience and therefore brackets the reality of possibility. Those who have *observed* Jesus and abandoned themselves to him in commitment should, as a consequence, be able to observe God and therefore also abandon themselves to God. Apparently Philip and his fellow disciples have not experienced the coincidence of observing God by observing Jesus. He is constrained therefore to accentuate his previous disclosure: "The one who *has seen* (ἑωρακως) me *has seen* (ἑώρακεν) the Father. Do you not believe that I [am] in the Father and the Father is in me?" The image that Jesus has projected in all that he has done and said is the face of God. While it is true, as 1:18 maintains, that no one has ever *seen* (ἑώρακεν) God, Jesus, the New Human Being as the enfleshment of the Logos-Sophia, manifests the image and likeness of God.[44] His works and his words originate from God who *remains* (μένων) in him. He submits to his disciples, as he submitted to the ruling elite in 10:25, 38, that his works are the basic premise that establishes "the mutual presence of Jesus and the Father in one another" and therefore also their faith.[45] "Believe me that I [am] in

incarnation, the empowerment by God's Spirit to engage in world transformation and accordingly continue the work that Jesus inaugurated. Jesus is the only Way into the continuation of incarnation in this world and the fulfillment of 14:12.

[43] It is the perfect active indicative, ἐγνώκατε, attested to by P^{66} and other mss. So also Barrett, *St. John*, 458; and Metzger, *A Textual Commentary on the Greek New Testament*, 243.

[44] As in 5:37, Jesus, as the incarnate Logos-Sophia is the εἶδος of God.

[45] Segovia, *Farewell*, 89.

the Father and the Father in me, and if not, believe on account of the works themselves!"

That faith that acknowledges the intimate union between "the Son" and "the Father" is simply an extension of their commitment to Jesus, and it is that commitment to him that bears momentous consequences in their discipleship. By another double asseveration Jesus warrants the awesome possibilities that their commitment to him will actualize (14:12).

> Amen, amen I say to you, "The one who believes into me will do the works that I do and greater things than these she/he will do because I am going to the Father."

This anticipation of their collaboration with him glorifies God by consummating the glorification of "the Son of the Human Being," as Jesus intimated in 13:31-32).[46] He will support them in their continuation of his apprenticeship by responding affirmatively to their prayers and intercessions, and that will perpetuate God's glorification in the Son (14:13).

In 14:15 Jesus returns to the new commandment that he issued to them in 13:34-35. The love that he anticipates from them, based on their commitment to him will be expressed in their obedience to his commandments. He is constituting a horizontal relationship with them for the continuation of his work, but he is nevertheless their Pioneer and also their Lord. What those commandments are will eventually be disclosed. As yet, only one has been articulated, and that on the basis of his own initiating love for them. Indeed, whatever commandments he will impose on them he has already observed in his own horizontally established relationship with God.

The love that binds them together in a mutuality of purpose will require their empowerment that will enable them to do his works and to do even greater things. In this eventuality their endowment with God's Spirit is essential.

> And I shall ask the Father and he will give you another Advocate/Paraclete so that it will be with you forever. (14:16)

The major features of the genre of a farewell discourse have been emerging in Jesus' last will and testament. He has announced his imminent departure. He has consoled and encouraged his disciples and promised their participation in the living Temple of God that he embodies. He has exhorted them to observe his commandment of love. Now as he begins to anticipate his return to the Father, beyond his going away into death and resurrection, he promises them a successor to serve in the role of a παράκλητος, an *intercessor*, an *encourager*, an *advocate*, the role in which he has been serving them. This Paraclete is "the Spirit of Truth," the Spirit that Jesus has embodied throughout his ministry as the Light of the

---

[46] Contrary to Segovia, *ibid.*, the grounding of Jesus' promise in 14:12 is the disciples' believing into Jesus. His disclosure of his return to the Father is the necessary cause to insure the continuation of his work.

world. It is the Spirit of God that descended and remained on him and blew into his face the primordial Logos at the time of his baptism by John the Witness.

The world, alienated and alienating by its own construction of reality, is unable to perceive the light of the first day of creation and therefore cannot receive the Paraclete. Those who surrender themselves to the world's social construction of reality cannot *behold/observe* (θεωρεῖ) the Spirit of Truth, and because they have not given themselves over to it, they have not experienced it and do not *know* (γινώσκει) it. The incapability of the world to *see* and *know* has already become apparent in the ministry of Jesus. The disciples, however, have *observed* it in the objectification of truth that Jesus has manifested as the enfleshment of the Logos-Sophia. They have *observed* it because God's Spirit has been residing in Jesus as "the Father's house," and therefore, as Jesus says in 14:17c, God's Spirit has been *remaining* (μένει) alongside of them and will be in them. That, as already indicated, will take place on Easter evening.

The second half of chapter 14 continues to develop the two levels of understanding that have been disclosed in the first half.[47] Jesus has announced his imminent departure, a departure, however, into death and resurrection in order to prepare a place for his disciples in the living Temple of God that he embodies. He will return to his disciples after his resurrection and preliminary ascension in order to give them the Paraclete, so that this Spirit of Truth will dwell within them and empower them for the continuation of his work. Accordingly, he assures them that they will not be orphaned; he will return to them: "I am coming *towards* (πρός) you." The preposition πρός, on the basis of its other uses in the Gospel, implies union. Although Jesus is going away into death and resurrection, he assures his disciples, "In a little while the world will no longer *see/observe* (θεωρεῖ) me, but you will *see/observe* (θεωρεῖτε) me." They will experience him, indeed, they will *see* (ἰδόντες) him; and by their participation in his resurrection they will begin to live: "Because I live, you also will live." Jesus will establish a permanent presence with them.[48] This promise is based on " a mystical union of awesome intimacy" that will emerge at that point in time, for as Jesus goes on to tell them, "In that day *you will know* (γνώσεσθε) that I in my Father and you in me and I in you."[49]

This "awesome intimacy" presupposes that the commandments that Jesus has issued to his disciples will be kept and fulfilled because they continue to love him. Their love to him guarantees God's love to them as well as Jesus' continued love to them, and Jesus pledges that in that intimacy of love he will continue to *make* himself *visible* (ἐμφανίσω) to them. That assurance must presuppose the ongoing reality of incarnation of the Logos-Sophia, now embodied in Jesus of Nazareth, but

---

[47] Ashton, *Understanding*, 466, is quite correct in differentiating two levels of understanding, and determining that the first level is "the mystical union of awesome intimacy." But he relegates the second level to the future life that believers can anticipate, and 14:2-3, therefore, in spite of his interpretation of 14:23, is "set in heaven." See pages 461-462.

[48] Ashton, *Understanding*, 463.

[49] The quoted phrase is taken from Ashton, *ibid.*, 466.

appearing within the fellowship and communion of the New Humanity that he is pioneering after his resurrection and preliminary ascension.

Still another interlocutor enters the dialogue between Jesus and his disciples, "Judas, not the Iscariot," who inquires, "Lord, what then has happened that you are going to make yourself visible to us and not to the world?" In his response Jesus not only repeats what he has already said in the first half of verse 21, but he returns to 14:2 in order to reinforce the privileged membership of those who acknowledge themselves to be the embodiment of "the Father's house." "If anyone loves me, she/he will fulfill my word, and my Father will love him, and we shall come *towards* (πρός) him/her and we shall make a room (μονήν) with him/her." The love that arises out of commitment to Jesus and the commitment to him that is energized by love will sustain the disciple's membership in this divine household. But where this animated love is absent, the fulfillment of his words will be precluded; and, lest it be forgotten, the word that he speaks originates from "the Father who sent him."

In the face of this disquieting note Jesus diminishes their apprehension by reintroducing the Successor he had promised earlier in 14:16. He is aware of the weaknesses of their humanity and therefore emphasizes that he has spoken all these things while remaining *alongside of them* (παρ' ὑμῖν). "But the Paraclete, the holy Spirit, whom the Father will send in my name," and who, according to 14:17c *will be in them*, "will teach all things and remind you of all the things I said to you." In this respect the Paraclete will serve as his Successor and as their Advocate. Jesus removes whatever trepidation or diffidence might remain by pronouncing a benediction of peace upon them, "Peace I leave to you, my peace I give to you. Not as the world gives do I give to you. Let your heart neither be agitated nor cowardly. You heard that I said to you, 'I'm going away and I'm coming *toward* (πρός) you'."[50] His return after Easter will draw them into union with him and with "the Father" by breathing God's Spirit upon them and incorporating them as individual rooms into "the Father's house."

Having mollified their anxiety, Jesus turns their attention to his ultimate destiny. While they relish the benediction of peace that he has pronounced upon then and trust him for the fulfillment of his promise to send his Successor, they can rejoice and take pleasure in his return to God: "If you love me, you would rejoice because I am going *towards* (πρός) the Father." Now, for the first time, Jesus alludes to his eventual ascension. The primordial movement of the Logos-Sophia, now incarnate in Jesus, is going to be consummated. The Son of the Human Being, who descended in order to be lifted up as a snake in the wilderness, is going to ascend and return to his heavenly origin where he, as God's apprentice will reenter his primordial glory in his subordination to God, "for the Father is greater than I."[51]

[50] See also 17:11.

[51] See C. K. Barrett, *Essays on John,* 19-36, for his discussion of the subordinationist christology of the Fourth Gospel over against the essential equality that the Nicene Creed attributes to the three

All that he has said so far in his dialogical interactions with his disciples has been intended to prepare them for the events that will soon begin to unfold. By voicing his motive in 14:29, he continues to convey his solicitude toward them, "And now I told you before it happens, so that when it happens you may believe once and for all." They have been committed to him, but the fulfillment of all that he has forewarned them should establish them decisively in their faith.

Jesus is now ready to conclude his dialogical exchange with them: "No longer *shall I speak* much *with you*" (λαλήσω μεθ' ὑμῶν). Ordinarily whenever he addresses them with his pronouncements and exhortations, the narrator employs the verb λαλεῖν (to speak) followed by the personal pronouns ὑμῖν (to you), αὐτοῖς (to them), σοι (to you) or αὐτῷ (to him) in the dative case.[52] There are two instances, however, in which the verb λαλεῖν is followed by the preposition μετά. In 4:27, after the Samaritan woman has left Jesus to return to her fellow Samaritans, the disciples ask Jesus, "Why are *you speaking with her*?" (Τί λαλεῖς μετ' αυτῆς?). The combination of the verb λαλεῖς and the prepositional phrase μετ' αυτῆς implies that he has been engaged in a conversation with the Samaritan woman. Here in 14:30, the other exception, Jesus is informing his disciples that he is delimiting their dialogue in which he and they have been engaged. They have interrupted his farewell discourse with their questions, and he has answered them with love and patience. But for the time being, at least, there will be no more exchanges between them, "For," as he continues, "the ruler of the world is coming, and he has nothing in me, but in order that the world knows that I love the Father, and even as the Father commanded me, so I am doing." There are no allegations or charges that Satan, in his role as accuser, can level against Jesus.[53] He has continued to discharge all that God commanded him to do, even in his farewell exchange with his disciples. Consequently, the world – and the implied readers of Alexandria – *should know* (γνῷ) on the basis of all that he has done and said in the narrative world of the Gospel that he loves "the Father."[54]

Because the ruler of the world is coming, there will be no more dialogue between Jesus and his disciples, at least not until 16:17.[55] But Jesus will continue his farewell discourse. John 15:1-16:16 is the longest monologue in the Gospel. To end this first unit of his last will and testament he summons his disciples – and the implied readers – "Arouse yourselves! Let us go from here!" Generally these

---

"persons" of the Godhead. The subordinationist christology of the Fourth Gospel does not support the formulation of the Nicene Creed.

[52] As in 6:63; 8:12, 25,; 10:6; 12:29; 14:25; 15:3, 11, 22; 16:4, 6, 25, 33.

[53] Satan serves as God's district attorney or accuser in Job 1:6-13; 2:1-7; Zech 3:1-2 and Rev 12:10. Contrary to Moloney, *Glory*, 51-52, "the ruler of the world" is not an "oblique reference to the Jews."

[54] Brown, *John* II, 656, has observed, "Verse 31 is the only passage in the NT that states that Jesus *loves* the Father."

[55] Segovia, *Farewell*, 323, aptly characterizes the two-fold command of 14:31d as "a distinctive concluding marker," but a marker by which Jesus' terminates, at least temporarily, his interchange with his disciples.

two imperatives, ἐγείρεσθε and ἄγωμεν have been construed as the conclusion of Jesus' original farewell address. Many interpreters have noted it as a parallel to Mark 14:42. It has the appearance of a seam between 14:31a and 18:1 that induces many interpreters to reach the conclusion that two or three traditions of Jesus' farewell speech have been redacted into a more or less cohesive unity.[56] On the basis of a diachronic source-redactional analysis, Fernando F. Segovia posits three stages of composition as "a process of accretion and expansion," 13:31-14:31, 15:18-16:4a and 16:4b-33, and 15:1-17, that served "as a repository for ongoing and developing messages to the community."[57]

A close reading of 14:30-31 opens the possibility that a diachronic source-redactional analysis of John 14-16 is unnecessary to explicate 13:31-14:31 as the original of two or three farewell speeches.[58] To resolve the problem of 14:31b as an element that a final editor allowed to stand because he "did not want to tamper with the text" is a surrender to the platonically oriented method of redaction criticism that prioritizes ideas instead of experience.[59] Jesus' concluding summons, "Arouse yourselves! Let us go from here!" is not a mustering call, "The ruler of this world is coming ... Up, let us be going!"[60] There is more that must be said! But Jesus is not going to continue his dialogical exchanges with his disciples. The ruler of the world is coming, and therefore it is essential that he concludes his last will and testament as a farewell to his disciples.

The initial verb that Jesus employs, ἐγείρειν, occurs in different contexts throughout the Gospel, usually in the active voice.[61] The form in 14:31b, ἐγείρεσθε, is distinctive as a present middle or present passive imperative, occurring only here in the narrative world of the Gospel. If it is to be construed as a present middle imperative, it should be translated, "Keep on arousing yourselves!" On the other hand, if it is a present passive imperative, it would be rendered "Keep on being awakened or aroused!" Either of these meanings would appear to be appropriate in this context.[62] It is night, according to 13:30, and,

---

[56] Bultmann, *John*, 631; German, 489. Brown, *John* II, 656; Schnackenburg, *St. John* II, 87-88; see also his discussion, pp. 89-93; Fortna, *Fourth Gospel*, 149; apparently also Keener, *John* II, 986. See Ashton's discussion on "The Community and its Book, *Understanding*, 162-174 . See Wayne Brouwer, *The Literary Development of John 13-17: A Chiastic Reading* (Atlanta: Society of Biblical Literature, 2000), 109-115 on "Displacement Theory" and "Multiple Sources Theory."

[57] *Farewell*, 319-328; Segovia, however, devotes most of his book to a synchronic analysis of the Farewell Discourse. See also Barrett, *St. John*, 454.

[58] Verse 31c does not necessarily reflect an earlier stage in the development of the discourse before chapters 15-17 were added. Brouwer, *The Literary Development of John 13-17*, 147-154, attempts to resolve the inconsistencies and disjunctures of the farewell speech by a macro-chiastic reading that locates the center of the discourse in the metaphor of the vine, 15:1-17. But disjunctures and inconsistencies are often more validly determined by a close reading of the text.

[59] Brown, *John* II, 656, and many others!

[60] See Dodd, *Fourth Gospel*, 409.

[61] As in 2:19, 20; 5:8, 21; 12:1, 9,17. In the passive voice only in 2:22; 7:52; 11:29; 13:4.

[62] The present active imperative is used to convey the command, ἔγειρε, "Get up" or "Rise," and that is how ἐγείρεσθε is translated by many commentators. See Brown, *John* II, 656.

before Jesus initiates his monologue – after the exchange that has taken place between them – it is imperative that his disciples *and the implied readers* are wide awake. The movement that is implied in his second imperative, "Let us go from here!" (ἄγωμεν ἐντεῦθεν) may seem to be a transition from the table fellowship that Jesus and his disciples have been sharing into a confrontation with those who are coming to apprehend him. But there is no physical movement reported by the narrator.[63] Moreover, no intrusive remark that might provide a transition interrupts the narration.[64] The imperative is simply enunciating a digression into a new topic, a subject matter that will require the disciples' – and the implied readers' – vital attention.[65]

Unit 2[66] • "I AM the authentic vine-stock!" 15:1-17[67]

Jesus proceeds with his farewell discourse by confronting his disciples – and the implied readers – with a startling **I AM** declaration, but without the narrator's frequently employed prefatory announcement of a direct discourse: "Jesus said" or "Jesus spoke, saying." His bold, perhaps even audacious enunciation of self-disclosure, " **I AM** (ἐγὼ εἰμί) the true Vine-stock and my Father is the farmer" introduces a predicate that bears profound implications for the self-understanding of his disciples – and especially the implied readers of Alexandria. He appropriates an agricultural metaphor that encompasses the annual cycle of viticulture and therefore enables him to identify its essential realities of the vine-stock, the farmer, and the branches with the tri-partite fellowship that he is constituting in his collaboration with God. More significantly, his attachment of the adjective ἀληθινή (true/authentic) to the metaphor ἄμπελος (vine-stock), "**I AM** the authentic Vine-stock," recalls Jeremiah's characterization of Israel as the *authentic vine-stock* (ἄμπελον ἀληθινήν) that God planted, but a vine-stock that retrogressed into bitterness (πικρία) and became an alien vine-stock.[68] Within this Alexandrian context of Judaism, Jesus declares that he is the genuine Vine-stock

---

[63] See Brouwer, *Literary Development of John 13-17*, 104-105, for a summary of the constructions of 14:31 that are oriented to "Delayed Physical Movement". Jesus uses the time during which the disciples are getting themselves ready "to explain further some of the matters that he had already begun to address."

[64] *Ibid.*, 107-109, on the "Transitional Movement," that maintains that at this point Jesus and his disciples are beginning their procession to Gethsemane."

[65] There is no need to posit "tension and delay" in the experience of the implied readers, as Moloney does, *Glory*, 52-53, neither is it correct to project this into an eschatology of living "in-between" the times.

[66] Segovia, *Farewell*, 125-135, divides the second unit of Jesus' farewell speech into two major sections: 15:1-8 and 15:9-17.

[67] John 15:1-17 may be the "turning point," the center of the macro-chiastic structure of the farewell discourse, as Brouwer, *Literary Development of John 13-17*, 167-170 contends, but it should be worked out more consistently in conjunction with the development of Jesus' thought.

[68] LXX Jer 2:21.

implying, therefore, that he has replaced the vine-stock that God originally planted but that already in Jeremiah's time had degenerated into a wild vine.

The vine-stock is a common metaphor for Israel, as Hos 10:1, Isa 5:1, Jer 2:21, and Ezek 17:6-8 attest.[69] Psalm 79(80):8-16 laments the ravaging of the vine-stock that God brought out of Egypt, planted and carefully tended.[70] The psalm, composed perhaps before the Babylonian captivity, possibly during the career of Jeremiah, expresses the misery of Israel, being despoiled by the beastly kingdoms that have broken down its walls, and implores God "to look from heaven and be mindful of the vine-stock." Verse 16 personifies Israel as υἱὸς ἀνθρώπου (son of a human being) "whom you made strong for yourself" and verse 18 petitions God: "Let your hand be upon the man of your right hand and upon a son of a human being (υἱὸν ἀνθρώπου) whom you made strong for yourself."[71] As the genuine Vine-stock and therefore the true Israel, Jesus may also be identified with the psalm's personification of Israel as υἱὸς ἀνθρώπου "whom [God] has made strong for himself."

Israel was represented as the vine-stock on the coins of the Maccabees. Of more immediate interest, however, is a Bar-Kokhba Temple coin that shows a curving line that appears to be a representation of the Temple façade that is described by Josephus in both *The Jewish War* and *Jewish Antiquities*.[72]

> The gate opening into the building was, as I said, completely overlaid with gold, as was the whole wall around it. It had, moreover, above it those golden vines from which were hanging grape-clusters as tall as a human being.[73]
>
> The entrance-doors, which with their lintels were equal (in height) to the sanctuary (ναός), he adorned with multi-colored hangings, with purple colors and with in-woven design of pillars. Above these, under the cornice, spread a golden vine with grape-clusters hanging from it, a marvel of size and artistry to all who saw it with what costliness of material it had been constructed.[74]

Evidently the representation of Israel as the vine-stock, indeed, a golden vine-stock with grape-clusters hanging from it, as it adorned the great entrance doors of the sanctuary, remained impressed on the memory of the Jewish people, not only into

---

[69] Also Schweizer, *EGO EIMI*, 39-41, but, he wrongly concludes that the vine in John 15 does not have its origin in the Old Testament but in the mythology of the tree of life, as it is encountered in the Mandaean parallels.

[70] Cited by Barrett, *St. John*, 472. See Brown's discussion, *John* II, 668-684.

[71] It is the Septuagint version that is quoted here, Psa 79:16 and 18.

[72] See Lawrence D. Sporty, "Identifying the Curving Line on the Bar-Kokhba Temple Coin," *BA* 46/2 (1983, 121-123. Sporty includes a picture of a sarcophagus from Mount Scopus showing a grapevine motif. Also John Pairman Brown, "The Mediterranean Vocabulary of the Vine," *VT* 19/2 (1969) 170.

[73] Josephus, *BJ* 5, 210, *Loeb Classical Library* III, 265.

[74] Josephus, *Ant* XV, 394-395, *Loeb Classical Library* VIII, 191.

the time of Bar Kokhba but into later centuries, as the gold-decorated glass plate of the Via Labina cemetery in Rome dramatizes.[75] Presumably it was inscribed in the memory of many of the Jews of Alexandria, who had made pilgrimages to Jerusalem before 70 C.E. and had seen these beautiful motifs. Jesus' self-disclosure, "**I AM** the authentic Vine-stock," without any introductory direct discourse formula would make a formidable impression on the implied readers. At the beginning of his ministry Jesus substituted his own body in place of the sanctuary (ναός) to become "the Father's house"(2:19-21). Now after the closure of his ministry, prior to his death and resurrection, he replaces the golden vine adorning the great doors of the Temple's sanctuary to become the authentic Vine-stock and therefore also the personification of the true Israel. He is both the living Temple of God and the Vine-stock that embodies the new people of God.[76]

"The Father" is the farmer, but in contrast to the work of planting that is ascribed to him in Jer 2:21 and LXX Psa 79 (80):8, he is engaged in tending the branches that are grafted into the Vine-stock. He removes the branches that are not bearing fruit, and he prunes or *cleans* (καθαίρει) the branches that are bearing fruit so that they will become more fruitful. In the face of this anxiety-raising ambiguity of God's engagement in viticulture as the farmer, Jesus re-assures his disciples, "You are already clean through the word which I have spoken to you." Earlier in 13:10 he had declared all of them to be clean, except Judas. However, persisting in that condition of being "clean" and therefore being fruit-bearing requires more than "believing into him." Throughout his ministry Jesus invoked his fellow Jews to make a commitment to him by "believing into him" as the Pioneer of a New Humanity. The preposition *into* (εἰς) is used deliberately in order to transcend simple intellectual assent and accentuate the personal involvement of commitment. Perseverance in that commitment requires "remaining in his word in order to be his authentic disciples," as he stressed to the ruling authorities who believed into him in 8:31. Beyond the discipleship of "believing into him" and "remaining in his word," however, is the "awesome intimacy" of union, *remaining* or *abiding in him*. Already in 6:56 Jesus laid down the condition for this intimacy: "The one who chews my flesh and drinks my blood *remains* (μένει) in me and I in her/him." Now, however, in view of the crisis of the coming of the ruler of the world, he endeavors to draw his disciples into this condition by charging them, "*Begin to remain* (μείνατε) in me and I in you." He

[75] Sporty, "Identifying the Curve Line on the Bar Kokhba Temple Coin," 121.

[76] According to Philo, *de Somniis* II, 169 and *de Mutatione Nominum*, 162-164, the vine is an ambiguous metaphor that he allegorizes as two ethical orientations: folly and gladness. Folly is represented by the vine of Sodom and Gemorrah that produced grapes of gall and clusters of bitterness. See *de Somniis* II, 191-211and *de Ebrietate*, 222-223. The great clusters of grapes that the Israelite spies brought back from the land of Canaan signify "the sprouting and fruit-bearing of noble living" resulting in gladness. Philo cites Isa 5:7, "The vineyard of the all-powerful Lord is the house of Israel;" which he interprets as: "Israel is the mind contemplating God and the world, for Israel is interpreted 'seeing God,' but the house of the mind is the entire soul; and this is the most holy vineyard, bearing the fruit of divine growth, virtue." See *de Somniis* II, 171-174. Also *de Josepho*, 91-92.

employs the aorist imperative in order to invoke an existential *entry* into this mutual indwelling. Only in that continuous dynamic union will the divine objective of fruit-bearing be actualized, that is, the possibility of doing the works Jesus has done and even exceeding them (14:12). "Even as the branch cannot bear fruit of itself, unless it *continues to remain* (μένῃ) in the vine-stock, neither you unless you *continue to remain* (μένητε) in me."

There are two different readings of both occurrences of the verb μένειν (to remain/abide) in the manuscript transmission of 15:4: μένῃ (continue to remain) and μείνῃ (begin to remain).

> Even as the branch is unable to bear fruit of itself unless it *continues remaining* (μένῃ)[77] in the vine-stock, so also you, unless you *continue remaining* (μένητε)[78] in me.
>
> Even as the branch is unable to bear fruit of itself unless it *begins to remain* (μείνῃ)[79] in the vinestock, so also you, unless you *begin remaining* (μείνητε)[80] in me.

The fruit-bearing of grape-vines occurs naturally in the grape-growing season, but only after the branches have sprouted from the vine-stock and the pollinated blossoms have formed into berries that gradually ripen into juice-filled grapes. Consequently it is necessary for the branches *to continue to remain* attached to the vine-stock if there is to be fruit at harvest time.

Jesus employs the **I AM** formula again in 15:5 in order to restate his self-disclosure as the Vine-stock, but now to identify his disciples metaphorically as the branches. Together, as the Vine-stock and the branches, Jesus and his disciples constitute the New Israel. They are the new people of God. By joining them together, the Vine-stock and the branches, Jesus accentuates the necessary, continuing union between himself and his disciples for the eventual production of fruit.

> **I AM** the vine-stock, you the branches! *The one continuing to abide* (ὁ μένων) in me and I in him/her, this one bears much fruit, because without me you cannot do anything at all. (15:5)

Bearing "much fruit" will occur only if the disciples *continue to remain* attached to Jesus as the Vine-stock of the new Israel. Should that necessary, continuing union be broken, they, like the detached branch that withers, will not reach that maturating season of bearing fruit, and God, as the tending but also exacting farmer, will remove the unproductive branches from the Vine-stock. The severe

---

77 This reading is found in ℵ B L 579 pc.

78 This reading occurs in ℵ A B L Θ* 579.

79 This reading occurs in $P^{66\ vid}$ A D Θ Ψ 0250 $f^{1\ 13}$ 33 M.

80 This reading is supported by D $Θ^c$ Ψ 0250 $f^{1.13}$ (33) M. Barrett, *St. John*, 474, considers the present tense to be more suitable to the context, yet acknowledges "for that very reason the aorists (if original) might have been changed." Nevertheless, he prefers the readings of B ℵ.

consequences of being separated from the Vine-stock, withering, and then being gathered together in order to be thrown into the fire and burned necessarily arise out of God's resolute determination to establish an Israel that finally will fulfill God's objective for humankind. God has generated the Vine-stock of the New Israel by the enfleshment of the Logos-Sophia in Jesus of Nazareth and by the empowering of the holy Spirit who descended and remained upon him. Accordingly, it is the function of the Vine-stock to be the source of God's Life and Power, and concomitantly it is the role of the branches to produce the fruit. Bearing "much fruit," therefore, is the divine requirement of discipleship.

On the other hand, the disciples' entry into this "awesome intimacy" that grafts them into the source of God's everlasting Life and Power and results in bearing fruit guarantees privileged benefits.

> If you begin to remain in me and my words continue to remain in you, ask for yourselves whatever you want, and it will happen to you. (15:7)

Jesus poses the possibility of unrestricted prayer and petitioning with the attendant promise of fulfillment, but categorically grounds it in the condition of continuous abiding. The aorist subjunctive is used in the protasis to express the condition of an existential *entry* into this mutual indwelling, while the apodosis conveys the guaranteed benefits. The use of the verb μένειν (to remain) in the second half of the protasis, however, is problematic. Once again the manuscript variants are divided between the present and the aorist tenses, but more specifically between the present indicative, μένει, and the aorist subjunctive, μείνῃ. The latter, μείνῃ, corresponds in both tense and mood to the first verb of the protasis, μείνητε: "If you begin to remain in me and my words begin to remain in you ..." Its use would appear to be a scribal effort at correlating the two tenses and moods. The former, however, the present indicative μένει, is the more difficult reading and should be regarded as the more original of the two.[81] If "the protasis is the only half [of a conditional sentence] in which the mood is variable," its verbs in two different tenses and moods would seem to be permissible.[82] Abiding in him as the Vine-stock and remaining in his words are not necessarily synonymous realities. In 8:31 Jesus informed the ruling authorities who had made a faith commitment to him, "If you begin to remain in my word, you truly are my disciples." The entry into remaining in his word should follow naturally from the initial act of "believing into him." In this context of chapter 15 Jesus has charged his disciples for the very first time "Begin remaining in me and I in you." This mutual indwelling is a consequence of the disciples being grafted, like branches, into Jesus the Vine-stock. The persistence of "remaining in his words" and therefore being obedient to his commandments, can precede as well as follow the entry into a relationship of

[81] The present indicative, μένει, is supported by P^{66} L 579, pc. The corrector of P^{66}, however, substituted μείνῃ, evidently to make it correspond in tense and mood to μείνητε at the beginning of the condition.

[82] C. F. D. Moule, *An Idiom-Book of New Testament Greek,* 150.

mutual indwelling. Here all three, the acts of "believing into him" and "remaining in his word," and the "awesome intimacy" of *remaining* or *abiding in him*, merge to constitute perfect discipleship.[83] It is that kind of discipleship, as Jesus stipulates in 15:8, that will be productive in bearing much fruit, and that in turn will engender God's glorification.

The Vine-stock is not only the source of Life; it is also the fountainhead of love. But it is the fountainhead of love only because that love originates from God the Creator: "Even as the Father loved me, I also loved you."[84] Being grafted into the Vine-stock is the only means by which this divine love can be experienced. "Begin to remain in my love!" Jesus commands his disciples.

Earlier in 14:15 he had laid down for his disciples the conditional basis of corroborating the love they have for him: "If you love me, you will keep my commandments." Again in 14:23, "The one who has my commandments and keeps them, that is the one who loves me, and the one who loves me will be loved by my Father, and I shall love her/him." Love that rises out of obedience to Jesus' commandments is an entry into the circle of love that establishes the solidarity of the tri-partite relationship that Jesus has been actualizing: the disciples, God the Creator, and Jesus, who is going away into death and resurrection to prepare a place for his disciples.

Now in 15:9, Jesus as the Vine-stock opens another access into the circle of love: "Begin to remain in my love!" The love that originates from the disciples is validated by obedience to his commandments. But there is also a love that originates from Jesus, and accordingly he charges them to enter into abiding in *his* love. This is the other factor of the dynamic circle of love that he is constituting. Indeed, this is the preeminent command: to abide in his love![85] On the one hand, they are keeping his commandments in order to express their love to him. On the other hand, because they are keeping his commandments, they are to enter into *his* love and continue to remain in *his* love. The love that originates from them, the love they will manifest by observing his commandments, will be authenticated and reinforced by *his* love, a love that originates from the Creator in whom he abides. Jesus offers himself as a model who keeps his Father's commandments while he abides in his Father's love. For the implied readers of the Jewish community in Alexandria this dynamic circle of love poses a stark contrast to the domineering legalism of the Pharisaic-oriented guardians of their society.

---

[83] Segovia, *Farewell*, 145-146, n. 33, reaches a similar conclusion, but evidently without considering the two variants of the protasis.

[84] Segovia, *ibid*., 150, identifies the two verbs of verse 9a, ἠγάπησεν (he loved) and ἠγάπησα (I loved), as constative aorists and comments, "... so both loves are presented from a fully completed or accomplished perspective."

[85] Segovia, *ibid*., 158 and also 162-163, accentuates the earlier command that Jesus issued to his disciples, namely, to love one another, as the preeminent command. But the disciples can only love each other as Jesus loves them by abiding in his love.

Jesus' objective in invoking his disciples to enter into abiding in him as the New Israel and attendantly to remain in his love is to communicate his joy to them, the joy that pervades the circle of love that he is forming, and ultimately to ensure that their joy is full as they participate in his tri-partite community. In their membership in this circle of love they are to love one another. That is his commandment, and, as he stated in 13:34, it is a new commandment. The range and magnitude of the love within this circle includes offering one's life on behalf of one's friends. Jesus himself is the measure of its range and magnitude, as he prepares to leave his disciples in order to fulfill God's will by establishing a new Exodus through his death and resurrection. On the basis of the enormity of his love and their participation in his circle of love, he acknowledges them as his friends.

Ironically, however, the friendship they share is dependent on their doing the things he has commanded (15:14). He has charged them to love each other (13:34), and he has directed them to abide in him *and* to abide in his love (15:3, 9). The fundamental purpose of these commands that he imposes on his disciples is to maintain the tri-partite circle of love for which he is offering up his life. Grafted into Jesus as the Vine-stock and entering into his community of love, they can finally be identified as his *friends*. In this climactic moment Jesus' work as the incarnate Sophia has reached its fulfillment! For Sophia, as she is characterized in the Wisdom of Solomon 7:27, "… is able to do all things and remaining in herself she renews all things, and in every generation passing over into holy souls she constitutes *friends of God* and prophets." Jesus as the incarnation of Sophia, however, surpasses the activity of Sophia in as far as he establishes a tri-partite circle of love in which all human beings – not only certain individuals – are destined to become friends of God and to experience the fulfillment of the human yearning for an intimate relationship with God.

His disciples, therefore, will no longer be slaves but friends, "for the slave does not know what his master is doing." The inter-dependence that the relationship between the Vine-stock and the branches establishes abolishes the hierarchical conjunction of master and slave and the oppressive dependency that it promotes. The friendship with Jesus into which the disciples are entering is confirmed by his entrusting them with the safekeeping of "all the things that I heard from my Father."[86] He initiated the horizontal relationship of interdependence between them, as he also originated their call to discipleship: "You did not choose me, but I chose you." Their inclusion in the community of the Son of the Human Being that he is constituting is ultimately attributable to the divine drawing power of the

[86] Contrary to Segovia, *ibid.*, 159, the disciples qualify as Jesus' friends not because they have received and accepted his teaching and his revelation. There is no indication of that in this part of Jesus' farewell speech. Earlier he commanded them to remain in him and his words to remain in them. They qualify as his friends because they are being drawn into the circle of love that he is constituting, and as participants in that circle, he has not hesitated to share "all the things I heard from my father".

Sophia that he incarnates and that is engaged in making human beings "friends of God."

But their participation in this tri-partite fellowship is not an end in itself, for as Jesus informs his disciples, "...and *I offered* (ἔθηκα) you so that you go forth and bear fruit and your fruit remains." The unusual employment of the verb ἔθηκα corresponds to Jesus' enunciation of the authority he has *to offer* (θεῖναι) his life and the authority he has to take it again (10:18).[87] Ironically, in the newly established horizontal relationship of interdependence, he, as the enfleshed Logos-Sophia, exercises that same authority *to offer up* his committed disciples for fruit-bearing so that the ministry he inaugurated may be continued and even arrive at its divinely appointed objective through their teaching and through their works.[88] That, in fact, must be his rationale for communicating to them "all the things I heard from my Father." They are to know what their commitment to Jesus encompasses as they are being prepared to participate in the work of transforming the social construction of reality for the salvation of the world.

The second ἵνα (so that) clause of 15:16, echoing 14:13 and 15:7, appears to be an unconnected afterthought joined to the necessity of bearing fruit, yet it reconfirms the necessary interdependence of the tri-partite fellowship of Jesus, the disciples and the Father. Bearing fruit requires continued remaining/abiding in the Vine-stock, and the Father, the vigilant farmer, is ever ready to respond to the disciples' requests for the fulfillment of their fruit-bearing activity.

The necessity of bearing fruit that remains is not only dependent on their participation in this tri-partite fellowship; it compels them to love one other. That mutuality of love that is to regulate their relationships in community is conveyed as a purposeful objective by the ἵνα clause of verse 17 that concludes Part Two of Jesus' farewell discourse, "These things I command you *so that* (ἵνα) you continue to love one another."[89] Here the charge is not "to love one another."[90] Jesus has voiced it already in 13:34. The independent clause of verse 17, "These things I command you ..." refers to the directives Jesus issued in 15:3, "Begin to remain in

---

[87] The awkwardness of the verb ἔθηκα is acknowledged by many commentators. Barrett, *St. John*, 478, following Lindars, explains it as a "Semitisizing" of the Hebrew נתן (give) but also proposes the possibility that it may be a rendering of the Hebrew סמך, a verb that was also used to convey "a laying on of the hands" or "to ordain." Also Brown, *John* II, 665.

[88] Segovia, *Farewell*, 160, n. 58, does not differentiate three roles for the disciples in Jesus' words, "so that you go forth and bear fruit and your fruit remains". He sees "these three components as pointing emphatically to the role of the disciples as a whole ..."

[89] The original scribe of P^{66*} deleted the adverbial conjunction ἵνα, so that15:17 would read, "These things I command you, keep on loving one another!" But the ἵνα is necessary in order to express the purpose of the commands Jesus has issued in 15:1-16 and thereby to serve as the conclusion of Part Two. Segovia, *Farewell*, 162, does not evaluate the omission of ἵνα and appears to interpret 15:17 in terms of its omission. Later, however, on p. 163 he recognizes that the disciples who abide in Jesus' love will carry out his commands and love one another.

[90] Brown, *John* II, 665 , vacillates between considering the ἵνα to be epexegetical or final. Of the two possibilities, the ἵνα clause almost certainly denotes purpose or finality.

me!" and 15:9, "Begin to remain in my love!"[91] Only by fulfilling these commands and experiencing the "awesome intimacy" of abiding in him as the Vine-stock and persisting in his love, will the disciples be able to continue to love one another and discharge their discipleship by bearing fruit.[92]

Unit 3[93] • *Adverse consequences of discipleship 15:18-16:4a*

John 15:18 introduces a new direction in Jesus' farewell speech that proceeds to disclose the adverse consequences of discipleship that his followers will necessarily encounter in the world, but only after Jesus has prioritized the benefits of being incorporated into the Vine-Stock of the new Israel and the "awesome intimacy" of the tri-partite fellowship that he is constituting. The glory that is intrinsic to a committed discipleship must be enunciated before the stark realities of opposition, hatred, and martyrdom that committed discipleship will experience are acknowledged.

Moreover, Jesus has waited until this moment to confront his disciples with the adversities of discipleship because, as long as he was with them, he was the lightning rod that attracted the hostility and persecution of the ruling authorities. "These things I did not say to you from the beginning because I was with you" (16:4b). But now he is on the verge of going away, not a going away into death and resurrection, as he announced in 13:33, but a "going away *towards* (πρός) the One who sent me," that is, a going away into ascension. Accordingly, it is vital that the disciples are aware that they, having become embodiments of his word as the result of his teaching remaining in them, will be opposed and maltreated as he was.[94] Almost from the beginning of their discipleship they have witnessed the animosity and antagonism that he has endured: "If the world (κόσμος) hates you,

---

[91] Bultmann, *John*, 546-547, rightly cites 15:3 and 9 in this context of 15:17 and concludes that they are essentially synonymous. But abiding in the Vine-stock is oriented toward bearing fruit, and abiding in his love" is the source of the love that the disciples are enjoined to have for each other. He introduces "faith" into this context as a summons inseparable from the command to love, but Jesus has said nothing about "faith" in this context of 15:1-17. German, 420-421.

[92] Segovia, *Farewell*, 165-167, concludes this section by claiming that the metaphor of Jesus as the Vine-stock functions polemically to differentiate Jesus and his disciples from "the Jews as the primary representatives of an unbelieving world". This is Bultmannian in origin! But the Gospel originated within the Jewish community of Alexandria and was addressed to the Jews of that community.

[93] Segovia, *ibid.*, 174, regards 15:18-16:4a as "the third self-contained and coherent unit of discourse" within Jesus' farewell speech. Its primary focus, according to his summary on p. 173, is on "the external affairs of the community, the relationship of the disciples to the world and the sustained emphasis on the opposition of the world to Jesus and his disciples." His analysis of the literary-rhetorical structure on pp. 174-179 claims a three-part division: 15:18-21, 15:22-25 and 15:26-16:4a.

[94] Barnabas Lindars, "The Persecution of Christians in John 15:18-16:4a," *Essays on John*, 131-152, interprets this Part Three of Jesus' farewell speech in a context of conflict between "the Church and the Synagogue". His source-critical presuppositions linked to his redaction-critical work, however, prevent him from interpreting the Gospel synchronically, yet he does offer some significant insights into an earlier state of the Gospel that intimated the presence of secret Christians among the Jews. See especially pp. 149-150.

you know (γινώσκετε) that it has hated me first."[95] The use of γινώσκετε intimates that this knowledge of the world's hatred is presupposed as an existential experience by the disciples – and the implied readers of the Gospel. The signifier κόσμος, as in all its other 75 occurrences, refers to society's construction of reality and its guardians, more specifically those in the Jewish community of Alexandria who regard themselves to be divinely ordained to safeguard it at all costs.

The disciples, however, as Jesus informs them for the first time, are not ἐκ τοῦ κόσμου (from within the world). The preposition ἐκ in 15:19ab indicates source or origin, and Jesus had employed it with the same phrase in 8:23 in order to differentiate his origin from that of the ruling elite. Like him, therefore, his disciples – and the implied readers – are to understand themselves as not originating from within the social construction of reality. Consequently, as Jesus continues, "If you were ἐκ τοῦ κόσμου (from within the world), the world would be loving its own kind, but because you are not ἐκ τοῦ κόσμου, but I have chosen you ἐκ τοῦ κόσμου, on account of this the world hates you." If Jesus has chosen them ἐκ τοῦ κόσμου (from within the world), and they are no longer ἐκ τοῦ κόσμου, they must be like him; they must be ἐκ τῶν ἄνω (from above).[96]

In spite of the equality of sharing the same heavenly origin that Jesus has established, the disciples must remember the word he spoke to them earlier in 13:16, "The slave is not greater than his/her lord." Although he called them into being as his "friends" in 15:14-15, his re-employment of an earlier proverb does not negate the new status he has imparted to them. They continue to be his friends! But in terms of the reality of the axiom, "The slave is not grater than his Lord!" their identification with Jesus will destine them to the same persecution that Jesus experienced.[97] "If they persecuted me, they will also persecute you." On the other hand, "If they guarded my word, they will also guard yours" (15:20). They will encounter what Jesus has experienced throughout his ministry, antagonists who do not know (οἴδασιν) the One who sent him.[98] Consequently, hatred and

---

[95] It is noteworthy that the personal pronoun ὑμῶν (you) was interpolated into 15:18 by ℵ D 579 it arm, and adopted by Tischendorf, most likely because πρῶτον (first) was construed as a preposition on the basis of its misunderstood employment as a preposition in 1:15, 30. Apparently Segovia, *Farewell,* 182-183, considers the pronoun ὑμῶν (you) to be original. He first interprets the perfect tense of the verb μεμίσηκεν (it has hated) as a "completed action," but on p. 183, n. 20, expands the sense of the verb to include "the enduring hatred of Jesus … after his departure or death only in terms of hatred for his disciples …" The use of the perfect tense of the verb μεμίσηκεν includes both levels of the narrative world: the time of Jesus and the circumstances of the Jewish community of Alexandria.

[96] Segovia, *ibid.*, 180-181, notes 16, 17, rightly differentiates between a genitive of source for the prepositional phrase ἐκ τοῦ κόσμου in 15:19ac and a genitive of separation in 15:19d, contending that the latter is logically prior to the former. While that may be true, it is their affiliation with Jesus as the result of his calling them *from within the world* that consequently results in their being transplanted into the origin that is identical to his: ἐκ τῶν ἄνω (from above).

[97] Segovia, *ibid.*, 184, notes 23, 24, acknowledges the axiom as a proverb, but he interprets it literally and concludes that the disciples are reminded that "they, as 'servants' are not greater than Jesus."

[98] Segovia, *ibid.*, 186, n. 26, expresses surprise that the persecution of the disciples by the world is already acknowledged at this point in the narrative. But this is a mirror reflection of the Alexandrian

persecution should be expected because they will be the bearers of Jesus' name and the embodiments of his teaching.

The disciples continue as Jesus' friends. Although they are no longer slaves, as Jesus declared in 15:14, they are nevertheless his apprentices, even as he is "the Father's" apprentice; and by abiding in him and his love as well as having his words abiding in them, they must begin to learn how to fulfill their apprenticeship in the world that will hate them and persecute them.

As Jesus' farewell speech moves into what may be considered as "the second major section" of 15:18-16:4a, he states more fundamentally why both he and the Father *have been hated* (μεμισήκασιν).[99] The use of the perfect tense of μισεῖν (to hate) is noteworthy because it embraces the two overlapping periods of history in the narrative world of the Gospel: the time of Jesus and the context of the Jewish community of Alexandria. Jesus has been hated fundamentally because his teaching exposed the human condition of ἁμαρτία: "If I had not come and spoken to them, they would not have *sin* (ἁμαρτία)". But Jesus did come and speak, and the world and all those who identify themselves with it were confronted with the fundamental diseased condition of its social construction of reality, the sickness of alienation that separates the human community by its economic, political, and social structures and maintains power and wealth in the hands of a minority at the top of the socio-economic pyramid of society. These are the fundamental realities of ἁμαρτία, that is, sin as the condition that engenders the acts of injustice, oppression and exploitation in society; and they are exposed through Jesus' healing ministry as well as through his teaching: "If I did not do among them the works that none other did, they would not have *sin* (ἁμαρτία)."[100] Before his ministry his people, the Jews, were well aware of the offenses and transgressions of the Law. The proverb that Jeremiah cites in 31:29 discloses a consciousness of an underlying sociological condition that generates the injustices that human beings perpetrate in society, and the prophet anticipated the termination of that generation-by-generation transmission of that condition, but apparently not the condition itself: "In those days it shall no longer be said, 'The fathers [and mothers] have eaten sour grapes, and the children's teeth are set on edge.' But all shall die for their own sins." The eradication of ἁμαρτία became the eschatological expectation of Jewish apocalypticism.[101] God's judgment would end the old moral order that had originated with Adam and Eve and with it the human infection of sin that engenders the many forms of living death in human

---

context of the first edition of the Gospel. There is a profound conflict within the Jewish community between those who want to replace the destroyed Temple with the Torah and those who advocate replacing it with the living Temple of a new people of God.

[99] This is Segovia's structuring of the Third Part of the farewell discourse; *ibid*., 189-196.

[100] Segovia, *ibid*., 191, n. 36, defines "sin" as the overall rejection of Jesus' coming and ministry. But that interprets ἁμαρτία as an act rather than the more fundamental condition out of which acts of transgression arise.

[101] See 1 Enoch 5:8, 69:29, 91:12-17.

society. Its termination is anticipated by John the Witness and proclaimed in his identification of Jesus as "the lamb of God that *removes* (αἴρων) the *sin of the world* (ἁμαρτία τοῦ κόσμου)."

Jesus' exposure of this fundamental condition of ἁμαρτία, has made it empirically visible: "But now they also *have seen* (ἑωράκασιν) ..." Although no direct object follows the verb ἑωράκασιν, the objectification of ἁμαρτία that he is referring to must be the paralysis, the blindness, and the living death that he has remedied during his ministry as well as the reactions of hatred and persecution that he has experienced. His exposure of this condition fulfills the purpose of God, yet because of it he has suffered hostility and malice: "... they have hated both me and my Father." And that too is a fulfillment, for as Jesus declares, "But in order that the word that is written in their Law is fulfilled, 'They hated me without reason.'"

It is generally agreed that this word of fulfillment in verse 25 is drawn from the Septuagint rendition of Psa 34 (35):19 and Psa 68 (69):5 or both. Since John 2:17 quoted LXX Psa 68 (69):10, it seems likely that Jesus is drawing from the same psalm. Moreover, as the aorist verb, κατέφαγεν (it devoured) of Psa 68 (69):10 was changed to the future καταφάγεται (it will devour) in John 2:17 in order to adjust the quotation to the objective of the implied author, in all likelihood the aorist ἐμίσησαν (they hated) of 15:25 was substituted in place of the substantive present participle, οἱ μισοῦντες (the ones hating), of Psa 68 (69):5 in order to accommodate this context.[102] The use of νόμος (law) here in verse 25 is probably to be construed as "Torah." Once again Jesus is differentiating himself from the Pharisaic law-oriented interpretation of the Torah by which the ruling authorities are reconstituting Judaism. For their hatred of Jesus they are condemned by their own Scripture.[103]

Jesus, however, will be vindicated, for, as he states in the last unit of this Third Part of his farewell (15:26-16:4a), "When the Paraclete comes, whom I shall send to you from the Father, the Spirit of Truth, who proceeds from the Father, that One will bear witness about me." This verse does not provide a rationale for 16:1-4a.[104] By identifying the Paraclete again as "the Spirit of Truth" and linking it to the Father, verse 26 refers back to verse 24 and the scriptural quotation of verse 25 in order to establish God's future justification of Jesus and his work. Moreover, the disciples themselves will have a role in Jesus' vindication by their continuation of his ministry of world transformation, doing his works and even greater works by the power of the same Spirit.

Jesus closes this Third Part of his farewell, 15:18-16:4a, by stating his rationale for informing his disciples of the adverse consequences of their discipleship, "so that you are not scandalized." Those among the implied readers of Alexandria who are already experiencing hatred and suffering persecution will be confirmed in

[102] It is, as Segovia claims, *ibid.*, 194, n. 40, "a deliberate and appropriate adaptation."

[103] Barrett, *St. John*, 482.

[104] Contrary to Segovia, *ibid.*, 198.

their discipleship because Jesus' predictions have been and are continuing to be fulfilled among them: "They will make you ἀποσυναγώγους (without a synagogue). Indeed, perhaps even for them "... the hour is coming when anyone who kills you *will suppose* (δόξῃ) that he/she is offering a service to God." These specific forecasts mirror the conflict and the factions that are embroiling the Jewish community of Alexandria. The deplorable reality is that "They do these things because they don't *know* (ἔγνωσαν) the Father or me." The great irony is that they are the elect people of God, but they do not have a personal knowledge of God that is nourished by a relationship with the Creator.

Unit 4[105] • *"None of you asks, 'Where are you going?'" 16:4b-33*

For a second time Jesus announces to his disciples that he is going away. Surprisingly, however, he adds, " ... and none of you asks, 'Where are you going?'" In response to his first announcement of his departure in 13:33, Simon Peter had inquired, "Lord, where are you going?" Why, then, at the second announcement does Jesus add, "... and none of you asks, 'Where are you going?'" Has the narrator of Jesus' farewell speech had a lapse of memory? Or does this second announcement have another reference that moves beyond the first announcement? Not all commentators note the contradiction between 13:33-36 and 16:5.[106] There are two announcements of departure, but they refer to two different goings-away. The first, 13:33-36, as 14:1-28a implies, is a departure into death and resurrection in order to prepare rooms for his disciples in "the Father's house" that Jesus has embodied throughout the Gospel.

In 16:5 Jesus is referring to a departure beyond his death and resurrection, and, to alert the implied readers to that departure, he remarks, "... and none of you asks, 'Where are you going?'" It is a rhetorical device that is intended to interrupt the attention of the implied readers in order to divert their focus to a prospect that he already has disclosed but which must now be elaborated. In a word in 14:28b he had looked beyond his initial leave-taking of his disciples to his return to God: "If you loved me, you would rejoice because I am going *towards* (πρός) the Father, for the Father is greater than I."

---

[105] Segovia, *ibid.*, 216, rightly contends for 16:4b-33 as the fourth unit of Jesus' farewell discourse. Because there is no major shift in Jesus' standpoint as the speaker of the discourse, he prefers to identify with the more frequently represented position that this passage is a unity without a major break at verse 15. At the same time, this fourth unit can be divided into three sections: 16:4b-15, 16:16-24 and 16:25-33.

[106] Generally the second announcement of 16:5 is considered to be a continuation of 13:33. Brown, *John* II, 704, ignores it all together. Segovia, *Farewell*, 217, asserts, "No major shift in the standpoint of Jesus as speaker of the discourse can be detected within 16:4b-33. As in the first unit, this is a Jesus who is both about to undergo the climactic events of "the hour" and who has already surpassed "the hour" except for the final events (the bestowal of the Spirit-Paraclete – Jesus' promised successor to and among the disciples – and Jesus' final return to the Father). Moloney, *Glory*, 81-82, recognizes the contradiction between 13:36 and 16:5 but concludes, " ... failure to understand Jesus' destiny is in question in both places."

The two departures, the first into death and resurrection and the second into an ascension, are adjoining events, the second occurring very soon after the first. Jesus' directive to Mary Magdalene in 20:17b indicates that his ascension will take place as she leaves to make her report to her fellow disciples. His subsequent return to breathe the holy Spirit upon his disciples and to confront Thomas with the reality of his resurrection must be construed as post-ascension appearances.

As Jesus announces his second departure "*towards* (πρός) the One who sent me," he is aware that his disciples are grieving over his earlier disclosures of his leave-taking. Yet this second departure is as necessary as the first one: "But I tell you the truth, it is expedient for you that I am going away, for if I do not go away, the Paraclete would not come *towards* (πρός) you, but if I go away, I shall send him *towards* (πρός) you." The first departure into death and resurrection will enlarge the Father's house by preparing a place for them. This going-away into ascension and returning to the Father will result in their empowerment by being divinely inbreathed by the Spirit that descended and remained on Jesus.

Through the indwelling of the Spirit, the Spirit of Truth, the disciples will continue the work of exposing the diseased condition of the world: "Coming that One *will expose/convict* (ἐλέγξει) the world about ἁμαρτία (sin)." The verb ἐλέγξει, already utilized by Jesus in 3:20 and 8:46, bears several different denotations: expose, convict, reprove.[107] In 3:20 the verb conveys the meaning of "expose"; in 8:46 the meaning "convict" is apposite. Both meanings appear to be appropriate in 16:8. If Jesus, as he declared in 15:22, exposed sin by coming and speaking to his people, God's Spirit, the Paraclete, by being sent into the world by Jesus will continue to expose the reality of this universal condition. But that will be done in an entirely new context! For by his death Jesus will have fulfilled John's witness as "the lamb of God who removes the ἁμαρτία (sin) of the world."[108] Consequently, in this post-Easter context those who do not follow Jesus into a new Exodus towards the promised land of health and salvation will remain in the diseased condition of sin. Through the ministry of the disciples, empowered by the Paraclete and continuing the work of Jesus, the fundamental condition of sin will be exposed.[109] But at the same time those who refuse to commit themselves to the New Humanity that Jesus has inaugurated and therefore repudiate the eradication of sin that has been actualized through his death will be convicted.

The Paraclete, in and through the ministry of the disciples, will also convict the world of injustice, "because," as Jesus says, "I am going away *towards* (πρός) the

[107] Also noted by Segovia, *Farewell*, 229. After examining all the possibilities of meaning, he chooses "convict" because it best conveys the "forensic dimension" of 16:8-10.

[108] Segovia, *ibid.*, 228, separates the role of the Spirit, as described in 16:8-11, from the role of the disciples in 16:12-15, but later, on p. 234, acknowledges that the work of the Spirit will be discharged by the disciples. If the Paraclete-Spirit is coming *towards* (πρός) them and therefore uniting with them, the resulting empowerment will enable the disciples to continue the work that Jesus fulfilled, according to 15:22-24.

[109] This is also the conclusion of Segovia, *ibid.*, 234-235, but without attention to the verb θεωρεῖτε and its implications.

Father and you are no longer going to *be-hold* or *observe* (θεωρεῖτε) me." As long as Jesus was in the world, present in its social construction of reality, his deeds and his words manifested the realities of God's justice, and the disciples who *observed* him, gave themselves over to him and to the Father who sent him on the basis of what they saw (12:45). By going to the Father and sending the Paraclete to unite with his disciples, Jesus is replacing his works of justice and healing with theirs. All who persist in the world and its structures of alienation will be exposed and convicted by the manifestation of God's justice as it will be actualized by the disciples.

Finally, the Paraclete, in and through the ministry of the disciples, will expose the reality of the judgment that has occurred "because the ruler of the world has been condemned". The transcendent Power that represents all the forms and forces of living death in the world will have been doomed. The disciples, empowered by the Paraclete, will disclose Jesus' victory over death in all its forms and forces by their preaching and by their life-giving and life-affirming works. Those, however, who reject this judgment that terminates this transcendent Power will be convicted by the same activity of the Spirit.

On the one hand, the world will be the objective of the Paraclete's activity through the disciples. On the other hand, the disciples themselves will be the groundwork of the Paraclete-Spirit.[110] At this moment, as Jesus stated earlier in 14:17, the Paraclete "remains *with* you ..." He still has many things to say to his disciples, but in the present circumstance they are not able to bear it. Later, when the Paraclete "...will be *in* you" after he breathes the Spirit upon them, the Spirit will guide them into all truth. Since Jesus has declared that he is "the Truth," the Spirit will not speak of its own things but will speak such things as it hears and will announce to them the things that are coming (16:13). The Paraclete, therefore, as the successor and therefore the representative of Jesus, will also continue their instruction. Because they have become Jesus' friends and potentially also prophets, according to the activity ascribed to Sophia in Wis 7:27, the Spirit will also reveal to them the things that are coming in the course of history. They will have the perspicuity of interpreting the actualities of the present as well as discerning the possibilities of the future.

The Paraclete in its role as the successor and representative of Jesus, is completely subordinate to Jesus, not only in as far as he is the incarnate Logos-Sophia, but also because he is fulfilling God's will in saving the world by eradicating the human affliction of ἁμαρτία (sin) and inaugurating a new

[110] *Ibid.*, 235, defines the second role of the Paraclete as "the essential change in the situation and status of the disciples that will allow them 'to bear' (to comprehend and endure) such disclosures. But he does not relate this change of status to Jesus' word of 14:17, that at this moment the Spirit is present *with* the disciples but eventually the Spirit will be *in* the disciples. When he breathes the Spirit upon them in 20:22, the Spirit will be *in* them, and not only will they comprehend his revelations, but they will also be empowered for their ministry.

creation.[111] Accordingly, as Jesus certifies to his disciples, "That One *will glorify* me, for he will take what is mine and will disclose to you." The activity of the Paraclete is subject to Jesus because he is the incarnate Logos-Sophia and therefore can claim for himself the totality of all that belongs to the Creator: "All the things that the Father has are mine." For as the enfleshment of the Logos, he is the agent of God's creativity, and in his enfleshment of Sophia, according to Wis 7:26-27, he is "a reflection of eternal light, a spotless mirror of God's activity [and] being but one, able to do all things." "On account of this," as Jesus recapitulates, the Paraclete "takes what is mine and will disclose to you." This is the awesome legacy that Jesus is bequeathing his disciples.

In this context it is to be remembered that Philo's Logos separates the creature from the Creator and therefore forecloses to human beings the actualizing of the divine possibilities that would result from being in union with God.

> To the Logos, chief messenger and most elderly, the Father, who generated all things, gave the special prerogative, so that standing [as] a border he separates the creature from the Creator. And he exults in this estate and magnifying it describes it saying, "And I stood between the Lord and you," neither uncreated as God, nor created as you, but [in the] middle of extreme limits, between the two extremes, having shares in both sides.[112]

Here, however, the Logos is not God's separating agent. There is no hierarchical ordering of power and privilege. All that Jesus claims for himself as the incarnate Logos-Sophia will be communicated to those who commit themselves to him by the Paraclete-Spirit.

After elucidating the objectives of his two departures, Jesus returns to a clarification of the existential effects that his leave-taking will have on his disciples. Earlier in 14:18-19, in the context of his initial announcement of his going away, he had promised, "I shall not leave you orphaned. I am coming *toward* (πρός) you. Still a little while, and the world will no longer *observe* (θεωρεῖ) me, but you will observe (θεωρεῖτε) me, because I live you also will live." Now, instead of the world no longer beholding or observing him and challenged to give itself over to him, it is his disciples who, *after a little while* will no longer *behold* him and be drawn into an involvement with him and his ministry. But again, *after a little while* they *will see* (ὄψεσθε) him.[113]

Two different verbs of seeing are employed in Jesus' promise: θεωρεῖν and ὁρᾶν, and, as has become evident, they denote two different kinds of visual experience. In a little while Jesus will no longer be with his disciples, and during his absence they will not be able to observe him in his movements and activities,

---

[111] Segovia, *ibid.*, 240-243, speaks of "the Spirit-Paraclete's ultimate and complete dependence on an external source," namely Jesus.

[112] See Philo, *Quis Rerum Divinarum Heres*, 205-206. Also 234-236.

[113] The difference between these two verbs of seeing is not analyzed by Segovia, *Farewell*, 247-251.

experience the magnetism of his presence and be drawn into the inspiration and power of his life. However, *after a little while*, specifically after his resurrection from the dead, they will see him again as an objective reality with their physical eyesight.

It is at this point that Jesus' monologue that began in 15:1, ends.[114] His renewed announcement about his leave-taking, however, proves to be problematic for his disciples, and the discussion that it engenders among them marks a return to the dialogical structure of the First Unit of his farewell discourse. Among themselves the disciples review the words that Jesus has addressed to them, but they are unable to construe their meaning. His earlier announcement, "I am going away *towards* (πρός) the Father," is drawn into their interaction, but it offers no key to unlocking their incomprehension. In spite of their frustration, "We don't know what he is speaking!" they are hesitant to question him.

Jesus *intuits* (ἔγνω) their inhibited desire to question him, and he proceeds to repeat his original words: "*Are you searching* (ζητεῖτε) about this with each other that I said, 'A little while and you will not *be-hold* (θεωρεῖτε) me and again a little while and *you will see* (ὄψεσθε) me'?" This threefold repetition of the time factors of his departure and return must be intended to accentuate its paramount significance – specifically to the implied readers. The two different verbs of seeing should prepare them for their imminent experience of loss and recovery.

The eventful character of his enunciated departure and return is reinforced by the double asseveration with which he projects the emotions that they will experience: "Amen, amen I say to you, 'You will weep and mourn, but the world will rejoice. You will grieve, but your grief will be turned into joy'." These will be the two dramatically opposed responses to Jesus' departure into crucifixion. All those who are dedicated to world maintenance will exult at his death; and since it is a death by crucifixion, the curse of Deut 21:23 will reinforce their self-justification. His disciples, however, will be reduced to a state of grief and mourning. Those who accompanied Jesus during his earthly career, according to his final words of farewell in 16:32, will be scattered, each to their own things, as they abandon him at the beginning of his passion. The implied readers, who will continue to inhabit the Gospel's narrative world and accompany Jesus into his arrest, trial, crucifixion and death will be constrained to choose between the abandonment of Jesus by his disciples or the commitment to Jesus that will be exemplified by the Beloved Disciple. It will be a time of lamentation, for the life and activity of the incarnate Logos-Sophia will be terminated by crucifixion and the curse that the Law of Deut 21:23 imposes. Although the implied readers will see Jesus in terms of eye-witnessing his passion, they will not be *observing* or *beholding* him in order to be inspired by his activity and accordingly give them-

[114] For a discussion of whether 16:15 is a major or a minor break in the Fourth Unit of Jesus' farewell speech, see Segovia, *ibid.*, 215-217. In any case, there is a return to a dialogical interaction between Jesus and his disciples; and, as Segovia acknowledges on p. 247, the Paraclete disappears completely in this final section of the discourse.

selves over to it. There will be nothing in the horrors of his crucifixion that would motivate them to emulate him.

But after a little while, that is, after his resurrection, their sorrow will be turned into joy for they will *see* (ὁρᾶν) him again. They will see him as an objective reality with their physical eyes. Jesus elucidates this movement in time from mourning to joy by utilizing the metaphor of a woman in labor anticipating the birth of her child, but suffering the pain of contractions until the child is born. The labor pains that she endured will no longer be remembered when she experiences "the joy of having brought a human being into the world." Analogously, Jesus reassures his disciples: "Now you have grief. But *I shall see* (ὄψομαι) you again, and your heart will rejoice, and no one is going to remove your joy from you."

That day will also bring with it an attendant eschatological reality of the great paradigm shift that Jesus is inaugurating: "And on that day," Jesus declares, "you will question me [about] nothing." There will be no need because, as Jesus stated in 16:12, "When the Spirit of Truth comes, it will conduct you in all truth."

But in the here and now, as they begin to experience the sorrow of his departure, they have the right to approach the Father and make their entreaties without qualification. To reinforce this prerogative, he utilizes his typical solemn formula, "Amen, amen I say to you, 'Whatever you ask the Father, he will give you in my name'." Up until this moment they have not petitioned for anything in his name, as he had urged in 14:13 and 15:7. Consequently he commands them with a present imperative and guarantees fulfillment: "Keep on asking, and you will receive, so that your joy is completed." In spite of the sorrow they will experience as a result of his departure, their open-ended relationship with the Father will be their source of joy.

The present has been a time of παροιμίαι (veiled sayings, enigmas, figures of speech). Jesus has been communicating with them in this mode of speech, and they have been forced to rely on him for elucidation. They have not reached the maturity of being able "to seek out the hidden meanings of veiled sayings (παροιμιῶν).[115] "But the hour is coming," Jesus promises, "when I shall no longer speak to you in figures of speech, but in openness I shall disclose to you concerning the Father." The coming of the Paraclete-Spirit will end the time of veiled sayings and their dependence on his explanations and clarifications, because, as Jesus said in 16:13, "[The Spirit] will not speak of itself, but such things as it will hear, it will speak, and the coming things it will disclose to you."

The restructuring of the world by his resurrection from the dead will also terminate his mediating role between God and his disciples: "In that day you will ask in my name, and I do not say to you that I shall ask the Father about you; for the Father himself loves you because you have loved me and believed that I came

[115] As Sirach 39:3 attributes to the wise and to those who study the Law. Kim Dewey, "*PAROIMIAI* in the Gospel of John," *Semeia* 17, ed. by John Dominic Crossan (Chico, CA: Scholars Press, 1980) 81-99, reviews all the proverbs in the Fourth Gospel as instances of παροιμίαι, apparently presupposing that all the words of Jesus in the Fourth Gospel are instances of this genre.

from the Father." Their love and their commitment to Jesus will draw them directly into a relationship of union with God as they engage in Jesus' work of interpreting God to the world. God will respond to the disciples directly because God loves them, and God loves them because they have loved Jesus and because they have believed that he came from the Father.

After validating God's love to his disciples, Jesus repeats the final clause of verse 27 that conveys their faith and adds an epitomizing statement of his self-understanding.[116]

> I came forth from the Father and I have come into the world. Again I am leaving the world, and I am going *toward* (πρός) the Father. (16:28)

Perhaps, as he reaches the end of his farewell discourse, he wants to reinforce the faith that he has attributed to his disciples but at the same time to amplify it with a more complete acknowledgment of his origin and destiny that has dominated the Gospel. He is the enfleshment of the Logos-Sophia who embodies the dynamic movement of union and differentiation in terms of his aporetic identity as "the Son of the Human Being" who descended from God and "the son of Joseph from Nazareth". By his ascension, after he has fulfilled God's will and work by saving the world, he will be reunited with God.

All that Jesus has said since verse 19, when he became aware of the necessity to elucidate what he had said to his disciples, evokes their enthusiastic response: "See, now you are speaking plainly, and no more are you uttering enigmas (παροιμίαι)." They claim to have grasped what he has said as plain speech, but their use of the adverb *now* (νῦν) indicates that they have not been listening! For he had continued to speak to them in figures of speech, as he explicitly informed them in 16:25. More significantly, by adding an eschatological promise, he had projected an end to speaking to them in enigmas: "An hour is coming when I shall no longer speak to you in figures of speech."[117] Obviously they have not understood. Yet, on the basis of concluding that he has spoken to them plainly, they claim that now *they know cognitively* (οἴδαμεν) that he cognitively *knows* all things.

---

[116] Whether verse 28 should be construed as a continuation of God's motive for loving them or whether it is intended to serve as an epitomizing declaration of Jesus' self-understanding depends on a critical judgment of the textual variants. Verse 27 ends with the clause: πεπιστεύκατε ὅτι ἐγὼ παρὰ τοῦ θεοῦ ἐξῆλθον. Verse 28 begins with the clause: ἐξῆλθον παρὰ τοῦ πατρός. The definite article τοῦ (the) is omitted in the manuscripts that substitute πατρός (father) in place of θεοῦ (God) in verse 27. At the same time, the clause that begins verse 28 and repeats the prepositional phrase that preceded it in verse 27, although in reverse order, is omitted by various manuscripts: ἐξῆλθον παρὰ τοῦ πατρός (I came forth from beside the Father). According to the judgment of Metzger and the editorial committee of *A Textual Commentary on the Greek New Testament*, 248-249, it probably is an accidental omission.

[117] As Metzger, *A Textual Commentary on the New Testament*, 248, has observed, the conjunction "but" (ἀλλά) that appears in various manuscripts probably was inserted by copyists in order to alleviate the abrupt beginning of the sentence.

> *Now* we *know* (οἴδαμεν) that you *know* (οἶδας) all things, and you have no need that anyone should question you. (16:30)

They had wanted to question him, but he had anticipated their inquiry and used the metaphor of a woman suffering labor pains to bring a baby into the world in order to facilitate their understanding. There is no indication that they comprehended the referent of that metaphor in relation to his imminent departure. Will the implied readers have understood? Ironically, it is only after he has spoken eschatologically about the day when it will no longer be necessary for him to mediate their relationship with God because they have entered into union with God by receiving the gift of the Spirit that they infer that he knows all things and therefore has no need to be questioned by anyone. Of course he intuited their questioning among themselves, and therefore they can conclude that he knows all things and has no need that anyone should question him.[118] But they have missed the point that he had made earlier in 16:13:

> When that One comes, the Spirit of Truth, it will guide you in all Truth, for it will not speak of itself but such things as it will hear it will speak and the things that are coming it will disclose to you.

In other words, it is they who will no longer be forced to ask questions because they will no longer be dependent on Jesus. When the "baby" of the New Creation is born, as the result of Jesus' death and resurrection, they will receive the Spirit of Truth, and, as Jesus said in 16:14, "That One will glorify me because it will take from what is mine and will disclose it to you. All the things the Father has are mine; on account of this I said that it will take from what is mine and will disclose it to you." This will be the interdependent relationship between Jesus and the Paraclete-Spirit, and this in turn will be the interdependent relationship between Jesus, the Paraclete-Spirit and the disciples. Then there will be no more enigmas and figures of speech. Consequently, as Jesus had informed them in 16:7, "… it is to your best interest that I go away, for if I do not go away the Paraclete will not come *towards* (πρός) you."

Because the disciples have inferred that Jesus possesses an all-encompassing knowledge, they readily acknowledge the confession that Jesus had attributed to them in 16:27, "By this we believe that you came from (ἀπό) God." Yet how ironic! Jesus has been communicating his origin *from the Father* (παρὰ τοῦ πατρός) throughout his ministry, both to the ruling authorities and to them. Now at last, prior to his imminent passion, they claim to comprehend what he has said

[118] This appears to be the interpretation of Segovia, *Farewell*, 271. "… although the disciples openly accept Jesus' origins with the Father, such acceptance is strictly based on a demonstration of his all-encompassing knowledge and does not really indicate whether they fully understand Jesus' origins at this point (that is, whether such an affirmation understands this provenance as the prologue of 1:1-18 presents it). As true as this is, the disciples' lack of understanding is not only christological but also soteriological in as far as they do not grasp what Jesus has said about their own future as recipients of God's Spirit.

and, on the basis of his all-encompassing knowledge, to believe that he came from God.[119]

Jesus, aware of their lack of understanding and their inadequate confession of faith, resignedly asks, "Do you just now believe?" He had announced to them that "the ruler of the world is coming"; and, in view of the great matters of consequence that he had to communicate to them, he had summoned them to arouse themselves to alertness (ἐγείρεσθε). But they appear to have understood little of the things he has conveyed to them in his farewell discourse. He knows, therefore, that at the critical moment of his arrest they will abandon him: "Look, the hour is coming and has come so that each of you will be scattered to your own things and you will leave me alone." This prediction applies to the time of Jesus' original disciples, but it also confronts the implied readers of the Jewish community of Alexandria. Have they comprehended the prodigious truths that he has transmitted? What is their confession of faith at this point in the narrative world of the Gospel?

Nevertheless, in spite of the abandonment by his disciples that he will experience, he confidently declares that he is not alone, "for the Father is with me." His final word to those who will leave him is the reassurance that he guaranteed to them earlier: "I have spoken these things to you so that in me you may have peace. In the world you have affliction, but be of good cheer, I have conquered the world."

[119] Noticeable in their confessional response is a slight change in their substitution of the preposition ἀπό (from) followed by the compound verb ἐξῆλθες (you came forth) in place of παρά (originating from the side of) that Jesus used in 16:28 and elsewhere. It corresponds to the narrator's christological summary in 13:3 in which the same combination of ἀπό (from) and the compound verb ἐξῆλθεν (he came forth) is used. In 3:2 Nicodemus told Jesus, "We know that you have come *from* (ἀπό) God [as] a teacher."

Chapter Sixteen

The Prayer of Consecration: John 17

After concluding his farewell discourse, Jesus enters into a prayerful communion with God that climactically attests to the profound intimacy of the "Father-Son" relationship that he has manifested throughout his ministry.[1] His prayer will convey to his disciples, who continue to be present, a preview of the "awesome intimacy" that they will experience when the Paraclete will be *in* them. As he had promised them in 14:20, "In that day you will *know* (γνώσεσθε) that I [am] in my Father and you in me and I in you."[2] As in 11:41, he lifts his eyes heavenward, perhaps as an expression of the straightforward and uninhibited communion that he experiences in the "Father-Son" communication that takes place between them. He is, it should not be forgotten, the Son of the Human Being, upon whom the heavenly ladder rests and upon which the divine messengers of God ascend and descend (1:51).

In Jesus' prayer of John 17 the circular movement implied in the Prologue reaches its climax. The epitomizing declaration of 16:28 in which he expressed the dynamic movement of his Logos-Sophia identity: coming from the Father, entering the world, and leaving the world to return to the Father, will soon be culminated in his ascension: κἀγὼ πρὸς σὲ ἔρχομαι (and I am coming towards you). The "Father-Son" relationship that he has enunciated in different contexts of the narrative world was voiced objectively by using the third person singular to refer to both sides of the relationship, as in the asseveration of 5:19, "Amen, amen I say to you, the Son by no means can do anything of himself, except whatever he sees the Father doing." Now, as he stands on the threshold of his καιρός (fixed time), he returns to the use of the second person singular that he employed in 11:41 and 12:27, and the implied readers are confronted with the profound intimacy which "the Father" and "the Son" share in their union and in their differentiation.

At the outset he acknowledges that the fixed time, the long awaited hour has come. It has been anticipated since he responded to his mother's appeal for wine at the Cana wedding with the word, "My hour has not yet arrived." The sign of transforming 162 gallons of water into a vintage superior to that which had been served will now be fulfilled.

Jesus first of all petitions the Father, "Glorify your Son so that your Son glorifies you." His crucifixion must convey a double glorification: that of "the Son" and that of "the Father." Here again the mutuality of interdependence is evident. Since the Son can do nothing apart from the Father (5:19), the latter must take the initiative, so that

---

[1] The structure of Jesus' prayer unfolds in three stages: 1-8, 9-19, 20-26. So also Moloney, *Glory*, 106-107.

[2] 14:17c.

the apprentice Son can respond in kind. If the Father glorifies the Son in the forthcoming crucifixion, the Son will also be able to glorify the Father. "Glory" is essential, so that this will not be another crucifixion like the thousands of crucifixions that the Romans carried out throughout their history. The glory, however, must be manifested ironically, for there is no dignity or grandeur in being "lifted up" on a stake like a poisonous snake. Only then will his being lifted up on a cross be his exaltation. It will be a coronation because his crucifixion will draw all human beings to himself (12:32), for his death will begin the termination of their participation in the old moral order of ἁμαρτία (sin). That achievement of deliverance will glorify God because that was the Creator's motivation to send the Son into the world.

Attendantly, therefore, his attestation to the ruling authorities will also be fulfilled, "When *you lift up* (ὑψώσητε) the Son of the Human Being, then *you will know* (γνώσεσθε) that **I AM** (ἐγώ εἰμί)." Accordingly, the consummation of his long-awaited hour will prove to be the supreme ironic event in human history.

In this opening petition for a double glorification, Jesus acknowledges "the authority of all flesh" which the Father gave him. This is not "power over all flesh," as some translations and commentators render the Greek text.[3] Nor is it a jurisdiction over all human beings. It is the authority which all flesh and blood human beings have been divinely destined to exercise on the basis of God's mandate at creation, as Ps 8:6 affirms. Jesus, the Son of the Human Being, the personification of the New Humanity, is the bearer of "the authority of all flesh," the One who through the exaltation of the cross will draw all human beings, the Many, to himself for healing and for the recovery of the authority which they have lost. No domination is implied here, only the restoration of freedom and life, or as Jesus prays, "so that all [flesh] which you have given him [the Son], he might give to them eternal life" (17:2).

Verse 3 offers a parenthetical observation that attempts to elucidate eternal life, but its content poses a number of problems that make it suspect as an editorial gloss. Simply knowing God and Jesus Christ in terms of an interpersonal involvement, as the verb γινώσκωσιν denotes throughout the Gospel, is not a definition of eternal life nor is it the means by which eternal life is conferred. Is this a trace of a Gnostic perspective?[4] Eternal life, as Jesus enunciates in the previous verse, is his gift to all those whom God has given him, namely those who are drawn into the New Humanity that he will establish by his death and resurrection. Equally unexpected is Jesus' use of "Jesus Christ" as the reference to the relative pronoun ὅν (whom) in the concluding clause of verse 3, "the one whom you sent, Jesus Christ." Jesus never refers to himself as "Jesus Christ" in the narrative world of the Gospel. As a name, "Jesus Christ" is encountered only in the Prologue (1:17) where it is juxtaposed with Moses in order to pose a contrast between the one through whom the grace of the Law was given and the one through whom "grace and truth happened". By deleting verse 3 as

[3] For example: the RSV, the NRSV and the NASV. Also Schnackenburg, *St. John* III, 171; Moloney, *Glory*, 109.

[4] See Brown's discussion of a possible Gnostic orientation, *John*, II, 752-753,

a later redaction, a more immediate continuity is established between verses 2 and 4, in as far as Jesus acknowledges his glorification of God by fulfilling the work of giving eternal life to all those whom God has given him.[5]

> Even as you gave him [the] authority of all flesh so that everything that you have given him he should give to them everlasting life. (17:2)
>
> I glorified you on the earth completing the work that you have given me that I should do. (17:4)

For a moment Jesus turns away from the imminent future and the prospect that awaits him and professes, "I glorified you on earth completing the work that you have given me that I should do." The work that lies behind him consists of actions and teaching, deeds and words; and together they form an integrated unity of revelation disclosing a new order of being, a transformed world, in which the injustices of racism and sexism can be eliminated, those blinded by the social construction of reality can begin to see the truth of things, the disabled and incapacitated human beings can recover their full humanness, and those trapped in living death can be resurrected.[6] Human brokenness is to be healed by the re-establishment of a relationship with the Creator; but, in contrast to the past, it is divinely willed to be a family relationship that is characterized by interdependent horizontality instead of a hierarchical and patriarchal dependence.

As the incarnate Logos-Sophia in union with God, Jesus has included the work of incorporating into himself certain external religious structures and formal ceremonies that determine the religious life of his society. As a result, he has become the embodiment of God's Temple from which rivers of living water will flow for the renewal of humankind. He has made himself the Passover meal of liberation. In the integration of his deeds and words he becomes the Light of the first day of creation. By his appropriation of the golden vine and its grape clusters of the Temple's entrance doors he identifies himself as the embodiment of the new people of God. And symbolically he will become the Door upon which the Passover rite of smearing the blood of the Lamb for the deliverance of God's people will be enacted.[7] The objective of this internalization is to integrate religious structures and religious activities into the flesh and blood existence of human beings so that the evaluation of every individual in society transcends the significance of any and every institution that a society's ideology might hold in greater veneration. As the result of this paradigm shift, God's presence is no longer mediated to human beings by the priestly role of broker operating within the temple cult of the hierarchical structures of patron/client relationships. God's residence is no longer a stone building that serves as an

[5] Schnackenburg, *St. John* III, 172, offers seven objections to support the rejection of verse 3 as a gloss.

[6] Against Käsemann, *The Testament of Jesus*, who throughout these Schaffer Lectures dissolves the paradox of the heavenly and the earthly. His projection of a "naïve docetism" onto the Fourth Gospel has blinded him to the work of world transformation that Jesus inaugurates and that his disciples are to continue to its completion. The Fourth Gospel is neither docetic nor Gnostic. If its theology is "dangerous," it is because it is aporetic and radical, not because it is unorthodox.

[7] See chapter 17.

architectonic center that establishes the boundary lines of the sacred and the secular. Human beings are now exhorted to offer themselves as living sacrifices to God instead of animals or things. God's Spirit, housed in the physical body of human beings, can generate a fountain or even rivers of living water by which others can be refreshed. The Passover meal of liberation becomes a giving of one's life and its energies as food to revitalize others. Resurrection can occur in present historical existence so that human beings can be extricated from the web of living death.

In as far as "the hour has come," and he has surrendered himself to it, Jesus is including his imminent death by which he will consummate his work when, in the final moments of his life, he announces, "It has been accomplished!" Before he enters into his passion, therefore, he wants this comprehensive work to be authenticated and certified by the Father in the culminating events of his life. Accordingly, he prays that the glory that he shared with the Creator even before creation will be manifested in his enthronement on the cross: "And now you, Father, glorify me with your own glory which I had with you before the world came into being." The union between Jesus of Nazareth and the Logos-Sophia, that resulted at his baptism, when God's Spirit descended and remained on him and breathed the divine Logos into him, is so consummate that he can identify himself with the Logos and claim its primordial glory for himself. As the enfleshment of the Logos-Sophia and the bearer of God's Spirit, he is the prototypical Human Being, the first final Human Being.

His work also has engaged him in *manifesting God's name* to those whom God gave him, both the disciples of his earthly career and the disciples among the implied readers of the Gospel. Accordingly, he has fulfilled the eschatological promise of Isa 52:6.[8]

> On account of this my people will know my name on that day because **I** myself **AM** the one speaking (ἐγώ εἰμι αὐτὸς ὁ λαλῶν). I am present.

In the narrative world of the Gospel Jesus has claimed that God has been present in his speaking ministry because, as the incarnate Logos-Sophia, he has been speaking God's word. But speaking God's word in and of itself does not necessarily endorse Jesus as the presence of God. How then are the people to know God's name through "the one speaking"? Even more to the point, how can God's name be *manifested* through the hearing of speech? God's name is identifiable with God's activity, and God's activity is directed towards creation and re-creation, towards the birth and rebirth of human beings, and towards the transformation of the world in which justice and peace will prevail. Consequently, God's name and therefore God's presence can only be manifested empirically by activity that corresponds to the will of God as it is disclosed in the Word of God. Throughout his ministry in the narrative world of the Gospel Jesus has manifested God's name by objectifying the truth of God through the integration of his words and deeds. Concomitantly the presence of God has been

[8] Barrett, *St. John*, 505, also cites Isa 52:6. But the verb ἐφανέρωσα (I manifested) is reduced to "revealing the name of God," which of course can be done orally. But the verb, to manifest, implies empirical experience that includes seeing. Jesus is the objectification of all that God's name implies.

authenticated by the activities that are metaphorically associated with the predicates of his self-disclosure as **I AM.**

> **I AM** the Bread of Life.
> **I AM** the Light of the world.
> **I AM** the Good Shepherd.
> **I AM** the Door.
> **I AM** the Resurrection and the Life.
> **I AM** the Way, the Truth and the Life.
> **I AM** Vine-stock.

Because the disciples belong to the work of his ministry, and he has manifested God's name and God's presence to them, it is only natural that he should intercede for them. They have been God's gift to him! "They were yours, and you gave them to me." Moreover, as he acknowledges, "They have guarded *your word* (τὸν λόγον σου)." In view of his subsequent use of τὰ ῥήματα (sayings/statements) in verse 8, his employment of the word λόγος seems to be directed towards the identification of *your word*, that is, God's word, with Jesus himself as the incarnate Logos. Through the conjunction of his words and deeds he has manifested the truth of God to his disciples. Their personal experience of that integrity that he has manifested throughout his ministry has induced in them the certainty that "all the things you have given me are from you." That includes the τὰ ῥήματα (sayings/statements) that God gave Jesus, and Jesus in turn gave them.

> And they received them, and *they* truly *knew* (ἔγνωσαν) that I came forth from (παρά) you and they believed that you sent me.

This testimonial, that his disciples knew from their personal grasp of Jesus' τὰ ῥήματα (sayings/statements) that he originated from God and was sent by God, poses a telling contrast to the response the ruling authorities have made as Jesus witnessed to them about his origin and his commission. More than an historical note, this condition of alienation is essentially a reflection of the divided community of Jews in Alexandria.

Accordingly, Jesus is interceding for those who know the only true God and Jesus whom God sent, not for the world and those who are promoting its dissension and conflict. He is praying for his disciples because they are God's possessions and God gave them to him. That is the mutuality of the union they share, and Jesus acknowledges it by recognizing first of all, "… all my things are yours," and then also, "and all your things are mine" (17:10). In view of this reciprocal interactive relationship, Jesus unhesitatingly affirms, "And I have been glorified by them." If, as he says in 5:19, he is imitating God's works, and there will be greater works that God will show him, so that "you," namely the ruling authorities, will marvel, then he, as God's apprentice, will be a partner in the splendor of their collaborative activities.

Jesus does not pray for the world, because he no longer considers himself to be in the world: "And I am no longer in the world, and they are in the world, and I am coming *towards* (πρός) you." Ironically, however, he is still very much in the world, and the world, in its alienation and with all of its hatred, will condemn him to death by crucifixion. But he construes all that he is going to suffer: his trial, condemnation and crucifixion, as the beginning of his return to God.

But his disciples are still in the world! Indeed, they are among the implied readers of the Gospel, and, according to 16:1, they are confronting the stark realities of exclusion from the synagogue (ἀποσυνάγωγος) and martyrdom. They are his successors! They have been called to continue his work of world transformation. A sense of anxiety seems to be conveyed in his intercession for them, for he repeats the mode of address that he employed at the beginning of his prayer, "Father," but now includes the epithet "holy" as he pleads for their safe-keeping. As an epithet, the adjective "holy" in the Philonic and Pharisaic context of the Gospel attributes to God a sanctity of apartness or separation that is established by the Logos. The very reverse, however, may be intended here! Jesus, as the incarnate Logos-Sophia, unites human beings with God as he himself is united with God. Consequently, Jesus' form of address, "Holy Father" may be intended to intimate a safe-guarding that prevents the disciples from losing their footing and slipping back into the world and its alienated construction of reality by a guardianship that is oriented towards union. That, in fact, is implied in the last subjunctive clause of verse 11.

> Holy Father, guard them *in/by* your name *which* you have given me, so that they are one even as we. (17:11e)

As the disciples have guarded God's word (λόγος), so God is petitioned to guard them *in/by* God's name. To be kept *in* God's name implies that they belong to God's province and therefore are under God's personal jurisdiction. To be kept *by* God's name signifies a guardianship that involves all that is associated with God's name, above all the authority and power that Jesus manifests in the garden when he identifies himself to the cohort of soldiers as **I AM** (ἐγὼ εἰμί) and they fall backwards to the ground helpless. This is the name that God gave Jesus! The referent of the dative singular relative pronoun ᾧ (which) is the dative singular ὀνόματι (name), and it indicates that the name in and by which the disciples are to be guarded is the name that God gave to Jesus, and the implication may be that God should share his name with them as well.[9] God's name includes all that God is as disclosed by the Hebrew Scriptures and, of course, for the Alexandrian Jews, the Septuagint. God's name also includes Jesus' work of interpreting God as the incarnate Logos-Sophia. But God's name is also to be associated with God's self-disclosure of God's name to Moses in

[9] The manuscripts, P^{66vid} ℵ L W 579 pc, support the reading of the dative singular relative pronoun ᾧ (which), referring to the dative singular ὀνόματι (name), over against the accusative plural of the relative pronoun οὓς (whom) that refers to the object of God's care-taking, namely the disciples. The former, ᾧ is almost certainly the more difficult reading. P^{66}, however, replaces the perfect tense, δέδωκας, with the aorist, ἔδωκας, and omits the remaining subordinate clause of verse 11.

LXX Ex 3:14, ἐγώ εἰμί ὁ ὤν (**I AM** the One who is). Throughout the narrative world Jesus has employed this formula of self-disclosure in its absolute form, ἐγώ εἰμί, as, for example in his self-identification to his disciples while walking on the Sea of Galilee. He also has connected this formula of self-disclosure with predicates, as in 6:48, 51: "**I AM** the Bread of Life." In 6:46, he used ὁ ὤν (the one who is) in conjunction with the prepositional phrase, παρὰ τοῦ θεοῦ (from God).

> Not that anyone has seen the Father, except *the one who is from God* (ὁ ὤν παρὰ τοῦ θεου). This one has seen the Father.

As already evidenced, the objective of this safe-keeping in and by God's name is unification: "so that they are one even as we." Jesus prays that the province and jurisdiction of God's guardianship will draw his disciples into the same union that they experienced while he was with them, as he himself lived in union with God. During that time he fulfilled his response-ability in keeping them.

> When I was with them, I was guarding them *in/by* your name which you have given me, and I protected [them] and none of them is lost except the son of destruction with the result that Scripture is fulfilled. (17:12)

He made himself accountable for their preservation by keeping them within the province and under the jurisdiction of God's name, the name, as he again acknowledges, that God gave him. Only one of the disciples is lost, destroyed by his own rejection and betrayal of Jesus. Judas is not named but referred to as "the son of destruction," an appellative that stands in opposition to the titles that Jesus bears in the Gospel, "the Son of the Human Being" and "the Son of God," and therefore characterizes Judas as an opponent of God's work who has destined himself to damnation.[10] Most likely the scriptural fulfillment that is acknowledged is Psa 41:10, a text that that Jesus quoted in 13:18, but here in 17:12 it is not clear whether he is alluding to it or whether it is the narrator's aside. Jesus' revision of Psa 41:10, as was indicated earlier, implies that Judas also has partaken of the Bread of Life. By chewing Jesus' flesh and drinking his blood, he has participated in the divine Life of the New Human Being. But his betrayal has negated his participation in it. Instead of crossing over from death into Life by entering into the New Humanity Jesus is pioneering, he has become "a devil." But he was not predestined by God or the Scriptures; his act simply results in scriptural fulfillment.[11]

Once again Jesus confidently affirms his already-here-and-now heavenward movement but acknowledging – in contrast to verse 11a – that what he has been saying has been spoken within the reality of the world: "But *now* I am coming *towards* (πρός) you, and *these things* I speak in the *world* so that they have my joy fulfilled in themselves." The *things* that Jesus is referring to, that will fulfill his joy in

---

[10] See Brown, *John* II, 760, and Barrett, *St. John*, 508, on Judas as "the son of perdition" and its parallels.

[11] This is also true of the subordinate clause of 13:18 that announces the fulfillment of Scripture. According to 6:71, Jesus foreknew that Judas would betray him, and, as a result Scripture was fulfilled. See Chapter 15.

them, is his petition that they should be guarded by God's name by becoming its co-bearers, as he himself was. Bearing the divine name is vital for two reasons. He has given them God's λόγος (word), the plan and meaning of the universe that Jesus as the incarnate Logos-Sophia embodies and that he has been engaged in establishing. And secondly, as he also acknowledges in 17:14, "... and the world hated them, because they are not ἐκ τοῦ κόσμου (from the world) even as I am not ἐκ τοῦ κόσμου."[12] Here Jesus repeats the words he spoke to the ruling authorities in 8:23, "ἐγὼ ἐκ τῶν ἄνω εἰμί (I from above **AM**) ... ἐγὼ οὐκ εἰμὶ ἐκ τοῦ κόσμου τούτου (**I** not **AM** from this world)." If the disciples, like Jesus, are not ἐκ τοῦ κόσμου, if they did not originate from that social construction of reality, then, like Jesus, they also must be ἐκ τῶν ἄνω (from above). They must have the same heavenly origin that he attributes to himself. Like him, they must be God's offspring, and therefore the implication must be that they too have descended from heaven.

Consequently, they too are strangers in the world. Yet he does not want them to be removed from the world but to be preserved from evil and from the evil one. They are the vines grafted into the Vine-stock that will bear fruit, indeed, fruit that will remain. Their forthcoming empowerment by God's Spirit, the Paraclete, will enable them to fulfill their commission to do the works that Jesus has done and, indeed, even greater works. Because he is leaving them, they must be safe-guarded in the world by being bearers of God's name that would place them in the province and under the jurisdiction of God's name. Again, for the sake of emphasis, he repeats the words of verse 14: "They are not ἐκ τοῦ κόσμου even as I am not ἐκ τοῦ κόσμου." For that reason Jesus charges God to consecrate (ἁγίασον) them, to set them apart for a sacred duty in the truth of God's λόγος (word): "Consecrate them in the Truth, your Word is Truth (ὁ λόγος ὁ σὸς ἀλήθεια). The phrase ὁ λόγος ὁ σὸς is simply the nominative form of the twofold earlier uses of the same phrase in the accusative case in verses 8 and 14: τὸν λόγον σου, but it is the former, ὁ λόγος ὁ σὸς that more immediately conveys a sense of identification with Jesus himself. Because he is the incarnate Logos, he is also God's Word and God's Truth by which the disciples are to be sanctified.

In anticipation of their consecration to the Truth of God's λόγος, Jesus sent them into the world, even as God sent him into the world. Correspondingly he is consecrating (ἁγιάζω) himself, setting himself apart for his appointed sacred task, so that they will be consecrated in Truth. The authentication of their consecration is directly dependent on his consecration. This is sacrificial language, as Edwyn Hoskyns has stipulated: "It is equally appropriate to the preparation of a priest and the preparation of a sacrifice; it is therefore doubly appropriate to Christ."[13] In his forthcoming passion Jesus will be both priest and sacrifice. His sacred commission, therefore, is to offer himself as a "snake lifted up on a stake" so that the New

[12] Here again, consistency building is vital! Moloney, *Glory*, 116, does not relate verses 14, 16 to 8:23.

[13] Hoskyns/Davey, *Fourth Gospel*, 503; Also Barrett, *St. John*, 511.

Humanity that Jesus embodies will be established foundationally. Only then will his disciples be able to enter into it, and only then will they be able to fulfill their consecrated commission in the world by communicating the Good News of this new era of salvation.

Finally, in the third and last section of his prayer Jesus intercedes for those who will become disciples in the future by the efforts of those who are his present disciples, namely those among the implied readers of the Gospel in Alexandria.

> I ask not only about these but also about the ones who are going to believe into me on account of their word (λόγου), so that all are one, even as you, Father, in me and I in you, so that they also are in us, so that the world believes that you sent me. (17:20-21)

The ultimate objective of Jesus' mandate is the unity of the Many: "so that all may be one." But that unity of the One and the Many can only be constituted by the multitude of human beings as they are drawn into the New Humanity that will be established ontologically by Jesus' resurrection from the dead. The eschatological outcome will be a cosmic living Temple of God in which the One, God the Creator, and the Many of the New Humanity will be united into everlasting life. All dualisms, all pollution systems, all the structures that divide the world of human beings into the two realms of the clean and the unclean, the good and the evil, will be terminated. Everyone living in the province and under the jurisdiction of God's name will have equal access to the domain of divine possibility and the grace of self-fulfillment. Human beings fully alive, without the infection of sin and no longer subject to the forms and forces of living death, will manifest the glory that Jesus bequeathed to his disciples.

> And the glory that you have given me I have given to them so that they are one, even as we are one. I in them and you in me, so that they are going to be *made complete/perfect* (ὦσιν τετελειωμένοι) into one." (17:22-23)

The use of the perfect passive participle, τετελειωμένοι, plus the present subjunctive, ὦσιν, implies a process that will be realized over a period of time. The effect of its fulfillment, as Jesus reiterates, is that the world will *know* (γινώσκῃ) by experience "that you sent me and loved them even as you loved me" (17:23).[14]

As he nears the end of his prayer in which he has offered up his petitions and intercessions as prescriptions to God, he addresses God once again as "Father." Now, in conclusion he gives voice to a consummate longing. It is a repetition of the promise he made in 12:26 and especially in 14:3:

> I want that *where* ***AM I*** (ὅπου εἰμὶ ἐγώ), those are with me so that they *observe/look on* (θεωρῶσιν) my glory which you have given me because you loved me before the foundation of the world. (17:24)

---

[14] It is noteworthy that only ἀγαπᾶν (to love) is employed in Jesus' prayer of consecration.

Jesus has employed the phrase ὅπου εἰμὶ ἐγώ (where **AM I**) on four previous occasions. Initially he spoke it to the ruling authorities (7:34), who repeated it in their efforts to understand what it means (7:36). He enunciated it as a condition in 12:26, "If anyone ministers to me, let her/him follow me and *where **AM I***, there also my minister will be." He uttered it to his disciples as a pledge in 14:3, "Again I am coming and I will receive you *towards* (πρός) myself so that *where **AM I*** you also are." Now, however, it forms a petition that he addresses to the "Father." He wants his disciples – including of course the implied readers of the Gospel! – to be located in his divine ἐγὼ εἰμί so that they will *observe* (θεωρῶσιν) his glory, the glory that God gave him, and that by observing or beholding they will be drawn into it and surrender themselves to it.[15] Nothing less than their eventual participation in his glory is his consummate desire. His acknowledgment of the glory that "the Father" gave him because he "loved him before the foundation of the world" echoes his earlier claim in 17: 5 on the primordial glory that he considers as his divine heritage as the incarnate Logos, the enfleshed prototypical Human Being.

As Jesus ends his prayer of consecration, he addresses God once more as "Father" but now with the accompanying epithet δίκαιε (just/righteous). It is an appeal to God's justice in view of the present status quo. Jesus delineates four basic realities:

1. The world did not know you.
2. But I knew you.
3. These disciples knew that you sent me.
4. I made known to them your name.

Unexpectedly and surprisingly he employs the past tense of γινώσκειν (to know), the verb denoting personal experience on the basis of interpersonal involvement that he consistently has used throughout his prayer. It would appear that Jesus is concluding his prayer as though he is looking back on his career, perhaps even as though he already has ascended to "the Father" and is now addressing him "face to face." That would correspond to the acknowledgment he made in verse 11a, "And no longer am I in the world." It is a summation of his ministry in retrospect, and it epitomizes the stark realities that he encountered and his consequent engagement with the social construction of reality and the human beings who inhabit it. The first statement, "The world did not know you" is an almost verbatim repetition of 1:10. It not only acknowledges the truth of the Prologue's declaration; it intimates that little has changed during the course of Jesus' ministry. The second assertion, "But I knew you" accentuates the intimate relationship of "the Father" and "the Son" and the mutuality that they shared throughout Jesus' ministry. The third and the fourth acknowledge the affirming response of his disciples to his exegesis of the Creator God that the concluding verse of the Prologue ascribed to the incarnate Logos-Sophia.

---

[15] See Hans Georg Gadamer, *Truth and Method*, 111. *Wahrheit u. Methode*, 140, on the Greek idea of *theoros* who engages in *theorein*. The Apostle Paul, in 2 Cor 3:18 expresses the same reality.

Jesus reminds the "righteous Father" of these four realities and commits himself to the completion of his divine commission and its fulfillment of LXX Isa 52:6 with his final acknowledgment: "And I made known to them your name, and I *shall make known* …" The objective of this continued engagement with the world through his disciples remains the same as it was throughout his ministry, "So that the love [with] which you loved me is in them and I in them." That, in effect, is almost a redundancy. For Jesus is the embodiment of God's love, and by being "in them," as they "begin to remain in his love," God's love will dwell in them, and they will become embodiments of God's love.

Chapter Seventeen

The Third Passover: Jesus' Trial, Crucifixion, and Burial

The arrest 18:1-12

The death and resurrection that culminate Jesus' career in the narrative world of the Fourth Gospel may be characterized in his own words, words that he uttered in different contexts of this ministry and particularly in his Prayer of Consecration to the "Father," "And now I am coming towards (πρός) you![1]

Having revealed the objectives of his imminent departures to his disciples – and the implied readers – in his Farewell Discourse and having laid claim to God's glorification as well as his own glorification in the crucifixion to which he will be condemned, Jesus commences his journey towards "the Father." Escorted by his disciples, he crosses the winter torrents of the Wadi Kedron and enters a garden that had served as a place of communion with his disciples.

Judas, his betrayer, knows the place and leads a σπεῖρα, a cohort of 600 soldiers, and the torch-bearing temple police of the chief priests and Pharisees into the garden.[2] Most likely Judas is simply serving as a guide to lead the military force to the garden and to an identification of Jesus.[3] Such a large arresting party is undoubtedly symbolic to augment the effect of the power that Jesus' self-identification to this alliance of Romans and Jews will have on the implied readers.[4] The implication of a Roman presence as a cohort under the command of a χιλίαρχος, (a leader of a thousand/tribune) would appear to be equally symbolic.[5] Their involvement along with the Jewish temple police would imply a collaboration between the chief priests and the Romans. Historically speaking, the

---

[1] 17:13, 11; 7:33; 13:1, 3; 14:12, 28; 16:5, 10, 17, 28

[2] Is the cohort a Roman detachment under the command of a χιλίαρχος, (leader of a thousand, a tribune) who is referred to in 18:12, or is the cohort a Jewish detail of Levitical temple police? The military designation, σπεῖρα, evidently Roman, is used in 2 Macc 8:23; 12:20,22, where it refers to Jewish divisions. But in *Ant* XVII, 215 and *BJ* 2, 11, Josephus refers to a cohort of hoplites under a χιλίαρχος sent out by the Herodian, Archelaus. Surely these must be mercenaries, not the temple police who would be under the authority of the chief priests. Brown, *John* II, 808, maintains that "A writer living under Roman domination would scarcely use a technical Roman military term for a Jewish force…"

[3] Judas plays no further role, as verse 12 indicates. Consequently, Judas is not in charge of the cohort; the tribune is. There is no discrepancy here. Contrary to Winter, *On the Trial of Jesus*, 44.

[4] Mark W. G. Stibbe, *John as Storyteller,* 170-171. Barrett, *St. John*, 516, surmises that the Romans are implicated "to show that the whole κόσμος was ranged against Jesus."

[5] Winter, *Trial of Jesus*, 45, contends that the temple police had only an auxiliary function. It was the Romans who arrested Jesus. More likely, however, the narrator wants to implicate both the Romans and the Jewish authorities.

chief priests would have cooperated with the Romans during the lifetime of Jesus, because, as the ruling power of the Jewish people, they were subject to the authority of Rome as it was invested in the Roman governor. The anachronistic inclusion of the Pharisees lends support to the symbolic character of this episode. They are mentioned here for the last time in the narrative world of the Gospel and may have been included in this context because of their collaboration with Rome under the leadership of Yochanan ben Zakkai during and after the destruction of Jerusalem.[6]

Jesus, very aware of what is happening and what the eventual outcome will be, takes the initiative and questions them, "Whom are you seeking?" He has no intention of being reduced to victimization.[7] The freedom that he begins to disclose on the verge of his arrest is a cardinal feature of the glory that he will manifest throughout his passion. He exhibits it immediately in and through the power of his divine self-disclosure as the bearer of God's name, **I AM** (ἐγὼ εἰμί). For when the answer is shouted, "Jesus the Nazoraios," he responds with the divine self-identification, ἐγὼ εἰμί, and, as the narrator observes, the effect is immediate.[8] "They went backwards and fell onto the ground!" Judas of course is there, and because of his earlier discipleship he, more than the others, must be dismayed, if not appalled at what he is experiencing. For a stunning moment the implied readers are confronted with the truth of Jesus' pronouncement to the Pharisees.

> No one takes my ψυχή (soul/life) from me, but I offer it of myself. I have authority to offer it, and I have authority to take it again. This command I received from my Father. (10:18)

As God's apprentice he has divine Life in himself, and the authority he exercises as the bearer of God's name conveys a power that his enemies are unable to oppose. They can apprehend him only because he surrenders himself to them. That

[6] Schnackenburg, *St. John* III, 222 may be correct in his insistence that Roman participation in Jesus' arrest is "as good as impossible." Yet in their respective historical periods, both the priests and the Pharisees collaborated with the Romans, and the implied author appears to intend to implicate them as co-conspirtors with the Romans.

[7] For an honor/shame analysis of Jesus' passion in the fourth Gospel, see Jerome H. Neyrey, "'Despising the Shame of the Cross': Honor and Shame in the Johannine Passion Narrative," *Honor and Shame in the World of the Bible. Semeia* 68 (Atlanta: Scholars Press, 1996) 113-137.

[8] The identification of Jesus as τὸν Ναζωραίον continues to be elusive in scholarly investigation. Here in John 18:5, 7 and 19:19 as well as in Matt 2:23 and 26:71 and Luke 18:37 it may denote "the Nazarene," the one from Nazareth and therefore would correspond to Philip's witness to Nathanael, "We have found the one Moses wrote about in the Law and [the one} the Prophets [wrote about], Jesus, the son of Joseph from Nazareth (ἀπὸ Ναζαρέτ). Efforts at unraveling the origin and significance of the term include: Bertil Gärtner, *Die rätselhaften Termini Nazoräer und Iskariot. Horae Soederblomianae* (Uppsala: C. W. K. Gleerup, 1957); Matthew Black, *The Scrolls and Christian Origins* (New York: Scribner's sons, 1961); Eduard Schweizer, "Er wird Nazoräer heissen," in *Judentum, Urchristentum, Kirche: Festschrift für Joachim Jeremias*, ed. by Walter Eltester (Berlin: Alfred Töpelmann, 1960) 90-93.

freedom is a glimpse of his glory and majesty as the New Human Being (ὁ υἱὸς τοῦ ἀνθρώπου)[9]

Jesus repeats his question, "Whom are you seeking?" He has already identified himself to them, so they should know who he is. But the second question is necessary in order to accentuate the sovereignty he is able to exercise as the bearer of God's name and therefore to confront his enemies with their own powerlessness. For a second time he identifies himself with the divine **I AM,** and with a command he exacts from them the freedom and safety of his disciples. Here too he shows himself to be the Good Shepherd who offers his ψυχή (soul/life) on behalf of his sheep. "If then you seek me, let these go." His reply in verse 8 is completed by the narrator's intrusive observation, "so that the word that he said is fulfilled, 'Those whom you have given me, I lost none of them'." Again and again the implied readers are confronted with Jesus' integrity as the incarnate Logos: his actions correspond to and indeed fulfill his earlier promises.

Apparently Simon Peter does not want to be included among his fellow disciples whose release Jesus has claimed from the military officers. Since he had enunciated a pledge earlier to offer his ψυχή (soul/life) on behalf of Jesus (13:37), he obviously intends to demonstrate the integrity of his avowal with his swordsmanship. He strikes the slave of the High Priest and cuts off his right ear.[10]

The narrator pauses momentarily to identify the slave to the implied readers: "His name was Malchus." Surely he is an insignificant participant in this drama. The narrator's pronounced reticence to name certain characters in the narrative world of the Gospel, such as: the Mother of Jesus, the Samaritan woman, the crippled human being of 5:5, the blind male of 9:1 and the Beloved Disciple, evokes an inquisitiveness as to why a slave is named, who may be one of the torch-bearers providing light in order to facilitate the arrest of Jesus. There is no necessity to identify him simply because the one who struck him is named.[11] It may be that the implied readers are to be tantalized into an active reflection on the significance of naming and not naming certain characters in the narrative world.

Peter's discipleship expresses itself in the style of a zealot who meets violence with violence. Somehow he has not grasped Jesus' repeated emphasis in his last will and testament that his departure is mandatory because its objective will enable his disciples to become participants in his empowerment and continue his work of world transformation. Jesus has no ambition to engage in a power struggle with

---

[9] Schnackenburg, III, 224-225, contrary to Bultmann, observes that this is not a "falling down as 'before the epiphany of Deity". For "the powerlessness of the enemies when confronted with the might of God," he cites 2 Kings 1:9-14, 2 Esd 13:3-4; and, for the words used by Jesus , Ps 27 (26):2 and Psa 35 (34):4.

[10] So also Arthur J. Droge, "The Status of Peter in the Fourth gospel: A Note on John 18:10-11," *JBL* 109/2 (1990), who discusses the question: why, of the four Gospels, does the Fourth Gospel identify Simon Peter as the one who drew his sword and cut off the ear of the high priest's slave? In his assessment of the Gospel's portrayal of Peter, he concludes that "Peter is not a "subject" of Jesus' heavenly kingdom" and that Peter's denial is really his *confession*."

[11] Contrary to Schnackenburg III, 227

the "ruler of the world," as he is represented here by a Roman cohort and the temple police of the chief priests. He rejects Peter's fierce interference and rebukes him openly before Judas and the military detachment that is on the verge of arresting him: "Thrust the sword into its sheath! The cup that the Father has given me, shall I by no means drink it?" This is the first and only reference to a cup in the Gospel. It echoes the metaphor of the cup that Jesus employs in the Synoptic tradition to represent the passion of suffering and death that he will endure.[12] Whether the Evangelist was familiar with one or more of the Synoptic Gospels or an oral tradition is difficult if not impossible to determine.

On the other hand, it may be that "the cup" in all four Gospels refers to the cup of LXX Psa 74 (75): 9. It is indeed a cup that connotes suffering and death, but more specifically it is God's cup of intemperate wine: that is, the wine of God's wrath that the boastful, the wicked, and all the sinners of the earth will drink.

> For a cup is in the hand of the Lord, full of a mixture of intemperate wine. And he turned aside from this [the boastful] to this [the wicked]. But dregs of his cup were not exhausted. All the sinners of the earth will drink (of it).[13]

In their place, however, Jesus, the incarnate Logos-Sophia, the New Human Being, (ὁ υἱὸς τοῦ ἀνθρώπου) will drink the dregs of the wine of God's wrath. Ironically, that too will be his glory as he forms or frames his crucifixion into the preposterous event of terminating the human infection of sin (ἁμαρτία). Any effort by Simon Peter will not frustrate Jesus' determination to fulfill his divine commission.

The interrogation before Annas and Simon Peter's denial 18:13-27

Jesus is arrested and bound by the military detachment, its commander and the temple police, and led away "to Annas first."[14] The narrator identifies him as "the father-in-law of Caiaphas, who was High Priest that year." The implied readers are reminded of the irony of Caiaphas' advisement to his fraternity of ruling authorities (οἱ Ἰουδαίοι) that it is advantageous that one human being die on behalf of the people. Annas, who, long after his deposition was still called High Priest, will conduct the initial interrogation.[15] There is no need to rearrange the text of 18:13-24 in order to remedy the apparent confusion of two high priests, as it was

---

[12] See Mark 14:36; Matt. 26:39; Luke 22:42.

[13] This is my own translation of a rather ambiguous Septuagint rendition of Psa 74 (75): 9.

[14] Unfortunately Schnackenburg *St. John* III, 228-233, devotes much space to the question of sources, without resolving any historical problems that the text poses. The Gospel, however, is not an historical document as such. It is a narrative world in which history, tradition and interpretation are combined and into which the implied readers are invited to enter for an existential experience.

[15] Josephus *Ant* XVIII, 34. Cited by Dodd, *Historical Traditions* 94,11.2. On Annas or Ananus, and the house of eight high priests that came from his family, see S. Safrai, "Jewish Self-Government," *The Jewish People in the First Century* I, 402-403; M. Stern, "The Province of Judea," *The Jewish People in the First Century* I, 349-350.

undertaken by the scribe of the Sinaitic Syriac or more recently by W. Randolf Church.[16]

Only two disciples follow Jesus as he is led away to the hearing before Annas. Like the others, they have not been detained, but unlike them, they are committed to supporting Jesus with their encouraging presence. Simon Peter is named first. In spite of Jesus' censure of his swordsmanship in the garden, he apparently intends to be true to his avowal to offer his life on Jesus' behalf. The other is not named but simply referred to as an "other disciple" but one known to the High Priest. His identification continues to be controversial. Many of the scribes who later produced copies of the Fourth Gospel inserted the definite article, ὁ (the) in front of the adjective ἄλλος (other) in order to convey their conviction that, on the basis of the phrase in 20:2, τὸν ἄλλον μαθητὴν ὃν ἐφίλει ὁ 'Ιησοῦς (the other disciple whom Jesus was loving), this must be the Beloved Disciple.[17] It is possible that the author of the Gospel deliberately omitted the definite article before the phrase ἄλλος μαθητής (other disciple) in order to challenge the implied readers to determine the identity of this disciple and subsequently in 20:2 to correct or reinforce that identification by being confronted with this same phrase, τὸν ἄλλον μαθητὴν (the other disciple), placed directly before the characteristic formula ὃν ἐφίλει ὁ 'Ιησοῦς (the one whom Jesus was loving.)

The narrator's identification of this "other disciple" who is "known to the High Priest" is equally enigmatic and probably also intended to challenge the implied readers to fill this tantalizing gap. Who, of all the disciples in the narrative world of the Gospel, would be known to the High Priest? It could not be John, the son of Zebedee, because he is not a disciple of Jesus in the first edition of the Gospel (chapters 1-20). It would have to be someone who, in contrast to Simon Peter, had the courage and commitment to *accompany* Jesus *into* (συνεισῆλθεν) the courtyard of Annas. That could only be the Beloved Disciple, and he is implied to be Lazarus whom Jesus had raised from the dead and who therefore no longer fears death even though the chief priests had also been planning to kill him. Moreover, it should not be forgotten that the presence of the ruling authorities at Lazarus' death and resurrection (11:31, 35) signified that he was recognized as a figure of importance in Jerusalem. Although he is a disciple of Jesus, it is probably on the basis of his stature and reputation that he is admitted to the interrogation before Annas. Evidently this is only a preliminary hearing; it is not a trial before the Sanhedrin.

---

[16] W. Randolf Church, "The Dislocations in the Eighteenth Chapter of John," 376-379, cites the changes that ancient writers made to alleviate the seeming confusion of the two high priests, Anna and Caiaphas in the text of 18:12-27. The Sinaitic Syriac offers another sequence of verses: 12, 13, 24, 14, 15, 19-23, 16-18, 25b-27, but Church presents a further alternative: 12, 13, 24, 14, 19-23, 15-18, 25b-27. Both re-orderings of these verses are attempts to improve upon what appears to be confusion, and what Church explains as "a replacement of folia" in the transmission of the text.

[17] The absence of the definite article before the phrase ἄλλος μαθητής (other disciple) in 18: 15 supported by P^{66} ℵ*AB and many other manuscripts, is very likely the more difficult reading.

Simon Peter has preferred to remain outside of the courtyard. Fear and apprehension may prevent him from entering Annas' courtyard. The narrator simply observes, "But Peter stood πρός τῇ θύρᾳ (towards the door) door outside." This would be the door of the courtyard. But the phrase may also imply a metaphorical reference to Jesus, who in 10:7-9 employed the **I AM** formula of self-disclosure to identify himself as ἡ θύρα τῶν προβάτων (the door of the sheep).[18]

It is the "other disciple," the Beloved Disciple, Lazarus, who intervenes by speaking to the porter, a female slave, and requesting Peter's admission into the courtyard. As he enters, she inquires, "You too aren't one of the disciples of this human being, are you?" Her question, that includes the negative particle μή and the additive sense of the conjunction καί, indicates that she knows that the Beloved Disciple is a disciple of Jesus but also that she is surprised that another disciple would want to be admitted to the hearing before Annas. Peter replies, "I am not (οὐκ εἰμί)." Ironically he has allowed himself to be brought into the courtyard by the intervention of the Beloved Disciple, the same person he had depended on to learn from Jesus the identity of the disciple who would betray him. Now, however, he disowns any connection with Jesus or the disciple who interceded for his admission, and instead of standing with Jesus, he joins the temple police and warms himself at the fire they have made.

The hearing before Annas is telescoped into two central issues: Jesus' disciples and his teaching. What precisely Annas wants to know about either matter is not indicated. Jesus ignores the question about his disciples and responds to the issue of his teaching by directing Annas to the ear-witnesses who heard his teaching in the public places of the synagogue and the Temple.

> I have spoken to the world (κόσμος) openly. I always taught in the synagogue and in the Temple where all the Jews gather, and in secret I spoke nothing. Why do you ask me? Ask those who *have heard* (ἀκηκοότας) what I spoke to them. See, these know what I said. (18:20-21)

Jesus emphasizes his public teaching in order to eliminate any accusation of sedition that might be brought against him. That should exclude the possibility of being put on trial on a charge of conspiracy against Rome and the Roman administration of Judea and Jerusalem. The use of the perfect participle, ἀκηκοότας, in Jesus' response is noteworthy. Its implication is addressed to the implied readers of the Gospel, namely that they too must judge Jesus on the basis of what they *have heard* about his teaching in the narrative world of the Gospel or in the synagogues of the Jewish community of Alexandria. Consequently, there is

---

[18] A kind of a parallel occurs in Mark 14:54. Peter entered into the courtyard of the high Priest and was warming himself "towards the light." It is not πῦρ (fire), the word the implied reader would expect, but φῶς (light) that is employed by the narrator. The phrase "towards the door" may be a metaphorical reference to Jesus. On Mark 14:54, see Waetjen, *A Reordering of Power,* 219.

no need for the narrator to expand on these two issues. The implied readers have encountered Jesus' disciples in their community, and they have heard Jesus' teachings in their synagogues. Moreover, they have been inhabiting the narrative world of the Gospel and therefore have been interacting with Jesus, his disciples and Jesus' teaching. At this point they should be ready to make their own judgment.

Jesus' audacious response to Annas, who, though he has been succeeded into the high priesthood by his son-in-law, Caiaphas, is nevertheless referred to as the High Priest, offers a glimpse of his ideological egalitarian perspective. In his self-understanding as "the Son," God's apprentice, to whom God gave the authority to do judgment (5:26-27), Jesus quite naturally does not subordinate himself to the prestige and authority of a High Priest who regards himself to be the divinely-appointed broker between God as Patron and Israel as Client. For that presumption he is given a slap in the face by one of the temple police with the reprimand, "Is that how you answer the High Priest?" Jesus, however, refuses to submit himself humbly to this spiteful rebuke and confronts the officer with his perpetrated injustice, "If I spoke wickedly, testify about the misdeed. But if well, why do you strike me?"

No preliminary verdict emerges from this hearing (18:19-23). Jesus is sent bound to Caiaphas without any indication of a determination of Jesus' innocence or guilt. But it is not needed! At an earlier session of the Sanhedrin Caiaphas already had pronounced sentence on Jesus, "... it is advantageous that one human being should die on behalf of the people (λαός) than the entire nation should be destroyed" (11:47-53). The hearing before Annas, therefore, was imperative. In view of the authority that he continued to exercise, it was politically expedient that he concur with the verdict of his son-in-law, and possibly also the Sanhedrin.[19] Consequently, this act of sending Jesus bound to Caiaphas could mean only one thing: Jesus was to be condemned to death. The judgment that Jesus must be killed had been approved within the fraternity of the ruling authorities from the time that he began to subvert the Jewish social construction of reality (5:8-18). Accordingly, no further session of the Sanhedrin was necessary. Whatever the duration of that hearing before Caiaphas may have been, it resulted, as 18:28 indicates, in the decision to deliver Jesus to Pilate, the Roman governor.

Simon Peter follows that procession from Annas' courtyard to the interrogation before Caiaphas, but he appears to want to remain incognito by waiting and warming himself with the temple police. They, like the slave girl at Annas' courtyard, are curious about his identity and question him, "You too aren't one of his disciples, are you?" Evidently they suspect that he is one of Jesus' disciples,

[19] Dodd, *Historical Tradition*, 95, writes, "... the aging Annas, formally deposed from the office of High Priest some fifteen years ago, continuing to hold the reins of power behind the scenes, while members of his family in succession received the titular dignity." Dodd also observes on p. 95, n. 1, "The house of Annas was, according to rabbinic tradition, guilty of worse misdemeanors than nepotism."

yet they have difficulty believing that he would be present at this teacher's inquisition. For a second time he denies with the same words, "I am not." However, one of the slaves of the High Priest, a relative of the one whose ear Peter had cut off, presses the issue, "Did I not see you in the garden with him?" For a third time he denies, and at that moment a cock crows; and the implied readers are confronted with the fulfillment of Jesus' prediction of Peter's three-fold denial in 13:38. Nothing more is said, and the implied readers may be left wondering how Peter reacted to his cowardice in view of the pledge he had made to Jesus.

The trial before Pilate 18:28 – 19:16

The chief priests are now acting alone, and therefore the responsibility of handing Jesus over to the Roman procurator is entirely theirs. There are no further references to any involvement of the Pharisees. On the basis of the High Priest's condemnation of Jesus, as recounted in 11:48-51, it is likely that the author is implicating Caiaphas and his fellow chief priests in the consequences of the destruction of Jerusalem and particularly the catastrophic loss of the Temple that they ironically attempted to avoid by advocating the death of Jesus.[20] No formal charges have been formulated against him, and no session of the Sanhedrin has been convened for a formal trial according to Jewish law. Caiaphas proceeds to have him delivered to the Praetorium, where Pilate will conduct his trial. The chief priests accompany the temple police to the Praetorium, but they decline to enter the Roman court because it is the morning of the Day of Preparation, and they do not want to be infected with any Gentile defilement or uncleanness that would prevent them from participating in the celebration of the Passover on the following day (18:28b). Pilate, therefore, is obliged to accommodate them.

It is curious, at least in contrast to the Synoptic Gospels, that it is Jesus' trial before Pilate that dominates the Passion narrative of the Fourth Gospel. Its rationale and its significance, as will become evident, are conditioned by the Alexandrian context of the Jewish community to whom the Gospel is addressed. The narrator's account, however, should not be read as an eye-witness transcription or an historical report. It is the construction of the author, and it has its own determined function, its psychological development and its theological integrity.

Pilate commences the trial by attempting to ascertain from the Jewish authorities, the chief priests, what accusation they are bringing against Jesus.[21] Significantly, they respond to Pilate's question defensively, "If this one were not doing wrong, we would not have handed him over to you." Up to this point no explicit charge has emerged from their previous deliberations, but it appears that one has been formulated in secret. At the same time, however, they are uncertain

[20] At the same time the Fourth Gospel does not "load the responsibility for the death of Jesus on the Jews". Contrary to Stibbe, *John as Storyteller*, 170.

[21] Generally speaking, Bultmann, *John*, 651-666, offers a fine construction of Jesus' trial before Pilate.

about the adequate grounds of the charge they want to lodge against Jesus. Their defensive indecision conveys to Pilate that whatever the accusation may be, it most likely belongs to their civil authority and its legal jurisdiction: "Take him and judge him according to your law." His initial refusal to accept the responsibility of this legal prosecution forces the Jewish authorities to reveal that their suit against Jesus involves a capital crime: "It is not legal for us to kill anyone." They are hesitant to state an accusation because they are uncertain of its tenability.

The narrator momentarily pauses to make an intrusive remark, "… so that the word of Jesus is fulfilled which he said signifying by what death he was going to die."

Returning to the Praetorium, Pilate calls Jesus and, although no charge has been stated, he surmises – it would seem – that it must involve sedition. His question appears to be expressed in the form of an allegation that anticipates an affirmative reply: "You are the king of the Jews?" But before he answers, Jesus wants to know who has defined this accusation, "Do you say this of yourself or did others speak to you about me?" Finally the truth of the matter emerges in Pilate's response: "I'm not a Jew, am I? Your nation and the chief priests delivered you to me. What did you do?" The charge originated from the Jewish authorities in spite of his insistence before Annas: "I always taught in the synagogue and in the sacred precinct of the Temple where all the Jews gather, and in secret I spoke nothing."

Although a cohort under the authority of a tribune has collaborated in apprehending Jesus, there is no indication that Pilate has been aware of this affair. His question: "What did you do?" reveals his ignorance of Jesus' arrest and the crime that he is accused of.[22]

Jesus' reply is unexpected and surprising. He does not deny that he is the king of the Jews, although his identity as "the son of Joseph from Nazareth" does not correspond to the messianic typology of the Scriptures. His defense implies that he is willing to acknowledge the truth of this accusation, but on his own terms by substituting "kingdom/reign" (βασιλεία) in place of "king" (βασιλεύς).[23]

> My kingdom/reign is not ἐκ τοῦ κόσμου τούτου (from this world). If my kingdom/reign were *from this world*, my retainers/servants would fight for me so that I would not be delivered over to the Jewish authorities. But now my kingdom/reign is not from here (ἐτεῦθεν). (18:36)

Nothing has been said about "kingdom" or "the kingdom of God" since Jesus confronted the Pharisee, Nicodemus, with the possibility of an empirical experience (*seeing*) of this eschatological reality in the here and now (3:3-5). In Jewish apocalypticism, from which this conceptuality is derived, "the kingdom" or

---

[22] There is no indication that Pilate is a co-conspirator with the Jewish authorities, nor that he already knows what the problem is. Consequently it is not necessary to read a tone of mockery or sarcasm into his words. Contrary to Howard-Brook, *Becoming Children of God*, 396.

[23] Contrary to Meeks, *The Prophet-King*, 63-67, who claims that Jesus is appropriating the prophet-king motif of the Moses typology.

"the reign of God" is a corporate reality that God delivers to "the saints of the Most High" in order to serve as God's surrogate and therefore to reign on God's behalf.[24] In all likelihood this is why Jesus has substituted βασιλεία (kingdom) in place of βασιλεύς (king). The reign or kingdom that he is establishing is not a hierarchical structure in which he alone is located at the pinnacle and exercises divine authority. That would be a kingship of domination, the kind that originates from within this world and its social construction of reality. But even as he and his disciples are not ἐκ τοῦ κόσμου τούτου (8:23, 17:14, 16), his reign does not originate from within the social construction of reality (κόσμος). His kingdom is horizontally constituted, and his disciples and all those who follow him into this new moral order will be drawn into a participation of this divine sovereignty that he is already exercising, first of all in their own lives and then also in the mutual collaboration of community and communion.

Ironically, however, Jesus will enter into a kingship when he is lifted up and exalted on the cross as "the King of the Jews". His crucifixion will be his coronation, and his reign, the reign that he will share with his followers, will be inaugurated from the throne of his cross when "the ruler of the world" will be expelled from his dominion.

Kingship is messiahship, and, in this context of Jesus' acknowledgment of a kingdom or reign, it is pertinent that the implied readers encountered the first confession of his messiahship in their early entry into the Gospel's narrative world. It is Andrew's disclosure to his brother Simon, "We have found the Messiah," a confession that somehow appears to have been derived from John's witness, "Behold the Lamb of God who removes the sin (ἁμαρτία) of the world." It is only in terms of John's witness that Jesus is willing to acknowledge a kingship that fulfills the work that God has commissioned him to consummate. For in and by his death the reality and power of ἁμαρτία, the contagious disease of sin, will be eradicated.

Pilate seems baffled by Jesus' response to the charge against him, "Are you not then a king?" he asks. The term "king" (βασιλεύς), Jesus replies, is Pilate's word, not his.[25]

> You say that I am a king. I for this have been born and for this I have come into the world so that I bear witness to the Truth. Everyone who is from the Truth hears my voice.[26] (18:37)

Jesus voices his aporetic self-understanding in his correction of Pilate. Both his physical birth as "the son of Joseph" and his descent from heaven as "the Son of

[24] See Dan 7:13-27.

[25] Jesus' reply, "You say that I am a king" is not an affirmative answer to Pilate, as Bultmann claims, *John*, 654, n. 6; German, 506, n. 7. Nor does Jesus confess himself to be a king, as Schnackenburg maintains, *St. John* III, 247-248, 254. It is certainly, as Brown, *John* II, 853, concludes "a qualified answer."

[26] This translation follows the Greek word order in order to capture the emphasis that is conveyed by the syntax.

the Human Being" are united in fulfilling God's purpose: to bear witness to the Truth. Pilate will not understand and will dismiss Jesus' witness with a derisive skepticism, "What is truth?" But will the implied readers grasp the uniqueness of his messiahship? A messiahship that, in contrast to all the kings who have preceded him, imitates God's works and attendantly speaks God's Truth! He is the Word that he speaks because his works correspond to the manifestations of God's justice in the history of Israel.[27] That congruity and all that it comprehends is the essence of his messiahship, a self-understanding that he has attempted to communicate to the ruling authorities in 10:24-25 without committing himself to their typology of messiahship.

This dialogue with Jesus has convinced Pilate that the accusation against Jesus is untenable, and he returns to the Jewish authorities who are waiting outside in order to inform them of his judgment: "I find in him no basis for a charge." Yet, in spite of his pronouncement of "not guilty," he continues to refer to Jesus as "the King of the Jews" and proceeds to introduce the custom of the Passover amnesty. If Jesus is innocent of the charge against him, his release should be immediate without any further mediation with his accusers. It has been proposed that Pilate wants to offer the Jewish authorities the possibility of avoiding a loss of face by opening to them a back door that would enable them to withdraw from their objective to have Jesus killed.[28] Implicit in this submission may well be Pilate's fear that the Jewish authorities might complain about his actions to the emperor. That possibility will emerge more concretely in 19:12.

At the same time, however, this custom of the Passover amnesty lends itself to the author's theological motive. The Exodus that the Passover celebrates occasioned deliverance, but also death; that is, the deliverance of the Israelites, and death to the first-born of the Egyptians. At this Passover memorialization of the Exodus one is to be released, the other sentenced to death. The chief priests, who soon will begin to slaughter the lambs for the Passover, choose Barabbas, who, according to the narrator's aside, was an outlaw, an insurrectionist. Jesus, like the first-born of the Egyptians, must suffer death. Ironically, however, his death will inaugurate a new Exodus. An Exodus from the power and slavery of sin!

Since the Jewish authorities reject the back door of saving face that has been offered to them, Pilate turns Jesus over to his soldiers to be flogged, and they in turn mock him by crowning him with a diadem of thorns and "throwing around him a purple robe." In this burlesque impersonation of a worldly kingship, Jesus, scourged and bleeding, is ridiculed as "the King of the Jews" and abused with slaps

[27] Philo ascribes this kind of integrity to Moses in *de Vita Mosis* I, 29; "He demonstrated his philosophical beliefs by his daily works, speaking such things as he thought and his deeds following the things he said so that word and life were in harmony."

[28] Schnackenburg, *St. John* III, 252. On the basis of the work of Ch. B. Chavel, "The Releasing of a Prisoner on the Eve of Passover in Ancient Jerusalem," *JBL* 60 (1941) 273-278, Schnackenburg is inclined to believe that the custom of the Passover amnesty did exist, and he concludes, "If that is right, the Johannine chronology of the passion is confirmed; the release would have had to take place before the eve of the Passover."

in the face. Jesus' flogging may represent the Roman practice of *verberatio*, an initial punishment that probably is intended to dissuade the Jewish authorities from their determination to have him crucified.[29] As Jesus is led out of the Praetorium in order to be viewed by the Jewish authorities, Pilate, for a second time, enunciates to them his innocence. But they remain unmoved as he stands before them, beaten and mocked, and in his wretchedness proves that their accusation against him is as ludicrous as this caricature of kingship that confronts them. In this despicable state of abasement Pilate introduces him to his adversaries: "Behold the Human Being!" (ἰδοὺ ὁ ἄνθρωπος).

To the implied readers of the Jewish community of Alexandria the incongruity between Jesus, the New Human Being (ὁ υἱὸς τοῦ ἀνθρώπου), who descended from heaven, and Jesus, flogged and ludicrously dressed up as a king and presented to the Jewish authorities as ὁ ἄνθρωπος must seem absurdly contradictory. Philo had differentiated between two types of human beings:

> For the one is the heavenly human being, but the other is earthy. The heavenly, having happened according to the image of God, is incorruptible and all together free of earthy substance, but the earthy is out of scattered matter, which he [Moses] called clay.[30]

The earthy human being, however, is a bearer of the Logos in as far as she/he is endowed with the reasoning power of the mind.

> So then the two natures, both that of the reasoning power in us and that of the divine Logos beyond us are indivisible.[31]

But in spite of this indivisibility of the human mind and the Logos, it is only the latter, the Logos, the heavenly human being, God's first-born, who, among the many names that he bears, is called ὁ κατ' εἰκόνα ἄνθρωπος (*the human being* according to the image).[32]

It is another feature of the immense irony of this moment that the narrator utilizes the Roman governor as the interlocutor to introduce Jesus as "the Human Being" to the Jewish authorities. There is no other individual in this context who can confront the implied readers with this stunning appellative that challenges Philo's dualism. This solitary use of ὁ ἄνθρωπος (the human being) in the narrative world of the Gospel intimates that Jesus of Nazareth, who is being presented to the Jewish authorities in this pitiful caricature of a king, is the embodiment of the heavenly and earthy human being. He is the Logos, the prototype of the humanity that the Creator willed at creation who has finally appeared in human history. Rudolf Bultmann has stated it eloquently, "The

---

[29] *Ibid.*, III, 254.

[30] Philo, *Legum Allegoria* I, 31.

[31] Philo, *Quis Rerum Divinarum Heres,* 234.

[32] Philo, *de Confusione Linguarum,* 146.

declaration ὁ λόγος σάρξ ἐγένετο has become visible in its extremest consequence."[33]

When the Jewish authorities see Jesus ludicrously crowned and cloaked as a king yet introduced as the Human Being, they respond to this ironic incongruity with shouts of crucifixion. Pilate, confronted with his failure to convince the Jewish authorities that Jesus should be released, has become a victim of his own maneuvering. He could have terminated the trial when he first pronounced Jesus "not guilty" of the charge of sedition. Now, in ironic desperation he attempts to end the trial by returning Jesus to his adversaries with a third pronouncement of his innocence: "You take him and you crucify, for I find no basis for a charge in him." Since the Jewish authorities, as they themselves stated in 8:31b, do not have the authority to execute a capital sentence, Pilate's rhetoric must be construed as an ironic move to reject their demand for Jesus' crucifixion.[34]

But the chief priests persist in their determination to force Pilate to condemn Jesus to death. Because their earlier accusation had proved to be untenable, they now introduce a new charge, the charge of blasphemy that they had raised in earlier contexts of his ministry.[35]

> We have a law, and according to the law he ought to die because he made himself God's Son. (19:7)

On the basis of this charge, and in accordance with the prescription of Lev 24:16, they had attempted to stone him to death twice but had failed. Why then introduce this earlier charge now, especially when it is an offense that belongs to their jurisdiction? At this moment Pilate has an opportunity to terminate this trial by returning Jesus to the Jewish authorities with the same response he had given them earlier in 18:31, "You take him and judge him according to your law."

But the new charge against Jesus has an unexpected effect on him. Instead of taking advantage of this moment to end the trial, he is disturbed by the religious character of the charge. "When therefore Pilate heard this word, he was all the more afraid and entered into the Praetorium again and says to Jesus, 'Where are you from?'" As the representative of the Roman emperor, he is aware of the religious titles and epithets that the Caesars appropriate and apply to themselves for propagandistic purposes. Now he is no longer confronted with a Jew who is accused of sedition but a Jew who is charged with the crime of making himself God's Son. Earlier he had dismissed truth with scornful cynicism, but now his spirituality, however weak it may be, is suddenly awakened, and he experiences within himself an existential dread of the numinous that evokes fear. What course of action should he take now? He returns to the Pretorium and asks Jesus, "Where are you from?" Jesus returns his question with silence. How could he possibly

[33] *John*, 659; German, 510.

[34] *Ibid.*

[35] See 5:18; 7:32; 8:37, 40, 48-59; 10:24-39.

give the Roman governor a reply that would be intelligible to him? Pilate, desperate for an answer, threatens Jesus with the power of his authority: "Don't you know that I have authority to release you and I have authority to crucify you?" But Jesus is unmoved. He is already free in his exercise of his own divinely given authority to offer his life in obedience to the command of "the Father," even though at this moment he has been handed over to the authority of the Roman governor. In that freedom he acknowledges the momentary authority that Pilate has over his life, authority that Pilate should recognize has been granted to him by God: "You would be having no authority against me at all, if it was not being given to you from above." The pronoun "it" that is contained in the past tense of the periphrastic, ἦν δεδομένον (it was being given), indicates that it is not the general power that Pilate has, but the power at this particular moment to release Jesus or sentence him to death.[36] Pilate, confronted by the truth that Jesus has verbalized and perhaps impressed by the authority with which he has expressed it, appears to acknowledge its validity and suddenly becomes more determined to release him.

But the Jewish authorities will not accede to it. They shout again, but now for the first time at Pilate and not against Jesus:

> If you release him, you are not a friend of Caesar. Everyone who makes himself a king is opposed to Caesar. (19:12)

This intimidating insinuation that his discharge of the case they are bringing against Jesus will evoke the disfavor of the emperor is the threat they now pose to coerce Pilate's cooperation. Their libel that Jesus promoted himself as a king in opposition to Caesar is a lie. But their intimidation of Pilate is successful, and abruptly the trial comes to an end. The peril of being discredited before Caesar motivates Pilate to lead Jesus out of the Praetorium into the Lithostroton – in Hebrew, Gabbatha – in order to take his place on the platform of the tribunal (βῆμα) and hand down his judgment.

To the implied readers of the Jewish community of Alexandria this would evoke no surprise. Philo, their philosophical theologian, has already acquainted them with Pilate. In his treatise, *The Embassy to Gaius* 299-305, Philo recounts Pilate's act of setting up gold shields in Herod's palace that provoked the multitude of Jerusalemites into appealing for their removal. Pilate refused and proposed that they write the emperor a letter to petition the emperor if they insisted on having them taken down. It is in this context that Philo goes on to state:

> It was this final point that particularly exasperated him, for he feared that if they actually sent an embassy they would also expose the rest of his conduct as governor by stating in full the briberies, the insults, the robberies, the outrages and the wanton injuries, the executions without trial constantly repeated, the ceaseless and supremely grievous cruelty. So with all his vindictiveness and furious temper, he was in a difficult position.[37]

---

[36] See also Schnackenburg, *St. John* III, 261.

This corresponds to the conduct Pilate displays throughout the trial of Jesus. As the representative of the colonial power of Rome, he is torn between the exercise of his authority and the necessity of pleasing and placating the Jewish authorities. They in their turn are equally schizophrenic in their servitude as Rome's clients while at the same time they hate both the domination imposed on them and their own ignominious groveling and their betrayal of their own people.

Pilate knows that Jesus is innocent. He has pronounced him innocent three times. But in this trial there has been no integrity in his practice of Roman jurisprudence. He and the Jewish authorities have been vying to out-maneuver each other in order to determine the outcome of the prosecution of this case. The briberies, insults, robberies, the cruelties and the wanton injuries and the executions without trial that Philo ascribes to him would force him to maintain a guarded relationship with the Jewish authorities. On the one hand, as is customary of the colonial governors of the empire, he is constrained to exploit the people and the province of Judea in order to augment the emperor's treasury while he also engages in self-aggrandizement. On the other hand, he is obliged to cooperate with the Jewish authorities in order to prevent them from reporting to Tiberius the atrocities he continues to commit during his procuratorship in Judea. Pilate was only an equestrian, and therefore, unlike the Romans of senatorial rank, he could not qualify as an *Amicus Caesaris*, a Friend of Caesar.[38] But he could not afford to antagonize the emperor. He was well aware of the *lex Julia maiestatis* decreed by Augustus that Tiberius enforced. Suetonius writes:

> About this time a praetor asked Tiberius whether, in his opinion, courts should be convened to try cases of lese majesté. Tiberius replied that the law must be enforced; and enforce it he did, most savagely, too. One man was accused of decapitating an image of Augustus with a view to substituting another head; his case was tried before the Senate and, finding a conflict of evidence, Tiberius had the witnesses examined under torture. The offender was sentenced to death, which provided a precedent for far-fetched accusations.[39]

Consequently, when the Jewish authorities exploit their advantage by threatening to expose him to the emperor, he surrenders weakly to their resolute objective to put Jesus to death by crucifixion.

The two levels of the narrative world of the Fourth Gospel are very evident in this singular account of Jesus' trial before Pilate. There is a general pre-70 historical dimension that is evident in the machinations of the colonial governor as he contrives to finesse the Jewish authorities into consenting to his judgment that Jesus is innocent of the charge against him and should be released. This level is

---

[37] Philo, *de Legatione,* 302-303. See also Josephus, *BJ* 2, 169-177 and *Ant* XVIII, 55-64, 85-87 on Pilate's rule in Judea and Jerusalem. Also Luke 13:1.

[38] Schnackenburg, *St. John* III, 262.

[39] Suetonius, "Tiberius," *The Twelve Caesars*, 58; from Brown, *John* II, 894.

also manifest in the political advantages the Jewish authorities can exploit as subjugated clients of Rome, especially in their self-serving efforts to retain their power and privilege and concomitantly to suppress any prophetic or messianic faction, like the Jesus movement, that might challenge their rule. In this proceeding they have cleverly coerced Pilate into acceding to Jesus' crucifixion.[40]

However, the more immediate narrative level of Jesus' trial before Pilate – as well as the entire Gospel – is the post-70 crisis of Judaism as it involves Jews and Christian Jews in a struggle to resolve the question of Jewish identity. The Pharisees, who, already before the destruction of the Temple, were attempting to cleanse the Temple cult by excluding all those priests who did not accept their rulings, are striving to dominate the Jewish people by imposing on them a program of ideological separation and loyalty. The narration of the trial of Jesus before Pilate, as a two-level construction of the author, is designed to confront the implied readers of the Jewish community of Alexandria with the spiritual and political destitution of the world, the world of Jesus' career and the world of post-70 Judaism in Alexandria.

Pilate is not exonerated in the narrative world of the Fourth Gospel, nor is the sole responsibility of Jesus' death attributed to the Jewish authorities.[41] Both are implicated! The world that the Romans and Jews have constructed, specifically by the men and women of the upper class, the dominators, who maintain the systemic structures that they and their predecessors have established, that world is destitute of the light of Truth to which Jesus has been bearing witness.

As Pilate takes his tribunal seat in order to pronounce his judgment, the narrator interrupts the scene in order to note the time of day: "Now it was the Preparation of the Passover, the hour was about the sixth."[42] At this moment, high noon on the Day of Preparation, the priests are beginning to slaughter the paschal lambs in the sacred precinct of the Temple for the Passover celebration on the following day. Jesus, "the Lamb of God who removes the sin (ἁμαρτία) of the world!" is being sentenced to death at the same time the lambs are being sacrificed for the Passover.

As Pilate prepares to hand down his judgment, he turns Jesus over to the Jewish authorities, and presents him to them on the basis of their original accusation of insurrection, the accusation they revived as the trial drew to a close. But his mood has changed! In view of his defeat by the chief priests, his professional bearing has been transformed into a smoldering rage that is unable to conceal his resentment and animosity. With scarcely disguised malice, he thrusts Jesus at them, "See, your King!"

---

[40] See Paul Winter's discussion of "Pilate in History and in Christian Tradition," *On the Trial of Jesus*, 51-61 and his extensive footnotes, 173-183. Winter is attempting to reconstruct the historical realities of Jesus' trial.

[41] Contrary to Winter, *Trial of Jesus*, 47, 60-61.

[42] This note of the time corresponds to the tractate *Sanhedrin* 43a in the *Babylonian Talmud*, "On the Day of Preparation of the Passover they hanged Jesus."

With a vitriolic aversion they repudiate Jesus: "Take away! Take away! Crucify him!" Pilate intensifies his virulent antagonism by confronting them with the prospect of what they are demanding, "Shall I crucify your king?" As the trial reaches its culmination the chief priests disclose their catastrophic spiritual desolation: "We have no king except Caesar!" In this climactic moment of their triumph over Pilate, they are not only rejecting Jesus as their king. By implication they are also renouncing their faith and commitment to God as the only true King. They are nullifying the first and the eleventh benedictions of the Shemone Esre, the eighteen petition Tefillah that they pray every day: "You are our King and Helper, our Savior and Protector" and "May you be our King, you alone!"[43]

Pilate terminates the trial by handing Jesus over to *them* (αὐτοῖς) in order to be crucified. The personal pronoun *them*, here in verse 16, must refer back to the chief priests of the previous verse. Is the narrator, in fact, informing the implied readers that Pilate handed Jesus over to his Jewish adversaries in order to let them carry out the crucifixion? The answer must be *No*. They have demanded it, but they do not have the legal authority to execute a capital sentence. Because the trials in the provinces of the Roman empire were *extra ordinem*, it may have been possible for Pilate to sentence Jesus to be executed by stoning on the charge of blasphemy. But it is the first accusation, not the second, that prevailed.[44] Pilate's hostility is manifested here in his motivation to hold the chief priests equally responsible for the sentence that he has imposed on the basis of the first charge, but the crucifixion itself will be carried out by the Romans.[45] Most likely the adverbial conjunction, ἵνα, is to be construed as an expression of result.

> Then, therefore, he delivered him to them so that (ἵνα - with the result) he is crucified. (19:16)

The verb that introduces verse 17 is equally ambiguous, "So *they* took Jesus."[46] Here again the pronoun of the verb, *they*, would also refer back to the chief priests; and it would indicate that they, the chief priests, are acknowledging their responsibility in the outcome of the trial. But, as verse 19 indicates, Pilate himself is in charge of the crucifixion, and verse 23 implicates the soldiers in carrying it out.

---

[43] Schnackenburg, *St. John* III, 266.

[44] See Brown's discussion of the principle of *extra ordinem*, *John* II, 884-885.

[45] Schnackenburg, *St. John* III, 267, rightly says, "But it is possible that John intentionally allowed the uncertainty to remain."

[46] The manuscript evidence for verse 19:16 is a hodge-podge of variants, indicating that ancient scribes experienced difficulty in construing the referents of the personal pronouns, particularly the subject, "they," in the verb παρέλαβον (they took). But the text of the 27th edition of Nestle-Aland, "Then they took Jesus" is the more difficult and therefore also the more original reading. The actors of the verb, "they took," are most likely the chief priests.

The crucifixion 19:17-27

Jesus carries his own cross to Golgotha.[47] There is no Simon of Cyrene in the narrative world of the Gospel to do this for him. He is crucified between two others who, in contrast to the Synoptic tradition, are not identified by the crime that has resulted in their crucifixion. They play no role in the crucifixion scene of the Fourth Gospel. According to the narrator, Pilate involves himself in the preparation of a superscription that is attached to the cross, publicizing both the identity of Jesus, "Jesus the Nazoraios," and the accusation that justifies his crucifixion: "The King of the Jews."[48] The narrator notes that the inscription was composed in three languages: Hebrew, Latin and Greek, and read by many of the Jewish people because the place of execution, Golgotha, was "near the city." The inscription itself may be an expression of Pilate's revenge against the Jews at being coerced into this sentence of death.[49] "The chief priests of the Jews" are dismayed at the wording of the text and attempt to have Pilate revise it, "Do not leave it written: the King of the Jews."[50] The present active imperative, γράφε (keep on writing), governed by the negative particle μή is intended to end the continuation of the wording of the inscription.[51] They want the superscription to read: "He said, 'I am King of the Jews'." But Pilate defiantly refuses, "What I have written, I have written!" What he ordered inscribed remains inscribed.[52] Ironically, the title is profoundly true.

The narrator now changes the scene to the four soldiers who, having stripped Jesus of his clothing and carried out his crucifixion, have divided his garments among them, "a part for each soldier." But the tunic or undergarment (χιτών), which was worn next to the skin, proves to be seamless "being woven from the top through and through." Affected by its quality and therefore also its value, they decide to gamble for it: "Let's not tear it apart but obtain for it by lot whose it will be." The narrator appends a scriptural quotation to their verbal agreement in order to pronounce fulfillment:

> ... so that the Scripture is fulfilled, "They divided my garments (ἱμάτια) for themselves, and for my apparel (ἱματισμόν) they cast lots." (19:24)

In contrast to the earlier citation of LXX Psa 40 (41):10 in 13:18, which is introduced by a fulfillment formula, this is a verbatim rendering of the Septuagint

---

[47] Very likely the "place of the skull" is named in Hebrew, Golgotha, because many of the implied readers of Alexandria, who had been in Jerusalem would know of the place.

[48] Here too, *Nazoraios*, should be construed as "from Nazareth" on the basis of 1:45.

[49] Bultmann, *John*, 669; German, 518.

[50] The subject of verse 21, "the chief priests of the Jews" is an unusual phrase, seemingly tautological, as Brown, *John* II, 902, observes. It may be intended to heighten the irony of Pilate's superscription, as he proposes. But, more likely, it may be intended to differentiate chief priests from "the Jews" of verse 20 who are to be regarded as the Jewish population of Jerusalem.

[51] Brown, *John* II, 902.

[52] Brown, *ibid.*, points to parallels in Strack-Billerbeck, *Kommentar* II, 573.

translation of Psa 21 (22):19 without any contextual adjustments, in spite of the difference between Jesus' undergarment, the χιτών, and the ἱματισμόν (apparel). Confronting the implied readers with the attestation of scriptural fulfillment continues to be mandatory for the author. But the accentuation throughout the Gospel is the fulfillment of Scripture and not simply the fulfillment of this or that text of prophecy.[53] Philip's witness to Nathanael underlines this disposition, "The one whom Moses in the Law and [the one whom] the prophets wrote about we have found."

But there is more of significance here than simply scriptural fulfillment! The soldiers' claim on Jesus' garments also confronts the implied readers with the theological relevance of the χιτών. The seamless weave of Jesus' undergarment that he has been wearing next to his skin in all likelihood is representative of the wholeness of his person that is finally revealed when he is stripped naked. Here is another expression of the paradox of his being. In contrast to Philo's metaphysical dualism of two human beings, the spiritual prototype and the physical copy, Jesus unites both in his primary identity as the New Human Being (ὁ υἱὸς τοῦ ἀνθρώπου).[54] The disclosure of his wholeness is also vital to his forthcoming role as "the Lamb of God who removes the sin of the world." The narrator closes this report by stating, "The soldiers therefore did these things."

Jesus' crucifixion is also attended by three women who had been standing (εἱστήκεισαν) beside the cross.[55] They are identified as "his mother," who, as in 2:1-5 is not named; the sister of his mother, "Mary, the wife of Clopas," and Mary Magdalene. Two of them, Mary, the wife of Clopas and Mary Magdalene appear for the first time in the narrative world of the Gospel. The use of the pluperfect active indicative, εἱστήκεισαν, indicates that they had been there for some time, perhaps even from the beginning of the crucifixion. As Jesus looks down from the cross, he sees his mother and "the one whom he loved" standing near (παρεστῶτα) her. He is not identified with the three women because first and foremost the narrator wants the implied readers to focus on them. They alone have followed Jesus to his execution, and they stand by the cross to demonstrate their love, embody their support and reinforce his courage. But it is natural that the Beloved Disciple also should be here, because he too, like the women, has proved his commitment to Jesus by following him into the initial interrogation at Annas' courtyard. He has not materialized suddenly and unexpectedly.[56] He has been

---

[53] So J. Beutler, "The Use of 'Scripture' in the Gospel of John,"147, 149.

[54] Again, see McGaughey, *Strangers and Pilgrims*, 213-240. Schnackenburg, *St. John* III, 274, offers two *symbolic interpretations* of this text that move in an entirely different direction. See also Bultmann, *John*, 671, n.2; German, 519-520, n. 10.

[55] Brown, *John* II, 904, contends that four women are present. He differentiates "the sister of his mother" from "Mary, the wife of Clopas." But there are only three, for the the narrator uses the conjunction καί to separates these women from each other.

[56] Sandra M. Schneiders, " 'Because of the Women's Testimony …'" 520-522, reads this text differently, contending that one of the three women must be the Beloved Disciple, in all likelihood, Mary Magdalene. But the Beloved Disciple includes other characters among Jesus' pre-Easter

standing apart but near Jesus' mother, most likely in order to minister to her with the reassurance of his love and strength. It is because Jesus sees them together, his mother and the Beloved Disciple, that he issues a last will and testament for them. He addresses his mother as he did in 2:4, "Woman, see your son!" Then to his disciple, "See your mother!"[57] In the final moments of his life Jesus entrusts his mother into the care of the Beloved Disciple.

The narrator draws the mother of Jesus away from the two other women in order to place her near "the one Jesus loved." Both of these two figures are among the unnamed characters in the narrative world of the Fourth Gospel. The contrast between those who are named and those who are not is provocative and elicits deliberate literary critical reflection. Malchus, for example, a slave of the high priest whose ear Simon Peter cut off, is identified by name. Nathanael plays a significant role at the beginning of Jesus' ministry, but never appears again in the first edition of the Gospel. But the crippled human being of 5:1-16 and the blind male of 9:1-39 are not named. Are they representative of the conditions of paralysis and blindness that are generated by the world and its socio-religious construction of reality? Is the Samaritan woman unnamed because she is the embodiment of the Samaritan community? Is it possible that the Mother of Jesus remains unnamed and the identity of the Beloved Disciple is only intimated because both of them represent two different communities? The mother of Jesus is Mother Israel, the personification of the Jewish community; the Beloved Disciple who emerged from the tomb of living death is Lazarus, and he represents the Christian Jews among the implied readers of Alexandria.[58] Jesus' last will and testament at the threshold of his death is to unite them as mother and son and to appoint the latter to carry on a loving and caring relationship with God's elect people, the Jews, that will protect them from any and every harm that others might want to inflict on them. The narrator notes that the Beloved Disciple fulfilled Jesus' last will and testament "from that hour" by taking his new mother "*unto* his

---

disciples as well as leading figures of the Johannine School, and therefore should be construed as a **textual paradigm**.(The bold text is hers.) Another close reading of the text construes the two verbs, εἱστήκεισαν and παρεστῶτα, to be differentiating those who are present from each other; the first informs the implied readers of the presence of the three women, and the second locates the Beloved Disciple near Jesus' mother and implies that he is at her side supporting her.

[57] *Ibid.*, 522-535. Schneiders calls attention to the absence of a masculine address in the words spoken to the Beloved Disciple. But Jesus cannot address him as "son" because he is not his son. The masculine gender has already been used when he referred his mother to the Beloved Disciple as "your son". Most certainly, the Beloved Disciple and the community that he represents are to serve Jesus in the role of son, the role in which he had served his mother. But in view of the emerging character of the Beloved Disciple since the resurrection of Lazarus, his gender can only be that of a male.

[58] Bultmann, *John*, 673, claims that the mother of Jesus represents Jewish Christianity, and the Beloved Disciple represents Gentile Christianity. Schnackenburg, *St. John* III, 278, considers that the mother of Jesus may be representative of "that part of Israel which is receptive to messianic salvation." The Beloved Disciple personifies the Johannine Church. See Brown, *John* II, 922-927 for a lengthy discussion on the various symbolic identifications of the two figures that have been proposed. Schneiders, *ibid.*, 521-522, poses the possibility of some kind of representation, but without reaching any final conclusions.

own possessions" (εἰς τὰ ἴδια). A masculine possessive pronoun is not contained in this neuter plural phrase τὰ ἴδια, but, as in the many parallels in 1:11; 10:3, 4, 12; 16:32, it is governed by the masculine gender of the subject to which it is related. The gender of the noun μαθητής is masculine, and that in and of itself would justify the insertion of the pronoun "his." But since the Beloved Disciple has been identified with Lazarus on the basis of consistency building, the masculine pronoun is doubly justified.[59]

Contemporary readers can only wonder if the Christian Jews of Alexandria were similarly motivated, while at the same time they are constrained to ponder, and probably with a profound sense of guilt, why Christians have not fulfilled that role as "son" to the Jewish community down through the centuries into the present time.

The death of Jesus 19:28-36

As Jesus approaches the threshold of death, he knows that "already all things have been completed (τετέλεσται)." Like the snake that Moses lifted up on a pole, Jesus, the New Human Being (ὁ υἱὸς τοῦ ἀθρώπου) has been lifted up on a cross (3:14), but there is as yet no exaltation that is apparent in his crucifixion. He has been lifted up on a cross, but his avowal to the ruling authorities in 8:28 awaits a final fulfillment: "then you will know (γνώσεσθε) that **I AM** (ἐγὼ εἰμί). He has been lifted up from the earth, but his promise is only beginning to be fulfilled in Alexandria and the world at large: "I shall draw all to myself" (12:32). He must still bring Scripture to its divinely appointed goal. Consequently, as the narrator states: " ... so that the Scripture reaches its final fulfillment (τελειωθῇ), he says, 'I thirst'!"[60] The completion of Jesus' work, as many commentators have observed depends on Scripture reaching its divinely appointed goal.[61] But how is that objective related to his cry of thirst? There is a large complex of contradictions that emerges here, and their resolution requires a careful reading of the text combined with "consistency building" and the interplay of intertextuality.

It is certainly true that there is no Scripture that is fulfilled merely by a cry of thirst. The ὄξος, the wine vinegar that Jesus is offered and drinks becomes the

---

[59] Schneiders, *Ibid.*, 523, calls attention to the lack of a masculine possessive pronoun in the phrase, εἰς τὰ ἴδια, but she does not consider the cited parallels which require the insertion of such a pronoun on the basis of the preceding subject. The case she is building is not immediately affected by this observation, but if the Beloved Disciple is identifiable as Lazarus on the basis of consistency building, the masculine pronoun is valid.

[60] The verb τελειόω (complete, finish, bring to an end) is encountered in other contexts of the Fourth Gospel: 4:34; 5:36; 17:4, 23. In three of the four instances, the verb is used by Jesus to express the completion of the work "the Father" has given him to fulfill. In 17:23, the meaning of the verb is directed towards the final completion of the work Jesus has undertaken: the union of Jesus, his followers and God.

[61] Bultmann, *John*, 674; German, 522-523; Brown, *John* II, 929. Robert L. Brawley, "An Absent Complement and Intertextuality in John 19:28-29," *JBL* 112/3 (1993) 427. Schnackenburg, *St. John* III, 283, notes that the verb τελειωθῇ is employed instead of the usual ἵνα πληρωθῇ, but dismisses it as a word derived from a dependent source.

content of the cup that "the Father has given him to drink" (18:11).[62] Whether the wine vinegar should be interpreted as an act of mockery or as a gesture of kindness is beside the point; it is "intended to signify the conclusive fulfillment of the entire content of the Scriptures."[63] Already he has begun to actualize the role of the Servant of Isa 52:13, who *will be lifted up* (ὑψωθήσεται) and *glorified* (δοξασθήσεται) as the one who "bears our sins and is caused pain for us," as the one who "was wounded on account of our lawlessnesses and weakened on account of our sins," and as the one whom "the Lord delivers ... up with respect to our sins."[64] But this is the perspective that the narrator would hope for from the implied readers. What Jesus achieves through his crucifixion, however, eclipses the sufferings of the Servant of Isa 53.[65]

The scriptural goal of completion that he fulfills is the scriptural significance of this final episode of his life and the objective of his cry, and both depend on the wine vinegar that is offered to him and also on the means that are employed to raise the wine vinegar to his mouth.

> A vessel was standing there, full of wine vinegar. Placing a sponge full of wine vinegar on hyssop they brought it to his mouth. (19:29)

There appears to be a general consensus that LXX Psa 68 (69): 22 is the more immediate reference towards the fulfillment of Jesus' cry of thirst: "And they gave me gall for my food and they gave me wine vinegar to drink for my thirst." This text alone, however, hardly qualifies for a scriptural fulfillment that completes the work of Jesus.[66] Nor does the suffering of a righteous human being that may be concretized in the offer of vinegar to a thirsty Jesus transform his crucifixion into a confirmation of his messiahship.[67] All of the intertextuality that is implied by the cry of thirst and the drinking of the wine vinegar establishes the exaltation of Jesus as "the king of the Jews" in disguise.[68]

The Septuagint version of Psa 68 (69) is quoted or alluded to at least three times in the Fourth Gospel. Jesus' disciples remember 68 (69):10 in 2:17. Jesus himself cites 68:5 (69:4) in 15:25; and 68:22 (69:21) is alluded to in 19:28-29. The first of these three, the text that the disciples remember, as Jesus engages in "cleansing the Temple," is being fulfilled at the moment that Jesus drinks the wine vinegar that has been offered to him. As already observed, the verb κατέφαγεν (it devoured)

[62] Contrary to Brawley, "John 19:28-29," the wine vinegar is not merely a metonymy for the opposition to Jesus at his crucifixion. Contrary to L. Th. Witkamp, "Jesus' Thirst in John 19:28-30: Literal or Figurative?" *JBL* 115/3 (1996) 494, the ὄξος is not merely water to which vinegar has been added; its identity as wine vinegar is critical for the significance of this culminating event.

[63] As Bultmann, *John*, 674, n. 2; German, 522, n. 3.

[64] As anticipated in LXX Isa 53:4-6.

[65] Contrary to George Carey, "The Lamb of God and Atonement Theories," *Tyn Bul* 32 (1981) 111, who combines the motif of the Paschal lamb with the suffering Servant passages of Isa 53.

[66] It cannot be "the target text," as Witkamp contends, "John 19:28-30," 503.

[67] Contrary to Brawley, "John 19:28-29," 440, 443.

[68] Also Witkamp, "John 19:28-30," 496.

was altered from the aorist to the future tense, καταφάγεται (it will devour) in order to correspond to the objective that Jesus' twofold action in the Temple anticipates. As he drinks the wine vinegar, he is being consumed by his zeal for the Father's house. No more sacrificial animals will be needed, for he is the Lamb of God who removes the sin (ἁμαρτία) of the world.

By receiving the wine vinegar, Jesus is drinking the cup that God has given him, as he had avowed to Peter in the garden at the time of his arrest. Drawn intertextually into this culminating moment on the basis of 18:11 is the Septuagint text of Psa 74:(75):9. "For a cup is in the hand of the Lord, full of a mixture of immoderate wine. And he turned aside from this [the boastful] to this [the wicked]. But the dregs of his cup were not exhausted. All the sinners of the earth will drink [of it]."[69] Even if this cup of wine vinegar is a "favorite refreshment," for Jesus it is a bitter cup. It is the dregs of the cup of God's wrath.[70] In obedience to God Jesus is drinking it instead of the boastful, the wicked and the sinners of the earth, for *it is his thirst to complete the work that God has given him to fulfill*. It conforms to his rejection of the food that his disciples had offered him after his dialogue with the Samaritan woman, "My food is that I do the will of the One who sent me and *I shall bring to completion* (τελειώσω) his work."[71]

Indeed, it is supreme irony that Jesus, who celebrated the new creation of a marriage by originating the heady vintage of 162 gallons at the wedding of Cana, is now drinking the dregs of the last wine of the old creation, the bottom of the wine barrel of the old moral order that stands under God's judgment. It is that "mixture of immoderate wine" that Jesus is drinking, and it is analogous to the cup of calamity that Jerusalem was compelled to drink at the divine judgment of the Babylonian destruction of her city and Temple.

> Be aroused, be aroused! Stand up Jerusalem, the one drinking the cup of wrath from the hand of the Lord. For the cup of calamity, the drinking vessel of wrath from which you drank and emptied, and there was none comforting you … (Isa 51:17)

Jesus terminates the old moral order by drinking the cup of God's wrath, the cup that signifies God's judgment of the world of the old creation and its ruler, Satan or the devil. At the same time that he suffers God's judgment on behalf of "all the sinners of the earth," he also eradicates the human infection of sin (ἁμαρτία) that dominated the humanity of the old creation.[72] Accordingly, he fulfills the initial identification of John the Witness in 1:29, "Behold the Lamb of God who *removes*

---

[69] See also LXX Jer 25:15-16

[70] Wine vinegar, ὄξος, according to the LXX text of Prov 25:20 is a "troublesome lacerating drink, [producing] a condition, that befalling the body, grieves the heart."

[71] Also Witkamp, "John 19:28-30," 500.

[72] Carey, "The Lamb of God and Atonement Theories," 119, interprets the verb *removes* (αἴρων) as a strong echo of Isaiah's Servant who "bears the sin of many." But Jesus is more than an expiation for "the sins of the world."

(αἴρων) the sin (ἁμαρτία) of the world." Like the snake that Moses lifted up on a pole that brought healing to the Israelites in the wilderness, Jesus' elevation on the cross originates the well-being of salvation. As more of the significance of his being lifted up on the cross emerges, his exaltation as the New Human Being and his glorification as the bearer of God's name, **I AM** (ἐγώ εἰμί) are manifested to the implied readers.

The significance of Jesus' cry of thirst that completes "the work of the Father" and brings Scripture to the realization of its goal has not yet been exhausted. Consequently, there is no paradox of an absent complement that perpetually withholds a complete meaning.[73] The means that are employed to raise the wine vinegar to his mouth intimates another dimension of meaning. In response to Jesus' cry of thirst, as 19:29 discloses, a sponge is soaked with wine vinegar, placed around hyssop and raised to his mouth. Hyssop, however, is the foliage of an aromatic plant that is used for ritual purposes, and it does not have the necessary inflexible strength or rigidity to raise a soak-filled sponge to the lips of a crucified human being. Ancient scribes, who were aware of this difficulty, substituted a rod (κάλαμος) or a javelin (ὕσσος) in place of hyssop (ὑσσώπος) in order to correct the supposed error.[74] The most difficult reading and therefore also the original of the three variants is easily identified as ὑσσώπος (hyssop).

Although hyssop is not rigid enough to bear the weight of a soak-filled sponge, it is used deliberately in order to alert the implied readers to a symbolic re-enactment of the ancient rite of Passover.[75] The narrator has already signaled that Jesus, the Lamb of God, was sentenced to death by crucifixion at the moment the priests have begun to slaughter the Paschal lambs in the sacred precinct of the Temple for the Passover celebration. The command that Moses received from God includes:

> You shall take a bundle of hyssop and dipping from the blood you shall touch by the door (θύρα) the lintel and on both of the doorposts from the blood, that which is by the door (θύρα). (LXX Ex 12:21-22)

As the wine vinegar is raised to the lips of Jesus to fulfill his thirst for the completion of God's work, it is also symbolic of the blood of the Passover lamb,

[73] It needs to be said that Brawley, "John 19:28-29" 443, is moving in the right direction. He is aware that there is a missing complement, but he does not seem to be able to locate it and therefore concludes that the text paradoxically withholds its meaning. Witkamp, "John 19:28-30," 509, advances the discussion a step further when he maintains, "This passage is not paradoxical but symbolic in nature in that it contains hidden meanings for those who have eyes to see and ears to hear." But by limiting his discussion to Psa 68 (69) he ignores the missing complement of Ex 12 that is linked to the symbolic act of smearing the Door with the hyssop.

[74] The sixteenth century text critic, J. Camerarius, conjectured that the original word was ὕσσος (javelin), and the very word appeared in the subsequently discovered late minuscules 476 and 1242. See *A Greek-English Lexicon of the New Testament*, 1043.

[75] Schnackenburg, *St. John* III, 284, dismisses the connection with Ex 12 as "far-fetched." Barrett, *St. John*, 553, in relation to the hyssop, refers to Ex 12:22 and concludes that the text sets forth Jesus "as the true Paschal lamb."

the blood of Jesus' sacrifice.[76] Attached to the bundle of hyssop, the wine vinegar soaking a sponge and symbolic of Jesus' blood as the Paschal lamb, smears his mouth and accordingly touches him in terms of his earlier self-disclosure, **I AM the Door** (ἐγώ εἰμί ἡ θύρα). But at this moment Jesus is not yet dead. After he dies, and a soldier pierces his side with a spear, the blood that flows out from this wound is the blood of the slain Paschal lamb that, symbolized by the wine vinegar, has been smeared on Jesus as the Door. He is both the Father's House and the Door to the Father's House, and in his death he has become the fulfillment of Ex 12:27, Θυσία τὸ πασχα τοῦτο κυρίῳ, *the Passover sacrifice to the Lord.* The result is, as Moses informed the elders of Israel in Ex 12:23, "The Lord will pass over the door and will not allow the destroyer to enter your houses to slay." Jesus, as the Passover Lamb whose blood is symbolically smeared on him as the Door, fulfills his promise of 10:9, "**I AM** the Door. If anyone enters through me, she/he will be saved, and he/she will go in and go out and find pasture." All those who are in the courtyard of the Temple and are on the threshold of entering through the Door into a New Exodus are spared, while Jesus alone suffers death. Accordingly, he is also the Shepherd of the sheep. Indeed, as he says in 10:11, "**I AM** the Good Shepherd. The Good Shepherd offers his life (ψυχήν) on behalf of the sheep." Finally, by being the Door of the Passover, he also opens the Way into the living Temple of God that he has embodied and that he will enlarge after his resurrection by breathing the holy Spirit upon his disciples so that they, like him, will house the divine presence of God.[77]

After drinking the wine vinegar, Jesus triumphantly declares, "It has been accomplished." The work of God and the goal of the Scriptures have been fulfilled. "The ruler of the world" has been cast out, and the infectious disease of sin has been terminated. By Jesus who, like Moses' snake, has been lifted up on a cross! But it is only in the ascertainability of the ironic significance of this culminating moment of quenching his thirst with the cup of God's wrath that his exaltation as the New Human Being and his glorification as the bearer of God's self-disclosure, **I AM**, become visible in his crucifixion. Their determination emerges through the interplay of intertextuality and the projections from the perceived relationship between the parts and the whole that are necessary in order to fill the blanks or the "no-thing" that are embedded in the text.[78]

---

[76] Also Bruce H. Grigsby, "The Cross as an Expiatory Sacrifice in the Fourth Gospel," *JSNT* 15 (1982) 57, who also relates the bundle of hyssop to Ex 12:22. By speaking of the Paschal lamb as a victim, he unfortunately imposes that perspective on Jesus. Jesus is indeed the Paschal lamb, but he is not a victim. His thirst expresses immense irony because he is thirsting to fulfill God's will by being consumed on behalf of God's house. See also Carey, "The Lamb of God and Atonement Theories," 97-122, who also identifies Jesus in these passages as the Paschal lamb.

[77] Also Witkamp, *ibid.*, 504.

[78] As Wolfgang Iser says in his analysis of the act of reading, *The Act of Reading: A Theory of Aesthetic Response* (Baltimore: The Johns Hopkins University Press, 1978) 166-167, "Now it is the very lack of ascertainability and defined intention that brings about the text-reader interaction, and here there is a vital link with dyadic interaction. …it is the gaps, the fundamental asymmetry between

Jesus, as the Passover lamb and the snake lifted up and exalted on the cross, bows his head and delivers up his spirit.[79] The narrator's employment of the phrase, παρέδωκεν τὸ πνεῦμα (he handed over the/his spirit) stands in contrast to LXX Isa 53:12, in which the same verb is used twice, but in the passive voice in order to convey the victimization of the Suffering Servant:

> On account of this he will inherit many and he will divide the spoils of the mighty, on account of whom his life/soul was delivered up (παρεδόθη) and he was counted among the lawless, and he offered up in sacrifice the sins of many and on account of their sins he was delivered up (παρεδόθη).

Jesus, in contradistinction to the Suffering Servant, actively handed over his spirit in accordance with his declaration of 10:18, "No one takes my life from me, but I offer it of myself. I have authority to offer it and I have authority to take it again." In this final act of sovereignty and freedom his prayer of 17:4 is fulfilled: "I glorified you on earth completing the work that you have given me that I should do."

Because it is the Day of Preparation that precedes the great celebration of the Passover, it is necessary to remove the three bodies from the cross. The following day, according to the narrator, is not only the Sabbath but "the great day of the Sabbath," that is, the beginning of the Passover. To avoid desecrating "the great day of the Sabbath" and polluting the land, the ruling authorities approach Pilate in order to request that the legs of the three crucified men be broken in order to hasten their death so that their corpses can be removed from the cross and buried. Pilate consents, and his soldiers carry out this pitiless charge.[80] After breaking the legs of the other two crucified individuals, they come *over to* Jesus' cross and discover that he is already dead.[81] They do not break his legs, but one of the soldiers thrusts his spear into Jesus' side, probably to make sure that he is dead, and, as the narrator observes, "immediately blood and water came out."

The interpretation of this confluence of blood and water that flows from the corpse of Jesus has resulted in a great diversity of constructions of meaning.[82]

the text and reader, that give rise to communication in the reading process; the lack of a common situation and a common frame of reference corresponds to the contingency and the "no-thing" which bring about the interaction between persons."

[79] Barrett, *St. John*, 554, suggests that the πνεῦμα was the Holy Spirit and not the spirit of Jesus, but in the light of 10:18 that would make no sense.

[80] Brown, *John* II, 934, cites the discovery of the skeletal remains of a crucified victim of the first century whose legs were broken.

[81] Schnackenburg, *St. John* III, 286, observers that the narrator has used the preposition ἐπί with the verb ἔρχομαι (come over to) instead of πρός (towards) and therefore relegates the verse to the Gospel's source. But this is an inadequate basis for source analysis. Πρός has a distinctive meaning in the Gospel and would not be appropriate in this context.

[82] The most extensive medical, historical, and theological review, is offered by Brown, *John* II, 946-952. For Bultmann, *John*, 677-678; German, 525, the blood and the water are the foundation of the two sacraments, baptism and the Lord's Supper, but he attributes this tradition to the final ecclesiastical editor. Barrett, *St. John*, 556-557, relates the blood and the water to various texts in the Gospel: water to 4:14, 7:38f., 3:5, 13:5; blood to 6:53ff., and 1 John 1:7. Schnackenburg, *St. John* III,

There is general agreement, in view of the narrator's intrusive remark of verses 35-36, that this episode holds immense significance:

> And *the one having seen* (ἑωρακώς) has testified, and his testimony is true, and *that one* (ἐκεῖνος) knows that he is speaking truthfully, so that you may begin to believe. For these things happened so that the Scripture is fulfilled: "A bone of it/his shall not be broken." And again another Scripture says, "They will look upon the one whom they pierced."[83]

Although the verse is omitted in the Old Latin text of "e" and a number of Vulgate manuscripts, in all likelihood it belongs to the first edition of the Gospel and is intended to confront the implied readers with the historical certainty of this event.[84] But it is difficult to determine if the author of the Gospel is referring to himself as this witness or if the testimony that is being cited was adopted from someone who is being validated as a reliable eyewitness. The demonstrative pronoun (ἐκεῖνος) seems to refer to someone other than the eye-witness *who has seen* (ὁ ἑωρακώς) the confluence of blood and water, and it is "that one," probably the Evangelist who is guaranteeing the truth of the received testimony "in order that you may begin to believe." *That one* (ἐκεῖνος), therefore, writing at a later time, specifically at the end of the first century C.E. is confronting the implied readers of Alexandria with the testimony of someone who was present at the crucifixion. That individual may be one of the four figures who have been identified at the crucifixion and probably is the Beloved Disciple to whom Jesus entrusted his mother. More specifically, that would be Lazarus whom Jesus raised from the dead and who has followed him all the way to the cross. Indeed, he would be a persuasive witness, if he were that unnamed disciple who, with Andrew, left John the Witness and has been present throughout Jesus' ministry in the narrative world of the Gospel.

The order of the effusion of blood and water is important. The blood must necessarily be prior to the water, because it has already been symbolized by the wine vinegar. The blood that flows from the dead body of Jesus, the slain Paschal lamb, has been smeared onto Jesus, the Door, symbolically by the wine vinegar lifted up to his mouth by a bundle of hyssop. The implication that is conveyed is the inauguration of a new Exodus that was foreshadowed by the events of the second Passover in the Gospel. Jesus, as 6:1-3 narrates, crosses the Sea of Galilee followed by a great crowd into the mountain (εἰς τὸ ὄρος), an architectonic center analogous to Mt. Sinai, and celebrates the imminent Passover with the multitudes by the multiplication of the loaves and the fish. At this imminent second Passover

291, on the basis of 1 John 5:7-8a is inclined to a symbolic interpretation referring to the sacraments.

[83] As in 20:31, two different verbs in the subjunctive mood are encountered in the manuscript tradition of this verse: the aorist subjunctive, πιστεύσητε (you begin to believe) and the present subjunctive, πιστεύητε (you continue to believe). The first edition of the Gospel, addressed to the Jews of Alexandria, would probably have employed the aorist subjunctive.

[84] Physiologically speaking, the flow of blood and water is not impossible. See Brown, *John* II, 946-947.

Jesus becomes the embodiment of the Passover meal. Now, at this imminent third Passover, that is, on the Day of Preparation, he becomes the Paschal Lamb.[85]

Even as Jesus disclosed himself as the Door, he also has embodied "the Father's House. Indeed, he has been the living Temple of God since 2:19 when he substituted his physical body of flesh and blood in place of the stone building of the sanctuary on the Temple Mount. The water that flows out of the body of Jesus as the Temple of God is an attestation of the truth of 7:38, "The one who believes into me, even as the Scripture said, rivers of living water will flow out of his/her belly." Furthermore, it is an affirmation of the promise that he addressed to the Samaritan woman in 4:14, "Whoever drinks of the water that I shall give to her/him, will by no means thirst forever, but the water that I shall give will become in her/him a fountain of water springing up into everlasting life." Even in death Jesus, the Paschal lamb of God, continues to be the source of living water, and the Life that it symbolizes.[86]

The adverbial conjunction γάρ, by which verse 36 is related to the narrator's intrusive remark of verse 35, implies a cause and effect linkage between the corroborating witness of the confluence of blood and water and the fulfillment quotations of Scripture. Two texts are cited successively:

> A bone of it/his shall not be broken. (Ex 12:46b)
>
> They will look upon the one whom they pierced. (Zech 12:10)

It is principally the first of these two fulfillment quotations that implies Jesus' identification as the Paschal Lamb. The author has edited Ex 12:46b in order to change the aorist imperative οὐ συντρίψετε (do not break/smash), the command that God gave Moses and Aaron, into the future passive indicative οὐ συντριβήσεται (it shall not be broken), so that it becomes a directive to future generations for the divinely-willed celebration of the Passover. More significantly, however, is the adjustment that the implied readers are required to make, for in the original context of Ex 12:46b the antecedent of the pronoun αὐτοῦ (it/his) is the neuter noun, τὸ πάσχα (the Paschal lamb).[87] Because Jesus is signified to be τὸ

---

[85] J. M. Ford, "'Mingled Blood' from the Side of Christ," *NTS* 15/3 (1969) 337-338, introduces a number of rabbinical texts that refer to "mixed blood" in order "to show that Jesus was not only the Paschal Lamb but the lamb that was כשר. On the basis of these rabbinical texts, she claims that John 19:34 conveys three allusions to the Passover: the hyssop, the unbroken bones and the mingled blood. But the narrator refers to "blood and water," not "mingled blood," and therefore these rabbinic texts contribute little of significance to the allusions of the Passover that are already in the context.

[86] Barrett, *St. John*, 557, says, "It is highly probable then that, in the effusion of blood and water from the pierced side of Christ, John saw a symbol of the fact that from the Crucified there proceed those living streams by which men are quickened and the church lives." Contrary to Grigsby, "The Cross as an Expiatory Sacrifice in the Fourth Gospel," 61-62, who concludes that the water is symbolic of "Christ, the cleansing Fountain." The living water is not a cleansing agent but the very source of life, the gift of the indwelling holy Spirit.

[87] Brawley, "John 19:28-29," 429, is quite right to observe that "John 19:36 violates the context of Exod 12:46." But in as far as the implied readers are to infer that Jesus is the Paschal Lamb (τὸ πάσχα) of Ex 12:27, the contextual violation is theologically legitimate.

πάσχα (the Paschal lamb), it would not be problematic for the implied readers to apply the ambiguous pronoun αὐτοῦ of Ex 12:46b to Jesus instead of the Paschal lamb (τὸ πάσχα).

Jesus dies on the Day of Preparation and becomes the Passover lamb. His corpse is removed from the cross in order to avoid polluting the land and desecrating the "high day of the Sabbath". Although the Passover is implied in 19:31, it is noteworthy that it is not named. It should be the third Passover, but in the narrative world of the Gospel it will not take place. Neither did the two previous Passovers in 2:13 and 6:4 actually occur. The narrator stipulated them to be *near* (ἐγγύς), *always near*, but neither of them was actually noted to have occurred. The same is true of the third and last Passover. Once again, in 11:55, the narrator announces that it is *near* (ἐγγύς). All of the Passovers in the Fourth Gospel are *near* but never here – until Jesus, the Paschal Lamb dies. At his death on the Day of Preparation the long-awaited Passover finally arrives. Jesus becomes the final, indeed, the ultimate Passover! He is the Paschal Lamb who by his death terminates the old moral order and inaugurates a new Exodus into everlasting life.

The second fulfillment quotation is more problematic in as far as it does not appear to have been derived from the Septuagint. The verb ὄψονται that denotes empirical vision in the Fourth Gospel has been substituted for ἐπιβλέψονται (gaze/look upon). Seemingly insoluble is the replacement of κατωρχήσαντο (treat spitefully) with the verb ἐξεκέντησαν (they pierced). Whether the author made use of a different Septuagint text remains indeterminable. But it is noteworthy that Rev 1:17, in its citation of Zech 12:10, employs the same verb ἐξεκέντησαν (they pierced). The observation that both Theodotion and Aquila used ἐξεκέντησαν (they pierced) in their translation of the Hebrew text of Zech 12:10 adds to the perplexity of resolving the source of this revised quotation in John 19:37.[88] The author's accessibility to their Greek versions seems unlikely since they were produced during the first third of the second century. The Gospel's distinctive fulfillment quotation of Zech 12:10 may have been derived from a tradition of testimonials, or the author himself may have translated the Hebrew text of Zech 12:10, rendering the verb דקר (to pierce) as ἐξεκέντησαν.

Nevertheless, the version of Zech 12:10 that is used is appropriate to this literary context as well as to the historical context of the first edition of the Fourth Gospel. The identity of the subject of the verb, "they" in the both the Hebrew and Greek version of Zech 12:10 would naturally be "the Jews". By placing this text as a fulfillment quotation at the very end of Jesus' passion, immediately prior to the episode of his burial, the author is confronting the implied readers of the Jewish community of Alexandria with the total theological significance of Jesus' crucifixion, as they look at the one whom they pierced.

[88] See Bultmann, *John*, 677, n. 2; German, 524-525, n. 9.

The burial of Jesus 19:38-42

Before the Day of Preparation ends, it is necessary to prepare Jesus' corpse for entombment. His burial is undertaken by Joseph of Arimathea, who approaches Pilate for permission to take the body of Jesus. This is the first and only appearance of Joseph, and he is characterized by the narrator as "being a disciple of Jesus but *kept-secret* (κεκρυμμένος) on account of the fear of the Jews." Like others within the narrative world of the Gospel, he reflects the context of the Jewish community of Alexandria and the threat of excommunication by the ruling authorities. Pilate gives his permission, and Joseph removes Jesus' corpse to a designated burial site. It is ironic that he, a disciple of Jesus in secret and therefore fearful of the Jewish authorities, is joined by Nicodemus, "a Pharisee and a ruler of the Jews". But it is the same Nicodemus who once again is identified by the narrator as "the one coming to him at night" and who in 7:51 manifested an integrity that will not tolerate any abuse of the Law. By confronting the implied readers once again with the note of Nicodemus' visit with Jesus at night, the narrator appears to be accentuating the contrast that is emerging in his relationship to Jesus. He, a ruler of the Jews, and Joseph, the secret disciple, are now manifesting a public discipleship by undertaking the burial of Jesus.[89] What might the implied readers have imagined of this collaboration between these two individuals, particularly when the narrator states that Nicodemus contributed one hundred λίτρας (pounds) of a mixture of myrrh and aloes, both aromatic substances, for the burial of Jesus?[90] That would be approximately seventy-five pounds of crushed spices to be strewn between the linen bandages that are to be wrapped around Jesus' body:

> Then they took the body of Jesus and bound it with bandages with the aromatic spices, to entomb according to the custom among the Jews. (19:40)

The narrator's aside, "to entomb according to the custom of the Jews," must be an interpolation by the editor of the second edition of the Gospel. Such a comment would be unnecessary for the implied readers of the Jewish community of Alexandria.

Together, the secret disciple of Jesus and the ruler of the Jews who came to Jesus by night work together to prepare Jesus' body for entombment. Noteworthy in this process is the narrator's use of the verb ἔδησαν (they bound). It was employed earlier in 11:44. Lazarus came out of his tomb bound (δεδεμένος) hands and feet, and he had to be unbound by the bystanders. The same verb is used here in 19:40 in order to prepare the implied readers for the sovereignty and

[89] Also Schneiders, *Written That You May Believe*, 119, who states, "The evangelist reminds the reader that this now public disciple is the same Nicodemus who first came to Jesus 'by night'."

[90] Martyn, *History and Theology*, 88, has concluded, "When John joins Nicodemus to this figure [Joseph], he tells the reader quite plainly that Nicodemus is to be understood as a secret believer."

freedom Jesus will be manifest in the empty tomb on Easter morning. In his resurrection Jesus will unbind himself in his tomb.[91]

One hundred λίτρας or seventy-five pounds is an immense quantity of crushed myrrh and aloes.[92] In faith it may be inferred that Nicodemus intends Jesus to be honored with a royal burial, in spite of the shame of his crucifixion.[93] The quantity of the aromatic spices, the linen cloths, and his burial in a new tomb are concrete expressions of the eulogy that is silently voiced in the hearts of Joseph and Nicodemus as they prepare Jesus' body for interment. The new tomb is suitable for the holiness of his body that during Jesus' lifetime incarnated the living Temple of God. Propitiously, in view of the imminent end of the Day of Preparation, the tomb in which he will be buried is nearby, in an unnamed garden. There, perhaps in order to emphasize the reality of his death, "they placed Jesus."

---

[91] Contrary to D. Sylva, "Nicodemus and his Spices (John 19:39)," *NTS* 34/1 (1988) 148-151, who maintains that the action of binding Jesus "shows that for Nicodemus and Joseph Jesus is held by the power of death; they have not understood Jesus' life beyond death." The binding is not "contrary to Jesus' function as the resurrection and the life."

[92] As Brown, *John* II, 941, notes, The Roman pound was about twelve ounces, so that this would be the equivalent of about seventy-five of our pounds, but the amount is still extraordinary."

[93] See Josephus, *Ant* XVII, 196-199, for his account of Herod the Great's extravagant funeral that ncluded five hundred servants carrying burial spices. In Strack-Billerbeck, II, 584, Billerbeck cites tory of the proselyte, Onkelos, burning more than 80 pounds of spices at the funeral of Rabbi l I, who died in the middle of the first century C.E. When asked why, he is quoted as saying, ie in peace, and someone will ignite body spices for you. Isn't Rabbi Gamaliel much better d kings?" Also cited by Brown, *John* II, 960.

Chapter Eighteen

The Resurrection of Jesus

Investigation of the empty tomb 20:1-10

The Sabbath and with it "the high day of that Sabbath," namely the Passover, have passed unnoted. They have been eclipsed by Jesus as he completed the goal of the Scriptures and inaugurated a new Exodus as the Passover Lamb.

A new week has begun! On its first day – the third day after Jesus' death as intimated by the earlier references in 2:1 and 2:19 – Mary Magdalene comes "unto the tomb" very early in the morning, and she comes alone. It would appear that she is more deeply attached to Jesus than any of the other disciples. She was present at his crucifixion, and, as though she cannot wait any longer, she comes to the tomb on the very morning after the Sabbath "while it is still dark." Since the Jewish day begins at 6 p.m. or after the sun has set, the implied readers may surmise that she set out for the tomb between 4 and 6 o clock in the morning. Whatever motive she may have is left to the imagination of the implied readers. Evidently it is in the darkness that "she *sees* (βλέπει), or discerns the stone removed from the tomb." The verb that is used generally denotes a seeing that includes but also moves beyond sense perception. Although nothing had been said in the context of Jesus' burial about a stone rolled into place in order to seal the tomb, perhaps it is to be presupposed. Mary apparently does not enter the tomb, yet she draws the conclusion that the body of Jesus has been taken away. Running, she reports to Simon Peter and the other disciple *whom* Jesus *was loving* (ὃν ἐφίλει), "They removed the Lord from the tomb, and we don't know where they placed him." There is no implication in her report that she believes that Jesus' corpse was stolen. She has concluded that it was removed, but without speculating by whom or for what reason. In this way Mary Magdalene first of all becomes the messenger of the empty tomb! But she does not infer from her limited experience of what she discerned in the darkness that Jesus has been raised from the dead. The empty tomb, therefore, demands an interpretation![1] In and of itself, it does not offer an epistemological basis of the truth of Jesus' resurrection.

Several aspects of the opening two verses of chapter 20 evoke puzzlement. Why does Mary approach Simon Peter first? There has been no intimation that he is the head of the community of disciples, and it should not be presupposed from one of the Synoptic Gospels.[2] Moreover, he was not present at the crucifixion.

---

[1] Also Bultmann, *John*, 681; German, 528.

[2] Schnackenburg, *St. John* III, 309, who contends that the evangelist's source presupposes that "Peter is the leading man in the group of disciples."

Consequently the natural expectation is that Mary would seek out the Beloved Disciple first because the two of them had been present at Jesus' crucifixion. She may be ignorant of Peter's three-fold denial, but the implied readers are well aware of his faint-hearted commitment to Jesus that he manifested at the hearings before Annas and Caiaphas.[3] Imminently, however, the perplexity of this prioritization of Simon Peter will be resolved in a chiastic reversal when both men stand side by side in Jesus' tomb, and only one of them will comprehend the origination of the reality they are experiencing.

The other question is raised by Mary's employment of the first person plural in her report to the two male disciples: "They removed the Lord from the tomb, and *we don't know* (οὐκ οἴδαμεν) where they placed him." The verb οἴδαμεν, plus the negative particle οὐκ, expresses a corporate ignorance of what has happened to Jesus' body? She alone went to Jesus' tomb, yet she says "we". This is all the more puzzling when she returns to the tomb and replies to the two angels who ask her why she is weeping, "Because they took my Lord and *I* don't *know* (οἴδα) where they placed him." Various explanations have attempted to resolve this dilemma, but none very satisfactorily.[4] Perhaps the pairs of two that are encountered in the first two Easter episodes of 20:1-18 may intimate a rationale: Simon Peter and the Beloved Disciple who investigate Mary's report and the two angels in the tomb. If their witness is to be established according to Num 35:30 and Deut 17:6, they must be at least two in number. Accordingly, it may be necessary for Mary to formulate her report by utilizing the plural "we" in order to motivate the two men to investigate the truth of her disclosure.[5]

Both disciples, in their "coming to the tomb" begin to run together, but "the other disciple" outruns Simon Peter and arrives at the tomb first (20:4).[6] It is not his youthfulness, as is often presupposed, that enables him to outrun Peter. He may in fact suspect that something extraordinary, something unexpected has happened, and in suspense and apprehension he races to the tomb. Stooping down he looks in and *sees* (βλέπει) the linen bandages lying there. The narrator's use of the verb βλέπει implies that the Beloved Disciple, like the blind male of 9:7 whose eyes Jesus opened, is not only able to see empirically but can also discern with the eyes of the mind.[7] But what he ascertains from the burial bandages is not

---

[3] Compare Brown, *John* II, 983, who offers a more positive appraisal of Peter.

[4] According to Hoskyns/Davey, *The Fourth Gospel*, 540, the Synoptic tradition may have been assumed; Howard-Brook, *Becoming Children of God*, 442, it may be that Mary is a representative figure; G. Dalman, "In Galilean Aramaic the first person plural was frequently used for the first person singular." Cited by Brown, *John* II, 984.

[5] Schnackenburg, *St. John* III, 310, who makes this proposal but without including the possibility ...at the use of the "we" may be due to the necessity of requiring more than one individual to establish ...imony.

...hrase, "the other disciple" was encountered in 18:15, and may identify the two as one and ...vidual, namely, the Beloved Disciple.

... on verbs of seeing.

indicated. Something, however, seems to be troubling him, for he does not enter the tomb.

When Simon Peter arrives, he enters the grave unhesitatingly and *observes* (θεωρεῖ) the linen strips (ὀθόνια) and the folded face cloth (σουδάριον). The separation of the two, the linen strips and the face cloth, and particularly the description of "the face cloth that was over his head, not lying with the linen strips but apart, having been folded into one place," indicates purposeful ordering within the tomb. But it is noticeably the face cloth (σουδάριον) that is distinguished by its having been folded and put into its own place, an indication that it will no longer be needed. The verb θεωρεῖ that is used to denote Peter's seeing is also significant, for, as in other instances of its occurrences, it denotes a *looking on* that gives itself over to what is being seen empirically. Will Simon Peter – and the implied readers – surrender themselves to the mystery of what they are observing?

But then "the other disciple" enters, " the one who arrived at the tomb first," and, according to the narrator, "*he saw* (εἴδεν) and he believed." Three different verbs of seeing have been utilized by the narrator in this initial Easter episode. The kind of seeing that is attributed to Mary Magdalene by the use of the verb βλέπει implies both empirical vision and a transparency of seeing beyond sense experience. Is it the latter, a seeing beyond sense experience, that enables her to discern the stone removed from the tomb even in the darkness of the morning? The Beloved Disciple is discomposed as he runs towards the tomb, for he not only outruns Peter but as he bends down to look inside, he also is able to *see* (βλέπει) with a clarity of vision beyond sense experience. He discerns an empty tomb and the *linen strips* (ὀθόνια), but he does not enter. What is it that Mary Magdalene and the Beloved Disciple have in common in as far as the narrator ascribes a perspicuity of sight to both of them, but they do not enter the tomb? Perhaps their seeing in these first moments at the tomb is limited to sense perception. Simon Peter, however, after entering the tomb, *observes* (θεωρεῖ) the burial bandages and the face cloth folded up and laid aside in its own place, but he does not give himself over to what he be-holds. He is a spectator who does not get involved.

It is the Beloved Disciple who, after entering, now *sees* what Peter was observing, and, as the narrator notes, *he saw* (εἴδεν) and *he believed* (ἐπίστευσεν). No objects are attached to either of the two verbs, and, therefore, the implied readers are compelled to fill in the blanks. Earlier, when the Beloved Disciple first peered into the tomb he discerned only the absence of Jesus' corpse and the *linen strips* (ὀθόνια), but after he entered the tomb he was able to *see* everything that Simon Peter had observed. He finally *saw* the face cloth (σουδάριον).[8] It was this object, folded and set apart in its own place, that

[8] This is Sandra Schneiders' keen observation based on her close reading of the text. But she concludes that the face cloth is a *sign* that elicits the beloved Disciple's faith. It is a sign in the sense of reminding Lazarus of his own σουδάριον, but not a *sign* like the Wedding at Cana that evoked the faith of Jesus' disciples. Schneiders misses the connection between the two resurrections. See her seminal essay, "The Face Veil: A Johannine Sign (John 20:1-10)," *BTB* 13 (1983) 94-97. Howard-

confronted the Beloved Disciple with a similar experience and enabled him to comprehend what had occurred in the tomb. The σουδάριον was not a sign that elicited his faith! It was the object that reminded him of his own resurrection. After he came out of his tomb, bound hands and feet and his face covered with a σουδάριον, the by-standers had been instructed by Jesus to unbind him and set him free (11:44). His face cloth also was removed, signifying that it would no longer be needed. The Beloved Disciple's personal experience of resurrection becomes the non-epistemic basis of his faith that Jesus has risen from the dead – without the empirical confirmation of seeing or touching him.[9] His Easter faith, therefore, grounded in the experience of his own resurrection, is prior to but at the same time confirmed by the Scriptures. To affirm this and at the same time to prevent the implied readers from assuming that the Scriptures were the source of both his comprehension and faith, the narrator inserts the intrusive remark of verse 9, "For they did not yet know the Scripture that it is necessary that he rises from the dead." Lazarus, therefore, must be the Beloved Disciple! No other possibility is tenable.

Jesus, however, is distinguished at his resurrection by unbinding himself. He ordered his burial garb, deliberately separating the linen strips from the face cloth, and, after folding the face cloth, he put it aside in a place by itself to signify that it was no longer needed.

What, then, is the significance of the σουδάριον? It appears unexpectedly in the resurrection stories of both Lazarus and Jesus, but only as an aspect of the event of resurrection. No reference is made to it to at the burial. As already noted, decisive differences separate the two resurrections: Lazarus was summoned out of his tomb by Jesus and subsequently unbound by the by-standers; Jesus unbound himself. Nevertheless, they have something in common! The σουδάριον that covered each of their faces was taken off, and the implication appears to be that they will have no further need of it, neither Lazarus nor Jesus.

Curiously, σουδάριον, a Latin loanword (*sudarium*) that was adopted into Greek and Aramaic, does not occur in the Septuagint nor in the writings of Philo.[10] The lexicons define it with a variety of meanings: a handkerchief to wipe away perspiration, a bride's dowry stipulated in a marriage contract, a handkerchief containing a charm that is placed over the head at night to promote dreams. But what meaning does it have in these two episodes of resurrection in the Fourth Gospel? Perhaps the Targum *Neofiti* and the Targum *Pseudo-Jonathan* offer a

---

Brook, *Becoming Children of God*, 444-445, draws upon Schneiders' work, but presents an interpretation that lacks clarity.

[9] As Moloney, *Glory Not Dishonor*, 163, has said, the Beloved Disciple believed without seeing Jesus. BUT he believed because his seeing reminded him of his own resurrection experience, and that became the basis of his faith.

[10] Schürer, *The History of the Jewish People in the Age of Jesus Christ* II, 70, lists σουδάριον as a clothing material of foreign origin, translates it as "the sweat rag," and cites its use in various texts of the Mishnah: Shabbat 3:3, Yoma 6:8, Sanhedrin 6:1, Tamid 7:3 and Kelim 29:1. Also in Luke 19:20 and Acts 19:12.

clue.[11] Inexplicably the translators of these two Targums used the Aramaic **סוּדָר**, derived from the Latin loanword *sudarium*, to translate the Hebrew word **מַסְוֶה**, the face covering or handkerchief that Moses wore to conceal the glory of the Shekinah that his face reflected as a result of his forty-day presence with Yahweh on Sinai (Ex 34:33-35).[12] It would appear, therefore that the Aramaic **סוּדָר** (veil) that translates **מַסְוֶה** (face covering) in the Targumic rendition of Ex 34:33-35 is the source of the Evangelist's employment of the Greek equivalent, σουδάριον.[13] Why the Septuagint's translation of **מַסְוֶה** as κάλυμμα (face covering) in Ex 34:33-35 was not employed is difficult, if not impossible to determine. Perhaps the Evangelist appropriated the term from the Targums because they were the texts that the ruling authorities of post-70 Judaism, specifically the rabbis of the Jamnia academy, were utilizing exegetically and liturgically. They, above all, are to be confronted with the ironic correspondence between the Targum of Ex 34:33-35 and the diverging outcome of the resurrections of Lazarus and Jesus.

The implication of the σουδάριον in the two resurrection episodes is that both Lazarus and Jesus are entering into a new state of being in as far as they are leaving behind a Moses-like face cloth or veil that has been concealing the glory that the Creator, according to Psa 8:6, willed for all humanity. The resurrected Jesus is returning to "the Father" imminently by ascension, and therefore he has no further use of the face veil that has been concealing his glory as the incarnate Logos-Sophia. Lazarus, on the other hand, having come out of his tomb of death, requires the intervening assistance of his community to remove his face cloth so that at last the divinely-willed glory of being created in the image and likeness of God will become visible. In 2 Cor 3:18 the Apostle Paul expresses the same process of transfiguration: "Now we all with unveiled face looking at the glory of the Lord as though in a mirror are being metamorphosed into the same image from [one degree of] glory into another."

The two disciples, Simon Peter and Lazarus, the Beloved Disciple, pose an ironic contrast in their responses to the empty tomb and Jesus' burial garb.[14]

---

[11] See *Targum Neofiti* 1: Exodus, trans. by Martin McNamara and *Targum Pseudo-Jonathan*: Exodus, trans. by Michael Maher (Collegeville, Minnesota: Michael Glazier, 1994) 141, n. z and 261, n. 33. The Evangelist's familiarity with the Genesis translations of these two Targums emerged earlier in probing the implication of the question that the Samaritan woman addressed to Jesus in 4:12. See chapter seven.

[12] It is notable that in the Hebrew Scriptures the word **מַסְוֶה** (face covering) occurs only in Ex 34:33-35.

[13] Schneiders, "The Face Veil," 96. But she seems uncertain, for she says, "...it appears to translate." In fact both Targums translate the Hebrew with the Aramaic **סוּדָר**. Also, no explanation is offered as to why the Hebrew **מַסְוֶה** is not an ordinary word for "veil" in the Hebrew Scriptures. That the Evangelist did not adopt κάλυμμα (head covering), the Septuagint rendering of the Hebrew **מַסְוֶה**, as the Apostle Paul did in 2 Cor 3:13-14, may remain indeterminable.

[14] As Schneiders, "The Face Veil," 94, has verbalized it, "In the tomb scene he is then played off, physically and spiritually, against Simon Peter in a way that has no parallel in the synoptics." See her analysis of "The priority of the Beloved Disciple" on pp. 95-96. The perspective that she presents in, "'Because of the Woman's Testimony...' Reexamining the Issue of Authorship in the Fourth Gospel,"

Simon Peter, who was renamed *Cephas* remains an enigma. He disappears from the narrative world of the Gospel's first edition, and it is left to the implied readers to judge his discipleship over against any traditions about him that may be known to them. The Beloved Disciple also disappears.

Because he had been a follower of John who bore witness to the Logos, and because he was raised from the dead as "the one whom Jesus loved," he is privileged to occupy a position of honor by reclining on Jesus' bosom. If the Logos, according to 1:18, is "into the bosom of the Father and interprets (the Father)," Jesus as the enfleshed Logos becomes the historical interpreter of "the Father;" for as he tells Philip in 14:9, "The one having seen me has seen the Father." Analogously, therefore, the Beloved Disciple, who reclines in the bosom of Jesus, is destined to become the interpreter of Jesus, the incarnate Logos. His fearlessness of death, as a result of his resurrection, will enable him to follow Jesus into his trial, to be present at his execution, and to become the first believer in his resurrection from the dead.[15] Consequently, he is the only disciple in the narrative world of the Fourth Gospel who is qualified to bear witness to the Logos and therefore to supersede John by becoming the interpreter of the incarnate Logos.

The implied readers are challenged by the model of ideal discipleship that he leaves behind as a legacy. Like Nathanael, indeed, more than Nathanael, he is a true Israelite. For, after leaving John, he responded to Jesus' invitation, "Keep coming and you will see!" and he *continued to come* (ἔρχεσθε) all the way to the Easter event until finally *he saw* (εἴδεν). In fact, it may be his witness that has served the Evangelist as the foundation of the construction of his narrative world.

The new Adam and the new Eve in the garden 20:11-18

Mary Magdalene is constrained to have her own experience of the mystery of the empty tomb. She returns alone, and, while standing outside of the tomb, she is overcome by her emotions and weeps. Simon Peter and the Beloved Disciple have left to rejoin the community of disciples (20:10). However, no testimony from either of them would be a sufficient and convincing attestation of the significance of the empty tomb. She must have her own experience. In her grief she looks into the tomb for the first time, and *she observes* (θεωρεῖ) two angels in white sitting there, one "towards the head and one towards the feet where the body of Jesus lay." Will she – and the implied readers – give themselves over to the disclosure that she is be-holding? For symbolically it is the substantiation of Jesus as the New Human Being (ὁ υἱὸς τοῦ ἀνθρώπου) upon whom the heavenly ladder rests and who therefore unites heaven and earth (1:51). The angels, of course, are

---

NTS 44/4 (1998), prevents her from identifying Lazarus as the Beloved Disciple.

[15] Schneiders, *ibid.*, 520-522, on the basis of her reading of 19:25-26 concludes that the Beloved Disciple is "a textual paradigm realized in the plurality of textual figures who are drawn from real historical characters in the life of Jesus and/or the community." It is above all Mary Magdalene who serves as an eye-witness and who more than any other disciple embodied the role of the Beloved Disciple in the Gospel.

the heavenly messengers who, by ascending and descending, facilitate the communication between heaven and earth. The placement of the two angels, "one towards the head and one towards the feet," implies a refutation of Philo's dualism by intimating the unification of the heavenly human being and the earthly human being that Jesus has embodied throughout his ministry and that he continues to embody spiritually in his resurrection.[16] On the one hand, he is the son of Joseph from Nazareth upon whom God's Spirit descended and remained (1:32-33). On the other hand, he is the New Human Being who descended from heaven (3:13) and at the same time the Bread of God who descended from heaven (6:33, 38, 41, 50, 51, 58). While her concentrated look takes all of this in, she obviously does not understand what she sees. When the angels ask her why she is weeping, she does not interact with them. She is not drawn into their reality to inquire about their representation of the paradox of the actuality of Jesus' personhood. She simply explains to them what she had said earlier to Simon Peter and the Beloved Disciple, "Because they removed my Lord, and I don't know where they put him."

At that moment she turns around and *she observes* (θεωρεῖ) Jesus standing behind her. Will she – and the implied readers – now become more than *looking on* spectators? She does not recognize him. In his resurrected state Jesus still is a body, but no longer a body of flesh and blood. The empty tomb, therefore, does not signify a physical resurrection. The flesh and body blood of Jesus' corpse was not resuscitated. A metamorphosis occurred in which Jesus was transformed into another kind of body, a body discontinuous with the flesh and blood body of his earthly life. A spiritual body, perhaps, but an objective and independent body![17] He is visible to Mary because he shows himself, but in his altered state Mary is unable to recognize him. Jesus repeats the angels' question but adds a second, "Whom are you looking for?" Remembering that she is in a garden, she ironically regards him to be "the gardener" and without indicating whom she is searching for, she ardently pleads, "Lord, if you carried him off, tell me where you placed him, and I shall take him away." At this moment, in this post-resurrection scene, a recapitulation of the primordial man and woman in the Garden of Eden is emerging before the eyes of the implied readers. But Mary is not yet ready to be drawn into this drama that is unfolding symbolically. She is still unaware that the one she thinks is "the gardener" is also the resurrected Jesus, the New Human Being, the New Adam. He calls her by name, "Mariam," and thereby calls her into being.[18] It is a creative act that finally discloses to her the identity of this presence she *looked*

[16] Barrett, *St. John*, 564, dismisses any significance the position of the angels might have as "an elaboration of a source, not an independent tradition."

[17] For a critical analysis of Jesus' resurrection, specifically vis a vis the major interpretations of the resurrection traditions in the New Testament in the first half of the twentieth century, see Richard R. Niebuhr, *Resurrection and Historical Reason*.

[18] Notable in this context is the parallel of Gen 3:20, "Adam called the name of his wife Ζωή (Life), because she is the mother of all the living."

on (θεωρεῖ) as "the gardener."[19] She not only recognizes him; she also fulfills the word spoken by Jesus in 10:3-4,

> ...and he calls his own sheep by name... and the sheep follow him because they know his voice. (10:3-4)
>
> **I AM** the Good Shepherd, and I know the ones that are mine and the ones that are mine know me. (10:14)

By being named, Mary ceases her *looking on* as a spectator and in her act of turning to him again she greets him as "Rabbouni" and abandons herself to him by throwing her arms around him in an embrace and honoring him with an Aramaic title of great distinction.[20] Like the appellation "Rabbi," that came into wide use after 70 C.E. as the designation for teacher, it is derived from רַב, meaning, "master." "Rabbouni," however, is higher than "Rabbi" and therefore the translation "Teacher" that the narrator gives in an aside is inadequate.[21] "Rabbouni" became a collateral form of "Rabban," a title that was limited to the "princes" among the rabbis: Gamaliel, Shimeon, Yochanan ben Zakkai, and a few others.[22] Mary's use of "Rabbouni," therefore, may distinguish Jesus as a prince among the rabbis; or, on the basis of its limited designation of Israel's great patriarchs in the Targums, it may be a title that ranks Jesus with Abraham and Moses.

In this second Easter episode of the Gospel, Mary, who is *be-holding* the risen Jesus by embracing him, is being drawn into Jesus' reconstitution of the old moral order. Her response, however, expresses a continuation of the curses that were pronounced by God before the expulsion from Eden, "... and *towards* (πρός) your husband your inclination will be and he will dominate you."[23] A man and a woman are together in a garden, and the woman, after referring to the man twice as "Lord" in 20:2, 13 and after addressing him as "Lord" when she mistook him for the gardener, continues to express the dependence and subordination that belong to the old moral order even at the moment she recognizes who he is. Jesus chides her with the imperative that belongs to the entry into the New Creation, "Stop clinging

---

[19]Mariam, rather than Maria, may be the original reading of her name. It corresponds to the spelling of Moses' sister in LXX Ex 15:20. The lack of vocalization in the *Targum Onkelos* makes it possible to read her name in both ways: *Maryam* and *Miryam*. See Israel, Drazin, *Targum Onkelos to Exodus* (Denver: Ktav Publishing House, 1990) 161. It is difficult to determine, therefore, whether the spelling of her name follows the Septuagint or is drawn from the Targums. See Brown's discussion, *John* II, 990-991.

[20] Schnackenburg, *St. John* III, 317, interprets Mary's second turning in another yet similar way, "She turns to him – an outward gesture, which at the same time expresses an opening up of her inner self and a believing openness to the risen Lord."

[21] Most likely the aside of the narrator at the end of verse 17 should be attributed to the editor of the second edition of the Gospel, the editor who added chapter 21.

[22] Gustaf Dalman, *The Words of Jesus* (Edinburgh: T. & T. Clark, 1902) 332-335. On p. 340 he observes that "Mary desires to resume the old attitude towards the 'Master' which is not permitted by Jesus."

[23] My translation of the LXX Gen 3:16.

to me!"[24] On this Easter morning, however, a New Creation is emerging in which the curses of Gen 3:16-19 are abolished. Jesus wants Mary – and the implied readers – to enter into a new relationship with him. There is to be no more patriarchy. The lordship of men over women is abolished forever. Mary must cease clinging to Jesus and begin to exercise the freedom and sovereignty that is hers by right of her participation in the New Creation. Jesus, the New Adam, the New Human Being, the incarnate Logos-Sophia, is returning to the Creator whose work he has fulfilled: "Do not keep on clinging to me, for I have not yet ascended to the Father."[25] Here at last Jesus' declaration to Nicodemus in 3:13 will be completed: "and no one has ascended into heaven except the one who descended, the Son of the Human Being."

The New Humanity that Jesus is inaugurating as a New Adam by establishing a new relationship with a New Eve also marks the beginning of a New Family of God.

> But continue to go *towards* (πρός) my sisters and brothers and say to them, 'I am ascending *towards* (πρός) my Father and your Father, my God and your God. (20:17)

Earlier, in his Farewell Discourse, in 15:14-15, Jesus had redefined the relational structures of the community he is constituting: "You are my friends if you do that which I command you. No longer do I call you slaves, because the slave does not know what his lord does. But I have called you friends because all the things I heard from my Father I made known to you." Ironically the horizontal relations of friendship are based on obedience, but obedience to the commandment that establishes genuine friendship, namely love. "This is my commandment that you love each other as I loved you" (15:12). In the New Creation that Easter originates, the relationship between Jesus and his followers is graduated from "friends" to "brothers and sisters." A New Family arises from a New Adam and a New Eve into which God the Creator wills all human beings to be incorporated. [26]

In his apprenticeship with "the Father" throughout his ministry, Jesus also has expressed and exemplified the horizontality of union with God into which his disciples – and the implied readers – are to be drawn. It was the objective of his going away into death and resurrection, as he disclosed to his disciples at the beginning of his Farewell Discourse:

---

[24]The verb ἅπτου is a present imperative and denotes continuous action. Accordingly Mary has thrown her arms around Jesus and is holding on to him until Jesus charges her "Do not keep on holding me." Dodd, *Interpretation*, 443, n. 2, suggests that the present imperative ἅπτου, on the basis of its relationship to the present infinitive, ἅπτεσθαι, and with the negative particle μή nay be translated as, "Stop clinging to me."

[25] Contrary to Schneiders, "The Face Veil," 96, who rightly contends that the glorification of Jesus takes place on the cross but goes on to state, "when Jesus goes to the Father and the resurrection by which the glorified Jesus returns to his own."

[26] So also Schneiders, *Written That You May Believe,* 112.

> Again I am coming and I shall receive you *towards* (πρός) myself, so that *where **AM I*** (ὅπου εἰμὶ ἐγώ) you also are. (14:3)

It was also a culminating petition in his prayer of consecration:

> But not only about these am I asking, but also about those who [will] believe into me through their word, so that all are one, even as you, Father [are] in me and I in you so that they also are one in us… (17:20-21)

On Easter morning in the New Creation that is emerging in the garden between a New Adam and a New Eve the sign of the wedding at Cana has begun to be fulfilled and the New Eve – and all those of the implied readers who are able to identify with her – are entering into the realization of Hosea's prophecy:

> And it will be on that day, says the Lord, you will call me "My husband," and you will no longer call me "Baalim." … And I shall betroth you to myself forever, and I shall betroth you to myself in justice and in judgment and in mercy and in compassion. And I shall betroth you to myself in faith and in the knowledge of the Lord. (Hos 2:18, 21-22)[27]

Hosea uses the metaphor of marriage to envision a new relationship between God and Israel. Even as Easter originates God's New Family into which Jesus draws his disciples – and the implied readers – as his sisters and brothers, the resurrection also extends to them the prerogative of the incarnation of the Logos-Sophia that Jesus has disclosed throughout his apprenticeship. It is the relationship of "a mystical union of awesome intimacy" with God the Creator.[28]

Mary Magdalene is the first disciple to experience the reality of the risen Jesus. She is the first to express to him her love and devotion and to enter into God's New Family with him. She is the first disciple Jesus commissions as his emissary and representative, to inform the community of her fellow disciples that he is ascending to "my Father and your Father, my God and your God" in order to unite them into one household and enable them to participate in Jesus' divine **I AM**. Accordingly, she becomes the earliest witness to Jesus' resurrection in the narrative world of the Fourth Gospel: "*I have seen* (ἑώρακα) the Lord." The verb that she employs denotes empirical experience and attests to the objectivity of the risen Jesus. The other disciples will encounter the presence of the risen Jesus before that day ends, but it is her testimony, based on empirical sight and touch, that will confront the implied readers with the truth of her revelation. The Easter experience of the Beloved Disciple that evoked the reality of his own resurrection, serves as the non-epistemic foundation of faith that Jesus rose from the dead. Mary Magdalene, on the other hand, serves as the foundational witness of the historical reality of the objectivity of his resurrection.[29] That will include what the

---

[27] My translation of the Septuagint of Hos 2:18, 21-22; the corresponding Hebrew text is Hos 2:16, 19-20.

[28] Ashton, *Understanding*, 463.

[29] As already stated, Jesus' bodily resurrection is not to be construed in terms of flesh and blood, but rather as a recreated human being who is still a body but a body that has transcended into the

narrator has appended to her witness as an intrusive remark, "...and these things he said to her." But in his charge to her Jesus utilized the present imperative, πορεύου, "*Continue to go* to my sisters and brothers..." Her commission, therefore, is forever! Implicit in her authorization as an apostle and a witness is a never-ending mission to communicate her Easter experience of the risen Jesus and "the things he said to her."

But why in her witness does Mary refer to the risen Jesus as "the Lord"? The new moral order, symbolized by the sign of the 162 gallons of "good wine" that Jesus produced at the Wedding at Cana, constitutes a paradigm shift by which the door to God's new household has been opened. Mary Magdalene, as the New Eve, is a founding member of God's New Family and its reconstituted relationships. Jesus, therefore is no longer her Lord but her brother! Consequently, like her brother in this New Creation, she is called to become God's apprentice, to participate in Jesus' divine **I AM** and to do the works that he did, indeed, perhaps even greater works than he did. Although she testifies to her fellow disciples, "I have seen "the Lord," it is noteworthy that she does not designate him as "my Lord" as she did earlier.

Her witness to Jesus as "the Lord" does not contradict the realities of the New Creation into which she has entered. Jesus is Lord! In his incarnation as the Logos-Sophia throughout his ministry he was Lord. By his resurrection from the dead and by his ascension and return to "the Father" he is Lord. As the New Human Being (ὁ υἱὸς τοῦ ἀνθρώπου), who unites heaven and earth, he is Lord. Lordship is an essential attribute of his paradoxical identity as the incarnate Logos-Sophia and the son of Joseph from Nazareth. Neither polarity of his aporetic being is dichotomized into a dualism.

Implicit in Mary's witness, "I have seen the Lord" is her own gradual transfiguration and attendant participation in his lordship. His lordship is her rightful inheritance as a member of God's new household, for without it she would be incapable of duplicating his works or even superseding them. Like him, she too bears an aporetic identity, although its scale in her life at this point may be diminutive. She is Mary of Magdala, but in as far as she now belongs to God's New Household, she is also a New Eve who in a triadic union with God and the risen Lord Jesus will begin to bear much fruit, as Jesus promised in 15:1-8. Moreover, in his Prayer of Consecration Jesus had interceded for her and her fellow disciples – and above all the implied readers:

> Father, that which you have given me, I want that *where **AM I*** (ὅπου εἰμὶ ἐγώ) those are with me so that they *observe* (θεωρῶσιν) my glory which you have given me because you loved me before the foundation of the world. (17:24)

---

dimension of spirit and, consequently, for lack of language, may be regarded as a spiritual body. See Richard R. Niebuhr, *Resurrection and Historical Reason*, 162-181.

By *be-holding* Jesus' glory as participants in God's New Family, Mary, her fellow disciples and the implied readers will give themselves over to it and absorb it into themselves in order to glorify God their Creator – as Jesus did throughout his career.

Becoming rooms in the "Father's house" 29:19-23

It is Easter evening of the first day of the disclosure of Jesus' resurrection, and, ironically, in spite of Mary Magdalene's witness, the disciples are gathered together behind locked doors.[30] Their fear of *the ruling authorities* (οἱ Ἰουδαίοι) mirrors the stark possibilities of exclusion from the Jewish community that confronts the implied readers of Alexandria on the grounds of confessing Jesus as Messiah. Unlike Mary or the Beloved Disciple, the remaining members of Jesus' community have not had their own Easter experience. Intellectual assent to her testimony, no matter how convincing it might be, does not relieve their anxiety.

Jesus suddenly appears, standing in their midst, and, evidently aware of their fear, pronounces a benediction upon them, "Peace to you!" In order to mitigate any possible apprehension that this stunning moment of his appearance may have engendered, he proceeds to authenticate himself to them – and the implied readers – by showing them the marks of his crucifixion in his hands and his side. This substantiation, it would seem, is necessary – perhaps especially for the implied readers. A figure has materialized before them, and identification is critical. Neither of the previous episodes of the Beloved Disciple and Mary Magdalene conveyed the necessity of establishing the continuity between the risen Jesus and the crucified Jesus. A motivated authentication is indispensable![31]

As the disciples are confronted at last with the reality of the risen Jesus, they rejoice. This moment of confirmation corresponds to the empirical experience that Mary's testimony implies, *I have seen* (ἑώρακα), and the narrator employs the participle of the same verb, ὡρᾶν, in order to certify this equivalence, "When they saw him, they rejoiced."

Jesus repeats his blessing of peace, perhaps intended to prompt them – and the implied readers – to remember the peace that he vouchsafed to them in his farewell discourse (14:27). As he stated in that context, it is not the kind of peace that the world gives, for it is not to be identified with the absence of war. It is not a state of being in which the Logos serves as "the guardian of peace" by pledging to the Creator that human beings will not rebel against the rein of the Law and choose

[30] Bultmann, *John*, 690; German, 535, interprets the locked doors as the essential means of showing forth the miraculous coming of Jesus. The essential means, however, may be to present the implied readers with the other aspect of Jesus' glorification in his resurrection. His is an aporetic being: both an objective body and a spiritual body that can appear to disciples behind locked doors. Authentication of identity in this circumstance is necessary.

[31] Contrary to Bultmann, *John*, 691; German, 535, who, of course, does not take the implied readers into account. The Fourth Evangelist appears to be treating all the necessary aspects of the problem of Jesus' resurrection from the dead.

disorder rather than order.[32] The peace that Jesus bestows is the wholeness of *shalom*, the reconciliation that his followers grow into within themselves and with their fellow human beings as they "begin to remain in his love" (15:9).

Jesus proceeds to delegate them to continue the work that he inaugurated in his fulfillment of "the Father's" commission. This is the realization of the petition he prayed in his Prayer of Consecration:

> Even as you sent me into the world, I also sent them into the world, and on their behalf I consecrate myself so that they also are consecrated in Truth. (17:18)

Jesus has set himself apart for the appointed sacred task of accomplishing God's work. He has died as the Lamb of God who removes the sin of the world. Having completed his consecration on behalf of his disciples – and the implied readers – he now proceeds to consecrate them for the continuation of the work of world transformation. To achieve that objective *he breathed* (ἐνεφύσησεν) upon them and says to them, "Receive [the] holy Spirit."[33] The verb ἐνεφύσησεν is a *hapax legomenon*; it is a word that is encountered only here in the entire New Testament. It occurs in the Septuagint translation of Gen 2:7 and Ezek 37:9, and also in Philo's interpretation of the creation stories of Gen 1 and 2.[34] Here at last the promise of John the Witness is being fulfilled: "This is the one baptizing *in/with* (ἐν) [the] holy Spirit." At this moment as Jesus breathes God's Spirit upon them, the Logos-Sophia also is becoming enfleshed in them! For Jesus' act of breathing God's Spirit upon them is analogous to his own receiving God's Spirit and simultaneously being made in the image of the One who sent the Spirit upon him. Consequently, as the Spirit not only descended but remained on him, the Spirit will also remain on them as they begin to serve as his surrogates.

At the same time as they receive the holy Spirit, they are also being constituted as rooms in "the Father's house." The living Temple of God that Jesus embodied throughout his ministry and continues to embody in his glorification is being enlarged as his disciples become the residence of God's Spirit. Jesus' promise of 14:2, therefore, has been fulfilled. He has gone away into death and resurrection in order to prepare a place for them. Moreover, he has come again and received them *towards* (πρός) himself, so that, as he declared in 14:3, " where **AM I** you also are."

Empowered by the holy Spirit and incarnations of the Logos-Sophia and members of the living Temple of God, they are authorized by Jesus:

---

[32] This is Philo's interpretation of one of the aspects of the mediation of the Logos in *Quis Rerum Divinarum Heres, 205-206*.

[33] The definite article is not used here in 20:22, perhaps because it was not utilized in 1:33, although P^{66} includes it in 1:33 but not in 20:22. However, the definite article appears before πνεῦμα (Spirit) in 1:32-33a.

[34] See Philo, *de Opificio Mundi,* 134, 135; *Legum Allegoria* I, 31, 33, 36; 3:161; *Quod Deterius Potiori,* 80.

> Whose sins you forgive, they have been forgiven to them, and whose you continue to withhold, they have been withheld. (20:23)

Jesus, as the Lamb of God, has removed the sin (ἁμαρτία) of the world. By being consumed with the zeal of "the Father's house," and therefore quenching his thirst with the wine vinegar of God's wrath, he has completed God's work. He has ended the old moral order, and with it he has terminated the human infection of sin. Although this condition has been eradicated, sins will continue to be committed because the world and its social construction of reality continue to be dominated by the old moral order in which human beings are incarcerated without knowing that their diseased condition can be healed. As they are being sent forth into the world, Jesus' disciples – and the implied readers – are being authorized to forgive sins as well as to withhold forgiveness.

Jesus' use of the aorist subjunctive, ἀφῆτε, in the opening clause, "Whose sins *you forgive* ..." implies that forgiveness will be readily granted and be immediately effective in closing the past and opening the future into the New Creation.[35] His employment of the perfect passive subjunctive, ἀφέωνται (they have been forgiven) in the apodosis denotes God's immediate validation of the disciples' pronouncement of forgiveness. On the other hand, those who reject forgiveness because they refuse to repent will remain unforgiven and therefore be left stranded in the old moral order and its realities of living death. The present subjunctive, κρατῆτε in the parallel clause intimates that the withholding will continue until repentance, a turning away from the old moral order, has been manifested. The world will be transformed when it is drawn into the eschatological reality of the eradication of sin by the disciples' pronouncement of forgiveness that opens the door into the New Creation and membership in God's New Family.

Unbelieving Thomas 20:24-29

The episode of unbelieving Thomas that closes the narrative world of the first edition of the Gospel culminates the trajectory of "seeing and therefore believing" and "believing in order to see" that runs through the entire narrative world of the Gospel.

"Thomas, one of the Twelve, the one called Twin (Didymus)," was not present on Easter evening when the risen Jesus consecrated his disciples for their apostolic ministry. His absence, however, does not exclude him from that corporate commission. The objective of this concluding event that focuses on him individually is to communicate Jesus' final benediction to the implied readers of the Gospel in Alexandria.

Although his fellow disciples continue to bear witness to him, "*We have seen* (ἑωράκαμεν) the Lord," echoing Mary Magdalene's earlier testimony, he refuses

---

[35] Brown, *John* II, 1023-1024. See also Lindars, *John*, 612

to accept their eye-witness endorsement. Like them, he must have his own experience of the risen Jesus, but he insists on a thorough empirical identification:

> Unless *I see* (ἴδω) in his hands the mark of the nails and cast my finger into the place of the nails and cast my hand into his side, I shall by no means believe. (20:25)

Jesus obliges him. Eight days later, while the disciples are gathered together again behind locked doors and Thomas is among them, he appears standing in their midst, and, as on Easter evening, he greets them with a benediction of peace: "Peace to you!" Evidently the blessing of peace continues to be indispensable because they are still behind locked doors, an indication – at least among the implied readers – that the disciples continue to encounter animosity and persecution within their community. But it is essential that Thomas' requirement is satisfied. For him as a Jew this is absolutely necessary in order to overcome the scandal of Deut 21:23: "Cursed by God is everyone hanged on a tree." Only the validation of resurrection, God's recreation of Jesus, can contradict and refute the curse of crucifixion. Consequently, the continuity of identity between the crucified Jesus and the risen Jesus is critical. Without hesitation Jesus proceeds to present himself to him for his inspection: "Bring your finger here and *see* (ἴδε) my hands and bring your hand and cast it into my side and do not keep on being faith-less but faith-full!" (20:27). If a true Israelite is one who sees, it is imperative that Thomas has the empirical experience that he covets.

Although Thomas' response to the reality of the Easter event poses a significant contrast to the Beloved Disciple, both are required for Easter faith. Thomas will not believe unless he has empirical evidence of the resurrected Jesus and therefore demands sensory validation. For him, however, it is vital in order to transcend the discredit of Deut 21:23. The Beloved Disciple finally saw (εἶδεν) the facial cloth folded and set apart in its own place in Jesus' empty tomb, and its recall in his own experience became the non-epistemic foundation of his own faith. It is not intellectual assent to the Scriptures or the testimony of others, but the subjective experience of one's own resurrection that lays down the only authentic ground of faith in the Easter event.

Thomas, convinced on the basis of his sensory experience that this objective reality of a body that he has examined is indeed Jesus, submits to his summons to be faith-full and voices his confession of faith, "My Lord and my God." It is a singular attribution of christological titles to Jesus in the Fourth Gospel, and because it is identical to the self-identification of the Caesars, particularly Domitian, at the end of the first century, it concludes the Gospel with a christological recognition that bears a far-reaching political significance. While Thomas may be representative of all those who insist on seeing before they are able to believe and make a commitment of faith, his confession at the conclusion of the original edition of the Gospel acknowledges that Jesus, the son of Joseph from Nazareth of Galilee, is the true *Dominus et Deus* (Lord and God) in the world, who, on the basis of his resurrection from the dead, has eradicated the human infection of sin and has conquered death.[36]

Jesus brings the narrative world of the gospel, the first edition of chapters 1-20, to a close with a benediction that culminates this trajectory of seeing and believing and believing in order to see.

> Blessed are *those not seeing* (μὴ ἰδόντες) and believing!

Thomas has believed because *he has seen* (ἑώρακα). The demand for empirical evidence, before a commitment of faith is expressed, may be fulfilled, and it can indeed elicit faith. Characteristic of this kind of faith, however, is that it is oriented to the past. It looks backwards and establishes itself on the basis of what has already happened and consequently is circumscribed by those actualities that define what is possible. But believing in order to see, its binary opposite, is oriented to the future and its limitless possibilities. That is the final and climactic benediction that Jesus enunciates as the narrative world of the Gospel ends. And that is the orientation of faith that will actualize the impossible possibilities of the New Creation.

The conclusion of the First Edition of the Gospel 20:30-31

John 20:30-31 is the original conclusion of the first edition of the Gospel that originated from within the Jewish community of Alexandria.

> Jesus, of course, did many other signs before the disciples which have not been written in this book. But these things have been written so that you begin to believe that Jesus is the Christ, the Son of God, and that continuing to believe you have life *in/by* (ἐν) his name.

If the Gospel according to John is not a book of signs, at least its first half, chapters 1-11, is designated by many commentators, possibly following the lead of C. H. Dodd, as "The Book of Signs."[37] Of the seventeen occurrences of the word σημεῖον (sign), fourteen are encountered in the first eleven chapters of the Gospel. Jesus performs many signs, but for the most part they are not told, only alluded to, as in 2:23, 6:2 and 11:47. Jesus performs many signs and, if seven have judiciously been selected, only two are numbered, 2:1-11 and 4:43-54. Most likely they are numbered because they introduce the trajectory of the aporia of seeing and therefore believing (2:11) and believing in order to see (4:50).

Signs tend to be a prerequisite of faith in the Jewish community, as the Apostle Paul stipulates in his characterization of his fellow Jews as sign seekers in 1 Cor

[36] See Rensberger, *Johannine Faith and Liberating Community*, 107-132, who, in relation to other texts in the Fourth Gospel, opens up the far-reaching anti-Roman perspective in many of the texts of the Fourth Gospel, especially in the trial before Pilate and the emphasis on Jesus' kingship. John 20:28 can be added to this orientation. Also Koester, "The Savior of the World," who identifies the same bearing toward Roman domination in John 4:4-42, especially in the Samaritan confession of Jesus as "the Savior of the world."

[37] Dodd, *The Fourth Gospel*, 297.

1:22, "For the Jews ask for signs …" The signs that Jesus performs are designed to elicit faith, as this concluding statement of purpose in 20:30-31 indicates. But the signs are not always interpreted validly in the narrative world of the Gospel. On the one hand, the transformation of water into wine at the Wedding at Cana may be the archetypal sign signaling a meaning that permeates the entire Gospel; and the disciples, to the extent that they perceive the reality to which it is directed, see and believe. On the other hand, the nobleman of Capernaum, in as far as he is representative of the Galileans – and the implied readers – who demand signs, is chided by Jesus, "Unless you see signs and wonders you will by no means believe." Jesus' feeding of the multitudes is perceived by the Galileans as a sign of a messianic king who is able to provide them with an unlimited supply of bread. Bread is vital for physical sustenance, but as a sign it does not refer to itself but ironically to the reality of a liberation that transcends Moses' deliverance from Egyptian enslavement. Jesus as the Bread from heaven is the flesh and blood body of the new Passover Meal that redeems Israel from the infection of sin and its resulting death.

Some signs that are first seen can evoke faith, such as the transformation of water into wine at the marriage at Cana. Other mighty works of Jesus become signs only after faith has risked acting in the face of impossible possibilities. Martha must believe and have the stone removed from the entrance to Lazarus' tomb before the impossible possibility of Lazarus' resurrection can be actualized. Jesus' signs point away from themselves to a reality that transcends the literal or material character of the sign itself, and it is this reality that is to be embraced in a faith that is inspired into action. The narrator, having concluded the story of Jesus, informs the implied readers that the signs, discriminatingly selected and purposefully elaborated in order to insure transparency of meaning, are designed to evoke faith: "so that you begin to believe that Jesus is the Christ, the son of God..."

Finally, at the end of the Gospel, Jesus is presented to the implied readers as "the Christ."[38] It is appropriate that he should be recognized and acknowledged by this christological title after his death and resurrection, indeed, perhaps only after his death and resurrection. It is the epithet that Andrew chose by which to identify Jesus in his testimony to his brother Simon after he and his unnamed fellow disciple had heard John the Witness, designate Jesus as "the Lamb of God." What could be the origination of this surprising confession? Typologically messiahship cannot be deduced from the cultic genre of the Paschal lamb. There is no historical or theological relationship between them. The implied readers have been compelled to continue to interact with the "moving viewpoint" of the narrator until

[38] During their movement through the narrative world of the Gospel, the implied readers have been confronted with the question that the Samaritan woman posed to her fellow Samaritans, "This isn't the Christ, is it?" They have also encountered Martha's confession, "I have believed that you are the Christ …" that was challenged by Jesus' command to have the stone removed from the entrance into Lazarus' tomb but then confirmed through Lazarus' resurrection. In both instances, however, the Christ title that these women employed had no relationship to Jesus as the Paschal Lamb.

they arrived at Jesus' ironic correlation of these two disparate appellations in his completion of God's work on the cross as God's Son. Only now, after he has united John's witness and Andrew's testimony, can Jesus be validated authentically to the implied readers as the Christ.

The implied readers, by believing and continuing to believe that Jesus is the Messiah, who used his death in the role of the Paschal Lamb to inaugurate the New Exodus, are united with the New Family of God that is destined to continue into everlasting Life. Consequently, it is his name Jesus, the name by which he moves through the narrative world of the Gospel, that is the bearer, the receptacle, of all that he has achieved and, therefore also all that he is. For his identity as the incarnate Logos-Sophia upon whom God's Spirit descended and remained is confirmed by his integration of his words and deeds. All that he has said and all that he has done are incorporated harmoniously into his aporetic identity as Jesus the son of Joseph and the New Human Being who descended from heaven to serve as God's apprentice and fulfill God's work. All the religious institutions that Jesus absorbed and embodied are projections for the future of God's people that his resurrection actualized: the constitution of God's New Temple in which the Spirit of God resides; the rivers of living water that flow out of this living Temple; the new Passover meal in which the members of the New Humanity, pioneered by Jesus, offer themselves as the Bread of Life; the New Humanity in which the curses of Genesis 3 have been canceled, and the potentiality of the termination of sin that Jesus' disciples are actualizing. By embodying these institutions Jesus glorified God, and this is how God is and will be glorified.

Abbreviations

ABR	Australian Biblical Review
ADB	Anchor Dictionary of the Bible
ANF	Ante-Nicene Fathers
Ant	Antiquities of Josephus
BA	Biblical Archeologist
Bib	Biblica
BJ	Bellum Judaicum of Josephus
BR	Biblical Research
BT	Babylonian Talmud
BTB	Biblical Theology Bulletin
CBQ	Catholic Biblical Quarterly
CH	Church History
ContempRev	Contemplative Review
EH	Ecclesiastical History of Eusebius
EvT	Evangelische Theologie
ExpT	Expository Times
GCS	Die griechischen christlichen Schriftsteller
HTR	Harvard Theological Review
ICC	International Critical Commentary
JAAR	Journal of the Academy of Religion
JBL	Journal of Biblical Literature
JLT	Journal of Literature and Theology
JSNT	Journal for the Study of the New Testament
JT	Jerusalem Talmud
JTS	Journal of Theological Studies
LXX	Septuaginta
M	Mishnah
MT	Massoretic Text
Neot	Neotestamentica
NovTSup	Novum Testamentum Supplements
NT	Novum Testamentum
NTD	Das Neue Testament Deutsch
NTG	Novum Testamentum Graece
NTS	New Testament Studies
PRSt	Perspectives in Religious Studies
SBLMS	Society of Biblical Literature Monograph Series
STZ	Schweizerische Theologische Zeitschrift
T	Tosefta
TDNT	Theological Dictionary of the New Testament
THzNT	Theologisches Handbuch zum Neuen Testament
TWNT	Theologisches Wörterbuch zum Neuen Testament
TynBul	Tyndale Bulletin
TZ	Theologische Zeitschrift
VD	Verbum Domini
VT	Vetus Testamentum
ZNW	Zeitschrift für neutestamentliche Wissenschaft

Bibliography

Ancient Sources

The Ante-Nicene Fathers: Translations of the Writings of the Fathers down to A.D. 325, ed. by Alexander Roberts and James Donaldson and rev. by A. Cleveland Cone, 10 vols. Grand Rapids: Eerdmans, 1975.

The Apocryphon of James, trans. by Dankwart Kirchner, *New Testament Apocrypha*, rev. ed. by Wilhelm Schneemelcher; English translation ed. by R. McL. Wilson. James Clarke & Co. and Westminster/John Knox Press, 1991.

The Apostolic Fathers. *Loeb Classical Library*. 2 vols. translated by Kirsopp Lake. Cambridge: Harvard University Press, 1959.

The Babylonian Talmud. Edited by Isidore Epstein. London: Soncino Press, 1948.

2 Baruch, trans. by A. F. J. Klijn, *The Old Testament Pseudepigrapha*, ed. by James. H. Charlesworth. Garden City: Doubleday & Co. 1983.

Biblia Hebraica. Edited by Rudolf Kittel. Stuttgart: Privilegierte Württembergische Bibelanstalt, 1949.

Clement of Alexandria, *Προτρεπτικος Προς Ελληνας* or *Exhortation to the Greeks.* Edited by M. Marcovich. Leiden: E. J. Brill, 1995.

Clement of Alexandria. *Loeb Classical Library*. Translated by G. W. Butterworth. Cambridge: Harvard University Press, 1960.

The Complete Text of the Earliest New Testament Manuscripts. Edited by Philip W. Comfort and David P. Barrett. Grand Rapids: Baker Books, 1999.

Corpus Papyrorum Judaicarum. Edited by Victor A. Tcherikover in collaboration with Alexander Fuks. Cambridge: Harvard University Press, 1957.

Diogenes Laertius, *Lives of Eminent Philosophers*. *Loeb Classical Library*. Translated by R. D. Hicks. Cambridge: Harvard University Press, 1965.

Documents of the Christian Church. Selected and edited by Henry Bettenson. New York: Oxford University Press, 1947.

Early Christian Fathers: The Library of Christian Classics. Translated and edited by Cyril C. Richardson. Philadelphia: Westminster Press, 1953.

Epistula Apostolorum. Translated by C. Detlef G. Müller, *New Testament Apocrypha*, Schneemelcher- Wilson. Louisville: Westminster/John Knox Press, 1991.

The Ethiopic Book of Enoch. A New Edition in the Light of the Aramaic Dead Sea Fragments. Translated and edited by M .A. Knibb and E. Ullendorff. Oxford: Clarendon Press, 2 vols., 1978.

The Book of Enoch or I Enoch, with commentary and textual notes by Matthew Black. *Studia in Veteris Testamenti Pseudepigrapha*. Leiden: E. J. Brill, 1985.

Eusebius, *Ecclesiastical History*. *Loeb Classical Library*. 2 vols. translated by Kirsopp Lake and J. E. L. Oulton. Cambridge: University Press, 1953.

The Fathers according to Rabbi Nathan. Translated and edited by J. Goldin. New Haven: Yale University Press, 1955.

The Gospel according to Thomas. Edited by A. Guillaumont, H. Puech, G.Quispel, W. Till, Y. A. Al Masih. Leiden: Brill, 1963.

Irenaeus, *Against Heresies*. *The Ante-Nicene Fathers*. Edited by Alexander Roberts and James Donaldson. Grand Rapids: Eerdmans, 1956.

The Isaiah Targum: Introduction, Translation, apparatus and Notes. The Aramaic Bible. Vol 11. Bruce D. Chilton. Collegeville, Minnesota: Liturgical Press, 1990.

Josephus, *Antiquities*. *Loeb Classical Library*. 9 vols. Translated by H. St. J. Thackeray and L. H. Feldman. Cambridge: Harvard University Press, 1961-1965.

Josephus. *Bellum Judaicum. Loeb Classical Library*. 2 vols. Translated by H. St. J. Thackeray. Cambridge: Harvard University Press, 1956-1957.

Justin Martyr, *Dialogue with Trypho*. *The Ante-Nicene Fathers*. Vol. 1, edited by Alexander Roberts and James Donaldson. Grand Rapids, Eerdmans, 1956.

The Midrash on Psalms. Translated from the Hebrew and Aramaic by William G. Braude. New Haven: Yale University Press, 1959.

Midrash Rabbah: Genesis. Translated by H. Freedman. London: Soncino Press, 1951.

Nestle-Aland, *Novum Testamentum Graece*. Stuttgart: Deutsche Bibelgesellschaft, 27 ed., 6th printing, 1999.

The Mishnah: A New Translation. Jacob Neusner. New Haven & London: Yale University Press, 1988.

The Nag Hammadi Library in English. Edited by James M. Robinson. San Francisco: Harper & Row, 1977.

New Testament Apocrypha. Initiated by Edgar Hennecke, revised edition by Wilhelm Schneemelcher. English translation edited by R. Mcl. Wilson. James Clarke & Co and Westminster/John Knox Press, vol. 1, 1991; vol. 2, 1992.

The Old Testament Pseudepigrapha: Apocalyptic Literature and Testaments. 2 vols. edited by James H. Charlesworth. Garden City: Doubleday & Co., 1983, 1985.

Origen, *Commentary on the Gospel according to John, Books 1-32*. Translated by Ronald E. Heine. The Fathers of the Church 80, 89 (Washington D. C.: Catholic University of America Press, 1989, 1993).

Philo, *Loeb Classical Library* (Cambridge: Harvard University Press, 1959)
de Opificio Mundi
Legum Allegoria
de Cherubim

de Sacrificiis Abelis et Caini
Quod Deterius Potiori insidiari solet
Quod Deus immutabilis sit
de Agricultura
de Plantatione
de Ebrietate
de Confusione Linguarum
de Migratione Abrahami
Quis Rerum Divinarum Heres
de Fuga et Inventione
de Mutatione Nominum
de Somniis
de Vita Mosis
de Abrahamo
de Iosepho
de Specialibus Legibus
de Virtutibus
in Flaccum
de Legatione ad Gaium
Quaestiones et Solutiones in Exodum

Plato, *The Republic. Loeb Classical Library*. 2 vols. translated by Paul Shorey. Cambridge: Harvard University Press, 1969-1970.

Pliny the Elder, *Natural History. Loeb Classical Library*. Cambridge: Harvard University Press, 1983.

Septuaginta id est Vetus Testamentum Graece. 2 vols. edited by Alfred Rahlfs. Stuttgart: Privilegierte Württembergische Bibelanstalt, 4th ed. 1950.

Siphre to Deuteronomy: An Analytical Translation. Trans. by Jacob Neusner, 2 vols., (Atlanta: Scholars Press, 1987).

Sophia Sirach or *Ecclesiasticus*. *Septuaginta*. Edited by Alfred Rahlfs. Stuttgart: Privilegierte Württembergische Bibelanstalt, 1935.

Suetonius. *The Twelve Caesars*. Translated by Robert Graves. Baltimore: Penguin, 1957.

Targum Neofiti 1: Genesis. Translated with Aparatus and Notes by Martin McNamara. Collegeville, Minnesota: Michael Glazier, 1992.

Targum Neofiti 1: Numbers. Translated with Apparatus and Notes by Martin McNamara. Collegeville, Minnesota: Michael Glazier, 1995.

Targum Pseudo-Jonathan: Genesis. Translated with Introduction and Notes by Michael Maher. Collegeville, Minnesota: Michael Glazier, 1992.

The Tosefta. Translated by Jacob Neusner et al. 6 vols. New York: Ktav, 1977-1986.

Wisdom of Solomon. Septuaginta. Edited by Alfred Rahlfs. Stuttgart: Privilegierte Württembergische Bibelanstalt, 1935.

Reference Works

Aland, Kurt & Barbara Aland. *The Text of the New Testament*. Grand Rapids: Eerdmans & Leiden: Brill, 1989.

Alexander, Philip S. "Targum, Targumim." *ABD*. Edited by D. N. Freedman. New York: Doubleday, 1992: VI 320-331.

The Anchor Bible Dictionary, 6 vols. ed. by David Noel Freedman with Gary A. Herion, David F. Graf and John David Pleins. New York: Doubleday, 1992

Blass F. and A. Debrunner. *A Greek Grammar of the New Testament and Other Early Christian Literature*, trans. and rev. by R. W. Funk. Cambridge: at the University Press, 1961.

A Dictionary of the Targumim, the Talmud Babli and Yerushalmi, and the Midrashic Literature, compiled by Marcus Jastrow. New York: Pardes Paublishing House, 1950.

Gesenius-Robinson, Brown, Driver & Briggs. *A Hebrew Lexicon of the Old Testament*. Oxford: Clarendon Press, 1951.

Greek-English Lexicon of the New Testament and Other Early Christian Literature, revised and edited by Frederick W. Danker, based on the sixth edition of Walter Bauer's *Griechisch-deutsches Wörterbuch* and previous English editions by W.F. Arndt, F.W. Gingrich, and F.W. Danker. Chicago: University of Chicago Press, 2000.

Hatch, Edwin and Henry Redpath. *A Concordance to the Septuagint and the Other Greek Versions of the Old Testament (including the Apocryphal Book)*. 2 vols. Oxford: Clarendon Press, 1897.

Kittel, Gerhard and Gerhard Friedrich, eds. 1933-1973. *Theologisches Wörterbuch zum Neuen Testament*. Stuttgart: W. Kohlhammer Verlag,

Kittel, Gerhard and Gerhard Friedrich, eds. *Theological Dictionary of the New Testament*, trans. and abridged in one volume by Geoffrey W. Bromiley. Grand Rapids: Eerdmans, 1985.

Liddell, H. G. and R. A. Scott. *Greek-English Lexicon*, Oxford: at the Clarendon Press, 9th ed., 1966.

Metzger, Bruce M. *A Textual Commentary on the Greek New Testament*. London, New York: United bible Societies, 1971.

Moule, C. F. D. *An Idiom-Book of New Testament Greek.* Cambridge: at the University Press, 1960.

Moulton, James Hope and George Milligan. *The Vocabulary of the Greek Testament illustrated from the Papyri and other non-literary Sources*. London: Hodder & Stoughton, 1957.

Modern Authors

Ashton, John. "The Identity and Function of the IOUDAIOI in the Fourth Gospel." *NT* 27/1 (1985): 40-75.

Ashton, John. *Studying John: Approaches to the Fourth Gospel*. Oxford: Clarendon Press, 1994.

Ashton, John. "The Jews in John." *Studying John: Approaches to the Fourth Gospel*. Oxford: Clarendon Press, 1994: 36-70.

Ashton, John. *Understanding the Fourth Gospel*. Oxford: Clarendon Press, 1991.

Aune, David E. *The Cultic Setting of Realized Eschatology in Early Christianity*. Leiden: E. J. Brill, 1972.

Bacon, B. W. *The Gospel of the Hellenists*. Edited by Carl H. Kraeling. New York: Holt & Co., 1933.

Bacon, B.W. "The Elder John, Papias, Irenaeus, Eusebius and the Syriac Translator." *JBL* 27/1 (1908): 1-23.

Bacon, B. W. "John and the Pseudo-Johns." *ZNW* 31 (1932): 132-150.

Barrett, C. K. "John and Judaism." *Anti-Judaism and the Fourth Gospel: Papers of the Leuven Colloquium, 2000*. Edited by R. Bieringer, D. Pollefeyt, and F. Vandecasteele-Vanneuville. Assen: Royal Van Gorcum, 2001.

Barrett, C. K. "The Lamb of God." *NTS* 1 (1954-55): 210-218.

Barrett, C. K. *Essays on John*. Philadelphia: Westminster Press, 1982.

Barrett, C. K. *The Gospel according to St. John: An Introduction with Commentary and Notes on the Greek Text*. Philadelphia: Westminster Press, 2nd ed. 1978.

Bassler, Jouette M. "Mixed Signals: Nicodemus in the Fourth Gospel," *JBL* 108/4 (1989): 635-646.

Bauer, Walter. *Rechtgläubigkeit und Ketzerei im ältesten Christentum*. 2d edition with a Postscript by Georg Strecker. Tübingen: J. C. B. Mohr (Paul Siebeck) 1964.

Becker, Heinz *Die Reden des Johannesevangeliums und der Stil der gnostischen Offenbarungsrede* Göttingen: Vandenhoeck & Ruprecht, 1956.

Becker, Jürgen. "Die Abschiedsreden Jesu im Johannesevangelium." *ZNW* 61 (1970): 215-246.

Becker, Jürgen. *Das Evangelium nach Johannes*. 2 vols. Ökumenischer Taschenbuchkommentar zum Neuen Testament 4. Würzburg: Gütersloher Verlagshaus, 1981.

Belo, Fernando. *A Materialist Reading of the Gospel of Mark*. Maryknoll, New York: Orbis Books, 1981.

Berger, Peter and Thomas Luckmann, *The Social Construction of Reality: A Treatise in the Sociology of Knowledge*. Garden City: Doubleday, 1966.

Berger, Peter L. "Religion and World Maintenance." *The Sacred Canopy: Elements of a Sociological Theory of Religion.* Garden City: Doubleday, 1969.

Bernard, J. H. *A Critical and Exegetical Commentary on the Gospel according to John*. Edited by A. H. McNeile. 2 vols. *ICC*. Edinburgh: T & T Clark, 1928.

Bernard, J. H. *A Critical and Exegetical Commentary on the Gospel according to John*. Edited by A. H. McNeile. 2 vols. *ICC*. Edinburgh: T & T Clark, 1953.

Beutler, Johannes. "Der altestamentlich-jüdische Hintergrund der Hirtenrede in Johannes 10." *The Shepherd Discourse of John 10 and its Context.* Edited with introduction by Johannes Beutler and Robert T. Fortna. Cambridge: at the University Press, 1991.

Beutler, Johannes. "The Identity of the 'Jews' for the Readers of John." *Anti-Judaism and the Fourth Gospel: Papers of the Leuven Colloquium, 2000*. Edited by R. Bieringer, D. Pollefeyt, and F. Vandecasteele-Vanneuville. Assen: Royal Van Gorcum, 2001.

Beutler, Johannes. "The Use of 'Scripture' in the Gospel of John." *Exploring the Gospel of John: In Honor of d. Moody Smith*. Edited by R. Allan Culpepper and C. Clifton Black. Louisville: Westminster John Knox, 1996: 147-162.

Black, Matthew. *The Scrolls and Christian Origins*. London: Nelson, 1961.

Blenkinsopp, Joseph. "John VII.37-9: Another Note on a Notorious Crux." *NTS* 6/1 (1959-1960): 95-98.

Boers, Hendrikus. *Neither on This Mountain nor in Jerusalem*: *A Study of John 4*. SBLMS 35. Atlanta: Scholars Press, 1988.

Borgen, Peder. *Bread from Heaven: An Exegetical Study of the concept of Manna in the Gospel of John and the Writings of Philo*. Leiden: E. J. Brill, 1965.

Bornhäuser, Karl. *Das Johannesevangelium: eine Missionsschrift für Israel*. Gütersloh: Bertelsmann, 1928.

Bornkamm, Günther. "Die eucharistische Rede im Johannesevangelium," *ZNW* 47 (1956): 161-169.

Bornkamm, Günther. "Towards the Interpretation of John's Gospel: A Discussion of *The Testament of Jesus* by Ernst Käsemann (1968)." *The Interpretation of John*. Edited with an Introduction by John Ashton. Philadelphia: Fortress Press, 1986: 79-98.

Botha, J. E. *Jesus and the Samaritan Woman: A Speech Act Reading of John 4:1-42*. Leiden: E. J. Brill, 1991.

Botha, J. E. "Reader 'Entrapment' and Literary Device in John 4:1-42." *Neot* 24/1 (1990): 37-47.

Botha, J. E. "The Case of Johannine Irony Reopened I: The Problematic Current Situation." *Neot* 25/2 (1991): 209-220.

Botha, J. E. "The Case of Johannine Irony Reopened II: Suggestions, Alternative Approaches." *Neot* 25/2 (1991): 221-232.

Botha, J. E. *Jesus and the Samaritan Woman: A Speech Act Reading of John 4:1-42*. Leiden: E. J. Brill, 1991.

Boyarin, "Justin Martyr Invents Judaism." *CH* 70/2 (2001): 427-461.

Brawley, Robert L. "An Absent Complement and Intertextuality in John 19:28-29." *JBL* 112.3 (1993): 427-443.

Brodie, Thomas L. *The Gospel according to John*. New York: Oxford University Press, 1993.

Brodie, Thomas L. *The Quest for the Origin of John's Gospel: A Source-Oriented Approach*. New York: Oxford University Press, 1993.

Brouwer, Wayne. *The Literary Development of John 13-17: A Chiastic Reading*. Atlanta: Society of Biblical Literature: 2000.

Brown, John Pairman. "The Mediterranean Vocabulary of the Vine." *VT* XIX/ 2 (1969): 146-170.

Brown, Raymond E. *The Community of the Beloved Disciple: The Life, Loves, and Hates of an Individual Church in New Testament Times*. New York: Paulist Press, 1979.

Brown, Raymond E. *The Gospel according to John. The Anchor Bible Commentary*. New York: Doubleday, vol. 1, 1966; vol. 2 1970.

Brown, Raymond E., Karl P. Donfried, & John Reumann, editors, *Peter in the New Testament*. Minneapolis: Augsburg and New York: Paulist Press, 1973.

Bruteau, Beatrice "Prayer and Identity." *Contemplative Review* 1982.

Büchsel, F. *Das Evangelium nach Johannes. NTD* 4. Göttingen: Vandenhoeck and Ruprecht, 1935.

Bultmann, Rudolf. "Hirsch's Auslegung des Johannesevangeliums." *EvT* 4 (1937): 115-142.

Bultmann, Rudolf. *Das Evangelium des Johannes* with the Ergänzungsheft 1967. Göttingen: Vandenoeck & Ruprecht, 1956.

Bultmann, Rudolf *The Gospel of John: A Commentary*. Translated by G. R. Beasley Murray, et al. Philadelphia: Westminster Press, 1971.

Bultmann, Rudolf. "The History of Religions Background of the Prologue to the Gospel of John." *The Interpretation of John*. Edited and translated by John Ashton (Philadelphia: Fortress Press, 1986), first published in *Eucharisterion: Festschrift für H. Gunkel II* (Göttingen: Vandenhoeck & Ruprecht, 1923).

Bultmann, Rudolf. *Theology of the New Testament.* 2 vols. New York: Scribner's Sons, 1955.

Burridge, Kenelm. *New Heaven-New Earth: A Study of Millenarian Activities*. New York: Schocken Books, 1969.

Burtchaell, James Tunstead. *From Synagogue to Church: Public Services and Offices in the Earliest Christian Communities*. Cambridge: at the University Press, 1992.

Busse, Ulrich "Open Questions on John 10," *The Shepherd Discourse of John 10 and its Context*. Edited. with introduction by Johannes Beutler and Robert T. Fortna. Cambridge: at the University Press, 1991.

Carey, George. "The Lamb of God and Atonement Theories." *TynBul* 32 (1981): 97-122.

Colson, F. H., G. H. Whitaker, Ralph Marcus. *Philo: Loeb Classical Library.* Cambridge: Harvard University Press, 1950.

Cairns, Douglas L. *Aidos. The Psychology and Ethics of Honour and Shame in Ancient Greek Literature*. Oxford: Clarendon Press, 1993.

Camp, Claudia V. "Honor and Shame in Ben Sira: Anthropological and Theological Reflections." in *The Book of Ben Sira in Modern Research*. Edited by Pancratius C. Beentjes. Berlin: Walter de Gruyter, 1997.

Cantwell, Laurence "Immortal Longings in Sermone Humili: A Study of John 4:5-26," *SJT* 36 (1983): 73-86.

Carson, D. A. "The Purpose of the Fourth Gospel: John 20:31 Reconsidered." *JBL* 106/4 (1987): 639-651.

Chance, John. "The Anthropology of Honor and Shame: Culture, Values and Practice." *Honor and Shame in the World of the Bible. Semeia* 68. Edited by Victor H. Matthews and Don C. Benjamin Atlanta: Scholars Press, 1996: 139-152.

Charles, R. H. *Revelation. ICC*. 2 vols. Edinburgh: T & T Clark, 1920, 1956.

Charlesworth, James H. *The Beloved Disciple: Whose Witness Validates the Gospel of John?* Valley Forge, Pennsylvania: Trinity Press International, 1995.

Charlesworth, James H. "The Gospel of John: Exclusivism Caused by a Social Setting Different from that of Jesus (John 11:54 and 14:6)." *Anti-Judaism and the Fourth Gospel: Papers of the Leuven Colloquium, 2000*. Edited by R. Bieringer, D. Pollefeyt, and F. Vandecasteele-Vanneuville. Assen: Royal Van Gorcum, 2001.

Chavel, Ch. B. "The Releasing of a Prisoner on the Eve of Passover in Ancient Jerusalem." *JBL* 60 (1941): 273-278.

Church, W. Randolf. "The Dislocations in the Eighteenth Chapter of John." *JBL* 59/4 (1930): 375-383.

Cohee, Peter. "John 1.3-4." *NTS* 41/3 (1995): 470-477.

Conway, Colleen M. "The Production of the Johannine Community: A New Historicist Perspective." *JBL* 121/3 (2002): 479-495.

Corssen, P. "Warum ist das vierte Evangelium für ein Werk des Apostels Johannes erklärt worden?" *ZNW* 2 (1901): 202-227.

Cotterell, "F. P. The Nicodemus Conversation: A Fresh Appraisal," *ExpT* 96 (1984-85): 237-242.

Cullmann, Oscar "The Meaning of the Lord's Supper in Primitive Christianity." *Essays on the Lord's Supper*. O. Cullmann and F. J. Leenhardt. Atlanta: John Knox, 1958.

Cullmann, Oscar. "The Infancy Story of Thomas." *New Testament Apocrypha*. Initiated by Edgar Henneke, revision edited by Wilhelm Schneemelcher and English translation by R. Mcl. Wilson. Cambridge, England: James Clarke & Co. and Louisville: Westminster/John Knox Press, 1991.

Cullmann, Oscar. *Peter: Disciple, Apostle, Martyr*. Philadelphia: Westminster, 1953.

Culpepper, R. Alan. "The Pivot of John's Prologue." *NTS* 27/1 (1980): 1-31.

Culpepper, R. Alan. *Anatomy of the Fourth Gospel: A Study in Literary Design*. Philadelphia: Fortress Press, 1987.

Culpepper, R. Alan. *John, the Son of Zebedee: The Life of a Legend*. Columbia: University of South Carolina Press, 1994.

Culpepper, R.Alan. *The Gospel and Letters of John*. Nashville: Abingdon Press, 1998.

Culpepper, R. Alan. "The Johannine *Hypodeigma*: A Reading of John 13." *Semeia* 53: 132-152.

Culpepper, R. Alan and C. Clifton Black. *Exploring the Gospel of John: in Honor of D. Moody Smith*. Louisville: Westminster John Knox Press, 1996.

Culpepper, R. Alan. "Reading Johannine Irony." *Exploring the Gospel of John: in Honor of D. Moody Smith*. Louisville: Westminster John Knox Press, 1996: 193-207.

Culpepper, R. Alan. "Anti-Judaism in the Fourth Gospel as a Theological Problem for Christian Interpreters." *Anti-Judaism and the Fourth Gospel: Papers of the Leuven Colloquium, 2000*. Edited by R. Bieringer, D. Pollefeyt, and F. Vandecasteele-Vanneuville. Assen: Royal Van Gorcum, 2001: 68-91.

Dahl, Nils. Alstrup. "Der Erstgeborene des Satans und der Vater des Teufels (Polyk. 7:1 und Joh 8:33)." *Apophoreta: Festschrift für Ernst Haenchen*. Edited by W. Eltester. Berlin: Alfred Töpelmann, 1964.

Dahl, Nils Alstrup. "The Johannine Church and History." *Current Issues in New Testament Interpretation: Essays in Honor of Otto A. Piper*. Edited by William Klassen and Graydon F. Snyder. New York: Harper & Brothers, 1962.

Daise, Michael A. "If Anyone Thirsts, Let That One Come to Me and Drink": The Literary Texture of John 7:37b-38a." *JBL* 122/4 (2003): 687-699.

Dalman Gustav. *The Words of Jesus*. Edinburgh: T & T Clark, 1902.

Dalman, Gustav. *Die Worte Jesu*. Leipzig: J. C. Hinrichs'sche Buchhandlung, 1930.

Dalman, Gustav. *Jesus-Jeshua: Studies in the Gospels*. Translated by Paul L. Levertoff. New York: KTAV Publishing House, 1971.

Dalman, Gustav. *Orte und Wege Jesu*. Gütersloh, C. Bertelsmann, 1921.

Dalman, Gustav. *Sacred Sites and Ways*. London: Society for Promoting Christian Knowledge, 1935.

Daube, David "Jesus and the Samaritan Woman: the Meaning of συγχράομαι." *JBL* 69/2 (1950): 137-147.

The Dead Sea Scrolls in English. Edited by Geza Vermes. New York: Penguin, 1997.

De Jonge, Marinus. "Nicodemus and Jesus: Some Observations on Misunderstanding and Understanding in the Fourth Gospel." *Jesus: Stranger from Heaven and Son of God*. Missoula: Scholars Press, 1977.

De Jonge, Marinus. "The Conflict between Jesus and the Jews and the Radical Christology of the Fourth Gospel," *PRSt* 20 (1993).

De Vaux, Roland. *Ancient Israel. Its Life and Institutions*. London: Dalton, Longman and Todd, 1961.

Dewey, Kim. "PAROIMIAI in the Gospel of John." *Semeia 17*. Edited by John Dominic Crossan. Chico: Scholars Press. 1980: 81-99.

Diefenbach, Manfred. *Der Konflikt Jesu mit den "Juden": Ein Versuch zur Lösung der johanneischen Antijudaismus-Diskussion mit Hilfe des antiken Handlungsverständnis*. Münster: Aschendorff Verlag, 2002.

Dodd, Charles.Harold. *The Interpretation of the Fourth Gospel*. Cambridge: at the University Press, 1960.

Dodd, Charles. Harold. *Historical Tradition in the Fourth Gospel*. Cambridge: at the University Press, 1963.

Doeve, J. W. *Jewish Hermeneutics in the Synoptic Gospels and Acts*. Assen: Van Gorcum, 1954.

Droge, Arthur J. "The Status of Peter in the Fourth Gospel: A Note on John 18:10-11." *JBL* 109/2 (1990): 307-311.

Duke, Paul D. *Irony in the Fourth Gospel: The Shape and Function of a Literary Device*. Atlanta: John Knox Press, 1985.

Dunn, James D. G. "John VI – A Eucharistic Discourse?" *NTS* 17/3 (1971): 328-338.

Dunn, James D. G. "The Washing of the Disciples' Feet in John 13:1-20." *ZNW* 61 (1970): 247-252.

Edwards, R.B. "Charin anti Charitos (John 1.16): Grace and the Law in the Johannine Prologue," *JSNT* 32 (1988): 3-15.

Eliade, Mircea. *Cosmos and History: The Myth of the Eternal Return*. New York: Harper & Brothers, 1959.

Eliade, Mircea. *The Sacred and the Profane. The Nature of Religion*. New York: Harper Torchbooks, 1961.

Eller, Vernard. *The Beloved Disciple: His Name, His Story, His Thought*. Grand Rapids: Eerdmans, 1987.

Eltester, Walter. "Der Logos und sein Prophet." *Apophoreta: Festschrift für Ernst Haenchen*. Berlin: Alfred Töpelmann, 1964.

Eslinger, Lyle. "The Wooing of the Woman at the Well: Jesus, the Reader and Reader-Response Criticism." *JLT* 1/2 (1987).

Farmer, W. R. "The Palm Branches in John 12,13," *JTS* 3 (1952).

Faure, A. "Die alttestamentlichen Zitate im vierten Evangelium und die Quellenscheidungshypothese." *ZNW* 21 (1922): 99-121.

Filson, Floyd V. "Who Was The Beloved Disciple?" *JBL* 68 (1949): 83-88.

Filson, "The Gospel of Life: A Study of the Gospel of John." *Current Issues in New Testament Interpretation: Essays in Honor of Otto A. Piper*. Edited by William Klassen and Graydon F. Snyder. New York: Harper & Brothers, 1962.

Ford, J. Massingberd. "'Mingled Blood' from the Side of Christ." *NTS* 15/3 (1969): 337-338.

Fortna, Robert T. *The Gospel of Signs: The Chief Narrative Source Underlying the Fourth Gospel*. Cambridge: at the University Press, 1970.

Fortna, Robert T. *The Fourth Gospel and Its Predecessor: From Narrative Source to Present Gospel*. Philadelphia: Fortress Press, 1988.

Freed, Edwin D. "The Son of Man in the Fourth Gospel." *JBL* 86/4 (1967): 402-409.

Funk, Robert W. "Papyrus Bodmer II (P^{66}) and John 8, 25." *HTR* 51 (1958): 95-100.

Gadamer, Hans Georg. *Truth and Method*. New York: Crossroad, 2nd rev. ed. 1989.

Gärtner, Bertil. *John 6 and the Jewish Passover*. Lund: C. W. K. Gleerup, 1959.

Garvie, A. E. *The Beloved Disciple: Studies of the Fourth Gospel*. London: Hodder & Stoughton, 1922.

Gaventa, Beverly Roberts. "The Archive of Excess: John 21 and the Problem of Narrative Closure." *Exploring the Gospel of John: In Honor of D. Moody Smith*. Edited. by R. Alan Culpepper and C. Clifton Black. Louisville: Westminster John Knox Press, 1996.

George, Larry D. *Reading the Tapestry: A Literary-Rhetorical Analysis of the Johannine Resurrection Narrative (John 20-21)*. New York: Peter Lang, 2000.

Girard, René. *Violence and the Sacred*. Baltimore: Johns Hopkins University Press, 1977.

Girard, René. *The Scapegoat*. Baltimore: Johns Hopkins University Press, 1986.

Graebbe, Lester, L. *Judaism from Cyrus to Hadrian*. Volume 1, *The Persian and Greek Periods* 1992 and volume 2, *The Roman Period*. Minneapolis: Fortress Press, 1992.

Grant, Robert M. *Theophilus of Antioch: Ad Autolycum*. Oxford: at the Clarendon Press, 1970.

Grässer, Erich. "Die antijüdische Polemik im Johannesevangelium." *NTS* 11/1 (1964): 74-90.

Grassi, J. A. *The Secret Identity of the Beloved Disciple*. New York: Paulist Press, 1992.

Griffith, B. G. "The Disciple Whom Jesus loved." *ExpT* 32 (1920-1921): 379-381.

Grigsby, Bruce H. "The Cross as an Expiatory Sacrifice in the Fourth Gospel." *JSNT* 15 (1982): 51-80.

Gruen Eric S. *Diaspora: Jews amidst Greeks and Romans*. Cambridge: Harvard University Press, 2002.

Guilding, Aileen. *The Fourth Gospel and Jewish Worship*. Oxford: at the Clarendon Press, 1960.

Grundmann, Walter. "κράζειν." *TWNT*. III: 898-904. *TDNT*. III: 898-903.

Grundmann, Walter. *Das Evangelium nach* Markus. *THzNT*. Berlin: Evangelische Verlagsanstalt, 1959.

Grundmann,Walter. "Das Wort von Jesu Freunden (Joh. XV, 13-16) und das Herrenmahl," *NT* 3 (1959): 62-79.

Gundry, Robert H. "In my Father's House are many Μοναί." *ZNW* 58 (1967): 68-72.

Gunther, J. J. "The Relation of the Beloved to the Twelve." *TZ* 37 (1981): 147.

Haenchen, Ernst. *A Commentary on the Gospel of John. Hermeneia*. 2 vols. Translated and edited by Robert W. Funk with Ulrich Busse. Philadelphia: Fortress Press, 1984.

Hamerton-Kelly,Robert G. *The Gospel and the Sacred: Poetics of Violence in Mark*. Minneapolis: Fortress Press, 1994.

Hartin, P. J. "The Role of Peter in the Fourth Gospel," *Neot* 24/1 (1990): 49-61.

Hengel, Martin. *The Johannine Question*. Philadelphia: Trinity Press International, 1989.

Hollenbach, Paul W. "Jesus, Demoniacs, and Public Authorities: A Socio-Historical Study." *JAAR* XLIX/4 (1981): 567-588.

Horbury, William. "The Benediction of the *Minim* and Early Jewish-Christian Controversy." *JTS* 33 (1982): 19-61.

Hornschuh, Manfred. *Studien zur Epistula Apostolorum*. Berlin: Walter de Gruyter, 1965.

Horsley, Richard A. with John S. Hanson. *Bandits, Prophets, and Messiahs: Popular Movements at the Time of Jesus*. San Francisco: Harper, 1988.

Hoskyns Edwyn. and Davey, F.N. *The Fourth Gospel*. London: Faber & Faber, 2nd ed. 1947.

Howard-Brook, Wes. *Becoming Children of God: John's Gospel and Radical Discipleship*. Maryknoll, New York: Orbis Books, 1994.

Instone-Brewer, David. "The Eighteen Benedictions and the *Minim* Before 70 CE." *JTS* 54/1 (2003): 25-44.

Iser, Wolfgang. *The Implied Reader: Patterns of Communication in Prose Fiction from Bunyan to Beckett*. Baltimore: The Johns Hopkins University Press, 1974.

Iser,Wolfgang. *The Act of Reading: A Theory of Aesthetic Response*. Baltimore: The Johns Hopkins University Press, 1978.

Jacob, Edmund. "ψυχή." *TWNT*. IX: 614-629; *TDNT*. IX: 617-631.

Jocz, J. *The Jewish People and Jesus Christ*. London: SPCK, 1962.

Johnson, Luke T. "The New Testament's Anti-Jewish Slander and the Conventions of Ancient Polemic." *JBL* 108/3 (1989): 419-441.

Jonas, Hans. *The Gnostic Religion: The Message of the Alien God and the Beginnings of Christianity*. Boston: Beacon Press, 1958.

Käsemann, Ernst. "Aufbau und Anliegen des johanneischen Prologs." *Exegetische Versuche und Besinnungen*. Göttingen: Vandenhoeck & Ruprecht, 1964, II, 155-180..

Keener, Craig S. *The Gospel of John: A Commentary*. 2 vols. Peabody, Mass.: Hendrickson, 2003.

Kirkendraht, K. "Ist Lazarus der Lieblingsjünger im vierten Evangelium?" *STZ* 31 (1914): 49-54.

Koester, Craig R. "'The Savior of the World' (John 4:42)." *JBL* 109/4 (1990): 665-680.

Koester, Craig R. *Symbolism in the Fourth Gospel: Meaning, Mystery, Community*. Minneapolis: Fortress Press, 1995.

Kovacs, Judith L. "'Now Shall the Ruler of This World Be Driven Out:' Jesus' Death as Cosmic Battle in John 12:20-36." *JBL* 114/2 (1995): 227-247.

Kragerud, Alv. *Der Lieblingsjünger im Johannesevangelium*. Oslo: Osloer Universitätsverlag, 1959.

Kreyenbühl, J. "Der Verfasser des Evangeliums," *Das Evangelium der Wahrheit: Neue Lösung der johanneischen Frage*. Berlin: C. A. Schwetschke und Sohn, 1900.

Kruse, H. "'Magni Pisces Centum Quinquaginta Tres' (Jo 21, 11)." *VD* 38 (1960): 129-148.

Kruse, H. "Jesu Seefahrten und die Stellung von Joh. 6." *NTS* 30/4 (1984): 508-530.

Kuhn, K. G. "Proselytes" and "God-fearers." *TWNT*. VI: 730-745.

Kysar, Robert. *John the Maverick Gospel*. Atlanta: John Knox Press, 2nd ed. 1979.

Kysar, Robert. *The Fourth Evangelist and His Gospel: An Examination of Contemporary Scholarship*. Minneapolis: Augsburg Publishing House, 1975.

Kysar, Robert. "Johannine Metaphor- Meaning and Function: A Literary Case Study of John 10:1-8." *Semeia 53: The Fourth Gospel from a Literary Perspective*. Edited by R. Alan Culpepper and Fernando Segovia. (1991): 81-111.

Lake, Kirsopp. "The Epistola Apostolorum." *HTR* 14/1 (1920):15-29.

Lietzmann, Hans. "Die Epistula Apostolorum," *ZNW* 20 (1921): 173-176.

Lieu, Judith. "Temple and Synagogue in John." *NTS* 45/1 1999: 51-69.

Lightfoot, R. H. *St. John's Gospel: A Commentary*. Oxford: at the University Press, 1960.

Lindars Barnabas. *Behind the Fourth Gospel*. London: SPCK, 1971.

Lindars Barnabas. *The Gospel of John. New Century Bible*. London: Oliphants, 1972.

Lindars, Barnabas. *Essays on John*. Edited by C. M. Tuckett. Leuven: University Press, 1992.

Lindars, Barnabas, Ruth B. Court, and John M. Court. *The Johannine Literature: With an Introduction by R. Alan Culpepper*. Sheffield: Sheffield Academic Press, 2000.

Lindars, Barnabas. "Rebuking the Spirit: A New Analysis of the Lazarus Story of John 11." *NTS* 38/1 (1992): 89-104.

Lindars, Barnabas. *The Gospel of John*. London: Marshall, Morgan & Scott, 1972.

Lowe, Malcolm. "Who were the IOUDAIOI?" *NT* 18 (1976): 101-130.

Macdonald, John. *The Theology of the Samaritans*. Philadelphia: Westminster, 1964.

McDonald, J. Ian H. "The So-Called *Pericopa de adultera*." *NTS* 41/3 (1995): 415-427.

MacRae, George W. "The Meaning and Evolution if the Feast of Tabernacles." *CBQ* 22 (1960): 251-276.

Mahoney R. "Two Disciples at the Tomb: The Background and Message of John 20:1-10." *Theologie und Wirklichkeit*. Bern: Herbert Lang, 1974.

Malina, Bruce J. *New Testament World: Insights from Cultural Anthropology*. Atlanta: John Knox, 1981.

Manson, T. W. "The Pericope de Adultera (Joh 7:53-8:11)." *ZNW* 44 (1952-53): 255-256.

Manson, T.W. "St. Paul's Letter to the Romans – and Others." *Bulletin of the John Rylands Library* 31/2 (1948).

Marcus, Joel. "A Note on Marcan Optics." *NTS* 45/2 (April 1999): 250-256.

Marcus, Joel. "Rivers of Living Water from Jesus' Belly (John 7:38)." *JBL* 117/2 (1998): 328-330.

Martyn, J. Louis. *History and Theology in the Fourth Gospel*. Louisville: Westminster John Knox Press, 3rd ed. 2003.

Martyn, J. Louis. "Source Criticism and Religionsgeschichte in the Fourth Gospel." *The Interpretation of John*. Edited by John Ashton. Philadelphia: Fortress Press, 1986: 99-121.

Martyn, J. Louis. "A Gentile Mission That Replaced an Earlier Jewish Mission?" *Exploring the Gospel of John: In Honor of D. Moody Smith*. Edited by R. Allan Culpepper and C. Clifton Black. Louisville: Westminster John Knox Press, 1996: 124-144.

Matsunaga, Kikuo, "Is John's Gospel Anti-Sacramental?" – A New Solution in the Light of the Evangelist's Milieu." *NTS* 27/4 (1981): 516-524.

Maynard, Arthur H. "TI EMOI KAI SOI (John 2:4)," *NTS* 31/4 (1985): 582-586.

Maynard, Arthur H. "The Role of Peter in the Fourth Gospel." *NTS* 30/4 (1984): 531-548.

McGaughey, Douglas R. *Strangers and Pilgrims: On the Role of Aporiai in Theology*. Berlin: Walter de Gruyter, 1997.

McGaughey, Douglas R. *Christianity for the Third Millennium: Faith in an Age of Fundamentalism and Skepticism*. San Francisco: International Scholars Publication: 1998.

Meeks, Wayne A. "Am I a Jew? Johannine Christianity and Judaism," *Christianity, Judaism, and Other Greco-Roman Cults. Studies for Morton Smith*. Edited by Jacob Neusner. Leiden: E. J. Brill, 1975.

Meeks, Wayne A. *The Prophet-King: Moses Traditions and the Johannine Christology*. Leiden: E. J. Brill, 1967.

Meeks, Wayne. A. "The Man from Heaven in Johannine Sectarianism," *JBL* 91/1 (1972): 44-72.

Menzies, Allan. "Introduction to the Commentaries of Origen," *The Ante-Nicene Fathers*. Grand Rapids: Eerdmans, 1956.

Meyer, Arnold. *Jesu Muttersprache: Das galiläische Aramäisch in seiner Bedeutung fur die Erklärung der Reden Jesu*. Freiburg & Leipzig: J. C. B. Mohr (Paul Siebeck), 1896.

Michaelis, Wilhelm. "πρῶτος." *TWNT* VI: 866-869. *TDNT* VI: 865-882.

Miller, E. L. *Salvation-History in the Prologue of John: The Significance of John 1:3-4*. NovTSup 60. Leiden: E. J. Brill, 1989.

Moloney, Francis J. *Signs and Shadows: Reading John 5-12*. Minneapolis: Fortress Press, 1996.

Moloney, Francis J. "Who is 'The Reader' in/of the Fourth Gospel." *ABR* 40 (1992).

Moloney, Francis J. *Belief in the Word: Reading John 1-4*. Minneapolis: Fortress Press, 1993.

Moloney, Francis J. *Glory not Dishonor: Reading John 13-21*. Minneapolis: Fortress Press, 1998.

Moore, George Foote. *Judaism in the First Centuries of the Christian Era: The Age of the Tannaim*. Cambridge: Harvard University Press, 1954.

Motyer, Stephen. "The Fourth Gospel and the Salvation of Israel: An Appeal for a New Start," *Anti-Judaism and the Fourth Gospel: Papers of the Leuven Colloquium, 2000*. Edited by R. Bieringer, D. Pollefeyt, and F. Vandecasteele-Vanneuville. Assen: Royal Van Gorcum, 2001.

Moule, C. F. D. "A Note on 'under the fig tree' in John 1 48,50." *JTS* 5 (1954): 210-211.

Moxnes, Halvor. "Honor and Shame," *The Social Sciences and New Testament Interpretation.* Edited by Richard Rohrbaugh. Peabody, Mass.: Hendrickson, 1996.

Muller, C. Detlef G. *Epistula Apostolorum. New Testament Apocrypha*. Initiated by Edgar Henneke, revision edited by Wilhelm Schneemelcher and English translation by R. Mcl. Wilson. Cambridge, England: James Clarke & Co. and Louisville: Westminster/John Knox Press, 1991.

Murphy-O'Conner, Jerome. "John the Baptist and Jesus: History and Hypotheses." *NTS* 36/3, (1990): 359-374.

Neirynck, F. "John 21." *NTS* 36/3 (1990): 321-336.

Neusner, Jacob. *From Politics to Piety: The Emergence of Pharisaic Judaism.* Englewood Cliffs: Prentice-Hall, 1973.

Neusner, Jacob. "Emergent Rabbinic Judaism in a Time of Crisis," *Judaism* 21 (1972): 313-327.

Neusner, Jacob. *The Fathers according to Rabbi Nathan: An Analytical Translation and Explanation*. Atlanta: Scholars Press, 1986.

Neusner, Jacob. *The Mishnah: A New Translation*. New Haven: Yale University Press, 1988.

Neusner, Jacob. *The Rabbinic Traditions about the Pharisees before 70.* Part 1, *The Masters*; Part 2, *The Houses*; Part 3, *Conclusions*. Leiden: E. J. Brill, 1971.

Neusner,Jacob. *First Century Judaism in Crisis*: *Yohanan ben Zakkai and the Renaissance of the Torah*. Nashville: Abingdon Press, 1975.

Neusner,Jacob. *Development of a Legend: Studies on the Traditions Concerning Yohanan ben Zakkai*. Leiden: E. J. Brill, 1970.

Neusner,Jacob. *There We Sat Down: Talmudic Judaism in the Making.* Nashville: Abingdon Press, 1972.

Neyrey, Jerome H. "Jacob Traditions and the Interpretation of John 4:10-26." *CBQ* 41 (1979): 419-437.

Neyrey, Jerome H. "Jesus the Judge: Forensic Process in John 8,21-59." *Bib* 68/4 (1987): 509-541.

Neyrey, Jerome H. "I said 'You are Gods:' Psalm 82:6 and John 10." *JBL* 108/4 (1989): 647-663.

Neyrey, Jerome H. "The 'Noble Shepherd' in John 10: Cultural and Rhetorical Background." *JBL* 120/2 (2001): 267-291.

Neyrey, Jerome H. "Despising the Shame of the Cross: Honor and Shame in the Johannine Passion Narrative." *Semeia 68. Honor and Shame in the World of the Bible.* Edited by Victor H. Matthews and Don C. Benjamin Atlanta: Scholars Press, 1996: 113-137.

Neyrey, Jerome H. *Honor and Shame in the Gospel of Matthew*. Louisville: Westminster John Knox Press, 1998.

Nicholson, G. *Death as Departure: The Johannine Descent-Ascent Schema*. Chico, CA: Scholars Press, 1983.

Nicklas, Tobias, *Ablösung und Verstrickung: "'Juden" und Jüngergestalten als Charaktere der erzählten Welt des Johannesevangeliums und ihre Wirkung auf den impliziten Leser. Regensburger Studien zur Theologie*. Frankfurt: Peter Lang, 2001.

Nicklas, Tobias. "'Unter dem Feigenbaum:' Die Rolle des Lesers im Dialog zwischen Jesus und Natanael (Joh 1.45-50)." *NTS* 46/2 (2000): 193-203.

Niebuhr, Richard R. *Resurrection and Historical Reason: A Study of Theological Method*. New York: Charles Scribner's Sons, 1957.

O'Day, Gail R. "John 7:53-8:11: A Study in Misreading." *JBL* 111/4 (1992): 631-640.

O'Day, Gail R. *Revelation in the Fourth Gospel: Narrative Mode and Theological Claim*. Philadelphia: Fortress Press, 1986.

Odeberg Hugo , *The Fourth Gospel: Interpreted in its relation to contemporaneous religious currents in Palestine and the Hellenistic-Oriental world*. Uppsala: Almqvist & Wiksells,1929; repr. Chicago: Argonaut, 1968.

Olsson, Birger. *Structure and Meaning in the Fourth Gospel*. Coniectanea Biblica. New Testament Series 6. Lund, Sweden: CWK Gleerup, 1974.

Overbeck, Franz. *Das Johannesevangelium.* Edited by C. A. Bernoulli. Tübingen: J. C. B. Mohr, 1911.

Pagels, Elaine H. *The Johannine Gospel in Gnostic Exegesis: Heracleon's Commentary on John*. Nashville: Abingdon Press, 1973.

Pagels, Elaine H. *Beyond Belief: The Secret Gospel of Thomas*. New York: Random House, 2003.

Painter, John. "Tradition and Interpretation in John 6." *NTS* 35/3 (1989): 421-450.

Painter, John. "The Farewell Discourses and the History of Johannine Christianity." *NTS* 27/4 (1981): 525-543.

Painter, John. "Tradition, History and Interpretation in John 10." *The Shepherd Discourse of John 10 and its Context*. Edited. with introduction by Johannes Beutler and Robert T. Fortna. Cambridge: at the University Press, 1991.

Phillips, G.L. "Faith and Vision in the Fourth Gospel." *Studies in the Fourth Gospel.* Edited by F. L. Cross. London: Mowbray, 1957.

Procksch, O. " Wort Gottes im AT." *TWNT*.IV: 89-100. *TDNT* IV: 91-100.

Puech, H. C., G. Quispel and W. C. van Unnik *The Jung Codex: Three Studies*. Translated and edited by F. L. Cross. London: A.R. Mobray, 1955.

Quast, Kevin. *Peter and the Beloved Disciple: Figures for a Community in Crisis. JSNT*: Supplement Series 32. Sheffield: Sheffield Academic Press, 1989.

Reicke, Bo. "πρό ." *TWNT* VI: 720-725. *TDNT*. VI: 720-724.

Reim, Günther "Joh. 8. 44 – Gotteskinder/Teufelskinder. Wie antijudaistisch ist 'Die wohl antijudaistischste Äusserung des NT'?" *NTS* 30/4 (1984): 619-624.

Reinhartz, Adele. *Befriending the Beloved Disciple: A Jewish Reading of the Gospel of John*. New York: Continuum, 2001.

Rensberger, David. *Johannine Faith and Liberating Community*. Philadelphia: Westminster Press, 1988.

Richter, Georg. "Zur Formgeschichte und literarischen Einheit von Joh 6. 31-58." *ZNW* 60 (1969): 21-55.

Richter, Georg. *Die Fusswaschung im Johannesevangelium*. Regensburg: Pustel, 1967.

Ricoeur, Paul. "The Hermeneutical Function of Distanciation." *From Text to Action: Essays in Hermeneutics,* II by Paul Ricoeur. Translated by Kathleen Blamey and John B. Thompson. Evanston: Northwestern University Press, 1991: 75-88.

Roberts, Colin H. *Manuscript, Society and Belief in Early Christian Egypt.* The Schweich Lectures 1977. London: Oxford University Press, 1979.

Robinson, J. A. T. "The Destination and Purpose of St. John's Gospel." *Twelve New Testament Studies. Studies in Biblical Theology* No. 34. London: SCM Press, 1962. Published earlier in *NTS* 6/2 (1960): 117-131.

Romeo, Joseph A. "Gematria and John 21:11 – The Children of God." *JBL* 97/2 (1978): 263-264.

Rowland, Christopher. "John 1:51, Jewish Apocalyptic and Targumic Tradition." *NTS* 30/4 (1984): 498-507.

Safrai, S. "Jewish Self-Government." *The Jewish People in the First Century*. 2 vols. Edited by S. Safrai and M. Stern. Assen: Van Gorcum, 1974: I, 377-419.

Sanders, J. N. *The Fourth Gospel in the Early Church*. Cambridge: at the University Press, 1943.

Sanders, J. N. *A Commentary on the Gospel according to St. John*. Completed by B. A. Mastin. New York: Harper & Row, 1968.

Schenke Ludger "Das johanneische Schisma und die 'Zwölf' (Johannes 6.61-70)." *NTS* 38/1 (1992): 105-121.

Schenke, Ludger. "Der 'Dialog Jesu mit den Juden' im Johannesevangelium: ein Rekonstruktionsversuch." *NTS* 34/4 (1988):

Schlatter, Adolf. *Der Evangelist Johannes*. Stuttgart: Calwer Verlag, 3rd ed. 1960.

Schmidt, Carl. *Gespräche Jesu Mit Seinen Jüngern.* Hildesheim: Georg Olms Verlagsbuchhandlung, 1967.

Schnackenburg, Rudolf. *Das Johannesevangelium: Einleitung und Kommentar zu Kap. 1-4.* Freiburg: Herder, 1965.

Schnackenburg, Rudolf. *The Gospel according to St. John* 3 vols. Vol. 1: translated by Kevin Smyth. and edited by J. Massingberd Ford and Kevin Smyth. New York: Herder & Herder, 1968. Vol, 2: New York: Seabury, 1980. Vol. 3: New York: Crossroad, 1982.

Schneiders, Sandra M. "The Footwashing (John 13:1-20): An Experiment in Hermeneutics." *CBQ* 43 (1981): 76-92.

Schneiders, Sandra M. "Women in the Fourth Gospel and the Role of Women in the Contemporary Church." *BTB* 12/2 (1982).

Schneiders, Sandra M. "The Face Veil: A Johannine Sign (John 20:1-10)." *BTB* 13 (1983): 94-97.

Schneiders, Sandra M. "A Feminist Interpretation of John 4:1-42," *The Revelatory Text. Interpreting the New Testament as Sacred Scripture*. San Francisco: Harper, 1991.

Schneiders, Sandra M. "'Because of the Women's Testimony…': Reexamining the Issue of Authorship in the Fourth Gospel." *NTS* 44/4 (1998): 513-535.

Schneiders, Sandra M. *Written That You May Believe: Encountering Jesus in the Fourth Gospel*. New York: Crossroad, 1999.

Schottroff, Luise. *Der Glaubende und die feindliche Welt*. Neukirchen-Vluyn: Neukirchener Verlag, 1970.

Schürer, Emil. *The History of the Jewish People in the Age of Jesus Christ*. Revised and edited by Geza Vermes, Fergus Millar, Martin Goodman. Edinburgh: T & T Clark, 1986.

Schwartz, Eduard. "Über den Tod der Söhne Zebedäi: ein Beitrag zur Geschichte des Johannesevangeliums." *Johannes und sein Evangelium*. Edited by Karl Heinrich Rengstorf. Darmstadt: Wissenschaftliche Buchgesellschaft, 1973.

Schwartz, G. "ΥΣΣΩΠΩ ΠΕΡΙΘΕΝΤΕΣ: (Johannes 19, 29)." *NTS* 30/4 (1984): 625.

Schweizer, Eduard. *EGO EIMI: Die religionsgeschichtliche Herkunft und theologische Bedeutung der johanneischen Bildreden, zugleich ein Beitrag zur Quellenfrage des vierten Evangeliums*. Göttingen: Vandenhoeck & Ruprecht, 2nd ed. 1965.

Schweizer, Eduard. "Das johanneische Zeugnis vom Herrenmahl." *EvT* 12 (1952/53): 341-363.

Schweizer, Eduard. "Er wird Nazoräer heissen." *Judentum Urchristentum, Kirche: Festschrift für Joachim Jeremias*. Edited by Walter Eltester. Berlin: Alfred Töpelmann, 1960.

Schweizer, Eduard. "ψυχή." *TWNT* IX: 635-657. *TDNT* IX: 637-656.

Segovia, Fernando. "The Final Farewell of Jesus: A Reading of John 20:30-21:25." *The Fourth Gospel from a Literary Perspective*. Edited by R. Alan Culpepper and Fernando Segovia. *Semeia* 53 (1991): 167-190.

Segovia, Fernando. *The Farewell of the Word: The Johannine Call to Abide*. Minneapolis: Fortress Press, 1991.

Sevrin, Jean-Marie. "The Nicodemus Enigma: The Characterization and Function of an Ambiguous Actor of the Fourth Gospel." *Anti-Judaism and the Fourth Gospel:Papers of the Leuven Colloquium, 2000*. Edited by R. Bieringer, D. Pollefeyt, and F. Vandecasteele-Vanneuville. Assen: Royal Van Gorcum, 2001: 357-369.

Smith, D. Moody. *The Theology of the Gospel of John*. New Testament Theology Series. Cambridge: at the University Press, 1995.

Smith, D. Moody. "The Contribution of J. Louis Martyn to the Understanding of the Gospel of John." J. Louis Martyn. *History and Theology in the Fourth Gospel*. Louisville: Westminster John Knox Press, 3rd ed. 2003: 1-23.

Snyder, Graydon. F. "John 13:16 and the Anti-Petrinism of the Johannine Tradition." *BR* 16 (1971): 5-15.

Söding, Thomas. "'Was kann aus Nazareth schon Gutes kommen?' (Joh 1.46). Die Bedeutung des Judeseins Jesu im Johannesevangelium." *NTS* 46/1 (2000): 21-41.

Sporty, Lawrence D. "Identifying the Curving Line on the Bar-Kokhba Temple Coin." *BA* 46/2 (1983): 121-124.

Staley, Jeffrey L. "Stumbling in the Dark, Reaching for the Light: Reading Character in John 5 and 9." *Semeia 53: The Fourth Gospel from a Literary Perspective*. Edited by R. Alan Culpepper and Fernando Segovia. (1991): 55-80.

Stemberger, Günther. *Introduction to the Talmud and Midrash.* Translated and edited by Markus Bockmuehl. Edinburgh: T & T Clark, 2nd ed. 1996.

Stern, M. "The Province of Judaea." *The Jewish People in the first Century*. 2 vols. Edited by S. Safrai and M. Stern. Assen: Van Gorcum. 1974: I, 308-376.

Stibbe, Mark W. G. *John as Storyteller: Narrative Criticism and the Fourth Gospel*. Cambridge: at the University Press, 1994.

Stibbe, Mark W. G. *John's Gospel*. London: Routledge, 1994.

Strack Hermann L. & Paul Billerbeck. *Kommentar zum Neuen Testament aus Talmud und Midrash*. 6 vols. München: C. H. Beck'sche Verlagsbuchhandlung, 1956.

Strathmann,H. *Das Evangelium nach Johannes: NTD*. Göttingen: Vandenhoeck & Ruprecht, 1963.

Sylva, D. "Nicodemus and his Spices (John 19:39)." *NTS* 34/1 (1988): 148-151.

Tcherikover,Victor. *Hellenistic Civilization and the Jews*. Philadelphia: Jewish Publication Society of America, 1966.

Thiselton, Anthony C. *The Two Horizons: New Testament Hermeneutics and Philosophical Description*. Grand Rapids: Eerdmans, 1980.

Thyen, Hartwig. "Das Heil kommt von den Juden," *Kirche: Festschrift für Günther Bornkamm zum 75.Geburtstag*. Edited by D. Lührmann and Georg Strecker. Tübingen: J. C. B. Mohr (Paul Siebeck) 1980.

Titus, Eric L. *The Message of the Fourth Gospel*. New York: Abingdon, 1957.

Tolmie, D. F. *Jesus' Farewell to the Disciples: John 13:1-17:26 in Narratological Perspective*. Leiden: E. J. Brill, 1995.

Turner, John D. "The History of Religions Background of John 10." *The Shepherd Discourse of John 10 and its Context*. Edited with introduction by J. Beutler and R. T. Fortna. Cambridge: at the University Press, 1991.

Van Belle, Gilbert. "'Salvation is from the Jews:' The Parenthesis in John 4:22b." *Anti-Judaism and the Fourth Gospel: Papers of the Leuven Colloquium, 2000*. Edited by R. Bieringer, D. Pollefeyt, and F. Vandecasteele-Vanneuville. Assen: Royal Van Gorcum, 2001: 370-400.

Van Unnik, W. C. "The Purpose of St. John's Gospel." *Studia Evangelica I*. Berlin: Akademie Verlag, 1959.

Von Campenhausen, Hans. *The Formation of the Christian Bible*. Translated by J. A. Baker. Philadelphia: Fortress Press, 1972.

Von Loewenich, W. *Das Johannes-Verständnis im zweiten Jahrhundert*. Giessen: Alfred Töpelmann, 1932.

Von Wahlde, Urban C. "The Johannine 'Jews': A Critical Survey," *NTS* 28/1 (1982): 33-60.

Von Wahlde, Urban C. "The Terms for Religious Authorities in the Fourth Gospel: a Key to Literary Strata," *JBL* 98/2 (1979): 231-253.

Waetjen, Herman C. "Logos πρὸς τὸν θεόν and the Objectification of Truth in the Prologue of the Fourth Gospel." *CBQ* 63/2 (2001): 265-286.

Waetjen, Herman C. *A Reordering of Power: A Socio-political Reading of Mark's Gospel*. Minneapolis: Fortress Press, 1989.

Waetjen, Herman C. *The Origin and Destiny of Humanness: An Interpretation of the Gospel according to Matthew*. San Rafael: Crystal Press, 1976.

Weiss, Johannes. "Zum Märtyrertod der Zebedäiden." *ZNW* 11 (1910): 167.

Wenham, J. W. "The Fig Tree in the Old Testament." *JTS* 5 (1954): 206-207.

Wiles, M. F. *Spiritual Gospel: The Interpretation of the Fourth Gospel in the Early Church*. Cambridge: at the University Press, 1960.

Wilkens, Wilhelm. *Die Entstehungsgeschichte des vierten Evangeliums*. Zollikon: Evangelischer Verlag, 1958.

Wink, Walter. *Engaging the Powers: Discernment and Resistance in a World of Domination*. Minneapolis: Fortress Press, 1992.

Winston, David. *Logos and Mystical Theology in Philo of Alexandria.* Cincinnati: Hebrew Union College Press, 1985.

Winter, Paul. *On the Trial of Jesus. Studia Judaica.* Berlin: Walter de Gruyter, 1961.

Witkamp, L. Th. "Jesus' Thirst in John 19:28-30: Literal or Figurative?" *JBL* 115/3 (1996): 489-510.

Wolff, Hans Walter. *Anthropology of the Old Testament.* Philadelphia: Fortress Press, 1974.

Wuellner, Wilhelm. "Putting Life back into the Lazarus Story and its Reading." *Semeia 53: The Fourth Gospel from a Literary Perspective.* Edited by R. Alan Culpepper and Fernando F. Segovia. Atlanta: Scholars Press, 1991: 113-132.

Index of Ancient Sources

Old Testament

Genesis

Exodus

Leviticus

Numbers

Deuteronomy

Joshua

Judges

2 Samuel

1 Kings

2 Kings

2 Chronicles

Nehemiah

Job

Psalms

Rabbinic Literature

New Testament Apocrypha and Early Christian Literature

Index of Modern Authors